AF847929

FIDUCIARIES AND TRUST

Systematic analysis of fiduciaries and trust is rare. The aim of this volume is to help fill this gap. The authors explore the interactions of fiduciary law and trust, drawing on literatures on trust that have been generated in a variety of disciplines. They do so with an eye to the full scope of extension claimed for the fiduciary principle, from its heartland in private law, to its frontiers in public law and government more broadly. Overall, the volume advances an integrated and wide-ranging understanding of the relation of fiduciaries and trust that illuminates key legal and political problems, and challenges and deepens our understanding of fiduciaries and trust themselves.

PAUL B. MILLER is Professor and Associate Dean for International and Graduate Programs, and Director of the Notre Dame Program on Private Law, Notre Dame Law School, Indiana, USA. He is a leading private law theorist specializing in fiduciary law, the law of trusts and corporate law. His other books include *Philosophical Foundations of Fiduciary Law, The Oxford Handbook of Fiduciary Law* and *Civil Wrongs and Justice in Private Law.*

MATTHEW HARDING is Professor and Deputy Dean at Melbourne Law School, University of Melbourne, Australia. He is a leading expert on fiduciary law and on trust, and has published extensively in both areas. More generally, he is considered a leading authority on equity and trusts and the law of charities and other not-for-profits.

FIDUCIARIES AND TRUST

Ethics, Politics, Economics and Law

Edited by

PAUL B. MILLER

University of Notre Dame

MATTHEW HARDING

University of Melbourne

CAMBRIDGE
UNIVERSITY PRESS

CAMBRIDGE
UNIVERSITY PRESS

University Printing House, Cambridge CB2 8BS, United Kingdom

One Liberty Plaza, 20th Floor, New York, NY 10006, USA

477 Williamstown Road, Port Melbourne, VIC 3207, Australia

314–321, 3rd Floor, Plot 3, Splendor Forum, Jasola District Centre, New Delhi – 110025, India

79 Anson Road, #06–04/06, Singapore 079906

Cambridge University Press is part of the University of Cambridge.

It furthers the University's mission by disseminating knowledge in the pursuit of education, learning, and research at the highest international levels of excellence.

www.cambridge.org
Information on this title: www.cambridge.org/9781108480420
DOI: 10.1017/9781108616225

© Cambridge University Press 2020

This publication is in copyright. Subject to statutory exception and to the provisions of relevant collective licensing agreements, no reproduction of any part may take place without the written permission of Cambridge University Press.

First published 2020

Printed in the United Kingdom by TJ International Ltd, Padstow Cornwall

A catalogue record for this publication is available from the British Library.

Library of Congress Cataloging-in-Publication Data
Names: Fiduciaries and trust (Conference) (2018 : University of Melbourne, Law School) | Miller, Paul B. (Law teacher), editor. | Harding, Matthew, 1974– editor. | University of Melbourne. Law School, host institution.
Title: Fiduciaries and trust : ethics, politics, economics and law / edited by Paul B. Miller, University of Notre Dame [and] Matthew Harding, University of Melbourne.
Description: Cambridge, United Kingdom ; New York, NY, USA : Cambridge University Press, 2020. | Includes index.
Identifiers: LCCN 2019048223 (print) | LCCN 2019048224 (ebook) | ISBN 9781108480420 (hardback) | ISBN 9781108727389 (paperback) | ISBN 9781108616225 (epub)
Subjects: LCSH: Trusts and trustees–English-speaking countries–Congresses.
Classification: LCC K795.A6 F53 2018 (print) | LCC K795.A6 (ebook) | DDC 346.05/9–dc23
LC record available at https://lccn.loc.gov/2019048223
LC ebook record available at https://lccn.loc.gov/2019048224

ISBN 978-1-108-48042-0 Hardback

DAMAGED

Cambridge University Press has no responsibility for the persistence or accuracy of URLs for external or third-party internet websites referred to in this publication and does not guarantee that any content on such websites is, or will remain, accurate or appropriate.

For my mentors, with gratitude:

Peter Lipton, Arthur Ripstein, Ross Stanway,
Charles Weijer and Cyril Welch.

PBM

For Clare, Isabel and Charlie, as always.

M.H.

CONTENTS

CONTRIBUTORS

ROB ATKINSON, Greenspoon Marder Professor of Law, Florida State University College of Law

BRIAN J. BROUGHMAN, Professor of Law, Indiana University Maurer School of Law

EVAN J. CRIDDLE, Cabell Research Professor of Law, William and Mary Law School

PAUL FAULKNER, Professor in Philosophy, Department of Philosophy, University of Sheffield

EVAN FOX-DECENT, Professor of Law, McGill University Faculty of Law

THOMAS P. GALLANIS, Allan D. Vestal Chair in Law and Associate Dean for Research, University of Iowa College of Law

ANDREW S. GOLD, Professor of Law, Brooklyn Law School

KIRSTY GOVER, Professor of Law, Melbourne Law School

MATTHEW HARDING, Professor of Law and Deputy Dean, Melbourne Law School

CAROLYN MCLEOD, Professor of Philosophy, Department of Philosophy, Western University

PAUL B. MILLER, Professor of Law and Associate Dean for International and Graduate Programs, Notre Dame Law School

JAMES PENNER, Kwa Geok Choo Professor of Property Law, Faculty of Law, National University of Singapore

ELIZABETH POLLMAN, Professor of Law, University of Pennsylvania Carey Law School

GERALD J. POSTEMA, Professor of Philosophy Emeritus, University of North Carolina at Chapel Hill

NICOLE ROUGHAN, Associate Professor of Law, Faculty of Law, University of Auckland

EMMA RYMAN, JD Candidate, University of Toronto Faculty of Law

D. GORDON SMITH, Dean and Glen L. Farr Professor of Law, J. Reuben Clark School of Law, Brigham Young University

LIONEL D. SMITH, Sir William C. Macdonald Professor of Law, McGill University Faculty of Law

TESS WILKINSON-RYAN, Professor of Law and Psychology, University of Pennsylvania Law School

ACKNOWLEDGEMENTS

This book follows a workshop on the themes of trust and fiduciaries held at the Melbourne Law School in December 2018. We received generous financial support for the workshop from the Melbourne Law School's international collaboration fund and from the Notre Dame Program on Private Law, and we are grateful for this support. We also thank those colleagues from the Melbourne Law School and elsewhere who joined us and the contributors for the workshop and who enriched our conversation and understanding in many ways as a result. Finally, thanks to our respective families for their patience through yet another book project. One of the greatest satisfactions of this project was that it enabled our families to meet and spend some time together in Melbourne, and it deepened a friendship as well as an ongoing academic collaboration.

Introduction

PAUL B. MILLER AND MATTHEW HARDING

We begin with two bibliographical observations. First, scholarly interest in trust is no recent phenomenon, but lately there has been a flowering of academic literature studying numerous dimensions of trust from the standpoints of philosophy, economics, sociology and psychology. The depth and richness of this literature is impressive but hardly surprising, given that trust itself is a notoriously complex, elusive and fact-specific phenomenon. Secondly, scholarly interest in the fiduciary principle that plays such a central role in common law legal systems with a tradition of equity was scarce until the late twentieth century. However, that situation has most definitely changed (for the better), and we now enjoy an abundance of scholarship exploring the fiduciary principle in private law. Moreover, there is a growing body of work exploring ideas of fiduciary government and international law. Scholars are puzzling over fiduciaries and trust as never before.

Given this, one might expect to see a flourishing of academic interest in the relation of fiduciaries and trust, especially as it is often assumed or asserted that such a relation exists and that it has descriptive or normative significance for fiduciary law and practice. Yet this is not the case. Systematic analysis of fiduciaries and trust is rare. The aim of this volume is to help fill this gap. Our contributors explore the interactions of fiduciary law and trust, drawing on literatures on trust that have been generated in a variety of disciplines. They do so with an eye to the full scope of extension claimed for the fiduciary principle, from its heartland in private law to its frontiers in public law and government more broadly. Overall, the volume advances an integrated and wide-ranging understanding of the relation of fiduciaries and trust that illuminates key legal and political problems, and challenges and deepens our understanding of fiduciaries and trust themselves.

1 Personal Trust and Fiduciary Relationships

It has been widely suggested that fiduciary law is significant to personal trust, and likewise that personal trust is salient to fiduciary law. And when this is said, it is often on the basis that fiduciary relationships are premised on personal trust, or that they invite or cultivate personal trust, or both. The notion that fiduciary relationships are premised on personal trust is sometimes framed as a characterization of – or assumption about – the motivations of the parties forming a fiduciary relationship. Thus, it might be suggested that a grantor or beneficiary was motivated to enter into the relationship because of his trust in the fiduciary, whether spontaneous or a response to the fiduciary's invitation to trust. In turn, it might be thought that fiduciaries are routinely motivated to solicit or undertake trust out of a desire to be seen as, and/or to prove, trustworthy. Alternatively, personal trust may be understood in terms of conduct, encompassing a position of dependence or vulnerability willingly accepted by the grantor or beneficiary, in which case the relationship is one of trust in the sense that its formation involves acts of entrustment. Finally, independently of concern over how trust factors in the formation of fiduciary relationships, some have argued that trust is significant to the ongoing performance of a fiduciary relationship, insofar as it factors in the moral regard that the fiduciary and beneficiary have for one another and the quality of cooperation achieved by them. Ultimately, however one conceives of trust and its bearing in fiduciary relationships, it is clear that there are many difficult questions to be addressed in sorting out the intuition that trust is important to fiduciary relationships and vice versa. The chapters gathered in Part I of this volume identify and address these questions.

In "Fiduciary Grounds and Reasons," Paul Faulkner aims to clarify the significance of consent and trust in fiduciary relationships. He focuses on two issues: first, the roles of consent and trust in grounding the transfer of power through which fiduciary relationships are formed; and second, their salience for the reasons fiduciaries have for acting on behalf of their beneficiaries.

Faulkner takes as his starting point Paul Miller's Fiduciary Powers Theory of the fiduciary relationship. As Miller explains, fiduciary duties are premised on the formation of a fiduciary relationship, which in turn arises upon the authorization of one person or group of persons to exercise discretionary legal powers for another person or group in pursuit of other-regarding purposes. Mechanisms of authorization include, Miller says, the mutual consent of a grantor and fiduciary and (more rarely) unilateral undertaking or legal decree. Faulkner aims to clarify the place of consent and trust in each of these modes of authorization. He also aims to clarify what this implies about the moral reasons fiduciaries have in acting for their beneficiaries.

Faulkner begins with relationships formed by mutual consent. He clarifies that consent here serves as a mechanism of authorization where expressed intentionally to another via a communicative act, and where recognized as such. In this sense, it is a second-personal mode of authorization (i.e., it is means by which one person intentionally confers authority on another). According to Faulkner, consent also gives fiduciaries second-personal reasons for acting in accordance with their mandate, where the consent includes specific requests or directions. Personal trust is salient to fiduciary relationships formed by mutual consent to the extent that it is presumed to factor in the beneficiary's willing acceptance of dependence on the fiduciary. Beneficiaries are, in consenting, presumed to have a trusting expectation that fiduciaries will act on their behalf, in accordance with the terms of their mandate, for the reason (in part) that they have been trusted with faithful execution of same.

Turning to relationships formed by unilateral undertaking or decree, Faulkner suggests that the grounds of fiduciary authority are here supplied by presumed consent. The presumption of consent is supposed by Faulkner to be premised on the beneficiary's filial bond with, and robust trust in, the fiduciary. In turn, Faulkner believes that in these circumstances, fiduciaries are inclined to serve in a fiduciary capacity because of a background relationship of robust personal trust that foregrounds the formation of the fiduciary relationship.

In "Trust and Advice," Andrew Gold takes on difficult questions about the justification for extension of fiduciary duties to relationships that do not have settled fiduciary status: advisory relationships, and ad hoc fiduciary relationships. As Gold recognizes, these relationships raise hard questions for fiduciary theory for different, but related, reasons. Advisory relationships are often, but not always, treated as fiduciary, and where they are, it is seemingly not on the basis that the fiduciary wields fiduciary power. Advisory relationships are thus outliers for leading theories of the fiduciary relationship. How can we make sense of the courts' willingness to hold that advisors are sometimes fiduciaries, if advice giving is not inherently fiduciary? Ad hoc fiduciary relationships raise other questions. Notably, what grounds (juridically) and justifies (morally) the imposition of fiduciary duties on relationships that do not fall into the presumptions generated by the attachment of fiduciary status to broad categories of relationship? According to Gold, in both cases, the answers turn on epistemic dependence and trust.

Gold begins by arguing that while trust is not an essential element of all fiduciary relationships, it does figure significantly in some of them. It factors in those advisory relationships that are fiduciary to the extent that thick trust may result in epistemic dependence, the latter being a strong form of cognitive dependency whereby advice recipients tend to accept and act uncritically on trusted advice. Gold builds on Paul Miller's observation that the law differentiates advisory relationships and his suggestion that it might sort fiduciary from non-fiduciary advisory relationships on the basis of epistemic dependence (the latter understood by Miller as entailing effective rather than formal authority to act for another). Gold explains that epistemic dependence can be a common and therefore predictable phenomenon within certain kinds of relationship, and is thus relied on at law to support the extension of fiduciary status to certain categories of advisor. Put briefly, where one can reasonably expect epistemic dependence in a kind of advisory relationship, one has a compelling reason to treat it as presumptively fiduciary, and the reason tracks that established by Miller's Fiduciary Powers Theory (fiduciary impositions should be borne by those with the power to decide for others).

Gold also sees a critical role for thick trust in ad hoc fiduciary relationships. Here, he explains, the key interpretive challenge is one of explaining and justifying the imposition of fiduciary duties ad hoc, on parties whose relationships don't conform to a general fiduciary type. Why allow for the recognition of fiduciary relationships on an ad hoc basis, and how can one address concerns about unfair surprise? Gold notes that the case law is replete with reference to trust and reliance. And he thinks that this is telling. Relationships can be differentiated, ad hoc as well as categorically, on the basis of trust giving rise to robust reliance, and thick trust of this sort generates moral expectations of regard that serve as a kind of moral constructive notice to fiduciaries. A person cannot claim unfair surprise – or, at least, not compellingly – if the nature of her involvement with the beneficiary is such that she ought to have known that she was to act in an other-regarding and self-restrained way.

In "Contracts, Fiduciary Relationships and Trust," Matthew Harding explains the significance of personal trust to contractual and fiduciary relationships. He argues that contractual and fiduciary relationships "orient and channel" trust in different ways, and likewise that these relationships are formed against different background levels of confidence in systems for enforcement of contractual and fiduciary duties.

Harding begins by stipulating the meaning of trust and confidence, respectively. Trust, he explains, is an "attitude of optimism" about the choices that one's object of trust will make, bearing in mind risks attendant in depending on those who have freedom of choice. Harding says further that trust is a protean concept, implying that trusting attitudes might be connected with any of a number of beliefs about the object of one's trust, whether of their good will, character or other matters. Confidence, by contrast, is marked by positive belief in, and reliance on, the predictable operation of systems, including, notably, legal and regulatory systems.

Harding argues that trust and confidence are both important to contractual and fiduciary relationships, but tend to figure differently in each. Because contractual duties of performance are not usually specifically enforced, a robust system of contract enforcement will support confidence in the availability of an adequate remedy for breach but *not* for an expectation of performance. By contrast, enforcement of strict prophylactic (no profit, no conflict) fiduciary rules will mean greater reason for confidence in performance by fiduciaries. Turning to trust, Harding argues that contractual relationships implicate trust, but in the thin sense of reliance on the tendency of persons to behave in rational self-interest. Fiduciary relationships, by contrast, tend to implicate thick trust, and so beliefs about the good will or virtuous character of fiduciaries, and fiduciary duties signal the importance of these qualities in a fiduciary while furnishing fiduciaries with legal reasons to meet more robust expectations of trustworthiness.

Harding acknowledges that these tendencies become complicated in practice by the fact that fiduciary and contractual relationships are often overlapping. And yet, he says, in case law on contracting out of, or within, fiduciary relationships, one can see the law aiming for a balanced accommodation of contractual and fiduciary norms.

In "Trust, Autonomy and the Fiduciary Relationship," Carolyn McLeod and Emma Ryman critically examine the conventional wisdom that the formation of fiduciary relationships, and the presence of trust within them, come at the expense of beneficiary autonomy. As the authors explain, some have argued that fiduciary relationships involve a "transfer of autonomy" inasmuch as the fiduciary is placed in a position of power over the beneficiary. Others have suggested that fiduciary relationships feature structural paternalism, to the extent that fiduciaries are granted authority to make decisions for others. McLeod and Ryman reject each of these claims on the basis that they assume a defective concept of autonomy and miss the sense in which the bearing of trust and fiduciary relationships on autonomy is contingent: they can be autonomy enhancing or inhibiting.

McLeod and Ryman acknowledge that, formally, the formation of a fiduciary relationship means a transfer of legal power to fiduciaries to be wielded relative to beneficiaries. Thus, fiduciaries assume positions of significant potential influence over beneficiaries. Trust of beneficiaries in fiduciaries is, on their view, instrumentally significant insofar as it is entailed by the formation of a fiduciary relationship, or is a significant motivational factor in the decision whether to enter into a fiduciary relationship. But whether trust and fiduciary relationships impair or enhance autonomy turns on the behavior of the parties, and how the law aims to shape that behavior. Where a beneficiary cedes all of her decision-making power in respect of a particular matter to, or relies blindly on, the fiduciary, there is clearly significant diminishment of her autonomy. But it needn't be this way. The beneficiary can assume an active role in a fiduciary relationship, asserting retained control rights, and, in turn, the fiduciary can support beneficiary autonomy by refusing broad delegation and blind reliance, and by providing the beneficiary with informational and other supports requisite to the realization of meaningful autonomy. In making these points, McLeod and Ryman explain that this contextual perspective is consistent with analyses of relational autonomy in moral philosophy.

In "The Psychology of Trust and Fiduciary Obligations," Tess Wilkinson-Ryan canvasses the results of psychological research on trust and highlights their implications for fiduciary law. Her chapter suggests that certain intuitions about trust and fiduciary relationships are well supported empirically – for example, our preference for delegating decision-making on financial matters to experts in trust that they will make decisions that are more competent, and that better reflect our risk preferences, than we could ourselves. But her chapter also challenges other beliefs – for example, the belief in the value of forced disclosure as a device for enhancing fiduciary accountability and integrity.

Wilkinson-Ryan begins by noting that trust, understood psychologically, is a matter of social perception. The person considering whether to trust has to determine, based on her perception of a possible object of trust, whether that person is trustworthy in respect of the subject matter of trust. In turn, one who wishes to invite trust must be concerned with social perceptions of their trustworthiness, and will show that concern through efforts – deliberate or otherwise – to shape these perceptions. While philosophers are often anxious to distinguish trust from reliance, Wilkinson-Ryan notes that psychologists view trust as a choice that arises in situations where one is confronted with the question whether to take a chance in relying on another, despite the risk of disappointment. Fiduciary relationships, she explains, instantiate this kind of situation (i.e., a situation calling for trust).

On the assumption that fiduciary relationships are relations of trust – or, at least, relations that call for trust – Wilkinson-Ryan focuses attention on the implications of various fiduciary obligations for trust and trustworthiness. She explains that psychological research provides support for the notion that the duty of loyalty promotes loyal behavior, on the basis that norms rich in moral content like that of loyalty tend to elicit conscientious responsiveness. That said, Wilkinson-Ryan argues that loyalty rules are sensibly given strict formulation in order to mitigate the effects of self-serving biases. Interestingly, Wilkinson-Ryan extrapolates concerns about the duty of disclosure from research on the effects of disclosure on trust. For example, ironically, disclosure might make a beneficiary *less* likely to question a fiduciary as a result of "insinuation anxiety," self-blame and fear of being judged foolish in one's questioning.

Additionally, disclosure might make a fiduciary more likely to disappoint reliance on the basis of their perception that disclosure licenses self-serving conduct.

Wilkinson-Ryan concludes by highlighting topics ripe for further research. She recommends research on the impact of role-related perceptions of fiduciaries on trust in fiduciary relationships. She notes also the need for research on the impact of sex stereotyping on role-related trust and perceptions of trustworthiness of fiduciaries. Finally, Wilkinson-Ryan suggests that it might be illuminating to place fiduciary relationships within psychological typologies of relationship. This would help us to better locate fiduciary relationships within the broader fabric of social and economic relations.

2 Personal Trust and Fiduciary Duties

Reflecting the belief that trust is consequential to the formation and flourishing of fiduciary relationships, it is also widely believed that fiduciary duties are – directly or indirectly – responsive to the value of trust. Thus, for example, it is said that a function of the duty of loyalty is to attract and sustain the trust of grantors and beneficiaries in their fiduciaries, and that the duty is justified in part by the inherent or instrumental value of trust. Similarly, it is said that trust is often reposed in fiduciaries on account of their superior expertise, and thus that the duty of care secures a trust-based expectation of competent judgment by fiduciaries. And one sees the suggestion from time to time that information-forcing rules help to ensure that trust in fiduciaries is warranted and that betrayals will be caught out and redressed.

These suggestions all have a ring of plausibility. But they are made without mind to finer-grained questions that we ought to be asking, and distinctions that we ought to be drawing. For example, to what extent does trust in fiduciaries suggest that the duty of loyalty should be articulated and enforced in conventional terms, as forbidding conflicts? To what extent might trust extend to expectations of good faith performance? Why, independently of threatened sanctions, might a fiduciary reasonably think she has trust-based reasons for proving worthy of a trust accepted? The chapters collected in Part II address these and other questions, sharpening our thinking about the normative significance of trust to fiduciary law.

In "Stakeholder Fiduciaries," Evan Criddle questions conventional wisdom about the fiduciary duty of loyalty. He does so by drawing attention to different ways parties to a fiduciary relationship form bonds of trust. Fiduciary relationships are, he explains, ordinarily established for the exclusive benefit of beneficiaries, in which case the bond of trust is an asymmetrical one under which the fiduciary is to act exclusively in the beneficiaries' interests. For relationships of this sort, the duty of loyalty reinforces trust by forbidding the fiduciary from entertaining his own interests or those of third parties when performing his mandate. But, Criddle observes, many fiduciary relationships have a different structure. In these relationships, the fiduciary has a lawful stake in the performance of his mandate, one that entitles him to a share in profits realized thereby. Here, fiduciary and beneficiary are allied to a common enterprise. Their bond of trust is one of solidarity, and in these circumstances the duty of loyalty reinforces solidarity in interest rather than exclusivity of interest.

Criddle's core aim is to establish that "stakeholder fiduciaries" are a properly distinctive subset of fiduciaries. According to Criddle, all stakeholder fiduciaries are alike in having a lawful stake in a common enterprise in which they are engaged in fiduciary administration for the common benefit of all beneficiaries, including themselves. The lawfulness of the stake held by fiduciaries is recognized, in part, through adjustment of fiduciary standards of conduct. Stakeholder fiduciaries are not required to forgo self-interest or to rigorously justify their actions. Rather, they are permitted to profit from their endeavors provided they maintain solidarity with other beneficiaries by ensuring that each receives their fair share. And courts are more willing to defer to the judgment of stakeholder fiduciaries in recognition of the bonding effect of their stake.

There are, Criddle says, a number of stakeholder fiduciary arrangements. General partnerships, structured through the reciprocal agency of partners, are just the most obvious example. Others include fiduciary relationships between joint venturers and members of other common enterprises. In each case, Criddle argues, the law is evidently concerned to vindicate trust and to promote loyalty, but it does so with mind to keeping the fiduciary to his commitment of solidarity; the fiduciary is permitted to share in profits in keeping with his stake but is forbidden from undermining the enterprise by taking more than he is due.

Trust is widely considered normatively salient to fiduciary loyalty. But it is also believed to be pertinent to expectations of good faith performance by fiduciaries. Indeed, it might be thought that trust in a fiduciary just is an expectation that the fiduciary will perform his mandate competently and in good faith, with *fides* being a matter of the fiduciary's commitment to the mandate. James Penner pursues questions about the relationship between trust, good faith and fiduciary duty in "Trustees and Agents Behaving Badly: When and How Is 'Bad Faith' Relevant?" In his chapter, Penner draws a number of striking conclusions. One is that the concept of "good faith" is empty; it merely signifies the absence of bad faith. Another is that good faith is not pertinent to fiduciary regulation of the exercise of powers by fiduciaries.

Penner begins by distinguishing good faith from other obligations that attend fiduciary relationships. Penner rejects the notion, once embedded in US corporate law, that good faith is a component of fiduciary loyalty. According to Penner, what are misleadingly framed "loyalty" norms can be tidily encapsulated within principles regulating conflicts. Penner also counsels against conflating good faith with the proper purposes doctrine. While a fiduciary might act for improper purposes in bad faith, regulation of propriety of purposes is aimed at ensuring adherence to purposes specified by a grantor for a mandate. Fiduciaries can and do act for improper purposes in ways having nothing to do with good (i.e., bad) faith, including mistake and inadvertence.

Having distinguished good faith from the foci of other modes of fiduciary regulation, Penner clarifies its significance. He argues that good faith is a matter of the motivation of fiduciaries, and in particular their honesty and integrity. According to Penner, good faith is presumed absent evidence of bad faith; that is, evidence that a fiduciary has been dishonest, exploitative, or corrupt. Finally, Penner notes that the legal consequences of bad faith by fiduciaries are hard to decipher because there are few cases in which liability has turned on it. However, he suggests that the law seems to respond to bad faith by limiting or denying compensation and by providing for summary removal or dismissal of fiduciaries.

Discussions of the significance of fiduciary norms to trust and vice versa sometimes trade on questionable claims about the norms' content and scope. Penner suggests that this is true of good faith; a chapter by Lionel Smith argues that it is also true of rules associated with the duty of loyalty. In "Conflict, Profit, Bias, Misuse of Power: Dimensions of Governance," Smith aims to disentangle and clarify these rules. Briefly, he suggests that private and public fiduciary relationships raise concerns about fidelity to the other-regarding purposes attached to discretionary powers. The trust requisite to these relationships is fostered by what is conventionally referred to as the "duty of loyalty." But there are several different rules that aid in ensuring abidance of other-regarding purposes, and distinctions between them are rarely kept in view.

Some accounts of the duty of loyalty suppose that it is exhausted by conflict rules. Smith urges greater care and precision in analysis. He notes that fiduciaries are subject to rules designed to prevent misuse of power – including the proper purposes doctrine – but explains that, accurately construed, they have nothing to do with conflicts or loyalty as such. They govern the exercise of all powers, fiduciary or otherwise, and are jurisdictional. Second, Smith suggests the need for greater clarity on conflict rules. He emphasizes, for instance, that it is not *being* in a conflict that is wrongful, but rather acting on a conflict or mishandling it. Third, Smith argues that it is important to distinguish no-profit from conflict rules, noting that the former is an attribution rule attaching to the occupation of a fiduciary role rather than a liability rule constraining the exercise of fiduciary powers. Finally, Smith situates conflict rules in the broader context of concern over bias in private and public administration. Smith shows that the law deploys a variety of methods to secure private and public trust in fiduciary administration, and that its primary focus is on ensuring adherence to the other-regarding purposes that fiduciaries are charged with pursuing.

3 Political Trust and Fiduciary Government

One of the more exciting recent developments in fiduciary theory has been scholarship exploring the idea of fiduciary government. Notions of trust promise to illuminate theories of fiduciary government in significant ways. Indeed, via doctrinal conceptions of public trust and the fiduciary Crown, the legal system has for many years sought to explain and justify the exercise of state authority through appeal to trust and fiduciary principles. But a range of questions remain underexplored. What is the relationship between political trust and authority? Are they mutually reinforcing, or in tension? What about the relationship between political trust and the rule of law? What roles do ideas of trust and fiduciary responsibility play in understanding the relationship between the state and Indigenous peoples? Does trust help us to grasp similarities and differences in the operation of fiduciary principles in private law and public law and, if so, how? The chapters collected in Part III of this volume explore these and other important questions.

Evan Fox-Decent's "Trust and Authority" examines the mutual relationship of trust and political authority. Fox-Decent begins by drawing a distinction between authorization, which he understands to be the process by which a decision maker comes to have authority, and authority itself, which for Fox-Decent is to be understood through reflection on the nature and effects of the legal power that a decision maker holds. Fox-Decent then applies this distinction to address an interpretive puzzle in the work of Thomas Hobbes. On the one hand, Hobbes famously thinks that people in a state of nature consent to subjection to sovereign power in exchange for peace and order; on the other hand, for Hobbes the power of the sovereign is to be exercised only within certain constraints set by the law of nature and is held on trust for the sovereign's subjects. How can these two seemingly conflicting positions be reconciled? For Fox-Decent, the answer lies in seeing that popular consent is a matter of authorization, and does not tell us everything, or even much, of what we need to know in order to understand the nature and limits of sovereign authority.

Deeper insight is, Fox-Decent thinks, found in Hobbes's account of mutual trust between sovereign and subject. The subject trusts the sovereign in the sense that the authorization brought about by popular consent is conditioned by a trusting expectation that the sovereign undertake and exercise that power for the purpose of securing peace and order for the benefit of subjects. The sovereign trusts the subject insofar as the subject enjoys liberty and is not ruled by coercive force alone. For Fox-Decent, this mutual trust helps to explain the nature and limitations of the sovereign's authority (it does not extend to exercising political power for purposes that are inconsistent with the trust in which it is held), including the conditions on the authority of the sovereign's law (governance by law is possible only where subjects enjoy liberty; slaves cannot be ruled by law, but only by brute force).

Fox-Decent concludes by arguing that the mutual trust necessary for the maintenance of political authority renders the sovereign's law gapless; even where rules and norms do not constrain the sovereign's power, the implications of mutual trust provide such constraints, demanding that power be exercised consistent with the trust in which it is held.

Kirsty Gover and Nicole Roughan explore the relation of the state and Indigenous peoples in "The Fiduciary Crown: The Private Duties of Public Actors in State–Indigenous Relationships." States around the world with a colonial legacy are grappling with this relation, working through the difficult questions of how to conceptualize it and to realize its political, moral and legal implications. Gover and Roughan take issue with the view of Evan Fox-Decent and others that the relationship of the settler state and its Indigenous peoples reveals the state in an archetypal public fiduciary role. They instead argue that it this relationship is better characterized as a private law relationship. In defending this claim, Gover and Roughan draw on leading decisions from Canada and New Zealand in which private law aspects of the relationship of the state and Indigenous peoples have been emphasized.

Alongside Gover and Roughan's interpretive argument is another of a more overtly political character. Conceptualizing the state–Indigenous relationship as a private law relationship enables an argument to be made that the legally recognized interests that Indigenous peoples bring to that relationship are insulated from third-party claims and competing public interests in the way that is typical of the protection afforded to beneficiary interests in private law. In public law, the balancing of Indigenous interests alongside such competing claims and interests might be achieved through principles such as proportionality or public policy. In private law, this is often thought to be impermissible. Gover and Roughan do not think that a private law characterization is entirely satisfactory. Rather, they think that the relationship is best conceived as a matter for international or "interpublic" law. But they see the private law characterization as a valuable staging post on the road to the international characterization that they think will best serve the political goals of Indigenous recognition, self-determination and sovereignty.

In "Political (Dis)Trust and Fiduciary Government," Paul Miller brings together two key ideas in modern political thought: political trust and fiduciary government. Much has been written about these ideas, but considerably less about the way they interact and whether indeed they are distinct.

Miller begins by reflecting on the idea of fiduciary government. He distinguishes "thick" from "thin" accounts of this idea. Thick accounts of fiduciary government lay substantial normative weight on the idea; for example, for Evan Fox-Decent, the idea of fiduciary government solves the problem of political authority. Thin accounts of fiduciary government make more modest demands of the idea. Miller's own thin account suggests that fiduciary government articulates conditions under which the conduct of government is truly representative; this account rests on Miller's more general theory of fiduciary relationships as relationships of representation.

Having clarified his thin conception of fiduciary government, Miller develops a conception of political trust to serve his analysis. Miller draws on the work of Phillip Pettit to argue that political trust is best understood as *particularized*, in the sense of being directed at a certain focal point, as well as *objective*, in the sense of being more a matter of externally manifested action than internal affective or cognitive states. Miller argues that particularized and objective political trust does distinct work in understanding public life that cannot be done by the idea of fiduciary government. Put briefly, Miller argues that political trust illuminates understanding of the political conditions and activity on which fiduciary government depends. That said, Miller also notes that the demands of fiduciary government enable the state and its officials to prove trustworthy in ways that promote political trust.

Miller concludes by introducing a seemingly counterintuitive proposition: that moderate citizen distrust in government is a desirable state of affairs. For Miller, the idea of fiduciary government helps to understand this proposition; citizen distrust tends to accompany active citizen engagement in democratic processes by which government is held accountable in light of fiduciary standards of representation. Bringing political trust and distrust together with the idea of fiduciary government thus grounds a vision of democratic and representative government that tells us much about where political systems the world over are currently falling short.

In "Trust, Distrust and the Rule of Law," Gerald Postema, like Miller, focuses on the working of trust and distrust in political life. Postema begins by introducing what he calls the "Trust Challenge" to the rule of law. To the extent that the rule of law depends on citizens holding each other and public officials accountable under law, the rule of law seems to entail a measure of citizen distrust of each other and of government, all of which seems inconsistent with the intuitive thought that the rule of law depends on political trust. Postema sets out to "draw the sting" of the Trust Challenge to the rule of law by showing that accountability is not inconsistent with political trust.

Postema spends some time developing a taxonomy of different types of trust. Among other things, he distinguishes between trust that entails a robust recognitional element and that which lacks this strong relational character. He also isolates what he calls "proleptic" trust, which is manifested in conduct inviting the sort of trust-responsive behavior that might then generate robust recognitional trust, distrust, which entails an intentional withholding of reliance, and mistrust, which is tentative and cautious but all the same open to trust-responsive behavior. Postema then moves to impersonal settings, where relationships are mediated by institutions and other frameworks. The operation of trust in such settings is elusive, running into system confidence on one side, and robust recognitional trust on the other. Nonetheless, Postema identifies civic and political trust as distinctive types of impersonal trust, civic trust arising when citizens deal with other in civil society, and political trust arising when citizens deal with government or government officials in institutionally mediated settings.

For Postema, overcoming the Trust Challenge is partly a matter of seeing that a practice of mutual accountability holding is a way of expressing civic trust, at least in a society where civic trust is otherwise sufficiently present. And against the background of a climate of civic trust, holding government to account is also a way of expressing institutionally mediated trust or, at least, a mistrust that is open to trust-responsive behavior on the part of government and public officials. At the same time, holding government and officials to account can entail the sort of proleptic trust that invites trust responsiveness that, in turn, can generate more robust and even recognitional forms of trust. Just like Miller, Postema offers us a compelling vision of civic and political engagement in which trust and trust responsiveness reinforce each other through mutual accountability practices and a certain public culture.

4 Trust and Fiduciary Law in Context

General theoretical work on trust and fiduciary law promises to inform our understanding of particular legal institutions and practices. In the case of some of these, there is already a substantial literature: take, for example, the literature on interpersonal trust and the institution of contract, or writings dealing with the interplay of contracts and fiduciary relationships. Other institutions and practices have been studied less. For example, the operation of interpersonal trust in express trusts has been seldom explored. And the ways in which interpersonal trust is mediated by forms such as the corporation deserve more attention. The burden of Part IV is to take up these sorts of questions about trust and fiduciary law in its institutional and social context. As the chapters collected here demonstrate, reflection on trust and fiduciary law in context prompts insights into the interaction of law's coercive order with the virtues, the interplay of legal and social norms and the relationship of law and morality.

Rob Atkinson's "For-Profit Managers as Public Fiduciaries" explores the fiduciary responsibility of the managers of for-profit organizations in light of three traditions of Western political philosophy: Lockean liberalism, utilitarianism and neoclassical republicanism. Starting with Lockean liberalism, Atkinson challenges the notion that this tradition's view of the fiduciary responsibility of for-profit managers is exhausted by Milton Friedman's assertion that the social responsibility of a business is to increase its profits. Atkinson argues that it in fact delivers a much more demanding understanding of fiduciary obligation, including responsibilities not to harm others and to support just government through taxes, as well as the cultivation of virtues fitting to the discharge of such responsibilities.

Atkinson then turns his attention to the utilitarianism most commonly associated with Jeremy Bentham and (more recently) classical economics. In this tradition, the contours of fiduciary for-profit management are differently understood and arguably more onerous than in the Lockean tradition. For example, Atkinson argues that in the Benthamite tradition, for-profit managers are required to pay such taxes as are required to optimize the production of desired goods, take into account the preferences of consumers when engaging in market transactions and refrain from discrimination in the provision of goods and services. Moreover, Atkinson argues that a utilitarian perspective subordinates private property and the interests of for-profit organizations to democratically expressed majoritarian preferences. The fiduciary responsibilities of for-profit managers must be adjusted accordingly.

Finally, Atkinson explores his preferred tradition, that of neoclassical republicanism. Building on previous work, Atkinson argues that in this tradition, for-profit managers are required to strive for the common good in everything they do. In this sense, they are public fiduciaries. Atkinson goes on to offer some thoughts on how a neoclassical republican state might ensure that for-profit managers are equipped to perform their roles well; he concludes that the key lies in the sort of liberal education that universities are especially well suited to providing. The academics who train professionals and managers are therefore critical to the realization of Atkinson's neoclassical vision of public fiduciaries striving for the common good.

In "Fiduciary Law and the Preservation of Trust in Business Relationships," Brian Broughman, Elizabeth Pollman and Gordon Smith consider the justification of fiduciary obligations in business relationships. With their eye to the start-up economy, they focus in particular on the relationship between entrepreneur and investor.

Broughman, Pollman and Smith begin by presenting their take on the notion that fiduciary law operates to guarantee the trustworthiness of fiduciaries. In law and economics, this idea is connected to the thought that fiduciary law enables parties to commercial contracts to minimize or avoid transaction costs. Broughman, Pollman and Smith suggest that fiduciary law adds value in another way as well: it enables parties to achieve desired contractual outcomes in circumstances of contractual incompleteness without signaling that they distrust each other. Broughman, Pollman and Smith note that the very act of drafting and negotiating a contract that seeks contractual guarantees of other-regarding conduct might signal distrust. Fiduciary law allows parties to avoid sending these signals by providing extracontractual security for expectations of other-regarding conduct. In this way, the fact that fiduciary law is imposed on contract parties by the state is one of its virtues.

Broughman, Pollman and Smith conclude by pointing out that fiduciary law is not a complete answer for a party who seeks other-regarding behavior from his counterparty. In the sort of horizontal business relationship that arises where an entrepreneur deals with an investor, conflicting interests are such that fiduciary law cannot guarantee other-regarding conduct in the way that it can in, say, a traditional agent–principal relationship. In these circumstances of relative complexity, fiduciary law is itself incomplete and must be supplemented by other risk-minimization strategies. Here, trust comes back into view. For Broughman, Pollman and Smith, the overall picture is one in which contract, fiduciary law and trust operate together to reduce uncertainty in commercial settings.

The final chapter of the book, "How Much Trust Do Trusts Require?," by Thomas Gallanis, looks at the extent to which the legal institution of the trust assumes or demands that beneficiaries and settlors repose trust in trustees. Gallanis focuses his attention on express trusts under US law, in which the trustee voluntarily undertakes her office.

Gallanis identifies three features of the trust that seem to demand significant trust in trustees. First, the trust separates out management from beneficial ownership of trust assets, and places responsibility for the former with the trustee and the enjoyment of the latter with beneficiaries. In this way, the trust generates problems of "agency costs"; the trustee's management of the trust assets is, to some extent, beyond the direct knowledge and control of beneficiaries and the settlor. Secondly, in many US trusts today, beneficiaries' interests are contingent on trustees' discretion, and indeed in some cases trustees are authorized to decant trust assets in ways that may interfere with and even extinguish those interests. Thirdly, US trusts often make provision for beneficiaries who are unascertained at the moment of the trust's creation, and in state law there has been a recent trend toward enabling settlors to establish perpetual trusts, in which unascertained beneficiaries may figure to a much greater extent.

For Gallanis, the characteristics of express trusts that call for trust are counterbalanced by further characteristics that promote or support the trustworthiness of trustees such that trust actually need not be reposed. Gallanis notes that duties of loyalty and care in trust law are relatively stringent compared with, say, the duties owed by directors and officers under US corporate law. American trust law specifies a "sole interest" rather than a "best interest" standard of loyalty and does not include anything like a business judgment rule. Furthermore, American trust law requires trustees to furnish beneficiaries with information about the trust and its administration, which helps to minimize agency costs. Traditionally, this duty has been conceived as mandatory, but Gallanis notes that in some states the duty operates as a default only. Finally, Gallanis discusses the use of trust protectors to monitor trustees and hold them to settlor expectations. Gallanis concludes that American trust law seems to move in two directions: on the one hand, assuming or calling for trust in trustees, and, on the other hand, trying to minimize the need for such trust.

* * *

While it has long been supposed that trust and fiduciary law are related in important ways, it has taken this volume to show precisely how fiduciary law and trust are, or can be, mutually sustaining. The expansive and multifarious perspectives provided by the chapters collected here show just how complex and contingent are the connections between fiduciary law and trusting attitudes and behaviors. Private and public fiduciary administration call for trust of various kinds – personal, civic and political. They place trust at risk and therefore ironically promise to deepen it through the trust-responsive behavior of fiduciaries. And yet, and without any contradiction, we have learned that fiduciary law can support trustworthiness in fiduciary administration while also supporting constructive distrust toward fiduciaries. All of this just goes to show that the connections between trust and fiduciary law defy simplistic analysis and reward analytical subtlety and nuance. Our contributors have proven as much in their analyses, and it is a testament to the genuine intellectual challenge of the topic and the depth of insight that our authors have provided that this volume may be counted as a first installment in charting the mutual bearing of trust and fiduciary law as a matter of ethics, politics, economics and law.

PART I

Personal Trust and Fiduciary Relationships

1

Fiduciary Grounds and Reasons

PAUL FAULKNER

The legal wisdom of judges, Paul Miller argues, takes the fiduciary relationship to be primary: for there to be fiduciary duties, there first needs to be a fiduciary relationship to ground these duties. Miller then offers the following characterization of the fiduciary relationship:

> A fiduciary relationship is one in which one party (the fiduciary) exercises discretionary power over the significant practical interests of another (the beneficiary).[1]

Two terms of this definition have specific legal meanings. First, the power exercised is fiduciary power, or power derived from the legal personality of the beneficiary; 'fiduciary power consists in the substitutive exercise of legal capacity'[2]. For example, as a legal personality, the beneficiary has the legal capacity to enter into contracts, hold property, make decisions that concern their welfare and so on; and the fiduciary can then do these things *on behalf of* the beneficiary (where the scope of the fiduciary relationship determines what fiduciary powers the fiduciary acquires). Second, the significance of such practical interests is not a matter of their significance to the beneficiary but a matter of the interest being recognized as the object of a legal power; it is a matter of legal significance. However, ordinarily these coincide: those interests the law recognizes as significant – the right to contract, property and control over decisions concerning one's physical welfare, for instance – should be significant to the beneficiary. Other points to observe about this definition include the following. Fiduciary power is over the practical interests, legally defined, of the beneficiary, which may range broadly over matters of personality, welfare and rights pertaining to persons. Tied to the practical interests of the beneficiary, fiduciary power is thereby relational: it is held with respect to a particular beneficiary. And the exercise of this power is discretionary in that the fiduciary is at liberty to make those decisions they judge to be best for the beneficiary.

Fiduciary duties, legal wisdom has it, are grounded in the fiduciary relationship. And the fiduciary power theory, which I take as my starting point, proposes that this relationship is constituted by the exercise of transferred legal powers. This chapter then pursues two questions: (1) what is it in the fiduciary relationship that grounds this transfer of legal power? And, given this grounding, (2) what kind of reason (e.g. practical, moral or otherwise) does the fiduciary then have to act on behalf of the beneficiary?

[1] Paul Miller, 'The Fiduciary Relationship' in Andrew Gold and Paul Miller (eds.), *Philosophical Foundations of Fiduciary Law* (Oxford University Press 2014), 69.

[2] Ibid., 71.

1 The Grounds of Fiduciary Authority

Fiduciary powers are grounded in fiduciary relationships. It follows, Miller argues, that different ways of forming these relationships amount to 'modes of authorization' of these powers; and he identifies 'three principle modes of authorization: mutual consent, unilateral undertaking, and legal decree'.[3]

In the next section, I am interested in exploring the grounds of mutual consent, where consent gives one answer to Question (1) above. In Section 3, I consider what reasons these grounds give for the fiduciary acting on the beneficiary's behalf, where this is Question (2). In Section 4, I then consider how the fiduciary relationship might be grounded on 'unilateral undertaking, and legal decree', which gives an alternative answer to Question (1); and consider what reasons these alternative grounds then support in answer to Question (2). In both cases, I identify trust as an essential component of these grounds and reasons. Section 5 concludes with a discussion of trust and loyalty, where loyalty has been taken to be 'a hallmark of the fiduciary relationship'.[4]

2 Consent

A beneficiary B consenting to a fiduciary F's φ-ing requires, on David Owens's account of consent, that B '(intentionally) communicate the intention of hereby making it the case that someone [F] would not wrong you [B] by φ-ing'.[5] Comment is needed on various parts of this definition.

First, consent is something that needs to *be expressed.* It is not enough that the beneficiary intends to authorize the fiduciary. In this respect, consenting is like promising or apologizing: the requisite internal state is not enough. You do not promise someone that you will do something just by intending to do it; and you do not apologize for doing something just by feeling sorry that you did it. Having this intention and this remorseful attitude are necessary for the sincere promise and apology, but they do not amount to either without expression. Moreover, the conjunction of the right internal state and the other party's knowledge of it is equally not enough. It is equally not enough that the beneficiary intends to authorize the fiduciary and the fiduciary knows this. Again, the comparison with promising and apologizing is apposite. You might feel sorry for what you did to me, and I might know that you feel this way but still want you to apologize. And you might intend to do something and I might know that you have this intention, but this does not amount to a promise. In this respect, Joseph Raz gives the example of John wanting to know whether he can get a lift into town with Harry tomorrow, and Harry telling him, 'I am almost certain to offer you a lift to town tomorrow. In the circumstances it would be far wiser for you to rely on me rather than make alternative arrangements, but remember I do not

[3] Ibid., 74.

[4] Andrew Gold, 'The Loyalties of Fiduciary Law' in Andrew Gold and Paul Miller (eds.), *Philosophical Foundations of Fiduciary Law* (Oxford University Press 2014), 176. See also Stephen Galoob and Ethan J. Leib, 'Fiduciary Loyalty, Inside and Out' 92 *Southern California Law Review.*

[5] David Owens, *Shaping the Normative Landscape* (Oxford University Press 2012), 166.

promise anything, I am merely advising you.'[6] In this case, John gets to know Harry's intention from Harry's advice, but there is explicitly no promise made. Similarly, knowledge that the beneficiary intends to authorize the fiduciary is not enough for consent; any attempt by the fiduciary to play a fiduciary role on the basis of this knowledge would be premature and illegitimate.

Second, consent requires not mere expression but *intentional expression*. We can express our beliefs and other mental states in different ways. 'Expression' can be used as a general term for the different ways that something can be made manifest; and it can be taken as a verb of intentional action. Richard Moran calls these respectively the *impersonal* and *personal* senses of expression.[7] Impersonal when one's mental state is made manifest in some way, say through one's behaviour, but is not expressed to anyone. Personal when one intentionally expresses one's mental state to someone. For example, you impersonally express your belief that it is raining when you pick up your umbrella on exiting the house; and you personally express the same belief when you tell your housemate as you leave, 'It's raining outside.' What consent, along with promises and apologies, requires is personal expression: the *intentional* expression of one's attitudes *to another*.

Insofar as consent requires the intentional expression of a consenter's attitudes, it should be included in Elizabeth Anscombe's list of actions that can only be intentional, which includes telephoning, greeting, groping, signing, paying, selling, hiring, marrying and contracting.[8] For Anscombe, saying that these actions can only be intentional means that these descriptions apply to the agent's actions only insofar as the agent is aware of what they are doing under this description. Anscombe then puts this in terms of the dictum from Aquinas that '[p]ractical knowledge is "the cause of what it understands"'[9]. The claim here is that the agent's practical knowledge – their knowledge of what they are doing – is necessary for them doing that thing. One cannot, for instance, marry someone without knowing that one is marrying someone. Marrying is not like talking in one's sleep. Similarly, consenting to someone's doing something – this is not something that can be done unwittingly. The epistemic relation here, Anscombe observes, is not that of 'speculative knowledge' such as our knowledge of external matters, seeing other parties greet one another or observing a marriage, for instance.[10] Again, the participant's knowledge is a constitutive element of the action itself.

Third, insofar as consent requires one to knowingly express one's attitudes *to* another, it *requires a communicative act*. How consent is communicated will be various, and, Owens notes, consent can even be communicated by silence.[11] But a paradigmatic formalization of the communicative act would be a declaration such as

6 Joseph Raz, 'Voluntary Obligations and Normative Powers' 46 *Aristotelian Society Supplementary Volume* 79, 99.
7 Richard Moran, *The Exchange of Words: Speech, Testimony and Intersubjectivity* (Oxford University Press 2018), 85.
8 G. E. M. Anscombe, *Intention* (Blackwell 1957), 85.
9 Ibid., 87.
10 Ibid.
11 Owens, 165.

'I hereby consent for you to act on my behalf' or 'I hereby authorize you to act on my behalf'. Of course, merely uttering the words is not enough for declaration, since one could do this unwittingly in one's sleep. Nor would merely uttering the words (awake and) intentionally be enough, since one could do this as an exercise in pronunciation. Rather, what is needed for declaration is that this utterance be an intentional communicative act addressed to someone – the person addressed as 'you'. Practical self-knowledge is necessary here: the beneficiary must know that the utterance is one of consenting. And in this respect, the beneficiary enjoys illocutionary authority, or the authority to decide that this is what the utterance is, and that it is not, say, a mere exercise in pronunciation. This authority is shown through the 'hereby': in this declarative form, consent is an illocutionary act that is enough, in normal circumstances, for its own truth. Similarly, it is enough for a promise to be made for a promisor to declare 'I hereby promise . . .' and enough for an apology to be made for a speaker to declare 'I hereby apologise . . .'. Thus Moran observes that a mark of the illocutionary 'is the possibility of naming the action in the very performance of it, with the inclusion of the demonstrative "hereby" before the performative verb'.[12]

One question raised is, then, what gets bundled into 'in normal circumstances'? Here Moran offers a quite particular answer. On his account of the illocutionary, while the speaker has the authority to determine that their speech act has a particular illocutionary force – that of a promise, an apology, an authorization, etc. – this authority is nevertheless limited in a specific way. This authority, as Moran presents it, manifests two freedoms. The freedom to confer a certain illocutionary status on their words; and the freedom in doing this to thereby make oneself subject to the freedom of another. However, this latter freedom, and so too the former, presupposes that the addressee recognizes the illocutionary act for what it is. Thus, no consent has been given, no apology or promise made, if the addressee thinks that the utterance is merely an exercise in pronunciation. It follows that in order for the 'hereby' of the illocution to be true there must be such recognition. This recognition is an essential component of the normal circumstances that define the communicative exchange. Thus Moran, who talks about asserting but could have equally been talking about any other illocutionary act, argues that '[f]or the act of asserting . . . to take place the two parties have to both understand and "know together" what it is that they are doing, for this shared knowledge is the formal cause of the reality of the act of illocution itself'.[13] The appeal here is to Anscombe's account of intentional action: just as the description of an arm raising as an act of greeting someone presupposes some knowledge – in this case, the arm raiser's knowledge that they are greeting someone – so too the description of an utterance as the act of asserting presupposes some knowledge. But in this case, the knowledge that is presupposed is a piece of *shared knowledge* comprising the speaker's knowing what they are doing in uttering and the audience's recognizing what the speaker is so doing. As Moran notes here, getting the right account of this shared knowledge has proved philosophically

[12] Moran, 134.
[13] Ibid., 167.

difficult.[14] But the idea of shared knowledge is fairly simple. In the particular case of consent, it involves two individual pieces of knowledge, *which depend for their existence on each other.*[15] That is, it involves (a) the beneficiary knowing what they commit themselves to in uttering 'I hereby consent . . .'. For this knowledge to be possible, there must be uptake by the fiduciary, which requires the fiduciary recognizing the illocutionary act for what it is, and so (b) the fiduciary knowing that it is the giving of consent. In a communicative exchange, 'in normal circumstances' both bits of knowledge will be present and so too will be the shared knowledge.

While shared knowledge might characterize successful communicative acts, an objection might be raised to making an addressee's recognition a necessary condition for an illocutionary act, or the truth of the 'hereby' claim. To think about this objection, consider the following case. Suppose that Jane consents to Peter taking a shortcut on his way to work that involves walking across her front garden. But unbeknownst to Jane when they had the telephone conversation about Peter doing just this, his attention was entirely occupied with the ongoing misdemeanours of his children so that the conversation finished with his having no idea whether or not Jane agreed to his request. Nevertheless, Peter proceeds to act as if consent has been given. In this case, does Peter wrong Jane? If there is a wronging, then consent has not been given, which means Moran is right to claim that uptake is necessary for consent. And if not, then not. Now hopefully it is fairly clear that Peter does something wrong. He shouldn't proceed to act as if he has consent when he doesn't know whether or not he has it. The question is then whether or not the wrong that Peter does in walking across Jane's garden wrongs Jane. Suppose that Jane comes to know that Peter was thoroughly distracted when they had their conversation so that he doesn't know what she said and is walking across her garden regardless. In this case, Jane will feel not merely that Peter is doing the wrong thing but also that Peter is not sufficiently respecting her – that she is being wronged. (How sharp is this feeling will depend, of course, on the nature of their relations.) And unless wrongings only come into being on being known, this suggests that Peter was wronging Jane all along; it was just that Jane was not aware of it. On this way of looking at things, Moran is right: insofar as Peter is wronging Jane in walking across her lawn, this must be because Jane has not in fact given Peter consent to do just this; one should not talk of Jane's having given consent to this while Peter is ignorant of what was communicated. And insofar as we do think of their conversation as involving Jane giving her permission, this is just because we take the perspective of the successful communicator and so 'hear' Jane's utterance as

[14] Ibid. P. Grice, 'Meaning' in P. Grice (ed.), *Studies in the Way of Words* (Harvard University Press 1957), suggested making A's intention the object of B's knowledge, i.e. B knows that A intends that B believe. Further, nested iterations were added by followers of Grice, e.g. S. R. Schiffer, *Meaning* (Clarendon Press 1972). David Lewis, *Convention – A Philosophical Study* (Harvard University Press 1969), used a notion of *common knowledge* that idealizes such nesting. Moran rejects this strategy of appealing to nested states and instead appeals to P. F. Strawson, 'Intention and Convention in Speech Acts' 73 *Philosophical Review* 439, 456), and the idea that the intentions behind an illocutionary act must be 'wholly overt or essentially avowable'.

[15] Thus Moran argues that the 'hereby', which expresses the speaker's illocutionary authority, is nevertheless dependent 'on the participants' shared knowledge'. Moran, 189.

the illocutionary act that it is. It is this necessity of recognition that then makes consent thoroughly second personal, since its being given 'simultaneously and reciprocally involves the perspective of addressing and being addressed'.[16]

Where the fiduciary relationship is established by mutual consent – the beneficiary performing some illocutionary act such as 'I hereby consent for you to act on my behalf', which is addressed to and recognized by some fiduciary – the fiduciary relationship is then grounded by second-personal facts. The next question – (2) above – is, when it is grounded in this second-personal way, what reason does the fiduciary thereby have for acting on behalf of the beneficiary?

3 Consent, Trust and Fiduciary Reasons

Insofar as fiduciary power is held relative to a specific beneficiary, the reasons that bear on a fiduciary's decisions should concern the beneficiary. (Decisions made on the basis of what lies in the fiduciary's self-interest are prescribed by conflict rules.) Two kinds of reasons can be identified. Consider, for example, a fiduciary's decision as to whether or not to sell the beneficiary's house (supposing that the fiduciary has a mandate to do this). First, the beneficiary might give the fiduciary reason to sell by referring to considerations of how the sale will benefit them (the beneficiary). Insofar as this set of considerations is a reason for the fiduciary to conclude that selling the house is the best thing to do, it would equally be a reason for anyone to reach this conclusion; a third party could also reach the same conclusion on their basis. Equally, the fact that these considerations are named by the beneficiary is irrelevant: insofar as these considerations support the decision to sell the house, they would do so if the beneficiary said nothing and the fiduciary lighted on these considerations themselves. These considerations thereby specify *third-personal reasons*. Second, and by contrast, suppose these third-personal reasons are perfectly balanced, neither favouring selling nor not, but the beneficiary gives the fiduciary reason to sell by requesting, or telling, the fiduciary to do just this. In this case, the fiduciary has a reason to sell only because and insofar as the beneficiary requests, or commands, this. The reason thereby exists only because this illocution has been made and recognized as legitimate. Reasons of this kind are *second personal* insofar as the reason involves the fiduciary and beneficiary standing in an 'I–you' or 'you–I' relation such that each might think 'I am selling for you' or 'you are selling for me', rather than the third-personal variant 'the fiduciary is selling for the beneficiary' (where neither might recognize the truth of this statement). Now insofar as the fiduciary relationship is grounded on consent, which transfers legal authority by virtue of certain second-personal facts holding, the natural assumption is that the reasons this ground gives are equally second personal.

Suppose, then, that a beneficiary B consents to a fiduciary F acting on his behalf. If this consent itself is to give F a reason to act in a certain way, then this is something that must be contained within the *knowledge that is shared* in a successful authorization. This knowledge is twofold. It is the knowledge that the communicative act is one

[16] James Conant and Sebastian Rödl, 'Introduction' 42 *Philosophical Topics* 1, 9.

of authorizing or giving consent; and it is the knowledge of the consent that is given. In the last section, we focused on the former piece of knowledge; the present question concerns the latter – the knowledge of the consent given. On Owens's account, this latter piece of knowledge is not knowledge of any obligation, which is to say it is not knowledge of any reasons for action. Consent is purely a *permissive* act; it is not prescriptive: it demands nothing of either the consentee or the consenter. Rather, it merely removes some action from the category of a wronging. Consider Owens's case of dentistry.[17] Consenting to dentistry does not oblige you to have dentistry. And consenting to dentistry does not impose any obligation on your dentist; having got your consent, the dentist is not obliged to practice dentistry on you. It is simply OK if the dentist proceeds to do so, where the knowledge of the consent given, on this account, is knowledge of what it is OK to proceed to do. Consenting can be contrasted with promising here, which is prescriptive and imposes obligations on both promisor and promisee. Consider Raz's case of Harry and John, described above, but suppose Harry *does promise* John a lift into town tomorrow. This puts Harry under an obligation: the obligation to do what he promised to do (excepting special circumstances – the need to attend to a sick child etc.). But it also creates an obligation for John: the obligation to release Harry from his promise if a lift is no longer wanted or needed. For suppose that Harry dutifully drives to John's flat to pick him up only to find that John got a lift into town earlier with someone else. Harry would feel rightfully put out, and were John to explain his absence by saying 'that Harry has promised him a lift', it would be seen as no excuse at all. Promising thus generates prescriptions on both parties. Consenting, on Owen's account, does so on neither.

An immediate objection here is that in consenting to dentistry, and booking an appointment, you do put yourself under obligation. This is shown by the practice of most dental surgeries of fining non-attendance. In response, Owens would argue that one needs to distinguish between the operation of consent and effect of choice, since both can change the normative landscape. For example, consider a boxing match. Having *chosen* to enter the ring, the boxer cannot blame his opposition for punching him. And the opponent is not responsible for any battering or knockout blow the boxer might suffer (provided play is fair and within the rules). Such a bruising is a predictable consequence of the boxer's choice. Choice, like consent, can then change the normative landscape since a subject can be held responsible for the consequences of the choices they made. The obligation to attend the dental appointment, and so undergo dentistry, is then a consequence of the choice of booking the appointment to this end; it is not a consequence of the consent.

Another feature of the knowledge of the consent given is that this knowledge can be dynamic because what is consented to can change. Consent, unlike a promise, can be revoked. And the revoking of consent does not wrong the consentee since consenting to their φ-ing is not a promise that they can φ. Owens's discussion of sex is illustrative here.[18] First, Owens identifies a notion of *bare wronging* – or a wrong in itself – where the action of φ-ing is a bare wronging if it satisfies two conditions: (1) it is possible for

[17] Owens, 165.
[18] Ibid., 177.

there to be a φ-ing that remains a (serious) wrong even though it has no consequences and (2) the wrongness of φ-ing contributes to the normative significance of any consequences that follow it. Breach of a promise is bare wronging. And so too, Owens argues, is rape. This is because, satisfying (1), it is possible for there to be a rape with no consequences – if the victim were unconscious, never found out or even suspected what happened, there was no physical trauma, the rapist died or otherwise disappeared shortly after, etc. – that remains a serious wrong. And satisfying (2), were the victim to discover what had happened, a multitude of consequences would follow whose severity would be informed by the fact that the act suffered was one of rape. What consent to sex does is that it stops the sex from being rape:

> Consent to sexual relations is a paradigm case of an exercise of the power of consent. Merely by intentionally communicating the intention of hereby authorizing you to have sex with me, I ensure that you do not commit the egregious wrong of rape, whatever other wrong you may do me.[19]

What needs to be added to this proposal is that consent can be revoked at will. It follows that consent to sexual relations is not consent to any form of sexual relations. Rather, it is consent to just those sexual relations that each party consents to. There is prescription here, not that the sex should be a certain way but that it should not move beyond what is mutually consented to, where this is something that can be both negotiated and changeable. Most sex does not involve safe words, but the model is the right one. It follows, given that it is the absence of consent that makes a bare wronging, that bare wrongings are not limited to rape. This is not to argue that rape is not a bare wronging or that Owens's two conditions don't identify bare wrongings but to argue that this class of wrongs is more extensive than rape.

Returning to the fiduciary relationship, the consent that establishes the fiduciary relationship, and with it the transfer of powers to the fiduciary, can be compared in one way to the consent given when signing a form at the dental surgery and in another way to the consent found in sexual relations. The first similarity holds because while it can still be revoked at any time, once it is given, there is thereafter a standing presumption of consent (a presumption that can be contractually supported by, for example, early termination penalties). Consent is not an ongoing negotiation because the fiduciary relationship is not a relationship between equals; in authorizing the fiduciary, the beneficiary consents to be dependent in specified ways. The second similarity holds because there is something of a prescription to the consent given. Not that the fiduciary should be sensitive to the potentially changing shape of consent but that the fiduciary should be sensitive to what lies in the best interests of the beneficiary, where the consent is given on the mutual understanding that there can be the presumption that this is how the fiduciary will proceed. These properties of the fiduciary relationship do not follow simply from the act of consent that establishes it. Consent need not create a relationship of inequality (it need not do so in sex, for instance). And it need not entail that the consentee have any further thoughts about the consenter (having got Jane's agreement that he can walk across her lawn, Peter

[19] Ibid.

doesn't need further worry about Jane's attitudes; he need merely pay attention if she withdraws this permission). But this is to say that when it comes to specifying the reasons that consent determines, consent can only be part of the picture. What needs to be further introduced is the fact that the relationship established through consent is one of trust.

That the fiduciary relationship is one of trust is something that is presumed in consent: authorization would only be given with this presumption in place. The characteristics of dependence and being other regarding in a certain way then follow not from consent itself but from the trusting nature of the relationship that consent establishes. The trust at issue here, like consent, is second personal in character. Let me now elaborate these two claims.

First, that the fiduciary relationship is one of trust. At a minimum trust is simply 'the willingness of one party to rely on another to act in certain ways'.[20] Trust is that attitude towards this dependence, or reliance, that explains its willingness. And the simplest attitude that could explain a willingness to rely would be belief. Thus, trust can be no more than a positive belief about outcome.[21] However, this rather thin – or, as I've called it, 'predictive' – sense of trust is inadequate for the present context.[22] To illustrate this, suppose that a fiduciary consistently abuses their power but that in this case, their interests and those of the beneficiary converge on selling the beneficiary's house, with the beneficiary needing the sale to raise money for care provision and the fiduciary wanting to profit. In such a case, if the beneficiary was aware of the history of their relations and the fiduciary's present interests, the beneficiary might believe there would be no hesitancy in the fiduciary pushing through the sale of their house and so rely on them to do this. But there would be no trust in this case (even if there is 'encapsulated interest')[23]. Rather, this is a case where the beneficiary might feel betrayed at having their vulnerability exploited, where the presence of this reactive attitude then marks the breakdown of trust. Trust in this thicker sense – which I've called 'affective' and which is the only notion of trust that will be employed hereafter – then involves a normative expectation, or an expectation placed on the trusted.[24] It is not merely a subjective expectation or belief about outcome but the expectation of a certain outcome. In relying on the fiduciary to sell their house, the beneficiary will expect it of the fiduciary that they will do this and do it because they need the house sold, which is to say for the reason of the beneficiary's benefit (and not for personal profit). On this proposal, one party X trusts another party Y to φ when X relies on φ-ing and expects it of Y that Y will φ because of this reliance. This expectation characteristic of trust then renders reliance willing because the attitude of trust is an

[20] Bernard Williams, *Truth and Truthfulness* (Princeton University Press 2002), 88.

[21] And in this respect, to the extent that legislation can support belief, it can engender trust (in this predictive sense). See Paul Faulkner, 'Finding Trust in Government' *Journal of Social Philosophy*; O. O'Neill, *A Question of Trust* (Cambridge University Press 2002), Frank B. Cross, 'Law and Trust' McCombs School of Business, Research Paper Series 1.

[22] Paul Faulkner, *Knowledge on Trust* (Oxford University Press 2011), 145.

[23] Where this identifies a form of predictive trust, see R. Hardin, *Trust and Trustworthiness* (Russell Sage Foundation 2002), 2.

[24] Faulkner, *Knowledge on Trust*, 146.

optimistic attitude, or a way of thinking well of the trusted. So in expecting it of the trusted that they will act in a certain way for a certain reason, the trusting party presumes, other things being equal, that the trusted will be moved by this reason and so act in this way. This presumption about outcome then rationalizes reliance in the same way that a belief about outcome does; it explains the willingness of reliance.

That the fiduciary relationship, when it is based on consent, is one of trust can then be seen by considering the expectation that the beneficiary has of the fiduciary when consenting to the fiduciaries acting on their behalf. Specifically, consider the beneficiary consenting to the fiduciary φ-ing (selling their house, say) when this is what the beneficiary needs to be done. The expectation is that the fiduciary will act on behalf of the beneficiary and do what is best for the beneficiary; moreover, the expectation is that they ought to do this for this reason. Specifically, the beneficiary's expectation will be just that the fiduciary will φ and φ because this is what the beneficiary needs, where this is the expectation characteristic of trust. That this expectation, which is characteristic of trust, is one of trust is then further shown by its carrying with it a thinking well of the fiduciary expressed in the presumption that the fiduciary will do what is expected of them.

Second, that the trusting relationship is second personal in character. This claim could be supported in a number of ways. To start, consider Darwall's account of second-personal reasons, or reasons 'whose validity depends on presupposed authority and accountability relations'.[25] There is a 'closed circle of concepts' here: the *authority* to make a demand; a *valid* (or *authoritative*) demand; a *second-personal reason* for acting as demanded; and *responsibility* (or *accountability*) to someone for acting as demanded.[26] For example, suppose that I park in such a way that you cannot move your car without me moving mine first. In this situation, you might demand that I move my car. In making this demand, you presuppose that you enjoy the authority to make this demand and invite me to recognise that you have this authority. In this respect, second-person address comes with, as Darwall says, 'an RSVP'.[27] In recognizing that you are in a position to ask me to move my car, I thereby recognize that your asking me gives me a distinctive reason to move my car – a reason that I have by virtue of your addressing this request to me. If I ignore your request, I fail to take responsibility for doing what I have a reason to do, and you will rightly resent me for this. Your resentment then expresses the view that I wrong you in ignoring your request, and a propensity to feel this is a way in which the demand that I move my car can be implicitly addressed.

Applying this circle of concepts to trust shows it to be second personal in this way, up to a certain point. Let me focus on a fiduciary F and beneficiary B trusting F to φ. B will feel betrayed by F, where this reactive attitude seems to be a species of resentment, were F not to φ or to φ for some other reason than φ-ing being to B's benefit – for instance, if F were to sell B's house in order to enjoy some profit. Any susceptibility to resentment

[25] Stephen Darwall, *The Second-Person Standpoint: Morality, Respect and Accountability* (Harvard University Press 2006), 8.

[26] Ibid., 11–12.

[27] Stephen Darwall, 'Reply to Korsgaard, Wallace, and Watson' 118 *Ethics* 52, 54.

shows that B's trust, with its characteristic expectation of F, in effect places a demand on F that F φ and φ for the reason of B's benefit. This demand then gives F a second personal reason to act in this way to the extent that F recognizes B's authority to make this demand. Trust thus seems second personal, in these terms, up to a point. But *only up to a point* because this closed circle of concepts is breached by the fact that in trusting, one is in a position of vulnerability rather than a position of authority. In trusting F to φ, B is thereby not in a position to demand that F act as B expects. This point is made and developed by Knud Ejler Løgstrup in his discussion of trust:

> The other person's interpretation of the implication of the trust offered [that is, the trusting party Y's interpretation] ... is one thing, and the demand which is implicit in that trust ... which I must interpret is quite another thing.[28]

Responding to trust cannot be 'merely a matter of fulfilling the other person's expectations and granting his or her wishes'.[29] This is because, in Løgstrup's terms, the trust situation contains 'a demand for love, not for indulgence'.[30] This demand on the trusted – what Løgstrup calls the *radical ethical demand* – is generated by the fact of the trusting party's dependence. That is to say, what F should respond to is B's needs, not B's expectations, which might be mistaken in various ways. What F needs to judge is how to act in a way that best benefits B, where this is to say that F's reasons for φ-ing, if this is what F does, are *third personal* – to do with B's welfare. Third-personal reasons exist independently of the trusting relation, and that fiduciary relations equally determine this kind of reason is shown by the fact that the beneficiary has a backstop of authority. This is not authority in the *second-personal* sense, an authority that is contained with the relation; rather, it is the standing of the beneficiary to assert that their legal rights have been violated by the fiduciary.

One response here, which preserves the idea that reasons grounded on trust are second personal, is suggested by Darwall's later work, which expands his conception of the second personal, compares trust with love and identifies both as second-personal 'attitudes of the heart'[31]. To begin, Darwall distinguishes between deontic and reciprocating second-personal attitudes. Deontic attitudes hold their objects, the second person, accountable – this is the closed circle of concepts involving authority just outlined – whereas reciprocating attitudes invite their object, the second person, to take a reciprocating attitude. Trust is second personal in this latter way. So it is not that trust is only second personal up to a point, as just argued, but that it is second personal in a different way. Here, Darwall observes that it is

> essential to my trusting you that I invite you to accept my trust and, indeed, that I invite you to trust that I am trusting you, to trust in my trust and in me, trusting you. It will turn out that trust is a reciprocating attitude to itself. Trust always necessarily invites trust in return.[32]

[28] Knud Eljer Løgstrup, *The Ethical Demand* (University of Notre Dame Press 1997), 21.
[29] Ibid., 21.
[30] Ibid., 21.
[31] Stephen Darwall, 'Trust as a Second-Personal Attitude (of the Heart)' in Paul Faulkner and Thomas Simpson (eds.), *The Philosophy of Trust* (Oxford University Press 2017).
[32] Ibid., 7.

The notion of trust in play has shifted here. We started by considering a trust situation where one party trusts another to do something, but now we are considering one party trusting another simpliciter – a shift from the three-place grammatical form, 'X trusts Y to φ,' to the two-place grammatical form, 'X trusts Y'. The claim is then that in trusting someone to do something, you invite them to see your relationship as trusting, where Darwall compares a trusting relationship to relations of friendship or love, wherein trust similarly identifies 'an "attitude of the heart", using "heart" in its customary metaphorical sense to refer to that aspect of the human psyche through which we are heartened or disheartened'.[33] This suggests that the invitation found in trusting someone to do something is to view the trust as a trust relationship, which is something substantial and ongoing. But this is certainly too strong, both as a claim about trust and as a claim about fiduciary relations, which need not be premised on a background relationship. But a much slighter interpretation is possible, which is just that in trusting someone to do something, you invite them to recognize that the reliance involved in trusting is trusting. Trust aims at being recognized by the trusted. Trust has this aim because it is a reciprocating attitude, or one that calls on its object to respond in kind, where the kind here is for the trusted to be trustworthy, or do the right thing. (In this respect, trusting is comparable to an illocutionary act, which aims at shared knowledge.) When this is so – when the trusted responds to trust with trustworthiness – the relation formed in the trust situation is trusting, which would be heartening. But so much can be agreed without this construal of the second-personal nature of trust undermining the claim that the reasons it grounds remain ultimately third personal.

To recap, then, the question we have been considering is, what reasons for acting does the fiduciary have when fiduciary power is second-personally grounded on consent? At first blush, the reasons looked to be second personal, or reasons that rested on the beneficiary's authority to request that the fiduciary act in certain ways. However, I have argued that insofar as consent involves the handing over of authority, the relationship that it establishes is one of trust, which is characterized by vulnerability. While trust involves a determinate expectation of the trusted, which implicitly places a demand insofar as it amounts to a propensity to experience various reactive attitudes, the proper characterization of these reactive attitudes would describe them as a tendency to be heartened or disheartened. They are no more prescriptive than this because the expectation can be no more specific than that the trusted (fiduciary) will do the right thing and the trusting party (beneficiary) does not have authority over what this thing is. At this point, we hit the limits of the second personal: the 'right thing' names that thing that the trusted (fiduciary) has greatest third-personal reason to do, the action that is best for the trusting party (beneficiary), which is not necessarily that action expected if this expectation is specifically formulated. The 'right thing' is something that can be third-personally identified and something that the beneficiary has some legal right to. In short, the fiduciary needs to act for the benefit of the beneficiary. So with respect to Question (2) – the reasons the fiduciary

[33] Ibid., 11.

has for acting when fiduciary power is second-personally grounded on consent – once the role of trust in determining these reasons is fully described, the answer, somewhat surprisingly, is third-personal reasons.

4 Presumed Consent and Fiduciary Reasons

Fiduciary powers are grounded in fiduciary relationships. In Section 2, we considered how a fiduciary relationship can itself be grounded in consent, where this is one of Miller's suggested three 'modes of authorization'.[34] In this section, I would like consider the other two 'unilateral undertaking, and legal decree'. These modes, Miller notes, can be 'made necessary by the incapacity of the beneficiary'.[35]

Where there is incapacity, consent in this case must be *presumed*. There are then two features of presumed consent that are important here. First, presumed consent can never be substituted for actual consent. While a doctor might perform an emergency operation on a patient to save their life, "[t]he doctor cannot argue that he didn't need to ask me when he had the chance because he knew I would have agreed'.[36] Second, the presumption here 'concerns what would have been communicated', were communication possible.[37] So acting on presumed consent requires knowledge of what would have been communicated. Knowledge requires grounds, so presumed consent requires knowledge-supporting grounds. The first question is then, what kinds of grounds are available? I would like to identify two broad grounds: *institutional* and *philial*. With respect to the former, grounds can be given by a background of knowledge that is institutionally held. This is the doctor and patient case, where the doctor can presume the consent of the patient they need to operate on in order to save the patient's life. The presumption made here will be supported by institutional protocols based on general assumptions about preferences, and so about what would be communicated. This institutional background establishes the doctor–patient relationship as having a pre-existing fiduciary character. With respect to the latter, the necessary background knowledge upon which to ground a presumption of consent is not given by general considerations but by particular known facts about the beneficiary, or presumed consenter. That is, the presumption of consent might be based on an existing relationship wherein the bonds and history are sufficient to ground knowledge of what the presumed consenter would have communicated. A situation where the incapacity of one partner leads to the other taking control of their estate would fit here.

Comparing the fiduciary relationship with trusting relationships is illustrative here. Trusting relationships can be established by acts of trust. Such acts, it has been noted, have an illocutionary character: the trusting party, up to a point, can decide to trust, or think well of the trusted in relying on them. And in doing so, the trusting party works on a presumption about the trusted's motivations that they invite the trusted to share.

34 Miller, 74.
35 Ibid., 74.
36 Owens, 170.
37 Ibid., 171.

Thus, trusting relationships can be grounded on second-personal facts or facts that only become visible when one takes 'the perspective of addressing and being addressed'.[38] Such a trusting relationship Wanderer labels *transactional* insofar as it based on an 'act directed towards another person that, if recognized as appropriate by that other person, alters the normative status of both parties'.[39] In the last section, I argued that this characterisation does not quite fit trust because while the grounds of a trusting relationship can be second personal, the trusted's reasons for action remain essentially third personal. But the fit is good enough for the contrast that Wanderer goes on to draw, which is between transactional trust relationships and *philial* trust relationships, where the latter are 'those relationships to other persons that involve some kind of reciprocal affective regard for each other'.[40] The claim is then that this same distinction applies to fiduciary relationships. When consent is given, these relationships are transactional in grounds. When consent is presumed, one set of grounds available supporting this presumption are philial, or those grounds that come with a background of knowledge about and affective regard towards the presumed consenter. Consider then what reason the fiduciary has when the presumption of consent has this ground.

This is to turn to Question (2): when the fiduciary relationship is thus grounded on presumed consent, what kind of reason does the fiduciary have to act on behalf of the beneficiary? Again following Owens, philial relationships can be divided into two kinds: those that are chosen – such as one's relationship with friends and partners – and those that are not – such as family relationships.[41] The former kind Owens calls *involvements*, and his account of how involvements can generate and sustain obligation can then be used to consider how these existing philial relationships, broadly conceived, determine the kind of reason the fiduciary has to act on behalf of the beneficiary in these cases.

The account Owens opposes is the *benefactor-plus model*. Taking the involvement that is friendship, the benefactor-plus model accounts for the obligations of friendship in two stages. First, there are no obligations that are *constitutive* of friendship: friendship is a matter of benevolent concern; friendship simply entails that you have a special concern for your friend's interests. Second, the obligations of friendship are then generated in the normal way that obligations are generated, e.g. by promise, reciprocation or due care of expectations. One might add that friendship might entail a greater willingness to be put under obligation; your concern for your friend's interests, for example, might mean that you are more willing to promise to help your friend in various ways, but your obligations still derive from your promises rather than the friendship as such.

This model applies naturally to the fiduciary case. It implies that your status as friend does not entail that you are under obligation to take on the role and

[38] Conant and Rödl, 9.

[39] Jeremy Wanderer, 'Testimony and the Interpersonal' 21 *International Journal of Philosophical Studies* 92, 94.

[40] Ibid., 94.

[41] Owens.

responsibilities of a fiduciary, and that these obligations follow only if you take on this role. It also implies that your concern for their friend's interests means that you do have a reason to take on the role of fiduciary when presented by your friend's incapacity to pursue their own interests. Your reason for acting as a fiduciary, which is your care for your friend's interests, is then turned into the obligation to act for your friend's benefit once the role of fiduciary is adopted, given your friend's presumed consent. This account of the reasons friendship generates then naturally extends to all philial relationships insofar as benevolent concern follows from 'reciprocal affective regard'. On this model, when presumed consent has philial grounds, fiduciary reasons are again third personal in being determined by the shape of the beneficiary's interests. The pressing question is then, why does Owens reject this account?

Owens rejects both planks of the benefactor-plus model. First, the principle concern of friendship is not concern for the friend's interests but concern for the friendship itself:

> Friends think about their friends, about how to help, advise or amuse them. Friends also think about their friendship, about how to become someone's friend, about how to cultivate, express, and deepen a friendship they already have and about how to preserve it from various threats.[42]

Second, there are obligations of friendship itself. What these obligations actually are is hard to say because the rules of friendship 'are dense and subtle'.[43] Importantly, we need to include permissions as well as obligations; for example, 'only my friends are permitted to ask personal questions or to call me outside of working hours'.[44] Moreover, and this is Owens's key claim, this complex set of rules is an essential part of what makes friendship valuable. We value our friends in part because we value being in relationships that are normatively structured. We have, as Owens puts it, *normative interests* alongside our ordinary (non-normative) interests.

It seems to me that Owens is right to claim that there are obligations of friendship; and so right to argue that the benefactor-plus model fails with its second, and central, claim. The observation that friends care about the status of their friendship also seems right. And these two points can be combined: sometimes, for instance, you can feel obliged to do things you don't want to do simply for the sake of friendship. But it seems wrong to infer from this that friendship is not a matter of benevolent concern (and the quote given above does not suffice for this conclusion). This is because these concerns do not seem to be exclusive. Moreover, in the fiduciary case, your reason, qua friend, for taking on a fiduciary role when confronted by your friend's incapacity would seem to be just your concern for your friend's interests, rather than your concern for your friendship. And if you took it on for the latter reason, you would seem to be acting for the wrong reasons. So, in the present context, the only issue raised by Owens's disagreement with the benefactor-plus model is whether a philial relationship entails that a first party is under obligation to take on a fiduciary role

[42] Ibid., 112.
[43] Ibid., 101.
[44] Ibid., 114.

when confronted by the second party's incapacity, or whether this is merely something that first party has a reason to do. If Owens is right, there will be cases of obligation; and this seems correct. But it does not alter the kind of reason there is for taking on this role, which remains a third-personal concern for the second party's (or beneficiary's) non-normative interests.

When a fiduciary relationship is based on presumed consent whose grounds are given by the knowledge contained within a pre-existing philial relationship, then the fiduciary's reason for acting for the benefit of the beneficiary will be concern for the beneficiary's interests. This leaves open what to say about those cases where the presumption of consent has institutional grounds; for example, as it does in the doctor–patient case, or when a court appoints guardians for incapable adults, appoints foster parents or when the state acts in loco parentis. In these cases, institutional protocols take the place of particular knowledge. But it is plausible to suppose, though this supposition would require defence that I do not attempt here, that such institutional protocols are legitimate only to the extent that they are guided by the kind of reasons for action that would structure the philial case. That is, and in short, by those reasons that focus primarily on what would be best for the beneficiary.[45]

5 Trust and Loyalty

A fiduciary relation, I argued above, can be grounded on either second- or third-personal facts, which is to say on either consent plus trust or the facts that support a presumption of consent. Putting institutional cases aside for the moment, fiduciary relationships, I argued, are thereby established as relationships of trust or piggyback on existing trust relationships. In trusting someone to do something, your expectation of them, in part, is that they will be moved by your needing them to do that thing. What you need them to do lies in your interests. So the expectation had in trusting someone to do something, in part, is that they will be moved by your interests. Thus, it is unsurprising that irrespective of the grounds of a fiduciary relationship, the reasons a fiduciary has for acting, qua fiduciary, concern the lie of the beneficiary's interests. It follows that trust is central to both the grounds of fiduciary relations and the reasons that these grounds provide. In conclusion, I want to consider a related claim put forward by Andrew Gold, who proposes that the fiduciary relationship can be defined in terms of loyalty and who then defines loyalty in terms of trust.[46]

[45] This chapter argues, in short, that trust is central to the grounds of fiduciary relationships, and so to the determination of the kind of reason that fiduciaries have, insofar as these relationships are formed on the basis of consent, given or presumed. In this respect, its argument is similar to that offered by Matthew Harding, who concludes that 'fiduciary relationships are likely to be characterized by relatively thick trust' from the premise that 'in all cases where fiduciary relationships arise, one person voluntarily allows another to exercise discretion in making choices that will affect the interests of the first person or at least interests that the first person cares about'. Matthew Harding, 'Trust and Fiduciary Law' 33 *Oxford Journal of Legal Studies*, pp. 85 and 86, respectively. Unfortunately, I came across this paper too late to adequately engage with it, but it is worth noting that the fact that a presumption of consent can be institutionally grounded falsifies this premise and so similarly poses a problem for this argument.

[46] Gold.

Fiduciary law is 'peculiarly concerned with loyalty', and, Gold continues, 'is a hallmark of the fiduciary relationship. Indeed, it is commonly thought that if a purported fiduciary does not owe a duty of loyalty to a beneficiary, then the relationship is not actually a fiduciary relationship.'[47] Gold then considers various characterizations of loyalty and finds them wanting. For example, loyalty could be defined in terms of *the avoidance of fiduciary conflicts.*[48] But the problem here is that there are cases where a fiduciary should be seen as loyal despite breaching non-conflict requirements, or seen as not loyal despite not breaking these requirements.[49] Or loyalty could be defined as *being true*, following Raz's claim that '[a]ll social forms involve being true to the project or to the relationship which they define'[50]. But the problem here is that loyalty might demand that one do something against the beneficiary's wishes (for example, Shiffrin argues that the fiduciary might be obliged to break a beneficiary's contract).[51] Now it is not clear that responding to a beneficiary's interests rather than wishes is a case of failing to be true. But the distinction is a good one; it is that made by Løgstrup, quoted above, when he says that the trust situation contains 'a demand for love, not indulgence', and it is this distinction that explains why reasons of trust are not second personal all the way down, but bottom out in third-personal reasons.

After rejecting these, and other, characterizations of loyalty, Gold then proposes that loyalty be defined in terms of trust; specifically, there is loyalty when there is trust and there has been no breach of it: '[S]uppose that loyalty condemns breaches of the trust that is characteristic of the relevant relationship. Different types of relationship may implicate different types of trust. . . . In turn, different types of conduct may count as a breach of trust in each case';[52] '[So that] loyalty means that a fiduciary must not breach the trust that is characteristic of a particular relationship.'[53] This idea that there are different types of trust relationship, where these differences offer different grounds for a fiduciary relationship, is an idea that has been worked through in the above. Thus, this chapter can be taken as supporting Gold's conjecture. There is one wrinkle, however, that needs to be observed, and again it follows from Løgstrup's point that the fiduciary ought to respond to the beneficiary's interest, not wishes. The wrinkle concerns how one identifies breaches of trust. A natural way to do this is by reference to the feeling of betrayal that it elicits. The problem is that our tendency to experience this reactive attitude when the expectation had in trust is disappointed. And trusting parties can have a tendency of being overly prescriptive in their expectations, to expect it of a trusted that they do such and such, rather than that they merely do the right thing. Thus, the definition of trust given above, which has it that X trusts Y to φ when X relies on Y φ-ing and expects this fact to motivate Y to φ, implicitly focuses on the successful case, where X knows what lies in their interest.

47 Ibid., 176.
48 Paul Miller, 'A Theory of Fiduciary Liability' 56 *McGill Law Journal* 235.
49 Gold, 184–5.
50 Joseph Raz, *The Morality of Freedom* (Clarendon Press 1986), 354, quoted Gold, 180.
51 Seana Shiffrin, 'The Divergence of Contract and Promise' 120 *Harvard Law Review* 708, 729.
52 Gold, 191.
53 Ibid., 194.

The problem is that we do not always possess this knowledge. And were X to lack this knowledge, Y might respond to X's trusting reliance by doing the right thing and still provoke feelings of betrayal associated with trust being let down through not doing what X expected, which is to say not φ-ing. So a natural way of identifying breaches of trust is fallible at best. But this wrinkle aside, it is plausible to propose, as I take the second quote from Gold above to be proposing, that the range of fiduciary responsibilities corresponds to the nature of the trust relationship that they are grounded on.

2

Trust and Advice

ANDREW S. GOLD*

1 Introduction

Trust is not an inevitable component of fiduciary relationships.[1] If there is a recognized categorical fiduciary relationship, it makes no difference if the fiduciary and her beneficiary wouldn't even trust each other to handle trivial tasks. Clients don't have to trust their lawyers, and shareholders don't have to trust their corporation's directors. Trust might even seem like an irrelevancy from the legal point of view; perhaps it is best seen as a positive or negative side effect of fiduciary relationships, but on this understanding, it is not a vital part of the field.

Even so, trust does make a difference in fiduciary law, and understanding how helps us to theorize fiduciary relationships. I will focus here on the way that trust helps to account for both categorical and ad hoc fiduciary relationships. In each instance, I will focus on examples involving advice. As we will see, trust helps to address what are otherwise puzzling features of advisory relationships.

In practice, trust is an interesting counterpart to conflicts of interest. While trust has many meanings, this paper will adopt the idea of "thick trust" developed in Matthew Harding's work.[2] As he develops this conception: "at the 'thick' end are wide-ranging beliefs about a person's character in relation to matters of central importance to the truster ('I trust him with my life; he's my best friend')."[3] Trust in this sense provides a setting where there is a predisposition to behave in a certain way, and the law takes note. This legal interest in such predispositions is part of a more general pattern in fiduciary law, which cares about contexts in which opportunistic behavior (or the effective equivalent[4]) are especially likely. In each case, the problem concerns vulnerability. As a beneficiary, we have a distinct source of vulnerability when there is a conflict of interest, beyond the vulnerability that results from being subject to another's discretion. Likewise, we have a distinct source of vulnerability when we trust someone who has this discretion.

* I am grateful to Evan Fox-Decent, Matthew Harding, Dan Kelly, Arthur Laby, Paul Miller, Gerald Postema, Henry Smith, Lionel Smith and Julian Velasco for helpful comments on the ideas in this paper. I am also grateful to participants in the conference on trust and fiduciaries held at the University of Melbourne. Any errors are my own.

1 *See* Matthew Harding, *Fiduciary Relationships, Fiduciary Law, and Trust* in D. Gordon Smith & Andrew S. Gold (eds.), RESEARCH HANDBOOK ON FIDUCIARY LAW 58 (Elgar Publishing 2018) ("A moment's reflection reveals that trust is not a necessary incident of fiduciary relationships; nor is it a sufficient one.").

2 *See, e.g.*, ibid., 60.

3 Ibid.

4 Note that good faith parties with conflicts can readily engage in distorted decision-making. They are not opportunistic, but the consequences are often similar.

The above point applies with particular strength in cases where we trust another person for their advice, at least if we trust them in a certain way. Often, the consequence of this trust is epistemic dependence. Judicial recognition of categorical relationships that implicate advice giving can be understood as a response to the likelihood of this type of trust and the resulting likelihood of epistemic dependence. From this perspective, the categorical relationship is recognized as a prophylactic measure. As such, it is also justified even in cases that lack epistemic dependence.

In the ad hoc setting, the same considerations regarding trust, vulnerability and epistemic dependence apply. Yet trust can also be relevant in an additional way. For at least some of these ad hoc relationships, trust is also a component of extralegal relationships of trust and confidence – and within that subset, these extralegal relationships are commonly *involvements*. Involvements are informal relationships with no obvious entry point; involvements characteristically develop over time. Trust helps in the identification of such extralegal relationships, and it does so with important implications for the appropriate behavior of a would-be fiduciary. A relationship of trust and confidence calls for certain types of loyalty and care, as a matter of morality and convention.

Relationships of trust and confidence are likewise recognizable for parties who participate in them. This means that, even if parties to an ad hoc fiduciary relationship – including an advisory one – are unaware that they have entered into a legal relationship, they can at least be expected to know of their extralegal, moral responsibilities. They can act to avoid the relationship, by means of disclaimers or potentially by avoidance of the obligation-related behavior. The result is that recognition of such relationships by the courts is less troubling in terms of notice to the fiduciary. Law has a duty-imposing role in this context, but the extralegal relationships that underpin the law's intervention are voluntary in nature and subject to avoidance or exit. In this context, then, trust is relevant to fiduciary law's fairness, and not only to its effectiveness.

This chapter will address each of these points in turn. It will begin with the difficulties posed by advisory contexts. Section 2 will indicate how advisory cases invite a skeptical challenge for leading theories of fiduciary relationships. Moreover, the most compelling response – that some advisory cases involve epistemic dependence – will only cover a limited area within the field. Section 3 will show how fiduciary law's prophylactic approach to a beneficiary's vulnerability can be extended to explain recognition of categorical fiduciary relationships that are classically advisory. Trust is central to this analysis. Section 4 will then address fact-based or ad hoc fiduciary relationships. It will indicate that recognition of these relationships builds on a certain kind of involvement that incorporates trust. Such involvements have bearing not only on a beneficiary's vulnerability but also on a fiduciary's awareness of his or her moral obligations. Section 5 will conclude.

2 The Adviser Challenge

A *Discretion and Epistemic Dependence*

Leading theories of fiduciary relationships take discretion to be a fundamental component of the relationship. The exact nature of that discretionary component varies somewhat. Gordon Smith, for example, understands fiduciary relationships to involve discretionary authority over a critical resource belonging to a fiduciary's beneficiary.[5] Paul Miller understands fiduciary relationships to involve discretionary authority over a beneficiary's practical interests.[6] Miller argues that the powers involved in these relationships are ordinarily considered fiduciary only if they are discretionary.[7] Ernest Weinrib likewise treats discretion as a central part of the fiduciary relationship, yet his account of fiduciary relationships is different from both Smith's and Miller's.[8] Notwithstanding variations in approach, discretionary power or authority is usually thought to be a crucial feature of fiduciary relationships.

Miller offers a recent account of how discretion extends to adviser relationships, despite what might seem to be conceptual difficulties in saying that advice involves discretionary power. Unsurprisingly, his view rules out adviser cases that involve advice and nothing more. On Miller's account, "advisers are not fiduciaries as such."[9] When advisers do qualify as fiduciary, the fact that they give advice is not what makes them fiduciary. Instead, the advice-giving component is "incidental to the exercise of discretionary power."[10] They might be fiduciaries, for example, where one party has effectively ceded power to another.

On the other hand, Miller notes an exception to the rule. Certain adviser cases look different:

> Save for the rare circumstance in which the advisee is so epistemically dependent on the adviser that he is incapable of exercising independent judgment in determining how to act in reliance on the advice. In cases characterized by total reliance the adviser enjoys *effective* discretionary power over the advisee; though there is no formal cession of capacity the advisee's exercise of it is effectively determined by the advice given.[11]

In other words, advisers are fiduciaries when their advice amounts to an exercise of the kind of discretionary power that exists in other fiduciary relationships.

B The Critique

Discretion-centered approaches to explaining fiduciary relationships have sparked a growing debate among fiduciary theorists, as several scholars have taken advisory relationships as counterexamples to the consensus on discretion. The classical understanding holds that discretion over a beneficiary's assets or person is a hallmark of a fiduciary relationship.[12] The dissenters suggest this perspective is overbroad.

[5] *See* D. Gordon Smith, *The Critical Resource Theory of Fiduciary Duty* (2002) 55 VAND. L. REV. 1399, 1447–48.

[6] *See* Paul B. Miller, *The Fiduciary Relationship* in Andrew S. Gold & Paul B. Miller (eds.), PHILOSOPHICAL FOUNDATIONS OF FIDUCIARY LAW (Oxford University Press 2014) 63.

[7] Ibid., 72.

[8] *See* Ernest J. Weinrib, *The Fiduciary Obligation* (1975) 25 U. TORONTO L.J. 1.

[9] *See* Miller (n. 6), 84.

[10] Ibid.

[11] Ibid., 84 n. 76.

[12] There is an important exception for cases involving abstract purposes. These cases, however, also involve discretionary authority – it is just that it is discretion regarding a different object. *See* Paul B. Miller & Andrew S. Gold, *Fiduciary Governance* (2015) 57 WM. & MARY L. REV. 513.

Arthur Laby has recently led the charge, contending that fiduciary theories that treat discretion as a necessary condition for fiduciary relationships are incorrect.[13] Myriad theories of the fiduciary relationship agree that such discretion is a necessary condition, despite differing significantly on the other core features and on the justifications for fiduciary status. Whichever theory is selected, Laby argues that a discretion-based approach fails to account for important examples.

Money managers are a leading illustration of where the problem lies. As Laby notes:

> Although it is true that many clients give discretionary authority to investment managers to invest and trade on their behalf, it is also true that other clients refuse to empower their investment advisers with discretion, and many investment managers refuse to assume discretion over client funds regardless of the customers' wishes. These money managers who lack discretion, are considered fiduciaries and subject to fiduciary liability enforced in private and public law.[14]

Despite a frequent absence of discretionary power, money managers still retain their fiduciary role.

Laby makes a similar point about other fiduciary professionals, such as lawyers and doctors. As he indicates: "In many instances, these professionals act in a purely advisory capacity – explaining potential courses of action or potential treatments."[15] Even so, Laby argues, "in those instances, these advisers are considered fiduciaries."[16] Laby thus emphasizes that there is no necessary connection between advice giving and control over the advisee. True, many advisory relationships are not fiduciary. But advisory relationships are apparently fiduciary in some cases despite the fiduciary lacking discretionary power over the advisee or her assets.[17] Not every jurisdiction may agree on the examples Laby offers (e.g., regarding doctors), but he marshals instances that pose a challenge in some settings.

Lawyers are particularly salient examples for this line of argument, and Laby is not alone in expressing concerns about the significance of lawyers that primarily give advice. Alice Woolley offers a related critique in her analysis of lawyers as fiduciaries.[18] While ultimately allowing for a type of discretion in lawyer–client cases, she critiques standard discretion-based accounts as inconsistent with legal doctrine and professional responsibility mandates.

Woolley notes that if "discretionary authority is defined as being about making decisions on another's behalf, . . . it does not easily apply to the lawyer–client relationship."[19] She emphasizes that "a lawyer's legal and ethical obligations leave

[13] *See* Arthur Laby, Book Review (2016) 35 LAW & PHIL. 123 (reviewing PHILOSOPHICAL FOUNDATIONS OF FIDUCIARY LAW (n. 6)).

[14] Ibid., 132.

[15] Ibid.

[16] Ibid.

[17] Adviser cases are also challenging for an account like Lionel Smith's, which sees loyalty as a requirement for the exercise of a power. For Smith's answer, see Lionel D. Smith, *Can We Be Obliged to Be Selfless?* in PHILOSOPHICAL FOUNDATIONS OF FIDUCIARY LAW (n. 6), 141, 157–58.

[18] *See* Alice Woolley, *The Lawyer as Fiduciary: Private Law Duties in Public Law Relations* (2015) 65 U. TORONTO L.J. 285.

[19] Ibid., 312.

decision-making power with the client."[20] That power could very well exist in cases involving the type of epistemic dependence that Miller points to. Yet, Woolley finds that this subset of cases falls short in the lawyer–client setting. As she concludes: "while it may be the case that sometimes clients have epistemic dependence on their lawyers or that lawyers have de facto discretionary authority over their clients, that dependence or authority is not a necessary or defining feature of the lawyer–client relationship."[21]

Woolley does not ultimately deny the significance of discretion in this context, but she says it needs to be understood differently.[22] On her account, the lawyer does not have discretionary authority regarding client ends but does have power respecting "the client's ability to determine and pursue his own ends."[23] She nevertheless concludes the existing fiduciary literature does not adequately explain how lawyers have discretion in these relationships.

As noted, Miller has a response that incorporates some advisory relationships. The apparent difficulty (from the critics' perspective) is that many categorical advisory fiduciary relationships do not involve epistemic dependence, and they commonly do not involve discretion over a beneficiary's assets or person. The challenge is thus a challenge of doctrinal fit – on this view, the epistemic dependence argument does not match up to a sufficient percentage of the cases (or of the core cases) to make it a satisfactory interpretive account.

3 Categorical Cases

Miller is right to indicate epistemic dependence cases as a special setting for advisory relationships, but I will suggest an extension of his argument that builds on the role of trust. Recall Miller's argument is that sometimes an individual will be so dependent on an adviser that they can't exercise independent judgment; the result is that the adviser has a de facto discretionary power. With that in mind, let's consider another angle on the problem of epistemic dependence.

A Trust and Vulnerability

Before proceeding, we will want to unpack the meaning of trust. That is by no means an easy task given the different meanings of trust, not just in society but also among scholars who study the subject. Trust also takes different forms depending on the context, so the answers can vary over time. Trust can even implicate different aspects of how we think and feel; it can be cognitive or affective, and these are very different things.[24]

[20] Ibid.

[21] Ibid., 315. Cf. Deborah A. DeMott, *The Lawyer as Agent*, (1998) 67 FORDHAM L. REV. 301, 304 (indicating that lawyers may be kept on "the tightest of leashes" by their clients).

[22] See Woolley (n. 18), 317.

[23] Ibid., 321.

[24] *See* Frank B. Cross, *Law and Trust* (2005) 93 GEO. L.J. 1457, 1464–68. Trust may also arise selectively. *See* Claire A. Hill & Erin Ann O'Hara, *A Cognitive Theory of Trust* (2006) 84 WASH. U. L. REV. 1717, 1740–44. On the relevance of these features in corporate fiduciary settings, see Andrew S. Gold, *The New Concept of Loyalty in Corporate Law* (2009) 43 U.C. DAVIS L. REV. 457, 509–14.

I will build on Matthew Harding's account of trust, which captures a particular type of trust that will have bearing on the present argument.[25] As Harding notes, trust can be "thin" or "thick."[26] On his account, the thin version covers "targeted beliefs about a person's basic rationality or consistency of action in some relatively trivial matter ('I'm trusting him not to be late for lunch; he never is')."[27] That type of trust does have some bearing on the function of fiduciary relationships, but it will not be our concern here. The thick version is more all-encompassing: "at the 'thick' end are wide-ranging beliefs about a person's character in relation to matters of central importance to the truster ('I trust him with my life; he's my best friend')."[28]

As the best friend example suggests in the above quotation, this kind of trust is "typical of the variety of enduring relationships that play a central role in most people's lives."[29] And, as Harding also indicates, such trust is closely linked to actions. Indeed, there is a need for certain actions if trust is to occupy a role in building relationships:

> [n]o one builds a relationship of any sort simply by having certain attitudes and beliefs; it is necessary to act, to show a person that you trust her, thus giving her an opportunity to show you that she can be trusted, at least to the extent necessary to keep the relationship going and quite possibly so as to broaden and deepen the relationship as well.[30]

And a key type of action in this category is reliance.[31] In short, while trust of various types may play a role in relationship building, it is reasonable to think that thick trust is vital to both the creation and development of close and lasting relationships.

As Harding rightly emphasizes: "Thick trust is . . . potentially very valuable. But it can also render a truster especially vulnerable . . . ."[32] This is a key point for present purposes; thick trust produces vulnerability, and particularly when it is demonstrated through reliance. Sometimes that vulnerability shows itself through entrustment of property; other times it shows itself through a failure to monitor. But in certain cases it shows itself through epistemic dependence; we follow another's advice unquestioningly if we trust them in the right way. It would overstate the case to say that thick trust inevitably means that epistemic dependence is going to arise. But we can adopt a more modest claim: where there is thick trust, the likelihood that epistemic dependence will arise (and lead to an effective discretionary authority) is increased. Thick trust need not include a belief in the trusted party's judgment, but it will characteristically include a belief in that party's integrity or at least reliability vis-à-vis the truster.

An adviser's expertise in a subject area is not enough to suggest epistemic dependence. I might know someone is far more expert than I am on a given topic yet refuse

[25] *See* Harding (n. 1). *See also* Matthew Harding, *Trust and Fiduciary Law* (2013) 33 OXFORD J. LEGAL STUD. 81, 83–84 (describing thick trust).

[26] *See* Harding (n. 1), 60.

[27] Ibid.

[28] Ibid.

[29] Ibid.

[30] Ibid., 60–61.

[31] Ibid., 61.

[32] Ibid. As Harding notes, reliance is an important part of this picture. Ibid., 60–61.

to let their advice alter my decisions because I expect they will lie to me. Or I might refuse to let their advice alter my decisions because I know I have idiosyncratic preferences, and, despite this other person's wisdom, I feel the need to do things my way. In either case I might wish for their advice yet discount it sufficiently that epistemic dependence is an implausible outcome. Matters are different in cases of thick trust; while epistemic dependence is not a foregone conclusion, it is substantially more likely to result (assuming that the truster also perceives the trusted party to be an expert). Recall that thick trust implicates beliefs about someone's character. When a trusting party holds the right beliefs about a trusted party's trustworthiness and expertise – and also doubts his own expertise – epistemic dependence is a foreseeable consequence.

But does that get us far enough to justify a categorical fiduciary relationship where advice giving occupies a central role? After all, not every case in these categorical fiduciary relationships will actually involve trust. The answer is to recognize that fiduciary law deals with probabilities. In this setting, the problem of trust is a mirror image of the problem of bias. Fiduciary law makes use of proxies and presumptions to prevent biased decision-making by a conflicted fiduciary. It also makes use of proxies to protect parties who are sufficiently likely to demonstrate thick trust toward someone who gives them advice.

B Fiduciary Law, Prophylactic Measures and Overinclusive Rules

Trust is not coextensive with epistemic dependence, as we might show trust regarding a non-advice-related area of conduct.[33] I might trust someone to whom I have given control over a prized possession while having no belief whatsoever in the quality of their advice. On the other hand, in the absence of such trust, epistemic dependence may still be unlikely even if the advice giver is truly expert in her subject. Experts can lie and shade the truth. Thick trust means we will count on the expert to be reliable, and that will not hold true for all experts.

Some relationships increase the odds of trust toward an advice giver (in her advice-giving capacity); they consequently increase the odds of epistemic dependence. Lawyer–client relationships are a good example. At least where a lawyer and client have worked together over a substantial period of time (and such relationships often last for years), this interaction – combined with dramatic information disparities – is fertile ground for epistemic dependence. This isn't to say that such relationships are trusting relationships in the vast majority of cases or even in most cases. If the likelihood of such trust is sufficiently high, however, and if it will often produce epistemic dependence of the right kind, we have a basis for a categorical fiduciary relationship that centers on advice. Where epistemic dependence would mean discretionary power over the advisee or her assets, a fiduciary relationship is justified – and the same can be true where such epistemic dependence is probable or even relatively

[33] Note also that one might have epistemic dependence on another party outside of advisory relationships and also outside of fiduciary relationships. I thank Paul Miller for emphasizing this point.

common.[34] As with many other prophylactic measures, the approach is overinclusive, but that can also be worth the cost.

A comparison to the conflicts setting may be helpful. Not every fiduciary with a conflict of interest will fail to act neutrally. The point to a broad-based measure designed to address bias, however, is not that every single conflicted fiduciary inevitably acts with bias; it is, rather, that the risk of such bias (even by well-meaning, good faith fiduciaries) is too great to take the chance. Indeed, not only is there a risk of bias when fiduciaries are conflicted; there is frequent obscurity as to what has really occurred and how bad it is. We can't always know when bias infects a decision, and we can't always know what an unbiased decision would have looked like by comparison. For conflicted fiduciaries, the risk of self-serving bias is nonetheless high, given the tempting combination of discretion and human nature.

As Henry Smith argues: "If equity seeks to ensure that one not profit from one's own wrong, traditional fiduciary law goes a step further in not allowing one to profit from a situation in which it is hard to tell whether one profited from one's own wrong."[35] Fiduciary law acts prophylactically, sweeping broadly so as not to take that risk.

There can be similarly heightened risks at the other end of the relationship and similarly troublesome uncertainty. When one person exercises discretion over another person or her assets, this makes the other party vulnerable in certain respects. That vulnerability may be compounded if they are also trusting of the party who exercises discretion. This admittedly won't be true for all types of trust, but it will plausibly be true for the "thick" trust that Harding identifies. The same point holds in cases of advice.

There is a structural difference in the way the law reacts in relationship recognition cases. The classic loyalty-related response occurs *within* fiduciary relationships, through the no-conflict rules; it is a measure to address the conduct of parties that are already understood to be fiduciary. Here, by contrast, the fiduciary category itself is at issue. Yet overinclusive responses are just as available (and plausible) at the relationship identification level. Accordingly, a concern with risks of bias can justify categorical fiduciary relationships in settings where epistemic dependence is likely, even if not guaranteed.[36]

Woolley offers a potential response, but it is not clear why it should rule out the present argument for such treatment. She notes that "not every aspect of the lawyer–client relationship is subject to fiduciary duties."[37] She then suggests that this is a problem for a prophylactic view:

[34] In other words, where there is a sufficient probability of the conditions described at Miller (n. 6), 84 n. 76. The threshold probability may be set lower given the stakes involved in legal representation.

[35] *See* Henry E. Smith, *Why Fiduciary Law Is Equitable* in PHILOSOPHICAL FOUNDATIONS OF FIDUCIARY LAW (n. 6), 261, 273.

[36] Note that if we understand these categorical relationships in proxy terms, there may be two levels at work. It is common in ad hoc cases for courts to assess whether the would-be beneficiary trusted the would-be fiduciary. Such trust can be a proxy for the kind of vulnerability that arises in cases of epistemic dependence; broad categorical relationships can then be a proxy for a more individualized analysis of whether that trust exists.

[37] *See* Woolley (n. 18), 315.

> This makes it more difficult to claim that the fiduciary status of the lawyer–client relationships is a broader, prophylactic measure designed to protect the sub-set of lawyer–client relationships that feature de facto authority. The [Supreme Court of Canada] itself has rejected the application of fiduciary obligations to lawyers except in circumstances where they ought to apply.[38]

I am not sure this conclusion follows. The fact that certain settings are marked off as nonfiduciary does not mean that a category-based approach is conceptually unavailable or normatively undesirable. What this may mean is that the overinclusiveness of the prophylactic measure is limited to some extent.[39] The same point holds true of rules against conflicts of interest, which are subject to various exceptions and limits in scope: such rules are still useful even if certain conflict cases are held permissible.

It is nonetheless true that individual cases of advice will fall outside the intended point of the fiduciary category. Do all lawyer–client relationships involve the kind of thick trust that heightens a client's vulnerability? Or all investment adviser cases? Certainly not. There are clients who can't stand their lawyers, accordingly believe very little of what their lawyers say and have only hired them because they feel a need to say that they obtained advice from counsel. Not every case of legal representation involves a thick type of trust, or any trust at all beyond reliance on reputation costs or malpractice claims to modify behavior. Nor, as Woolley notes, do all cases of lawyer–client relationships involve the kind of discretion that many fiduciary theorists emphasize. The same holds true for investment advice, doctor–patient relationships and various other advisory settings – at least some of the time.

But these cases don't need to involve epistemic dependence in order to justify a fiduciary category. If a categorical relationship is a prophylactic measure designed to take into account the odds (and the gravity of what is at stake), we have enough basis to justify categorical treatment of lawyer–client relationships and other advisory contexts as fiduciary. Proxies can function quite well even if they sweep in a large number of exceptions to the rule. A similar point holds for categorical relationships that focus very substantially on advice.

This argument may extend Miller's argument beyond its original scope, for it suggests that advisory relationships can appropriately be understood as fiduciary even in cases where there is no epistemic dependence. Yet my claim reinforces Miller's broader point that such dependence matters. Epistemic dependence may still be what best justifies categorical fiduciary relationships that center on advice. Even where the prophylactic measure applies to cases that don't specifically have features that merit fiduciary treatment, their inclusion in the broader category makes sense in light of the many hard-to-capture cases in which those features are present.

[38] Ibid.

[39] This may also be understood as a scope of mandate concern. That reading, however, does not preclude a prophylactic interpretation. I thank Paul Miller for noting this issue.

4 Ad Hoc Adviser Cases

Fiduciary relationships extend more widely than categorical cases such as trustee–beneficiary, guardian–ward, principal–agent or lawyer–client. They also include fact-based, or ad hoc, fiduciary relationships. This is not a difficulty. To the contrary, the concern with epistemic dependence is just as much a consideration in these ad hoc settings as it is for categorical fiduciary relationships – in fact, in ad hoc settings we can largely avoid the concern that trust may be lacking in individual cases. It is characteristic of many ad hoc fiduciary relationships that the beneficiary trusts her fiduciary, often considerably.

Yet trust is now playing more than one role, or so I will argue. There is another respect in which trust is important when we turn to ad hoc fiduciary relationships, as it is part of what makes it legitimate for courts to recognize such relationships. Ad hoc fiduciary relationships raise policy concerns that categorical relationships do not, for ad hoc fiduciary relationships are more likely to involve fiduciaries who were unaware that they owed fiduciary obligations. Trust, and more specifically relationships of trust and confidence, can alleviate this concern.[40]

A *The Judicial Approach*

The fact patterns that give rise to ad hoc fiduciary relationships vary considerably, as do the tests courts apply in determining whether such fiduciary relationships exist.[41] There are, however, certain features that commonly matter for legal analysis, and trust is one of them. Granted, trust on its own is not enough to determine whether an ad hoc fiduciary relationship exists. As one court nicely expresses the point:

> One party cannot transform a business relationship into one which is fiduciary in nature merely by placing trust and confidence in the other party. There must be additional circumstances, or a relationship that induces the trusting party to relax the care and vigilance which he would ordinarily exercise for his own protection.[42]

Trust is a common part of the determination that an ad hoc fiduciary relationship exists, but it is only part.[43] When an ad hoc fiduciary relationship is found, there is

[40] Alleviate this concern, but perhaps not remove it entirely. Indeed, lingering worries about surprise impositions of fiduciary relationships may be one (among several) of the reasons why the law should not accept certain expansive arguments for recognizing involvement-based fiduciary relationships, such as the argument that friends should be treated as fiduciaries. Other reasons include the damage that recognizing such relationships as legally fiduciary could inflict on valuable extralegal relationships.

[41] *See generally* Daniel B. Kelly, *Fiduciary Principles in Fact-Based Fiduciary Relationships* forthcoming in Evan J. Criddle, Paul B. Miller & Robert H. Sitkoff (eds.), THE OXFORD HANDBOOK OF FIDUCIARY LAW (Oxford University Press 2019).

[42] *See* Daktronics, Inc. v. McAfee, 599 N.W.2d 358, 363 (S.D. 1999) (quoting Ainsworth v. First Bank of South Dakota, 472 N.W.2d 786, 788 (S.D. 1991)). *See also* Harding (n. 1), 65–66 (noting that one person trusting another in some matter is not enough to constitute a fiduciary relationship).

[43] Indeed, there is a parallel to contract law. A would-be contracting party cannot bind another party to a contractual obligation just by relying on what the other party has said. Moreover, without more they should not be able to. As Charles Fried asks: "[W]hy should my liberty be constrained by the harm you would suffer from the disappointment of expectations you choose to entertain about my choices?" *See*

ordinarily something more that is present in the fact pattern; this is as true for advisory relationships as it is for fiduciary relationships in general.

Consider, then, what an ad hoc fiduciary case involving advice can look like. *Burdett* v. *Miller* is a famous example of an ad hoc fiduciary relationship that was also an advisory one.[44] There, Judge Richard Posner confronted the problem of advice giving within a friendship, in a context where the beneficiary was particularly likely to trust the advice she received. The court had no hesitation in finding a fiduciary relationship, and the analysis that led to that conclusion is instructive. To be clear, a number of ad hoc fiduciary cases look different from *Burdett*. They may involve reasonable expectations and reliance invited by one to the detriment of another, in largely arms-length commercial settings. But *Burdett* is nonetheless an important subtype within the ad hoc category, and its significance is worth developing.

In that case, Patricia Burdett was a successful sales representative for a typography firm who sought tax-related advice from her friend Robert Miller. Miller was a professor of accounting at Northwestern University and also an owner of an accounting firm. Burdett had been friends with Miller for years, ever since she took a course that Miller taught in 1979. In 1983, she asked Miller for advice on tax shelters, and he made various suggestions. Over the next couple of years, he suggested a series of tax shelters sponsored by corporations that he and three of his acquaintances controlled. Unfortunately, there were serious problems with the investments, and key facts were left undisclosed. The investment failed, the three acquaintances fled to Canada, and Burdett ultimately lost $200,000 before tax benefits were factored in.

In addition to a claim under the RICO statute, Burdett claimed that Miller had breached his fiduciary duties to her. In assessing the latter claim, the court indicated that investment adviser is not a categorical fiduciary relationship but allowed for the possibility that fiduciary duties could be "imposed on an ad hoc basis."[45] Trust also figured prominently in the legal test for this ad hoc imposition. As the court explained: "If a person solicits another to trust him in matters in which he represents himself to be expert as well as trustworthy and the other is not expert and accepts the offer and reposes complete trust in him, a fiduciary relation is established."[46] That test was readily applicable to the interactions between Burdett and Miller.

> Miller cultivated a relation of trust with Burdett over a period of years, holding himself out as an expert in a field (investments) in which she was inexperienced and unsophisticated. He knew that she took his advice uncritically and unquestioningly and that she sought no "second opinion" or even – until the end, when at last her suspicions were aroused – any documentary confirmation of the investments to which he steered her.[47]

CHARLES FRIED, CONTRACT AS PROMISE: A THEORY OF CONTRACTUAL OBLIGATION (Harvard University Press 1981) 10. In similar fashion, we cannot bind another person to a fiduciary obligation just by trusting them. People rely on others when it is unreasonable to do so, and they trust others when it is unreasonable to do so. Even when it makes sense to rely, or to trust, it needn't be the case that this supports an enforceable duty. The law appropriately finds that something more is necessary in each case.

44 957 F.2d 1375 (7th Cir. 1992) (Posner, J.).

45 Ibid., 1381.

46 Ibid.

47 Ibid.

As the court noted, "[i]t is true he did not ask her simply to sign over all her wealth to him to be invested in his sole discretion."[48] But Judge Posner concluded that the district court was entitled to find Burdett did the next best thing:

> That was to invite her to accept his advice with no questions asked or answered, in reliance on his professional and professorial status, on his insight in the arcana of tax shelter investments – a technical area about which she was ignorant – and on a continuing business relationship shading into a social friendship.[49]

In other words, it was the overall context that suggested something equivalent to handing over discretion.

Notice that part of what the court focuses on is a circumstantial indication of epistemic dependence – Burdett took Miller's advice "uncritically and unquestioningly." She simply did what he suggested, no second opinions required. But the court also emphasizes a continuing relationship between parties, one that was "shading into a social friendship." Burdett was relying not only on Miller's superior knowledge of the technical subject area but also on the relationship between them as an indicator that it was appropriate to trust him.

As cases like *Burdett* demonstrate, there is not necessarily a clear moment at which the fiduciary is formally alerted that a fiduciary relationship is in play.[50] Even so, there may still be a relationship that is recognizable to the parties and to outside observers as the kind of relationship that implicates trust and confidence. If so, this has bearing not only on the likelihood of epistemic dependence but also on the likelihood that both parties will act in light of knowledge regarding that epistemic dependence. It is this latter feature I will focus on below.

B *The Notice Concern*

A central puzzle is posed by the connection between trust and the other factors that add up to recognition of an ad hoc fiduciary relationship. In advice cases, one answer is simply that if the right kind of trust exists in combination with these other factors, there is a good case for epistemic dependence. That answer may suffice, but there is potentially another way that trust matters in this context. Trust is a component of a relation of "trust and confidence," and its presence is part of how we identify such a relation. In turn, the existence of such relations can play an important role in legitimizing the legal recognition of a fiduciary relationship, in light of the informality of ad hoc fiduciary relationships.

It is generally considered vital that legally recognized fiduciary relationships be identifiable as such by the participating parties. People must be able to know ex ante if

48 Ibid.

49 Ibid., 1382.

50 Note also that *Burdett* is not unique in recognizing the importance of social relationships between the parties for recognition of a fiduciary relationship. *See, e.g.*, Patsos v. First Albany Corp., 741 N.E.2d 841, 851 (Mass. 2001) ("Social or personal ties between a stockbroker and customer may also be a consideration because the relationship may be based on a special level of trust and confidence."). For further discussion of *Patsos*, see Kelly (n. 41).

they are fiduciaries, given the huge potential liability this status entails and the stringency of the duties the relationship calls for. This is a basis for hesitancy in recognizing ad hoc, fact-based fiduciary relationships. As Henry Smith observes:

> As with equity, scholars have criticized fiduciary duty for being unpredictable around the edges. And, as with equity, courts and commentators often state that fiduciary law is not closed, but nervousness about its open-endedness probably explains why courts try to hew to the established categories based on known status relationships.[51]

This point has bearing both on new status relationship categories and on the recognition of ad hoc fiduciary relationships in individual settings.

Ad hoc fiduciary relationships raise concerns about notice to the fiduciary parties. Status-based fiduciary relationships are voluntary to varying degrees, but whatever their mode of formation, a fiduciary generally understands when she has entered into one of these relationships. This is admittedly not true for all categorical fiduciary relationships. For example, individuals may enter into a general partnership without recognizing that this is the type of relationship they formed; it is enough if they simply intended to co-own a business for profit.[52] Still, in the usual case, people know when they enter into a status-based fiduciary relationship.

Ad hoc fiduciary relationships are different – the fiduciary may have no idea that he is party to a set of legal obligations that govern him as a fiduciary. No filings with the state are required; no contracts or formal documents need be signed. Indeed, he may rightly ask when it is that he undertook to be a fiduciary, or when it is that he undertook to have fiduciary obligations.[53] There is often no precise moment when a promise was made or even an offer made to act as a fiduciary, let alone any clear language in which the fiduciary has held himself out as occupying such status. As a consequence, the ad hoc fiduciary may fail to realize he took on any legal obligations, and certainly not the strict legal obligations that govern a fiduciary.[54]

And yet we may still see ad hoc relationships as the product of a choice. Just as with the general partnership, hasn't the ad hoc fiduciary chosen to be part of a relationship that calls for moral obligations that roughly track the legal obligations that courts impose? He may not have realized he was a fiduciary, but didn't he realize he owed his

[51] *See* Smith (n. 35), 278.

[52] *See* Byker v. Mannes, 641 N.W.2d 210, 215 (Mich. 2002) ("That is, if the parties associate themselves to 'carry on' as co-owners a business for profit, they will be deemed to have formed a partnership relationship regardless of their subjective intent to form such a relationship.").

[53] Some argue that fiduciary relationships are understandable in light of the fiduciary's undertaking. That there are fiduciary relationships that fall outside this picture can be shown by focusing on parent–child relationships and other exceptional cases. *See* Lionel D. Smith, *Contract, Consent, and Fiduciary Relationships* in Paul B. Miller & Andrew S. Gold (eds.), CONTRACT, STATUS, AND FIDUCIARY LAW (Oxford University Press 2016) 117, 133. To say that ad hoc fiduciary relations need not involve a fiduciary undertaking is not to deny that such undertakings can assist in recognizing such relations. *Cf.* ibid., 134 n. 65 (recognizing this role).

[54] A related problem is that fiduciary status may be ascertainable, but figuring out its implications will impose high information costs. *Cf.* Robert H. Sitkoff, *An Economic Theory of Fiduciary Law* in PHILOSOPHICAL FOUNDATIONS OF FIDUCIARY LAW (n. 6), 197, 205 (noting import of clear lines of demarcation across fiduciary types).

beneficiary a certain kind of behavior in light of their interactions and their relation to each other? In short, the relation that underpins the legal relationship is voluntary, even if the legal ramifications come as a surprise.

C The Import of Choice at the Extralegal Level

Ad hoc fiduciary relationships thus raise questions as to whether they are the product of power-conferring or duty-imposing legal rules. In fact, they reflect the duty-imposing aspects of fiduciary law but in a somewhat unusual way. This is because they are generally the product of a voluntary choice vis-à-vis the nonlegal relationship between the parties, but often not the product of a voluntary choice when viewed at the level of their *legal* relationship.

This divergence is not unique, for contract law implicates the same basic structure (albeit with important differences). In the contract setting, it is a doctrinal fact that one may end up with legal obligations despite no intent or even awareness that the underlying promises would trigger legal obligations. As Gregory Klass suggests, "[i]f the fiduciary obligations that attach to … non-legal voluntary relationships are similar to contractual obligations, they are similar to contract law's duty imposing aspect – the fact that one can acquire contractual obligations unawares."[55] This is precisely how ad hoc fiduciary relationships operate, for the legal recognition of ad hoc fiduciary relationships can surprise the parties.

But if the duty-imposing aspects of contract law sometimes catch the parties unaware, there is an important mitigating factor. People who enter into promises generally know that they have done so, and their promise is a form of consent to the resulting moral obligations. Promising is a classic exercise of a normative power, and it is characteristically a voluntary practice.[56] It is also a voluntary practice with broadly understood import, even if at the margins promissory obligations are contested. While a contractual promise will have legal ramifications that the promisor is sometimes unaware of, at least she will generally be aware of the promissory obligations that result, and those promissory obligations are often a close fit for the contractual obligations that the law imposes.

This relationship between promises and contracts can help mitigate concerns with notice. Promisors may not be aware of their legal ramifications, but they generally know about their closely aligned promissory responsibilities. They can't say that there was no performance obligation from a moral point of view.

Note also that a contractual promise is ordinarily something that occurs at a specific moment in time and usually such that both parties can easily point to the promise at issue. Outside of certain difficult cases, the existence of a promise is usually clear-cut, and its bindingness is well recognized in the relevant community. People know whether they have promised and when it took effect. They know when it bound them, and they know that their moral obligations changed in that instant. In other

[55] *See* Gregory Klass, *What If Fiduciary Relationships Are Like Contractual Ones?* in CONTRACT, STATUS, AND FIDUCIARY LAW (n. 53), 93, 102.

[56] This is so even if one holds the view that promises are capable of being made without intending to do so.

words, they have timely notice with respect to what they morally owe, and this has bearing on the fairness of imposing legal obligations.[57]

How can a fiduciary's choices play a similar role for ad hoc fiduciary relationships? Some fiduciary relationships begin with contracts or promises, but many fiduciary relationships do not – and this is commonly so with respect to ad hoc fiduciary relationships.[58] In the adviser setting, the same concern applies with equal force. Indeed, in a case like *Burdett* v. *Miller*, there may be no precise moment where an ad hoc fiduciary suddenly took on fiduciary obligations in a way that is recognizable to a neutral observer. It is also difficult to claim that the fiduciary in a case like *Burdett* consciously undertook to be a legal fiduciary, notwithstanding the importance of undertakings to some other fiduciary relationships.[59] It is thus fair to ask how an ad hoc fiduciary is able to make a choice that is analogous to the choice made by a contractual promisor.

To make the relevant distinctions clearer, it may help to differentiate types of voluntariness. Drawing on David Owens's work, Klass notes that fiduciary relationships could be voluntary relationships in three ways.[60] To begin, they could be "first grade choice dependent."[61] A first-grade choice-dependent obligation is "the result of [the individual's] prior choice, but without regard to whether she knew she was incurring the obligation."[62] As Klass argues, "[b]y driving a car, . . . I incur a legal and moral obligation not to drive drunk, whether I know I am incurring it or not."[63]

A second-grade choice-dependent obligation arises "where someone's choice puts them under [the] obligation only when they make this choice in the knowledge that it might have the effect of putting them under this obligation."[64] This is true of friendship. One who knows the obligations of friendship will acquire them through certain forms of conduct, while someone who knows nothing of what it is to be a friend does not take on the obligations of a friend by acting as a friend would act.[65] She needs to know what friendship is first. By contrast, third-grade choice dependence arises "when a person not only must know that her choice will result in a new obligation, but must intend or

57 Granted, some contractual cases do involve difficulties in determining the precise moment of formation. I thank Greg Klass for noting this possibility.

58 On the significance of such cases, see Daniel Markovits, *Sharing Ex Ante and Sharing Ex Post: The Non-contractual Basis of Fiduciary Relations* in PHILOSOPHICAL FOUNDATIONS OF FIDUCIARY LAW (n. 6), 209. For a related argument against contractual reductivism, see JOHN GARDNER, FROM PERSONAL LIFE TO PRIVATE LAW (Oxford University Press 2018) 45–46.

59 Such cases are, accordingly, a challenge for an undertakings-based view of fiduciary relationships. *But cf.* James Edelman, *The Role of Status in the Law of Obligations: Common Callings, Implied Terms, and Lessons for Fiduciary Duties* in PHILOSOPHICAL FOUNDATIONS OF FIDUCIARY LAW (n. 6), 21. On the other hand, undertakings can also contribute to the recognition of an ad hoc fiduciary relationship. *See* Smith (n. 53), 117, 134 n. 65.

60 Klass (n. 55), 107 (discussing DAVID OWENS, SHAPING THE NORMATIVE LANDSCAPE (Oxford University Press 2012) 3–6).

61 Klass (n. 55), 107.

62 Ibid.

63 Ibid.

64 Ibid.

65 *See* OWENS (n. 60), 4.

appear to intend the obligation if she is to incur it."[66] These obligations result from the exercise of normative powers like the power to promise.

With respect to *legal* obligations, ad hoc fiduciary relationships do not generally resemble either second-grade choice-dependent or third-grade choice-dependent obligations (though they may qualify as first-grade choice dependent). These relationships implicate legal obligations even if the parties have no idea that this will occur (or even that a legal relationship now exists between them). On the other hand, with respect to *moral* obligations, the ad hoc fiduciary is often in a second-grade choice-dependent relationship.[67] That relationship (be it friendship or some other relation of trust and confidence) is voluntary, and it is generally recognizable to the parties who participate in it, even in the absence of a precise moment when the relationship is chosen.[68] And this has import for the appropriateness of judicial recognition of the legal relationship.

D The Voluntariness of Involvements

Is it problematic that people can become legally recognized ad hoc fiduciaries without knowing it? As noted, the same surprise outcome can occur with contracts. As Klass recognizes: "Parties acquire contractual obligations simply by entering into exchange agreements, which are not distinctively legal acts. It is therefore possible for persons to acquire contractual obligations unwittingly."[69] This can also occur with partnerships. While the remedies differ in fiduciary settings, the notice concern that arises here is accordingly not peculiar to ad hoc fiduciary relationships. What is more unusual is the absence of a clearly delineated moment of choice regarding the nonlegal counterpart.

Still, even if there is no precise moment that we can recognize someone officially entering into an ad hoc fiduciary relationship (or an underlying nonlegal relationship), adequate notice regarding the type of moral obligations that are owed in these cases may still exist. To see how this can be, we will want to think further about how nonlegal relationships form.

Ease of recognition is commonplace for a range of nonlegal relationships that have no precise moment of creation. Friendships are famous for this; people do not become friends simply by announcing they will be friends.[70] The development is necessarily

66 *See* Klass (n. 55), 107.

67 As noted, not all ad hoc fiduciary relationships resemble *Burdett*. This chapter emphasizes cases in which the extralegal relationships at issue do bear some similarity to the type described in that case. It is an interesting question whether and when other ad hoc fiduciary relationships also involve moral obligations that stem from second-grade choice-dependent relationships. I leave those questions open here.

68 While this chapter has focused on involvements, there may also be interesting cases that implicate attachments (and these may not be voluntary at the entry point). The possibility that attachments play a role is beyond the scope of this chapter, but it merits further exploration. I am grateful to Gerald Postema for noting this issue.

69 *See* Klass (n. 55), 100.

70 For helpful discussion, see OWENS (n. 60), 106 (noting that "one cannot take on obligations of *friendship* simply by communicating the intention to do so"); Joseph Raz, *Respect for Law* in THE AUTHORITY OF LAW: ESSAYS ON LAW AND MORALITY (Oxford University Press 1979) 257 ("The friendship itself, involving an intricate web of reciprocal dispositions and attitudes, cannot be created by an act of commitment. It has to grow, develop, and cement over time.").

gradual. Granted, fiduciary loyalty obligations are not usually arrived at gradually; these fiduciary obligations may spring into existence at the moment a given categorical relationship is entered into, even if the parties have just met each other.[71] But the ad hoc fiduciary relationship is an exception to the rule; fiduciary loyalty in this context comes into play at approximately the same point that extralegal loyalty comes into play – and that development is the result of a gradual process.

To better see how this is possible, we need to recognize that relations like relations of trust and confidence (and perhaps other relationships that contribute to recognition of ad hoc fiduciaries) are a special kind of relationship; these relationships are typically *involvements*.[72] As involvements, they bring two or more parties together in a way that is not formally announced but that is readily apparent to the parties involved and to third parties in the relevant community.

David Owens helpfully introduces the idea of an involvement in his book *Shaping the Normative Landscape*, and it is this idea that we need in order to understand what is at stake. Owens begins with the acquaintanceship, drawing on the sociological work of Erving Goffman.[73] As Owens notes, people don't just count as acquaintances because they happen to know about each other; they must know each other in a way that involves social recognition. They must have certain behavioral dispositions toward each other. An acquaintanceship is not something that happens through a specific moment of choice. A past history, such as a long conversation at a party, can bring about the necessary change in social relation, with the result that each acquaintance will now have social expectations regarding the other's behavior.

As Owens explains, "[a]n involvement is a dynamic syndrome of attitudes, of behaviour that expresses (or purports to express) those attitudes and of norms that govern both attitudes and behaviour."[74] They build over time, but once we are established in such relationships, we also find characteristic obligations attach. Different involvements will have different kinds of obligations. In some cases – as with rivals – the obligations are quite narrow; in others – as with close friendships or loving relationships – the obligations are broad. In each case, involvements are chosen, *voluntary* relationships.

Like acquaintanceships, friendships are involvements, and they are particularly relevant here.[75] Friendship clearly plays a major role in the legal analysis for cases like *Burdett* v. *Miller*. This is part of what convinces the court that Miller is a fiduciary.

71 *See* Stephen A. Smith, *The Deed Not the Motive: Fiduciary Law without Loyalty* in CONTRACT, STATUS, AND FIDUCIARY LAW (n. 53), 213, 214–15 (contrasting loyalty's development over time with the instant appearance of legally recognized fiduciary obligations).

72 I would not claim that they are *necessarily* involvements. That would be hard to demonstrate for the nonlegal relationships at issue and perhaps also inconsistent with individual legal cases.

73 *See* OWENS (n. 60), 97 (citing ERVING GOFFMAN, INTERACTION RITUAL ch. 7 (1963)).

74 *See* OWENS (n. 60), 97.

75 I would by no means suggest that friends as such are fiduciaries. That would distort both friendships and the law of fiduciary relationships. *Cf.* Paul B. Miller, *Dimensions of Fiduciary Loyalty* in RESEARCH HANDBOOK ON FIDUCIARY LAW (n. 1), 180, 191 (noting that "the law rarely, if ever, requires of fiduciaries the kind of devotion that we expect of persons with moral loyalties."). Fiduciaries often owe something less than what friends owe, and friendships would often be ruined if their obligations were enforceable in the way fiduciary obligations are.

To the extent it is friendships that courts draw upon, they are recognizable, voluntary relationships that have no readily identifiable moment of origination. And we are also dealing with relationships that implicate thick trust, such that there is a genuine potential for epistemic dependence. Indeed, such trust is part of what tells us that a friendship is genuine.

One might question whether trust is a sine qua non for a friendship, and perhaps it isn't always. Imagine someone saying about a claimed friend: "I would trust him with my life, but when we play tennis, I don't trust him to give accurate line calls." This can be a genuine friendship, but it does not include trust in all cases.[76] On the other hand, if someone doesn't trust a purported friend in any context, it can reasonably be asked if they are really friends. On the usual understanding, friendships require trust (and something more than thin trust), even if they do not require trust in all contexts.

Relations of trust and confidence can also help support a case for recognition of an ad hoc fiduciary relationship. They likewise appear to be involvements in the ordinary case (whether or not they are friendships), and given the way that trust develops over time, they probably have to be if they are to exist at all. A cannot tell B to adopt an attitude of thick trust toward A and expect this will occur all at once.[77] Even if B wants to have that kind of trust, trust is not just a matter of willpower: trust builds up over time.

Granted, extralegal relations of trust and confidence are not enough on their own to support imposition of fiduciary liability. What matters is their (potential) link to epistemic dependence, which, under the right circumstances – notably, where there is an effective discretionary power over the significant practical interests of another – supports legal recognition of a fiduciary relationship. Relations of trust and confidence are settings in which thick trust is par for the course, and they offer the right backdrop for epistemic dependence to develop. What also matters is the voluntariness and recognizability of such relationships, and they are characteristically both voluntary and recognizable.

Is a relation of trust and confidence a distinct kind of involvement? Or is it just a special kind of friendship or acquaintanceship or other independently existing involvement? Outside of the law, people don't often refer to relations of trust and confidence in their social interactions. That makes identification by name somewhat more difficult, even if the relationship and what it entails is recognizable on reflection. This kind of relationship might just be a subset of friendships, but it is less clear that it must be. Perhaps sometimes we have relations of trust and confidence with non-friends. We might imagine cases where we lack the affection and well-wishing attitude toward certain individuals that is required to view them as friends while still feeling the requisite trust and sharing the requisite confidences with them.

Yet it doesn't matter for our purposes whether relations of trust and confidence are sometimes an independent category or always a subset of the friendship relation or

[76] *Cf.* Hill & O'Hara (n. 24), 1740–44 (describing selective trust).

[77] It is a disputed question whether trust can arise instantly (or nearly so) or instead requires a substantial period of time. Much depends on the definition of trust at issue. For discussion, see RUSSELL HARDIN, TRUST & TRUSTWORTHINESS (Russell Sage Foundation 2002) 79–81.

another involvement type. Friendships are indicative of the relevant kind of trusting relationship, and in combination with other evidence, they can appropriately convince a court that thick trust exists between the parties.[78] Other supporting (but nonfriendship relationships) can suffice. If relations of trust and confidence present their own category, trust is still a necessary component, and it will need to be thick trust if the relation is to provide strong support for recognition of an ad hoc fiduciary relationship.

These nonlegal involvements thus show how trust can have an additional function in the ad hoc fiduciary setting. Trust is central to nonlegal relationships that underpin legally recognized fiduciary relationships. Yes, trust results in a certain type of vulnerability, but trust is also a component of certain crucial nonlegal voluntary relationships – and this has bearing on concerns regarding notice to would-be fiduciaries. That these nonlegal relationships exist should not surprise their participants, at least not in the contexts where courts tend to pick them out. Trust is part of how we identify those nonlegal relationships that merit treatment as ad hoc fiduciary, and the widespread social understanding of these nonlegal relationships mitigates what would otherwise be substantial concerns about the fairness of imposing fiduciary duties on unknowing parties.

5 Conclusion

Trust is significant for fiduciary relationships in multiple ways. It is unquestionably important in cases involving advice. This chapter focuses on settings where this holds true: categorical fiduciary relationships and ad hoc fiduciary relationships. The reasons why trust matters in each setting overlap, but they are not identical.

For categorical relationships, a strong form of trust is closely linked to epistemic dependence. Recognition that such trust is likely can help justify a relationship's recognition as a categorically fiduciary relationship. So understood, the fiduciary category is adopted for prophylactic reasons. Seeing the law in this way can also help to address a skeptical challenge raised against the leading accounts of fiduciary relationships. It is argued that to the extent these accounts incorporate a fiduciary's discretion over her beneficiary's assets or person, they fail to adequately address various advisory settings in which a fiduciary lacks such discretion. Seeing categorical relationships as a prophylactic measure calls this skeptical challenge into doubt.

Ad hoc fiduciary relationships that center on advice can similarly be justifiable in light of epistemic dependence. Yet trust is important here for another reason: trust plays a part in the formation of certain nonlegal relationships that ground duties of loyalty outside the law. These nonlegal relationships are involvements, and accordingly they develop gradually rather than reflect a specific moment in which they are undertaken. Like other involvements, these nonlegal relationships are nonetheless voluntary, and to the extent their conventions are broadly recognizable, they mitigate concerns with notice and fairness to the would-be fiduciary.

[78] Note that there are also special relationships in tort law that implicate involvements. *E.g.*, friendship-linked affirmative duty cases, such as *Farwell v. Keaton*, 240 N.W. 2d 217 (Mich. 1976). The significant features of involvements may bear on other fields within private law.

Ad hoc fiduciary relationships involve the duty-imposing aspects of fiduciary law – and thus these relationships can be entered into unwittingly – but the underlying nonlegal relationships generally reflect a fiduciary's choice. This represents a relatively unusual private law case. Fiduciary law is not the only setting in which the law takes note of involvements, but involvements are rarely a source of legal liability. However, in advisory settings, involvements may be an especially important step along the way to recognition of a fiduciary relationship. The reasons why are closely tied to the importance of trust. Trust helps us to recognize the existence of the underlying involvement, and the involvement renders legal obligations a more appropriate consequence of the parties' interactions.

Some adviser relationships do not involve epistemic dependence or more than a minimum of trust, but the likelihood that they will is enough to support fiduciary recognition on a categorical basis. As in other areas of fiduciary law, prophylactic rules sweep broadly but sensibly in these cases. In ad hoc fiduciary settings, trust can do something more. Trust can help us pick out circumstances in which a fiduciary and a beneficiary are part of an involvement. And while trust and advice are not always found within our involvements, it matters morally and legally when they are.

3

Contracts, Fiduciary Relationships and Trust

MATTHEW HARDING*

1 Introduction

In this chapter, I consider the operation of trust in contracts and fiduciary relationships. Much has been written about how trust might figure in each setting, but there is little academic literature comparing the profile and workings of trust against the backdrop of the two legal forms. The gist of my argument is that contracts tend to orient and channel trust in one set of ways, and fiduciary relationships in a different set of ways. I begin in Section 2 by drawing a distinction between interpersonal trust and what, informed by work in sociology, I call 'confidence' in the predictable functioning of social or technological systems. I then argue that confidence is likely to develop differently in contracts than in fiduciary relationships, and that this has implications for how trust is likely to develop in each legal setting. In Section 3 of the chapter, I argue that there are reasons to think that the content of trusting beliefs might be different in fiduciary settings than in contractual settings. These reasons look to key differences between the contract form and the form of fiduciary relationships. I then explore some types of cases in which contract and fiduciary forms interact in ways that might affect the content of trusting beliefs. Section 4 concludes.

At the outset, I want to acknowledge that contracts and fiduciary relationships often overlap; for example, many relationships recognized in law as fiduciary are formed by contract. By drawing a distinction between contracts, on the one hand, and fiduciary relationships, on the other, I do not intend to deny this undeniable truth. Rather, I draw the distinction for analytical purposes, to illuminate features of contracts and fiduciary relationships as distinct legal forms. Indeed, such analytical work stands to deepen understanding of precisely those circumstances in which contract and fiduciary relationships overlap, and I have more to say about such circumstances in Section 3 of the chapter.

2 Trust and Confidence in Contracts and Fiduciary Relationships

In previous work, I have argued for an expansive understanding of interpersonal trust as an attitude of optimism directed at the freedom of other people to make

* My sincere thanks to Farrah Ahmed, Rob Atkinson, Michael Bryan, Carolyn McLeod, Paul Miller, Jeannie Paterson, Julian Sempill, Jason Varuhas and Yip Man, each of whom helped me in important ways in preparing this chapter.

choices and, to that extent, a response to the risks associated with human agency, usually in matters that implicate interests of the truster or about which the truster cares.[1] Thus understood, trust is protean in character, capable of taking on a variety of situation-specific forms. In some cases, trust is nothing but an attitude, as evidenced by the trust of young children in their parents.[2] However, in many cases, and certainly in cases of interest for the present paper, a trusting attitude is combined with certain beliefs.[3] Because of the protean character of trust, the beliefs with which it combines might refer to a range of matters bearing on human agency: for example, trust might come packaged with a belief that the trusted has good will towards the truster, or it might combine with a belief that the trusted is a person of a certain character, for example a person of moral integrity or virtue.[4] Trust might also inform a belief that the trusted will faithfully perform some social role that she occupies, and it might even combine with nothing more remarkable than a belief that the trusted will act in some matter from self-interest. This latter type of belief reveals what might be called 'thin' trust, as opposed to the manifestations of 'thicker' trust entailed in beliefs about good will, character or even role performance. Nonetheless, insofar as they respond to the risk associated with human agency, optimistic beliefs about a trusted's self-interested performance count as trusting on my understanding of trust.

Thus understood, trust may be contrasted with other combinations of attitude and belief, for example hope or faith. For present purposes, I want to concentrate on a different contrast, highlighted by sociologists who have worked on trust: the contrast between trust on the one hand, and confidence in social or technological systems on the other.[5] Both trust and confidence may be marked out as optimistic attitudes that typically combine with beliefs. But confidence may be distinguished from trust based on its primary concern or preoccupation. Confidence abstracts from human agency itself and takes as its subject matter the social or technological systems within which people make choices; such systems are defined by generalized norms or mechanisms the successful operation of which deliver predictable outcomes.[6] In contrast, trust focuses on people and the choices they make within or against the backdrop of systems. In the case of confidence, it is typically settled and generalized beliefs about what may be predictably expected from systems that enable confidence to form and, at the same time, express it. Trust, on the other hand, is an attitude that, while optimistic, entails some degree of acknowledgement that the exercise of human agency might

[1] Matthew Harding, 'Manifesting Trust' (2009) 29 *OJLS* 245.

[2] On the trust of young children, see Annette Baier, 'Trust and Antitrust' (1986) 96 *Ethics* 231, 240–4.

[3] Such beliefs are typically resistant to evidence, sometimes significantly so: Karen Jones, 'Trust as an Affective Attitude' (1996) 107 *Ethics* 4, 16–17.

[4] Jones, ibid., emphasises beliefs about good will and character in her account of trust.

[5] See, e.g., Niklas Luhmann, *Trust and Power* (trans. H. David et al., John Wiley and Sons 1979); Niklas Luhmann, 'Familiarity, Confidence, Trust: Problems and Alternatives' in Diego Gambetta (ed.), *Trust: Making and Breaking Cooperative Relations* (Basil Blackwell 1988) 94; Adam Seligman, *The Problem of Trust* (Princeton University Press 1993); Adam Seligman, 'Trust and Sociability: On the Limits of Confidence and Role Expectations' (1998) 57 *Am. J. Econ. Sociol.* 391.

[6] Of course, systems can fail, for example if participants in them do not understand and adhere to their constituent norms. Rule of law pathologies affecting legal systems are good examples.

disappoint: to this extent, trust recognizes that people can be unpredictable.[7] The perspective entailed in confidence seems a valuable one in a complex, post-industrial society in which people encounter each other as strangers but within relatively well-defined and well-understood systems. Nonetheless, the perspective entailed in trust seems equally important, especially in circumstances where clear definition and shared understanding in relation to systems is unavailable.[8]

When thinking about how trust operates within some system, then, it is important to consider how confidence might operate within that system as well. The interaction of trust and confidence against such a backdrop is a subject on which different views might be formed. For example, the sociologist Adam Seligman argues that trust arises only at 'system limits' where confidence cannot take root.[9] The overall picture for Seligman is one in which trust is a 'gap filler' within systems whose predictable functioning generates confidence. The implication of this analysis is that where we might expect to see confidence, we should not also be looking for trust. But arguably this understanding pays insufficient attention to the different perspectives entailed in trust and confidence, and the different concerns of the two phenomena. Thus, when considering the operation of trust within systems, I think we should be open to the possibility that a person might trust another within or against the backdrop of such a system while at the same time maintaining confidence in one or another aspect of the system itself. I might have confidence in the mechanical workings of my wife's car, while at the same time trusting her to drive the car safely. And I might have confidence that my lawyer has received rigorous training and continuing professional education while also trusting her to be a person of good character. There is no inconsistency in these different packages of attitude and belief, each of which depends on which matters I foreground in my thinking.[10]

I think there is a lesson here for how we approach the interplay of trust and confidence in the settings of contracts and fiduciary relationships. Theoretical work on both legal forms has tended to assume that in circumstances where confidence forms, trust is not present, and vice versa. Some argue that law is a substitute for trust, implying that trust is not present in any legally constituted relationships.[11] Many writers on trust assume that the distinction between informal modes of interaction and formal contracts entails a distinction between trusting and confident attitudes and beliefs.[12]

[7] This aspect of trust is emphasised by Luhmann, 'Familiarity, Confidence, Trust' (n. 5), 97–8; see also Diego Gambetta, 'Can We Trust Trust?' in Diego Gambetta (ed.), *Trust: Making and Breaking Cooperative Relations* (Basil Blackwell 1988) 213, 218.

[8] Luhmann, for example, views the two as symbiotic: 'Familiarity, Confidence, Trust' (n. 5), 102–3.

[9] Seligman, *The Problem of Trust* (n. 5), ch. 1.

[10] In saying this, I do not mean to suggest that a person chooses to trust or have confidence in circumstances where both attitudes might form. I tend to the view that trust cannot be willed. On this, see Baier (n. 2), 244, and Jones, (n. 3), 18; but cf. Richard Holton, 'Deciding to Trust, Coming to Believe' (1994) 72 *Aust. J. Phil.* 63.

[11] Larry Ribstein, 'Law v. Trust' (2001) 81 *BUL Rev.* 553. Cf. Frank Cross, 'Law and Trust' (2005) 93 *Geo. LJ* 1457.

[12] See, e.g., Francis Fukuyama, *Trust: The Social Virtues and the Creation of Prosperity* (Penguin Books 1995) 63; Russell Hardin, 'Distrust' (2001) 81 *BUL Rev.* 495; Edna Ullmann-Margalit, 'Trust, Distrust, and In Between' in Russell Hardin (ed.), *Distrust* (Russell Sage Foundation 2004) 60.

And a similar tendency may be observed in contract theory, in debates about whether contracts, like promises, enable trust to be invited and accepted or whether they enable parties who do not trust each other to cooperate nonetheless on the basis of confidence in enforceable law.[13] Theorists who assume that in contractual settings confidence and trust are mutually exclusive rather than potentially overlapping set up the two phenomena in opposition to each other when in many circumstances the reality is likely to be more complex. Equally, by focusing too much attention on the question whether fiduciary relationships truly are, as is often claimed, relationships characterized in some special way by trust, we risk neglecting the possibility that such relationships typically entail not only trust, but also confidence in the legal system and in particular the distinctive rules of fiduciary law.[14] I think it is important when developing the idea that confidence is present in some way in a contract or a fiduciary relationship not to assume that because of this trust is not present, and I try to heed this lesson in what follows.

What, then, can be said about how confidence might form and develop in contractual and fiduciary settings, and what are the possible implications for trust in each of those settings? To begin with, I want to consider confidence in two systems that are obviously in view whenever a contract or a fiduciary relationship is formed: the systems of contract law and fiduciary law. In the case of a contract, a party to that contract may form confidence in the rules of contract law quite apart from any beliefs (trusting or otherwise) she has about the counterparty; indeed, it may be a confident belief in the predictable functioning of contract law that enables her to overcome the risks associated with non-performance by the counterparty and causes her to enter into the contract. Of course, in the ordinary case, contract law is not designed to ensure performance; rather, as is well known, it is designed to ensure the payment of expectation damages in the event of non-performance.[15] To that extent, confidence in the rules of contract law is not confidence that the counterparty will be compelled to perform; it is confidence that sufficient remedial consequences will flow from non-performance, where sufficiency is measured against the performance interest.[16] Where a party enters into a contract on the basis of this sort of confidence, any risk associated with an assurance of expectation damages rather than performance itself

[13] Contrast Charles Fried, *Contract as Promise* (Harvard University Press 1981); Dori Kimel, *From Promise to Contract: Towards a Liberal Theory of Contract* (Hart Publishing 2003); Anthony J. Bellia Jr, 'Promises, Trust and Contract Law' (2002) 47 *Am. J. Juris.* 25.

[14] My own previous work has fallen short in this regard: see, e.g., Matthew Harding, 'Trust and Fiduciary Law' (2013) 33 *OJLS* 81.

[15] *Robinson* v. *Harman* (1848) 1 Exch. 850 (Parke B), 855. Two notes should be entered in relation to the statement in the text. First, equity's operation on contract law ensures that assurances of performance are available in some circumstances: see generally ICF Spry, *The Principles of Equitable Remedies: Specific Performance, Injunctions, Rectification and Equitable Damages* (9th ed., Lawbook Co. 2014). And contract law itself has developed assurances of good faith in matters of performance (for a recent example, see *Bhasin* v. *Hrynew* [2014] 3 SCR 494 (SCC)) although the scope and implications of these remain contested.

[16] This does not mean, however, that the performance interest is invariably fully recognised: see, e.g., *Ruxley Electronics and Construction Ltd* v. *Forsyth* [1996] AC 344 (HL).

will presumably be reflected in the contract price.[17] And perhaps it will be the occasion for the formation of trusting beliefs about the counterparty alongside confidence in the workings of contract law, a thought to which I return below.[18]

In contrast to contract law, key rules of fiduciary law seem designed to ensure performance. For example, the 'no conflict' rule aims to prevent a fiduciary from being in a position in which her personal interests (or other duties) can improperly influence the discretionary decision-making in her principal's interests that is at the heart of her fiduciary responsibility.[19] It is a rule designed to maximize the likelihood of due performance. Equally, the 'no profit' rule operates to deliver to the principal unauthorized profits made within the scope of fiduciary responsibility, thus guaranteeing performance of the fiduciary's commitment to serve the principal's interests in relation to profits derived within that scope.[20] The principal who is weighing up whether to enter into a fiduciary relationship and who forms confident beliefs about the application of these rules to her circumstances is thereby able to achieve confidence about performance itself and not only about the application of satisfactory remedial rules in the event of non-performance.

To the extent that contract law is not designed to ensure performance, contract law seems to offer less than fiduciary law to the party who seeks to deal on the footing of confidence in the legal system. Does this mean that where parties form contracts notwithstanding contract law's lack of assurances of performance, those parties are more likely to trust each other than parties seeking to form fiduciary relationships who enjoy such assurances? The suggestion might seem odd to those whose intuition is that fiduciary relationships are more, not less, likely than contracts to be characterized by trust.[21] However, the suggestion should be viewed with suspicion, because it exhibits the oppositional thinking about trust and confidence against which I warned earlier. It fails to account for the possibility that a principal's confidence in fiduciary law's assurances of performance might be consistent with her trusting her fiduciary, and indeed that those assurances might even contribute in important ways to the formation of the principal's trust. Equally, the suggestion neglects the possibility that

17 See Daniel Markovits, 'Sharing *Ex Ante* and Sharing *Ex Post*: The Non-contractual Basis of Fiduciary Relations' in Andrew S. Gold and Paul B. Miller (eds.), *Philosophical Foundations of Fiduciary Law* (Oxford University Press 2014) 209, 212. It may also be addressed by a liquidated damages clause, rendering certain ex ante the quantum of damages payable in the event of breach.

18 As Paul Miller and Rob Atkinson have each pointed out to me, this analysis is complicated to the extent that parties mistakenly think that contract law is designed to ensure performance: see further Matthew A. Seligman, 'The Error Theory of Contract' (2018) 78 *Md. L. Rev.* 147. Patterns of confidence and trust in such circumstances do not align with contract law as it truly is.

19 See *Bray* v. *Ford* [1896] AC 44 (HL), 51–2, referring to 'human nature being what it is' and noting the 'danger in such circumstances, of the person holding a fiduciary position being swayed by interest rather than by duty, and thus prejudicing those whom he was bound to protect'. See also Paul B. Miller, 'Dimensions of Fiduciary Loyalty' in D. Gordon Smith and Andrew S. Gold (eds.), *Research Handbook on Fiduciary Law* (Edward Elgar 2018) 180.

20 See Lionel Smith, 'Fiduciary Relationships: Ensuring the Loyal Exercise of Judgement on Behalf of Another' (2014) 130 *LQR* 608, 625–32.

21 Note *Norberg* v. *Wynrib* (1992) 92 DLR (4th) 449 (SCC), 488 (McLachlin J): 'The fiduciary relationship has trust, not self-interest, at its core.'

the absence of assurances of performance in contract law might tend to inhibit trust in contracts rather than be the catalyst for such trust to form.

To understand this better, notice that key rules of contract law and fiduciary law, such as the rule that expectation damages are the standard remedy for breach of contract and the 'no conflict' and 'no profit' rules that apply to fiduciaries, are operative not only in adjudicative settings when findings of liability are being made and remedies being ordered. Such rules also signal to relevant communities of practice what is expected of them when they utilize the contract or the fiduciary relationship as a legal form. Viewed from this ex ante perspective, fiduciary law's assurances of performance take on the character of clear statements about what that performance consists in, statements that are supplemented on occasion by rhetorical flourishes indicating the qualities and virtues that are entailed in being a good fiduciary.[22] The effect of this is to give to the fiduciary who seeks to be worthy of her principal's trust a road map indicating how to do so. The trustworthy performance of such a fiduciary might then trigger trust on the part of the principal who started out only with confidence in fiduciary law's assurances of performance.[23] In contrast, the rule of contract law that expectation damages are the standard remedy for breach of contract, while firmly rooted in the performance interest, nonetheless expresses no clear message about what trustworthy performance looks like; to an opportunistic party, it might be interpreted as indicating that efficient breach is acceptable.[24] It seems, to that extent, unlikely to promote the development of trust between parties. In fiduciary relationships, inter-party trust and confidence in fiduciary law may thus develop in a virtuous interaction; in contracts, matters are arguably different.

The next point to notice is that a party to a contract or a fiduciary relationship might form confidence in regulatory systems other than contract law or fiduciary law. For example, a party to a consumer contract may have confident beliefs about performance grounded in her understanding of the protections of consumer law. The customer of a bank may form similar beliefs based on knowledge of a regulatory scheme governing the provision of banking services.[25] In the fiduciary setting, regulatory oversight might inform confident beliefs on the part of beneficiaries of pension trusts or other managed funds; similarly, the client of a law firm might be confident in relation to performance because of known facts about the duties of lawyers to the court and the administration of justice. In the modern administrative state, in which

[22] Perhaps the best-known such statement is that of Judge Cardozo in *Meinhard v. Salmon* (1928) 249 *NY* 458, 464 ('A trustee is held to something stricter than the morals of the market place. Not honesty alone, but the punctilio of an honor the most sensitive, is then the standard of behaviour. . . . Only thus has the level of conduct for fiduciaries been kept at a level higher than that trodden by the crowd.').

[23] My understanding of trustworthiness is set out in Matthew Harding, 'Responding to Trust' (2011) 24 *Ratio Juris* 75, 81–5.

[24] See, e.g., the High Court of Australia's description of the appellant's position in *Tabcorp Holdings Ltd* v. *Bowen Investments Pty Ltd* (2009) 236 CLR 272, [13].

[25] In Australia at the present time, it seems unlikely that bank customers possess this sort of confidence to a high degree: Royal Commission into Misconduct in the Banking, Superannuation and Financial Services Industry, Final Report (1 February 2019).

contract law and fiduciary law sit alongside numerous regulatory schemes governing different roles, practices and institutions, it seems plausible to suggest that confident beliefs about those regulatory schemes might be present in many contractual and fiduciary settings.[26] But it seems difficult to draw, from the facts of regulation, specific conclusions about the likelihood of trust in cases where regulation is present. In some cases, confidence in regulation might take the place of trust in a contract or a fiduciary relationship; in others, via the signalling function to which I alluded above, regulation might inform trustworthy performance, which in turn generates trust.[27] To the extent that contract law lacks assurances of performance, regulation might have some special value in contractual settings insofar as it triggers confident beliefs about performance. But the extent to which it does so in fact is another question, the answer to which depends on empirical investigation.

A different account might be given of cases where the performance of contracts and fiduciary responsibilities itself entails the functioning of systems. In such cases, confidence might take the form of optimistic beliefs about the systems on which performance depends. An example in contract might be my confidence that the payroll system at the University of Melbourne works predictably and dependably and that as a result I will be paid each fortnight. Another might be my confidence that the theatre tickets that I ordered online will be delivered to the address I provided when filling in the online order form. In the fiduciary setting, I might believe that risk management practices within a professional services firm will protect my interests as a client of that firm. Or I might be confident that a 'robo-adviser' to which I turn for financial planning advice has been programmed consistent with fiduciary responsibility to serve my interests.[28]

I think there are reasons to believe that confidence in systems on which contract and fiduciary performance depends is a widespread phenomenon. For one thing, in many contractual and fiduciary settings, the counterparty or fiduciary will not be a human being but rather a corporate entity that depends in key ways on the functioning of systems.[29] And even in cases where the counterparty or fiduciary is a human being, the contract or fiduciary relationship may sit in a complex institutional structure that is the natural focal point for the attitudes and beliefs of those who deal within it. When I think about my superannuation fund, I think not of the individual trustees of the fund who have fiduciary responsibility in relation to it; indeed, I do not

[26] This is an important theme of Roger Cotterrell's seminal article on the interaction of trust and confidence in the setting of (legal) trusts: 'Trusting in Law: Legal and Moral Concepts of Trust' (1996) 43 *Current Legal Problems* 75. And see also Michael Bryan, 'Trusts Law and the Problem of Moral Distance' in Nick Piska and Hayley Gibson (eds.), *Critical Trusts Law: Reading Roger Cotterrell* (Counterpress forthcoming 2020).

[27] This seems especially likely where a regulator's remit extends to educating those it regulates about aspects of contractual and fiduciary performance. A good example, drawn from my home jurisdiction, is the online guidance issued for charities by the Australian Charities and Not-for-Profits Commission about the 'governance standards' in Subdivision 45-B of the Australian Charities and Not-for-Profits Commission Regulation 2013 (Cth): www.acnc.gov.au/for-charities/manage-your-charity/governance-standards.

[28] On the fiduciary responsibilities of 'robo-advisers', see Simone Degeling and Jessica Hudson, 'Financial Robots as Instruments of Fiduciary Loyalty' (2018) 40 *Syd. LR* 63.

[29] See Bryan (n. 26) for further discussion.

even know their names. Rather, I think of the fund as an organization based on what (little) I know of how it operates. Another reason to think that contract parties and principals are likely to focus on systems when forming optimistic beliefs about performance is that technological systems play a significant role in the performance of many contracts and fiduciary responsibilities. Indeed, in some settings – 'smart contracts' come to mind – performance just is the smooth functioning of a technological system and nothing more.[30]

Earlier, I cautioned against assuming that where confidence is present trust cannot be, and vice versa. Nonetheless, it does seem arguable that in many cases where parties are likely to form confidence in systems by which contracts and fiduciary responsibilities are performed, those parties are unlikely to form trust. Earlier, I argued that one of the characteristics of trust that helps to render it a distinctive attitude is its concern with people and the choices that they are free to make. For trust to form, then, the would-be truster must be able to adopt a perspective about the trusted as a person with agency. To adopt such a perspective, the would-be truster must at least have a sense that she is dealing with a specific person; and depending on the circumstances, it may also be necessary for the would-be truster to have a sense of the sort of person she is dealing with. In circumstances where systems are interposed between people in such a way that their attention is drawn to those systems rather than to each other, trust is unlikely to take root. And in ways I have outlined above, this is what happens in many cases where contract or fiduciary performance is system dependent, for example where trustee companies administer large mutual funds or where people seek legal or financial advice from online services. Where the party to a contract or the principal in a fiduciary relationship thinks about performance as a question of the effective functioning of systems, she not only orients herself towards forming confident beliefs (to the extent that she has optimism about her circumstances); she also orients herself away from being able to form trust.

A further point might be made at this juncture. While there is enormous variety in contracts, the performance of many, especially simple, contracts depends more or less entirely on the smooth functioning of systems. Consumer contracts formed online offer some of the clearest examples. In these contracts, it seems exceedingly unlikely for trust as opposed to confidence to inform beliefs about performance. In contrast, while in many cases systems play an important role in the performance of fiduciary responsibilities, they rarely if ever make up the whole story of that performance. One reason for this is that in social and economic life, fiduciary responsibility is often – although not invariably – undertaken by individual people: company directors, solicitors, partners, guardians, employees and so forth. Even trusteeship continues in some respects to follow the nineteenth-century model of

[30] For critical analysis of 'smart contracts' that refers to the social norms surrounding contract practice: Karen E. C. Levy, 'Book-Smart, Not Street-Smart: Blockchain-Based Smart Contracts and the Social Workings of Law' (2017) 3 *Engaging Science, Technology, and Society* 1; Eliza Mik, 'Smart Contracts: Terminology, Technical Limitations and Real World Complexity' (2017) 9 *Law, Innovation and Technology* 269.

individual personal service.[31] Another reason why fiduciary performance is rarely if ever just a matter of the functioning of systems is that fiduciary responsibility entails the making of choices; indeed, in one view, to exercise discretionary powers in ways that serve the interests of others is part of what it means to be fiduciary.[32] These facts suggest that in fiduciary settings it is unlikely that a principal's focus will be solely or even primarily on the functioning of systems when questions of fiduciary performance are in view. Rather, the principal is likely to foreground her fiduciary's agency to some extent, at least where the fiduciary is a human being, and especially in circumstances where the principal has met her fiduciary and has some relevant beliefs about the fiduciary's character.

What seems more likely in a fiduciary setting is that the principal's attitudes and beliefs about fiduciary performance will engage in some way with her understanding of a social role. Some fiduciary relationships entail the fiduciary discharging a social role, such as guardian, solicitor or even trustee. And where a fiduciary occupies a social role constituted by a well-defined and well-understood system of norms,[33] a principal's optimism about the fiduciary's performance might take the form of confident beliefs about that system. I should say straight away that this does not distinguish fiduciary relationships from contracts; after all, the performance of many contracts entails one or both contract parties discharging a social role, and indeed the repeated performance of similar contracts over time helps in substantial ways to constitute social roles. For example, my own contractual obligations as an employee of the University of Melbourne both require that I discharge the role of university professor, and in their own small way contribute to the maintenance of 'university professor' as a distinct social role.

However, while both contracts and fiduciary relationships engage social roles in important ways, contract law seems less engaged with such roles than fiduciary law. As is well known, fiduciary law marks out certain categories of relationship and identifies these as prima facie fiduciary in character.[34] It thereby contributes to the systems of norms constituting the social roles entailed in the categories of relationship in question. Most notably, it is because of fiduciary law that roles such as guardian and solicitor are associated with the norms of other-regarding service that lie at the core of

[31] For a historical account of the model: Chantal Stebbings, *The Private Trustee in Victorian England* (Cambridge University Press 2002). And for a sociological insight into the persistence of the model: Brooke Harrington, *Capital without Borders: Wealth Managers and the One Percent* (Harvard University Press 2016).

[32] Thus in his influential judgement in *United States Surgical Corporation* v. *Hospital Products Ltd* (1984) 156 CLR 41 (HCA), 97, Justice Mason of the High Court of Australia referred to an undertaking to serve the interests of another 'in the exercise of a power or discretion which will affect the interests of that other person in a legal or practical sense'. See also Ernest Weinrib, 'The Fiduciary Obligation' (1975) 25 *UTLJ* 1; Paul B. Miller, 'A Theory of Fiduciary Liability' (2011) 56 *McGill LJ* 235.

[33] On social roles as constituted by systems of norms, see Manfred Rehbinder, 'Status, Contract and the Welfare State' (1971) 23 *Stan. L. Rev.* 941, and the discussion of Rehbinder's work in Hanoch Dagan and Elizabeth S. Scott, 'Reinterpreting the Status-Contract Divide: The Case of Fiduciaries' in Paul B. Miller and Andrew S. Gold (eds.), *Contract, Status, and Fiduciary Law* (Oxford University Press 2016) 51, 57–8.

[34] In *United States Surgical Corporation* v. *Hospital Products Ltd* (1984) 156 *CLR* 41 (HCA), Justice Mason referred (at 96) to trustee-beneficiary, solicitor-client, agent-principal, company director-company, partner-partner and (perhaps more controversially) employee-employer.

fiduciary responsibility;[35] in addition, fiduciary law, in its expressive dimension, gestures to other norms associated with such roles and provides role occupants with resources to utilize when reflecting on how best to discharge the roles in question.[36] In contrast, contract law tends not to organize itself around categories of relationship; rather, contract law tends to presuppose parties that use contract terms to craft bespoke arrangements tailored to their particular circumstances.[37] To this extent, contract law does not contribute to systems of norms that constitute social roles, nor does it tend to exert any particular influence on the meaning of social roles, even if many contracts entail the performance of such roles.[38]

What are the implications of fiduciary law's interest in social roles for the ways in which trust operates in fiduciary relationships, and how (if at all) does this distinguish the operation of trust in fiduciary relationships from its operation in contracts? I think the answer to this question lies in an argument along the lines I offered above: by helping to constitute and inform certain social roles, fiduciary law signals to fiduciaries what is entailed in performance of those roles; and due performance from a fiduciary who has correctly interpreted fiduciary law's signals might then trigger trust on the part of a principal who previously lacked it. Where a principal responds to the facts of due performance by forming optimistic beliefs about future performance that engage with the system of norms constituting her fiduciary's social role, her beliefs are best described as confident rather than trusting. But where a principal's response to the facts of due performance concerns itself with the fiduciary as a human being with choices to make in the performance of her role, then trust may form. In contrast, while a contract party might well form trusting beliefs about her counterparty's performance of some social role, such beliefs will not respond to signals about role performance in contract law, because contract law sends no such signals. To this extent, it might be said that fiduciary law tends to orient parties more towards forming trusting beliefs about role performance than does contract law.

3 The Content of Trusting Beliefs in Contracts and Fiduciary Relationships

This is a good point at which to leave the distinction between trust and confidence and turn to the content of trusting beliefs that might form – alongside or instead of confidence, depending on the circumstances – in contracts and fiduciary

[35] See P. D. Finn, 'Fiduciary Reflections' (2014) 88 *Aust. LJ* 127, 136: 'It is accepted as axiomatic that a consequence of concluding that a relationship is fiduciary in whole or in part is that, to that extent, the fiduciary is obliged to act in the interests of the beneficiary, or in their joint interest (as, for example, in the case of a partnership) to the exclusion of his or her own self interest.'

[36] For a fuller treatment of this topic, see Matthew Harding, 'Fiduciary Law and Social Norms' in Evan J. Criddle, Paul B. Miller and Robert H. Sitkoff (eds.), *The Oxford Handbook of Fiduciary Law* (Oxford University Press 2019) 797. See also Edward B. Rock, 'Saints and Sinners: How Does Delaware Corporate Law Work?' (1997) 44 *UCLA L. Rev.* 1009; Gregory S. Alexander, 'A Cognitive Theory of Fiduciary Relationships' (2000) 85 *Cornell L. Rev.* 767.

[37] See John Gardner, *From Personal Life to Private Law* (Oxford University Press 2018), 41–7, emphasizing the extent to which contract parties control the 'deontic content' of their relationship.

[38] Note, however, that other bodies of law regulating contract types might well contribute to the constitution and understanding of social roles: employment law seems a clear example.

relationships. Earlier I alluded to the protean quality of trust as an optimistic attitude that might potentially combine with a range of different beliefs depending on the circumstances. Thus, for example, trust might combine with a belief that the trusted has good will or is a person of a certain character, or will reliably discharge some social role, or (at the thin end of the spectrum) will act in some matter from self-interest. Trust's protean quality, along with the great diversity that exists in contracts and fiduciary relationships, suggests that we must view with caution any argument that the content of trusting beliefs formed by contracting parties may be reliably distinguished from the content of trusting beliefs formed by parties to fiduciary relationships. Nonetheless, in what follows I do want to suggest some reasons for thinking that trusting beliefs might have different content in contractual settings than in fiduciary settings. These reasons look to certain distinctive characteristics of the contract form that set it apart from the form of fiduciary relationships.

In talking about contract and fiduciary 'forms', I have in mind something along the lines described by Larissa Katz in recent work on legal forms in property law theory.[39] For Katz, legal forms are ways of framing thinking about interpersonal relations for legal purposes. One form might therefore treat as salient certain normative and conceptual features of such relations, and another form might pick out different normative and conceptual features of those same relations. The normative and conceptual commitments that animate a legal form constitute that form as a 'regulative ideal', to use Katz's phrase.[40] Whether such a regulative ideal should, in a given set of circumstances, operate undisturbed, or be qualified or overridden, stands to be answered in light of the full range of moral and policy considerations that bear on the legal system; in this sense, acknowledging facts about legal forms is not the same as subscribing to formalism (the view that legal forms should operate unaffected by such 'extrinsic' moral and policy considerations).[41] But for present purposes, my interest is in a different question: what implications might different legal forms have for the people who use them in planning their affairs?

In an important paper, Daniel Markovits supplies theoretical resources that enable us to address just this question with reference to contract and fiduciary forms. Markovits identifies some key ways in which those forms orient parties into 'distinct deliberative postures' in their dealings with one another.[42] In the case of a contract, argues Markovits, parties are assumed to deal with one another on the basis of self-interest, within parameters set by the bargain that they have struck. Thus, a contract may be viewed as a mechanism for drawing together self-interested parties and harnessing their self-interest to achieve outcomes that will benefit each of them individually. Moreover, the contract form invites parties to look to the terms of their contract in working out what they must do over the course of time. Their stance is

[39] Larissa Katz, 'Legal Forms in Property Law Theory' in James Penner and Michael Otsuka (eds.), *Property Theory: Legal and Political Perspectives* (Cambridge University Press 2018) 23.

[40] Ibid., 26.

[41] One of the best known examples of formalism in private law theory is Ernest J. Weinrib, *The Idea of Private Law* (2nd ed., Oxford University Press 2012).

[42] Markovits (n. 17). The reference to 'distinct deliberative postures' is on 210.

thus directed to their ex ante agreement. Finally, Markovits argues that the contract form contemplates parties dealing with each other as abstract persons – 'through their general intentional capacities and for their generic moral personalities' – rather than as individual people with particular interests, qualities and virtues.[43] The overall understanding of the contract, then, according to Markovits, is of a form that enables and emphasizes ex ante commitment to coordinated but self-interested action on a basis that abstracts to a substantial degree from parties' knowledge of each other's circumstances.

For Markovits, once these features of the contract form are properly understood, the contrast with the fiduciary form is evident. Markovits argues that, while contract parties are expected to deal with one another on a self-interested basis bounded by the terms of their bargain, fiduciaries are expected to advance the interests of their principals within the scope of the fiduciary relationship. Thus, a contract party who operates entirely on the basis of self-interest might thereby discharge her contractual obligations in full; in contrast a thoroughly self-interested fiduciary will fail to perform her fiduciary responsibilities. To the extent that fiduciary responsibility entails the fiduciary being other regarding, we might say it demands a sort of altruism.[44] Moreover, for Markovits, while contracts orient parties to their ex ante agreement, fiduciary relationships demand that fiduciaries be responsive to the changing circumstances of their principals over the course of time. In this sense, fiduciary commitment is dynamic whereas contractual commitment is not.[45] Finally, Markovits argues that fiduciary relationships tend not to presuppose parties that lack knowledge of each other's individual circumstances; rather, fiduciary responsibility typically requires that the fiduciary acquire knowledge of her principal beyond a sense that she is dealing with another morally free, self-directed agent.[46] At the same time, the fiduciary form invites a principal to respond to her fiduciary not only as self-directed and morally free, but also as a person who has undertaken to serve her interests and has discretionary powers to affect those interests.

Arguably, Markovits overstates the differences between the contract form and the fiduciary form. There are reasons to think that the contract form might, in certain types of case, orient parties towards an ongoing ex post consideration of the position of their counterparties understood as particular individuals. For example, courts in some jurisdictions recognize an implied contractual duty of mutual trust and confidence in contracts of employment,[47] demanding dynamic engagement with a

[43] For Markovits's arguments about contract: ibid., 211–14. The quotation is on 214. See also Daniel Markovits, 'Contract and Collaboration' (2004) 113 *Yale LJ* 1417, especially part II.

[44] On altruism in fiduciary settings, see further Harding, 'Fiduciary Law and Social Norms' (n. 36).

[45] The degree to which a fiduciary is required to be responsive in this way depends on the nature and scope of her fiduciary responsibilities. 'Fiduciary relations are of many different types; they extend from the relation of myself to an errand boy who is bound to bring me back my change up to the most intimate and confidential relations which can possibly exist between one party and another where the one is wholly in the hands of the other because of his infinite trust in him': *In re Coomber* [1911] 1 Ch. 723 (Fletcher Moulton J), 728–9.

[46] For Markovits's arguments about fiduciary relationships: Markovits (n. 17), 214–18.

[47] *Malik* v. *Bank of Credit and Commerce International SA* [1998] AC 20 (HL).

counterparty after entry into the contract; that said, in Australia at least the High Court has rejected any such implied contractual duty in the employment setting,[48] revealing anxiety about departing too far from the archetype of ex ante self-interest when developing the contract form. Perhaps the most that should be drawn from Markovits's analysis – and all that needs to be drawn from that analysis for present purposes – is that the contract form typically or centrally situates parties in the ex ante self-interested deliberative posture described by Markovits, while the fiduciary form typically or centrally situates parties in the different stance to which he alludes. Focusing on the typical or central cases stands to illuminate the two forms in useful ways when thinking about patterns of trust and confidence, all the time acknowledging that the forms are not exhausted by the typical or central cases.

What are the implications of Markovits's analysis – now interpreted in this qualified fashion – for our understanding of the operation of trust in contracts and fiduciary relationships? One point that immediately stands out is that the contract form, as understood by Markovits, seems to orient parties towards forming relatively thin trust in relation to performance; parties who adopt the 'deliberative posture' of contract, to use Markovits's phrase, are thereby invited to channel their trust into beliefs about self-interested adherence to ex ante commitments unaccompanied by specific knowledge of the circumstances of the counterparty.[49] In contrast, fiduciary relationships seem to orient parties away from forming such thin trust. No doubt a principal might form beliefs that her fiduciary will be self-interested in matters of performance, and such beliefs might be trusting in a thin sense. For example, a principal might trust her fiduciary to advance her interests because the fiduciary is concerned to maintain a professional reputation or craves the approbation of her peers. However, insofar as fiduciary performance entails advancing the principal's interests, a principal who understands the nature of that performance is likely to seek to form trusting beliefs that take her fiduciary to be other regarding, beliefs that render it thicker. Equally, the fact that a fiduciary is committed to respond to her principal's changing circumstances over time, and the associated fact that in order to do so she must come to know her principal's circumstances in some concrete way, suggests that a principal who understands the nature of fiduciary performance might well combine trust with relatively thick beliefs about aspects of the fiduciary's character that bear on the discharge of this ongoing commitment.

It must be stressed that neither contract parties nor principals in fiduciary relationships need form trust; as I argued earlier, parties who do not trust each other may

48 *Commonwealth Bank of Australia* v. *Barker* (2014) 253 CLR 169 (HCA).

49 The sort of trust I have in mind here is akin to what Russell Hardin calls 'trust as encapsulated interest': see Russell Hardin, *Trust and Trustworthiness* (Russell Sage Foundation 2002), ch. 1; Russell Hardin, 'Distrust: Manifestations and Management' in Russell Hardin (ed.), *Distrust* (Russell Sage Foundation 2004) 3; Russell Hardin, 'The Street-Level Epistemology of Trust' (1993) 21 *Politics and Society* 505. In trust as encapsulated interest, the truster believes that the trusted believes that it is in the trusted's interest to take seriously the interests of the truster. On Hardin's account, the trusted has such a belief because she values an ongoing relationship with the truster. The contract form seems well suited to facilitating trust as encapsulated interest, especially in settings where contract parties hope to deal with one another on an ongoing basis or repeatedly.

nonetheless deal with each other in either setting on the footing of confidence in relevant systems.[50] At the same time, contract parties and principals in fiduciary relationships may form trust, whether thin or thick, quite apart from the existence of a contract or a fiduciary relationship. Such trust might combine with beliefs about aspects of the parties' relations that have little to do with the legal form in which their dealings have come to be manifested.[51] Indeed, as Lisa Bernstein shows in her celebrated study of the diamond industry, in some cases parties eschew legal forms altogether and deal solely on the basis of trust that refers to elements of their extralegal relations.[52] My argument here is not that parties to contracts or fiduciary relationships necessarily form trusting beliefs with any particular content; nor is it even that such parties are likely to form such beliefs. Rather, my argument is that the contract form, at least in typical or central cases, tends to orient parties towards forming trusting beliefs that render trust relatively thin, and that the form of the fiduciary relationship tends to orient parties towards forming trusting beliefs that render trust thicker. All else being equal, this argument might suggest a conclusion that contracts are typically accompanied by thin trust while fiduciary relationships are typically accompanied by thicker trust. But of course all else is not equal.[53]

In the remainder of this section, I want to consider some types of case in which contract and fiduciary forms interact in ways that might affect the content of trusting beliefs. To begin with, I return to an observation I made early on: many relationships recognized as fiduciary in law are formed by contract. In some cases a party is committed by contractual terms to perform some role or function recognized as fiduciary in law; in other cases, specific contractual undertakings may place a party in a position that is characterized factually by the incidents of a fiduciary relationship.[54] Where a contract generates a fiduciary relationship, two legal forms apply to the parties' dealings. Thus the principal is invited by the contract form to develop thin trust combined with beliefs concerned with the self-interested performance of ex ante commitments, and at the same time invited by the fiduciary form to develop thicker trust combined with beliefs about ongoing other-regarding

[50] Such parties may have no relevant attitudes about human agency or they may even have an attitude of distrust: for an exploration of these alternatives to trust see Edna Ullmann-Margalit, 'Trust, Distrust and in Between' in Russell Hardin (ed.), *Distrust* (Russell Sage Foundation 2004) 60.

[51] See Stewart Macaulay, 'Non-contractual Relations in Business: A Preliminary Study' (1963) 28 *Am. Sociol. Rev.* 55.

[52] Lisa Bernstein, 'Opting Out of the Legal System: Extralegal Contractual Relations in the Diamond Industry' (1992) 21 *J. Leg. Stud.* 115.

[53] In this regard, much may be learned from the 'relational contract theory' most powerfully articulated by Ian MacNeil. (See, e.g., Ian R. MacNeil, 'Relational Contract Theory: Challenges and Queries' (2000) 94 *Nw. UL Rev.* 877.) MacNeil's emphasis on the complex relations within which contractual dealings occur helps us to see the manifold ways in which trust might develop between contract parties. I do not, however, accept MacNeil's further claim that our conceptual understanding of the contract form is incomplete unless it accounts for these complex relations. The inability to isolate the contract form from other aspects of the relations between contract parties seems to me a theoretical loss rather than a theoretical gain.

[54] Whether a contract generates a fiduciary relationship in this way is a notoriously difficult interpretive question: see further *United States Surgical Corporation* v. *Hospital Products Ltd* (1984) 156 CLR 41 (HCA).

engagement with the principal's interests. That said, it seems unlikely, at least over time, that a principal will maintain thin trust directed at the self-interested performance of contractual obligations insofar as her counterparty is also her fiduciary. The longer a fiduciary relationship formed by contract endures, the more likely it seems that the principal's trust will cease to be concerned with the ex ante commitments of the contract and become concerned instead with the ongoing performance of the fiduciary responsibilities owed to her. Correspondingly, it seems plausible that such a principal's trust will thicken over time, shifting away from beliefs about self-interested performance and attaching to beliefs about, say, the character of the fiduciary.

Contrast this with the situation where a contract confers on a party a non-fiduciary discretionary power to affect the interests of the counterparty.[55] Contract law has developed an approach that, in theory, enables parties to form and maintain thin trust notwithstanding that their counterparties enjoy discretionary powers to affect their interests. Specifically, contract law recognizes an implied term demanding that the party who exercises a discretionary power must in doing so achieve a standard of lawfulness, good faith and reasonableness, and must take into account relevant considerations and set aside irrelevant considerations.[56] This approach enables parties to view the exercise of discretionary powers as a matter of self-interested performance of ex ante commitments, where those commitments include the obligations to which the implied term refers. However, the fact that contract law enables this perspective does not mean that parties are likely to adopt it. Parties may never have adverted to the implied term.[57] Moreover, it seems plausible to suggest that when forming attitudes and beliefs about the exercise of a discretionary power, a potentially affected party will be primarily concerned with matters that are pertinent at the time the power is to be exercised, rather than at the time the power was conferred. Non-fiduciary discretionary powers conferred by contract thus seem to create circumstances in which, notwithstanding the contract form, it is difficult for thin trust to develop. However, neither is the fiduciary form available to point the party in the direction of the thicker trust that I earlier associated with that form. In such circumstances, if the party potentially affected by the exercise of the discretionary power is to form relatively thick trusting beliefs about, say, the character of the power holder, those trusting beliefs are likely to develop quite apart from any applicable legal form.

In addition to cases in which fiduciary relationships are formed by contract, there are cases in which contract and fiduciary forms interact because a contract is entered into within the scope of an extant fiduciary relationship. For example, in the Australian case of *United Dominions Corp. Ltd* v. *Brian Pty Ltd*, parties who were negotiating a joint venture agreement had started to perform their anticipated contract even

[55] For insightful analysis of contract law's regulation of non-fiduciary contractual discretionary powers: Stephen Kos, 'Constraints on the Exercise of Contractual Powers' (2011) 42 *VUWLR* 17; Michael Bridge, 'The Exercise of Contractual Discretion' (2019) 135 *LQR* 227; Jason N. E. Varuhas, 'Contractual Powers' (unpublished paper on file with the author).

[56] *Braganza* v. *BP Shipping Limited* [2015] UKSC 17.

[57] Indeed, Varuhas suggests that the implied term should be considered implied in law not in fact, reflecting the fact that it responds to general concerns and not to the circumstances of individual bargains: (n. 55).

before entering into it.[58] In light of that fact, along with the fact that the parties expected the anticipated contract to create a fiduciary relationship between them, the parties' pre-contractual relationship was recognized as fiduciary.[59] A side agreement between two of the three negotiating parties could not be relied on as it was entered into in breach of fiduciary obligation. In this sort of case, an extant fiduciary relationship constrains parties who seek to utilize the contract form and, to that extent, deal on the basis of the 'deliberative posture' of contract, to once again use Markovits's phrase. Fiduciary law refuses to allow such parties to frame their relations according to their chosen legal form, framing those relations instead according to a different legal form that acknowledges and enables the thick trust that is likely to be present on the facts. In this regard, it is noteworthy that in *United Dominions Corp.*, members of the High Court of Australia referred explicitly to the likelihood of 'mutual trust and confidence' in the pre-contractual setting in view.[60]

Matters are different where a fiduciary relationship arises against the backdrop of an extant contract without being generated by the terms of that contract. In the partnership case *Birtchnell* v. *Equity Trustees, Executors and Agency Co. Ltd*, Justice Dixon of the High Court of Australia recognized this possibility in a well-known passage: '[t]he subject matter over which fiduciary obligations extend is determined by the character of the venture or undertaking for which the partnership exists, and this is to be ascertained, not merely from the express agreement of the parties, whether embodied in a written instrument or not, but also from the course of dealing actually pursued by the firm'.[61] Justice Dixon had in mind cases in which the scope of a fiduciary relationship formed by contract changes over time because of factors not contemplated by the contract terms; nonetheless, his logic extends also to cases in which a contract establishes a non-fiduciary relationship and the ongoing dealings of the contract parties generate a superimposed fiduciary relationship after the contract is entered into. Earlier, I suggested that in fiduciary relationships formed by contract, parties are likely over time to shift their attention away from the contract terms and towards the ongoing performance of fiduciary responsibility. This creates conditions under which relatively thick trust can form. In the same way, in cases where parties' ex post dealings cause a fiduciary relationship to be superimposed on an extant contract, the law recognizes that parties have ceased to frame their relations according to the contract form and have instead begun to frame those relations according to the fiduciary form. Here, far from overriding the parties, fiduciary law follows their lead, framing their relations according to the legal form that most accurately reflects their own understanding and the likely patterns of their trust.

Another way in which the contract and fiduciary forms interact so as to affect the content of trusting beliefs is via the 'contractualization' of fiduciary relationships.[62] By this I mean the use of contract terms to confine or eliminate a fiduciary relationship

[58] (1985) 157 CLR 1 (HCA).
[59] Ibid., 7–8 (Gibbs CJ), 12 (Mason, Brennan and Deane JJ), 16 (Dawson J).
[60] Ibid., 8 (Gibbs CJ), 12 (Mason, Brennan and Deane JJ), 16 (Dawson J, referring to 'mutual confidence').
[61] (1929) 42 CLR 384 (HCA), 407–8.
[62] For discussion of this phenomenon, see further Bryan (n. 26).

that might otherwise be present on the facts.[63] Examples abound in modern commercial practice. For example, in the Privy Council case of *Kelly* v. *Cooper*, the scope of a fiduciary relationship between a firm of real estate agents and its client was limited by the implied terms of the agency.[64] In Australia, in *Australian Securities and Investments Commission* v. *Citigroup Global Markets*, a contract for the provision of investment banking services provided bluntly that the investment bank was engaged 'as an independent contractor and not in any other capacity including as a fiduciary'.[65] And in the English case of *Citibank MA* v. *MBIA Assurance SA*, a trust instrument in a transactional setting authorized a third party to direct the trustee in the exercise of various powers, thus overriding any fiduciary responsibility that the trustee might otherwise have had in the exercise of those powers.[66]

In cases such as these, the contract form is deployed to override or displace the fiduciary form. In many instances – although query whether all the cases to which I just referred are good examples – this deployment of the contract form is successful because contract terms clearly demonstrate that neither party is committed to advance the interests of the other, and there are no other indicia present that might point to such a commitment. Where parties utilize the contract form to achieve this result, they thereby create conditions under which they are positioned to develop the relatively thin trusting beliefs about performance that I earlier associated with the contract form. However, in some exceptional circumstances, a deployment of the contract form to forestall or thwart a fiduciary relationship might fail because, on the facts, the relationship between the parties clearly reveals a commitment on the part of one or both to advance the other's interests in just the way entailed in a fiduciary relationship, notwithstanding contract terms that stipulate otherwise. In this sort of case, no degree of contractual stipulation can render the relationship other than what it truly is. There are implications here for law, for example in relation to the interpretation of contract terms.[67] But of more interest for present purposes are the implications of such a failed deployment of the contract form for the content of trusting beliefs that parties might develop. On the one hand, contract terms seem to point in the direction of thin trust; on the other hand, the fact that the parties' relationship is fiduciary in character seems to point in the direction of thicker trust.

[63] I leave to one side a different sort of 'contractualization' of fiduciary relationships, that in which contracts and fiduciary relationships are viewed as instances of the same underlying form. Against these contractualists (for example, James Edelman, 'When Do Fiduciary Duties Arise?' (2010) 126 *LQR* 302; James Edelman, 'The Importance of the Fiduciary Undertaking' (2013) 7 *J. Eq.* 128), I side with Markovits. Another well-known example of contractualist thinking focuses not on legal form but rather legal function: John Langbein, 'The Contractarian Basis of the Law of Trusts' (1995) 105 *Yale LJ* 625. I have nothing to say here about this functionalist contractualism except that my arguments in the text suggest that the contract and fiduciary forms may serve different valuable functions insofar as they orient and channel trust in different ways.

[64] [1993] AC 205 (PC).

[65] (2007) 160 FCR 35 (Jacobson J), [16].

[66] [2006] EWHC 3215.

[67] See further Paul Finn, 'Contract and the Fiduciary Principle' (1989) 12 *UNSWLJ* 76; Mark Leeming, 'The Scope of Fiduciary Obligations: How Contract Informs, but Does Not Determine, the Scope of Fiduciary Obligations' (2009) 3 *J. Eq.* 1.

If the parties form thin trusting beliefs associated with the contract form, their trust seems to misunderstand the true character of their relationship. But if the parties' attitudes to their relationship engage with factors other than applicable legal forms, then the fact of their unsuccessful contractual effort to eliminate the fiduciary form may turn out to be irrelevant to explaining their trust in matters of performance.

A more troubling type of case entails the unilateral use of contractual methods to minimize or eliminate a fiduciary relationship that might otherwise arise. I use the term 'contractual methods' to indicate that, although the cases I have in mind are not cases in which the contract form is invoked – they are, rather, cases of unilateral action – they nonetheless entail the crafting of bespoke terms that is a hallmark of the contract form. They are, to that extent, instances of 'contractualization'. A good example is the New Zealand case of *Clayton* v. *Clayton*.[68] There, a settlor expressed his intention in terms that enabled him, as the donee of a power of appointment, to distribute assets to himself as an object of that power. In doing so he could defeat entirely the interests in those assets of beneficiaries of a trust whose operation was contingent on the non-exercise of the power. The settlor in *Clayton* purported to render thoroughly self-interested what would otherwise be an archetypal fiduciary relationship.[69] It seems arguable that in *Clayton* the beneficiaries of the trust received mixed signals in relation to performance. On the one hand, their trustee was to an extent situated in a typically fiduciary position, holding discretionary powers the exercise of which might substantially affect the beneficiaries' interests. On the other hand, and critically, the trustee in *Clayton* did not undertake to advance the beneficiaries' interests when exercising his powers and so was not a fiduciary.[70] Moreover, the trustee's purpose in *Clayton* seemed to be to enable himself to act self-interestedly in respect of the assets while at the same time enjoying some of the asset protection benefits of the trust form. What sort of (interpersonal) trust might fit this peculiar arrangement?

The arrangement in *Clayton* seems analogous to a contract under which one party holds a non-fiduciary discretionary power to affect the interests of the other. As I suggested earlier, a contract party that stands to be affected by the exercise of such a power might, despite the contract form, develop relatively thick trusting beliefs about performance recognizing that the power holder is likely to have regard to factors other than ex ante contractual commitments when exercising it. Beneficiaries in a case such as *Clayton* might form similar beliefs. However, beneficiaries who know that their trustee's whole purpose has been to enable himself to exercise discretionary powers self-interestedly may not be disposed to form relatively thick trusting beliefs, for example about the trustee's character. It seems more likely that such beneficiaries, if they are optimistic at all, will form beliefs characterized by confidence in the rules of trusts law that spell out the constraints that apply to trustees' exercise of discretionary

[68] [2016] NZSC 29. See also *JSC Mezhdunarodniy Promyshenniy Bank* v. *Pugachev* [2017] EWHC 2426; *Webb* v. *Webb* [2017] CKCA 4.

[69] For the view that an express trust is an archetypal fiduciary relationship: Peter Birks, 'The Content of Fiduciary Obligation' (2000) 34 *Israel L. Rev.* 3.

[70] *Clayton* v. *Clayton* [2016] NZSC 29, [57]–[58].

powers. That said, trust law's rules constraining trustees' exercises of discretionary powers are obscure and unclear and may not justify a high degree of confidence on the part of beneficiaries. Overall, to the extent that the legal form of the parties' relationship in a case such as *Clayton* is ambiguous, beneficiaries lack reliable epistemic channels into which trust or confidence might flow. And this arguably increases the likelihood that other, less optimistic, attitudes might form in the minds of beneficiaries. But the implications for trust are not the most pressing concern raised by ambiguous legal form in a case such as *Clayton*. More urgent is the question whether the settlor of a *Clayton*-like arrangement has manifested sufficient intention to create something that even counts in law as a trust.[71] If not, then such arrangements have no legal effect, and questions about how interpersonal trust operates within them should not arise.

4 Conclusion

The short answer to almost any question about the operation of trust in contracts and fiduciary relationships is: 'it depends'. The contingency of this answer is driven by several considerations: the protean character of trust itself; the presence of normative and technological systems in contractual and fiduciary settings; and the multitude of contextual and relational factors that bear on contract and fiduciary forms when people utilize those forms in their dealings with one another. I hope this chapter has highlighted at least some of that complexity. But at the same time, I hope to have shown that something of sociological interest might be said about contracts, fiduciary relationships and trust, given that fiduciary relationships appear on the whole to be less system dependent than contracts. And I hope to have identified theoretical arguments, grounded in the distinctive characters of the contract form and the fiduciary form, for thinking that trusting beliefs in a contract setting might have different content than in a fiduciary setting.

[71] See further Mark Bennett, 'Competing Views on Illusory Trusts: The *Clayton v Clayton* Litigation in Its Wider Context' (2017) 11 *J. Eq.* 48; Charles Rickett and Jessica Palmer, 'The Revolution and Legacy of the Discretionary Trust' (2017) 11 *J. Eq.* 157; Lionel Smith, 'Massively Discretionary Trusts' (2017) 70 *Current Legal Problems* 653. In *Clayton* itself, the New Zealand Supreme Court recognized that this question was a live one on the facts but declined to answer it, preferring to determine the dispute on other grounds: see [2016] NZSC 29, [85]–[98] and [118]–[127].

4

Trust, Autonomy and the Fiduciary Relationship

CAROLYN MCLEOD AND EMMA RYMAN

According to most accounts of (bilateral) fiduciary relationships,[1] trust is an important element of a well-functioning fiduciary relationship.[2] Without trust, the fiduciary's ability to act in her beneficiary's interests would be at best significantly hampered, and at worst entirely thwarted. Placing one's trust in someone as one's fiduciary is, at least in the typical case, what gets the fiduciary relationship started and what allows it to function well. However, in entrusting a fiduciary with discretionary power over one's interests, one also makes oneself vulnerable to that person's misuse or abuse of one's trust.

The above description highlights the oft-discussed risks of harm that beneficiaries face as a result of placing their trust in disloyal or avaricious fiduciaries. However, some authors suggest that trust exposes beneficiaries to another, less widely acknowledged, type of risk: namely a threat to their autonomy. These writers put forth theories that place trust and autonomy squarely at odds with one another, such that trusting a fiduciary to act on one's behalf directly reduces one's ability to be self-governing. Our purpose in this chapter is to challenge this view, mainly by delving into philosophical work on autonomy and by explaining how autonomy, understood relationally – that is, as *relational autonomy* – requires trust.

This chapter has three main sections. Each one, for simplicity, focuses on bilateral fiduciary relationships (hereafter, simply 'fiduciary relationships'): in other words, relationships in which the fiduciary has a mandate to serve the interests of a particular

[1] We recognize that a widely agreed-upon understanding of what makes a relationship fiduciary remains elusive. While we endorse a view of the fiduciary relationship that emphasizes the fundamental role played by discretionary authority, our discussion is intended to be compatible with a range of views about the nature of the fiduciary relationship. On the discretionary authority of a fiduciary, see, for example, Paul Miller, 'A Theory of Fiduciary Liability' (2011) 56 *McGill LJ* 235. We endorse Miller's theory of the fiduciary relationship in Emma Ryman, 'Fiduciary Duties and Commercial Surrogacy' (PhD thesis, Western University 2017), https://ir.lib.uwo.ca/etd/4728, accessed 1 April 2019; and in Carolyn McLeod, *Conscience in Reproductive Health Care* (forthcoming in 2020 with Oxford University Press).

[2] This is the case even for theorists who deny that trust is a necessary component of the fiduciary relationship. (See, for example, Matthew Harding, 'Trust and Fiduciary Law' (2013) 33 *Oxford J. Legal Stud.* 81.) What trust is – that is, the nature of it – is a subject of intense discussion in moral philosophy; there are many different kinds of theories of trust in this literature. We use the concept here in a way that is compatible with most of these theories, with the exception of those that fail to distinguish between trust and reliance (what are called 'risk-assessment' theories) or to acknowledge that trustworthiness has a discretionary element. On different philosophical theories of trust, see Carolyn McLeod 'Trust', *The Stanford Encyclopedia of Philosophy* (3rd ed., 2015), http://plato.stanford.edu/entries/trust/, accessed 1 April 2019.

person.[3] In Section 1, we describe the view that these relationships are ones of trust but not autonomy (i.e. for the beneficiaries), and we also introduce an example that we use throughout the chapter to critique this idea. Section 2 draws on our background in moral philosophy to explain in general terms why trust and autonomy are *not* incompatible with one another, and why instead autonomy depends on trust in relationships like the fiduciary one. 'Autonomy' in this discussion is understood relationally and in terms of self-governance. Finally, Section 3 outlines how fiduciaries can use the trust their beneficiaries place in them to support their beneficiaries' autonomy.

1 Trust at Odds with Autonomy

As an example of a theory that describes the fiduciary relationship as inimical to autonomy, consider the following from Lionel Smith: 'When one person acquires the authority to make decisions *on behalf* of another person, there is a partial transfer of autonomy. One person is now authorized to act, not just in a way that *affects* another person, but rather *for* that other person.'[4] In Smith's view, the fiduciary relationship appears to inherently diminish the beneficiary's autonomy. He elaborates further:

> In every fiduciary relationship, the fiduciary acquires control over a part (or in some cases, all) of another person's autonomy. Autonomy is a person's ability to control what happens in his or her life. Autonomy itself cannot be transferred, in whole or in part. But the law does contemplate the transfer of certain levers by which autonomy is realised. That happens, for example, when the law allows one person to make legally effective decisions (say, regarding the disposition of property, or regarding medical care) that do not affect the decision maker, but only affect another person. In these cases, the decision-maker holds the legal controls of part or all of the other person's autonomy.[5]

Beneficiaries do transfer authority to fiduciaries to make certain kinds of decisions. In doing so, according to Smith, they also relinquish part of their autonomy – or at least, the legal controls over a part of their autonomy. To put the matter in terms of trust, when beneficiaries trust fiduciaries to act on their behalf, they 'hand over' part of their autonomy. This view seems to imply, in fact, that the more trust beneficiaries place in their fiduciaries, the more control over the 'levers' they give up, and hence the more compromised their autonomy becomes.

This tension between trust and autonomy in the fiduciary relationship also appears in Daniel Markovits's work, particularly when he explains:

3 For an account of fiduciary service mandates, see Paul Miller and Andrew Gold, 'Fiduciary Governance' (2015) 57 *Wm. & Mary L. Rev.* 513, 519–21. Other types of fiduciary relationships, such as those involving fiduciary governance mandates, also pose interesting questions concerning trust and autonomy. However, a thorough discussion of these issues would require, among other things, an account of collective agency, which is beyond the scope of this paper. For such an account, see, for example, Tracy Isaacs, *Moral Responsibility in Collective Contexts* (Oxford University Press 2011).

4 Lionel Smith, 'Fiduciary Relationships: Ensuring the Loyal Exercise of Judgement on Behalf of Another' (2014) 130 *LQR* 608, 613 (emphasis in original).

5 Ibid., 614.

> [F]iduciary loyalty and care build a measure of paternalism into every fiduciary relationship. . . . [E]ven where paternalism is not specifically required or permitted by law, it remains woven into the fabric of the fiduciary relation [because] the beneficiary has sought precisely the fiduciary's independent and (in commensurate measure) unreviewable judgment, and thus also the paternalism that the exercise of this judgment inevitably involves.[6]

Thus, in Markovits's view, there is something inherently paternalistic about a fiduciary's exercise of discretionary power. Paternalism is widely seen as anathema to autonomy, however fiduciary relationships therefore cannot be supportive of beneficiaries' autonomy.

The paternalism that Markovits sees as inherent to the fiduciary relationship exists because beneficiaries typically lack the technical knowledge or skill to effectively evaluate their fiduciaries' choices and actions. Beneficiaries are also rarely in a position to monitor the majority of the decisions that fiduciaries make while acting in their fiduciary role. As Markovits puts it: 'A fiduciary relation [is] appealing partly because a principal requires her agent to act in ways that she cannot substantially specify *ex ante* or cannot directly evaluate *ex post*.'[7] In this sense, fiduciary power is 'unreviewable' according to Markovits. While major decisions are usually left to beneficiaries (for example, a doctor allowing her patient to make the final choice about which medical treatment to receive), countless lower-level decisions (for example, about what information to present to her patient in order to obtain informed consent) are left to the fiduciary.

To be clear, fiduciary law does offer some protections for beneficiaries' autonomy. In the context of estates and trusts law, for instance, an executor has a duty to account to the beneficiaries of an estate, which provides a mechanism for beneficiary oversight.[8] Fiduciary power is therefore not *completely* unreviewable. Nonetheless, in most fiduciary relationships, where there are stark asymmetries in knowledge and power, it remains challenging for a beneficiary to review her fiduciary's exercises of authority in any meaningful way. Also, if a beneficiary were to closely monitor and direct the majority of her fiduciary's decisions, the relationship between them would cease to be a fiduciary one. Exercises of power by the fiduciary would no longer be discretionary, which is the hallmark of fiduciary authority.[9]

If a beneficiary stripped her fiduciary of any discretion, she would also no longer be *trusting* the fiduciary to act on her behalf, at least not in the robust sense of trust employed by many moral philosophers.[10] There is broad (though not complete)

[6] Daniel Markovits, 'Sharing Ex Ante and Sharing Ex Post' in Andrew S. Gold and Paul B. Miller (eds.), *Philosophical Foundations of Fiduciary Law* (Oxford University Press 2014) 217.

[7] Ibid., 215.

[8] Fiduciary power is limited more generally through rules on the permissible delegation of power, the enforcement of terms of fiduciary mandates, duties to account and disclose, etc. Thanks to Paul Miller for this point.

[9] See Miller (n. 1).

[10] The beneficiary may still *rely* on the fiduciary to achieve certain ends, because she has no choice but to do so. Perhaps the course of action she needs to take (e.g., acquiring prescription medications) can only be legally enabled by someone who holds a professional license.

consensus within moral philosophy that in a relationship of trust, as opposed to mere reliance, the person who is trusted has some freedom to act on her own judgement in living up to the trust that is placed in her. The actions of this person cannot be compelled by the watchful eyes of others or by the force of social constraints,[11] not without removing the 'special vulnerability' that comes with trusting another person.[12] For this reason, Annette Baier claims that there is a 'discretionary element' to trust, and more specifically, to trustworthiness.[13] Her theory suggests that upon taking away the discretionary power of a fiduciary, one ceases to trust her. Notice Markovits implies that removing this power has the opposite effect on one's autonomy: it preserves this quality. If both views are correct, then trust and autonomy truly are at odds with one another in the fiduciary relationship; they cannot exist together so long as the fiduciary exercises discretionary authority.

To better understand how the apparent tension between trust and autonomy plays out in the context of a fiduciary relationship, and also whether the tension is real or just apparent, it is useful to consider a detailed example. Imagine a relationship, then, between a lawyer and her client. Unlike the doctor–patient relationship (the fiduciary nature of which is subject to some debate), the relationship between lawyers and their clients is indisputably fiduciary.[14] In our example, the lawyer – call her Ada – works at a legal aid clinic. The clients she serves are all below the poverty line and are, generally speaking, highly vulnerable.

One of Ada's new clients – call her Bea – has been charged with assault for an alleged incident arising out of a house party, which Bea vehemently denies. Bea is an especially vulnerable client due to her health concerns and lack of education. Having left school very early, she is functionally illiterate and relies on Ada to read and explain to her all of her legal documents. Despite Ada's best efforts, Bea gets extremely frustrated and overwhelmed when discussing her case. On more than one occasion, Bea has told Ada that she trusts her completely and just wants to do whatever Ada thinks is best. Bea says she will happily sign anything that Ada tells her to.

In this example, Bea has given an enormous amount of discretionary power to Ada. She has made it clear that she wants to defer to Ada's judgement because she doesn't feel she can handle making legal decisions for herself. Bea's position appears to be one of compromised autonomy. The outcome of her criminal case could have a huge effect on her life, and she has handed over the decision-making reigns to another person. On the other hand, Ada appears to be in a position where she must act

[11] See McLeod (n. 2). For disagreement, see Diego Gambetta, 'Can We Trust Trust?' in D. Gambetta (ed.) *Trust: Making and Breaking Cooperative Relations* (Blackwell 1988), and Russell Hardin, 'Trustworthiness' (1996) 107 *Ethics* 26.

[12] Annette Baier, 'Trust and Antitrust' (1986) 96 *Ethics* 239. The 'special vulnerability' that Baier mentions is identical to what Paul Miller calls the 'structural vulnerability' of the beneficiary; Miller (n. 1), 254, 279.

[13] Baier (n. 12). Not all philosophers agree with Baier. In particular, Karen Jones says that Baier 'rather overstates the case in claiming that trust always involves discretionary powers'. See Jones, 'Trust as an Affective Attitude' (1996) 107 *Ethics* 8 n. 3.

[14] On the dispute about the fiduciary nature of the doctor–patient relationship, see, for example, Marc Rodwin, 'Strains in the Fiduciary Metaphor: Divided Physician Loyalties and Obligations in a Changing Health Care System' (1995) 21 *Am. J. Law Med.* 241.

paternalistically. Given the trust that Bea has placed in her, she must decide on Bea's behalf what course of action she thinks will produce the best outcome for Bea – for instance, whether it would be better for Bea to proceed to a criminal trial (an option that risks a harsher penalty but could also lead to full exoneration) or instead to try to negotiate a peace bond (an option that is much less risky but may impose behavioural requirements on Bea that would be difficult for her to adhere to, and would also require Bea to admit that her accuser's fear was reasonable). The more trust Bea places in Ada to make legal decisions for her, the less autonomy Bea appears to have.[15]

For those like Markovits, who deem all fiduciary relationships to be inherently paternalistic, or Smith, who think that fiduciary relationships necessarily involve a partial 'transfer' of autonomy (or of 'levers' for autonomy), there may be nothing wrong with Ada simply deciding for Bea. According to such views, Bea is allowing an expert to act on her behalf because that will provide her with the best outcome. So long as Ada is an upstanding and competent lawyer, and she exercises her discretionary power solely in the pursuit of Bea's best interests, then this is simply the fiduciary relationship functioning as it should. Although her relationship with Ada reduces her liberty in some regards – Bea isn't the one calling the shots when it comes to which legal strategy to pursue in her own case – this is presumably for her own good.

Some philosophers, such as Sarah Conly, have openly questioned whether autonomy, in and of itself, is important when compared to other potential gains (or reductions) in well-being.[16] As Conly puts it, 'autonomy is not all that valuable; not valuable enough to offset what we lose by leaving people to their own autonomous choices. ... Those who say we should respect autonomy by letting people hurt themselves irreparably do not, on my view, show as much respect for human value as they purport to.'[17] If compromised autonomy is the price that beneficiaries must pay to receive the benefits of a fiduciary relationship, then perhaps that is a fair cost. After all, without the assistance of a (competent, upstanding) lawyer, Bea's legal prognosis would probably be dismal.[18]

Yet, we are not entirely satisfied with such an explanation. Autonomy, we contend, *is* inherently valuable and deserving of protection, even in the context of a fiduciary relationship, where one party is acting on behalf of the other. Moreover, the benefits of a fiduciary relationship should not, we claim, be obtainable only at the expense of one's autonomy. The understanding of autonomy we wish to uphold, however, is not

[15] Admittedly, this example is unusual. Many, if not most, clients want to make legal decisions for themselves, and would never trust their lawyers to pick between a trial and a peace bond for them. We use this example not because it is illustrative of most lawyer–client relationships, but because it allows us to show that running roughshod over a beneficiary's autonomy – even one who asks her fiduciary to do what she thinks is best – is problematic and unnecessary.

[16] Sarah Conly, *Against Autonomy: Justifying Coercive Paternalism* (Cambridge University Press 2013) 1–2.

[17] Ibid.

[18] In general, while it is challenging to study whether having counsel 'makes the outcomes of adjudication "better" in the sense of making them more legally accurate or substantively just', research indicates that '[l]awyer-represented people are more likely to prevail than people who appear unrepresented, on average'. See Rebecca Sandefur, 'The Impact of Counsel: An Analysis of Empirical Evidence' (2010) 9 *Seattle J. Social Sci.* 50, 62, 69. With respect to Bea, given her vulnerabilities, she would likely fare worse than the average self-represented litigant.

autonomy as the 'ability to control what happens in [one's] life', which is Smith's view, or as the mere ability to 'live one's life according to one's decisions', which is Conly's view.[19] Rather, it is autonomy understood in a relational sense. Not only is relational autonomy not threatened by the fiduciary relationship, in our opinion, but where a beneficiary is capable of autonomy,[20] a trustworthy fiduciary can – and indeed should – serve as a relational support for this person's autonomy. In that case, autonomy would not be transferred or compromised in the fiduciary relationship. Instead, it would be enhanced.

2 Trust Together with Autonomy

In moral philosophy, 'autonomy' is generally understood to mean self-governance or self-direction.[21] This definition serves as a useful starting point for an argument in favour of our position about trust and autonomy. Let us build on it in an effort to show that rather than transfer any autonomy, beneficiaries maintain or even gain autonomy by trusting in fiduciaries who are committed to supporting their autonomy. Along the way, we will refine this definition of autonomy so that the capacity for self-governance is understood in relational terms.

Being self-governing is not equivalent to having control over what happens in our lives. To see why, consider that self-governance involves acting on reasons, values or ends 'that are [our] *own*'.[22] Such reasons or ends can encourage us to be dependent on others: for care, love, security, education, advice, etc.; in short, for many of the things that allow us, if we're lucky, to flourish. So long as we rely on others for these things, we do not control what happens to us, not completely anyway. Rather, some of this control lies with other people, namely those who will shape how much we are able to flourish. It follows that autonomy is not identical to controlling things in our lives. For the opposite to be true, the ideal of autonomy would have to be one of self-sufficiency, but self-governance does not require self-sufficiency. Autonomy would have little value if it did require that, moreover, given how much we rely on others for our lives to go well.[23]

To say that autonomy is not equivalent to control is not to say that control is never important for autonomy. We usually need some control over our bodily movements, for example, in order to be able to act on reasons or values that are authentic to us. What is more, assuming that reasons and values become authentic to us through some process of critical reflection and endorsement – as they do on most

[19] Conly (n. 16), 2.

[20] Our focus is on cases where the beneficiary has this capacity. Also, as is clear from our discussion of Bea's case, we believe that conditions such as illness or illiteracy tend not to pose insurmountable barriers to autonomy.

[21] Natalie Stoljar, 'Feminist Perspectives on Autonomy', *The Stanford Encyclopedia of Philosophy* (2015), https://plato.stanford.edu/entries/feminism-autonomy/, accessed 1 April 2019.

[22] Ibid., her emphasis.

[23] For more on why autonomy should not be identified with control, see Jennifer Nedelsky, 'Relinquishing Control: Autonomy, the Bodymind, and the Psyche' in *Law's Relations: A Relational Theory of Self, Autonomy, and Law* (Oxford University Press 2011).

philosophical accounts of autonomy[24] – then we require some control over our mental lives to be autonomous. More specifically, we need the control that is necessary to engage in the mental procedures that autonomy demands, including that of evaluating the options available to us to see which of them coheres best with our values (authentic ones). The control that we need to satisfy this particular procedural requirement is control over how we view our options; at the very least, our perception of them cannot be under the control of someone who is intent on deceiving us. These points about how control can be essential for autonomy explain – together or on their own – why conditions like the following undermine our autonomy: automatism, feeling 'out of control',[25] and being gaslighted.[26]

Thus, autonomy can require certain types of control; but at the same time, being autonomous is compatible with us being in relationships with people who have some control over what happens to us. Now, what about relationships in which people have substantial discretionary power over us? Above, we suggested that fiduciaries exercise discretionary power in deciding what information to offer their beneficiaries. They also use this power when choosing how to present the relevant information, whether to recommend particular courses of action and how to act on decisions their beneficiaries have made in light of the information they have received. Do any of these actions by fiduciaries inevitably compromise their beneficiaries' autonomy? We think the answer is clearly no: that so long as fiduciaries act in a way that furthers their beneficiaries' own values or objectives (e.g. in seeking their assistance), they respect their beneficiaries' autonomy. Fiduciaries can have their beneficiaries' autonomous goals in mind when choosing what information to present to them, for example, or how to present that information. Similarly, when acting on choices their beneficiaries have made, fiduciaries can direct their discretionary judgement towards carrying out their beneficiaries' will, rather than their own will or that of a third party.

To put the point from the perspective of the beneficiaries and in language used by Smith: in authorizing their fiduciaries to act on their behalves, beneficiaries may give up 'levers' of control, specifically over the means with which their goals are achieved; but that is not the same as giving up their autonomy. In addition, while this transfer of control puts their autonomy at risk – that much is true – this risk needn't materialize. In other words, the fiduciary relationship needn't be paternalistic (and normally shouldn't be that way either, as we discuss below).

The upshot in terms of autonomy (i.e. self-governance) is that autonomy does not require that we always act on our own behalves; we can trust others to act for us and still be autonomous so long as they are guided by our will. What our will is may be inferred, moreover, by the circumstances. For example, the will of a patient who goes to an emergency room writhing in pain is surely to have the pain treated. Fiduciaries

24 See, e.g., Catriona Mackenzie and Natalie Stoljar, 'Introduction: Autonomy Reconfigured' in C. Mackenzie and N. Stoljar (eds.) *Relational Autonomy: Feminist Perspectives on Autonomy, Agency, and the Social Self* (Oxford University Press 2000) and Andrea Westlund, 'Selflessness and Responsibility for Self: Is Deference Compatible with Autonomy?' (2003) 112 *The Philosophical Review* 483.

25 Nedelsky (n. 23), 277, 280.

26 See Paul Benson, 'Free Agency and Self-Worth' (1994) 91 *J. Phil.* 650.

needn't always have probing discussions with their beneficiaries about which ends they want to achieve in the relationship, for sometimes the ends will be patently obvious. At all other times, however, the fiduciaries will need to suss out what their beneficiaries' objectives are, that is, if they hope to further their beneficiaries' autonomy. Beneficiaries, in turn, need to divulge what their autonomous wishes are to their fiduciaries.

What about circumstances, however, where the beneficiary doesn't know what to wish for, and what is more, doesn't feel that she has the capacity or the desire to figure that out? She is reluctant to understand her situation fully and decide what to do in it, perhaps because it is overwhelming to her or everything else in her life is overwhelming and she can't handle yet another difficult choice. There is someone else who could make that choice for her, and so she decides to defer to them. She does so by saying, 'Just do what you think is best.' This is Bea's situation. The main question that her case raises about autonomy is whether we relinquish our autonomy if we grant this much discretionary power to others. In other words, can we allow others to act on our behalves so completely and still be autonomous?

Before moving forward, it will be useful to distinguish between what we'll call 'complete' and 'partial' deference. The latter is the act we just discussed, of letting others do what they think is best without them knowing what we want in our circumstances. By contrast, 'partial deference' occurs when those to whom we defer have this information and are expected to use it. Thus, allowing a fiduciary to choose for us with our autonomous goals in mind is an act of partial deference. We have already seen that such acts are compatible with autonomy. So, what about complete deference?

One might think that so long as autonomy means self-governance – again, acting on reasons or values that are our own – complete deference is consistent with autonomy. The reason why is plain: the values or reasons motivating us to be this deferential to others can be authentic to us.[27] In that case, we can *willingly* have others dictate how our lives will go, which they would do if the relevant decisions are serious enough. This view is the very opposite of the one found in Smith and Markovits, who suggest that giving others any discretionary power or control over us compromises our autonomy. The question before us now is this: why, when resisting their account of autonomy in the fiduciary relationship, should we avoid going to the opposite extreme and accepting that complete deference is compatible with autonomy?

Our answer is that when exercising complete deference, our values or reasons do not influence the decisions made on our behalf by the person we defer to. Although we may autonomously decide to be deferential in the first place,[28] we are not self-directing from that point onwards in our relationship with this person. For example, Ada does not know whether Bea would reject a peace bond because of what it suggests about the accusation against her. Ada would have to be motivated by her own values in deciding for Bea – or by what is best for Bea according to those values – which means she would not be respecting Bea's autonomy. In short, with complete deference, there is a loss of autonomy.

[27] See Stoljar (n. 21); Westlund (n. 24).

[28] We may not make that decision autonomously, for our deference could be self-abnegating; see below and Westlund (n. 24).

Some philosophers may disagree with us on this point. Consider the following from Andrea Westlund, who illustrates what she calls 'prudential deference' using the example of deference to experts:

> We would not normally think . . . that a patient who defers to her doctor regarding the appropriateness of some course of treatment lacks a mind of her own. So long as she is duly attentive to the expert's qualifications and character, we take her to be appropriately prudentially rational in seeking and abiding by such advice – she quite reasonably judges that she is likely to do better by deferring in this case. This motive to comply with expert advice . . . seems not to undermine but rather to express the agency of the one who defers.[29]

In other words, it promotes the patient's agency, understood by Westlund as autonomous agency. We agree with her that deference to experts may not be self-abnegating – one can engage in it and still have 'a mind of [one's] own'. Yet we insist that such action *can* diminish, if not undermine, our autonomy. In particular, if the experts are not aware of what is valuable to (or possible for) us in our circumstances, then their advice can easily compromise our autonomy. It can send us down a path that we would never choose for ourselves: that could throw our lives into chaos even. Experts can get things wrong – sometimes terribly wrong – when they lack guidance from the people they serve, because of the limits to their experiential knowledge of the lives of people who have different social positions or backgrounds than theirs.[30] For instance, Ada's social position and background may be *so* different from Bea's that she can't easily empathize with Bea with the aim of understanding what Bea would or should decide for herself. And if that were true of Ada, then Bea's deference to her would be both *non*-prudential and autonomy undermining.[31] Westlund seems to ignore such cases when she suggests that being 'duly attentive' to experts' 'qualifications and character' alone can make our deference to them prudential. What needs to happen as well, in our opinion, is that the experts themselves are duly attentive to what we, their patients or clients, want for ourselves, making our deference to them partial rather than complete. Deference of the former kind, not the latter, *is* prudential and autonomy enhancing. What is more, it is probably common in fiduciary relationships, because of the asymmetries of knowledge and information in these relationships.

[29] Westlund (n. 24), 486. Nana Kongsholm and Klemens Kappel refer to this phenomenon, of accepting expert advice, as 'consent based on trust' as opposed to 'consent based on information'; see their 'Is Consent Based on Trust Morally Inferior to Consent Based on Information?' (2017) 31 *Bioethics* 432. The patient agrees to what the doctor recommends because she trusts him, having some idea of the doctor's qualifications and character. Like Westlund, Kongshold and Kappel believe that this level of trust can further our autonomy, but we are not convinced that this is true, for the reasons given below.

[30] See, e.g., Susan Sherwin, 'A Relational Approach to Autonomy in Health Car' in the Feminist Health Care Ethics Research Network (ed.), *The Politics of Women's Health: Exploring Agency and Autonomy* (Temple University Press 1998).

[31] To be clear, we're not saying that deference or imprudence always conflict with autonomy. We can defer to others by letting them decide on our behalf and still be autonomous, so long as they are guided by our values, rather than just their own. We can be imprudent – for example, by 'hurt[ing ourselves] irreparably' (Conly (n. 16), 1) – and still be autonomous, so long as the reasons or values that motivated us to act are authentic to us.

To recap what we've argued so far, autonomy is compatible with being in relationships with people who exert some control over us, including by exercising discretionary power over us. The control or power simply needs to be channelled in a way that fosters or protects our autonomy. Where that is not possible, however – perhaps because those with the power lack a clear sense of what we value – any actions they take on our behalf will not promote our autonomy. These actions might instead be paternalistic (or be merely coercive or the like). While paternalism can occur in such circumstances, it is not inevitable in every fiduciary relationship. Contra Markovits, what determines whether a fiduciary's judgement is paternalistic or respectful of autonomy is whether it aligns with what the beneficiary wants for herself, not whether it is discretionary or 'unreviewable'. Beneficiaries *can* trust their fiduciaries to make discretionary, unreviewable judgements while also respecting their autonomy.

The trust of beneficiaries therefore needn't diminish their autonomy. Having argued for that point, we now want to go further and say that the trust of beneficiaries can enhance their autonomy and can even be essential for it. These claims bring us finally to a discussion about relational autonomy. The primary insight of philosophers who have relational understandings of autonomy is that autonomy does not occur in the absence of relationships that are supportive of it. Theories of relational autonomy originated within feminist philosophy among philosophers who wanted to explain how oppression can 'erode agents' autonomy'.[32] As a consequence of undergoing traditional and harsh forms of gender socialization, for example, women can be deferential in a way that *is* self-abnegating and therefore non-autonomous.[33] They can also simply lack options that cohere with what they value or experience as women (more specifically, as women of a particular race, class, level of ability, etc.), because the options made available to them do not take their needs or values into account.[34] This problem about options occurs when society is so oppressively structured that it serves men's needs (more specifically, privileged men) and their needs only. In response to barriers to autonomy like these – those that exist because of oppression – many feminists insist not just that the barriers should be removed, but also that they should be *replaced* with relationships and structures that promote people's autonomy equally. For these feminists, the experiences of oppressed people in having their autonomy eroded have revealed that autonomy is relational. It requires, in other words, not just that oppressive relations are absent, but also that supportive relations are present: those that foster our autonomy by ensuring that we develop 'a mind of our own', that we have options that cohere with what we value most, etc.

If autonomy is relational, then being able to trust well in others to support our autonomy is essential to it.[35] Rather than being at odds with one another, trust and *relational* autonomy go hand in hand. There are different conceptions of relational autonomy in the literature (e.g. those that are 'procedural' versus 'substantive', or

[32] Stoljar (n. 21), 11.
[33] Westlund (n. 24).
[34] Sherwin (n. 30).
[35] See Carolyn McLeod, *Self-Trust and Reproductive Autonomy* (MIT Press 2002).

'causal' versus 'constitutive'[36]), and depending on the conception, different kinds of trust relationships will be important for our autonomy. Although we cannot defend a particular account of relational autonomy here, we will appeal to one that fits with our intuitions about trust and autonomy in fiduciary relationships (one that is constitutive in nature).

For beneficiaries to be autonomous, it is important that they can trust their fiduciaries. More specifically, they need to be able to trust them to do the following sorts of things: generate a list of options or perhaps a recommendation for them, which makes sense given their (the beneficiaries') values; help them to understand their options or the recommended course of action well enough that they can choose autonomously; and act on the autonomous choices they make in the spirit in which they made them – in other words, with their motives in mind. Trust is essential here because beneficiaries normally cannot do these things for themselves and cannot, because of their lack of expertise, confirm whether their fiduciaries are doing them either. Thus, their relationship of trust with their fiduciary is a 'defining condition' of their autonomy, which is relational (constitutively so).[37]

In short, because of the vulnerability of beneficiaries that is inherent to the fiduciary relationship (i.e. their 'structural vulnerability'[38]), their autonomy in this relationship is possible only if they can trust in their fiduciaries in the ways just described. Their autonomy therefore must be relational. In our view, if fiduciary law is to have a philosophical conception of beneficiary autonomy, which we believe it should, then the conception must be a relational one.[39] Luckily such an understanding of autonomy is well developed in feminist philosophy and is also perfectly reasonable; surely it is reasonable to think that by trusting others to help us achieve our ends, we can become more self-governing as a result. We can come closer, in other words, to living the life that we envision for ourselves.

3 Fostering Relational Autonomy

To show how the fiduciary relationship can enhance a beneficiary's autonomy in practice, let us return to the case of Ada and Bea. In the face of Bea's deference, it appears that Ada has a choice. On the one hand, she could accept the authority Bea gives to her without further question and agree to 'just do what she thinks is best'. Perhaps Ada, based on her own educational and class privileges, simply assumes that Bea would be better off if she made such decisions on Bea's behalf. This belief, although misguided, may be held in good faith; Ada could genuinely think that the best way to promote her client's legal interests would be to accept her deference and forge ahead with seeking the 'best' legal outcome (that is, what Ada deems to be the

36 Stoljar (n. 21); Mackenzie and Stoljar (n. 24).

37 See John Christman, 'Relational Autonomy, Liberal Individualism, and the Social Constitution of Selves' (2004) 117 *Phil. Stud.* 147; cited in Stoljar (n. 21).

38 Miller (n. 1).

39 Jonathan Herring makes a similar claim in *Relational Autonomy and Family Law* (Springer 2014); he argues that the conception of autonomy that informs family law should be a relational one.

best outcome). In this scenario, Bea's autonomy would very likely be compromised (i.e. even if Bea decided autonomously to defer to Ada). Imagine Ada chooses, for instance, to pursue a peace bond without becoming better informed about Bea's goals and capacities. A peace bond, though potentially in Bea's legal interests narrowly construed, could be a bad decision for Bea. For suppose that Bea was intoxicated at the time of the alleged house party incident, and that a condition of the proposed bond is that Bea abstains from consuming alcohol. Without understanding Bea's orientation towards alcohol, it would be impossible for Ada to know if Bea would be able to live up to this condition. Or, even if Bea was able to abstain, doing so may be extremely difficult for her, and therefore have an overall negative impact on her life and on her autonomy.

On the other hand, Ada could refuse to accede to Bea's request, and instead explore ways to better inform and involve Bea in the decision-making process without overwhelming her.[40] For instance, when Bea expresses how overwhelmed and frustrated she is when discussing her case, Ada could shift the conversation away from the specifics of the legal matter and towards a more general discussion about Bea's life: the struggles she regularly experiences, her long-term goals, or what things are most important to her. Discussing this sort of information could then enable Ada to make a recommendation about which avenue to pursue that is informed and guided by Bea's values and abilities. This type of discussion might even reveal facts about Bea that are relevant to building her legal case. Perhaps in the course of their conversation, Bea discloses some information, which she didn't realize could be legally relevant, that evinces a motive the complainant has for lying about the events at the house party.

In making the latter choice – of refusing to be deferred to – Ada could be guided by work in clinical legal education about models of the lawyer–client relationship that are designed to enhance client autonomy and deter paternalism. Take the model of 'client-centred counselling' or 'client-centred lawyering', which grew out of work conducted in the 1970s by David Binder and Susan Price.[41] One formulation of this approach frames client-centred counselling as being premised upon four primary goals: '(1) recognizing the importance of non-legal aspects of the client's case [such as clients' social and economic circumstances], (2) limiting the role of lawyers' professional expertise, (3) giving primacy to client decision-making, and (4) understanding the client's perspective and values'.[42] Such a model discourages lawyers from over-relying on their legal expertise and under-relying on their clients'

[40] It is worth noting that there are other circumstances in which a lawyer may rightfully refuse to accede to her client's requests. If a client asks her lawyer to do something that would actively mislead the court, for instance, then the lawyer would be obligated to refuse that request. In some cases, a fiduciary may need to consider exiting the fiduciary relationship entirely. Fiduciaries do not need to act to further any and all autonomous ends their clients may have if those values or ends are contrary to the fiduciaries' other duties (e.g. as an officer of the court) or are otherwise obnoxious (e.g. racist).

[41] David Binder and Susan Price, *Legal Interviewing and Counseling: A Client-Centered Approach* (1st ed., West Publishing Company 1977).

[42] Jonah Siegel, Jeanette Hussemann and Dawn Van Hoek, 'Client-Centered Lawyering and the Redefining of Professional Roles among Appellate Public Defenders' (2017) 14 *Ohio St. J. Crim. L.* 579, 584.

expertise on their own life. The approach recognizes that, given the nexus between the legal and non-legal facts of a client's life, it is crucial both to consider a client's social situation, goals and values, and also to effectively involve them in decision-making. A decision that, from a lawyer's perspective, appears suboptimal may in fact be the best decision for a client given her particular social location and values. As Siegel et al. put it, '[c]lient-centered lawyering ... shifts the focus from cases to clients, emphasizing clients' stories and encouraging lawyers to assess clients' legal needs within the broader context of their lives'.[43]

Although legal work on client-centred lawyering does not typically align itself with philosophical work on relational autonomy, the same sorts of insights animate the two. As a result, client-centred lawyering, or the like (e.g. patient-centred doctoring), can enable fiduciaries to respect their beneficiaries' relational autonomy, and overall to act in their beneficiaries' best interests. It can allow them, in other words, to discharge their fiduciary duties better than they otherwise would. That is particularly true for a fiduciary like Ada, whose position in society is very different from her beneficiary.

4 Conclusion

We have argued in this chapter that the fiduciary relationship need not present a threat to beneficiaries' autonomy. On the contrary, fiduciaries can, and should, act as relational supports for their beneficiaries' (relational) autonomy. Although beneficiaries often place enormous trust in their fiduciaries, a well-functioning fiduciary relationship allows beneficiaries to pursue ends that are authentic to them. It does so by ensuring that these ends inform the actions fiduciaries make on their beneficiaries' behalves. Fiduciaries who centre their practice on their beneficiaries' autonomy in this way can still be trusted by their beneficiaries to exercise their discretionary authority. They *must* be trusted to do so, in fact – that is, to decide using their discretionary judgement how best to serve their beneficiaries' ends. This trust is not simply compatible with autonomy in the fiduciary relationship; rather, it is necessary for it.

[43] Ibid., 585.

5

The Psychology of Trust and Fiduciary Obligations

TESS WILKINSON-RYAN

1 Introduction

This chapter addresses the question of trust in fiduciary relationships, but more specifically the *psychology* of trust in fiduciary relationships. Unlike economics or sociology, disciplines that locate the notion of trust largely in terms of institutional or social facts, psychology asks about internal states. What are the cognitions and attributions that constitute trusting, on the one hand, or being regarded as worthy of trust, on the other?

Fiduciary relationships are characterized by one party who is trusting (the beneficiary) and another who is trustworthy (the fiduciary). As a practical matter, a fiduciary makes judgments on behalf of another person. This is a distinct moral and cognitive task, and research suggests that it is both more rational in some ways – less prone to biases like hyperbolic discounting or excessive risk aversion – but more fraught in others, especially when the fiduciary's interests are in conflict with the beneficiary's. The demands of being trustworthy pose cognitive, as well as social and emotional, challenges. Such challenges also arise for parties on the other side of the relationship, deciding not whether to be fulfill an expectation of trustworthiness but whether to form such an expectation. This is the psychology of trusting, and it too offers important insights for regulation.

Interpersonal trust is not often considered core to doctrinal analysis, and this is a chapter fundamentally about fiduciary law, not something separate like organizational behavior or even "order without law."[1] For present purposes, I preface the chapter by articulating my presumption that trust and trustworthiness are foundational to law, and indeed foundational to human social life. Entire accounts of child development – from Erik Erikson, for example – revolve around the early dawning of trust in caretakers. Psychologists describe trust as the "psychological state comprising the intention to accept vulnerability based upon positive expectations of the intentions or behavior of another"[2] or "an expectancy held by an individual or a group that the word, promise, verbal or written statement of another individual or group can be relied upon."[3] We might shorthand this formulation as subjective, normative expectations of reliability. Those expectations and reliances are at the core of our

[1] Robert Ellicskon, *Order without Law: How Neighbors Settle Disputes* (Harvard 1991).
[2] Denise Rousseau and others, "Not So Different After All: A Cross-Discipline View of Trust" [1998] 23 *Academy of Management Review* 393, 395.
[3] Julian Rotter, "Generalized Expectations of Interpersonal Trust" [1971] 26 *American Psychologist* 443, 444.

understanding of ourselves as social creatures in a social compact. As a society, institutional and interpersonal trust are widely understood to be required for functioning democracy.

Scaling those claims (way) down, I would just make the simpler point that I am assuming here that interpersonal trust is a necessary, integral feature of fiduciary law. The humans involved will make attributions and develop expectations, and the law cannot and should not make informal, interpersonal trust irrelevant. Matthew Harding has made the case more systematically that not only is trust relevant, but thick trust is naturally implicated by "reliance on discretion": "First, the voluntary yielding up of interests that characterizes an act of reliance is widely understood, according to a complex of social conventions and meanings, to be a fitting way to manifest relatively thick forms of trust; moreover, thick trust is widely understood to be a fitting attitude to manifest in circumstances of reliance."[4] Although legal sanctions can make the material consequences of selfishness worse or more salient, they are inadequate to the task of policing every small-stakes slip or even high-stakes judgment call. Breaches of trust can be hard to detect and even harder to prosecute. Legal remedies are rare and undercompensatory. Efficient, legitimate relationships require trust and foster trust in return.

This chapter will ask how a psychological account of trust might inform our understanding of the doctrines of fiduciary duties.[5] The remainder of this chapter proceeds as follows. Section 1 sets out the basic vocabulary and methodology of the psychology of trust. Section 2 considers the implications of the psychological evidence on trust and trustworthiness for the fiduciary duty of loyalty. Section 3 offers evidence to suggest that fiduciary decision makers may be more competent (i.e., prudent) investors but may have systematically biased empathy for the beneficiaries in whose interests they are meant to be acting. Section 4 outlines the psychological function of accounting and being accounted to, and Section 5 suggests avenues for future research.

2 Introduction to the Psychology of Trust

A Measuring Who Trusts Whom and When

What do we mean when we ask if someone can be trusted? Imagine that I have cause to tell an embarrassing secret about myself to a colleague. There is some reason to do this, but not such a good reason that it's worth doing it if he's going to tell my secret to other people. I know that he would derive mild pleasure from having good gossip but otherwise has no strong incentive to disclose my confidence. How do I decide whether to trust him with my information? Presumably I would need to know two things. First, does he like or at least respect me enough to take my preferences seriously? And second, is he someone who is capable of keeping a secret? If the answer to either is no, then presumably I should keep my cards close to my chest.

[4] Matthew Harding, "Trust and Fiduciary Law" [2012] 33 *Oxford Journal of Legal Studies* 81.

[5] Although my hope is that some of the insights described here are relevant to fiduciary duties across doctrinal domains, the implicit referent relationship here is between adviser and advisee or trustee and beneficiary outside of the corporate governance or shareholder context.

In the psychology of social perception, this is described as the warmth-competence model.[6] The notion, drawn in broad terms from evolutionary psychology, is that the fundamental task of perceiving another person is to figure out if she is friend or enemy and whether she is any good at those roles – a helpful ally or a fearsome enemy versus a useless friend or a toothless antagonist. These assessments in turn yield action imperatives – fight, run away, recruit, ignore, help or, indeed, trust.[7] At the most basic level, then, trust is predicted by attributes of competence and good intentions.[8] Psychological research has dedicated thousands of pages to studying attribution theory – how we figure out what inferences to draw from others' behaviors.

What attributes or roles foster or predict trust? Do you trust your intimate partner? How about your financial broker? How about the online retailer to whom you are giving your credit card number? You might respond that even those questions are not right – the question is not whether or not I trust my intimate partner but whether I trust him to be kind to my sister (yes) or to file our taxes on time (no). Similarly, I might trust my stockbroker to choose good investments for me when she has no material interests adverse to mine because she is basically competent and well meaning, but I might not trust her when her interests diverge substantially from mine. Because psychology is at based a highly context sensitive, psychological descriptions of trust largely reflect what philosophers have conceptualized as a three-part trust relation:[9] trust in *someone* to do *something*.

Fostering trust between parties has predictable consequences for their behavior and their expectations. Trust occurs in a dyadic model, meaning that when we talk about trust, there is a subject who is deciding whether or not to trust in part based on whether or not the object appears trustworthy and an object deciding whether or not to be trustworthy in part based on whether or not she feels trusted. Or, to paraphrase the following more precise explanation, trust develops in a feedback loop.[10] Philosophers and psychologists alike have described the propensity for trustingness to foster trustworthiness as a descriptive matter; its normative status, though, is perhaps less obvious, which I discuss in my concluding thoughts.

B Methods

The question of whether or not people trust in any particular context asks about their attitude/expectations of the decision maker given the nature of the decision task. As such, psychologists conceptualize the trust *context* in terms of three features:

[6] Susan Fiske, Amy Cuddy and Peter Glick, "Universal Dimensions of Social Cognition" [2007] 11 *Trends in Cognitive Sciences* 77.

[7] Amy Cuddy, Susan Fiske and Peter Glick, "Warmth and Competence as Universal Dimensions of Social Perception: The Stereotype Content Model and the BIAS Map" [2008] 40 *Advances in Experimental Social Psychology* 61.

[8] F. David Schoorman, Roger Mayer and James Davis, "An Integrative Model of Organizational Trust: Past, Present, and Future" [2007] 32 *Academy of Management Review* 344.

[9] See, e.g., Russell Hardin, "Conceptions and Explanations of Trust" in K. S. Cook (ed.), *Russell Sage Foundation Series on Trust, Vol. 2: Trust in Society* (Russell Sage Foundation 2001).

[10] Victoria McGeer, "The Empowering Theory of Trust" in Paul Faulkner and Thomas Simpson (eds.), *The Philosophy of Trust* (Oxford University Press 2017).

interdependence, risk and choice. Trust matters when (1) an outcome requires reliance (interdependence), (2) there is a downside risk if one's partner acts selfishly (risk) and (3) vulnerability is optional (choice).[11]

But how do we study these moments? Questions about voluntary vulnerability and voluntary reciprocity have driven a large body of research, some of which I will review here and much of which I consider in more specific contexts in later sections of this chapter. What psychologists are doing in this research is asking what independent variables have effects on the dependent variables of trust and trustworthiness. There are a few ways to study these questions, some of which are intuitive – some research just asks "do you/would you trust this person?" But we also have ways to measure trust and trustworthiness without having to ask individuals to report on their subjective state, and the canonical method is with a trust game.[12] In a trust game, a lab-based experimental protocol used in economics and psychology, two players are each randomly assigned one of two roles: an investor and a trustee. The investor is allocated an endowment – say, ten dollars – and can pass any amount of it to the trustee. Whatever the investor passes to the trustee is tripled, and the trustee, who makes the final "move" of the game, can choose how much of the tripled transfer to send to the investor. In this game, the investor both creates the trust relationship and benefits from it. The trustee has the ultimate power to determine their respective outcomes and makes a calculation taking into account preferences for material wealth along with preferences for social or moral goods.

The trust game is the protocol that launched a thousand papers. In the broadest strokes, many of the studies confirm commonsense intuitions about trust – that trust is based on information, that it is sensitive to the incentives of the trustee to be trustworthy and that humans can use language to convince one another to trust or to be trustworthy. In different papers, researchers find that trust increases over repeated interactions,[13] that trustworthiness is accounted for by reciprocity norms but as well as by preferences for unconditional kindness,[14] that trust is reliably fostered by negotiation[15] or communication even when it is just "cheap talk,"[16] that opportunities for retaliation increase ex ante trust,[17] and that trustworthiness is a socially valued trait but trustingness is not.[18]

[11] Francesca Righetti and Catrin Finkenauer, "If You Are Able to Control Yourself, I Will Trust You: The Role of Perceived Self-Control in Interpersonal Trust" [2011] 100 *Journal of Personality and Social Psychology* 874.

[12] Joyce Berg, John Dickhaut and Kevin McCabe, "Trust, Reciprocity, and Social History" [1995] 10 *Games and Economic Behavior* 122.

[13] Luke J. Chang and others, "Seeing Is Believing: Trustworthiness as a Dynamic Belief" [2010] 61 *Cognitive Psychology* 87.

[14] Nava Ashraf, Iris Bohnet and Nikita Piankov, "Decomposing Trust and Trustworthiness" [2006] 9 *Experimental Economics* 193.

[15] Davide Barrera, "The Impact of Negotiated Exchange on Trust and Trustworthiness" [2007] 29 *Social Networks* 508.

[16] Avner Ben-Ner and Louis Putterman, "Trust, Communication, and Contracts: An Experiment" [2009] 70 *Journal of Economic Behavior and Organization* 106.

[17] Kiridaran Kanagaretnam and others, "The Impact of Empowering Investors on Trust and Trustworthiness" [2012] 33 *Journal of Economic Psychology* 566.

[18] Cristina Bicchieri, Erte Xiao and Ryan Muldoon, "Trustworthiness Is a Social Norm, but Trusting Is Not" [2011] 10 *Politics, Philosophy and Economics* 170.

The trust game and other dependent variables measuring trust are also sometimes used to measure stable traits. Although this will not be a focus of the chapter, it is worth noting that trust is so core to the conception of human psychology that it is also studied as a measurable feature of individual personality. Some personality questionnaires include items such as "Most elected public officials are really sincere in their campaign promises" or "In dealing with strangers, one is better off to be cautious until they have provided evidence that they are trustworthy."[19] And, indeed, there are social and behavioral correlates of trust. An influential retrospective analysis in 1980 argued that those higher in baseline interpersonal trust were more likely to have a cluster of positive, adaptive traits. The study found trusters to be more trustworthy (less prone to lying, cheating and stealing), more personally satisfied (happier and with more friends) and no more gullible or easily suckered.[20] Although trait trust may not be central to the discussion of fiduciary obligations, at least in an overview like this, the overall picture is in line with the sense that interpersonal trust has a facilitative role to play in our sociolegal system.

In the fiduciary relationship, there are at least two important instantiations of the trust dynamic. In this chapter, I will motivate most of my discussion with consideration of the traditional trust structure. A settlor chooses a trustee to manage assets on behalf of a beneficiary. In some cases the settlor and the trustee are the same person, and in some cases the settlor and the beneficiary are the same person. As the name suggests, the person in whom the parties must place trust is the trustee. The beneficiary trusts the trustee to make decisions in his best interests. The settlor trusts the trustee to make competent decisions in keeping with the settlor's intent. The former relationship is the most intuitive example, and of course the one governed by fiduciary duties, but I will also consider the role of the settlor, whose internal trust state is often overlooked but is the motivating source of the resulting legal trust structure.

3 Warmth and Loyalty

A *Moral and Social Norms*

In Justice Cardozo's famous formulation, a trustee "is held to something stricter than the morals of the market place. Not honesty alone, but the punctilio of an honor the most sensitive, is then the standard of behavior."[21] The duty of loyalty is the trustee's moral obligation toward the beneficiary, to act fairly and in good faith and to administer the trust solely in the interests of the beneficiary. This is the requirement that the trustee avoid temptations for selfishness when those temptations arise. It is worth noting here that the moral sense of selfishness and loyalty is not coterminous with the fiduciary obligation; it is both under- and overinclusive. Scholars have observed that the legal rule may in fact go further than the moral rule – that the

[19] Julian Rotter, "A New Scale for the Measurement of Interpersonal Trust" [1967] 35 *Journal of Personality* 651, 654.

[20] Julian Rotter, "Interpersonal Trust, Trustworthiness, and Gullibility" [1980] 35 *American Psychologist* 1.

[21] *Meinhard* v. *Salmon* 164 NE 545 (NY 1928).

punctilio of an honor most sensitive may in some cases be insufficient to satisfy a legal rule that requires more than good faith. Stephen Smith has observed that "the most loyal of fiduciaries may run afoul of the no-conflict rule."[22] Paul Miller has argued that the moral dimensions of fiduciary obligations are somewhat misunderstood, insofar as fiduciary duties implicate a circumscribed set of goals specified by the grantor rather than the agent's own sense of moral loyalty.[23]

It bears introducing this duty with the observation that behavioral research supports the proposition that people who believe themselves to be constrained or guided by a moral norm will often forgo material benefits in order to avoid norm violations. In many well-studied contexts, people evince strong preferences for promise keeping, equity and reciprocity.[24] The predecessor laboratory result to the trust game is the well-known dictator game. The dictator game asks two players in a study to be a sender and a receiver. The sender is allocated money, and the receiver is passive. The modal transfer is not zero, as we might expect given that the players do not meet one another and have no obligations – it's half of the initial endowment. Subjects behave as if they've been asked to share a fair amount, and the default fair allocation is fifty-fifty. Perhaps even closer to the fiduciary context is the contract context, where there is ample evidence to support the idea that people prefer to keep their contractual obligations, even when they could make a small premium via breach.[25] As a baseline proposition, it is reasonable to think that fiduciaries will try to do their role justice. The question for the remainder of this section is what psychological factors might disrupt those intentions and how the law can or should respond.

B Self-Dealing and Self-Serving Biases

In re Gleeson's Will is the dispute between a trustee, Con Colbrook, and the estate of his landlady, Mary Gleeson. Gleeson died two weeks before Colbrook's lease was set to expire. Colbrook inherited the land as trustee for the benefit of Gleeson's children. With few renters available to take the land on short notice, Colbrook increased the rent and renewed the lease to himself for another year before finding a new tenant. It is undisputed that had he vacated the property, it would most likely have remained empty for all or part of the year.

The case involves three basic rules of loyalty: the trustee must act in the "sole interest" of the beneficiaries; fiduciaries may not privilege loyalty to one beneficiary at the expense of another; and once a court identifies a case of self-dealing or a conflicted transaction, it makes "no further inquiry." The sole-interest rule essentially says that a

[22] Steve Smith, 'The Deed, Not the Motive' in Paul Miller and Andrew Gold (eds.), *Contract, Status, and Fiduciary Law* (Oxford University Press 2017).

[23] Paul Miller, 'Dimensions of Fiduciary Loyalty' in D. Gordon Smith and Andrew S. Gold (eds.), *Research Handbook on Fiduciary Law* (Edward Elgar 2016).

[24] Ernst Fehr, Urs Fischbacher and Simon Gächter, "Strong Reciprocity, Human Cooperation, and the Enforcement of Social Norms" [2002] 13 *Human Nature* 1.

[25] Tess Wilkinson-Ryan, "Incentives to Breach" [2015] 17 *American Law and Economics Review* 290; see also Tess Wilkinson-Ryan, "Do Liquidated Damages Encourage Breach – A Psychological Experiment" [2009] 108 *Michigan Law Review* 108.

party in Colbrook's position can be a tenant or a trustee, but not both, because acting in both capacities raises the specter of self-dealing. The no-further-inquiry rule essentially prevents the trustee from defending herself with evidence of her good faith or reasonable judgment.

On the one hand, this case seems quite egregious – the estate overall almost certainly benefited from Colbrook's choice to stay on the land. On the other hand, the case may simply confirm a strong view that it is too easy to convince oneself, and maybe others, of transactional fairness. The body of literature in psychology devoted to motivated judgments of fairness falls under the umbrella of "self-serving biases."[26] The self-serving biases studies illustrate the difficulty of assessing the *fair* allocation when the assessor has a material or psychic interest in the allocation. Linda Babcock and George Loewenstein demonstrated the basic principle by simply asking subjects to put themselves in the role of the plaintiff or the defendant in a car accident and to estimate both the party's preferred settlement as well as the range of objectively fair settlements. While it is perfectly predictable that opposing parties should disagree about the ideal outcome, what was surprising was that the subjects disagreed about the range of fair outcomes, even when instructed to try to be objective. They often had little to no overlap, leading to frustration when they tried to negotiate with one another. Especially where the standard might otherwise be "good faith" or "reasonableness," one can imagine that conflicted transactions would tend on the whole to be biased, even where courts could discern no intentional or obvious wrongdoing on the part of the self-dealing trustees. The rule chooses to enforce a second-best world – transactions chosen from a smaller number of overall transactors and thus with a smaller market, but the beneficiary gets the benefit of being able to trust.

C *Effects of Disclosures on Trust*

Once the principal has announced his trust in an agent, how are his incentives changed? Research suggests that, first, he might be less likely to complain about unfair dealing. This is a straightforward cognitive dissonance phenomenon, which just suggests that when evidence is in tension with a cherished belief, the interpretation of the evidence often changes rather than the belief itself. It is embarrassing to be taken in or duped, and one way to avoid the experience is to believe that the duping is not happening.

Some of the canonical work in the psychology of advising has come from three professors of judgment and decision-making: Sunita Sah, George Loewenstein and Daylian Cain. Together and in separate work, they have studied the effect of disclosing conflicts of interest on beneficiary behavior. A brief description of their most famous study helps to illustrate the paradox. The researchers recruited participants to an adviser/advisee task. The roles were randomly assigned, and advisers were asked to give advisees advice about which one of two die would yield better outcomes for the experimental game. Advisers had information about the possible prizes associated

[26] Linda Babcock and George Loewenstein, "Explaining Bargaining Impasse: The Role of Self-Serving Biases" [1997] 11 *Journal of Economic Perspectives* 109, 111.

with each die, and advisees did not. The participants were randomly assigned to a no-conflict condition, a conflict condition with no disclosure and a conflict condition with disclosure. In the disclosure condition, the advisers had to explain that one of the choices, die B, yielded a better payoff for the adviser. The disclosure almost doubled the rate – from 42% to 76% – at which advisees receiving conflicting advice chose the inferior roll.

What explains this result? We might think that it is caused by an increase in trust. Someone who discloses their conflict of interest in an upfront manner might be perceived as more trustworthy. This does not appear to account for the pattern, though. In facts, subjects in the experiment (and in a cascade of follow-up work and replications) reported that their trust in the adviser was decreased but that they felt pressure to comply. This has been reported in other work as "insinuation anxiety," or the worry that turning down advice after a disclosure of a conflict will be perceived as an insult.

It is also the case that advisers who behave in a transparent manner about conflicts of interest may actually become more rather than less likely to make decisions in their own interest. Cain, Loewenstein and Don Moore found that disclosing advisers were more biased than nondisclosing advisers, in part because of "moral licensing." They found evidence that disclosures may "backfire" because the disclosure itself is experienced as a moral good that racks up some points, as it were, to be used against future moral decision-making. Or the disclosure may be understood as the fulfillment of the moral obligation rather than a warning – I told you that I may give you bad advice, thus placing you on fair warning to expect my (now morally permissible) bad advice. Thus in this arena, the psychological evidence is surprisingly pessimistic about the ability of disclosures, or transparency, to improve fiduciary relationships.

4 Competence and Prudence

A Competence: Maximizing Wealth

One of the most compelling reasons to encourage fiduciary delegation is that there are some tasks for which humans are generally better at deciding for others rather than deciding for themselves. Of course, a core reason to delegate is because the delegee is more expert – if I choose a financial adviser to invest for me or a trustee to manage money on behalf of my minor children, the choice is between the more and the less sophisticated decider. But even holding sophistication constant, there appears to be a substantial advantage to delegation simply because some of the most important financial decision-making biases – namely loss aversion, risk aversion and hyperbolic discounting – appear dampened or absent when the choice does not affect the decision maker directly.

Some of the original authors of prospect theory studies showed early in their work that agents were less likely to exhibit the endowment effect than principals. The researchers had subjects play a game with lottery tickets and asked sellers and buyers for their willingness-to-accept price and willingness-to-pay price, respectively.

As expected, sellers deciding for themselves wanted to overcharge compared to what their counterparts would pay; this is the endowment effect.[27] However, they saw no endowment effect at all in subjects setting prices as agents for other subjects.[28] The endowment effect, the status quo bias and the default bias – each manifestations of prospect theory's value function – are reduced in agents.[29]

The prudent investor rule is essentially a codification of the observed phenomenon, which is that agents are less likely to adhere to the status quo investments in defiance of long-standing expert financial advice requiring a diverse portfolio. In the risk context, psychologists have found that emotional distance is key to diminishing irrational risk aversion.[30] The negative emotional response to the risk of loss is acute, but people tend to experience less emotionally intense responses to risk when they are deciding for others.[31]

A similar emotional mechanism predicts the reduced salience of the "here and now" that otherwise drives impulsive and short-sighted financial choices for principals. Studies of intertemporal trade-offs show that many people appear to be "hyperbolic" discounters – that is, that their discount function is implausibly steep between now and now plus one but very flat between future moment and future moment plus one.[32] The mechanism of emotional salience of immediate reward is simply diminished, thus yielding a more calculative and less urgent response.

In sum, a substantial literature now suggests an increased competence for agents making financial decisions on behalf of an otherwise competent principal.

B Competence: Assessing Someone Else's Needs

Of course, the ability to manage money for another requires not just an understanding of wealth maximization in the given time frame – it ideally requires *utility* maximization, or welfare maximization. Looking after the welfare of a beneficiary entails knowing something about her life. Where does she live, how does she live, and what does she need? Indeed, many trust structures are explicitly intended to be support trusts, keeping the beneficiary in some basic state of comfort and well-being, oftentimes through difficult life transitions. Achieving prosperity is a straightforward goal, but facilitating another person's flourishing is not, and there are reasons from the case law and from the psychology literature to suspect that the challenges are systematic.

27 Daniel Kahneman and Amos Tversky, "Prospect Theory: An Analysis of Decision Under Risk" [1979] 47 *Econometrica* 263.

28 See James D. Marshall, Jack L. Knetsch and J. A. Sinden, "Agents' Evaluations and the Disparity in Measures of Economic Loss" [1986] 7 *Journal of Economic Behavior and Organization* 115.

29 See Evan Polman, "Self-Other Decision Making and Loss Aversion" [2012] 119 *Organizational Behavior and Human Decision Processes* 141.

30 Yaacov Trope, Nira Liberman and Cheryl Wakslak, "Construal Levels and Psychological Distance: Effects on Representation, Prediction, Evaluation, and Behavior" [2007] 17 *Journal of Consumer Psychology* 83.

31 Qingzhou Sun and others, "Increased Social Distance Makes People More Risk-Neutral" [2017] 157 *Journal of Social Psychology* 502.

32 George-Marios Angeletos and others, "The Hyperbolic Consumption Model: Calibration, Simulation, and Empirical Evaluation" [2001] 15 *Journal of Economic Perspectives* 47.

Let us consider a modern chestnut of the wills and trusts course: *Marsman* v. *Nasca*.[33] Sara Marsman, who had substantial wealth in part from her first marriage, had married her second husband, Cappy, a horse trainer of more modest means. Marsman left Cappy one-third of her estate in trust, for his "comfortable support and maintenance." The trustee, a family attorney named Farr, was rather reluctant to distribute principal to Cappy, even when it came to pass that retirement and hard times forced him to sell the family home. At one point Cappy requested additional funds and was met with a request that he justify the disbursement in writing. He demurred, and the disbursement was never made. On his death, Cappy's second wife sued the estate, claiming in part that she would have inherited the family home had Farr been appropriately attentive to Cappy's lifestyle.

What happened in this case? Why was Farr apparently so stingy, especially when he personally benefited very little from his own failure of generosity? Trustee decision-making requires assessing another person's utilities in intimate and granular ways rarely required in nonfamily relationships. How do we differentiate between indulgence and comfort, especially when the person who has to predict the utility of a particular choice is not the person who will experience the utility? Evidence from psychology suggests that we should worry that failures of estimation will be systemically biased toward stinginess. It is easy to underestimate the seriousness of another person's pain and the value of someone else's pleasure.

The psychological literature on the hot–cold empathy gap offers a glimpse into this set of problems. In a "cold" state – that is, unaffected by the visceral drives that often underlie the urgency or intensity of consumption choices – decision-making is more calculated and rational. In a "hot" state, hunger, thirst, fatigue, pain, sexual arousal, drug cravings or other physical drive states are highly salient and highly motivating. The normative status of these decisions is not inherent to the underlying drive state. If I am trying to cut down on sugar, I may prefer my cold-state decision stance and thus keep sweets out of the house even though I know I will be miserable come time for my next snack. On the other hand, my failure to bring along extra food on a long hike truly decreases my overall well-being.

The "empathy gap" describes the consistent difficulty of accurately predicting the preferences and utilities of the hot state. An evocative example comes from Sayette, Loewenstein & Griffin, who asked smokers to estimate the value of a particular smoke break to a group of people with whom they should have been quite expert at empathizing: themselves.[34] The smokers were told that they would have to wait two hours until the next smoke break, at which point they would have the option of receiving a small payment to delay the break another ten minutes. Some smokers were allowed to precommit to accept the delay, and the payment, in advance; many of them did. Others were told of the option but not permitted to decide until the smoke break arrived. Those who had to decide whether or not to accept money for the delayed smoke break under the influence of nicotine craving (that is, hours after their last

[33] *Marsman* v. *Nasca* 573 NE 2d 575 (1991).

[34] Michael A. Sayette and others, "Exploring the Cold-to-Hot Empathy Gap in Smokers" [2008] 19 *Psychological Science* 926.

cigarette) were substantially less likely to take the payment than those who decided under conditions of satiation. One way to understand this result is that subjects choosing their smoking schedule in advance, and in a cold state, underestimated the value of satisfying an urgent nicotine craving.

The basic notion of the empathy gap explains a number of real-world phenomena. In addition, there is ample evidence that there are some consumption patterns that we clearly pursue for ourselves but undervalue for others. It turns out, for example, that dental care is extraordinarily important for quality of life but is frequently underfunded. The particular examples do not cover the field, of course, but they serve to evoke the concern that there are some ways in which we may be unable to apprehend others' discomfort as we would our own.

5 Accounting and Accountability

The duty to inform and account requires a trustee to keep beneficiaries apprised. Accounting and informing are supportive mechanisms – they constitute the verification in the old adage to "trust but verify."

On its face, the duty to communicate and keep records may seem clerical rather than psychological; these are duties that do not obviously invoke a lot of judgment calls or fraught interpersonal dynamics. Indeed, this obligation is essentially about improving decision-making via the transfer of information. In this section, I want to consider the role of the accounting separate from its information benefits. What are the behavioral implications of explaining, and what are the implications of receiving notice?

A Psychological Consequences of Accounting

The psychological construct of accountability mirrors its role in legal analysis:

> Accountability refers to the implicit or explicit expectation that one may be called on to justify one's beliefs, feelings, and actions to others. Accountability also usually implies that people who do not provide a satisfactory justification for their actions will suffer negative consequences ranging from disdainful looks to loss of one's livelihood, liberty, or even life. Conversely, people who do provide compelling justifications will experience positive consequences ranging from mitigation of punishment to lavish rewards that, for example, take the form of political office or generous stock options.[35]

The canonical work on accountability comes from cognitive psychologist Phil Tetlock, who hypothesized that expectations of accountability – expecting that one will be required to justify a decision to another – leads to more deliberative and less heuristic/motivated information processing. In his 1983 study, he gave subjects eighteen pieces of evidence in a murder prosecution. Subjects were randomly assigned according to a two-by-two design – they saw either pro- or antidefendant information first, and they either did or did not expect to justify their verdict. Nonaccountable subjects showed a strong primacy bias – whichever verdict they

[35] Jennifer Lerner and Philip E. Tetlock, "Accounting for the Effects of Accountability" [1999] 125 *Psychological Bulletin* 255.

saw evidence for first was the verdict they were more likely to vote for. But subjects in the accountability condition did not differ based on order of information. Accountability even improved subject recall of the information. It looked like accountability improved information-processing vigilance.

This seems particularly helpful for combating competence issues and perhaps also for decision-making involving conflicts of interest. However, there is another layer to accountability research that asks not just *what* is being accounted but also *to whom*. This research draws on the intuition that accounting is essentially a formal acknowledgment of the social context of the decision. In some cases, we may "account" without a clear sense of who we are accounting to. But in others, we know exactly who will hear or read the explanation – and this is certainly true in the fiduciary context. Research by Phil Tetlock and Jennifer Lerner, among others, argues that the decision-changing mechanism of accounting is social approval. If you know what will make your audience happy or proud or at least accepting, you prefer decisions with those outcomes. One experiment is particularly relevant for the fiduciary context. In this experiment, subjects were "hired" by a temp agency and asked to allocate financial aid among applicants to a university program. They were randomly allocated to be either unaccountable, accountable to the financial aid recipients or accountable to the financial donors.[36] As it turned out, the most efficient (i.e., welfare-maximizing – maximizing the number of applicants who would be able to afford to attend) allocation of aid was done by those in the unaccountable condition. Those in the accountable conditions resorted to essentially an equity heuristic and divided the aid evenly among applicants, even though that meant underfunding needier applicants. There was a sense among the subjects that it would be easier to defend that decision. In the fiduciary context, we can imagine this distorting some forms of expert judgment for risky decisions when expectations are that the client will have a strong sense of the default norm – for example, naive diversification or an omission bias – making the better choice harder to explain if it goes poorly.

B Psychological Consequences of Being Informed

In many contexts, the duty to inform will boil down to a trustee telling the beneficiary how she is handling assets being managed on behalf of the beneficiary. Notice serves an essential function for the obvious reason that it is hard to know if you should object to decisions you don't know have been made.

Let's imagine for a moment, though, that many such disclosures are largely pro forma – that in fact many beneficiaries will fail to read the accountings carefully enough to fully apprehend all of the details. Or that even if they are fully read and comprehended, there may be a variety of reasons that a beneficiary might not decide to challenge the decision right away. As a legal matter, disclosures, if not objected to in a timely manner, protect the trustee. But I would argue that this is likely exacerbated by the psychology of disclosure.

[36] Ibid.

Experimental research suggests that contract-like notice mechanisms depress challenges to unfair policies or deals, because disclosees blame themselves for failing to pay attention.[37] In one experiment, subjects read about an unexpected fee being charged on a rental car. They were informed either that all of the company policies were available online or that the company policies had been provided via a term sheet hidden in a sheaf of papers not otherwise marked as including terms of the rental. Those in the term-sheet condition were significantly more likely to report that the fee was legally enforceable and that indeed the fee was reasonable. That is, the mechanism of disclosure affected their perception of the quality of the company's behavior.[38] This was not so much because the company seemed more trustworthy when it affirmatively provided a (hidden) term but rather because subjects reported that consumers on notice of contractual terms should be held responsible for protecting themselves.

Thus one concern we might have is that beneficiary disclosees may come to realize that they've been exploited or neglected, and the notices may serve as a deterrent to complaint even when they would not actually prevent a claim in court.

6 Future Research: The Fiduciary Schema

What is the psychological prototype of the fiduciary? What is the commonsense understanding of what fiduciary means, and who it refers to? In this last section, I briefly consider two broader questions for the psychology of fiduciary obligations.

A Trust and Group Stereotypes

My first question for future research is, what does the schema of a fiduciary look like? A schema is a mental model, or a prototype. It often tells us a lot about a particular role or concept to ask about its prototypical form – what do we expect, and what violates those expectations? As such, I am ending this chapter by revisiting the basic psychology of social judgment from the introduction. In this conclusion, though, I want to reconsider the question of trust and distrust at the group level – what *kind* of person is more likely deemed trustworthy in context, based on group characteristics?

Psychological research on stereotyping has mapped group stereotypes onto the warmth-competence quadrants with rather robust replication over time. Some of the articles read like a very politically incorrect parlor game. Can you guess which groups are viewed by Americans as incompetent but friendly (the elderly, housewives), competent but cold (Asians, Jews, feminists), competent and warm (soldiers, Christians)?

In keeping with the proposal that this chapter may serve as the seeds of a research agenda, drawing connections and making suggestions, I think it is worth bringing attention to the possibility that fiduciary obligations are stereotypically male sex typed. The central intuition is that leadership is stereotypically male. Laurie Rudman

[37] Tess Wilkinson-Ryan, "The Perverse Consequences of Disclosing Standard Terms" [2017] 103 *Cornell Law Review* 117.

[38] Ibid.

and Stephen Kilianski explored this phenomenon empirically in their research on gender authority and identified a strong descriptive and normative association of men with leadership: "These findings suggest that negative reactions to female authority may stem, in part, from an implicit prototype for male leaders and the attendant belief that it is more natural for men to take control. Individuals may be comforted by male leadership for the simple fact that they are accustomed to viewing men as authority figures and women as subordinates." Of particular note for our purposes here is that some of the questions measuring gender attitudes were explicitly about fiduciary relationships:

1. If I were in serious legal trouble, I would prefer a male to a female lawyer.

. . . .

7. If I were having a serious operation, I would have more confidence in a male surgeon.

. . . .

12. In most areas, I would rather take advice from a man than from a woman.[39]

Fiduciaries make decisions on behalf of others, particularly financial decisions. Outside of the childcare context, being in charge of other people and making financial decisions have historically and stereotypically been male roles. Although these are rather obvious observations, the psychology of women in the workplace is somewhat subtle. Susan Fiske and her coauthors (including Rudnick and Glick) have written about the trade-off between competence and warmth. Women may be warm but not particularly powerful (stay-at-home mothers) or powerful but distrusted (female professionals). Evidence from psychology studies suggests a very tight trade-off[40], with women in the workplace who become mothers docked for competence even as they are seen as warmer. (Men do not face this trade-off when they encounter fatherhood.)

Many, many fiduciaries are in historically male occupations (law, medicine) or male-stereoptyped fields (finance). One potentially fruitful avenue of research would ask how gender stereotyping affects trust in the fiduciary context, perhaps granting some (male) fiduciaries latitude but raising skepticism when women are in that role.

B Typology of the Fiduciary Relationship

My second question for future research is, what does the schema of a fiduciary relationship look like? Finally, I would propose that one of the fundamental destabilizers of fiduciary relationships is an underlying confusion, to the parties involved, about their stance. In the early 1990s, an anthropologist named Alan Fiske proposed a model of relationships that proved to be enormously influential in psychology.

[39] Laurie Rudman and Stephen E. Kilianski, "Implicit and Explicit Attitudes toward Female Authority" [2000] 26 Personality and Social Psychology *Bulletin* 1315, 1326.

[40] Charles M. Judd and others, "Fundamental Dimensions of Social Judgment: Understanding the Relations between Judgments of Competence and Warmth" [2005] 89 *Journal of Personality and Social Psychology* 899.

The original paper proposed that there are basically four types of interactions between humans. By "types of interactions," here we are thinking not about, say, arguing or agreeing but rather what kind of understanding individuals have about the constraints and possibilities of their kind of relationship. The four types of relationship are communal sharing, authority ranking, equality matching and market pricing. For the purposes of brief exposition, I will try to shorthand each of these modes and then sketch out the confusion that I suspect. Communal sharing is prototypically members of a family, but it is characterized by any task for which a group understands themselves to be joined by a shared goal – focused on what the individuals have in common. Authority ranking is essentially hierarchical – any relational stance that is focused on rankings, like age, gender, seniority, meritocracy, etc. The relationship between management and workers, for example, would fall in this category. Equality-matching relationships are those defined largely by reciprocity: "Examples include turn-taking, lottery or coin-flip; voting; eye-for-an-eye, tooth-for-a-tooth vengeance; rotating credit associations; baby-sitting coops; balanced in-kind reciprocity such as exchange of favors or dinner invitations; matching contributions; distributions divided into equal shares; symmetrical playing fields and even numbers of players in sports; and equal starting points and resources in games and contests."[41] Finally, market pricing is the mode that "yields such cultural coordination devices as prices, wages, rents, interest, dividends, tithes and taxes, efficiency calculations, and cost–benefit analyses."[42]

To grasp the intuition about how these frames operate in a meaningful way, imagine going to a dinner party and, at the end of a meal, offering the host fifty dollars as thanks for a lovely time. That would be quite taboo – the way one "pays" for a dinner invitation is with a reciprocal dinner invitation. Alan Fiske and Phil Tetlock offer the example of a marine in boot camp, or a novice in a monastery, suggesting that everyone vote about when to wake up in the morning. Which leads to the question for the present topic of fiduciary obligations: What kind of relationship does a fiduciary bear to the beneficiary? I would posit that the relationship is an uneasy combination of market pricing and communal sharing. Fiduciaries are typically paid for their services, but they are not employees, per se – it does not seem right that the trustee and the beneficiary are in a hierarchical relationship. Similarly, there is no sense at all of tit for tat – oftentimes the beneficiary has nothing at all to offer the trustee, for example. This is an opportunity both to understand the fiduciary relationship; we may learn, for example, that it is especially fraught precisely because it purports to cross relational categories.

7 Conclusion

Psychological literature on trust offers a complex picture. It is reasonable to infer from the existing research that people have a baseline preference for interpersonal trust in their relationships and even a propensity for being trustworthy. But those are

[41] Nick Haslam, *Relational Models Theory* (Routledge 2004) 5.

[42] Ibid. at 6.

complicated settings involving multiattribute judgment and decision-making, which behavioral research tells us should be predictably fraught. What stands in the way of loyalty when loyalty is the goal or undermines proficiency with agents trying their hardest to maximize wealth? What makes agents *seem* fair or *seem* smart? And finally, what are the conditions under which trust deteriorates, and when does that deterioration lead to confrontation? There are some reasons to be optimistic about fiduciary performance, especially when fiduciaries are not conflicted. Deciding on behalf of others often produces more efficient thinking, with fewer cognitive distortions. On the other hand, we might be more pessimistic about the ability of fiduciaries or beneficiaries to police violations, especially where the evidence is ambiguous. And finally, we know remarkably little about where fiduciary relationships fit in the mental model of our social world. Investing in empirical research on the psychology of the fiduciary relationship is valuable because it has promise for policy making but also for the basic social science of trust and trustworthiness.

PART II

Personal Trust and Fiduciary Duties

6

Stakeholder Fiducaries

EVAN J. CRIDDLE*

1 Introduction

Legal scholars and judges often assert that fiduciaries bear a duty of "undivided loyalty" that precludes concern for self-interest.[1] Indeed, the expectation that fiduciaries will abjure self-interest when exercising fiduciary power is so broadly accepted and applies to so many fiduciary relationships that it is sometimes mistaken for a universal principle of fiduciary law.[2]

This chapter explores the limits of selfless loyalty in American fiduciary law by showing that the duty of loyalty does not always demand disinterested service. Contrary to conventional wisdom, fiduciary law often permits parties to serve as fiduciaries while also maintaining a beneficial interest in their own exercise of fiduciary power. A fiduciary's beneficiary status may be a fixed structural feature of a particular type of fiduciary relationship (e.g., partnership), or it may depend on contingent features of specific relationships (e.g., spouses who acquire community property). Some fiduciary relationships have a symmetrical structure in which every party is simultaneously a fiduciary and beneficiary of every other party (e.g., joint ventures), while others have an asymmetrical structure in which certain parties are singled out to serve as fiduciaries for a group of beneficiaries that includes them (e.g., public officials). Regardless of such differences, the key point for present purpose is that these relationships all share a distinctive feature: in each case, the fiduciary is also a beneficiary of the fiduciary relationship.

In this chapter, I coin the term "stakeholder fiduciary"[3] to describe fiduciaries who are legitimate beneficiaries of their own exercise of fiduciary

* The author expresses appreciation to Matthew Harding, Paul Miller, Nate Oman and workshop participants at Hong Kong University and University of Melbourne for comments that have informed this paper, as well as to the Social Science and Humanities Research Council for supporting this project.

1 *Meinhard* v. *Salmon*, 164 N.E. 545, 546 (NY 1928).

2 Gregory S. Alexander, "A Cognitive Theory of Fiduciary Relationships" (2000) 85 *Cornell L. Rev.* 767, 776; Larry E. Ribstein, "Fiduciary Duty Contracts in Unincorporated Firms" (1997) 54 *Wash. & Lee L. Rev.* 537, 542. Some scholars have disputed the sole interest conception of fiduciary loyalty, but on different grounds than this chapter. D. Gordon Smith & Jordan C. Lee, "Fiduciary Discretion" (2014) 75 *Ohio St. LJ* 609, 633–34.

3 The term "stakeholder" carries a different meaning in corporate law jurisprudence and scholarship, where it refers to parties who have practical interests that may be affected by corporate decision-making and lack a direct legal interest in the performance of corporate fiduciaries (e.g., employees, customers). *Revlon, Inc.* v. *MacAndrews & Forbes Holdings, Inc.*, 506 A.2d 173, 182 (Del. 1986); Kent Greenfield, 'Proposition: Saving the World with Corporate Law' (2008) 57 *Emory LJ* 948, 975–83.

power.[4] I argue that stakeholder fiduciaries should be accepted as genuine "fiduciaries" despite the fact that they claim a beneficial interest in their own performance. But I also make the case that fiduciary law does – and should – treat stakeholder fiduciary relationships differently than nonstakeholder fiduciary relationships in a variety of important respects.

In previous writings, I have argued that fiduciary law safeguards beneficiaries against domination by ensuring that a fiduciary cannot betray her beneficiaries' trust with impunity by exercising entrusted power without due regard to her beneficiaries' interests.[5] A fiduciary betrays trust in nonstakeholder fiduciary relationships if she exercises entrusted discretionary power for self-regarding gain. In contrast, self-dealing is not antithetical to stakeholder fiduciary relationships. For example, when parties form a partnership, they authorize their copartners to share in the burdens and benefits of their collective undertaking. Partners may therefore attend to their own interests when conducting partnership business without betraying trust, provided that they also attend to other beneficiaries' interests in a fair and evenhanded manner. As legitimate stakeholders, partners are not expected to abjure self-interest when they exercise fiduciary power.

The fiduciary duty of loyalty therefore applies differently to stakeholder fiduciaries. For stakeholder fiduciaries, the duty of loyalty does not require that a fiduciary practice complete *self-abnegation* but rather *solidarity* with other beneficiaries. This means that a stakeholder fiduciary may retain an equitable share of the profits she generates through her position – even when those profits are the product of conflicted transactions or misappropriated opportunities. More striking still, when stakeholder fiduciaries exercise voting rights in collective governance, they are free to vote solely on their own interests as long as they do not misuse their voting power to undermine the purposes of the fiduciary relationship or dominate other beneficiaries. In each of these respects, stakeholder fiduciary law departs sharply from the conventional model of fiduciaries as selfless servants.

Courts also repose a different kind of trust in stakeholder fiduciaries, as reflected in the prudential limits they have established for judicial review of fiduciary discretion. When a nonstakeholder fiduciary is alleged to have violated her duty of care, courts do not necessarily give the fiduciary's decision any special deference.[6] The same cannot be said of stakeholder fiduciaries: as long as a stakeholder fiduciary's interests are plausibly in tune with the interests of other beneficiaries, courts will allow the

[4] Significantly, this definition excludes fiduciaries who are not formal beneficiaries but have other legal or practical interests in their own performance (e.g., lawyers with contingent-fee agreements). In a broad sense, every fiduciary has a "stake" of some kind in their own performance, whether it be a financial interest in receiving compensation for their services (e.g., agents, trustees) or a reputational interest in being perceived as loyal and careful (e.g., investment advisers, guardians). What distinguishes stakeholder fiduciaries from nonstakeholder fiduciaries, on the account offered here, is that the former are formal beneficiaries of their own fiduciary mandate.

[5] Evan J. Criddle, "Liberty in Loyalty: A Republican Theory of Fiduciary Law" (2017) 95 *Texas L. Rev.* 993.

[6] Deborah DeMott, "Fiduciary Principles in Agency Law" in Evan J. Criddle, Paul B. Miller & Robert H. Sitkoff (eds.), *The Oxford Handbook of Fiduciary Law* (Oxford University Press 2019); Robert H. Sitkoff, 'Fiduciary Principles in Trust Law' in Criddle, Miller & Sitkoff, *supra*.

fiduciary to decide for herself how much time and energy she should devote to a particular decision. Accordingly, when courts review stakeholder fiduciaries' decisions for compliance with the duty of care, they tend to grant relief only if unusual conflicts of interest or other exceptional circumstances furnish a compelling reason to question the fiduciaries' commitment to the beneficiaries' common good. Taking into account the fiduciary character of some fiduciary relationships thus enables us to better appreciate why courts apply a highly deferential standard of review to the decisions of some fiduciaries (e.g., business partners) but not others (e.g., investment managers). The best explanation, I will argue, is that courts trust stakeholder fiduciaries to exercise reasonable care without intrusive judicial oversight precisely because these fiduciaries have a direct personal stake in their own performance.

The stakeholder model also reveals a variety of other important insights for fiduciary theory and practice. As we will see, it strengthens the case for recognizing the fiduciary character of certain roles, such as majority shareholder and legislator, which scholars and policy makers sometimes call into question. It also challenges influential theories of fiduciary law that envision the duty of loyalty as protecting fiduciaries from being caught in positions where they would have to balance their own interests against others' interests.[7] For stakeholder fiduciaries, this balancing act is part and parcel of their fiduciary role.

Although the chapter covers a good deal of ground in a relatively short space, its scope is constrained in two respects. First, the chapter focuses on American law; it does not offer a general theory of stakeholder fiduciary law across all legal systems. Second, even as limited to American law, the chapter does not afford the space necessary to explore important differences in how various US jurisdictions have applied fiduciary principles to stakeholder fiduciaries. Instead, the chapter highlights general themes in American law for the purpose of showing that stakeholder fiduciaries (a) qualify as genuine fiduciaries, (b) are subject to distinctive legal requirements under the fiduciary duty of loyalty and (c) qualify for deferential judicial review under the fiduciary duty of care.

The balance of the chapter proceeds in two parts. Section 1 uses partnership law to illustrate and clarify how stakeholder fiduciaries are part of the wider family of fiduciaries while also differing fundamentally from nonstakeholder fiduciaries. Section 2 shows how fiduciary law's stakeholder model illuminates the juridical structure and legal duties associated with a variety of other relationships that are governed by private and public law. Rather than construe stakeholder fiduciary relationships as peripheral deviations from fiduciary law's "core,"[8] this chapter lays the groundwork for embracing stakeholder fiduciary relationships as a distinctive – but no less foundational – model for fiduciary law.

7 Matthew Conaglen, *Fiduciary Loyalty: Protecting the Due Performance of Non-Fiduciary Duties* (Hart Publishing 2011); Sung Hui Kim, "Fiduciary Principles and Corruption" in Criddle, Miller & Sitkoff (n. 6); Lionel Smith, "Fiduciary Relationships: Ensuring the Loyal Exercise of Judgement on Behalf of Another" (2014) 130 *LQR* 608, 623–25; Stephen A. Smith, "The Deed, Not the Motive: Fiduciary Law without Loyalty" in Andrew S. Gold & Paul B. Miller (eds.), *Contract, Status, and Fiduciary Law* (Oxford University Press 2016).

8 Charlie Webb, "The Philosophy of Fiduciary Law" in Criddle, Miller & Sitkoff (n. 6).

2 Trust and Loyalty among Stakeholders

This section explains how stakeholder relationships can trigger fiduciary duties despite the fact that the fiduciaries in these relationships are their own beneficiaries. It begins by identifying the defining features that all fiduciary relationships share. It then compares and contrasts nonstakeholder fiduciary relationships with the paradigmatic stakeholder fiduciary relationship: the general business partnership.

A Understanding Fiduciary Relationships

Fiduciary duties arise in relationships where a party has been entrusted with power over another's legal or practical interests.[9] Fiduciaries hold power in "trust" (*fides*) in the formal sense that their role is defined, at least in part, by entrustment: they are subject to a mandate that governs how they may legitimately exercise fiduciary power. In some cases, a fiduciary's mandate is limited to advancing the interests of particular beneficiaries. In other cases, a fiduciary's mandate may call for the fiduciary to pursue specific objectives or advance broader purposes.[10] However defined, a fiduciary's mandate triggers both social norms and formal legal requirements that she take others' interests or purposes into account when exercising fiduciary power. A fiduciary violates these justified expectations of loyal conduct if she exercises fiduciary power in a manner that is inconsistent with her mandate.[11]

Although entrusted power is a necessary criterion for the creation of a fiduciary relationship recognized under the law,[12] interpersonal trust is not. In practice, of course, fiduciary relationships are commonly premised upon interpersonal trust – i.e., an attitude or belief that the fiduciary will exercise discretion in a manner consistent with her mandate.[13] Few people would retain a lawyer, doctor or an investment manager if they were not already predisposed to expect loyalty from their fiduciary. Yet, fiduciary duties also apply to such relationships in the absence of interpersonal trust. Lawyers bear fiduciary duties to mentally disabled clients who are incapable of exercising interpersonal trust. Doctors are fiduciaries for unconscious strangers who receive their care. And investment managers owe fiduciary duties to pension fund beneficiaries who distrust their judgment. In short, the law does not care whether beneficiaries subjectively trust their fiduciaries. The relevant legal inquiry is, instead, an objective one: Has power been committed to a party under an other-regarding or purposeful mandate, such that the power holder is not entitled to determine

[9] For discussion of the fiduciary relationship as the foundation for fiduciary duties, see Criddle (n. 5); Tamar Frankel, *Fiduciary Law* (Oxford University Press 2011) 7–12; Paul B. Miller, "The Fiduciary Relationship" in Andrew S. Gold & Paul B. Miller (eds.), *Philosophical Foundations of Fiduciary Law* (Oxford University Press 2014) 63.

[10] Paul B. Miller & Andrew S. Gold, "Fiduciary Governance" (2014) 57 *Wm. & Mary L. Rev.* 513.

[11] Deborah A. DeMott, "Breach of Fiduciary Duty: On Justifiable Expectations of Loyalty and Their Consequences" (2006) 48 *Arizona L. Rev.* 925, 936.

[12] Criddle (n. 5) at 1036.

[13] Bernard Barber, *The Logic and Limits of Trust* (Rutgers University Press 1983) 14; Russell Hardin, *Trust and Trustworthiness* (Sage Publishing 2002) 1.

unilaterally how the power will be exercised?[14] If the answer to this question is yes, fiduciary duties apply to the relationship.

Keeping trust with a fiduciary mandate entails a variety of legal requirements, including compliance with the general fiduciary principles of solicitude, integrity, fairness, evenhandedness and prudence. Under the principle of *solicitude*, a fiduciary must exercise entrusted power in a manner that she believes will best advance her mandate. The principle of *integrity* prohibits a fiduciary from exercising fiduciary power for her own benefit or the benefit of third parties unless contemplated by the nature of the fiduciary relationship or with the consent of either the entrustor or the beneficiaries. When a fiduciary has multiple beneficiaries, the principles of *fairness* and *evenhandedness* dictate that she must exercise entrusted power in a manner that reflects due regard for her beneficiaries' respective equitable interests. Keeping trust also entails a requirement of *prudence*: a fiduciary must exercise the level of effort and skill that is necessary to fulfill her mandate. Failure to satisfy any of these principles would constitute a betrayal of the trust on which fiduciary relationships are predicated.

B Nonstakeholder Fiduciaries

In many fiduciary relationships, fiduciaries do not have a legitimate claim to benefit personally from their exercise of fiduciary power. These nonstakeholder fiduciary relationships are asymmetrical in two respects. First, they are *formally asymmetrical* in the sense that parties to these relationships hold different legal entitlements: one party (the fiduciary) is authorized to exercise power, while another party (the beneficiary) holds an exclusive entitlement to benefits generated by the power's exercise. Second, these fiduciary relationships are *practically asymmetrical* because the entrustment of power to fiduciaries exposes beneficiaries to heightened vulnerability. An untrustworthy fiduciary may abuse her power for self-serving purposes, or she may neglect her responsibilities and waste her beneficiary's resources and opportunities. Information asymmetries between the fiduciary and beneficiary may further exacerbate the beneficiary's vulnerability by frustrating her efforts to monitor and hold her fiduciary accountable. These formal and practical asymmetries pose a threat to beneficiaries insofar as fiduciaries have the capacity to betray trust by failing to practice solicitude, integrity, fairness, evenhandedness and prudence.

To safeguard beneficiaries from breaches of trust within nonstakeholder fiduciary relationships, fiduciary law imposes a variety of requirements. The duty of loyalty obligates nonstakeholder fiduciaries to exercise their entrusted powers without regard to their own interests or the interests of third parties. Fiduciaries are prohibited from concluding conflicted transactions without their beneficiaries' consent (the "no-conflict rule"), and they are required to relinquish any profits they accrue through their exercise of fiduciary power to their beneficiaries (the "no-profit rule"). When

[14] Entrustment may be inferred either from a party's formal status (e.g., agent, trustee, guardian) or from case-specific facts indicating that a relationship is premised on an other-regarding or purposive mandate. *Burdett* v. *Miller*, 957 F.2d 1375, 1381 (7th Cir. 1992); Daniel Kelly, "Fiduciary Principles in Fact-Based Fiduciary Relationships," in Criddle, Miller & Sitkoff (n. 6).

fiduciaries have multiple beneficiaries, the duty of loyalty also requires that they treat each beneficiary in a fair and evenhanded manner. Complementing these loyalty obligations, the duty of care obligates fiduciaries to use reasonable effort and skill whenever they exercise entrusted power. Collectively, these requirements affirm that nonstakeholder fiduciaries must exercise their entrusted power exclusively for the purposes specified in their other-regarding mandates.

C Partnership Fiduciary Law

The fiduciary duties of loyalty and care apply differently to stakeholder fiduciaries. Conventional wisdom suggests that the no-conflict and no-profit rules constitute fiduciary law's irreducible core,[15] but these rules do not apply to stakeholder fiduciaries. Fiduciary law permits stakeholder fiduciaries to conclude conflicted transactions and to profit from partnership business without other beneficiaries' consent. When fiduciaries can engage in such activities without breaching trust, fiduciary law does not stand in the way.

Partnership law illustrates how and why fiduciary duties apply differently to stakeholder and nonstakeholder fiduciary relationships. American law defines a partnership as an "association of two or more persons to carry on as co-owners a business for profit."[16] Unlike a traditional agency or trust relationship, partnerships have a distinctively egalitarian structure: unless partners decide otherwise, every partner is equally entitled to vote in governance decisions, to represent the partnership in conducting partnership business and to lay claim to partnership assets and profits.[17] Partners also presumptively share liability relative to any losses and debts the partnership accrues. Thus, each partner is both a fiduciary subject to duties of loyalty and care and also a beneficiary with a legitimate stake in partnership business.

The fact that partners are beneficiaries of their own performance has prompted some authorities to question whether partners can properly be described as fiduciaries. The Revised Uniform Partnership Act (RUPA) expresses concern that "the term 'fiduciary'" may be "inappropriate when used to describe the duties of a partner because a partner may legitimately pursue self-interest . . . and not solely the interest of the partnership and the other partners."[18] The Supreme Court of Kansas has asserted that the fiduciary characterization of partners "is somewhat misleading"[19] because a partner "is not held to the same strict standards of self-abnegation as a trustee."[20] State legislatures in Colorado and Texas have gone so far as to strike the word "fiduciary" from legislation codifying partners' duties of loyalty and care.[21] Although most jurisdictions in the United States continue to affirm that partners

[15] Conaglen (n. 7).

[16] Uniform Partnership Act s. 102(11); Rev'd Uniform Partnership Act (1997) (last rev'd 2013) s. 202(a).

[17] *Latta* v. *Kilbourn*, 150 US 524, 543 (1893).

[18] RUPA (n. 16) s. 404 cmt. The RUPA does acknowledge, however that "partners have long been characterized as fiduciaries." Ibid. s. 404 cmt.

[19] *Welch* v. *Via Christie Health Partners, Inc.*, 133 P.3d 122, 140 (2006).

[20] Ibid. 139.

[21] Colo. Rev. Stat. Ann. s. 7-64-404(1); Tex. Bus. Orgs. Code Ann. s. 152.204.

are fiduciaries,[22] the growing skepticism about partnership fiduciary law poses an important challenge: Is it meaningful to characterize partners as "fiduciaries" if they are also their own beneficiaries?

As we consider this question, it may be helpful to keep our sights trained on fiduciary law's core function: redressing breaches of trust. Like other fiduciary relationships, partnerships arise when parties entrust one another with power to conduct business on behalf of the group for the group's collective benefit. A partner therefore betrays her copartners' trust if she takes business opportunities of the partnership for her exclusive personal gain, if she wastes partnership assets or opportunities or if she fails to share profits and losses with her copartners in a fair and evenhanded manner.[23] The fact that partnerships are based on entrusted power makes them well suited for regulation under fiduciary law's paradigmatic duties of loyalty and care.

Yet, partnerships are also fundamentally different from nonstakeholder fiduciary relationships, such as garden-variety agent–principal, trustee–beneficiary and guardian–ward relationships. Unlike beneficiaries in nonstakeholder fiduciary relationships, a partner cannot reasonably expect her copartner to renounce self-interest when conducting partnership business. The ultimate purpose of a general business partnership, after all, is to advance the financial interests of each and every partner. Hence, a partner's fiduciary role is premised not on self-abnegation but solidarity: her entrusted role is to exercise fiduciary power in a manner that respects all partners (including herself) as rightful cobeneficiaries.[24]

The fiduciary duty of loyalty thus applies differently to partnerships than to nonstakeholder fiduciary relationships. A partner does not violate the duty of loyalty merely because she profits from her fiduciary role.[25] Instead, an aggrieved partner must show that her copartner failed to practice solidarity by, for example, diverting business opportunities away from the partnership or reserving a disproportionate share of partnership gains for herself.[26] Although a partner's duty of loyalty does not preclude concern for self-interest, it does require that a partner devote equal concern to her copartners' equitable interests, consistent with the principles of fairness and evenhandedness.

To better appreciate how fiduciary principles apply to partnerships, however, we need to dig a bit deeper into the partnership's relational structure. In the sections that follow, I argue that partners occupy two distinct fiduciary roles, which we might describe, respectively, as "partnership management" and "partnership governance."

22 *Meisel* v. *Grunberg*, 651 F.Supp.2d 98, 114 (SDNY 2009); J. William Callison & Maureen A. Sullivan, *Partnership Law & Practice* (Thompson 2017) s 12.1.

23 *Gossett* v. *St. Paul Fire and Marine Ins. Co.*, 427 So. 386, 387 (Fla. 4th Dist. 1983).

24 To be clear, a stakeholder fiduciary's duty of solidarity – like the duty of self-abnegation that applies to nonstakeholder fiduciary relationships – requires *conduct* consistent with solicitude, not pure *motivations*. Evan J. Criddle & Evan Fox-Decent, "Keeping the Promise of Public Fiduciary Theory: A Reply to Leib and Galoob" (2016) 126 *Yale LJ F.* 192.

25 RUPA (n. 16) s 404(e).

26 Ibid. s. 404 cmt.2; Paul Finn, *Fiduciary Obligations: 40th Anniversary Republication with Additional Essays* (Federation Press 2016) 53. Delaware permits partners to limit liability for breach of fiduciary duty. Del. Code Ann. (2005) tit. 6, s. 15-103(f).

In partnership management, partners conduct business on behalf of the partnership. Partnership governance refers to a partner's authority to participate in collective governance decisions. Both of these roles trigger fiduciary duties that safeguard partners' justified expectations of solidarity.

a Partnership Management

As a general default rule, American law empowers all partners to conduct business on behalf of their partnership while sharing equitably in the partnership's profits and liabilities. Accordingly, the partnership's formal structure is presumptively symmetrical. In practice, however, the actual conduct of partnership business immediately generates asymmetries of power and vulnerability: whenever a partner conducts partnership business, her actions have the potential to harm other partners' interests without their participation or consent. Hence, the actual conduct of partnership business generates role differentiation between the acting partner (as fiduciary–beneficiary) and passive partners (as beneficiaries). Partners sometimes choose to formalize this role differentiation by designating a single managing partner to conduct all business on the partnership's behalf. For ease of exposition, therefore, in the discussion that follows I refer to a partner who conducts business on behalf of the partnership – whether by formal designation or not – as the partnership's "managing partner."

Courts have developed two theories for conceptualizing the relational structure of partnership management. The "aggregate theory" envisions a managing partner as receiving power directly from, and owing fiduciary duties directly to, each of the partners individually. The "entity theory," in contrast, considers the partnership a distinct legal entity that stands between individual partners and the managing partner.[27] The two theories can be visualized as follows:

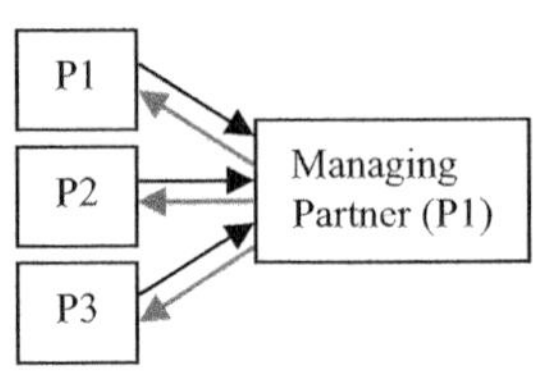

Figure 6.1 The aggregate theory

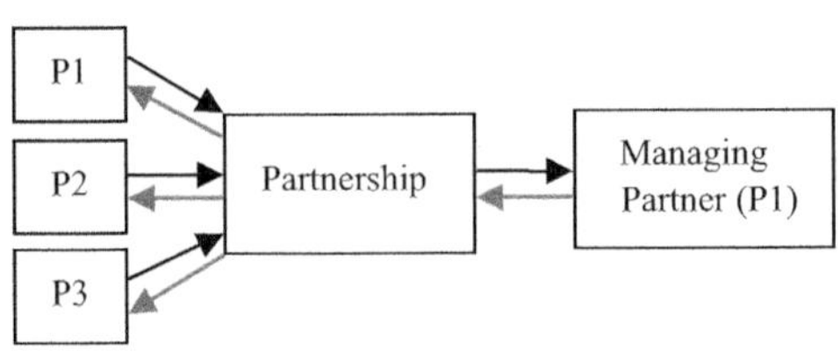

Figure 6.2 The entity theory

[27] The common law traditionally endorsed the aggregate theory, but the RUPA explicitly endorses the entity theory. Callison & Sullivan (n. 22) s. 3.1.

The formal distinction between these models is important for a variety of reasons, including whether partners may claim limited liability against the partnership's creditors.[28] On first impression, the distinction might also seem important in assessing whether a managing partner is a stakeholder fiduciary or a nonstakeholder fiduciary. Under the aggregate theory, the managing partner is clearly a stakeholder fiduciary: she receives power directly from the partners and acts, in part, for her own benefit. The entity theory, in contrast, purports to establish two nonstakeholder fiduciary relationships: one between the managing partner and the partnership, and a second between the partnership and each of the individual partners. As a legal matter, however, this formal distinction between the aggregate theory and the entity theory collapses on closer inspection. In practice, a managing partner exercises such complete domination and control over the partnership's day-to-day business and the distribution of partnership profits that the partnership entity effectively becomes the managing partner's alter ego for these purposes.[29] Thus, even under the entity theory, a managing partner is better understood as a stakeholder fiduciary whose duties of loyalty and care for all intents and purposes run directly to herself and her copartners.

Judges and legal scholars often assert that a managing partner serves as an "agent" of the partnership subject to ordinary principles of agency law,[30] but this is only partly true. While agency law does supply some rules for managing partners (e.g., actual and apparent authority, vicarious liability), the nonstakeholder fiduciary duties of agents do not apply to partners. Agency fiduciary law is premised on self-abnegation: an agent is expected to refrain from using entrusted power for her own ends. For this reason, an agent ordinarily must relinquish all profits and opportunities that flow from her exercise of entrusted power.[31] Partnership fiduciary law, in contrast, is premised on a managing partner's status as a cobeneficiary of her own performance. As such, managing partners are not prohibited from commingling their assets with the assets of other beneficiaries; nor must they refrain from entering conflicted transactions without their copartners' authorization. The duty of loyalty demands only that they not misappropriate partnership opportunities and that they divide profits and losses with their copartners in a fair and evenhanded manner.[32]

Courts apply a deferential "good faith" standard when reviewing a managing partner's conduct for compliance with the fiduciary duty of care.[33] This good faith

[28] Ibid.

[29] *Wallace* v. *Wood*, 752 A.2d 1175, 1183–84 (Del. Ch. 1999); *Outokumpu Eng'g Enters., Inc.* v. *Kvaerner Enviropower, Inc.*, 685 A2d 724, 729 (Del. Superior Ct. 1996).

[30] *Wash.* v. *Kass Mgmt. Serv.*, 2011 WL 1465581, at *3 (ND Ill. 2011).

[31] Restatement (Third) of Agency (Am. Law Inst. 2006) ss. 8.02, 8.05.

[32] *Latta* (n. 17); *Liggett* v. *Lester*, 390 P.2d 351, 354 (Or. 1964); *Welch* (n. 19) 142; UPA (n. 16) ss. 21–22. Some might argue that stakeholder fiduciaries should be required to relinquish all profits generated by conflicted transactions because the prevailing rule does not adequately deter bad faith self-dealing. Elsewhere, I have joined Lionel Smith in arguing that fiduciary norms and remedies are not designed for deterrence. Criddle (n. 5) 1051–55; Lionel Smith, 'Deterrence, Prophylaxis and Punishment in Fiduciary Obligations' (2013) 7 *J. Equity* 87. To the extent that deterrence is an important concern, however, other remedies such as punitive damages might be an appropriate response.

[33] Callison & Sullivan (n. 22) s. 12.2.

standard, like the "business judgment rule" (BJR) in corporate law,[34] restrains courts from holding partners liable for honest mistakes in the exercise of business judgment.[35] This does not mean that a managing partner is free to conduct partnership business with less than reasonable care; it simply means that courts won't second-guess a managing partner's decisions under the duty of care absent strong evidence of bad faith.[36]

Why such a deferential standard? Conventional justifications focus on several factors: respect for the partners' choice to repose trust in the managing partner, deference to the managing partner's superior expertise, and a recognition that partners often have strong market-based incentives to avoid developing a reputation for negligent or wasteful management.[37] None of these factors, however, adequately explains why courts have chosen to apply the deferential good faith standard to partners but not to various other categories of fiduciaries who possess special expertise and have similar incentives to practice loyalty and care (e.g., investment advisers).

Corporate law offers an additional rationale for its BJR. Courts assume that diversified shareholders want corporate officers and directors to take calculated risks when formulating corporate business strategy, but they recognize that officers and directors would be unlikely to take such risks without the BJR's protection because the duty of care could expose them with catastrophic personal liability if the risks do not pay off.[38] This rationale makes sense in the corporate context, where the threat of personal liability to shareholders ordinarily dwarfs an officer or director's own equitable stake in the corporation. It is much less persuasive as applied to partnerships, however, where investment diversification cannot be presumed and beneficiaries are likely to be more risk averse.

The stakeholder model offers a more compelling justification for partnership law's deferential "good faith" standard of review. Because managing partners are beneficiaries of their partnerships, they have a direct financial incentive to ensure that their business decisions reflect prudent effort and skill. This furnishes a reasonable basis for courts to presume that managing partners will be in a better position to decide both how much effort their partnership should devote to making a business decision and how aggressively the partnership should court risk in pursuit of greater profit. Thus, when managing partners make business decisions in good faith, courts wisely refrain from imposing liability under the fiduciary duty of care.

b Partnership Governance

Partners arguably perform a second fiduciary role when they participate in governance functions. Much like directors in a corporation, general partners are collectively

[34] Section 2 discusses the corporate law BJR in greater detail.

[35] *Rosenthal* v. *Rosenthal*, 543 A2d 348 (Me. 1988); *Wyler* v. *Feuer*, 85 Cal. App. 3d 392, 402 (1978).

[36] *Rosenthal* (n. 35), at 353–54.

[37] Ibid. I emphasize these two factors – entrustment and expertise – in "Fiduciary Law's Mixed Messages" in Andrew S. Gold & D. Gordon Smith (eds.), *Research Handbook on Fiduciary Law* (Edward Elgar 2018). Reliance on expertise can be understood, in part, as ensuring that decisions are made at a level where decision costs will be lowest.

[38] *Gagliardi* v. *Trifoods Int'l, Inc.*, 683 A.2d 1049, 1052 (Del. Ch. 1996).

responsible for establishing a partnership's general business strategy and making other major decisions. Most partnership-level decisions, including those that concern potential amendments to the partnership agreement and the sale of core partnership assets, require a unanimous vote.[39] Less consequential decisions regarding "ordinary matters connected with the partnership" may qualify for approval by a simple majority.[40]

Partners bear relatively thin legal duties to one another when they participate in partnership governance.[41] Generally speaking, individual partners may use their voting rights to further their own personal interests without according equal weight to other partners' interests.[42] Courts will intercede in partnership voting only when confronted with flagrant abuses of trust, such as when individual partners use their vote to thwart the partnership's core purposes, misappropriate partnership opportunities or undercut other partners' equal voice in governance decisions.[43]

Based on these features of partnership law, some scholars have disputed the idea that fiduciary duties apply to partnership governance. They argue that partners interact as principals, not as fiduciaries, when they cast votes in partnership governance. Proponents of this view offer two accounts of the ostensibly nonfiduciary character of partnership governance. For ease of exposition, I will refer to these models as the "property model" and the "contract model."

The property model connects partners' governance powers to their interests in partnership property. When partners cast votes in partnership governance, it is suggested, they exercise legal powers that emanate from their own beneficial interests in partnership property. The property model plausibly explains why partners might be legally entitled to control the use and disposition of their own personal stake in the partnership.[44] The model's primary weakness is that it cannot explain why partners would be entitled to exercise authority over the *partnership entity* as a whole (under the entity theory) and the beneficial interests of *other partners* (under the aggregate theory). A partner's authority over those interests is not merely incidental to her control over her own beneficial interests. Whenever a partner votes in partnership governance, she exercises a form of directorial authority over the entire enterprise. It makes little sense, therefore, to characterize partnership voting as a straightforward exercise of partners' individual property interests.

A more plausible model for partnership governance focuses on the partnership's contractual foundations. Under this contract model, partners relinquish their proprietary rights over property that they contribute to the partnership in exchange for

[39] RUPA (n. 16) § 401(j); Robert W. Hillman, "Private Ordering within Partnerships" (1987) 41 *U. Miami L. Rev.* 425, 450.

[40] RUPA (n. 16) § 401(j); Hillman (n. 39) 450.

[41] RUPA (n. 16) § 404(d) & 404 cmt. 5.

[42] RUPA offers, as an example, that "a partner who, with consent, owns a shopping center may … legitimately vote against a proposal by the partnership to open a competing shopping center." Ibid. s. 404 cmt. 5.

[43] *CBIF Limited Partnership* v. *TGI Friday's Inc.*, 2017 WL 1455407, at *23 (Tex. App. 2017).

[44] The model is only "plausible" in this respect because, as reflected in trustee-beneficiary relationships, there is no necessary relationship between having a beneficial interest in property and holding an entitlement to control the use or disposition of property.

receiving: (1) a beneficial interest in partnership business and assets, (2) management powers to conduct business on behalf of the partnership and (3) governance powers to vote on major questions regarding the partnership's strategy and core assets. Since partnership voting rights are conferred by contract, partners are arguably free to exercise these rights as they see fit as long they respect the implied contractual duty of "good faith and fair dealing,"[45] which proscribes actions "that would destroy or injure another party's right to receive the fruits of the contract."[46]

Proponents of the contract model tend to assume that if partnership voting rights are conferred by contract, then partners cannot also be fiduciaries in partnership governance. But these options are not mutually exclusive. Indeed, at least one US court has concluded expressly that the "contractual rights" partners owe one another when they vote in partnership governance "do not operate to the exclusion of fiduciary duties" but rather "must be exercised in a manner consistent with fiduciary duties."[47]

Why might courts conclude that fiduciary duties apply to partnership governance? For the same reason that fiduciary duties apply elsewhere: partners exercise entrusted power over others' legal and practical interests when they cast votes in partnership governance.[48] By entering into a partnership, each partner entrusts the others with power to vote on business decisions for the collective benefit of the partnership as a whole and respective benefit of the individual partners. Thus, partners do not stand at arm's length from one another when they vote on major business decisions; they exercise power within a fiduciary relationship that is premised on solidarity.

Some might object that this fiduciary model would impose more robust legal requirements than partnership law actually provides. If partners are fiduciaries for one another in partnership governance, why have courts allowed them to favor their own individual interests when they vote on major partnership decisions?

A possible response to this objection is that it fails to grasp how partnership voting itself is responsive to the fiduciary duty of loyalty. Rather than enlist individual partners to determine what would constitute a fair and evenhanded result, partnerships address these questions at the collective level through voting procedures. The expectation is that if every partner is free to vote in her own interest, the sum total of their votes will fairly and evenhandedly represent the interests of the partnership as a whole. Proceduralizing the requirement of fair and evenhanded treatment in this way makes good sense for major business decisions, which are likely to have complex and uncertain ramifications for the partnership. Furthermore, individual partners are often in a poor position to evaluate how major partnership decisions will impact

[45] RUPA (n. 16) s. 404 cmts. 4–5; *Continental Insur. Co.* v. *Rutledge & Co., Inc.*, 750 A.2d 1219, 1234 (Del. Ch. 2000); Larry E. Ribstein, "The Evolving Partnership" in Joseph A. McCahery et al. (eds.), *The Governance of Close Corporations and Partnerships: US and European Perspectives* (Oxford University Press 2004) 179 n. 108.

[46] *Kelly* v. *Skytell Comm'ns, Inc.*, 32 Fed. Appx. 283, 285 (9th Cir. 2002).

[47] *CBIF* (n. 43) *15, *23. The RUPA, in contrast, speaks somewhat cryptically of a need to balance "the partner's rights as an owner and principal in the enterprise, . . . against his duties and obligations as an agent and fiduciary." RUPA (n. 16) 404 cmt. 5.

[48] Criddle (n. 5) 1036.

their copartners' interests. Given these considerations, partners generally do not violate their duty of loyalty if they cast votes in partnership governance based exclusively on their own self-interest while relying on the collective voting process to ensure that other partners' interests receive equal weight in the final outcome.

In some settings, however, partners may violate their fiduciary duty of loyalty if they cast votes exclusively in their own self-interest. Such would be the case, for example, if a majority of the partners voted in favor of a measure that would prevent a minority from obtaining their fair and evenhanded share of partnership profits. The duty of loyalty would also prohibit a single partner from using her veto power to prevent the partnership from complying with legal requirements or to extort other partners into giving her an extra share of partnership profits.[49] The problem with using voting power in these ways is not that such actions are self-interested per se, but rather that a partner cannot reasonably rely on the aggregative process of partnership voting to safeguard the partnership's overarching purposes and ensure fair and evenhanded treatment for other partners in these settings. As courts have recognized, these abuses of voting power are incompatible with the "generalized [fiduciary] duty of good faith and utmost loyalty."[50]

D Partnership's Stakeholder Model

In sum, partnership law offers a model for fiduciary relationships that is distinct from the "undivided loyalty" that applies to nonstakeholder fiduciaries. Like nonstakeholder fiduciaries, partners hold power pursuant to an other-regarding and purposive mandate. And like nonstakeholder fiduciary relationships, partnerships are premised on the justified expectation that partners will practice loyalty and care when exercising entrusted power. In partnerships, however, practicing loyalty requires solidarity with other beneficiaries, not complete self-abnegation. Accordingly, partners are free to use the partnership as a vehicle for their own personal profit, as long as they also respect the terms of the partnership agreement (solicitude), refrain from misappropriating partnership assets and opportunities (integrity) and share profits and losses equitably (fairness and evenhandedness). Partnership law thus illustrates how parties may be genuine fiduciaries while still having a legitimate stake in their own exercise of fiduciary power.

3 Stakeholder Fiduciaries in Private and Public Law

Reflecting on partnership law's peculiar features, Robert Hillman once mused that "[i]f partners truly are fiduciaries, they are a unique species of this group and cannot be subjected to traditional standards applicable to other types of fiduciaries."[51] Section 1 offered support for Hillman's suggestion that the traditional fiduciary requirement of "undivided loyalty" is not well suited for partnership law. In the discussion that

[49] *CBIF* (n. 43) *14–15.
[50] *Petricca Development Ltd. Partnership* v. *Pioneer Development Co.*, 214 F.3d 216, 220 (1st Cir. 2000).
[51] Hillman (n. 39) 458.

follows, however, I want to challenge Hillman's assertion that partners are "a unique species" of fiduciaries who are subject to unique legal duties. As this section will show, stakeholder fiduciary relationships are ubiquitous and include some of the most consequential relationships governed by private and public law. Moreover, the legal duties and standards of judicial review that govern other stakeholder fiduciaries have striking parallels to partnership law. Although this chapter does not afford the space for a comprehensive survey of stakeholder fiduciary relationships, the examples provided in this section suggest that fiduciary law's stakeholder model may rival the nonstakeholder model in the breadth of its influence.

A Joint Ventures and Joint Enterprises

The fiduciary relationships that most closely resemble partnerships are joint ventures and joint enterprises. A joint venture is essentially a partnership established for a limited purpose: undertaking a single business venture for profit.[52] Joint enterprises are collective undertakings that do not require a profit motive, just a common purpose.[53] Under the general default rules of joint venture and joint enterprise law, members of joint ventures and joint enterprises are empowered to act on behalf of their association, and they are entitled to share gains and bear liability for losses in proportion to the extent of their investment.[54] They also exercise joint control over governance. Indeed, so close are the parallels between joint ventures and joint enterprises, on the one hand, and general partnerships, on the other, that some jurisdictions treat them all as a single legal category.[55]

One of the classic cases of the American fiduciary law canon, *Meinhard* v. *Salmon*, describes the fiduciary duties of joint ventures. In an opinion authored by then chief judge Benjamin Cardozo, the New York Court of Appeals explains that joint venturers, "like copartners," owe one another a kind of loyalty that is "stricter than the morals of the marketplace."[56] By undertaking to serve as managing coventurer, Salmon "put himself in a position where the thought of self was to be renounced, however hard the abnegation. . . . For him and those like him, the rule of undivided loyalty is relentless and supreme."[57]

Taken out of context, these statements can easily be misconstrued to suggest that managing coventurers bear a duty of strict self-abnegation. As the opinion continues, however, Cardozo clarifies that Salmon was not, in fact, required to practice the kind of undivided loyalty that precludes self-regard; rather, Salmon's duty was to give his coventurer, Meinhard, *equal* regard. Accordingly, when Salmon learned of an opportunity to lease property, he should have either (a) concluded the transaction on behalf of the joint venture and shared the profits equitably with Meinhard or (b) afforded

52 Noah J. Gordon, "Joint Ventures" in (2007) 46 *Am. Jur. 2d Joint Ventures* ss. 1, 6.

53 Ibid. s. 5.

Ibid.

54 Ibid. ss. 5, 10, 15, 18, 23–24.

55 Ibid. s. 3.

56 *Meinhard* (n. 1) 546.

57 Ibid. 548.

Meinhard an opportunity to bid against him for the lease.[58] Because Salmon failed to do either of these things, the court awarded Meinhard an equitable share of the leased property in an amount equal to "the value of half of the entire lease."[59] Thus, far from subjecting the coventurers to a "relentless" rule of "undivided loyalty," *Meinhard* confirms that coventurers, like partners, must practice solidarity when exercising fiduciary power.[60]

In subsequent cases, courts have continued to hold that joint venturers and members of joint enterprises are subject to duties of solidarity. Joint venturers are entitled to share in their association's profits without having to seek special approval from their coventurers. If a managing joint venturer acquires secret benefits, fiduciary law's classic accounting remedy can be used to compel equitable distribution,[61] but the disloyal coventurer, as a legitimate stakeholder, is still entitled to keep a proportional share of her secret profits unless the joint-venture agreement expressly provides for complete forfeiture.[62] When exercising governance powers, joint venturers also bear a partnership-style duty of good faith and fair dealing, under which they must refrain from misappropriating opportunities or otherwise freezing out their coventurers.[63] Moreover, courts will not hold joint venturers liable for the exercise of ordinary business judgment, only for a "breach of trust" tantamount to bad faith.[64] In each of these respects, the law governing joint ventures and joint enterprises mirrors partnership's stakeholder model.

B Corporate Officers and Directors

Under Delaware law, corporate officers and directors owe fiduciary duties to the corporation and its shareholders.[65] The fact that officers and directors are often their own beneficiaries has not been widely emphasized, however, in legal scholarship on corporate fiduciary duties. This oversight may be attributable, in part, to the fact that the stakeholder status of officers and directors depends upon firm-specific compensation packages and the personal investment decisions of individual officers and directors. Unlike a partnership or joint venture, there is no reason why a corporation must be governed or managed by stakeholder fiduciaries. And although corporate law permits officers and directors to hold equity in the firms they serve, it does not affirmatively require such investment. In practice, however, officers and directors so often hold stock in their corporations (particularly in closely held corporations, which

[58] Ibid. 547.
[59] Ibid. 548.
[60] Julian Velasco, "The Role of Aspiration in Corporate Fiduciary Duties" (2012) 54 *Wm. & Mary L. Rev.* 519, 564.
[61] Gordon (n. 52) s. 34.
[62] Ibid.
[63] *Bohler-Uddeholm America, Inc.* v. *Ellwood Group, Inc.*, 247 F.3d 79, 102–05 (3d Cir. 2001).
[64] *Ferguson* v. *Williams*, 670 S.W.2d 327, 331 (Tex. Ct. App. 1984).
[65] *North Am. Catholic Educ. Programming Foundation* v. *Gheewalla*, 930 A.2d 92, 101–02 (Del. 2007); *Malone* v. *Brincat*, 722 A.2d 5, 9 (Del. 1998).

represent at least 90 percent of American businesses[66]) that it has become easy to take their stakeholder status for granted.

In the past, some courts have characterized the corporate law duty of loyalty as imposing a requirement of strict self-abnegation. For example, in the oft-cited 1939 case *Guth* v. *Loft*, the Delaware Supreme Court asserted that corporate fiduciaries owe "undivided and unselfish loyalty to the corporation."[67] Although the court recognized that corporate officers and directors are "not technically trustees," it nonetheless declared that they "are not permitted to use their position of trust and confidence to further their private interests."[68]

Whether or not this formulation accurately captured American corporate fiduciary law in the 1930s, it is now woefully outdated. Far from being required to abjure self-interest, officers and directors are free to profit from their equity holdings as long as they accord fair and evenhanded treatment to other shareholders.[69] Corporate officers may even engage in conflicted transactions without the board's approval, provided they can demonstrate that the transactions were entirely "fair" to the corporation.[70] Courts refrain from intervening in corporate management and governance under the duty of loyalty as long as an officer or director "had an incentive to make the corporation more profitable," saving "intrusive" review for contexts "where the fiduciaries were conflicted and stood to gain *at the expense* of the company" and its shareholders.[71]

Courts also defer to officers and directors when reviewing corporate practice for compliance with the fiduciary duty of care. Under the BJR, courts in Delaware apply a strong "presumption that in making a business decision the directors of a corporation acted on an informed basis, in good faith and in the honest belief that the action taken was in the best interests of the company."[72] The BJR reflects the courts' belief that shareholders with diversified investment portfolios want (or should want) officers and directors to take calculated risks in pursuit of maximizing profits, as well as a concern that vigorous judicial enforcement of the duty of care would deter prudent risk taking.[73] Without the BJR, the thinking goes, corporate officers and directors would adopt overly conservative risk-management strategies in order to avoid the threat of catastrophic personal liability under the fiduciary duty of care.[74] By taking this threat of personal liability off the table except in cases of flagrant bad faith, the BJR liberates corporate officers and directors to take calculated risks in order to advance shareholders' interests.

[66] F. Hodge O'Neal & Robert B. Thompson, *O'Neal's Close Corporations* (3d ed. 2002) s. 1.19, at 108.

[67] 5 A.2d 503, 510 (1939).

[68] Ibid.

[69] *Katz Corp.* v. *T. H. Canty & Co.*, 362 A2d 975 (1975).

[70] *Weinberger* v. *UOP, Inc.*, 457 A.2d 701, 710–11 (Del 1983).

[71] Lawrence Hamermesh & Leo Strine Jr., "Delaware Corporate Law: Searching for the Optimal Balance" in Criddle, Miller & Sitkoff (n. 6) 871, 876 (emphasis added).

[72] *Aronson* v. *Lewis*, 472 A.2d 805, 813 (Del. 1984); Dennis J. Block et al., *The Business Judgment Rule: Fiduciary Duties of Corporate Directors* vol. 1 (Aspen Law & Business 5th ed. 1998) 4–5.

[73] *Gagliardi* (n. 38) 1052.

[74] Ibid.

The BJR assumes that officers and directors can be trusted to decide how much time and energy to devote to evaluating risky business opportunities. Is this assumption reasonable? Conventional wisdom suggests that corporate officers and directors have strong incentives to act prudently in order to retain their current employment and attract other professional opportunities. The stakeholder model suggests another reason for courts to trust officers and directors: when officers and directors are shareholders in their firms, they have a direct financial incentive to exercise appropriate care. Although this factor might not be sufficient to justify the BJR in every case,[75] it offers a supplementary justification for courts deferring to corporate officers' and directors' business judgments.

C *Shareholders*

Under American law, shareholders are also fiduciaries for one another in some contexts. Controlling shareholders in public corporations bear fiduciary duties to minority shareholders.[76] Many states also impose fiduciary duties on shareholders in closely held corporations.[77] Courts justify extending fiduciary duties to the relationship between shareholders based on the dominating power that certain shareholders would otherwise hold over others.[78] In particular, courts have intervened to prevent controlling shareholders from using their voting power to oppress minority shareholders.[79]

Some might question whether shareholders can properly be considered "fiduciaries" when they are also principals and beneficiaries of the corporation.[80] Yet, shareholders are fiduciaries for one another for precisely the same reasons that partners are fiduciaries for one another in partnership governance: both are entrusted with power

[75] Some corporate officers and directors do not hold equity in their corporation, and most others "can expect relatively little direct personal gain from devoting time and energy to overseeing the firm." Lynn A. Stout, "In Praise of Procedure: An Economic and Behavioral Defense of *Smith* v. *Van Gorkom* and the Business Judgment Rule" (2002) 96 *Nw. U. L. Rev.* 675, 679. Officers and directors with only minor equity holdings might be willing to take risks with corporate business strategy that would be unacceptable to a majority shareholder for whom firm-specific risks are more salient. Where corporate managers' financial incentives are misaligned with the incentives of other shareholders in this way, extrajudicial bonding mechanisms might be necessary to safeguard shareholder interests. Conversely, a corporate officer or director whose "holdings comprise a large percentage of her portfolio" might avoid risky investments that are attractive to "more-diversified shareholders" precisely "because she is exposed to the 'firm-specific' risks to which they are indifferent." Ibid. 679 n. 15. In such cases, the BJR alone is unlikely to persuade corporate managers to take the kinds of risks that might be more attractive to more diversified shareholders.

[76] John C. Carter, "The Fiduciary Rights of Shareholders" (1988) 29 *Wm. & Mary L. Rev.* 823, 831–36.

[77] *Crosby* v. *Beam*, 548 NE2d 217, 220 (Ohio 1989); *Donahue* v. *Rodd Electrotype Co. of New England, Inc.*, 328 N.E.2d 505, 513–15 (Mass. 1975); *Hollis* v. *Hill*, 232 F.3d 460 (5th Cir. 2000). In Delaware and some other states, majority shareholders do not owe fiduciary duties to minority shareholders in close corporations. *Nixon* v. *Blackwell*, 626 A2d 1366, 1379–81 (Del. 1993).

[78] *Donahue* (n. 70) at 513–15.

[79] *Crosby* (n. 70) at 221.

[80] D. Theodore Rave, "Two Problems of Fiduciary Governance" in Evan J. Criddle et al. (eds.) *Fiduciary Government* (Cambridge University Press 2018).

over others' legal interests.[81] Just as partnership agreements entrust individual partners with power over the partnership and other partners' beneficial interests, so too corporate charters and bylaws entrust shareholders with power over the corporation and other shareholders' interests.

The duty of loyalty also applies in a similar fashion in both contexts. Although corporate law generally permits shareholders to favor their own interests when they exercise voting powers,[82] this rule is premised on an expectation that the voting process itself will represent shareholders' interests, thus ensuring that all shareholders will receive fair and evenhanded treatment in the corporation's collective decision-making. This presumption does not apply, however, when controlling shareholders wield their voting power as an instrument of oppression. For example, a majority shareholder in a public corporation would violate her fiduciary duty of loyalty if she sought to "squeeze out" minority shareholders by instructing directors under her control "to approve a merger in which . . . [she] forcibly acquires the shares held by minority stockholders" at an inequitably low price.[83] Likewise, a controlling shareholder in a close corporation could violate her duty of loyalty by "denying employment to minority shareholders and eliminating dividends, so that they have no easy way to earn a return on their investments."[84] Such practices betray the trust that shareholders repose in one another when they participate in the collective corporate enterprise.

Recognizing these threats, states have developed rules to promote the equitable treatment of minority shareholders. Under Massachusetts law, a majority shareholder's attempt to freeze out minority shareholders in a close corporation from salary and dividends is governed by "substantially the same fiduciary duty . . . that partners owe to one another"; i.e., a duty of fair and evenhanded treatment.[85] Delaware protects minority shareholders against squeeze out mergers by limiting the BJR to cases where controlling shareholders have secured "*both* the approval of an independent, adequately-empowered Special Committee that fulfills its duty of care; *and* the uncoerced, informed vote of a majority of the minority stockholders."[86] In a similar spirit, the Supreme Court of Pennsylvania has held that the fiduciary duty of loyalty

> prevents [majority shareholders] from using their power in such a way as to exclude the minority from their proper share of the benefits accruing from the enterprise. This does not mean, of course, that majority shareholders may never act in their own interest, but when they do act in their own interest, it must be also in the best interest of all shareholders and the corporation.[87]

The common thread that unites these features of American corporate law is a commitment to ensuring that shareholders lack the capacity to abuse their entrusted power over corporate governance.

[81] *Pepper* v. *Litton*, 308 US 295, 306 (1939).
[82] *Ringling Bros.-Barnum & Bailey Combined Shows* v. *Ringling*, 53 A2d 441, 447 (Del. 1947).
[83] Hamermesh & Strine (n. 71) at 879.
[84] Julian Velasco, "Fiduciary Principles in Corporate Law" in Criddle, Miller & Sitkoff (n. 6).
[85] *Donahue* (n. 70) 515.
[86] *Kahn* v. *M&F Worldwide Corp.*, 88 A3d 635, 644 (Del. 2014) (emphasis added).
[87] *Ferber* v. *American Lamp Corp.*, 469 A2d 1046 (Pa. 1983).

D Stakeholder Trustees

In some US jurisdictions, even trustees can be stakeholder fiduciaries.[88] When settlors in these jurisdictions appoint a beneficiary to serve as trustee, courts treat the appointment as "authoriz[ing] the trustee to make distributions for the trustee's own benefit."[89] A stakeholder trustee is not expected to renounce self-interest, but she is required to treat other beneficiaries "equitably in light of the purposes and terms of the trust."[90] Courts apply an abuse-of-discretion standard when reviewing a trustee's efforts to balance her own beneficial interests against the interests of other beneficiaries.[91] A trustee who violates this standard is subject to removal.[92]

Trustees are subject to a strict "duty of prudence." Defenders of this approach have argued that BJR-style deference should not apply to trusts because trust beneficiaries are less likely to hold diversified trust portfolios and therefore may be more vulnerable to market risk on average than shareholders in publicly traded companies.[93] This argument is persuasive, as far as it goes. But facilitating risk taking in the interests of diversified investors is not the only reason to embrace BJR-style judicial abstention. As discussed previously, diversification cannot be presumed in partnerships and joint ventures, yet courts routinely apply BJR-style review to these fiduciary relationships. Stakeholder trustees arguably qualify for a similarly deferential standard of review, and for the same reasons: like partners and joint venturers, stakeholder trustees have a financial incentive to exercise prudence in the selection and management of trust investments.[94] Moreover, courts should recognize that a settlor's choice to entrust power to a specific stakeholder trustee may reflect an implicit endorsement of that trustee's judgment and tolerance for risk.[95] Thus, even if the BJR is not a good fit for most trust relationships, there might still be sound reasons for applying a deferential BJR-style standard of review to stakeholder trustees.

E Spouses

Spouses assume fiduciary duties to one another with respect to their administration of family-owned property.[96] In community property states, where property acquired

88 Uniform Trust Code s. 802 cmt. (Am. Law Inst. 2010); Austin Wakeman Scott, William Franklin Fratcher & Mark L. Ascher, *Scott and Ascher on Trusts* (Wolters Kluwer 5th ed. 2018) s. 11.10.01. In other jurisdictions, statutes or case law prohibit the appointment of beneficiary-trustees. Ibid. s. 11.10.01 n. 5, s. 18.2.5.

89 UTC (n. 88) s. 803.

90 Ibid. s. 803 & cmt.

91 Scott et al. (n. 88) s. 18.2.5.

92 Ibid s. 17.15.

93 Robert H. Sitkoff, "An Agency Costs Theory of Trust Law" (2004) 89 *Cornell L. Rev.* 621, 657.

94 Melanie Leslie resists extending the BJR to trust law on the ground that trustees lack an independent financial incentive to exercise prudence, but this argument lacks force when applied to stakeholder trustees. Melanie B. Leslie, Trusting Trustees: Fiduciary Duties and the Limits of Default Rules" (2005) 94 *Geo. LJ* 67, 99.

95 Courts will not approve a stakeholder trustee without settlor appointment. Scott et al. (n. 88) s. 11.10.01.

96 For purposes of this discussion, I will bracket the fiduciary roles that spouses play when exercising other entrusted powers, such as the authority to make medical decisions for an incapacitated spouse.

during marriage is owned by spouses jointly, both spouses become stakeholder fiduciaries in the management and disposition of their shared community property.[97] Spouses bear symmetrical rights, powers, duties and liabilities with respect to community property. In contrast, when a spouse manages property that belongs exclusively to the other spouse, she serves as a nonstakeholder fiduciary and must exercise her discretionary power for the other spouse's exclusive benefit.[98] Thus, determining whether a spouse is a stakeholder or nonstakeholder fiduciary, and whether the relationship is formally symmetrical or asymmetrical, depends on contingent features of particular marital relationships.

When spouses administer community property, their duties of loyalty and care track the duties of general business partners. Each spouse bears a fiduciary "duty of the highest good faith and fair dealing," which precludes either spouse from "tak[ing] any unfair advantage of the other."[99] As in partnerships, this is a duty of solidarity, not wholesale self-abnegation. Courts also apply a more deferential standard of review to duty-of-care claims involving community property than they would for similar claims that arise in nonstakeholder fiduciary relationships, such as ordinary trusts. For example, the California legislature has gone out of its way to specify that in community property jurisdictions marriage "is a fiduciary relationship subject to the same rights and duties of nonmarital business partners."[100]

F *Public Officials*

The stakeholder model also offers valuable insights for public law. The idea that public officials and institutions are fiduciaries is a familiar theme in American legal and political discourse.[101] US courts have affirmed that public officials bear fiduciary duties, including requirements to maintain confidentiality and account for bribes.[102] When judges and legal scholars invoke fiduciary principles in public law, they tend to compare public officials and institutions to agents and trustees, with the implication that they are subject to a strict requirement of self-abnegation. Yet, the stakeholder model suggests that this implication is not always warranted.

Many relationships governed by public law do fit congenially within the nonstakeholder model of fiduciary loyalty. Legislatures, courts, administrative agencies and other public institutions hold entrusted power over others' legal or practical interests,[103] but

[97] *In re Marriage of Fossum*, 192 Cal. App. 4th 336, 343–44 (Cal. Ct. App. 2011); *Loaiza* v. *Loaiza*, 130 SW3d 894, 900–01 (Tex. Ct. App. 2004).

[98] *Conigliaro* v. *Conigliaro*, 659 A2d 227 (Del. 1995); *Peterson* v. *Larson*, 225 SW 704, 706–07 (Mo. S. Ct. 1920); *In re Marriage of Walker*, 42 Cal. Rptr. 3d 325, 332 (Ct. App. 2006).

[99] *In re Marriage of Georgiou & Leslie*, 160 Cal. Rep. 3d 254, 259 (Ct. App. 2013).

[100] Cal. Family Code s. 721(b); *In re Marriage of Walker*, 42 Cal. Rptr. 3d 325, 336 (2006).

[101] James Madison, *The Federalist No. 46* (New American Library 1961).

[102] *United States* v. *Drumm*, 329 F2d 109 (1st Cir. 1964); *Snepp* v. *United States*, 444 US 507 (1980).

[103] Paul Finn, "The Forgotten 'Trust': The People and the State" in Malcolm Cope (ed.), *Equity: Issues and Trends* (Federation Press 1995) 131; Evan Fox-Decent, *Sovereignty's Promise: The State as Fiduciary* (Oxford University Press 2011); Criddle et al. (n. 93); Evan J. Criddle, "Fiduciary Administration: Rethinking Popular Representation in Agency Rulemaking" (2010) 88 *Texas L. Rev.* 441; Ethan J. Leib, David L. Ponet & Michael Serota, "A Fiduciary Theory of Judging" (2013) 101 *Calif. L. Rev.* 699.

like ordinary agents and trustees, they are not legitimate beneficiaries of the powers they exercise.[104] Public officials also bear strict duties of self-abnegation when they exercise entrusted power for the benefit of a discrete group that does not include them (e.g., children, refugees). Accordingly, public officials and institutions are often well suited for nonstakeholder fiduciary duties.[105]

In other contexts, public officials are legitimate beneficiaries of their own public service. Consider, for example, the fiduciary duties that apply to legislators by virtue of their assumption of entrusted public powers. Like partners or joint venturers, legislators are expected to practice solidarity with their constituent beneficiaries. Legislators typically reside among their constituents and therefore partake with them in the burdens and benefits of the laws they coauthor. As long as legislators' concerns for self-interest serve to align their performance with the interests of their constituents, attending to these concerns does not constitute a betrayal of the public's trust.[106]

To be sure, not all forms of legislator self-dealing are so innocuous. Legislators may betray constituents' trust in a host of ways, including by accepting secret commissions, supporting discriminatory laws, or exploiting confidential information for personal gain.[107] Legislators may also violate their duty of loyalty if they support redistricting plans or voter-suppression initiatives that are designed to insulate them or their political parties against electoral challenge.[108] Yet, the mere fact that legislators have a personal stake in their own official acts by virtue of their positions as residents, citizens and taxpayers does not disqualify them from serving as fiduciaries; nor does it represent a betrayal of their constituents' trust. Legislators are stakeholder fiduciaries.

G A Typology of Stakeholder Fiduciary Relationships

The foregoing examples demonstrate that stakeholder fiduciary relationships are remarkably widespread in public and private law, and they come in a variety of forms. Some of these relationships have a formally symmetrical structure, with practical asymmetries arising only when certain parties exercise power relative to the others' interests (e.g., partnerships). Others are formally asymmetrical, with some parties exercising special authority on behalf of the collective (e.g., stakeholder trustees). In some cases, a fiduciary's beneficiary status is a fixed structural feature of the type of fiduciary relationship (e.g., public officials), while in other cases a fiduciary's beneficiary status is a contingent feature of the specific relationship (e.g., spouses with community property[109]). These considerations suggest possible criteria

[104] Tara Leigh Grove, "Government Standing and the Fallacy of Institutional Injury" (2019) 167 *U. Pa. L. Rev.* 611.
[105] *Drumm* (n. 102) 112–14.
[106] James Madison, *The Federalist No. 52* (New American Library 1961); Michael Serota & Ethan J. Leib, "The Political Morality of Voting in Direct Democracy" (2013) 97 *Minn. L. Rev.* 1596, 1597 n. 3.
[107] Sung Hui Kim, "The Last Temptation of Congress: Legislator Insider Trading and the Fiduciary Norm against Corruption" (2013) 98 *Cornell L. Rev.* 845; Donna Nagy, "Owning Stock While Making Law: A Fiduciary Solution to an Agency Problem in Politics" (2013) 47 *Wake Forest L. Rev.* 845.
[108] D. Theodore Rave, "Politicians as Fiduciaries" (2013) 126 *Harv. L. Rev.* 671.
[109] *Fossum* (n. 97) 343–44.

for organizing stakeholder fiduciary relationships into subcategories, as reflected in the following table:

Table 6.1 *Stakeholder fiduciary relationships*

	Stakeholder status is a fixed feature of the type of relationship	Stakeholder status is a contingent feature of the specific relationship
Stakeholder relationship is formally symmetrical	Partners Joint venturers Members of joint enterprises	Spouses with community property
Stakeholder relationship is formally asymmetrical	Majority shareholders Public officials	Corporate officers and directors Stakeholder trustees

No doubt further study would suggest additional criteria that could lend greater nuance to this provisional typology. For present purposes, however, this exercise is sufficient to demonstrate that the universe of stakeholder fiduciary relationships is both broad and diverse, embracing some of the most important relationships in private and public fiduciary law.

4 Conclusions

This chapter has shown that the duty of loyalty does not always require fiduciaries to abjure self-interest when exercising fiduciary power. In the past, legal scholars have sometimes assumed that "the law does not trust fiduciaries" to "balance their own interests in the outcome against those of their supposed beneficiaries."[110] Nothing could be further from the truth. When fiduciaries are legitimate beneficiaries of their own performance, the law not only trusts them to balance their interests against the interests of other beneficiaries; it affirmatively *requires* that they do so. Balancing self-interest against regard for others' interests is part and parcel of a stakeholder fiduciary's role. More remarkable still, courts tend to give stakeholder fiduciaries considerable latitude when performing this role, interceding only when a fiduciary's conduct reflects bad faith.

These features of stakeholder fiduciary law offer important lessons for fiduciary theory. First, the stakeholder model strengthens the case for accepting the fiduciary character of some relationships, such as partner–partner and shareholder–shareholder, that are sometimes dismissed as poor candidates for fiduciary duties. The duty of loyalty properly applies to these and other stakeholder fiduciary relationships; it simply applies differently, calling for solidarity rather than complete self-abnegation.

[110] Rave (n. 80).

Second, the stakeholder model provides a novel justification for extending BJR-style deference to fields outside corporate law. If the BJR were concerned solely with liberating expert fiduciaries to take calculated risks, we might expect courts to extend BJR-style deference to other fiduciaries, such as investment advisors, who are tasked with making similarly challenging risk assessments. The fact that courts have been reluctant to take this step suggests that they often do not trust nonstakeholder fiduciaries to decide how much time and effort they should invest and how much risk they should assume in particular business decisions.[111] In contrast, when fiduciaries are also beneficiaries of their own performance, courts tend to trust fiduciaries' discretionary judgments.

Third, the stakeholder model offers new resources for testing prevailing theories of fiduciary law. By showing that parties can be genuine fiduciaries without renouncing self-interest, the stakeholder model calls into question proscriptive theories of fiduciary law, which treat the no-conflict and no-profit rules as the alpha and omega of fiduciary loyalty.[112] The model also challenges theories of fiduciary law that describe the duty of loyalty as applying prophylactically to prevent fiduciaries from being placed in positions where they might be tempted to use fiduciary power to advance their own self-interest.[113] Fiduciary law does not steer stakeholder fiduciaries away from positions where they would have to balance self-interest against concern for others' interests; rather, it directs how fiduciaries may legitimately exercise their discretion when they operate within these conflicted positions. Other theories of fiduciary law are better equipped to deal with the special features of stakeholder fiduciary relationships. Indeed, the idea that fiduciaries are sometimes entitled to profit from their own performance is plausibly consistent with a wide variety of legal and philosophical theories that emphasize fiduciary law's role in establishing a rightful relationship between a fiduciary and her beneficiaries.[114]

111 Arthur B. Laby, "Fiduciary Duties of Broker-Dealers and Investment Advisers" (2010) 55 *Vill. L. Rev.* 701, 717 n. 14.

112 Conaglen (n. 6); Smith (n. 6).

113 Kim (n. 6); Lionel Smith, "The Motive, Not the Deed" in Joshua Getzler (ed.), *Rationalizing Property, Equity and Trusts* (Oxford University Press 2003) 53, 74.

114 Criddle (n. 5); Arthur B. Laby, "The Fiduciary Obligation as the Adoption of Ends" (2008) 56 *Buff. L. Rev.* 100, 103; Ethan Leib & Stephen Galoob, "Intentions, Compliance, and Fiduciary Obligation" (2014) 20 *Legal Theory* 106; Paul B. Miller, "Justifying Fiduciary Duties" (2013) 58 *McGill LJ* 969.

7

Trustees and Agents Behaving Badly

When and How Is 'Bad Faith' Relevant?

JAMES PENNER[1]

1 Introduction

I shall contend that 'bad faith', as a legal concept, is very closely related, if not identical, to our common-sense notion of breaching the trust, or faith, or confidence that one person has reposed in another.

Before getting to grips with that, a few preliminary investigations are in order. First we have to address the diversity of the norms that apply to trustees and agents. This makes us confront directly fiduciary norms and fiduciary relationships, and the extent to which different trustees and agents are subject to those norms. Then we shall have to compare good faith with some similar ideas in order to sharpen our understanding of what good faith amounts to. The upshot of this investigation will be, in some respects echoing Conaglen,[2] that the duty of good faith is not particularly related to the core rules governing fiduciaries, though trustees and agents, amongst others, are always subject to this duty.

2 The Diversity of Norms Applying to Trustees and Agents

Outside the United States, it is trite law that not every duty a trustee or agent owes is a fiduciary duty.[3] But it seems to me that the discussion about this has not been as clear as it might, so in this first part I want to set out what I think is the diversity of legal

[1] I have benefited enormously from many helpful discussions with Lionel Smith and Rob Chambers on this and related topics, and from very helpful comments from Paul Miller.

[2] Conaglen, M., *Fiduciary Loyalty: Protecting the Due Performance of Non-fiduciary Duties* (Hart 2007), 40–4. I have elsewhere said that I disagreed with Conaglen's views on whether the duty to act in good faith was 'distinctive' of the fiduciary relationship: Penner, J. E., 'Fiduciary Law and Moral Norms' in Criddle, E. J., and others (eds.), *The Oxford Handbook of Fiduciary Law* (Oxford University Press 2019). My basic point was that whilst the duty of good faith was not a distinguishing feature of (a necessary and sufficient condition for) the fiduciary relationship, it was still a *distinctive* feature of the relationship that helped to characterize it. As the present text indicates, I now think this is not quite right. The duty of good faith really has nothing to do with fiduciary powers per se, even when these fiduciary powers are held by trustees or agents. Being subject to the duty of good faith is distinctive of the trust or agency relationship itself, whether or not the trustee or agent in question has any fiduciary powers.

[3] Regarding the array of duties that are considered 'fiduciary' in the United States, see, e.g., Gold, A. S., 'The Loyalties of Fiduciary Law' in Gold, A. S., and Miller, P. B. (eds.), *Philosophical Foundations of Fiduciary Law* (Oxford University Press 2014).

norms[4] that apply to agents and trustees. In particular I want to distinguish those norms that are properly styled 'fiduciary' and those that concern good or bad faith.

A *The Duty to Comply with Voluntarily Undertaken Obligations*

Trust and agency obligations are typically voluntarily undertaken. This is true of the express trust and the standard contractual agency. I shall not be concerned in this chapter with such relations that might be imposed by operation of law so, for example, I shall not be concerned with constructive and resulting trusts and whether they give rise to fiduciary obligations or obligations of good faith.

The primary obligation of the trustee is to carry out the terms of the trust that he has undertaken, and the primary obligation of the agent is to carry out the instructions given by her principal and that she has accepted. Just as is the case with common law contracts, the primary obligation is to give effect to the other's 'performance' interest – the settlor's interest in creating the trust so that it is performed for the beneficiaries, the principal's interest in having his instructions carried out, the promisee's interest in receiving the intended benefit of the contract. The default rule in each of these cases is that the trustee, agent or promisor is strictly liable for failing to perform these 'performance' obligations, simply for the reason that they undertook the obligation to do so. Of course the default rule can be departed from by the inclusion of liability limitation provisions in the trust or contract, and trustees may also be relieved of liability under s. 61 of the Trustee Act 1925 (England and Wales) and similar provisions in other jurisdictions. But the default rule suggests the nature of the obligation: unless otherwise so provided, these obligations are strict. *Why* the obligation was breached is irrelevant, as is the 'blameworthiness' of the duty ower. These breaches are breaches whether innocent, negligent or intentional. Moreover, sins of omission are no different from sins of commission. A trustee who fails to pay over the income to the life tenant, or the agent who fails to carry out his instructions, is just as much in breach as a trustee who transfers the trust assets to a non-object, or an agent who exceeds his actual authority but nevertheless binds his principal because of his ostensible authority.

Express trustees are always accounting parties,[5] in that they are strictly bound to keep records as to the disposition of the trust assets, and can be called to account for what they have done with the trust by the beneficiaries as of right. The same is true of agents who are accounting parties. The accounting rules cover cases where a trustee has wrongfully disposed of trust assets, and where through the trustee's negligence, for example in making investment decisions, the value of the trust assets is less than it otherwise should be. All of this applies to trustees and accounting agents whether or not under the terms of the trust or agency the trustee or agent has any discretionary powers that must be exercised exclusively in the interests of beneficiaries or principals – whether or not, that is, the agent or trustee has any 'fiduciary powers'.

[4] Including equitable norms, of course. Unless the context makes clear otherwise, I am not concerned with whether a norm is classified as one of common law or equity.

[5] For general discussion of the accounting relationship, see Penner, J. E., 'Distinguishing Fiduciary, Trust, and Accounting Relationships' (2014) 8 *Journal of Equity* 202.

B Fiduciary Powers and the 'No-Conflict' Principle

The fiduciary relationship is founded upon the fiduciary's voluntary undertaking to exercise powers, the exercise of which will involve his making judgements, judgements that require him to take into consideration only the principal's interests. This is sometimes called the 'discretionary theory' of the fiduciary relationship.[6] It responds to the fact that the voluntary obligation (or 'contract', loosely speaking), which underlies the relationship, is 'incomplete' in the important following sense: the actual exercises of the fiduciary's powers to enter into contracts on her principal's behalf, or in making investment decisions regarding the trust assets, or in exercising a dispositive discretion under a trust, cannot be specified in advance under the objective legal terms of the agency or trust. The now classic judicial formulation of this view in the United States is found in Justice Breyer's judgment in the US Supreme Court decision *Varity Corp* v. *Howe*:[7]

> [T]he primary function of the fiduciary duty is to constrain the exercise of *discretionary* powers which are controlled by no other specific duty imposed by the trust instrument or the legal regime. *If fiduciary duty applied to nothing more than the activities already controlled by specific legal duties, it would serve no purpose.*

Although 'discretion' and 'discretionary' are the standard terms used to describe the 'leeway' the fiduciary has in exercising her powers, the better word for describing this 'leeway' is 'judgement', not discretion, at least in so far as the word 'discretion' suggests that the fiduciary has any sort of personal freedom in these cases. The fiduciary is required to choose that course of action that, in her judgement, is in the best interests of her principal.[8] Following Smith and Miller, we can call these powers 'fiduciary powers'.[9]

6 See Conaglen, *supra* n. 2, at 39–40; Miller, P. B., 'A Theory of Fiduciary Liability' (2011) 56 *McGill Law Journal* 235; Miller, P. B., 'Justifying Fiduciary Duties' (2013) 58 *McGill Law Journal* 969; Miller, P. B., 'The Fiduciary Relationship' in Gold, A. S., and Miller, P. B. (eds.), *Philosophical Foundations of Fiduciary Law* (Oxford University Press 2014); Penner, J. E., 'Is Loyalty a Virtue, and Even If It Is, Does It Really Help Explain Fiduciary Liability?' in Gold, A. S., and Miller, P. B. (eds.), *Philosophical Foundations of Fiduciary Law* (Oxford University Press 2014); Penner, 'Distinguishing', *supra* n. 5; Smith, L. D., 'Fiduciary Relationships: Ensuring the Loyal Exercise of Judgement on Behalf of Another' (2014) 130 *Law Quarterly Review* 608; Smith, L. D., 'Can We Be Obliged to Be Selfless?' in Gold, A. S., and Miller, P. B. (eds.), *Philosophical Foundations of Fiduciary Law* (Oxford University Press 2014); Smith, S. A., 'The Deed, Not the Motive: Fiduciary Law without Loyalty' in Miller, P. B., and Gold, A. S. (eds.), *Contract, Status, and Fiduciary Law* (Oxford University Press 2016); Valsan, R., 'Fiduciary Duties, Conflict of Interest, and Proper Exercise of Judgment' (2016) 62 *McGill Law Journal* 1; Weinrib, E. J., 'The Fiduciary Obligation' (1975) 25 *University of Toronto Law Journal* 1; see also Sitcoff, R. H., 'An Economic Theory of Fiduciary Law' in Gold, A. S., and Miller, P. B. (eds.), *Philosophical Foundations of Fiduciary Law* (Oxford University Press 2014), on the same issue from the perspective of economic theory.

7 516 U.S. 489, 504 (1996) (first italics in the original, second italics mine). See also *Perez* v. *Galambos* [2009] SCC 48 (Canadian Supreme Court) at [50]–[84] & [83]–[84]; *Hospital Products Ltd* v. *United States Surgical Corporation* (1984) 156 CLR 41 (High Court of Australia) at 96–7 (Mason J).

8 See, e.g., Smith, 'Fiduciary Relationships', *supra* n. 6; Smith, 'Can We Be Obliged?', *supra* n. 6; Valsan, 'Fiduciary Duties', *supra* n. 6. See also Penner, 'Is Loyalty a Virtue?', *supra* n. 6, at 168–9; Penner, 'Distinguishing', *supra* n. 5, at 204–6.

9 Miller, P. B., 'Fiduciary Representation' in Criddle, E. J. (ed.) *Fiduciary Government* (Cambridge University Press 2018), 27; Smith, this volume.

Lionel Smith[10] has helpfully distinguished different norms that govern fiduciaries. We can notice, for example, the self- and fair-dealing rules, the no-unauthorized-profit rule, the rule prohibiting a fiduciary from competing with his principal's business, the 'corporate opportunity' doctrine,[11] the rule that an agent in breach of his fiduciary relationship with his principal loses his right to commission, and so on. In my view, all of these rules operate under a general umbrella norm that might be called the 'no-conflict' principle,[12] although I also agree with Smith that a refined notion of conflict of interest may require us to frame these rules in better ways.[13]

It is clear that not all the powers that a trustee[14] or agent has are fiduciary powers on the discretionary theory of the fiduciary relationship. The inescapable logic of this is that if we can find cases of trustees or agents without fiduciary powers, then not all agents and trustees are properly classified as fiduciaries. Moreover, this logic requires us to distinguish the agency and trust relationships *as such* from fiduciary relationships *as such.*

Any power the exercise of which is controlled by objective duties – 'already controlled by specific legal duties', as Justice Breyer put it – is not a fiduciary power. So, for example, where a trustee's power to invest is exercised negligently, determining this involves applying an objective standard – the appropriate standard of care. Where a trustee has an obligation to exercise his power of title over the trust assets so as to pay the income beneficiary the trust income each month, whether the trustee discharges this obligation is objectively determined – was the payment made or not?

[10] This volume; Smith, L., 'Prescriptive Fiduciary Duties' (2018) 37 *University of Queensland Law Journal* 261. See also Finn, P., *Fiduciary Obligations: 40th Anniversary Republication with Additional Essays* (Federation Press 2016).

[11] Construed properly, I think this is really just a manifestation in the corporate context of a mixture of the rule that a fiduciary, e.g. a managing director, cannot compete with his principal and the 'first' no-profit rule; see n. 13. If the fiduciary in such a context has a positive obligation to find and secure corporate opportunities for his principal (i.e. his company), a failure to do so is not a breach of any aspect of his fiduciary relationship to the principal but an actionable legal wrong, just a breach of contract, which would turn on a breach of the contractual duty of skill and care or 'best efforts'. As a matter of his fiduciary role, the corporate opportunity doctrine falls under the 'second' no-profit rule, which proscribes taking benefits that put his interests in conflict with the company.

[12] Where, of course, the principal in question, or a term of the trust or agency, authorizes, or indeed imposes, a duty upon the fiduciary to exercise a power in a situation of conflict, the rule does not apply, but only of course to the extent of the authorized or imposed conflict.

[13] Smith, this volume. Where I differ from Smith is in the categorization of the 'no-unauthorized-profit' rule. Smith regards the rule as entirely separate from the no-conflict principle. My own view is more complicated: I think that the no-profit rule is actually two rules; the first rule, which Smith is correct to identify as having nothing to do with the no-conflict rule, is nothing more than an elaboration of the accounting principles applying to accounting parties, whether they have any fiduciary powers or not. See Penner, 'Distinguishing', *supra* n. 5. This requires accounting parties to account for any benefit acquired in the course of carrying out their trust or agency duties. The second rule is, however, intimately connected with the no-conflict rule; this rule requires a fiduciary power holder to disgorge any gain the taking of which would give rise to a conflict between his own personal interest and his duty to exercise his fiduciary powers exclusively in the interests of his principal. The classic example of such an unauthorized profit is a bribe.

[14] It is worth noting that the question whether a *non-trustee* power under a trust is a fiduciary power or a 'personal' power always concerns discretionary powers. See Penner, J. E., *The Law of Trusts* (11th ed., Oxford University Press 2019), [3.15]–[3.23].

More precisely, any power the exercise of which does not require the very specific kind of judgement associated with fiduciary powers, i.e. the judgement of what is in the best interest of the beneficiary or principal, is not a fiduciary power. The exercise of a power may well involve some kind of judgement, such as the judgement involved in acting with care and skill. Yet this kind of judgment in exercising a power does not make the power fiduciary under the discretionary theory just described; otherwise all negligent tortfeasors would be regarded as fiduciaries in breach. Similarly, the judgements required in deciding how to keep the trust accounts, how much effort to spend on the trust,[15] and so on, are not the sorts of judgements that indicate the status of a fiduciary. This is so because the breach of the duties in respect of which these judgements are made is objectively determined, as with other non-fiduciary duties. True it is that I may negligently injure you, or breach my contract, because I made an error of judgement as to the precautions I should have taken or the preparations I should have made. But that is irrelevant to my liability. What makes a judgement relevant for the purposes of finding a fiduciary power is that the judgement in question concerns the interests of the principal, whose interests must be considered to the exclusion of all other persons' interests.

I have elsewhere provided a number of examples of trustees with no fiduciary powers.[16] To consider just one: under the typical co-ownership trust of land in England, where A and B hold their title as joint tenants at law for themselves as joint tenants or tenants in common in equity, as co-owners of the legal title they are not required to exercise any of the powers of title they each have as co-owners taking into account the interests of both of themselves, and only those interests. If A wishes to sever the joint tenancy in equity, she does not have to consider the interests of B and may perfectly legitimately do so in order to pursue the interests of a third party – likewise in deciding whether to join B in selling the property, or in licensing someone to enter, or anything else she is entitled as a co-owner to do.

The absence of fiduciary powers is common with many agents. Take the example of my bank. My bank is a paying and collecting agent for me. It may have some discretion in how it follows my instructions, but it has no fiduciary discretion in which it judges whether it should exercise its powers to pay or collect on my behalf on the basis of what it judges to be in my exclusive best interest. Agents whose instructions are clear, like my bank, have no fiduciary discretion.

Under the discretionary theory of the fiduciary relationship, to claim that all trustees and all agents are fiduciaries must mean that all trustees and agents have fiduciary powers – that is, discretionary powers that they must exercise for the benefit

[15] Smith, this volume, Section 3.A.

[16] Penner, 'Distinguishing', *supra* n. 5, at 214–16, 219–23. It is an interesting question whether most trustees have what might be called contingent, 'residual', fiduciary powers because all trustees have some discretionary powers simply in virtue of their role as trustees and their relationship to the court. For example, trustees of a family wealth management trust universally have the power to apply to the court – but since these implicit, contingent powers are rarely if ever taken to be central or germane to the discussion of the nature of fiduciary powers, we can happily leave them to one side. Even if it is true that because of such powers one can say that most trustees are fiduciaries, it does nothing to establish that any of the other powers a trustee has is fiduciary. See ibid., 221.

of beneficiaries or on behalf of their principals – and, as we have just seen, this is straightforwardly false. You either have to give up the discretionary theory or the claim that all trustees and agents are fiduciaries. You simply cannot have it both ways.

Of course, it is perfectly plausible to claim that having the status of trustee or agent makes one *presumptively* a fiduciary,[17] where the nature of a power the trustee or agent has is in question, specifically the question of whether the power is fiduciary or personal – the terminology is from the law of trusts – 'personal' in the sense that the power can be exercised for the power holder's own benefit. So, for example, where a trustee is given a power under the trust instrument to change the governing law of the trust, the very, very strong presumption is that this is a fiduciary power to be exercised with only the beneficiaries' interests in mind. It is not inconceivable that such a power could be granted to the trustee to exercise in her own interests, to make her life more convenient in certain ways, but this would have to be explicitly and clearly specified before any court would draw that conclusion.[18]

Turning now specifically to the issue of good faith and having the status of a fiduciary: although, as we shall see, fiduciaries are always subject to a duty of good faith in the exercise of their fiduciary powers, simply being under a duty of good faith does not make one a fiduciary. Nevertheless, it is easy to find examples of people thinking so. Consider Fletcher-Moulton LJ's famous observation in *In re Coomber*:[19]

> Fiduciary relations are of many different types; *they extend from the relation of myself to an errand boy who is bound to bring me back my change up to the most intimate and confidential relations* which can possibly exist between one party and another where the one is wholly in the hands of the other because of his infinite trust in him. All these are cases of fiduciary relations, and the Courts have again and again, in cases where there has been a fiduciary relation, interfered and set aside acts which, between persons in a wholly independent position, would have been perfectly valid.

If the discretionary theory is correct, then the italicized passage cannot be. An errand boy has no fiduciary powers of any kind. He is just an employee/agent with strict instructions, but one who has been placed in a position of trust and confidence, so if he, in bad faith, keeps the change, he has breached the employee's duty of good faith, or loyalty[20] – that is, has wronged his employer in a way that shows bad faith and is liable to summary dismissal.[21] This sort of misclassification has consequences. If one begins by saying that anyone who owes a duty of good faith is a fiduciary, then it would seem prima facie obvious that all the rules governing fiduciaries are, in principle, applicable. Then one will have to resort to the tedious business of explaining why, for example, though a 'fiduciary', an employee is not subject, say, to the no-profit rule. So I agree, then, with what Fletcher-Moulton immediately went on to say:

[17] See, e.g., Miller, P. B., 'The Identification of Fiduciary Relationships' in Criddle, E. J., and others (eds.), *The Oxford Handbook of Fiduciary Law* (Oxford University Press 2019), 35–9, 45–9.
[18] A similar presumption applies to trust 'protectors'; see Penner, 'Law of Trusts', *supra* n. 14, at [3.30].
[19] [1911] 1 Ch 723 at 728–9, my italics.
[20] See, e.g., *Nottingham University* v. *Fishel* [2001] RPC 22 at [92].
[21] Ibid., [96].

> 'Thereupon in some minds there arises the idea that if there is any fiduciary relation whatever any of these types of interference is warranted by it. They conclude that every kind of fiduciary relation justifies every kind of interference. Of course that is absurd. The nature of the fiduciary relation must be such that it justifies the interference.'

But it would have been better if he had just said that the errand boy was not a fiduciary in the first place.

Paul Finn, in his famous 1977 *Fiduciary Obligations*, denied that there was any such thing as a fiduciary relationship per se.[22] He later changed his mind[23] and viewed the fiduciary relationship as one in which the fiduciary principle applies, a principle that has two emanations:[24] the first concerns the classic 'no-conflict' concern, i.e. the concern regarding the exercise of powers in conflict of interest, or conflict of interest and duty, etc. The second concern relates to the possibility of a fiduciary's 'misuse of fiduciary position, or of knowledge or opportunity arising from it'.[25] Pertinent to our discussion here, we shall later ask whether 'misuse' of a fiduciary position is really just a breach of the duty of good faith by an agent or trustee, irrespective of whether they happen to be fiduciaries.[26] Trustees and agents, when they are fiduciaries, are the classic examples of fiduciaries, though as we shall see at Section 3.A below, they act in relation to their principals in different ways. Arguably, all other well-recognized fiduciary relationships are derivative from these two, trustee-like or agent-like, in one or more ways.[27]

C The 'Proper Purposes' Doctrine and Fiduciary Powers

As Smith points out,[28] the 'proper purposes' doctrine actually incorporates two separate rules. The first, objective, rule is concerned with the proper scope of a power, and, in a particular case, whether the power was purportedly used to do something beyond that scope. This limb of the rule involves the purely objective exercise of determining the scope of the power under the terms of the trustee or agent's voluntary undertaking, and the general law (as for the case of determining the scope of a power of 'maintenance' in general trust law). The second, subjective, limb concerns the subjective reasons for which the power was exercised. The exercise of the power may be flawed, and held invalid, on three broad 'subjective grounds': (1) though acting in good faith, the power holder's reasons were inadequate/inappropriate. For example, in innocent fraud on a power cases, the trustee may have exercised the

[22] Finn, 'Fiduciary Obligations', *supra* n. 10, at [3]–[4].

[23] Ibid., [770]–[791].

[24] Ibid., [773] et seq.

[25] Ibid., [773]

[26] 7.5 *infra*.

[27] That would certainly be my prima facie position; it would explain why company directors are fiduciaries. For a good start on looking at the particular context in which company directors operate, see Ho, L., 'Good Faith and Fiduciary Duty in English Law' (2010) 4 *Journal of Equity* 29; Langford, R. T., 'Best Interests: Multifaceted but Not Unbounded' (2016) 75 *Cambridge Law Journal* 505; Sale, H. A., 'Fiduciary Law, Good Faith and Publicness' in Criddle, E. J., and others (eds.), *The Oxford Handbook of Fiduciary Law* (Oxford University Press 2019).

[28] This volume, at Section 2.

power in a way that in fact was primarily for the benefit of a third party.[29] Or the trustee might simply have been seriously mistaken about the relevant facts or law.[30] (2) Though acting in good faith, the fiduciary's decision-making was impaired because he exercised a fiduciary power in a conflict of interest. Objectively, the exercise of the power may have been perfectly within the scope of the power, and objectively the exercise might have very much benefited the principal. But in such cases, the objective finding of conflict means the subjective reasoning in the exercise is regarded as flawed. (3) The power may be exercised in bad faith.

D The Duty Not to Breach Any Voluntarily Undertaken Obligations in Bad Faith

Now, turning to good faith, it is trite law that the application of the 'no-conflict' rules does not turn on any finding of bad faith and that acting in good faith is no defence at all.[31] So, for example, a court can set aside a transaction under the no-conflict rule, as where a fiduciary enters into a self-dealing transaction, or strip a fiduciary of an unauthorized profit, *whether or not the fiduciary was acting in good faith.*[32] Elsewhere[33] I have sought to explain this on the basis that fiduciaries in the exercise of their fiduciary powers are subject to two different legal norms, each of which is basic and morally sound. The first concerns conflicts of interests; the second concerns bad faith breaches of duty. The problem of conflicts of interest concerns the law's regulation of a fiduciary's judgement in the exercise of her powers, which must only be exercised in the interest of her principal. I have described this by saying that the fiduciary owes her principal 'deliberative exclusivity', which I think is more precise, and less moralistic (not to say prissy), than saying that the fiduciary must act 'selflessly', or 'altruistically'.

Good faith or bad faith has nothing to do with this sort of regulation of the fiduciary's judgement. This is not to say that fiduciaries cannot act in bad faith in exercising their judgement, or that trustees cannot act in bad faith in procuring an unauthorized profit by taking advantage of their position, for example voting trust shares to install themselves on the board of directors just for the purpose of obtaining directors' fees. Of course they can. The point is that nothing about the trustee's liability in such cases seems to *turn on* good or bad faith. When does liability turn upon good faith's absence or presence? I think we can begin our inquiry by considering how good faith or bad faith has to do with what might be called the 'problem of

29 *Re Pauling's Settlement Trusts* [1964] Ch 303; *Wong* v. *Burt* [2005] 1 NZLR 91.

30 *Pitt* v. *Holt* [2013] UKSC 26.

31 Though it may be, in some cases, relevant at the remedial stage, most notably in *Boardman* v. *Phipps* [1967] 2 AC 46 (but see *Guiness plc* v. *Saunders* [1990] 2 AC 663). A notable exception is *Holder* v. *Holder* [1968] 2 WLR 237, where the defendant was held to technically have remained an executor of his father's estate despite his apparently effective renunciation of the role but who had 'acted in complete innocence' (per Danckwerts LJ at 253), which I take to be equivalent to 'acted in good faith'. See further below, 'Consequences of Acting in Bad Faith'.

32 See, e.g., *Boardman* v. *Phipps, supra* n. 31; *In re Will of Gleeson*, 124 N.E.2d 624 (Ill. App. Ct. 1955).

33 Penner, 'Fiduciary Law and Moral Norms', *supra* n. 2.

representation', and this takes us first to the diversity of fiduciary and non-fiduciary relationships, where a duty of good faith is said to lie.

3 The Diversity of Representational Relationships: 'Acting as', 'Acting for'/'Acting for the Benefit of' and 'Acting on Behalf of/in the Place of' Another

There exists in the background to all questions of good and bad faith the issue, or problem, of representation.[34] Very broadly, others may, in law, represent us in various ways. Drilling down into the concept of representation, we can find three basic cases, although there are overlaps between them.

A 'Acting as' Another

The only clear, undisputed legal example of acting as another I can think of is the case of a general meeting of the shareholders of a company; in this case, the shareholders act *as* the company. The significance of acting as the company is that the shareholders are acting in their own right as the company, or in right of the company itself. In other words, they do not act as agents or trustees of the company in such a case, and so therefore they are not in a fiduciary relationship with any others, or inter se. It is disputed whether and in what circumstances a company's board of directors acts *as the company* rather than merely as (co-)agents of the company.[35]

A non-legal example may be the absolution of sins by a Catholic priest. Theology is not my strong suit, but as I understand the position, only God can absolve sins, but the priest, in absolving sins *in the name of* the Father, of the Son and of the Holy Spirit, in a way acts *as* God, 'channelling' as it were the power to absolve.[36]

Another, 'political theory' example is provided by Miller's discussion of Hobbes's notion of the representation of the sovereign.[37] The coming into existence of the sovereign at the same time constitutes the body of its subjects. In this sense, when the sovereign acts, it acts *as* that body of subjects.

B 'Acting for*'/'acting* for the Benefit of *' Another*

Trust and contract law provide a host of examples here. The typical family non-agent trustee is a classic example. Trustees can be agents as well as trustees, but are not so simply in virtue of their trusteeship. Parents and legal guardians are other examples. These latter have the power to act for the benefit of their children in legally significant ways. They have the power, for example, to license what would otherwise be a trespass to the person when they hand the baby to the babysitter or authorize a doctor to

34 I have benefited in this section very much from reading Miller, 'Fiduciary Representation', *supra* n. 9.

35 Watts, P., 'Directors as Agents – Some Aspects of Disputed Territory' in Busch, D., and others (eds.), *Agency Law in Commercial Practice* (Oxford University Press 2016).

36 See, e.g., https://en.wikipedia.org/wiki/Absolution.

37 Miller, 'Fiduciary Representation', *supra* n. 9, at 24–25.

examine their child. Bailees for the interest of the bailor (cleaners, repairers, warehousers, etc.) undertake their bailment to provide services to the bailor, and in that sense act for the bailor's benefit, as opposed to bailees who are hirers, who undertake the bailment to use their possession for their own benefit. Finally, solicitors, even if they are not acting as trustees or agents of their clients, when, for example, they are merely providing legal advice, provide that advice for/for the benefit of their client. Employees, more generally, by discharging their contractual duties, are acting generally for/for the benefit of their employer.

C *'Acting* on Behalf of/in the Place of*' Another*

The classic example here is, of course, the agent. We could call this 'representation by attribution': the agent's acts, entering into contracts, performing services that discharge the duties of their principal and so on, are *attributed* to their principal. Note the difference with trustees. A trustee acts in his own name, albeit for the benefit of the beneficiaries, but not on behalf of or in the place of the beneficiaries. His acts are not attributed to them, though these acts are *for* them, i.e. for their benefit.

Representation by attribution is a much broader phenomenon than that encompassed by trust and agency relationships, and has particular importance in the case of companies, which obviously cannot act in person. Many employees have agential functions without being agents in the traditional legal sense, just to the extent that their actions implicate their employer's legal relations with third parties. Three examples suffice.

First, custody. In order for title to tangible property to be acquired, factual possession must (generally) be acquired. So when an employee obtains factual possession of a chattel, his possession is attributed to his employer. The employee is not a bailee; he has *custody* of the chattel, which is best defined as representative possession of it. His act of taking possession (and his retaining possession) is attributed to his employer.[38] His factual possession is attributed to his employer, who is regarded as the possessor in law.

Second, in many cases where an employee discharges his obligations to his employer, he also discharges his employer's obligations to third parties. Take the case (one could choose from a multitude of examples) of an employer engaged to do building works for a householder. When his employees complete the job, thereby discharging (one or more) obligations to the employer, they also *thereby* discharge the employer's obligations to the householder. A third example comes from the law of torts. Certain tortious acts of one person can be attributed to another. Following Stevens, I hold that it is not the liability of the actor that is attributed to another, typically her employer, but the act itself.[39] So 'vicarious *liability*' is, strictly speaking, a misnomer.

A final example is our errand boy. Unlike the mere employee with custody, he is also an agent in the strict sense of entering into a contract on behalf of his

[38] Bridge, M., *Personal Property Law* (4th ed., Oxford University Press 2015), 39–40.
[39] Stevens, R., *Torts and Rights* (Oxford University Press 2007), ch. 11, 'Attribution'.

employer. He takes custody of his employer's money, buys the champagne from a seller according to his instructions and receives the change.[40] But the contract of sale is not only one between himself and the seller, but also between the seller and his employer.[41]

4 What Good Faith Is Not: Trustworthiness and Good Will

I can grant you powers and liberties over my property for your own benefit, whether by lease, or bailment, or otherwise, but these are not cases of trust or agency; it is definitive of these relationships, as we have seen, that the person in whom the powers and liberties are reposed *represents* the principal in one way or another. It follows by definition that the liberties or powers can only be used in the principal's interests – the fiduciary acts as a kind of instrument of and for the principal.

A Good Faith and Trustworthiness

My belief that a person is likely to act in good faith is a reason to trust him to do something for me, but acting in a trustworthy fashion concerns more than acting in good faith. Obviously, a person can be trustworthy or untrustworthy for all sorts of reasons having nothing to do with good faith; the person may be trustworthy because he is efficient, attentive, energetic and so on, and untrustworthy because he lacks those qualities or indeed has their opposites.

B Good Faith and Good Will

Good faith is not good will. Good faith concerns the 'faithful' discharge of one's obligations, or at least, not the bad faith breach of one's obligations. Good will is largely about adopting, and acting upon, a positive attitude towards someone. It can relevantly arise in the legal context. 'Working to rule'[42] is a good example in the contractual context. Employees working to rule punctiliously fulfil their contractual obligations but do no more. I think this is a good example of the withdrawal of good will from the employer, which may be entirely justified. In the trusts context, the breakdown of trustee–beneficiary relations leading to a court application seeking the replacement of a trustee strikes me as a case of this sort.[43] In particular, where beneficiaries 'lose all faith' in their trustees and will not cooperate with them, this can accurately be framed as a withdrawal of good will towards their trustees. But this has nothing to do with bad faith on the part of anyone.

[40] As explained immediately above, the errand boy only ever has custody of the initial coins and notes he takes from his employer, the bottle of champagne and the change he receives.

[41] So long as the employer can intervene on the contract under the doctrine of undisclosed agency, but there would appear to be no reason why that would not be the case here. See Watts, P., and Reynolds, F., *Bowstead and Reynolds on Agency* (21st ed., Sweet & Maxwell 2018), article 76.

[42] See https://en.wikipedia.org/wiki/Work-to-rule.

[43] See, e.g., the dicta in *Letterstedt* v. *Broers* (1884) 9 App. Cas. 371 at 385–90.

5 What Good Faith Is

A A Lack of a Certain Kind of Dishonesty; Colloquially, 'Disloyalty'

The philosophical literature on the phenomenon of 'trust' is extensive, and it seems to me clear that the writers are often not talking about the same thing.[44] Annettte Baier, the pioneer in this literature, got the ball rolling with the following preliminary definition:[45] 'Trust then, on this first approximation, is accepted vulnerability to another's possible but not expected ill will (or lack of good will) toward one'. Although Baier here speaks in terms of 'trust', it seems to me that 'good faith' is illuminated by what she says. One who colloquially reposes trust, confidence or faith in another by hiring them, or making them their agent or trustee, puts themself in a position of vulnerability. In particular they are vulnerable to the person acting with what she calls 'ill will'. But by far the most relevant paper that I have found for the purposes of looking at good faith is Collin O'Neil's 'Betraying Trust'.[46]

In the first place, O'Neil is concerned with the kind of trust, faith or confidence that is reposed in an employee when she is hired. He rightly distinguishes this sort of case from that, for example, of friendship.[47] It seems to me that this sort of reposing of trust is more or less identical with that reposed in agents or trustees. I have an unromantic view of trustees and agents; they just hold a particular kind of job, after all. Insofar as they have fiduciary powers, they have a special job to do, viz. consider the interests of their beneficiaries or principals in exercising their discretion. So be it. But it doesn't take them out of the realm of those trustees or agents who exercise non-fiduciary powers or comply with other duties they owe in so far as trust or confidence has been reposed in them.

The other important insights O'Neil offers are two. First of all, this trust doesn't itself generate any new first order obligations; it merely requires you to fulfil obligations you otherwise have. This seems right. An employee, agent and trustee all have obligations in the general law and under their particular role. Each of them, for example, should not misappropriate their principal's property. If they do so, it is a breach of trust because they have been treated, upon being offered the role, as being trustworthy, and the principal is usually made more vulnerable to wrongs by those in these roles because of the opportunities, liberties and powers these roles confer. Second, the obligation not to breach the trust or faith reposed in one has a particular scope – it is not like the general obligation to respond in any number of ways to a gift; rather, it only goes so far as the matter upon which trust is reposed, typically as far the task or job or role goes.[48]

The only place I differ from O'Neil's account is in his terminology. He says, 'What is morally significant about this form of trust is that it confers an *honour*, albeit

[44] For a good introduction to this literature, see Faulkner, P., and Simpson, T. (eds.), *The Philosophy of Trust* (Oxford University Press 2017).

[45] Baier, A. C., 'Trust and Antitrust' (1986) 96 *Ethics* 231, 235.

[46] O'Neil, C., 'Betraying Trust' in Faulkner, P., and Simpson, T. (eds.), *The Philosophy of Trust* (Oxford University Press 2017).

[47] Ibid., 73, 79, 85.

[48] Ibid., 85.

limited in scope, on the trusted person.'[49] I think the terminology of honour overeggs the pudding. I would prefer to put the point this way: when I trust you as an employee, agent or trustee, I *do you the credit of* treating you as, or *credit* you with being, the kind of person who would not deliberately take advantage of me because of the role I have offered to you.[50] Breaching an obligation 'in bad faith', on this account, is just that sort of breach by which you fail to properly respond to the trust in your honesty, integrity and so on that I credited you with. With these thoughts in hand, we can explore some other aspects of good faith.

B Good Faith Has No Genuine Positive Valence; We Mistakenly Think It Does because We Mistake Good Will for It

The relations between good faith and honesty and bad faith and dishonesty are intricate, and I cannot hope to spell all of them out here. But I shall suggest two things: first, that good faith is simply the lack of bad faith in context. There is no really substantial positive good faith that is really distinct from good will. The concept of bad faith is doing all the real work.[51]

Consider the following thought. In order to give good faith some genuine content, i.e. that acting in good faith makes some genuinely relevant contribution when assessing someone's actions, we would have to show how it matters both in cases where a duty is complied with and where a duty is breached.

Take the first case, where a duty is actually discharged. Trustees have positive trust obligations, agents must follow their instructions and so on; can we overlay, in these cases, a duty of good faith to support the claim that where an agent or trustee carries out his duties, that he acts in good faith, where good faith is something fulfilled that is distinct from the mere fact that the obligations were actually discharged? To think so seems to me to rest on a conceptual confusion; to wit: it seems to me that if one discharges one's duties, as a trustee by complying with the terms of the trust or as an agent by complying with one's instructions, in cases where the discharge is a matter of objectively doing what the trust terms require or what the agent's instructions require, good faith/bad faith is irrelevant so long as the person actually discharges the obligation in question. One can make the point by asking whether a person can *discharge* his obligations *in bad faith*. In my view, there is just no room for the invocation of bad faith, and if that is so, there is similarly no room for the invocation of good faith. Galoob and Leib, however, pose a counterexample,[52] which I shall

[49] Ibid.

[50] O'Neil himself at one point uses the terminology of 'credit'. Ibid., 84.

[51] In J. L. Austin's terminology, good faith is a 'trouser' word. With these words, the 'negative' use of the term 'wears the trousers', to employ Austin's sexist and dated terminology. Austin's own example is 'real'. His claim is that 'real' derives its meaning from the slew of different cases where things are 'unreal', variously 'fake', 'decoy', 'toy', 'makeshift' and so on: Austin, J., *Sense and Sensibilia* (Oxford University Press 1962), 70–2. For detailed discussion, see Coval, S., and Forrest, T., 'Which Word Wears the Trousers?' (1967) 76 *Mind* 73. I thank Rob Atkinson for reminding me of Austin's terminology.

[52] Galoob, S. R., and Leib, E. J., 'Intentions, Compliance, and Fiduciary Obligations' (2014) 20 *Legal Theory* 106, 113. I thank Paul Miller for drawing this example to my attention.

slightly modify though it doesn't alter their point. Consider a trustee who is clear about what his obligation is and what he must do to discharge it. He then makes it a matter of chance whether he complies, by flipping a coin: heads, do his duty, or tails, breach the trust. Galoob and Leib argue that even if the coin comes up heads and the trustee discharges his obligation, he does so disloyally.

I accept the counterexample. In particular if these facts could be proved, then this would justify removing this trustee from his office, which, as I claim below, is the standard response to someone who breaches his obligations in bad faith. But I think the counterexample proves the general point. In general, bad faith involves a deliberate breach of an obligation, not compliance with it. In general we are not concerned with a person's attitude, in terms of their subjective motivations, when they do their duty. It requires this sort of fanciful, not to say far-fetched or engineered, sort of case to show otherwise. I cannot see how this counterexample generalizes in any significant way so as to show that the 'faithful' discharge of an obligation requires any particular substantive attitude beyond the mere willingness to comply with whatever duties one has. In particular, so doing does not import any general attitude of conscientiousness in which particularly figures any cognitive attitude to the *vulnerability* of the principal, which is the source of the worry in the first place.

The same line of reasoning applies to honesty and dishonesty. It is senseless to speak of a dishonest yet valid discharge of an obligation. Of course a person can lie about having discharged an obligation, but that doesn't implicate anything about the discharge itself. Similarly, telling the truth about discharging an obligation also does nothing to alter the facts of the discharge itself. So just as in the case of the idea of good or bad faith, there is no conceptual room here for the application of the concepts of honesty and dishonesty either.

It is, however, perfectly right to observe that a person may discharge even perfectly objective obligations with good or ill will. A trustee or agent may have a positive attitude of good will towards her principal or, conversely, an attitude of ill will towards them, hence the expression 'she *grudgingly* performed her obligations'. But unless the latter attitude gets in the way of the functioning of the trust, as mentioned above, it is irrelevant to assessing the trustee's discharge of his obligations. A trustee who has a good will towards his beneficiaries may, besides punctiliously observing his obligations under the trust, go above and beyond the call of duty, sending his beneficiaries Christmas cards or attending their weddings and so on. Nice perhaps,[53] but legally irrelevant.

In *Boardman*, Lord Cohen said:[54] 'I desire to repeat that the integrity of the appellants is not in doubt. They acted with complete honesty throughout.'

In *Holder* v. *Holder*,[55] Danckwerts LJ said that the defendant 'acted in complete innocence'. It seems to me that in both these cases, these characterizations of good

[53] Possibly very much perhaps.

[54] Boardman, *supra* n. 31, at 104EF.

[55] *Holder, supra* n. 31, at 253.

faith do not give it anything by way of positive substance. What they indicate was that the court could find no improper motive, no dishonesty, no wrongful intent.[56]

C Bad Faith and Dishonesty

The relations between bad faith and dishonesty are intricate, and I can only make such connections as I can muster with the use of examples where they seem to come together and those where they seem to come apart. For a start, it seems right to say that bad faith concerns more than dishonesty; it concerns a kind of dishonesty that also reveals a breach of faith, or breach of trust or loyalty in the colloquial sense.

Honesty, of course, applies primarily to statements. Someone who tells the truth is honest, and a lie is the paradigm case of a dishonest statement. The concept has, of course, been extended to cover conduct, as in the Theft Act 1968:

> S.1 Basic definition of theft.
>
> (1) A person is guilty of theft if he dishonestly appropriates property belonging to another with the intention of permanently depriving the other of it; and 'thief' and 'steal' shall be construed accordingly.

Bad faith is a kind of dishonesty in a deed; the central element is a knowing or deliberate breach of faith by breaching a duty owed to the other, and in that sense all bad faith breaches of duties can be characterized as dishonest.

According to my criterion of breach of faith or trust, it is clear that not all acts of dishonesty are bad faith breaches of a duty. A thief who steals from a stranger acts dishonestly but not in bad faith, for bad faith requires a breach of 'faith' or trust, and no faith or trust has been reposed in the thief by the victim of his theft.[57] Consider also the case of a robber, who arguably is neither dishonest or acting in bad faith: when the robber demands money by threatening physical violence, his behaviour is certainly wrongful, but it seems strained to say he is acting dishonestly – where is any deceit or deception? – and similarly, assuming his victim is a stranger, it is difficult to see where any bad faith in the sense of disloyalty, breach of faith or breach of trust lies.

Bad faith and dishonesty would also seem to come apart in the fiduciary context. *Klug* v. *Klug*[58] provides an example. The relevant part of the judgment reads:[59]

> When the summons was previously before me I decided that the trustees could in the exercise of their discretion under the powers of advancement, if they thought fit, advance out of capital a sum sufficient to pay this legacy duty. The Public Trustee thinks that their discretion should be so exercised, but his co-trustee, the mother, declines to join him in

[56] See also the formulations of acting 'not in good faith' in the company law context *In re Walt Disney Co. Derivative Litig.* 731 A.2d 342 (Del. Ch. 1988), cited in Sale, 'Fiduciary Law', *supra* n. 27.

[57] Unless one wants to say that the thief breaches faith by breaching the faith his entire community confers upon him to act honestly, but this view turns on the view that a thief is never really a stranger to his victim, which I think is implausible. In small-knit communities, or other groups like sports teams or travelling expeditions, it seems plausible, however, to consider one person's thieving from the other as a breach of faith.

[58] *Klug* v. *Klug* [1918] 2 Ch 67.

[59] Ibid., 71.

> so doing, not because she has considered whether or not it would be for her daughter's welfare that the advance should be made, but because her daughter has married without her consent, and her letters show, in my opinion, that she has not exercised her discretion at all.

It seems to me that this was a bad faith breach of duty,[60] but it is not clear how we could characterize it as dishonest. The mother was apparently perfectly willing to be truthful that she was acting in bad faith, for an irrelevant reason, to deny her daughter the advancement. A person can be quite open about their acting wrongfully.

A person can also be dishonest whilst acting in good faith. The classic example is the 'white lie'. When I was a pupil, I was involved in a family trust matter where the trustees were required by the settlor to choose one of his two grandsons to take the bulk of the trust estate. The trustees made their choice and, very foolishly it must be acknowledged, wrote to the disappointed grandson giving reasons for their choice. The letter was untruthful, giving reasons other than the ones upon which they chose; they hoped the reasons given in the letter would soften the blow and help the disappointed grandson to move on.[61] Though dishonest, I would not describe the act as one of bad faith; there was no improper motive.

One last, non-legal example: I can act in bad faith, I think, by saying something perfectly truthful. I could, for example, damn a friend with honest but faint praise.

To summarize: to act in bad faith is deliberately, or knowingly (which includes cases of wilful ignorance or sincere suspicion that the act is not proper), though not necessarily dishonestly in the sense of intending to deceive, to act in a way that the actor knows is a breach of his duty towards another who is not a stranger to him in the relevant sense: 'Not a stranger in the relevant sense' expresses the idea that the person towards whom the dutyower acts has reposed trust, confidence, or faith, in him or her.

6 Paul Finn's Discussion of a Good Faith Standard

At this point I must notice Paul Finn's recent discussion of 'a good faith' standard, and the differences between his view and mine. In the first place, Finn uses the concept of good faith as a standard of other-regardingness that lies between an 'unconscionability' standard and the fiduciary one. Roughly, in some cases a party can be liable for acting unconscionably, but otherwise can act entirely in their own interests. In others a good faith standard applies. Here an actor may act primarily in their own interest but must take into some reasonable account their counterparty's

[60] In personal communication, Lionel Smith tells me that he doubts that this is a case of bad faith; rather he sees it as a case of someone just acting for the wrong reasons. I agree that a person who acts for the wrong reasons is not necessarily acting in bad faith, for one can do so innocently. However I would maintain that in this case the mother was consciously or deliberately acting for the wrong reasons, a finding that could easily be inferred from the facts.

[61] Indeed, if anything was improper, it seems to me, it turned on a genuine conflict of interest: by writing the letter, the trustees (though they did not realize it, perhaps) were protecting their own position, because there was a good chance that their choice of the other grandson might be challenged, and the letter might be seen as an effort to forestall this. Of course the letter had the opposite effect, ensuring the engagement of many expensive barristers and solicitors.

interests, for example the case of a mortgagee in exercising its power of sale, based upon the counterparty's reasonable reliance, legitimate expectations and so on, and this standard arises particularly in cases where the issue in question is the disclosure of information known to him, relevant to the transaction but unknown to his counterparty. Finally, the fiduciary standard requires the fiduciary to act only with the interests of her principal in mind.

For my purposes here, I cannot draw much assistance from Finn's discussion of good faith (though I commend it as a discussion of the issues he examines under his 'good faith' rubric), for two reasons. The first is that he uses good faith as an umbrella term under which to discuss a standard of legal review of an actor's 'neighbourliness' regarding his counterparty. Finn does not go through cases in which good faith or bad faith are discussed in those terms. Secondly, in the cases Finn discusses, the faulty actor cannot usually be seen as acting in bad faith in what I hope I have captured to be its normal sense. For example, a mortgagor who proceeds with the sale of the mortgagee's estate heedless of the legitimate interest of the mortgagor does not per se show bad faith. Mere disregard of another's interest is not bad faith. The same is the case with the actor who fails to disclose information. Of course, the failure to observe any duty whatsoever may be done deliberately or knowingly and then would appropriately be characterized as a bad faith breach of duty where the victim of the breach had reposed faith, confidence and trust in the wrongdoer, but none of this is relevant to Finn's discussion of 'good faith'.

One final note on this. Paul Finn's description of a good faith standard *does* entail a positive, prescriptive, 'good faith' duty in the cases to which the standard applies: the duty to consider the interests of one's counterparty alongside one's own interest in cases where one would normally need only consider one's own. It would be a positive obligation *to balance* in some suitably sensitive way one's own interests against those of the counterparty. Of course no such duty to balance interests applies to a fiduciary; indeed, he is positively prohibited from engaging in such a balance; he owes his principal his deliberative exclusivity.

7 Consequences of a Trustee's or Agent's Acting in Bad Faith

Cases where it actually appears that the court's holding as to an agent's or trustee's liability turned on a finding of bad faith are few and far between. Doubtless this is in part because of the court's reluctance to sully the character of a party unless it is absolutely necessary to do so. But a finding of good faith or bad faith is relevant in some bits of the law governing trustees and agents.

A *Giving a Fiduciary an Allowance Although Rightly Stripped of a Profit*

In the well-known case of *Boardman*,[62] the self-appointed agents were stripped of their profits, but in the taking of the account of profits, the court directed that they were to be given, 'on a liberal scale', an allowance representing their extensive efforts

[62] Boardman, *supra* n. 31.

in seeing the transaction through to completion. In awarding such an allowance, the finding that they acted in good faith – referring to their integrity and honesty – seems to have been essential to the granting of the allowance.

By contrast, in *Murad* v. *Al-Saraj*,[63] a joint venturer dishonestly failed to disclose his private arrangements with a seller of a hotel that was to be run for the benefit of the joint venture. He was found liable to account for all of his profits in the business, principally under the 'no-profit rule', though 'conflict of interest' and a 'fiduciary duty to disclose' also entered into the reasoning. In all three judgments in the Court of Appeal, it was made clear that the defendant's breach was 'fraudulent', 'deliberate', 'dishonest', 'deceitful' and showed a 'lack of good faith'.[64] Arden LJ, with whom Jonathan Parker LJ agreed, argued that in the right case the strict no-profit rule might be relaxed so that a fiduciary in breach might be given an allowance when rendering the account where the trustee has acted in perfect good faith, but this was not such a case.[65] Clarke LJ dissented to the extent of saying that such an allowance might be awarded even in such a case 'where a court of equity might well conclude that justice required that, *despite his fraud*, he should be allowed to retain some share of the profits and not to account for them all.'[66]

B *Agents and Their Commissions*

There are some fine-grained rules about when an agent in breach of her duties to her principal may 'forfeit' (that is the actual word used) her right to be paid commission or salary. A mere breach of contract will not generate such a result, but a fiduciary breach may. In these cases the courts have often distinguished dishonest and bad faith breaches from innocent, good faith breaches, so this does seem like an area of law where good faith or bad faith will go to liability, viz. the liability of an agent to the forfeiture of his commission or salary.[67]

C *Summary Dismissal of Employees and Agents, Removal of Trustees*

Merely because an employee or agent breaches a term of their contract does not necessarily entitle the employer or principal to other than a claim for breach of contract. But it is clear that a bad faith breach may allow an employer to summarily dismiss an employee[68] or a principal to dismiss his agent.[69] As regards the principal–agent case, it is to be remembered that save in cases of irrevocable agency, where the principal's grant of authority to the agent is for the benefit of the agent to secure the principal's contractual performance,[70] a principal may peremptorily terminate the

[63] [2005] EWCA 959.
[64] Variously, ibid., [4], [12], [13], [14], [15], [46], [68], [84], [97], [125], [142] and [159].
[65] Ibid., [82]–[84].
[66] Ibid., [142], my italics.
[67] For a review of the authorities, see *Imageview Management Ltd* v. *Jack* [2009] EWCA Civ 63.
[68] Fishel, *supra* n. 20.
[69] *Boston Deep See Fishing and Ice Company* v. *Ansell* (1888) 39 Ch.D 339, at 357 per Cotton J.
[70] See, e.g., *Re Hannan's Empress Gold Mining and Development Co.* [1896] 2 Ch 643.

agency relationship as of right, even if in breach of contract. The basic rationale for the rule is that no one is required by law to be represented by another. Since the principal has this peremptory power, no finding of bad faith on the part of the agent is necessary for its exercise, though it will enter into further remedial issues, such as whether the withdrawal of authority was a breach by the principal of his contract with the agent, or whether the agent loses the right to his salary or commission, as discussed at Section 7.B.

A similar principle applies to trustees. In the words of Lord Blackburn in *Letterstedt*:

> Story says, s. 1289, 'But in cases of positive misconduct, Courts of Equity have no difficulty in interposing to remove trustees who have abused their trust; it is not indeed every mistake or neglect of duty, or inaccuracy of conduct of trustees, which will induce Courts of Equity to adopt such a course. But the acts or omissions must be such as to endanger the trust property or to shew a want of honesty, or a want of proper capacity to execute the duties, or a want of reasonable fidelity.'[71]

Cases of trustee removal are few, probably for the reason stated in *Letterstedt*:[72]

> The reason why there is so little to be found in the books on this subject is probably that suggested by Mr. Davey in his argument. As soon as all questions of character are as far settled as the nature of the case admits, if it appears clear that the continuance of the trustee would be detrimental to the execution of the trusts, even if for no other reason than that human infirmity would prevent those beneficially interested, or those who act for them, from working in harmony with the trustee, and if there is no reason to the contrary from the intentions of the framer of the trust to give this trustee a benefit or otherwise, the trustee is always advised by his own counsel to resign, and does so. If, without any reasonable ground, he refused to do so, it seems to their Lordships that the Court might think it proper to remove him; but cases involving the necessity of deciding this, if they ever arise, do so without getting reported.

Klug[73] arguably stands as such a case, though to a more limited extent. The mother having shown a bad faith refusal to make an advancement to her daughter, the court stepped in and exercised the power itself. In a sense, then, the mother was removed and replaced as a trustee, but only to the extent of the exercise of the power in question in this particular instance.

Another example may be provided by *Re Representation of Centre Trustees (CI) Ltd.*[74] The protector of a trust, whose powers the court accepted were fiduciary, refused to resign as protector even though he was in his personal capacity suing the trustees in respect of certain trust assets. The court regarded his refusal to resign as 'wholly unreasonable and in flagrant breach of his duty as Protector and Appointor to the beneficiaries', and he was ordered personally to pay the costs of the suit initiated by the trustees, following which he was removed as protector.[75] Arguably, to find a

[71] *Letterstedt, supra* n. 43, at 385–6. See also *Kain* v. *Hutton* [2007] NZCA 199, [267].
[72] Ibid., *Letterstedt, supra* n. 43, at 386.
[73] *Klug, supra* n. 58.
[74] [2009] JRC 109, (2009) 12 ITELR 720.
[75] Ibid., [38], [39].

protector acted in a 'wholly unreasonable' way in 'flagrant' breach of duty can be construed as his acting in bad faith.

D *Agency Dishonesty and the Withdrawal of Instructions*

Bad faith may be relevant in certain cases where the agent breaches his instructions. Such a case was *Target Holdings* v. *Redferns.*[76] A solicitor acted as a trustee agent in the completion of a sale of land. The vendor was a company, which may have been associated with the principal interested party on the purchaser side, a Mr Kohli. Kohli controlled three companies, call them A, B and C. A entered into a sale and purchase agreement with the vendor. A entered into a sub-sale with B, and B entered into a sub-sale with C. At the time of completion, in clear breach of his instructions (as well as in clear breach of trust), the solicitor paid the moneys in different amounts to *Kohli's companies, not to the vendor's company*. One somewhat unremarked-upon[77] aspect of the case is that when the solicitor paid the moneys to Kohli's associated companies, he *lied* to the mortgagee, Target, who had advanced essentially all of the funds for the purchase, about what he had done, claiming that he had followed his instructions to the letter. For those whose intuitions are that the case is inadequately analysed, this fact deserves emphasis. By lying in this way, the solicitor clearly acted in bad faith. Given the fact that bad faith breaches of instructions immediately entitle the principal to dismiss the agent, it is strongly arguable that the solicitor, as happened in this case, by acting in bad faith, lost his authority to act further in pursuit of his principal's interests unless his principal, in full possession of the facts, authorized him to do so, in which case the solicitor's 'getting in' the relevant charge on the vendor's property would not have bound the principal.[78]

E *Bad Faith and 'Misuse of Position'*

As we have seen, Paul Finn's second basic rule governing the fiduciary relationship, distinct from the rules governing conflicts, relates to the possibility of a fiduciary's 'misuse of fiduciary position, or of knowledge or opportunity arising from it'. It seems to me the term 'misuse' resonates with 'abuse' or 'bad faith' in this context, given the distinctiveness Finn sees in the two rules. Acquiring a gain in conflict of interest that did not manifest bad faith could be framed as a gain acquired in misuse of position, but on that reading the two distinct rules would largely overlap, or, rather, the latter would swallow the former. An interesting US decision, *Mennen v Wilmington Trust*

76 [1996] AC 421.

77 Though see Watts, P., 'Agents' Disbursal of Funds in Breach of Instructions' (2016) 2016 *Lloyd's Maritime and Commercial Law Quarterly* 118, 120; he treats the point as 'important' but does not clearly elaborate on why it is.

78 Cf. Watts, ibid.; Edelman, J., 'Money Awards of the Cost of Performance' (2010) 4 *Journal of Equity* 122; Conaglen, M., 'Explaining *Target Holdings v Redferns*' (2010) 4 *Journal of Equity* 288. Unfortunately, as the case was one of summary judgment, no issue of fraud could be taken into account, nor any issue of bad faith. As to assuming good faith on an action for summary judgment, see *Guinness* v. *Saunders, supra* n. 31.

Company,[79] seems to suggest that the relevant sort of misuse for the rule would require a finding of bad faith.

In *Mennen* there were two trustees, a company trustee and an individual, 'Jeff', who was brother to one of the beneficiaries and uncle to the rest. Jeff embarked on a series of preposterously hazardous investments that he had no genuine skill to assess, and some of the investments involved collateral benefits to himself. These endeavours had the consequence of reducing the value of the trust assets from about $100 million to about $15 million. He also acted dishonestly in charging the trust for his expenses, and deliberately concealed the true value of the assets from his co-trustee and one of the beneficiaries. To top things off, he kept almost no records of his investment dealings.

The judge held that Jeff had acted in bad faith, which he treated 'as synonymous with the absence of good faith', and said that '[t]here is some conduct that is so far beyond the bounds of reasonable judgement that it seems essentially inexplicable on any other ground than bad faith'.[80] The judge also held that where investment decisions were motivated by Jeff's preference for his own interests, that would, 'by definition', amount to bad faith.[81] A further element of Jeff's bad faith was the employment of the trust assets to prove himself to be an investor of acumen.[82] The case is nothing if not a misuse of a fiduciary position, and it is no surprise, to my mind, that the judge held that Jeff's actions were throughout riven with bad faith.

8 Conclusion

A bad faith breach of a duty is a breach that betrays the trust – the credit given to one as an 'upstanding' moral actor – when one is offered the role of employee, trustee or agent. For obvious reasons, the typical legal response to bad faith breaches by agents or trustees is their removal from that role. This, as we have seen, has nothing to do with whether they have fiduciary powers, nor with whether the bad faith breach in question was a bad faith exercise of a fiduciary power. Bad faith is equally bad faith whatever the breach.

79 2015 WL 1914599.
80 Ibid., 16.
81 Ibid., 17.
82 Ibid., 18.

8

Conflict, Profit, Bias, Misuse of Power

Dimensions of Governance

LIONEL D. SMITH*

1 Introduction

It may be that we hear more about conflicts of interest these days than we ever have.[1] Policies about conflicts of interest are proliferating in public and private institutions, including universities.[2] But the expression 'conflict of interest', often shortened to 'conflict', is not used consistently. It is deployed as if it is a technical term with a precise meaning, and yet jurists rarely stop to say what they mean by it. Express policies are more likely to attempt to formulate clear definitions, but some of them may be of questionable quality.

Conflicts are a concern whenever a person holds power but not for his or her own benefit. Subjective trust may or may not be part of the story of how such a situation came into being;[3] but we often use the language of 'trust', 'entrustment', 'fiduciary (that is, trust-like) relationship' or 'public trust' to describe these situations. When someone holds power for and on behalf of another, we may say that they have been entrusted with that power precisely as a way of saying that it does not belong to them personally, which in turn implies that they may not turn it to personal advantage or indeed use it in any way that contravenes the trust. When norms – both legal and non-legal – are designed with those goals in mind, they may cultivate trust where it might otherwise be lacking, by providing a mandatory framework for the proper exercise of other-regarding powers.

The regulation of conflicts is, therefore, at the heart of governance in a broad sense, whether in corporate or trust law, whether in government or the administration of justice. A proper understanding of conflicts, and of other problems that are related but

* I am grateful for helpful suggestions to Michael Davis, Paul Miller and Alexandra Popovici. This research is part of a project on 'Conflicts of Interest and Fiduciary Obligations', funded by a Killam Research Fellowship during 2014–16. I acknowledge with gratitude the support of the Killam Trustees.

1 'Trump Lashes Out at Mueller for Alleged Conflicts of Interest', *The Hill*, 29 July 2018, https://thehill.com/homenews/administration/399427-trump-says-he-and-mueller-had-nasty-business-relationship; 'President Trump Has a Massive Conflict of Interest on Saudi Arabia', *Washington Post*, 18 October 2018, www.washingtonpost.com/outlook/2018/10/18/president-trump-has-massive-conflict-interest-saudi-arabia; and so on.

2 See, for example, McGill University, *Regulation on Conflict of Interest*, www.mcgill.ca/secretariat/files/secretariat/conflict-of-interest-regulation-on_0.pdf; see also 'Recognizing Conflicts', www.mcgill.ca/secretariat/files/secretariat/recognizing-conflicts-jan_2015.pdf.

3 See the chapter by Thomas Gallanis in this volume.

different, is essential to clarifying our discourse on these issues. A proper understanding can only exist in the presence of a sound theory of the problems that rules about conflicts of interest aim to address.

2 Misuse of Power

Power held in an other-regarding capacity may only be used for the advancement of the purposes for which it was held. This is true in private law and for holders of public powers. This has nothing to do with conflicts of interest. If power has been used improperly, the exercise of power is reviewable for that reason of improper use.

Private law examples abound in the field of what the common law calls fiduciary relationships, especially in trust law and corporate law, where fiduciaries have wide-ranging discretions but must use them for proper purposes. In private law we may say that this is an application of the 'proper purposes doctrine' or the rules about 'fraud on a power'. These expressions are potentially ambiguous as possibly referring to at least two distinct inquiries. First, a power may be restricted to use for some objective purpose, and then it can only be so used, whether it is held in a fiduciary capacity or not. Thus a 'power of maintenance' held in relation to trust property does not allow trust property to be used to assist an object of the power to buy a share in a law partnership, while a 'power of advancement' probably does. This involves a purely objective inquiry as to the scope of the power. Similar reasoning may be deployed even if a power does not have an express limitation as to its objective purpose, if it is thought that the proper interpretation of the power implicitly limits its use to certain objective purposes. Thus in corporate law we might say that the power of a board of directors to issue new shares can be used to raise capital – its primary use – but cannot be used to affect the control of the corporation.[4] If by that we mean it can never be used to affect the control of the corporation, *even if the board thinks that this would be in the best interests of the corporation*, it is just like the case of power of maintenance mentioned above: we are saying that the power, according to its correct interpretation, is not available for that objectively defined purpose.[5] This is not so much misuse of power as absence of power.

But even where a power does objectively extend to authorize what was done with it, there may be a further inquiry which may also be treated under the label 'proper purposes' or in some contexts 'fraud on a power'. A version of this type of review can apply to non-fiduciary powers, such as a bank's power unilaterally to change interest rates[6] or an employer's power to decide whether an employee committed suicide, disentitling his family to benefits.[7] It may be concluded that the proper interpretation of the non-fiduciary power shows that it cannot be used dishonestly or arbitrarily or unreasonably. If the power is a fiduciary power, this further inquiry is differently

[4] This is one reading of *Howard Smith Ltd* v. *Ampol Petroleum Ltd* [1974] AC 821 (PC) and *Whitehouse* v. *Carlton Hotel Pty Ltd* (1987) 162 CLR 285.

[5] Whether this is or should be the law is a separate question not addressed here.

[6] *Paragon Finance plc* v. *Nash* [2001] EWCA Civ 1466, [2002] 1 WLR 685 (CA).

[7] *Braganza* v. *BP Shipping Ltd* [2015] UKSC 17, [2015] 1 WLR 1661.

framed and may be called 'proper purposes' or 'fraud on a power'. A fiduciary power can only be used in the furtherance of the purposes for which it was created.[8] In many fiduciary contexts, this means it can only be used in what the fiduciary believes is the furtherance of the best interests of the beneficiary.[9] In relation to fiduciary powers that are dispositive (as opposed to administrative), it usually means that the power can only be used in what the fiduciary believes is the best way to further the purpose for which the power was created.[10] Either way (and also in the non-fiduciary context), this is a subjective inquiry in the sense that it looks at the actual reasons for decision that operated on the mind of the decision maker.[11]

My suggestion is that 'the' proper purposes doctrine therefore includes an objective aspect involving the interpretation of the power and a subjective aspect involving the reasons for action of the particular decision maker.[12] Those exercising fiduciary powers must comply with both the objective and subjective aspects (and they must comply with other norms as well).

Similar principles apply to the exercise of public powers: they must be used for the purposes for which they were granted. Such powers have to be interpreted as to their limits and cannot be used beyond them. As in private law, an apparently unrestricted power may be found, as a matter of interpretation, to be subject to implicit limitations as to the reasons for which the power can be used.[13] Thus, and also as in private law, even if the power holder had the power to do what they did, there may be judicial

[8] On the separateness of the objective and subjective inquiries, see Paul D. Finn, *Fiduciary Obligations* (Law Book Co. 1977), reprinted in Paul Finn, *Fiduciary Obligations: 40th Anniversary Republication with Additional Essays* (Federation Press 2016) [82]–[83] (the original monograph and the reprint employ the same paragraph numbers).

[9] Since there can be review for 'proper purposes' outside of fiduciary powers, some argue that the review of fiduciary powers for proper purposes is not part of fiduciary law (e.g. Matthew Conaglen, *Fiduciary Loyalty: Protecting the Due Performance of Non-fiduciary Duties* (Hart 2010), 44–50). But since the grounds of review in fiduciary law are quite different (requiring, for example, decision-making in the other person's interests, which is not required in non-fiduciary contexts), and since those grounds grow out of the fiduciary relationship, it is not surprising that courts have always treated the review of fiduciary powers as part of fiduciary law.

[10] *Vatcher* v. *Paull* [1915] AC 372 (PC) 378; *Klug* v. *Klug* [1918] 2 Ch 67 (ChD) 71; *McPhail* v. *Doulton* [1971] AC 424 (HL) 449, 457; *Re Hay's Settlement Trusts* [1982] 1 WLR 202 (ChD) 209; *Turner* v. *Turner* [1984] Ch 100 (ChD) 109–10; *Re Beatty* [1990] 1 WLR 1503 (ChD) 1506; *Hayim* v. *Citibank NA* [1987] AC 730 (PC) 746.

[11] *Eclairs Group Ltd* v. *JKX Oil & Gas plc* [2015] UKSC 71 [15].

[12] It also seems to me to make sense that where there has been purported action that is objectively not authorized by the power, the purported exercise is void because there was simply no authority; but where the action was within the objective authority granted by the power but was taken for the wrong reasons, the purported exercise is voidable, since here the authority was present but was misused. See *Pitt* v. *Holt* [2013] UKSC 26, [2013] 2 AC 108 [62], [93].

[13] In *Roncarelli* v. *Duplessis* [1959] SCR 121, the defendant, premier and attorney general of Quebec, ordered the revocation of the plaintiff's liquor licence in order to punish and make an example of the plaintiff who supported a minority religious group. This caused the plaintiff's restaurant business to fail. The court held by a majority that the defendant's action was unlawful, even though the statutory framework gave the liquor commission an apparently unfettered power to revoke a licence. Five of the six majority judges expressed the view that the power to revoke could not be exercised for reasons unrelated to the purposes of the licencing regime. See Geneviève Cartier, 'L'héritage de l'affaire *Roncarelli c. Duplessis* 1959–2009' (2010) 55 *McGill LJ* 375, and the other articles in this special issue devoted to the decision, and compare the decision in *Willcock* v. *Muckle* [1951] 2 KB 844 (DC).

supervision of the reasons on which they acted. In relation to many public powers, the courts may be able to articulate lists of considerations that must or must not be taken into account, and if the power is exercised in violation of those rules, it has been misused.

Misuse of power has nothing to do with conflict of interest, but an example from public law illustrates the creeping nature of conflict of interest terminology. Rule XXXVII of the ethics rules of the US Senate is entitled 'Conflict of Interest' and provides: '1. A Member, officer, or employee of the Senate shall not receive any compensation, nor shall he permit any compensation to accrue to his beneficial interest from any source, the receipt or accrual of which would occur by virtue of influence improperly exerted from his position as a Member, officer, or employee.'[14] What is described here is not a conflict of interest but corrupt influence peddling. If the person has 'improperly exerted' his position, he has misused his power.[15] Calling this a 'conflict of interest' is like characterizing a gangland murder as a 'failure to take proper care with a firearm'. It may be true, in a way, but it uses the label of a precautionary rule to describe the actual occurrence of the harm that the precautionary rule aims to avoid.

Similarly, in 2002, the Australian federal minister responsible for insurance wrote on her ministerial letterhead to her personal insurer about a personal insurance claim. An opposition politician was quoted as saying, 'It's a conflict of interest for the Minister for Insurance to be using her ministerial office and ministerial letterhead to be pursuing a $200,000 claim from an insurance company.'[16] There is no reason to call this a conflict of interest; it is simply a misuse of the ministerial role, for the minister's own benefit. One could add that it is also a misuse of government property, being the stationery and the time of any staff involved in the preparation of the letter.

I will argue in the next section that these situations are not what is meant by a conflict of interest when that term is used properly. These problems are better described as misuses of power.

Why do some people, and some rules and policies, call this kind of problem a conflict of interest? It is an inappropriate action by a person – a senator, or a minister – who needs to avoid conflicts of interest. But that does not mean that this action was done in a conflict of interest. In Canada, the issue is partially regulated by a statute called the Conflict of Interest Act; in that statute, the rules about misuse of power are in part 1, entitled 'Conflict of Interest Rules'.[17] This reveals the same terminological confusion as the ethics rules of the US Senate. Some, but not all, of the rules in that part are about conflicts of interest, and all of the rules in that part

[14] www.ethics.senate.gov/public/index.cfm/conflictsofinterest.

[15] The conduct forbidden by the quoted text also reveals an unauthorized profit, which is discussed below in Section 3 and which also is not a conflict of interest properly understood. The conduct forbidden by subsection 4 of the rule also reveals misuse of power: 'No Member, officer, or employee shall knowingly use his official position to introduce or aid the progress or passage of legislation, a principal purpose of which is to further only his pecuniary interest.'

[16] *The Age*, 13 December 2002, www.theage.com.au/national/coonan-defends-letterhead-use-for-personal-mail-20021213-gduxay.html.

[17] Conflict of Interest Act, SC 2006, c. 9, s. 2.

apply to people who must avoid conflicts of interest. But that does not mean that all of these rules are about conflicts of interest.[18] The official who oversees the act is called the conflict of interest and ethics commissioner. Some, but not all, of the rules that this official oversees are about conflicts of interest and about ethics. Others are legal (not ethical) rules that are not about conflicts.

As we will see, this problem is not confined to the norms governing politicians. The same thing may happen when codes of conduct are drawn up in other contexts, possibly through using the political codes as starting points.[19] And something very similar happens in private law scholarship and case law around the world: loose definitions of conflicts of interest are used to cover distinct problems that are more or less closely related to conflicts of interest.[20]

If misuse of power is caught in the act, so to speak, it can be remedied in various ways, including by removing the relevant person, permanently or in relation to a particular decision.[21] If the misuse is in the past, it may have been used to constitute a juridical act, which is a civilian expression referring to a manifestation of intention of one or more persons that is designed to produce effects in law.[22] When a power has been so misused, the juridical act is liable to be set aside. The effect is similar to the effect of fraud or duress on a juridical act: it is a vitiation or vice in the constitution of the juridical act that leads to its being voidable or, in civilian terminology, null. Thus in private law, when powers have been misused. the courts have set aside a transfer or appointment of property,[23] the making of a contract,[24] the issuance of corporate shares[25] or the adoption of a resolution by a board of directors.[26] In public law, the juridical act to be set aside may be the rendering of a decision in the exercise of public power, as where the decision of a minister or his or her delegate is set aside for failing to consider some relevant matter.[27]

18 For example, s. 9 of the act is about misuse of power: 'No public office holder shall use his or her position as a public office holder to seek to influence a decision of another person so as to further the public office holder's private interests or those of the public office holder's relatives or friends or to improperly further another person's private interests.'

19 The McGill *Regulation on Conflict of Interest* (n. 2), for example, covers conflicts of self-interest and duty and also aspects of care and diligence and, in a way that seems somewhat bolted on, certain post-retirement conduct (para. 2.1). The document 'Recognizing Conflicts' (n. 2), the juridical status of which is unclear but which purports to be an aid to understanding the *Regulation,* lists fifty-five situations that are said to be conflicts of interest. Many of them are, in my terminology, cases of misuse of authority, conflicts of duty and duty, and unauthorized profit.

20 The most prominent example in private law, to which I will return in Section 4, is that unauthorized profits are frequently referred to as conflicts of interest.

21 *Klug* (n. 10).

22 France Allard et al., *Private Law Dictionary and Bilingual Lexicons – Property* (Les Éditions Yvon Blais 2012), s.v. 'juridical act'.

23 *Turner* (n. 10); *Fox* v. *Fox* (1996) 28 OR (3d) 496 (CA).

24 *Lee Panavision Ltd* v. *Lee Lighting Ltd* [1991] BCC 620, [1992] BCLC 22 (CA) (although reasoned on the basis that the board did not have the power to make the contract, in my view the better explanation is that it was misused).

25 *Howard Smith Ltd* (n. 4).

26 *Eclairs Group Ltd* (n. 11).

27 For discussion of the effects of nullity in this context, see Paul Craig, *Administrative Law* (8th ed., Sweet & Maxwell 2016) 738–49.

In both private and public law, misuse of power can be simply misguided and thus in good faith, it can be careless or it can be deliberate, even corrupt. In some cases, therefore, the facts may reveal a wrongful act that may give rise to a right to compensation.[28] Compensation may be in order because the *consequences* of a misuse may be impossible to set aside: a letter written on the wrong letterhead cannot be unwritten, and the bankruptcy of a business, caused by the wrongful use of public power, cannot be set aside. Regardless of whether there is a breach of a legal duty, a misuse is a misuse; a power is improperly used if it is not used for the purpose for which it was granted. Such a vice in the exercise of a power is analytically separate from whether any wrong was committed.[29]

And that vice is not, as such, a conflict.

3 Conflict

A *Definition*

Jurists in the common law tradition have not produced a record of excellence in relation to the definition of conflicts. The expression 'conflict of interest' is often treated as having a self-evident connotation. It does not. It is striking that most academic discussions of this field of law do not even attempt a definition of conflict of interest; nor do the vast majority of judgments.

A fiduciary conflict of interest is not merely a feeling of being conflicted or torn; nor is it merely a difficult decision; nor is it even merely a decision between interests that are in conflict.

John Langbein argued that we should erode fiduciary conflict norms, partly by suggesting that '[c]onflicts of interest are endemic in human affairs, and they are not invariably harmful'.[30] But his attempt to prove this included a number of examples, some of which were not fiduciary conflicts of interest at all. One example was the decision faced by a parent when considering how much of his or her own wealth to enjoy personally and how much to leave to children and charity on death. This may be a difficult decision, but it has nothing to do with what fiduciary law identifies as a conflict of interest. Langbein's hypothetical parent owes no fiduciary duty in relation to his or her decision about what to do with his or her own assets.

Furthermore, a fiduciary conflict of interest is not simply a situation in which the fiduciary's interests are in conflict with those of the beneficiary. This has been called a conflict of *interests*, in order to distinguish it from a fiduciary conflict of interest.[31] Conflicts of *interests* arise in almost every interaction between persons who have each

28 *Roncarelli* (n. 13).

29 In *Turner* (n. 10), the exercises of powers by trustees were set aside in proceedings that they themselves brought. They were not accused of wrongdoing (although they might have been in breach of their duty of care and skill).

30 John H. Langbein, 'Questioning the Trust Law Duty of Loyalty: Sole Interest or Best Interest?' (2005) 114 *Yale LJ* 929, 935.

31 Michael Davis, 'Conflict of Interest' in Ruth Chadwick (ed.), *Encyclopedia of Applied Ethics* (2nd ed., Elsevier 2012) 571, 571, 576; Remus Valsan, 'Fiduciary Duties, Conflict of Interest, and Proper Exercise of Judgment' (2016) 62 *McGill LJ* 1, 16.

their own interests. Conflicts of *interest* are phenomena particular to those situations in which one person must exercise duty-bound judgement for other-regarding purposes. Take the case of a professional fiduciary who is paid by time on a profitable basis, like many lawyers and some professional trustees. This person's financial self-interest is always in conflict with the interests of the beneficiary, since the fiduciary's self-interest is in billing as much time as possible. This conflicts with the beneficiary's self-interest in paying as low a bill as possible. But we do not say that lawyers are always, at all times, in a conflict of interest. They are in a conflict of *interests*, and a proper definition of conflict of interest helps clarify this.

An example of the confusion of these situations is the definition of conflict of interest adopted by Matthew Conaglen, who claims that fiduciary law imposes a legal duty on a fiduciary not to be in a situation in which his non-fiduciary duties towards the beneficiary are in conflict with the fiduciary's self-interest.[32] But this does not seem possible, because the fiduciary is always in such a situation. The fiduciary's self-interest, narrowly defined, is to spend *as little time or effort as possible* acting on behalf of the beneficiary in relation to whatever remuneration the fiduciary receives. This is true whether the fiduciary is paid (by time, or by asset value, or in any other way) or is acting gratuitously.[33] Spending less time on behalf of the beneficiary would give the fiduciary more time to pursue his own choices, whether for profit or leisure. That self-interest always conflicts with whatever duties the fiduciary owes to the beneficiary to act on his behalf.[34] What Conaglen has described is not the fiduciary norm regarding conflict of interest but rather the different situation of a conflict of interests.

It is easy to criticize. What is my definition? We can start by thinking about what is common to all situations where we have concerns about conflicts of interest. These can arise in private law, in contexts of holders of public powers and even in situations where there is no relevant legal norm. If a university faculty is considering the admission of a prospective student, and one member of the admissions committee is the applicant's parent, we might well say that this person is in a conflict of interest even though there may be no legal norm that is applicable. What is common to all situations where we have concerns about conflicts of interest is that (1) a person holds some kind of power (possibly as a member of a group) that requires the exercise of judgement, but (2) that judgement needs to be exercised not selfishly but rather in a selfless or other-regarding way. It needs to be exercised in the pursuit of the mission or assignment for the achievement of which the power was granted.

32 Conaglen, *Fiduciary Loyalty* (n. 9) 63 and passim. For Conaglen, the fiduciary's duty of care and skill, which requires him to do more than nothing on behalf of the beneficiary, is a non-fiduciary duty (35–9). So (and here I would agree) are any contractual duties that the fiduciary owes to the beneficiary to expend effort on the beneficiary's behalf.

33 This does not imply that the fiduciary produces inaccurate bills; Conaglen's definition is satisfied by the conflict, without regard to whether the fiduciary breaches any other duty.

34 One of the other examples in Langbein (n. 30, 935) is similar: 'How much time should a board member or an officer or an employee of a business corporation or a charity devote to the affairs of that entity, as opposed to his or her personal business?' The legal answer to that question is given by the duty of care and skill, and by relevant terms of any contract of employment. This situation reveals a conflict of interests, but not a fiduciary conflict of interest.

Let us take these in the opposite order. If the person can rightly use the power in their own interests, there is never a concern about conflicts of interest. This is why a 'conflict of interest and duty' means a conflict of self-interest with the *fiduciary* duty to exercise judgement properly.[35] In the public law context, it means a conflict of self-interest with an analogous other-regarding duty owed to the public in relation to a public power.

The reason the exercise of judgement is also essential to understanding the concern about conflicts is that it creates a situation in which there is no single legally correct answer as to what the duty-bound person should do. They have to make a decision, using their judgement and using it in an other-regarding way. We can tell objectively whether non-fiduciary duties have been fulfilled or not. If a person owes another $100, they have either paid or they have not. Some duties may be rather vague, couched in terms of reasonableness, but that is treated as a factual issue. Even these duties are either breached or not. There is no need for rules about conflicts. But the proper exercise of judgement has a subjective element, as we have seen.[36] It requires a fiduciary (for example) to act in what he thinks are the best interests of his beneficiary. If he does not so act, he misuses his power. But if a person's self-interest is implicated, it becomes impossible to know whether the power has been properly exercised. This is not just because it is difficult to prove the reasons for which a person acted; it is, but courts do this a lot.[37] The crux of the problem is that even the fiduciary cannot be sure of the effect of the self-interest, or of the efficacy of their efforts to exclude it from their mind.[38]

A norm that is called upon to regulate situations where one person holds powers that must be exercised in an other-regarding way needs to be formulated so as to focus on the exercise of those powers. In 1987, a royal commission in Canada was required to produce a definition of conflict of interest, in the context of allegations of conflicts of interest in relation to a cabinet minister. After argument and submissions, and discussion of case law, here is what the commissioner (who was the chief justice of the

[35] As it has been articulated by the High Court of Australia: *Chan* v. *Zacharia* (1984) 154 CLR 178, 198; *Warman International Ltd* v. *Dwyer* (1995) 182 CLR 544, 557; *Howard* v. *Federal Commissioner of Taxation* [2014] HCA 21, 253 CLR 83 [33], [108].

[36] At the beginning of Section 2.

[37] As shown by the cases discussed above, Section 2, relating to 'proper purposes'. Part of Langbein's (n. 30) argument for weakening fiduciary norms about conflicts is that those norms exist because of historical difficulties of fact-finding, which does not trouble modern courts. My argument is that this is not correct; they exist because no amount of evidence can solve the relevant problem.

[38] *Furs Ltd* v. *Tomkies* (1936) 54 CLR 583, 592 per Rich, Dixon and Evatt JJ: 'The consequences of such a conflict are not discoverable.' E. R. Hoover, 'Basic Principles Underlying Duty of Loyalty' (1956) 5 *Cleveland–Marshall L. Rev.* 7, 10: 'Conflict destroys an essential ingredient without which a fiduciary relation cannot function – disinterested judgment.' See also Matthew Conaglen, 'Public–Private Intersection: Comparing Fiduciary Conflict Doctrine and Bias' (2008) *Public Law* 58, 67–8; Valsan, 'Fiduciary Duties, Conflict of Interest, and Proper Exercise of Judgment' (n. 31) 26–40, citing ethical and psychological research; Remus Valsan, 'The No-Conflict Fiduciary Rule and the Rule against Bias in Judicial Review: A Comparison' (2019) 6 *European J of Comparative Law and Governance* 1, 27–40. Note also the comment of A. L. Smith LJ in *Re Lamb* [1894] 2 QB 805 (CA) 820: 'It is obvious – everybody knows it who has any knowledge of life – that when a man has a pecuniary interest, his mind is naturally warped in favour of his own interest. It is human nature, and no one can doubt it.' See also the chapter in this volume by Tess Wilkinson-Ryan, discussing the psychological effects of both conflicts of interest and conflicts of interests.

High Court of Ontario) came up with: 'A real conflict of interest denotes a situation in which a minister of the Crown has knowledge of a private economic interest that is sufficient to influence the exercise of his or her public duties and responsibilities.'[39] The strengths of this definition are that it addresses both the conflict and the interest, anchoring them to the exercise of other-regarding power, and it addresses the problem that is created by the conflict and the interest: they make it foreseeable that the other-regarding power will be exercised inappropriately. In other words, a conflict creates a threat of a misuse of power. The conflict, as such, is not a misuse of power; it is a situation in which such a misuse is foreseeable and impossible to control for.

In a similar vein, the ethicist Michael Davis has proposed this definition, a wider one that will cover a range of contexts: 'A conflict of interest is a situation in which some person P (whether an individual or corporate body) is (1) in a relationship with another requiring P to exercise judgment on the other's behalf and (2) P has a (special) interest tending to interfere with the proper exercise of judgment in that relationship.'[40] This definition includes the private law fiduciary context, since fiduciaries have discretionary powers that require the exercise of judgement, and that judgement must be exercised on behalf of the beneficiary. It might need a small tweak to cover public law contexts such as those involving judges or members of the executive. The reason is that public powers of that kind are rightly exercised, not on behalf of 'another' but for a public purpose, such as the administration of justice according to law or the fulfilment of some statutory mandate. It also needs to be remembered that in an advisory relationship that is fiduciary, the giving of advice is itself an example of the duty-bound exercise of judgement, even though the adviser may not have any juridical power.[41] Subject to that, I adopt Davis's definition, although I will further qualify it below.

B A Duty Not to Be in a Conflict? or Other Juridical Effects

Even with a better definition of conflicts, it is impossible in my view to say that a person has a legal (or other) duty to avoid *being in* a conflict situation.[42] That is an

[39] Commission of Inquiry into the Facts of Allegations of Conflict of Interest Concerning the Honourable Sinclair M Stevens (The Commission 1987), http://publications.gc.ca/site/eng/9.818247/publication.html, 35 [hereafter 'Parker Commission']. Part of this strange story is that although the commissioner was mandated by the federal cabinet to make findings whether the minister had been in any actual or apparent conflict of interest, the relevant codes of conduct did not define those terms, which is why the commissioner had to produce definitions. An even stranger part of the story is that many years later, the findings of the commission were quashed by a court on the basis that the commissioner did not have the jurisdiction to produce his own definitions, even after hearing counsel: *Stevens* v. *Canada (Attorney General)* 2004 FC 1746. For a non-legal account of the story leading up to the Royal Commission, see Rod McQueen, *Blind Trust: Inside the Sinclair Stevens Affair* (Macmillan 1987).

[40] Davis (n. 31) 571. Davis does not specifically explain his qualifier '(special)' but implies (at 573) that he only means that his definition refers to an interest that is not of a kind that is always or inevitably present. See also Michael Davis, 'Conflict of Interest' (1982) 1 *Business & Professional Ethics Journal* 17.

[41] See Lionel Smith, 'Fiduciary Relationships: Ensuring the Loyal Exercise of Judgement on Behalf of Another' (2014) 130 *LQR* 608, 618–19.

[42] This is how the fiduciary norm about conflicts is sometimes described, particularly by those who take the view that fiduciary duties are only proscriptive. See, for example, *Breen* v. *Williams* (1995) 186 CLR 71,

imprecise formulation of the norm. If a person offers a bribe to a fiduciary agent, the agent is in a kind of conflict, but the agent has not done anything wrong (yet). In my view, the agent now has a duty to disclose the offer to the principal and will do wrong if that duty is breached; such a duty only arises when the person becomes aware of the conflict. Taking the bribe would be unlawful as against the principal (and possibly criminally unlawful). Whether or not the bribe is taken, the agent's use of his powers (to make contracts for and on behalf of the principal) for an (actual) improper purpose is unlawful. The agent's use of those powers while in a conflict (for example, with the prospect of a secret payment) is also unlawful. But merely *being in* a conflict is not legally wrongful as such. You cannot stop someone from speaking before you know what they are going to say, and *you* do not commit a wrong in virtue of the fact that *they* offer you a bribe. Many other examples could be given: a judge might find out, as a proceeding begins, that she has an indirect financial interest in one of the litigants. A trustee selling trust property calls for written offers, and when he opens the offer letters, he finds to his surprise that the only offer is from his brother. These people are in conflicts, but they have not done anything wrong (yet).

Conflicts need to be managed or eliminated. Part of this is often through a requirement of disclosure, which may be a legal duty in private fiduciary law[43] and in other private law settings,[44] may arise under statute in corporate law[45] or public law,[46] and may also be required by non-legal codes.[47] In addition to requirements of disclosure, a person in a conflict may be disqualified in advance of the exercise of their duty-bound judgement, either voluntarily or in another way, and either generally or in relation to the particular decision.[48] In private law, fully capacitated beneficiaries who are fully informed of the conflict can consent to the use of the power despite the conflict.[49] But when a power is improperly used in a conflict situation to constitute a

113 (Gaudron and McHugh JJ): an obligation 'not to be in a position of conflict'. This was an adoption of an argument in Paul D. Finn, 'The Fiduciary Principle' in Timothy G. Youdan (ed.), *Equity, Fiduciaries and Trusts* (Carswell 1989) 1, 27–8, reprinted in Paul Finn, *Fiduciary Obligations: 40th Anniversary Republication with Additional Essays* (Federation Press 2016) 308, 330–1. See also Conaglen, *Fiduciary Loyalty* (n. 9) 39–40 and passim.

43 Lionel Smith, 'Prescriptive Fiduciary Duties' (2018) 37 *UQLJ* 261 Section VI.E.

44 McGill, *Regulation on Conflict of Interest* (n. 2) paras. 2.1(iii), 3.

45 Canada Business Corporations Act, RSC 1985, c. C-44, s. 120.

46 Conflict of Interest Act (n. 17) ss. 22–6.

47 The codes that require members of legislative bodies to declare financial and other interests are typically resolutions of the relevant body and not statutes. For the UK, see the Codes for the Houses of Commons and of Lords, at www.parliament.uk/mps-lords-and-offices/standards-and-financial-interests/ See also the UK Ministerial Code, https://assets.publishing.service.gov.uk/government/uploads/system/uploads/attachment_data/file/672633/2018-01-08_MINISTERIAL_CODE_JANUARY_2018__FINAL___3_.pdf, para. 7. This code is governmental policy, not law.

48 E.g. *Re Lamb* (n. 38), in which a person was disqualified from appointment to a fiduciary role by foreseeable conflicts. Corporate law may disqualify conflicted directors from voting in addition to requiring them to make disclosure (e.g. Canada Business Corporations Act (n. 45) s. 120(5)); trust instruments may have similar systems (see, e.g., *Society of Trust and Estate Practitioners Standard Provisions* (2nd ed.), www.step.org/, cl 9.

49 Such consent may be implicit, as in *Kelly* v. *Cooper* [1993] AC 205 (PC). For an example of implicit statutory authorization of a conflict, see *Sun Indalex Finance, LLC* v. *United Steelworkers*, [2013] 1 SCR

juridical act, the act can be set aside.[50] This is the same remedy as that which arises when actual misuse of power is shown. This confirms that the danger against which the conflict rules guard is the possibility of misuse, even inadvertent misuse. But the duty of disclosure is an independent duty, and in private law, a breach of it can give rise to a claim for compensation for loss caused by the breach.[51]

Thus finding that someone is in a conflict does not on its own mean they have done anything wrong, nor does it necessarily impugn their integrity. The crucial question becomes how the conflict is managed once the person who is in the conflict becomes aware of it. Why, then, do people often treat an allegation of conflict of interest as a serious allegation of improper behaviour? I can think of two different, overlapping reasons, both of which might be at play. One is that the label 'conflict of interest' has been conflated with the danger against which it protects, which is misuse of power. This phenomenon was discussed above.[52] The other is that failing to manage a conflict that one is in once one is aware of it – doing nothing, for example – may itself be wrongful behaviour, as we have seen in the previous paragraph; moreover, this failure to manage may create concerns about integrity. If someone who is interested in the matter learns of the conflict otherwise than through the conflicted person's voluntary disclosure, this may well create a concern not only about the conflict and the effects it might have in the future, but about why the conflicted person did not disclose the conflict.

C *Different Kinds of Conflicts*

The phrase 'conflict of interest' now appears in a wide range of contexts. In its private law origins, it is shorthand for 'conflict of self-interest and fiduciary duty of loyalty'.[53] The fiduciary duty is the requirement to exercise the relevant power for and on behalf of another.[54] The self-interest is the external, improper and potentially corrosive influence. In this perspective, it is not surprising that it is also traditional in fiduciary law to distinguish a 'conflict of self-interest and fiduciary duty' from a 'conflict of

271, 2013 SCC 6, [64]–[66], [197]–[202]. As the latter case shows, the authorization of a conflict does not, as such, relieve the fiduciary of their other duties.

50 For example, in private law, a contract: *Aberdeen Ry Co.* v. *Blaikie Brothers* (1854) 1 Macq 461, 1 Paterson 394 (HL); in public law, the judgment of a court: *Ex Parte Pinochet (No. 2)* [1999] UKHL 1, [2000] 1 AC 119.

51 *Nocton* v. *Lord Ashburton* [1914] AC 932 (HL), as interpreted in *Hodgkinson* v. *Simms* [1994] 3 SCR 377, 415, for the majority, in *Swindle* v. *Harrison* [1997] 4 All ER 705 (CA), 732 per Mummery LJ, and in *Maguire* v. *Makaronis* (1997) 188 CLR 449, 495 per Kirby J; *London Loan & Savings Co.* v. *Brickenden* [1934] 3 DLR 465 (PC), 469; *Canson Enterprises Ltd* v. *Boughton & Co.* [1991] 3 SCR 534, 542, 558; *Hodgkinson*, 393–4. In *Swindle* all the judges agreed that the defendant had breached a fiduciary duty to disclose a conflict (718 (Evans LJ), 720 (Hobhouse LJ), 732–3, 735 (Mummery LJ)), but the plaintiff had not proven that the breach caused the loss that was suffered.

52 In Section 2.

53 The earliest occurrence I know of 'conflict of interest' in this sense is in the argument in *York Buildings Co.* v. *Mackenzie* (1795) 8 Brown PC 42, 3 ER 432 (HL) 66, 447. See *Aberdeen Ry Co.* (n. 50) at 471 (Macqueen), 399 (Paterson) per Lord Cranworth LC; see also n. 35.

54 I use the word 'requirement' here because I do not consider this to be a duty in the strictest sense, for reasons that are explained in Smith, 'Fiduciary Relationships' (n. 41) 609–12.

fiduciary duty and (another) duty'.[55] Many cases involving the disqualification of lawyers for 'conflicts of interest' are actually about allegations of conflicts of this latter kind.[56] Also of this kind are concerns, reflected in rules of law and of professional conduct, relating to lawyers and real estate agents who act for both sides of a transaction such as a sale of land. In these cases, there may be no relevant self-interest at play, but from the perspective of the beneficiary, the problem of improper influence on duty-bound judgement is just as serious.[57]

If in exercising judgement, I am bound to act in what I perceive to be the interests of one person, and yet in the same transaction I am bound to exercise judgement in what I perceive to be the interests of some other person, there is obviously a serious risk that in relation to one (or both) exercises of judgement, I will fall short of what my duty demands.[58] As with conflicts of interest, it will be impossible to know whether and to what extent my judgement was compromised. The difference is that the problem here is not introduced by a self-interest but by a conflicting requirement to consult the interests of another.[59]

Distinguishing conflicts of interest from conflicts of duty and duty allows us to say that a conflict of interest – a conflict of self-interest and duty relating to the exercise of judgement – must definitionally involve some interest of the person exercising

[55] *Moody* v. *Cox* [1917] 2 Ch 71 (CA) 81; see Finn (n. 8), chs. 21, 22.

[56] For example, *Canadian National Railway Co.* v. *McKercher LLP* [2013] 2 SCR 649, 2013 SCC 39. These cases are also complicated by the dimension of the potential misuse of confidential information. Note also that the conflict in *Canson* (n. 51) is probably best described as a conflict of duty and duty.

[57] There is no relevant self-interest inasmuch as typically the lawyer and the real estate agent are not personally parties to the transaction, directly or indirectly. There may be self-interest inasmuch as the lawyer and the real estate agent are paid for their services; that is a conflict of interests. It might become a conflict of interest if, for example, a lawyer was giving advice on the best way to proceed in a case, and some options would inevitably be more profitable for the lawyer, while others would be less so. Usually this is a conflict of which the client is fully aware, since they know they are billed by time and advice as to the options should include a comparison of expected costs.

[58] This formulation of the problem suggests that a conflict of duty and duty arises when both duties are duties relating to the proper exercise of judgement (as seems to be assumed in Finn (n. 8), ch. 22). This seems correct, although it is sometimes suggested that a fiduciary may be disqualified from acting when the fiduciary duty relating to the loyal exercise of judgement conflicts with *any* other duty owed to another. The problem with this wider view is encapsulated in a comment that was made to me by Michael Davis, that although a person exercising duty-bound judgement must not be influenced by the *interests* of third parties, he should not ignore their *rights*. The rights of third parties may, of course, be duties on the decision maker, and a decision-maker exercising discretionary powers, whether in private law or public law, must act lawfully. In *Ahmed Anguillia bin Hadjee Mohamed Salleh Anguillia* v. *Estate and Trust Agencies (1927) Ltd* [1938] AC 624 (PC), it was held that an estate administrator (who is a fiduciary) might not breach a contract with a third party, even if the administrator thought that such a breach was in the best interests of the estate beneficiaries. The administrator's duty of loyalty to the beneficiaries conflicted, in a sense, with its contractual duties to the third party, but this was not a disqualifying conflict of duty and duty. In line with the label 'conflict of *interests*', we might say this was simply a conflict of *duties*. It must be resolved, but it does not raise the same problems of unknown effects on other-regarding judgement.

[59] Here I differ from Davis, who has a wide definition of 'interest' ((n. 31) 572) as '. . . any influence, loyalty, concern, emotion, or other feature of a situation tending to make P's judgment (in that situation) less reliable than it would normally be (without rendering P incompetent)'. Since this definition includes a loyalty to another, 'conflict of interest' subsumes what the law traditionally calls 'conflict of duty and duty'. Similarly wide is the definition of 'actual conflict of interest' in the McGill *Regulation on Conflict of Interest* (n. 2) para. 1.2(i).

judgement, using that word in its normal sense of something that is of value to the person in question.[60] Self-interest, of course, may be pecuniary or non-pecuniary; my interests include the welfare of those who are important to me. Preserving conflict of duty and duty as a separate category allows us to label correctly a serious problem that may arise in relation to duty-bound exercises of judgement even where the one exercising judgement cannot be said to have any relevant self-interest in play. The problem is that the person is bound to act in the interests of persons whose interests diverge. It is thus a different problem from a conflict of self-interest and duty, and deserves its own label.

Distinguishing conflicts of interest from conflicts of duty and duty does not exclude the possibility that both may be present in a single case or that a single case may be hard to classify. Take the case of a trustee selling trust property, and the potential buyer is his cousin. If we consider this a problem, is it because the trustee's cousin is dear to him, so the trustee has a self-interest in favouring the cousin? Or because the trustee may feel duty-bound towards the cousin, albeit not by a legal duty (just as interests do not have to be legally protected interests to create conflicts of interest)? The answer might depend on the trustee, but if either or both is present, there is a potential problem.

The concern about labelling leads us to the question of bias. Take this case: a mechanic is criminally accused of defrauding customers of his garage by telling them their cars needed unnecessary work. A person who will potentially decide the case – the judge or one of the jurors (it does not matter) – has had a series of bad experiences with mechanics and thinks many of them are corrupt. Let us assume that we can agree that this person should not be involved in the case; the question is, how do we label the problem? Would we say they are in a conflict of interest? In my view, we should not; rather, this person has a bias against a class of people of which the accused is a member.[61] We will return to bias below.

In summary, a conflict of interest (conflict of self-interest and duty) does not arise unless there is a self-interest that may exert an improper effect on the exercise of duty-bound judgement. A conflict of duty and duty arises where duty-bound judgement may be improperly affected by the presence of a duty owed by the one exercising judgement to some other person.

[60] *Property Law Dictionary* (n. 22), s.v. 'interest[2]': 'That which is of import or benefit to a person, to a group or to society in general.'

[61] Davis's wide definition of interest (n. 59) would lead him to call this a conflict of interest. He distinguishes it from bias in this way (n. 31, 573): 'Bias (in a person) is a deflection of judgment in a definite direction. … Conflict of interest is not bias but a tendency toward bias.' The distinction is between knowing that the decision maker will be affected and knowing only that they might be. In law, we tend to draw a distinction between actual bias and appearance of bias, both of which may disqualify. Thus (and we will return to this below, Section 5) the lawyer's category of apparent bias is for Davis not bias but conflict of interest. Davis also says: 'Bias, whether conscious or unconscious, is relatively easy to correct for. For example, we can discount for the bias (e.g., "take his opinion with a grain of salt").' This may show that he is here only considering the context of relatively informal advisers; bias is more difficult in the context of decision makers or those giving formal views about, for example, a candidate for a prize or promotion. In such cases, it is not possible simply to correct mathematically for bias; the person must be disqualified or not from the role.

D Apparent Conflict

In the formulation of both legal and non-legal rules about conflicts, a concern is often expressed about apparent conflicts of interest. In some contexts, apparent conflicts are treated as seriously as real ones. The Parker Commission, which was charged with the application of a non-legal code of conduct for ministers of the Crown, had to decide whether the relevant minister was in a 'real or apparent' conflict of interest. The commission arrived at the following definition, in addition to the definition of 'real conflict of interest' that was set out above: 'An apparent conflict of interest exists when there is a reasonable apprehension, which reasonably well-informed persons could properly have, that a conflict of interest exists.'[62] Similarly, the policy at McGill University has a definition of 'conflict of interest' that is in two parts, actual and apparent; they are treated as two species of a genus.[63]

Now contrast this with what Davis says: 'Apparent conflicts of interest (strictly so-called) are no more conflicts of interest than counterfeit money is money.'[64] This is because 'a conflict of interest is (merely) *apparent* if, and only if, P does not have the conflict of interest (actual or potential) but someone other than P would be justified in concluding (however tentatively) that P does'.[65] Davis suggests that the phrase 'apparent conflict of interest' is often used to describe (actual) conflicts of interest, 'out of politeness or timidity'. He is probably right. The reason this may be thought to be necessary is that people may assume that saying that a person is in a conflict of interest impugns that person's integrity, in a way that does not arise by saying they are in an apparent conflict. I have suggested above that saying that someone is in an actual conflict does not necessarily impugn their integrity. But if Davis is right, it may be that when some people use the phrase 'apparent conflict', they really mean to refer to a situation that is, simply, a conflict.

As we saw above (in Section 3.A), the conflict rules themselves exist to protect against misuse of power, but they operate without regard to whether an actual misuse of power is proven. In this sense, one might say (although I would not) that they are about appearances rather than reality.[66] And we also saw (in Section 2) that some people might use the phrase '(actual) conflict of interest' to mean 'actual misuse of power'; on that terminology, 'apparent conflict of interest' has to do the work of '(actual) conflict of interest'.

The two definitions of apparent conflicts set out above, however, do not conflate actual and apparent conflicts in that way. On the contrary, they carefully define apparent conflicts as situations that can arise when the definition of actual conflict is not satisfied. Davis goes on to say that apparent conflicts, while not conflicts on his

62 Parker Commission (n. 39) 35.

63 McGill, *Regulation on Conflict of Interest* (n. 2) para. 1.2.

64 Davis (n. 31) 576.

65 Michael Davis, 'Introduction' in Michael Davis and Andrew Stark (eds.), *Conflict of Interest in the Professions* (Oxford University Press 2001) 3, 18.

66 The reason I would not say this is that the unknowable effect of the conflict on the exercise of judgement is a proven reality, of which judges and others who have formulated the relevant norms have been well aware; see n. 38 and the experimental evidence cited by Valsan, 'Fiduciary Duties, Conflict of Interest, and Proper Exercise of Judgment' (n. 31) 28–33.

terminology, are problematical: they mislead people about their security and create unnecessary anxiety.[67] This can be resolved without necessarily using the tools that are suited to managing conflicts; if the conflict is *only* apparent, then it is not real, and providing the right information will show it to be non-existent. Thus if a trustee called Amartya Butler proposed to sell trust property to a company called the Amartya Butler Co., this certainly looks like a conflict of interest. If it turns out that there is absolutely no connection between the trustee and the company except a coincidental name, then the apparent conflict is revealed to be no conflict at all.

To this point, it seems that Davis is correct, and it would be a serious mistake to treat apparent conflicts in the same way as actual conflicts. Disclosure of relevant information may be crucial in an apparent conflict, but disqualification is not appropriate.

Another hypothesis is that when people use the phrase 'apparent conflict of interest', what they mean is a 'potential conflict of interest'.

E Potential Conflict

This is an important part of the story. A conflict as I have defined it is a situation that relates to the exercise of duty-bound judgement. But the relationship between the conflict and the exercise can be near or far. Assume as Case One the case of a trustee who is proposing to sell an estate in land, which is trust property, to a property development corporation, Greenacre Ltd, in which the trustee has a financial interest but over which she does not have control. This trustee is in a conflict of interest, and if the sale is made, it will be voidable (unless there is fully informed consent from all beneficiaries). Now rewind the tape a little bit and consider Case Two. The trustee calls for written offers, receives ten and on opening them finds that there is an offer from Greenacre Ltd. Is this a conflict of interest? The conflict in this scenario is a little more remote from the duty-bound exercise of judgement. Many offers are on the table, only one of which is potentially problematic. There is time to manage the conflict, by full disclosure, and possibly resignation or recusal.[68] Now rewind the tape even more to Case Three. The trustee is considering selling the estate in land, but has not yet decided whether to do so. She knows that if she decides to sell the estate, Greenacre Ltd may well wish to make an offer. Is this a conflict of interest? I would say not. But it might be called a potential conflict. Here is Davis again:

> A conflict of interest is potential if and only if P has a conflict of interest with respect to a certain judgment but is not yet in a situation in which he must make that judgment. Potential conflicts of interest, like time bombs, may or may not go off. A conflict of interest is actual if and only if P has a conflict of interest with respect to a certain judgment and is in a situation in which he must make that judgment.[69]

[67] Davis (n. 65) 18.

[68] Simply disqualifying Greenacre Ltd might remove the conflict but is not necessarily in the best interests of the beneficiaries, since Greenacre Ltd might be willing to pay the highest price.

[69] Davis (n. 31) 575.

Here is what the Parker Commission said: 'Potential conflict is the situation that arises between the moment the public office holder realizes that he or she has a private economic interest in some matter at hand and the moment the public office holder exercises a public duty or responsibility and places himself or herself in a position of real conflict of interest.'[70] One reading of both Davis and the Parker Commission is that both of them would classify Case Two as only a potential conflict of interest. But a potential conflict may well require management; in private fiduciary law, for example, it may activate a duty of disclosure. Case Two, as I suggested above, arguably requires not only disclosure but recusal or resignation, unless the beneficiaries give fully informed consent.

It is, I think, a matter of judgement where the line falls between potential and actual conflicts of interest. One reason is that the decision maker himself may be the one who decides when to exercise the relevant duty-bound judgement. The decision maker who puts off the decision may think that the conflict remains potential, but if the decision to put it off is itself an exercise of duty-bound judgement, the conflict has already become actual. But if I am correct that even potential conflicts may need to be disclosed, the question of where the line falls is less important.

F Conflict and De Minimis

If a judge has a financial interest in one of the litigants, this has been said to be an automatic ground for disqualification, for obvious reasons.[71] It is a conflict of interest within the definition given above (although in the law, it is called 'apparent bias', to which we will return[72]). But what if the judge has a small investment in a mutual fund, in which the investments are chosen by a financial manager, and the fund holds shares in one of the litigants, with the result is that the value of the judge's financial interest in that litigant is $4?[73] A trustee selling trust property to his wife would be said to be in a conflict of interest; what if he was selling trust property to his second cousin once removed, whom he had never met?[74]

Since the concern about conflict is with the risk of improper influence on judgement, rather than actual misuse of authority, conflict is a matter of degree; and since it is a matter of degree, it seems that there must be room for a de minimis limit.[75] This consideration may also be relevant to preventing the *misuse* of conflict rules in order

[70] Parker Commission (n. 39) 29.

[71] *Pinochet* (n. 50) 132–3.

[72] Section 5.

[73] Valsan, 'The No-Conflict Fiduciary Rule and the Rule against Bias in Judicial Review' (n. 38) 26, notes that English law has, since *Pinochet*, adopted a de minimis rule for financial interests of judges, in *Locabail (UK) Ltd* v. *Bayfield Properties Ltd* [2000] QB 451 (CA) [8][10].

[74] To take another example: in the film *The Empire Strikes Back* (1980), Darth Vader famously tells Luke Skywalker: 'I am your father.' In the satire *Spaceballs* (1987), Dark Helmet tells Lone Star: 'I am your father's brother's nephew's cousin's former roommate.'

[75] Michael Davis indicated to me that on his terminology, an interest that does not reach the de minimis threshold is not a 'special' interest and so not problematical (see n. 40).

to disqualify people whom one wishes to disqualify.[76] By analogy to the law of bias, the kind of test we might use to decide whether there is a genuine problem would be to ask whether a reasonable and informed observer would have a concern.[77]

4 Profit

It is perhaps universally the case that a person who should not exercise duty-bound judgement while in a conflict is not permitted to extract unauthorized profits from their other-regarding role. This leads to a frequent error: that an unauthorized profit *is* a kind of conflict of interest. The Parker Commission cited an earlier report into conflicts of interest in public life:

> Private and public interests need not be in competition or conflict for an ethical problem to exist; the public interest could be abused equally where the private interests of the office holder coincide with the public interest so as to mesh together, with the result that in serving the public purpose the individual benefits privately as well. ... Conflict of interest can in some cases mean compatibility of interest.[78]

I agree with the opening of this, but the final sentence is nonsense. In order to have a conflict of interest, there must be some conflict of interest. The same conflation of unauthorized profit with conflict of interest happens constantly in private law.

One consequence of having a careful definition of the rules against conflicts is that it becomes obvious that the rules about conflicts are distinct from the rule against unauthorized profits, which applies to private law fiduciaries and in public law as well.[79] Very often conflicts go with profits: if a trustee sells trust property to a company in which he has a financial interest, he is in a conflict, and he may well derive a personal profit. But it is clear that there can be a conflict of interest without profit, as I have defined conflict of interest; and a conflict produces its legal effects without any need to show that any profit was extracted.[80] Conversely, it is perfectly possible to acquire an unauthorized profit without being in a conflict as I have defined conflict; in particular, because I have defined it by linking the definition of conflict to the exercise of powers. In the foundational case of *Keech* v. *Sandford*,[81] a trustee held a

[76] Which may be a phenomenon in some contexts (e.g. 'Trump Lashes Out at Mueller for Alleged Conflicts of Interest', n. 1).

[77] *Yukon Francophone School Board, Education Area #23* v. *Yukon (Attorney General)* [2015] 2 SCR 282, 2015 SCC 25. This is one reading of why the McGill *Regulation on Conflict of Interest* (n. 2), even in its definition of *actual* conflict, refers to whether the interest is sufficient to call into question the exercise of judgement 'in the opinion of a reasonably informed and well advised Person'.

[78] Parker Commission (n. 39) 26, citing Michael Starr and Mitchell Sharp, *Ethical Conduct in the Public Sector: Report of the Task Force on Conflict of Interest* (Minister of Supply and Services 1984) 29.

[79] For public law examples see *Bowes* v. *Toronto (City)* (1858) 11 Moo PC 463, 14 ER 770; *Reading* v. *Attorney-General* [1951] AC 507 (HL); *Attorney-General for Hong Kong* v. *Reid* [1994] 1 AC 324 (PC); Conflict of Interest Act (n. 17), s. 11; UK Ministerial Code (n. 47) para. 7.22.

[80] A contract created through the use of a fiduciary power in a conflict situation can generally be set aside without any inquiry into its fairness (see Finn (n. 8) [403], [518]); thus, regardless of whether the fiduciary profited.

[81] *Keech* v. *Sandford* (1726) Sel. Cas. T. King 61, 25 ER 223, 2 Eq. Cas. Abr. 741, 22 ER 629 (L.K.). See Joshua Getzler, 'Rumford Market and the Genesis of Fiduciary Obligations' in Andrew Burrows and Lord Rodger

lease in trust and on the expiry of the lease was unable to obtain a renewal as trustee. He took the renewal for himself and made a profit. Note that this means he did not use his fiduciary powers in a conflict of interest. There was no legal act to be set aside.[82] There was no wish to set aside the lease, since it was the source of his profit. There is no reason to analyse this case in terms of conflict of interest. It is only necessary to say that the profit was acquired through acting in the fiduciary role.

This is how many courts have formulated the rule: that a fiduciary is obliged to surrender a profit if it was acquired through acting in the fiduciary role.[83] It is important to observe that this formulation makes no reference to conflicts. It does not even describe the rule as operating through the breach of a duty.[84] This is because it creates a primary right in the beneficiary.[85] The foundation of the rule against unauthorized profits is *not* directly to protect duty-bound exercises of judgement. It is simply that you are acting for and on behalf of another. When you are acting for and on behalf of another, if you properly incur expenses, you can generally pass them on to that other. That right of reimbursement, of course, does not arise because of any wrongdoing. Conversely, if you acquire profits, you must also pass them on to that other. If you acquire relevant or valuable information, you must again pass it on, which creates duties of disclosure.[86]

An even clearer example of unauthorized profit without conflict is in the leading case of *Regal (Hastings) Ltd* v. *Gulliver*.[87] The defendant directors embarked on a kind of joint venture with the beneficiary, the company of which they were directors. They invested their own money in the new subsidiary company that their company invested in. Their interests were *aligned* with the interests of their company.[88] The

of Earlsferry (eds.), *Mapping the Law: Essays in Memory of Peter Birks* (Oxford University Press 2006) 577, contextualizing *Keech* as part of the development of the rule against unauthorized profits in multiple other-regarding contexts.

[82] Of course we might wonder whether he tried hard enough to get a renewal as trustee; he might be charged with an *omission* made in a conflict of interest, something that as a matter of logic cannot be set aside. The point of the case, however, is that we do not have to speculate. He was liable to account for the profit regardless of how hard he tried to get it for the beneficiary, which makes the conflict-of-interest analysis quite superfluous.

[83] *Furs Ltd* (n. 38) 598; *Regal (Hastings) Ltd* v. *Gulliver* (1942) [1967] 2 AC 134 (HL) 139, 145, 153, 159, 156; *Chan* (n. 35) 198; *Warman International Ltd* (n. 35) 557; *O'Donnell* v. *Shanahan* [2009] EWCA Civ 751 [52]; *Howard* (n. 35) [37], [62]–[63]. None of these formulations refers to conflict of interest.

[84] In *Regal (Hastings)*, ibid., 153, Lord Macmillan said that the issue was not '. . . whether they had acted in breach of their duty. They were not said to have done anything wrong.' Lord Porter said (159): 'Their liability in this respect does not depend upon breach of duty.'

[85] Smith, 'Prescriptive Fiduciary Duties' (n. 43) section VI.F.

[86] The English Court of Appeal linked the no-profit rule to the duty to disclose in *O'Donnell* (n. 83) [55].

[87] *Regal (Hastings) Ltd.*

[88] See Eilís Ferran, *Company Law and Corporate Finance* (Oxford University Press 1999), 190: '*Regal* is the apotheosis of the application of a strict no-profit rule which is not dependent on a conflict requirement or which treats any possibility of conflict as sufficient (in cases of profiting from position this comes to much the same thing as an independent no-profit rule since there is always a possibility of some conflict of interest in a situation where a director has acted for personal rather than corporate benefit).' Her reference to the wide idea of 'any possibility conflict' is to a conflict of *interests* (see text at n. 31), which is always present, not a conflict of interest as I have defined it. In his discussion of the case, Richard Nolan seems to agree that the case was decided, and rightly so, by an application of the rule against profits: Richard Nolan, '*Regal (Hastings) Ltd v Gulliver*' in Charles Mitchell and Paul Mitchell (eds.), *Landmark*

speeches formulate the rule about unauthorized profits without invoking conflicts.[89] The House of Lords did a better job here than in *Boardman* v. *Phipps*,[90] where the facts were quite similar inasmuch as the interests of the defendant fiduciaries were aligned with those of their beneficiaries; they all held profit-making shares in the same company. The two dissenters convinced themselves that there could be no remedy without a conflict.[91] The three majority judges correctly realized that this was not true under the law laid down in *Keech* and *Regal (Hastings)*. Lord Guest did not even mention conflicts, holding that the only question was whether the profit had been acquired from the fiduciary role.[92] There was no need even to look for a conflict in *Boardman*.[93]

Another situation in which there is unauthorized profit without conflict is where the fiduciary turns to profit some information acquired from the fiduciary role, but does so only after having resigned.[94] Since the person no longer has fiduciary powers, they cannot be in a conflict, but they must account for the profit even if the original acquisition of the relevant information was perfectly lawful.

This shows the wisdom of articulating two separate rules. They have overlapping rationales: both arise out of the fiduciary relationship, being a relationship in which one acts for and on behalf of another.[95] But the conflicts rules are about how

Cases in Equity (Hart 2012) 499, 519–20, 521. He goes on, however, to argue that the rules about conflicts are more 'central' and that there were 'significant' conflicts in the case itself. He does not offer a definition, but must be understood to be thinking of conflicts of interests.

89 n. 83. Lord Wright mentioned conflicts (154) but seemingly in obiter and only to dismiss an argument that the profits could be retained.

90 *Boardman* v. *Phipps* [1967] 2 AC 46 (HL).

91 Viscount Dilhorne (88–9) and Lord Upjohn, who expressed the view (123) that the rule about unauthorized profits is 'part of the wider rule' about conflicts.

92 Lords Cohen and Hodson both made it clear that the rules on conflicts were not necessary to decide the case, although they went on to discuss them. As mentioned at the beginning of this section, those who deny that the rules are distinct (such as Lord Upjohn, ibid.; see also Conaglen, *Fiduciary Loyalty* (n. 9) 120–5, tentatively expressing the same view) must think that every unauthorized profit reveals a conflict (since it is clear that there can be a conflict without profit (n. 80)). But as Ferran (n. 88) shows, the only definition of 'conflict' that could cover every case of unauthorized profit would be a definition of a conflict of *interests*, which is too wide as a workable definition for conflicts of interest (see text at n. 31).

93 Michael Bryan, '*Boardman v Phipps*' in Charles Mitchell and Paul Mitchell (eds.), *Landmark Cases in Equity* (Hart 2012) 581, 589–92, noting (589) that it was not even part of the plaintiffs' pleaded case.

94 *Industrial Development Consultants Ltd* v. *Cooley* [1972] 1 WLR 443; *Canadian Aero Services Ltd* v. *O'Malley* [1974] SCR 592.

95 This also shows why courts and commentators have had difficulty articulating the limits of the doctrine of 'corporate opportunities': the reason is that more than one principle is at play (Smith, 'Fiduciary Relationships' (n. 41) 629 n. 90). The fiduciary norm against unauthorized profits is triggered when rights or information are acquired through the fiduciary role; conversely, it does not matter, as the leading cases show, whether the beneficiary would or even could have enjoyed the right if the fiduciary had not acquired it (which is why it extends, for example, to corrupt bribes). Some corporate fiduciaries are subject to a different rule that is both wider and narrower (e.g. *Bhullar* v. *Bhullar* [2003] EWCA Civ 424, [2003] 2 BCLC 241). It is wider because it extends even to information and rights that were acquired *independently* from the fiduciary role. It is narrower because it *does* matter here whether the opportunity was in the 'line of business' of the beneficiary (these fiduciaries are not simply required to hand over everything of value that they come across). The key to this puzzle is that the fiduciaries subject to this second principle are not only fiduciaries; they are also subject to wide-ranging non-fiduciary duties to confer benefits on the beneficiary. Typically, and unlike many fiduciaries, including non-executive

other-regarding powers are properly exercised, while the rule about profits is simply a direct application of the role in which one acts. The rules have different rationales and generate different remedies.

In a similar way, when a loss is caused by non-disclosure of a conflict, the plaintiff's recovery is for breach of the duty of disclosure.[96] The conflict is part of the plaintiff's case because it gave rise to the duty of disclosure, but the claim is not founded on simply *being in* a conflict.[97] It is an analytical mistake to try to make the rules on conflicts do everything.

A profit that has been acquired in an other-regarding role, although it is not itself a conflict of interest, may *create* a conflict, or a potential conflict. Take the case of a fiduciary who accepts a gift from someone who wants the fiduciary to exercise his powers in a certain way. If the fiduciary agrees so to exercise them, then such an exercise of power is a misuse of power. Even without any agreement, gifts require reciprocation as a matter of social practice.[98] Thus, on a later occasion on which duty-bound judgement must be exercised, there may be a conflict if the decision maker feels indebted to the giver.[99] Regardless of what happens later, however, the rule against unauthorized profits, where it applies, requires such profits to be surrendered at the moment they are received, without any need for a finding of conflict or potential conflict.

5 Bias

In law, bias is a term that is used especially in relation to public law decision makers, such as judges and administrative decision makers. They should not be biased because they are supposed to be impartial.

One kind of bias arises from not coming to the question with an open mind. To a greater or lesser extent, actually or potentially, the decision maker has prejudged the case before hearing it. A 'prejudice' literally means a judgement made in advance. My example of the decision maker who is suspicious towards all mechanics is an example of potential bias of this kind.[100] The problem here is not created by an interest or a duty. It is created by a characteristic, which might be considered a weakness since the prejudice is unjustifiable. It can be positive or negative: a person who thinks all aristocrats are superior persons should not sit in judgement if one is charged with a

directors, they are the most senior kind of employee (who may be called officers or managing directors or executive directors in different places). They are full-time employees whose (contractual) job description precludes them from competing with the corporation and instead requires them to steer towards it any business opportunities in the corporation's line of business.

96 See the cases in n. 51.

97 It is important to note also that in these cases, simply being in a conflict is not typically a but-for cause of the plaintiff's loss, while failure to disclose the conflict may well be: Smith, 'Prescriptive Fiduciary Duties' (n. 43) Section VI.E.

98 Jacques Godbout and Alain Caillé, *The World of the Gift*, trans. D. Winkler (McGill-Queen's University Press 1998).

99 See Nicholas Bakalar, 'The More Lavish the Gifts to Doctors, the Costlier the Drugs They Prescribe', *New York Times*, 25 October 2017, www.nytimes.com/2017/10/25/well/live/the-more-lavish-the-gifts-to-doctors-the-costlier-the-drugs-they-prescribe.html.

100 Text at the end of Section 3.C. As Michael Davis suggested to me, if the decision maker actually thought all mechanics were dishonest wrongdoers, this would be actual prejudice.

crime. Like a conflict of interest, it has the potential to affect the proper exercise of the decision maker's judgement. Even a decision maker who tries in good faith can never be sure whether the effect of the prejudice has been excluded (or indeed whether he has overcompensated for it).

As late as the early nineteenth century, it was considered acceptable in English law for a judge to be part of a panel hearing an appeal from that judge's own decision.[101] Today's law is much stricter. The Privy Council has said this kind of previous involvement leads to disqualification for the 'appearance of bias as a result of pre-determination or pre-judgment'.[102]

Most problems of bias are not like this, but rather arise because the decision maker is not fully independent from one of the parties to a dispute, or from the person or persons in relation to whom he has to make a decision. And this problem *is* potentially created by an interest or a duty. If a judge is financially interested in one of the litigants, he is automatically disqualified for apparent bias.[103] This is exactly analogous to the disqualification of a private law fiduciary for conflict of self-interest and duty.[104] If a judge has non-financial but genuine affiliations with one of the litigants, the same result may follow.[105] This is analogous to the example mentioned above of a trustee proposing to sell trust property to his relative.[106] There is no financial interest, and as with that example, we may be unsure whether to say that our concern is with self-interest or duty; but there is a problem. Partiality can be negative, as in the case where prior interactions have created enmity between a decision maker and a person in relation to whom the decision must be made.[107]

101 For examples in Chancery, see James R. Atkin, 'Appeal in English Law' (1927) 3 *Cambridge LJ* 1, 4; in the common law courts, see Lionel Smith, 'Tracing in Taylor v. Plumer: Equity in the Court of King's Bench' [1995] *LMCLQ* 240, 12–13, 15.

102 *R.* v. *Stubbs* [2018] UKPC 30, [2018] 1 WLR 4887. In this case, Isaacs J presided over the second trial of the three accused persons; during the proceedings, he made certain interim rulings against them. The second trial was abandoned without a verdict and before Isaacs J completed his summing up to the jury. The accused were convicted on their third trial before another judge, and they appealed. The appeal was heard seven years after the end of the second trial, and the question was whether Isaacs JA (as he now was) could be a member of the panel. The Judicial Committee of the Privy Council held that he was disqualified by apparent bias. Although I classify this type of bias as prejudgement and not as conflict of interest, it is arguable that there is an element of conflict of interest, since we could say that a judge who has given judgment has a self-interest in being correct and not incorrect in law.

103 *Pinochet* (n. 50) 132–3, subject to a de minimis threshold (n. 73).

104 We do not generally call it bias in fiduciary law, because the fiduciary is not in a role where he needs to be neutral in a dispute or towards someone in relation to whom a decision is being made. The problem is similar, however, being an actual or potential interference with other-regarding judgement. See Conaglen, 'Public–Private Intersection' (n. 38); Valsan, 'The No-Conflict Fiduciary Rule and the Rule against Bias in Judicial Review' (n. 38), giving (at 32) some examples of the language of bias in fiduciary law. In *York Buildings Co.* (n. 53) 63, 446, explaining why an agent to sell property could not buy it himself, counsel said, '[t]he ground on which the disability or disqualification rests, is no other than that principle which dictates that a person cannot be both judge and party'.

105 *Pinochet* (n. 50).

106 Section 3.C.

107 This is the allegation levelled by Donald Trump against Robert Mueller ('Trump Lashes Out at Mueller for Alleged Conflicts of Interest', n. 1). Compare the film *Footnote* (2012; original Hebrew title: *הערת שוליים*), in which an academic serves on a prize committee over a period of years in part to be able to thwart his enemy's aspiration to win the prize.

Bias (of either kind) can be actual or apparent, in the sense that it can be known to have affected the decision maker's judgement, or only seen as potentially affecting it. It seems that bias is not identical to conflict, because some types of bias (such as what I have called prejudice) do not arise out of conflicts. But as mentioned in the previous paragraph, what the law calls 'apparent bias', where it arises from a connection to one of the parties, corresponds to an (actual) conflict of interest. In the law of bias, 'apparent' does not mean that it disappears when you look more closely; it only means the decision maker has not been proven to have been partial in making the decision. Rather, some facts have been established that make it a realistic possibility that that the decision maker was partial. Proof after the fact of 'actual' bias is proof of not having been neutral, which corresponds not to conflict but to (actual) misuse of power.[108]

Since bias is similar to conflicts of interest and conflicts of duty in raising concerns about improper influences on judgement, it is not surprising that bias also needs a de minimis filter, such as asking whether a reasonable and informed observer would have a concern.[109]

6 Conclusion

In 2004, a motion was brought in the Supreme Court of the United States, asking Scalia J to recuse himself from a case to which Vice President Dick Cheney was a party in his official capacity. They were old friends, and Scalia J had gone hunting with Cheney while the case was pending, flying to the lodge in Cheney's government aircraft. Scalia J denied the motion.[110] The opening of his judgment is taken up by statements that during the hunting trip, he and Cheney were not alone together and so could not have discussed the case.[111] Later he mentions that even though he and his son and son-in-law flew to the lodge on Air Force Two, it did not save them any money because they had to buy round-trip tickets anyway to get home, and that the inclusion of his relatives was not a favour to Scalia but to his relatives.[112] As he concluded, he said: 'If it is reasonable to think that a Supreme Court Justice can be bought so cheap, the Nation is in deeper trouble than I had imagined.'[113] To me, what this shows is that even a justice of the Supreme Court of the United States failed to understand the distinctions I have drawn. An allegation of conflict is not an allegation of corruption, and for a judge to treat it so is indefensible, because the implication is

108 Valsan, 'The No-Conflict Fiduciary Rule and the Rule against Bias in Judicial Review' (n. 38) 25.

109 *Yukon Francophone School Board, Education Area #23* (n. 77).

110 *Cheney* v. *United States District Court for the District of Columbia* 541 US 913 (2004). It has been said that the principle that one may not be judge in one's own cause is 'the first and most fundamental principle of natural justice': *Report of the Committee on Ministers' Powers* (1932) Cmd 4060, 76. It is curious that the practice of the Supreme Court of the United States on a motion for recusal is that the motion is decided by the judge in question, with no possibility of appeal. For an attempt to defend this, see Chief Justice John G. Roberts Jr, '2011 Year-End Report on the Federal Judiciary', www.supremecourt.gov/publicinfo/year-end/2011year-endreport.pdf, 7–10.

111 Ibid., 913–15.

112 Ibid., 920–1.

113 Ibid., 929.

that if there is no corruption, there can be no conflict.[114] This is a failure, deliberate or not, to take seriously the concerns that we rightly have with conflicts of interest.[115] Conversely, strict rules about conflicts may be used strategically to remove unwanted decision makers. This is itself a potential misuse of authority, depending on how and by whom the decision to remove is made.

Actual misuse of power is different from conflict of interest, including the kind of bias that arises from conflict of interest. Conflict of interest and duty is different, in an important way, from conflict of duty and duty. Some bias is not about conflict, while some is. And all of these are different from unauthorized benefits. It is time to stop calling all of them 'conflicts of interest'.

Perhaps more importantly, it is a mistake to think that pointing out a conflict (actual or potential) is an assault on integrity. Properly understood, the rules on conflicts are not about corruption, temptation or weakness. They exist because processes of reasoning are inscrutable, and the human mind can be affected in ways of which it cannot be aware.

Some people trust their politicians, their judges, their police officers, their trustees, their agents and their lawyers. Others may not. The norms discussed in this chapter aim to require that those who hold other-regarding powers conduct themselves in a way that is consonant with their position and role. Paradoxically, this kind of normative framework, if it is seen to be effective and enforceable, may help to cultivate trust and confidence that they will indeed do so.

[114] In *Pinochet* (n. 50), Lord Hoffman was held to be disqualified after participating in the judgment, on the grounds of apparent bias because of non-financial connections with a party in the case. He is reported by the BBC to have said, '[t]he fact is I'm not biased'. http://news.bbc.Couk/2/hi/uk_news/235456.stm. He too missed the point.

[115] See Don A. Moore, Lloyd Tanlu and Max H Bazerman, 'Conflict of Interest and the Intrusion of Bias' (2010) 5 *Judgment and Decision Making* 37, 47. This is one of the experimental sources cited by Valsan, 'Fiduciary Duties, Conflict of Interest, and Proper Exercise of Judgment' (n. 31) 27. The authors, who are psychologists, invoke the story about Scalia J to underline that even judges do not always understand the undetectable effects of conflict of interest on human reasoning. For an important empirical study based on the behaviour of elected judges in relation to litigants who contributed to the judges' election campaigns, see Vernon V. Palmer, 'The Recusal of American Judges in the Post-*Caperton* Era: An Empirical Assessment of the Risk of Actual Bias in Decisions Involving Campaign Contributors' (2010), available at SSRN: https://ssrn.com/abstract=1721665.

PART III

Political Trust and Fiduciary Government

9

Trust and Authority

EVAN FOX-DECENT*

1 Introduction

In the days of politically effective monarchy in France and England, the succession of one monarch by another was sometimes proclaimed with the announcement 'The king is dead! Long live the king!' The point of this superficially contradictory claim was to signal that the sovereign powers of public authority were not interrupted by the death of one monarch and the succession of another, but rather flowed seamlessly from one sovereign to his or her successor. Implicit to this conception of succession is the idea that the monarch holds an office that both pre-exists and survives any particular monarch's occupation of it. Kings and queens come and go, but the sovereign's office, in principle, is immortal, and so can explain how sovereignty and law can persist seamlessly over time and across the transition from one governing regime to the next. More generally still, the idea of an office denotes a quality of *temporal* seamlessness, since in the ordinary case, the powers and features of an office persist through time independently of the person who occupies it at a given moment. This chapter asks whether law's *spatial* dimension – the conceptual and normative space law constructs within and across legal regimes and doctrines – is also in some sense seamless and pervaded by law, or whether, by contrast, this dimension is punctuated by legal gaps and voids within which law does not operate.

Consider, for example, the spaces established within the various kinds of limits law sets for its subjects and officials, and within which subjects and officials appear largely at liberty to do as they please. In private law, reciprocal limits on interaction are present in every field. Reciprocal limits frame the scope of our power to contract with one another, the permissible ways of acquiring and using property, the kinds of associations we can lawfully create and the powers they may have, and the forms that marriage can take as well as the duties it produces and the consequences on dissolution. Under criminal law, individuals are generally understood to enjoy equal liberty within capacious limits that permit them to do as they please so long as their actions do not injure or create a substantial risk of harm to others. Within administrative law, judges sometimes say that a tribunal with discretionary power is 'within its province ... a law unto itself'.[1] On this view of discretionary decision-making, the

* I am indebted for comments and discussion to the participants of the workshop Fiduciaries and Trust: Ethics, Politics, Economics and Law, held at the Melbourne Law School, 17–18 December 2018, and to Matthew Harding in particular.

1 *Roncarelli* v. *Duplessis* [1959] SCR 121, 167 (Cartwright J, citing *re Ashby et al.* [1934] OR 421, 428 (Masten JA)).

space within which discretion operates is a legal void, and therefore is considered a space wholly without the discipline of legal principles. Judges who take this position hold that administrative discretion, within legal limits, is exercised on the basis of 'policy and expediency' rather than law.[2]

In this chapter I challenge the legal void view of legal space. I argue that law operates within the spaces created by legal limits and frameworks. As a consequence, law can be understood to assert a spatial as well as temporal seamlessness. Well-ordered legal regimes can govern the interstitial spaces that exist within legal limits, I argue, through their possession and assertion of legitimate authority. Importantly, their spatially seamless possession of legitimate authority relies on a relationship of mutual trust between lawgiver and legal subject.

I develop the argument in several stages. Drawing on recent work on international law with Evan Criddle,[3] Section 2 sets out the distinction between a decision-making entity's authorization (i.e. the process that led to it having authority) and its authority per se (i.e. the nature and effects of its legal power). Section 3 builds on the authorization/authority distinction and introduces the idea of mutual trust through the writings of Thomas Hobbes.[4] Hobbes suggests that public authority may be understood to have arisen from an original covenant to which all subjects consent and by which the sovereign comes to enjoy the subjects' authorization. Yet once legal institutions are in place, Hobbes tends to use the language of trust to characterize the position of the sovereign and other public officials. And Hobbes thinks the very possibility of being a subject rather than a captive slave depends on the sovereign trusting the subject with liberty, thus making the trust relationship between sovereign and subject mutual. Section 4 sketches the conception of trust on which I rely. I then explain how mutual trust informs law's authority such that law can be understood to pervade the spaces it creates for the liberty of its subjects and officials.

2 Authorization and Authority

The concepts of authorization and authority are distinct but easily confused. Typically, authorities are created through a deliberate conferral of legal power (e.g. through a delegation of power, an agency contract or the creation of a trust). There is in these cases an intimate connection between the entity's authorization and its resulting authority. The authorization may stipulate the power's scope, its purpose, the identity of the power holder, the terms of the power holder's tenure, the identity of beneficiaries or parties amenable to the power's exercise, and the relative autonomy of the power holder's decision-making authority (e.g. must the power holder consult her

[2] *Roncarelli* (n. 1) 167 (Cartwright J).

[3] Evan J Criddle and Evan Fox-Decent, *Fiduciaries of Humanity: How International Law Constitutes Authority* (Oxford University Press 2016).

[4] Thomas Hobbes, *Leviathan* (first published 1651, Edwin Curley ed., Hackett 1994). Unless otherwise indicated, italics in subsequent references are from the original. Subsequent references to Hobbes are from *Leviathan* and are to chapter (or R&C for the 'Review and Conclusion'), paragraph and page number from the Hackett edition.

beneficiaries, and if so, do they have a veto?). Authorization may seem to exhaust the possible content of authority.

Consider the case of Minerva – an omniscient but officious god devoted to wisdom who is set on creating a university, Minerva University. Minerva uses a charter to create and delegate to the requisite institutions the legal powers necessary to establish and run Minerva University. Because Minerva is omniscient with respect to the future as well as the present, she can anticipate every possible decision the relevant authorities might ever face and need to make. And because she is an officious intermeddler, she dictates within the authorization charter every decision the university's institutions will be required to make. Even with an authorization as comprehensive and ministerial as this, we can still distinguish Minerva University's authorization from its authority.

There is significant normative content to authority that authorization cannot capture. This content consists in the legal system's power-conferring rules that provide for the legal validity and effect of official decisions taken by Minerva University's institutions. I have assumed that Minerva the god is omniscient but she is not omnipotent. She is not a law unto herself nor has, I stipulate, extraordinary legal powers. Like natural persons who must abide by the relevant power-conferring rules if they wish to form a valid contract or execute a valid will, Minerva must abide by the legal system's rules on delegation and public decision-making for her wishes to become legally effective. The law may limit the scope of delegated powers and determine the manner in which they may be exercised (e.g. impartially and reasonably). The law might also require procedures such as a hearing to ensure procedural fairness in cases involving disciplinary action or other matters suitable for adjudication. In sum, even with every last decision dictated in advance within Minerva University's authorization charter, it is nevertheless the law that both provides for and conditions the scope, validity and legal effect of delegated decisions. Put differently, Minerva is the source of Minerva University's authorization, but it is the law embodying and governing the power-conferring rules relevant to university charters that explains the nature of the legal authority enjoyed by Minerva University's decision makers.

The familiar parent–child relationship is also a helpful foil for illuminating the authorization/authority distinction. An inquiry into the source of a parent's legal authorization to be a parent, I suggest, is plainly different than an inquiry into the nature of parental authority.[5] Parents ordinarily gain legal authority over their children when they are born to them or through adoption. Usually, the state authorizes biological and adoptive parents to have exclusive custody of their children. The state's authorization carries responsibilities related to the children's health and welfare, and may be suspended or even terminated. But to understand the nature of a parent's authority over her children, we need to consider the legally salient features of the relationship between parents and children. Criddle and I have argued that those features include the child's legal incapacity and her status as a legal person.[6] Parental

[5] For discussion of this case and the trustee–beneficiary case in the context of the authorization/authority distinction, see Criddle and Fox-Decent (n. 3) 323.

[6] Ibid., 25.

authority must account for both of these features, and does so, we say, through its incorporation of a fiduciary obligation to exercise power over children in what the parent reasonably perceives as the child's best interest. We claim that the parent's fiduciary obligation and her discretionary power together constitute parental authority. But even if one rejects our account of parental authority, on any plausible conception the authority relation between parent and child is interpersonal, and so to understand it we must interrogate the nature of that interpersonal relationship. This inquiry is entirely separate from the question of how a parent comes to have legal authority over a child through a process of authorization.

As a final example of the authorization/authority distinction, compare the authorization process of international courts and tribunals to the authority they possess and assert.[7] Generally, states and international organizations create international courts through multilateral treaties. States do not transfer international adjudicative authority to these courts because they have no such authority to transfer. Instead, states bind themselves through treaty to submit to the jurisdiction and decisions of the relevant courts. This authorization process is made effective by the international power-conferring rule pacta sunt servanda, an international rule that makes treaties effective in a manner akin to the power-conferring rules of contract in national legal orders.

As in the parent–child case, however, to understand the authority of international courts, we need to understand their relationship to litigants and the wider public amenable to their jurisdiction. Crucially, courts supply a remedy to the threat of unilateralism inasmuch as the parties before them are subject to their public authority rather than the will of the other party. On the fiduciary view Criddle and I defend, international law authorizes international courts to resolve disputes within a legal framework that treats the parties as equals under the law. Courts in effect are trustees of this framework on behalf of all within their jurisdiction. The overarching duty of these courts is to exercise their adjudicative power in a manner consistent with their institution's constitutive principles. These principles include a duty of impartiality or even-handedness, a duty to respect the norms of due process or natural justice, and a duty to interpret and apply the law in a manner that is reasonable, taking into account all relevant factual considerations as well as all relevant legal norms, doctrines and jurisprudence.

The legal power of international courts to issue rulings of an authoritative nature, then, is not explained by the process of treaty making and authorization through which those courts come into existence. The mandate arising from this consensual process will usually specify a court's subject matter jurisdiction, the composition of its bench, the terms of its judges' tenure and the process under law through which they take office.[8] An international court's treaty mandate also typically includes

[7] Ibid., 320–31.

[8] One could imagine that there are two moments of authorization. The first occurs when the office is established. The second is when an individual is appointed to the office and thereby authorized to exercise its powers. Arguably there is a closer relation between the first moment of authorization and authority than there is between the second moment and authority. The first moment partially constitutes the office

specification of the territory and parties over whom it has jurisdiction. But the consent that underwrites the authorization process does not explain the constitutive and regulative dimensions of a court's authority. The constitutive aspect of an international court's authority consists in its standing and legal power as an independent and impartial adjudicator that is duty-bound to abide by the procedural and substantive requirements of its office. These procedural and substantive requirements, in turn, are the regulative aspect of an international court's authority; they govern the court's exercise of its legal power. When courts comply with the constitutive and regulative requirements of their office in the execution of their mandates, they exercise legitimate authority.

Notice that it makes no difference to the nature of judicial authority whether parties properly before a court consent to its authority or were required to do so to trigger jurisdiction, as is often the case in international law. Instead, judicial authority takes its constitution from the norms of impartial adjudication. And yet, there is arguably a moral precept that connects the judiciary to litigants and the wider public, a precept that we now look to Hobbes to help unearth: mutual trust.

3 Hobbes and Mutual Trust

Conventional readings of Hobbes make him an unlikely champion of the idea that sovereign power is in some sense held in trust for the people, much less a proponent of reciprocal or mutual trust.[9] Hobbes's orthodox interpreters construe him as an authoritarian who prized peace and order above all else. On their reading, Hobbes commandeered liberal ideas of liberty, equality, voluntarism and social contract to assemble a process of authorization that would result in a legally unlimited sovereign with absolute and undivided public power. The sovereign's subjects are deemed to agree on an original covenant that authorizes him to do whatever he believes is best for his people's welfare.[10] Moreover, it follows from Hobbes's account of authorization that subjects are to recognize themselves as the ultimate authors of all the sovereign's actions, and therefore they are barred from accusing the sovereign of causing them injury. As Hobbes puts it, 'he that complaineth of injury from his sovereign complaineth of that whereof he is the author, and therefore ought not to

by attributing a substantive mandate to it via authorization. The mandate implicitly limits the office holder's exercise of power simply by being a pubic mandate directed towards the public good, so the power cannot be used for private ends but rather must be used for the purpose for which it was conferred. Yet, as the examples discussed in the text reveal, the terms of a mandate alone cannot provide a complete account of an office's authority. Power-conferring rules are also necessary.

9 See, e.g., Norberto Bobbio, 'Hobbes Political Theory' in Norbert Bobbio (ed.), *Thomas Hobbes and the Natural Law Tradition* (University of Chicago Press 1993) 53 ('By holding that the sovereign power is irrevocable, Hobbes opposes the theory of trust'); Jean Hampton, *Hobbes and the Social Contract Tradition* (Cambridge University Press 1988) 124–6 (arguing against reading Hobbes as an agency theorist because sovereign power is irrevocable). Some of the material in this section is culled from Evan Fox-Decent, 'Hobbes Relational Theory: Beneath Power and Consent' in David Dyzenhaus and Thomas Poole (eds.) *Hobbes and the Law* (Cambridge University Press 2012).

10 For convenience and ease of exposition, I will generally follow Hobbes and refer to the sovereign as 'he', though Hobbes plainly thought the sovereign could be a woman or an assembly.

accuse any man but himself; no nor himself of injury, because to do injury to one's self is impossible'.[11] Thus, Quentin Skinner, a leading orthodox interpreter of Hobbes, concludes dourly that the original covenant 'is not a means of limiting the powers of the crown; properly understood, it shows that the powers of the crown have no limits at all'.[12] Skinner, however, is only able to draw this conclusion because he neglects to take account of the authorization/authority distinction in Hobbes, assuming wrongly that authorization exhausts the content of authority. Or so I shall argue.

Throughout *Leviathan*, Hobbes expressly insists that the sovereign has no authority to violate various principles – many of them legal principles – he calls laws of nature.[13] Hobbes's legal principles in particular are intended to guide the operation of legal institutions such as adjudication. They include the idea that judges must treat the parties who come before them equally, and that judges must not be party to nor have an interest in the cases they adjudicate. These principles are part of both the constitutive and regulative aspects of the judge's authority, since they regulate how the judge is to perform her task while also being partially constitutive of what it means to occupy the role of judge.[14] If a judge with a financial interest in the outcome of a case before her refused to recuse herself, we would be tempted to think she was corrupt. If in apparent good faith she defended her decision to stay on as judge in these circumstances, we would be tempted to conclude that she did not understand what the role of judge involved. Ordinarily, to remain as judge while conflicted would subvert the rationale for establishing a system of impartial adjudication, because by hypothesis our judge cannot claim to be impartial. Nowhere does Hobbes say that the sovereign or his judges are entitled to disregard or override the no-conflicts principle, suggesting that it is partially constitutive of legality. A judge who refuses to recuse herself in the face of a conflict subverts legality by depriving her office of the authority it could otherwise possess.[15] As we shall see now, however, a judge upholds her office's authority by recognizing that she occupies a privileged position of trust whose authority depends on her fidelity to legal principles partially constitutive of her office's authority.

[11] Hobbes (n. 4) ch. xviii, para. 6, 112–13.

[12] Quentin Skinner, 'Hobbes and the Purely Artificial Person of the State' in *Visions of Politics: Hobbes and Civil Science*, vol. 3 (Cambridge University Press 2002).

[13] Hobbes (n. 4) ch. xv, para. 38, 100; ch. xxii, para. 7, 147; ch. xxvi, para. 41, 188; ch. xxix, para. 9, 213.

[14] For extended treatment of the laws of nature and the way they are constitutive of law's authority in Hobbes, see David Dyzenhaus, 'Hobbes and the Legitimacy of Law' (2001) 20 *Law and Philosophy* 461; David Dyzenhaus, 'Hobbes' Constitutional Theory' in Thomas Hobbes, *Leviathan: Or The Matter, Forme, & Power of a Common-Wealth Ecclesiasticall and Civill* (first published in 1651, Ian Shapiro ed., Yale University Press 2010); David Dyzenhaus, 'Hobbes on the Authority of Law' in David Dyzenhaus and Thomas Poole (eds.), *Hobbes and the Law* (Cambridge University Press 2012).

[15] To the extent that offices are independent of their occupants, one might think that they always possess some measure authority, and that the corrupt judge simply abuses her office's authority, which nonetheless survives as part of the independent office. In my view, offices may be thought to have *potential* authority independent of their occupants, but for them to have *actual* authority requires *someone* to occupy them and have at their disposal the office's legal powers. Otherwise, the institution cannot exercise judgement or the powers necessary to perform its mandate. Moreover, in the standard case the office-holder's fidelity to her mission will be a necessary condition of her office actually possessing authority, since departures from fidelity denote a misuse or abuse of power.

When Hobbes posits equity as a law of nature, he describes the judge or arbitrator as one who is '*trusted to judge between man and man*'.[16] Having accepted this trust from the parties, the adjudicator must '*deal equally between them*', since without equal treatment, 'the controversies of men cannot be determined but by war'.[17] Similarly, Hobbes says that the arbitrator who distributes 'to every man his own' is someone who can be said to 'perform his trust'.[18] The arbitrator could not be said to 'perform his trust' unless he in fact held in trust, for the parties, the power of adjudication. Trust also surfaces in Hobbes's justification of the no-conflicts principle discussed above. If the judge or arbitrator would gain from one side's victory in the dispute, such a gain would be equivalent to a bribe, and therefore 'no man can be obliged to trust him'.[19] Hobbes implies that there is a good sense in which the office of the judge is constituted by the judge's trustworthiness in relation to his role: in order for the parties to be bound by the judge's decision, they cannot have reason to believe that the judge will decide their case on the basis of an interest he has in the outcome rather than on the merits. In other words, a person subject to judicial authority cannot be obligated to take the judge's decision as binding if the judge has a conflict: the conflict destroys the judge's authority to issue a valid and binding judgment. It is a jurisdictional validity condition of adjudication that the judge must exercise judgement without the infection of conflict.

Hobbes is equally explicit in his discussion of the relationship between the sovereign and his people. 'Monarchs or assemblies', Hobbes claims, are '*entrusted* with power enough for [their people's] protection'.[20] The office of the sovereign arises from the people's trust: 'The office of the sovereign . . . consisteth in the end, for which he was *trusted* with sovereign power, namely, the procuration of *the safety of the people*'.[21] Similarly, a monarch dealing with succession 'is obliged by the law of nature to provide, by establishing his successor, to keep those that had *trusted* him with the government from relapsing into the miserable condition of war'.[22] Hobbes elsewhere acknowledges that 'a sovereign monarch, or the greater part of a sovereign assembly, may ordain the doing of many things in pursuit of their passions, contrary to their own consciences', and qualifies this as 'a breach of trust, and of the law of nature'.[23] While Hobbes insists that such a 'breach of trust' would not justify rebellion, the sovereign could not be said to have committed a *breach* of trust unless he had violated a duty or requirement intrinsic to the constitution of public offices held in trust, which is to say, offices held for the benefit of his people.

It is not until his discussion of punishment of the innocent in chapter 28 of *Leviathan*,[24] however, that Hobbes arguably makes an explicit attempt to reconcile

[16] Hobbes (n. 4) ch. xv, para. 23, 97.
[17] Ibid.
[18] Ibid., ch. xv, para. 15, 95.
[19] Ibid., ch. xv, para. 32, 98.
[20] Ibid., ch. xx, para. 15, 132 (emphasis added).
[21] Ibid., ch. xxx, para. 1, 219 (emphasis added to '*trusted*').
[22] Ibid., ch. xix, para. 11, 123 (emphasis added).
[23] Ibid., ch. xxiv, para. 7, 162.
[24] Ibid., ch. xxviii, para. 22, 208.

the absolutist character of his theory of authorization with his highly juridical theory of authority. Hobbes claims that punishment of the innocent offends the laws of nature concerning 'revenges' (retribution should always look to a future good) and equity considered as 'an equal distribution of justice'.[25] More interestingly still, Hobbes says that punishing the innocent violates the law of nature that prohibits ingratitude. For Hobbes, the sovereign is the only entity entitled to exact punishment, and so the only entity to which the bar on punishing the innocent could apply. The implication is that the sovereign is not a party to the original covenant, but instead receives sovereignty as a gift from the people. The original covenant is the means through which the multitude jointly bind themselves to regard a certain person or assembly as sovereign, and likewise jointly agree to treat the sovereign's commands as binding. The sovereign, however, receives sovereignty as a gift.

Hobbes equates gift with grace, and spells out the relevant law of nature concerning ingratitude as the principle '*that a man which receiveth benefit from another of mere grace endeavour that he which giveth it have no reasonable cause to repent him of his good will*'.[26] Without gratitude appropriate to a gift received, 'there will be no beginning of benevolence or trust; nor, consequently, of mutual help, nor or reconciliation of one man to another; and therefore they are to remain still in the condition of war'.[27] That is, gratitude is necessary for social or civic trust to develop, which in turn helps us avoid the state of nature.[28] Ingratitude, Hobbes says, 'hath the same relation to grace that injustice hath to obligation by covenant'.[29] With the structure and nature of ingratitude in view, Hobbes can draw the lesson with respect to punishment of the innocent: 'For seeing all sovereign power is originally given by the consent of every one of the subjects, to the end they should, as long as they are obedient, be protected thereby, the punishment of the innocent is a rendering of evil for good'.[30] Were the sovereign to render 'evil for good' by punishing the innocent and breaching the prohibition on ingratitude, he would undermine the rationale of his authorization and the purpose of his authority, which are one and the same: the subject's well-being and protection.

More constructively, the gift model of sovereignty helps illuminate the structure of a trusteeship account of Hobbesian legal order. When subjects jointly make a gift of sovereignty to the sovereign, they do so by renouncing as much of their right of nature as possible, i.e. each individual renounces all alienable aspects of her liberty right to govern herself as she thinks best ensures her self-preservation.[31] Through this joint

[25] Ibid.
[26] Ibid., ch. xv, para. 16, 95.
[27] Ibid.
[28] For helpful discussion of civic or social horizontal trust between citizens that is characteristically interpersonal rather than impersonal, see Gerald J. Postema's contribution to this volume, 'Trust, Distrust and the Rule of Law'. Hobbes's view of the importance of social trust to civil peace tracks Postema's view (ibid.) that widespread civic trust (what he calls a climate of trust) is an indispensable background condition to maintaining legal order under a conception of the rule of law premised on mutual accountability.
[29] Hobbes (n. 4) ch. xv, para. 16, 95.
[30] Ibid.
[31] There are certain aspects of one's liberty right of nature that Hobbes thinks an individual cannot renounce, such as the right to resist violence: see ibid. ch. 21, paras. 11–15, 141–2.

renunciation, they thereby strengthen the appointed sovereign 'to use his [right of nature] as he should think fit, for the preservation of them all . . . and (excepting the limits set him by natural law) as entire as in the condition of mere nature'.[32] In summary, the gift of sovereign power is delivered by the people and received by the sovereign 'for the preservation of them all' – not for the sovereign's personal benefit – and subject to 'the limits set him' by the laws of nature.

Now, on Arash Abizadeh's interpretation, Hobbes is said to believe that 'it is the sovereign who owns the sovereign power.'[33] Thus the sovereign, Abizadeh claims, 'has the right to determine his own successor – indeed, the right to transfer sovereign power whenever and to whomever he wishes – precisely in virtue of his proprietary right in the sovereign power'.[34] One way to reconcile the sovereign's putative ownership of sovereignty with the condition that sovereignty is received as a gift 'for the preservation of them all' is to conceptualize sovereignty using the structure of the common law trust. That is, the sovereign owns bare legal title to sovereignty, but the equitable or beneficial title belongs to the people. On this interpretation, the sovereign holds sovereignty in trust for the people, notwithstanding the fact that as trustee he holds legal title to it irrevocably.

Hobbes's pervasive use of the language of trust is significant. If the sovereign really were legally unlimited and empowered to rule howsoever he pleased without compromise to legal order, one would not expect Hobbes to insist consistently that the sovereign is not entitled to violate the laws of nature. Given the constitutional crises of his day, it is surprising that Hobbes did not carve out an exception to this principle for times of emergency. Hobbes's characterization of the sovereign's violations of the laws of nature as a 'breach of trust' is also in tension with the sovereign-as-legally-unlimited interpretation. Hobbes may have adopted the language of trust because once sovereignty is established, sovereignty can be held in trust on an ongoing basis, whereas acts of consent – such as those that produce the original covenant and gift of sovereignty – are discrete and datable. Hobbes's suggestion that the sovereign holds public power in trust affirms that for the ongoing relationship between the sovereign and his subjects to be legitimate, it must be a moral relationship in which the subjects' legal obligations are matched by a commitment on the part of the sovereign to respect the constitutive and regulative requirements of offices held in trust. Moreover, Hobbes thinks that trust runs in the other direction too, from sovereign to subject.

In his discussion of sovereignty by acquisition or conquest, Hobbes claims that a necessary condition of a conquered person becoming a subject and thereby having a duty to obey the law is that 'the victor hath *trusted* him [the captive] with his corporal liberty',[35] which is why slaves in chains or prison are not under obligation. A subject is

32 Ibid., ch. xxviii, para. 2, 204.

33 Arash Abizadeh, 'Sovereign Jurisdiction, Territorial Rights, and Membership in Hobbes' in Al P. Martinich and Kinch Hoekstra (eds.) *The Oxford Handbook of Hobbes* (Oxford University Press 2016) 408. But see Quentin Skinner, *Visions of Politics: Renaissance Virtues*, vol. 2 (Cambridge University Press 2002) 402–4 (arguing that one of Hobbes's signal contributions to modernity was the attribution of sovereignty to the state rather than the sovereign).

34 Abizadeh (n. 33) 407.

35 Hobbes (n. 4) ch. xx, para. 12, 131 (emphasis added).

someone who 'hath corporal liberty allowed him, and upon promise not to run away, nor do violence to his master, is *trusted* by him'.[36] The conquering sovereign thus allows the subject life and liberty, trusting that the subject will obey the law and not use his liberty to do violence to the sovereign. Running through Hobbes's conception of sovereignty, then, is an idea of mutual trust. The subject entrusts the sovereign with the gift of sovereignty; the sovereign entrusts the subject with liberty. Both acts make the trusting party vulnerable to predation by the trusted party. The familiar Hobbesian justification for entrusting the sovereign with public powers is that doing so is the only way to avoid the state of nature. But why should liberty be a condition of being or becoming a legal subject? If an imprisoned captive wishes to submit to a conquering sovereign, why must the sovereign entrust the captive with liberty for her to become a subject? Why isn't an express submission to the sovereign's authority enough? These questions matter because the answer, I suggest, lets us explain how the legitimacy and stability of sovereignty is necessarily a joint endeavour of sovereign and subject premised on mutual trust.

One reason for Hobbes to insist on corporal liberty as a condition of subjecthood is that doing so helps him equate the liberty under a monarchy with liberty in a democracy. Under both regimes, Hobbes says, the corporal liberty the subject enjoys is 'the same' (i.e. in neither regime is the law-abiding subject in chains or prison),[37] and in neither regime is there (nor should there be) exemption from the law.[38] Yet this is hardly a principled argument. It is vulnerable to the charge that it presses the liberty condition into polemical service without providing an explanation of why the condition is there in the first place.

Another possible explanation is that liberty is intrinsically or instrumentally valuable (or both), so making it part of subjecthood will help secure and promote liberty's value. Liberty's intrinsic value for Hobbes is suggested by the fact that the one right we possess in the state of nature – the right of nature – is not a claim right but a *liberty* right, i.e. the right to do whatever we think best to secure our self-preservation. On entering civil society, we are to insist on retaining no more liberty than we would allow to others.[39] This injunction can be interpreted to suggest that liberty has intrinsic value because its unequal distribution alone, Hobbes thinks, is liable to produce resentment and discord. Nowhere does Hobbes suggest that individuals in the state of nature are free to trade off or waive the liberty rights they could otherwise expect to enjoy in civil society.[40]

Liberty's instrumental value for Hobbes is revealed by his generous conception of 'the safety of the people', by which he means not merely 'a bare preservation, but also all the

[36] Ibid., ch. xx, para. 10, 131 (emphasis added).
[37] Ibid., ch. xx, para. 8, 140.
[38] Ibid., ch. xx, para. 6, 138.
[39] Ibid., ch. xiv, para. 4, 80.
[40] On one theory of Hobbesian conflict, Hobbes's view could be that equal liberty is necessary because people are intractably prickly, and so they will become rancorous if denied an equal share of something held in high esteem. See Arash Abizadeh, 'Hobbes on the Causes of War: A Disagreement Theory' (2011) 105 *American Political Science Review* 298. Still, prickliness doesn't explain why Hobbes declined to entertain the possibility of waiving or bartering away (some) liberty rights.

other contentments of life, which every man by lawful industry, without danger or hurt to the commonwealth, shall acquire to himself'.[41] Liberty is an all-purpose means to preservation and 'the other contentments of life', and therefore is instrumentally valuable. If an important part of sovereignty's justification is that legal order makes possible a regime of secure and equal liberty, then it is perhaps incongruous to think that one can be a legal subject but not enjoy equal and significant corporal liberty.

This argument, however, provides at best weak support for making liberty a condition of subjecthood. The more obvious, supple and effective way to safeguard liberty is through the creation of robust legal institutions and the adoption of policies supportive of liberty (e.g. economic policies that ban indentured servitude, criminal law policies that use custodial sentences as a last resort). Respect for the moral value of liberty implies, let us assume, that *some* policy should be adopted that protects liberty. But it is far from clear that making liberty a condition of subjecthood is either necessary or optimal to achieve this purpose. Unshackling captives is a blunt measure that without other supportive policies in place is unlikely to protect the liberty of the weak from the strong or otherwise guarantee equal liberty.

A better explanation of making liberty a condition of subjecthood proceeds by addressing the question from the standpoint of subjecthood rather than liberty. Investing subjecthood with liberty is worthwhile because doing so lends the value of liberty to subjecthood. The result is that subjecthood is valuable, in part, because it denotes the legal status and position of someone who is free. Chattel slaves who work solely 'to avoid the cruelty of their task-masters', or 'whose bodies are not in their own power, their lives depending on the will of their masters in such manner as to forfeit them upon the least disobedience', Hobbes claims, do not enjoy the corporal liberty that being a subject entails.[42] This distinction between slaves and subjects points to a further conceptual reason for thinking that subjecthood demands liberty.

Even if chattel slaves in principle could be subjects, they could not in any meaningful sense be subject to legal obligation. They cannot perform positive obligations because they are in irons. And their compliance with negative duties is trivial: they cannot help but comply with such duties precisely because they do not have the liberty necessary to breach them. In short, law and legal obligation cannot guide the action of a slave held in chains because the slave's lack of liberty leaves her incapable of performing actions to which law might apply. Chattel slavery deprives law of the material conditions necessary for its application to human affairs, revealing that at least some measure of liberty enjoyed by some of the ruled is a condition of legal order as well as subjecthood. It is thus only when the conquering sovereign trusts the captive with liberty that the sovereign can govern her through law rather than mere coercive force. In this sense, liberty makes legal order possible. Indeed, for Hobbes, the subject's liberty is a necessary condition of the existence of law – i.e. a necessary condition of the existence of a relation of legal authority between sovereign and subject.

There is also an important sense in which the subject's liberty helps to make legal order stable and enduring. Although Hobbes is firmly of the view that an

[41] Hobbes (n. 4) ch. xxx, para. 1, 219.
[42] Ibid., ch. xx, para. 12, 121; ch. xlv, para. 13, 443.

awe-inspiring sovereign is needed for internal and external security, he thinks that the grounds of sovereignty 'need to be truly and diligently taught, because they cannot be maintained by any civil law or terror of legal punishment'.[43] In *Behemoth or The Long Parliament*, Hobbes's account of the English Civil War, he writes that 'the power of the mighty hath no foundation but in the belief and opinion of the people'.[44] His argument is that eventually the sovereign's commands will have to be enforced by an executive institution of last resort, an institution behind which there are no swords or pointy sticks to compel obedience. In a discussion of legal obligation, Hobbes asks the following series of rhetorical questions: 'For if men know not their duty, what is there that can force them to obey the laws? An army, you will say. But what shall force the army?'[45] Ultimately, subjects need to be convinced of their regime's legitimacy, which for Hobbes involves equal liberty and security so that subjects can adopt the position of 'the just man' – someone whose will is framed by justice – while not making themselves 'a prey for others'.[46]

If sovereignty rests on 'the belief and opinion of the people', then the sovereign is in a relationship of dependence with his subjects; he depends on them to maintain civil society. Implicit to the sovereign trusting the subject with liberty, then, is the sovereign entrusting the subject with the maintenance and stability of legal order. Hobbes thinks it is a law of nature that 'every man is bound by nature, as much as in him lieth, to protect in war the authority by which he himself is protected in time of peace'.[47] Thus, much as the subject entrusts the sovereign to use the gift of sovereignty to govern legitimately, the sovereign entrusts his subjects to use their liberty to support the commonwealth. Subjects have motivation for doing so because, as subjects, they enjoy liberty and security. But the important structural point that emerges from this analysis is that the sovereign and subject have separate but interlocking responsibilities with respect to the maintenance of public authority, all of which is held together within a framework of reciprocal and mutual trust.

I turn now to elaborating a conception of mutual trust apposite to authority relations. I will then explain how a relational structure of mutual trust can supply a conceptual scheme for law's authority so as to fill with legal norms and principles the spaces within legal limits and across legal frameworks that law's positive norms create.

4 Trust and Law's Authority

The conception of trust I deploy is drawn from Annette Baier's work. Baier contrasts relations based on consent and agreement with relations based on trust. As she avers, 'Whereas it strains the concept of agreement to speak of unconscious agreements and unchosen agreements . . . there is no strain whatever in the concept of automatic and

[43] Ibid., ch. xxx, para. 4, 220.

[44] Thomas Hobbes, *Behemoth or The Long Parliament* (first published in 1682, Ferdinand Tönnies ed., Chicago University Press 1990) 16.

[45] Ibid., 59.

[46] Hobbes (n. 4) ch. xv, para 10, 93; ch. xv, para 36, 99.

[47] Ibid., ch. R&C, para. 5, 490.

unconscious trust, and of unchosen but mutual trust.'[48] In the case of decent public authorities and their subjects, the relationship in practice may be one of 'unchosen but mutual trust'. Let's consider what this might mean, and how authority relations connect to trust.

Part of the structure of trust relations involving authorities, I contend, is conditional and dispositional in nature. Hobbes's laws of nature are again instructive. Hobbes thought that the laws of nature had normative purchase, or a capacity to bind, in two distinct domains: *in foro interno* and *in foro externo*. By '*in foro interno*', Hobbes means that the laws of nature bind on conscience, or 'a desire they should take place'.[49] As precepts of reason, Hobbes thought that the laws of nature '*oblige in Conscience always*', in the state of nature as well as in civil society, when the individual enjoys security and when she does not.[50] However, he thought these same laws bind *in foro externo* – on action, or in effect – '*only where there is Security*', since no one can be obligated to make herself 'a prey to others'.[51] For a law of nature to bind on action means that it creates a full-fledged legal obligation.

The dispositional aspect of the laws of nature is the *in foro interno* element that is always binding on conscience, even when there is no security. The conditional aspect of the laws of nature is located in the structure of the *in foro externo* element, and has the form 'If security obtains in a given context, then the laws of nature applicable to that context bind on action and are legal obligations.' Consider now a law of nature applicable to a public authority, and how its dispositional and conditional aspects map onto the authority relation between public office holder and subject when that relation is viewed as one of mutual trust.

As set out in Section 3, the law of nature prescribing equity dictates that someone in the position of a judge must treat the parties before her equally. The dispositional aspect of this law would be a conscientious desire on the part of the judge to use her role to guarantee fair and even-handed treatment of the parties who come before her. The conditional element would ordinarily be satisfied because the very existence of a judge suggests the existence of a commonwealth, and therefore security.[52] Consequently, the judge would have a legal obligation to treat the parties equally and in a manner consistent with the customary norms of adjudication (taking the relevant facts and law seriously, not being swayed by irrelevant considerations, treating the parties with respect, etc.). A similar structure can help illuminate what it means for a judge to exercise her powers as the occupant of a position of trust.

I will assume that a position of trust held by a public official is a public office or role that comes with an other-regarding mandate and the powers necessary to enable its execution. In the case of a judge, the basic mandate is to decide cases impartially and in accordance with the relevant facts and law. Judges have various powers to help

[48] Annette Baier, 'Trust and Antitrust' (1985) 96 *Ethics* 231, 2445.

[49] Hobbes (n. 4) ch. xv, para. 36, 99.

[50] Ibid.

[51] Ibid.

[52] An interesting question that won't detain us is whether the security condition could ever fail in ordinary circumstances where the laws of nature embodying legal principles apply, since the ordinary conditions of application presuppose the existence of a commonwealth and (therefore, presumptively) security.

them fulfil this role, such as the powers to issue subpoenas or hold individuals in contempt. And there are numerous principles that guide their work, including the principle of legal equality. From the position of trust that judges and other office holders occupy, decision-making authority can be seen to have the following dispositional and conditional features.

The dispositional element is a preparedness to act exclusively for reasons that reflect the terms of an authority's mandate and any requirements or duties that regulate how entrusted powers are to be exercised in its discharge. The appropriate disposition of a trustworthy judge is one of solicitude and fidelity towards her mandate and the permissible means of its fulfilment, including a desire to respect the principle of legal equality. The trustworthy judge's reasons for acting qua judge are reasons that reflect the underlying purpose and mandate of her office as well as the legal principles that partially constitute it. For instance, the judge who decides in favour of the party whose case is best supported by the law displays an appropriate commitment to both the principle of legal equality and the substantive law.

We would not think the same of a second judge who reached the same verdict in an identical case but who had taken a bribe from the eventual 'winner'. The second judge is not trustworthy. Much like Hobbes's faithless sovereign, he is in breach of trust, since he is selling for private gain a judicial decision that is supposed to be made on the basis of publicly avowable reasons. His actual reasons for the decision fail to track his office's purpose. Indeed, the judge subverts his office from within by untethering his role as judge from the rationale for its existence. Put another way, the second judge is untrustworthy because his decisions treat the law, at best, as camouflage for his actual and corrupt reasons for decision, making a mockery of the institution and the individuals it is designed to serve. On the assumption that well-ordered public institutions make decisions transparently (barring special reasons for confidentiality), a corrupt disposition on the part of a judge would undermine the possibility of the subject having reasonable grounds to trust that the court will function as a well-ordered institution. This remains the case even if the corrupt judge on every occasion were to reach the same outcome as an honest judge. There is a sense in which corruption is the public embodiment of betrayal; the corrupt judge betrays her oath of office as well as the public's trust in her.

Trust in the context of an assessment of the legitimacy of authority relations, on the account defended here, is complicated by the fact that the ultimate object of trust – the public entity trusted by its subjects, or which in some way stands in a trust relation to them – is an office or institution rather than a natural person. Although offices and institutions are artificial persons to whom words and actions can be imputed, they cannot act and speak for themselves, but only through their representatives. That is, the only words and actions that can be imputed to them are the words and actions of their representatives acting as their representatives. This may lead one to conclude that there cannot be trust relations of a morally significant kind with institutions because institutions, shorn of their representatives or officials, cannot apprehend or respond to trust, nor engage in the act of trusting themselves. This sceptical conclusion is too quick.

What the sceptical line of reasoning gets right is that trust relations with institutions are at least partially impersonal and objective. The kind of trust in play is impersonal in the sense that, strictly speaking, it involves public institutions and therefore an artificial person on (at least) one side of the relationship rather than natural persons on both sides, as when two individuals are in a trust relation with one another in their private, moral capacities. As discussed above, office holders can undermine the possibility of subjects having reason to trust institutions, through corruption and other forms of misfeasance. Yet, in this context the proper object of the trust inquiry is the public institution, since it is the institution that ultimately stands in an authority relation to the subject. In my view, the key to explaining actual trust relations between public institutions and their subjects is conceptualizing the institution so that its representatives qua representatives are part of it. That is, the institution's representatives are not constitutive elements of it as natural persons (as Sally, Ari, Sonia, etc.), but they are part of those institutions as office holders responsible for the execution of the institution's mandate (as occupants of the role of judge, legislator, minister, administrative decision maker, etc.).[53]

This understanding of the connection between offices and their occupants helps explain various features of offices. First, it lets us make sense of the idea that offices are independent of their specific occupants while still affording a constitutive place within them for role-guided judgement and decision-making. That is, offices on this conception are independent of Sally, Ari, Sonia, etc., but they are partially constituted by office holders who must exercise powers and make decisions to carry out the office's mission. Second, including the occupant within the concept of office provides access to the decision maker's reasons for decision, and thus access to the reasons for decision of the office itself. To appreciate the significance of gaining access to an office's reasons for decision, however, we first need to have in view two distinct normative consequences that can follow from the attribution of an office holder's decisions to her office: responsibility and legal validity.

In the standard case, the decisions of an office holder may be attributed to her office in virtue of the combination of the office's personhood and the office holder's status as representative. From that attribution alone, one can infer responsibility, i.e. ordinarily the office will be morally or legally accountable for decisions the office holder makes in the office's name. A sovereign who enters into a treaty on behalf of her state makes the state liable under treaty law. An officer of a corporation who enters into a contract on behalf of her corporation makes the corporation liable under contract law. The personhood of state and corporation entails that words and actions can be attributed to them, while the representative status of sovereign and officer implies that *their* words and actions qua representatives are attributable to the state and corporation, respectively. A direct consequence of these attributions is legal responsibility.

In other contexts, however, the decisions of office holders are intended to have effects that depend in the first instance on an assessment of their legal validity. The

[53] For Hobbes, unlike the way we tend to think of artificial persons today, as artificial entities to be represented (e.g. corporations, states), the primary sense of artificial person denotes someone occupying a representative role (e.g. sovereign, judge, legislator). Hobbes (n. 4) ch. xvi, para. 2, 101.

decisions of administrative agencies, boards and tribunals are characteristically of this nature. For example, if a regulator grants a company a permit to engage in a commercial activity that requires the use of public resources (e.g. natural resource extraction), the validity of the decision to grant the permit may be challenged on a variety of grounds. Of central concern would be the regulator's reasons for the decision. Her reasons would have to attend to the publicly avowable considerations she was entitled or required to take into account, considerations usually found within the text and purpose of her enabling statute. And her reasons could not be contaminated by corruption, conflict or consideration of irrelevant factors. The presence of such factors invalidates the decision, rendering it of no legal effect. Whether or not these factors ultimately lead to civil liability is a separate inquiry (a legally invalid exercise of power may cause harm but not injury, or the public office holder may enjoy immunity from suit). The immediate point for present purposes is that assessments of validity depend on access to the reasons for decision.

Assessment of an institution's contractual liability to third parties does not typically depend on the office holder's reasons for legally binding her institution to a third party. Inquiry into liability in this context typically concerns whether the office holder is or reasonably appears to be a duly authorized representative empowered to change the legal position of the institution. Determinations of responsibility likewise call for an assessment of whether the office holder has satisfied the relevant formal requirements to bind her institution to a third party (e.g. the requirements of contract or treaty law). Although conflict or corruption in decision-making may render an office holder's decision void or voidable, this is (to reiterate) a separate matter from whether the office holder is a bona fide or ostensible representative who has complied with the formal requirements that would ordinarily bind her institution to a third party.

Let's now draw out the significance of the responsibility/validity distinction for the place and nature of trust within authority relations between public institutions and legal subjects. The sceptic, I suggested, may be tempted to think that public institutions do not stand in relations of morally significant trust with their subjects because institutions cannot act or speak (and therefore cannot trust or respond to trust) except through their representatives. And even then it may seem that the only plausible participants in a trust relationship, from the side of officialdom, are representatives rather than institutions, since representatives alone, it may seem, can trust and respond to trust. Although institutions can have words and acts imputed to them through their representatives, if all that is generally required of institutions is that potentially they can be held liable for the acts imputed to them, then as with contract and tort law, we don't generally need to inquire into their reasons for action. And if their reasons for action are irrelevant or unavailable, then it may seem that the sceptic is right to doubt the coherence of meaningful trust relations with public authorities, since acting for the right reasons does seem to matter when one party is trusted to act for another.

Suppose, however, that a public institution's representatives qua representatives are part of the institution, and that a fortiori the representatives' official acts are not merely attributed to the institution but are of the institution itself. That is, the office of the representative, its decision-making power and its actual decision-making are partially constitutive of the institution. Under this conception of an office or institution, the representative's decisions are the decisions of the institution, and, crucially, so too are her reasons for decision. In administrative law, it is sometimes the reasons for decision themselves that demonstrate and even produce the decision's validity (e.g. a discretionary decision to relieve an individual from a deportation order based on humanitarian and compassionate considerations).[54] This analysis explains the core practice of judicial review of administrative action where reviewing judges assess closely the reasons and decisions of public decision makers. Judges routinely attribute these reasons and decisions to the Crown, state, ministry or public agency to which the decision maker belongs. In other words, administrative law treats public institutions as entities capable of having reasons for decision, and as subject to rulings of invalidity if their decisions fail to reflect the right reasons (e.g. reasons tainted by corruption, conflict or irrelevant factors). Some courts have said that in high-stakes circumstances, the reasons must be 'responsive written reasons'.[55] The idea that public institutions can have reasons for decision, and that those reasons must be the right sort of reasons and responsive, suggests that some form of trust relation with public institutions is possible.

This is not to deny that the kind of trust in play with public institutions is impersonal. The legal subject's trust relation is not with specific, natural persons, but rather with institutions that are legal and artificial persons. Relations with agents within institutions are relations with person as occupants of official or representative roles. Yet the trust relation at stake is not *apersonal* either; it is not akin to the relation one might have with a reliable bike or car. One might rely on and develop confidence in these chattels, but one cannot have a moral trust relationship with them.

The conception of trust in the context of a legitimacy inquiry is also objective because, as a conceptual matter, the existence of trust does not depend (or at least does not depend exclusively) on the subject's actual beliefs about the integrity, fidelity, solidarity or associative closeness the authority may or may not possess in relation to either her office or the subject. The subject's actual beliefs about a seemingly trustworthy official (e.g. the corrupt judge discussed above) may be false, with the implication that an apparent case of mutual trust would really be an instance of false trust. I will suggest below that we can avoid this difficulty by distinguishing two dimensions of authority relations: (i) the legitimacy dimension, which concerns the conceptual requirements of legitimate authority in relation to trust and (ii) the stability dimension, which specifies the ways mutual trust can contribute to the stability of legitimate authority. First, however, consider how a public institution's authority may be thought to possess a conditional as well as dispositional element when her office is assumed to be a position of trust.

[54] See, e.g., *Baker* v. *Canada (Minister of Citizenship and Immigration)* [1999] 2 SCR 215 (articulating a comprehensive framework for the assessment of discretionary decisions based on humanitarian and compassionate grounds).

[55] *Suresh* v. *Canada (Minister of Citizenship and Immigration)* [2002] 1 SCR 3, para. 127 (applying the principle where deportation carried a risk of eventual torture).

The conditional element of an institution's authority may have both intrinsic and extrinsic aspects. Intrinsic elements refer to the institution's legal mandate and the conditions that must be met within that mandate for the office holder to exercise power. In the case of a good judge deciding a criminal law matter, for example, she generally will enter a conviction against an accused only if the Crown proves the actus reus and mens rea beyond a reasonable doubt, and there are no applicable defences. These features of the criminal law process are doctrines intrinsic to her role as a criminal law judge. Their application calls for the use of judgement and discretion in pursuit of other-regarding criminal law purposes, reflecting an important sense in which they are held in trust for public purposes.

The extrinsic side of the conditional aspect of an institution's authority concerns matters that are outside or external to the usual legal or factual considerations an authority would take into account in the exercise of her power. Perhaps the most capacious statement of this idea is Carl Schmitt's infamous dictum with which he launched his polemic *Political Theology*: 'Sovereign is he who decides on the exception.'[56] Schmitt was writing about emergencies, such as those provoked by war or civil unrest. The 'exception' is a period of time during an emergency when the sovereign suspends public law in order to contend with the emergency. For Schmitt, the sovereign has (and should have) unfettered discretion to decide to suspend public law because the nature and extent of a given emergency cannot be predicted.[57] For this reason too, Schmitt thought, the sovereign has (and should have) unfettered discretion to select the measures necessary to deal with emergencies and restore order. Thus, the ordinary constitutional legal order characterized by the usual operation of legal norms, for Schmitt, always depends on a prior implicit decision of the sovereign, i.e. a decision that the present state of affairs is not a crisis calling for the suspension of public law. In my view, Schmitt's theory reveals the danger of an approach to law that essentially calls on the subject to trust without a more legally unlimited sovereign.

Evan Criddle and I have argued that there is a more attractive and non-Schmittian way to acknowledge that sovereigns sometimes have to declare emergencies and exercise prerogative powers to deal with them.[58] Schmitt subscribes to an impoverished conception of legal order, one comprised of norms and decisions only. If one holds instead that legal principles too are constitutive of legal order (principles such as formal legal equality and proportionality in public decision-making), one can explain, we argue, how a sovereign's authority can be constituted and constrained by law during an emergency. On this understanding, which I can here only assert, sovereigns are always subject to ex post review and scrutiny of their decisions in light of principles such as proportionality. They are subject to this kind of review with respect to the decision to declare an emergency and with regard to exercises of prerogative powers during it. Accordingly, the validity of derogable legal norms may be

[56] Carl Schmitt, *Political Theology: Four Chapters on the Concept of Sovereignty* rev. ed. (first published in 1934, George Schwab trans., University of Chicago Press 2005) 5.

[57] Ibid., 6–10.

[58] Evan J. Criddle and Evan Fox-Decent, 'Human Rights, Emergencies, and the Rule of Law' (2014) 34 *Human Rights Quarterly* 39.

conditional on the absence of crisis, but their validity is not conditional on a legally unlimited decision of the sovereign, since the sovereign, properly understood, is always subject to law. The good and trustworthy sovereign acknowledges that extrinsic as well as intrinsic conditions on the exercise of authority are mediated by legal principles that serve the legal subject's interest in the rule of law.

To summarize, thus far I have followed Hobbes and most contemporary moral philosophers in supposing that, typically, if trust is present in a relationship, it emerges or has a close connection with the act of trusting; ordinarily one party trusts another with the care of something of value to the trusting party. I have also assumed that relations involving trust may have a legal or non-legal character, and may or may not involve public authorities. Interpersonal and morally thick relations involving trust between individuals (and not involving public authorities) are generally understood to involve a 'robust recognitional' element.[59] This involves a special kind of responsiveness to trust on the part of the trusted party (the trusting party's act of trusting is a reason to perform as trusted), and entails that 'when the trusted party does not act as expected, does not perform as trusted, the trusting party is not merely disappointed, but rather she legitimately feels betrayed'.[60]

It may be that this claim is too strong and that one's trust can be disappointed in some cases without one having a sense of betrayal. Suppose as your friend I undertake to manage your assets for your exclusive benefit. In an emergency I find that I cannot communicate with you, but nonetheless borrow funds from your portfolio to pay for a critical medical procedure. Shortly thereafter I replace the borrowed funds with interest. As a matter of law, I have wronged you. And I may have disappointed the trust you placed in me. But you may not feel betrayed given the circumstances. Indeed, you may insist that you would have felt aggrieved and in some sense betrayed had I *not* borrowed the money in these circumstances, since the bonds of friendship here weigh heavier than the law. Yet there are many cases in law involving disappointed trust where the appropriate response is a sense of betrayal, because in these cases the main duty is a duty of loyalty. The duty of loyalty is the central duty in private fiduciary law cases involving a fiduciary on one side (e.g. a parent, corporate director, agent, trustee) and a vulnerable beneficiary on the other (e.g. a child, corporation, principal, beneficiary). The faithless fiduciary's breach of her duty of loyalty is by definition an act of disloyalty – a failure to act for someone when so acting is required – and therefore an appropriate response to that failure is betrayal. One's bike or car can disappoint but not betray, because things cannot owe duties of loyalty that characteristically attend trust relations.

I have suggested that we can build on Hobbes's insights with respect to trust within authority relations to infer that trust in this context also has a dispositional element – the authority in whom trust is reposed must act for the right reasons, and a failure to do so is a betrayal of the office. Similarly, I have suggested that authorities understood to occupy positions of trust hold their power subject to intrinsic and extrinsic conditions that temper its exercise. Compliance with those conditions is a mark of

59 Postema (n. 26).
60 Ibid.

an authority's trustworthiness and legitimacy. I will now turn to sketching the role trust can play in the justification of legitimate authority and will distinguish that role from the conditions under which acts of mutual trusting productive of mutual trust can lend stability to well-ordered public institutions.

I have previously argued that the state and its institutions stand in a fiduciary relationship to the persons subject to their authority, and that one way (though not the only way) to understand the state's authority to establish legal order is that the state must be presumed to act on the basis of its people's trust.[61] Culling indicia from legal doctrine, I claimed that fiduciary relations exist whenever one party holds discretionary power of an other-regarding, limited and institutional nature in relation to the practical or legal interests of another, and that the other party is particularly vulnerable to the fiduciary's discretion. Trustees, for example, hold discretionary and other-regarding power in favour of the beneficiary, the power is limited to the uses permitted by the trust mandate, the power is institutional in that it is located within the institution of a trust and trust law generally, and the beneficiary is especially vulnerable to the trustee's discretion (ordinarily, the beneficiary cannot veto a trustee's lawful decision). While the source or origin of the trustee's authority typically comes from the trust instrument created by the settlor, the nature of her authority and its features, I argued, is to be gleaned from the fiduciary or trust-like nature of her office. Mutatis mutandis, a similar story can be told for the state–subject relation of public authority.

The immediate difficulty facing such an account is that many people, often for good reason, distrust or at least mistrust state institutions, and cannot plausibly be understood to have reposed trust in the state. To respond to this challenge, I adopted a non-voluntarist account of fiduciary relations, looking to the parent–child case and agency of necessity to support the idea that fiduciary authority was possible in some cases without the prior consent of the persons subject to fiduciary power. But I took on board the voluntarist's major premise that there must be some kind of 'appropriate moral relationship' between public authority and the subject for authority to be legitimate.[62] I inferred the basis of that relationship from legal practice and scholarship that consistently referred to fiduciary relations as trust or trust-like relations, and which referred to fiduciaries as persons occupying positions of trust. My methodology was not to postulate in the abstract that fiduciaries hold positions of trust and then derive implications from that assumption. My aim, rather, was to offer the best explanation of the law's own characterization of the fiduciary's position as one of trust, a characterization made even when the beneficiary does nothing to repose trust in or even entrust the fiduciary with anything.

While part of the explanation includes the special duties and remedies of fiduciary law (duties and remedies that generally are more onerous than the duties and remedies of contract law), this is far from the most important or salient aspect of the explanation. The most significant feature of fiduciary relations that their trust quality helps to explain is the authority of the fiduciary to act in the name of or on

[61] Evan Fox-Decent, *Sovereignty's Promise: The State as Fiduciary* (Oxford University Press 2012) ch. 4.
[62] See A. John Simmons, *Justification and Legitimacy* (Cambridge University Press 2001) 130.

behalf of the beneficiary. How is such authority possible if the beneficiary (or subject) distrusts the fiduciary (or state)? It is possible, I argued, if we recognize that it is the law itself, through fiduciary power-conferring rules, that ultimately entrusts the fiduciary (or state) with discretionary power to act on behalf of the beneficiary (or subject). Just as power-conferring rules underlie contract law so as to convert bilateral wishes into enforceable agreements, power-conferring rules also underpin fiduciary law so as to convert a de facto relation of power and dependency into a rightful relation of entrusted authority.[63] When the law posits the fiduciary's position as one of trust, it is in part because the law entrusts the fiduciary with power to which the beneficiary is especially vulnerable, and therefore the fiduciary is held to strict duties. But the more important aspect of the explanation of the law's treatment of the fiduciary's position as one of trust (even if the beneficiary has done nothing to repose trust) is that the fiduciary is empowered to act exclusively for the beneficiary, and often with legal powers capable of changing the beneficiary's legal position.

If the law is not confused and the fiduciary's position is one of trust, does this trust pertain or belong to someone, or is it a merely adjectival quality of the fiduciary's position? In my view, for the law to apprehend fiduciary relations as relations of authority premised in some way on trust, as it seems keen to do, the law must be taken to authorize the fiduciary to act on the basis of the beneficiary's trust, even when the beneficiary distrusts the fiduciary. The law might do so, for example, when it compels the recalcitrant subject to respect the norms of a regime of secure and equal freedom, notwithstanding the recalcitrant subject's anarchist desire to go it alone. In this context, where the bare legitimacy of the state's legal authority is at issue, the subject's trust is best conceived as a moral disposition that operates on two levels.

On the primary or object level, the act of trusting and the trustworthiness of public institutions coalesce to lend stability to legal order, as discussed further below. At a secondary level, however, trust is a moral disposition in the sense that it denotes a moral preparedness to accede to the secondary or constitutional power-conferring rules of legal order that enable public authorities to establish a regime of secure and equal freedom.[64] Trust at the secondary level is the normative substrate that underlies and explains the authority legal institutions claim when they use power-conferring rules on behalf of their people to establish legal order. While subjects need not trust the state at the factual or primary level, they nonetheless have a moral duty to relate to others on equal terms that they themselves are not entitled to set unilaterally. They can satisfy this duty while factually distrusting the state by possessing, at the secondary and moral level, Baier's 'unchosen but mutual trust', a form of trust understood as a moral preparedness to be the subject of a legal order.

[63] The theory I defend here is essentially G. H. L. Fridman's power/liability theory of agency extended to fiduciary relations generally, a theory that explains the agent's powers as powers vested in her by the law as a result of 'the way in which the *law* regards the relationship that has been created' (G. H. L Fridman, *The Law of Agency*, 7th ed, (Butterworths 1996) 15 (emphasis in original)).

[64] I adopt the idea of power-conferring rules from Hart but supplement it with ideas of equal freedom and representation that together provide a standard of adequacy for assessing the claim to legitimate authority legal systems necessarily make. See H. L. A. Hart, *The Concept of Law*, 3rd ed. (Oxford University Press 2012).

The moral disposition at this secondary level is expressly normative and representational. It is normative because ultimately it denotes an ongoing authorization of public power structured and mediated by legal principles. The disposition is representational because it implicitly requires the state to exercise power exclusively in a manner that can be understood to be in the name of or on behalf of the subject – i.e. on the basis of the subject's trust – even if the state's action ultimately sets back the subject's interests. By adhering to this criterion of legitimacy, the fiduciary state respects the demands of the moral relationship of trust that sustains its claim to have standing as a legitimate authority.[65]

All things being equal, the legitimacy of public authority is plausibly made more perspicuous and stable over time when public institutions demonstrate fidelity to their mandates and solicitude to the individuals subject to them. In relatively decent societies where civic or social trust is at least moderately present, and where public institutions generally 'perform as trusted', there are reasonable grounds for subjects to view their institutions as trustworthy, and to repose a measure of trust in their ability to bring about and respect the rule of law.

Postema's climate of trust together with reasonably trustworthy institutions offer fertile soil for Lon L. Fuller's conception of the rule of law and the idea of reciprocity within it. Fuller claimed that 'there is a kind of reciprocity between government and the citizen with respect to the observance of rules. Government says to the citizen in effect, "These are the rules we expect you to follow. If you follow them, you have our assurance that they are the rules that will be applied to your conduct."'[66] Fuller thought that reciprocity was important because 'maintaining a legal system in existence depends on the discharge of interlocking responsibilities – of government towards the citizen and of the citizen towards government', and so 'the citizen's voluntary cooperation must be matched by a corresponding cooperative effort on the part of the government'.[67] In a decent society with a climate of trust and trustworthy institutions, Fuller's idea of reciprocity under the rule of law provides a congenial framework for the development of mutual trust between public institutions and legal subjects, which in turn contributes to the health and stability of legal order.

It remains for me to weave together various strands of the foregoing discussion to explain how viewing public authorities as occupants of positions of trust can help reveal how legality fills the spaces law creates for itself by establishing limits within and across legal frameworks. The linchpin to this theory is the idea that trust mediates the dispositional and conditional features of authorities understood to hold positions of trust. Because authorities who hold positions of trust and other-regarding powers are required always to act for the right reasons – other-regarding reasons derived from the norms of fiduciary law or their particular mandates – the space within which they are authorized to exercise power is saturated with this obligation. There are no legal voids, but rather spaces permeated with an ongoing duty to respect the fiduciary's

[65] Evan Criddle and I develop and deploy this criterion in the context of international law: Criddle and Fox-Decent (n. 3) 3, 99–100, 131, 217, 240, 268, 288.

[66] Lon L Fuller, *The Morality of Law*, rev. ed (Yale University Press 1969) 39–40.

[67] Ibid., 216.

terms of office by acting only for reasons consistent with the purposes for which power was conferred. The duty to act for the right reasons is ongoing and perpetual for the duration the office is held. For the entirety of that period, the office holder is under an obligation to act on the basis of the trust of the people immediately affected by the official's exercise of power as well as on the basis of the public trust. In a decent society, mutual trust and Fuller's sense of reciprocity animate interpretation and application of legal principles apposite to context.

Similarly, the conditions of office holding are mediated by the intrinsic legal norms governing the fiduciary's position as well as more general principles relevant to extrinsic conditions (e.g. an emergency) that could frustrate the ordinary execution of her mandate. As the discussion of Schmitt revealed, the sovereign who must contend with an emergency unscripted can still answer to legal principles such as proportionality and legal equality. The sovereign who understands that she holds her position in trust for her people will also understand that her legitimacy depends on her being able to say that her actions are taken in their name or on their behalf, which is precisely what the constitution of her office through the norms of trust and legal principles makes possible.[68]

[68] Of course, things can go awry, and badly so. While authorities can, in my view, implement policies that bring with them a measure of injustice without calling into question their bona fides as legal authorities of a legal order, the fiduciary criterion of legitimacy sets a limit. If policies systematically abuse or dominate subjects such that no interpretation of them is possible that could make them intelligible as policies made and implemented in the name of or on behalf of the people subject to them, then the powers that be govern through mere force rather than law. Slavery is one such limit case. See Evan Fox-Decent, 'Jurisprudential Reflections on Cosmopolitan Law' in Jacco Bomhoff, David Dyzenhaus and Tom Poole (eds.) *The Double-Facing Constitution* (Cambridge University Press 2019, forthcoming).

10

The Fiduciary Crown

The Private Duties of Public Actors in State–Indigenous Relationships

KIRSTY GOVER AND NICOLE ROUGHAN[1]

1 Introduction

A line of Canadian jurisprudence beginning with *Guerin* v. *the Queen* [1984] 2 SCR 335 (*Guerin*) characterizes the relationship between Indigenous peoples and the state as a fiduciary relationship, in which certain duties arise, responsive to context, that are 'in the nature of private law dut[ies]'.[2] The Supreme Court of New Zealand recently followed the Canadian approach in *Proprietors of Wakatū* v. *Attorney General* [2017] 1 NZLR 423 ('*Wakatū*'), upholding the Crown's fiduciary duty with respect to the property interests in dispute while leaving open the question of whether the relationship between the Crown and Māori is 'generally' a fiduciary one.[3] These cases are part of a line of jurisprudence departing from earlier cases characterizing state–Indigenous relationships as non-justiciable 'political trusts', having a moral but not legal character.[4]

The approaches taken by courts in both countries raise broader normative, doctrinal and ontological questions about whether parties to state–Indigenous relationships, and the duties they owe, are best regarded as public or private. Our particular concern in this chapter is the use of state–Indigenous examples in two ongoing and interconnected debates: legal theories debating the coherence or content of 'public fiduciary

[1] Thanks to participants at the Fiduciaries and Trust: Ethics, Politics, Economics and Law workshop (Melbourne Law School, 17–18 December 2018) for thoughtful comments and suggestions, and especially to Matthew Harding for very helpful editorial notes. Thanks also to Robyn Gardner and Stuart Dixon of the Melbourne Law School Academic Research Service for expert assistance with final edits. Collaborative work on this project was also supported by Nicole's Rutherford Discovery Fellowship from the New Zealand Royal Society Te Apārangi.

[2] *Guerin* v. *the Queen* [1984] 2 SCR 335, 388–9 (*Guerin*).

[3] *Proprietors of Wakatū* v. *Attorney General* [2017] 1 NZLR 423 (*Wakatū*). In shifting from 'the Crown' to 'the state', we adopt the terminology preferred in fiduciary political theory, notwithstanding work theorizing the Crown and the state as conceptually separate entities. See especially Janet McLean, 'Crown, Empire and Redressing the Historical Wrongs of Colonisation in New Zealand' [2015] *NZL Rev.* 187. See also Janet McLean, *Searching for the State in British Legal Thought: Competing Conceptions of the Public Sphere* (Cambridge University Press 2012). These differences are immaterial to our arguments about the applicability of fiduciary theory to relationships between the state or Crown with its subjects or Indigenous peoples.

[4] See, e.g., *Tito* v. *Waddell (No. 2)* [1977] Ch 106.

law',[5] and political theories advancing or resisting a general fiduciary model of statehood.[6] In both debates, fiduciary accounts of public authority seek to show that states can (and in some cases should) bear fiduciary duties to individual subjects or to a notional 'public'. We argue in this chapter that assimilating state–Indigenous fiduciary relationships into either fiduciary political theory or an emerging public fiduciary law obscures the importance of the authority and distinctive private rights of Indigenous parties to those relationships that are protected by fiduciary duties. It may imperil Indigenous rights by stripping the relationship of its private law features. This could leave Indigenous interests to be weighed alongside those of third parties and the public using public law methods that have proven to be not only inhospitable to Indigenous rights but virtually incapable of securing Indigenous interests in the face of competing claims. The duties and rights at stake are distinct from those owed and held between subjects and authorities in public law, and the utility of the relationship for Indigenous peoples lies precisely in the fact that it is not generalizable.

We argue that, contrary to the positions expressed in much of the case law discussed in Section 2 of this chapter, and in academic commentary, the duties discussed are private and need not be described as 'analogous' to private duties, even given the public character of the parties. This characterization has doctrinal, analytical and normative implications. Doctrinally, it would preserve the usual protections for private rights against contending public or third-party interests, and enable recourse to the package of private law claims, remedies and defences that are not typically on offer for claimants relying on public law rights and obligations.[7] Analytically, the private characterization affirms that fiduciary duties owed to Indigenous peoples are not generalizable to non-Indigenous interest holders, third parties or 'the public'. Moreover, it positions such duties as structurally (and at times substantively) opposed to the more general relationship between state and subjects that underpins both liberal political theory and public law. The private characterization thus pushes back against efforts to use the state–Indigenous example to ground analytic theories of public fiduciary law or political theories of a fiduciary state.

We are of the view that state–Indigenous relationships are best characterized as having an inter-public or international character. Leaving open the prospect and promise of wholesale constitutional and conceptual renovations that would be required to give effect to an international model, we contend that that an 'inter-public' approach to state–Indigenous relations can be achieved by shifts in judicial reasoning. We further contend that understanding the state–Indigenous fiduciary relationship as one that entails private duties is a progressive step towards the

5 For a concise explanation, see Evan Fox-Decent, 'Challenges to Public Fiduciary Theory: An Assessment' in D. Gordon Smith and Andrew S. Gold (eds.), *Research Handbook on Fiduciary Law* (Edward Elgar 2018).

6 See, e.g., Evan Fox-Decent, 'The Fiduciary Nature of State Legal Authority' (2005) 31 *Queen's LJ* 259, 265; Evan Fox-Decent, *Sovereignty's Promise: The State as Fiduciary* (Oxford University Press 2011); Evan J. Criddle and others (eds.), *Fiduciary Government* (Cambridge University Press 2018).

7 See Nicole Roughan, 'Public/Private Distortions and State–Indigenous Fiduciary Relationships' (2019) *NZL Rev.* (forthcoming).

realization of such an inter-public approach. A private conception of state–Indigenous fiduciary relationships protects certain Indigenous interests without necessitating recourse to the problematic and limited mechanisms of the state's extant public law, and thus preserves the prospect of developing a genuine and effective *inter*-public law.

While we remain wary of the apparent paternalism and monism of fiduciary conceptions of state–Indigenous relationships,[8] we recognize that fiduciary doctrine provides Indigenous peoples with recourse to rights and remedies that are otherwise not available in public law (yet which, as private relationships, would be readily available in equity). As the cases below illustrate, fiduciary duties have produced concrete protections for some groups and are viewed by some commentators (Indigenous and non-Indigenous) as important legal toeholds for Indigenous peoples pursuing independent self-government.[9] In this chapter we take aim specifically at the conceptions of the duties entailed in the Indigenous–state relationship as 'analogous' to private law duties. We think there are doctrinal and normative reasons to conceive of and apply such duties within the forms of private law, without the kinds of qualification that are expressed in deference to the public statuses of the parties.

This chapter defends five claims. In Section 1 we argue (1) that a private duty is one owed directly between parties to a relationship and not to others outside that relationship, where the interest protected by the duty belongs or attaches only to its holder and is not generalizable to non-parties; (2) given that both Indigenous peoples and the state claim and exercise public authority vis-à-vis members of their polities, we argue that the tools of singular or monistic public law are ill-suited to upholding mutual relational duties in their inter-public relationship and (3) the specific duties owed in that relationship can include those arising from the creation, transfer, undertaking or injury of interests that are the objects of private duties according to the conception outlined in (1). In Section 2 we draw on the key cases of *Guerin*, *Wewaykum Indian Band* v. *Canada* [2002] 4 SCR 245 (*Wewaykum*) and *Wakatū* to argue (4) that the specific state–Indigenous fiduciary duties upheld by the courts in Canada and New Zealand are private duties. In Section 3 we explain that the duties identified in these cases require the state to protect Indigenous interests against the competing interests of non-Indigenous third parties and the public. In Section 4 we argue (5) that these features of judicially recognized state–Indigenous fiduciary relationships mean that they should not be used as exemplars in accounts of fiduciary political theory or public fiduciary law. Section 5 concludes.

2 Fiduciary Relationships in the Public, Private and Political Spheres

An emerging literature on public fiduciary duties draws upon fiduciary political theory to argue that public authorities (including the state, its agencies and representatives) owe fiduciary duties to those subject to their powers. While theoretical

[8] Ibid.

[9] See, e.g., Patricia Monture-Angus, *Journeying Forward: Dreaming First Nations' Independence* (Fernwood 2000) 44–5.

foundations differ between accounts,[10] their shared core is a supposed correlation of public authority and subjection on the one hand, with fiduciary discretion and the vulnerability of principals on the other. For our purposes, the key aspect of these accounts is their avowedly public character, by virtue of which whatever duties the state owes to its subjects are owed to all in the same way, and for the same reasons. Expressly, the duties are owed by public authorities to subjects because of their subjection.

In order to evaluate those accounts, we embark here on an outline of the anatomy of the public and private spheres within which state–Indigenous fiduciary relationships are situated. For our purposes it is crucial that the public and private spheres (in politics and in law) be understood in relation to each other, even if they cannot be fixed with a bright distinction. We understand that what is private is protected or carved out from public interest or interference, while what is public is thought to be of general application and importance, justifying the interventions of the collective notwithstanding private preferences. Others have offered demarcations emphasizing private law's core bilateral relational structure, where rights and interests are contested and protected 'between you and me', thereby situating other actors as third parties to our relationship.[11] That basic structural characterization is contested in private law theory, where trilateral relations challenge the primacy of bilateral relationality, or where sets of bilateral relations cannot, without distortion, be distinguished amidst complex networks of duties. Both of those tensions feed into our characterization of state–Indigenous duties as private duties but do not detract from the core structuring idea we offer here: that private duties are owed 'between you and me *and not others*', protecting interests that I hold *in distinction from others*. We will use this core idea to differentiate a set of directly relational state–Indigenous duties from duties the state owes to the wider public.[12]

A private conception of fiduciary duties offers a structural and not necessarily a substantive demarcation and protection of private rights and duties from public interference. As matters of both doctrine and justification, private rights are often

[10] For instance, a fiduciary conception of public authority may avoid the Kantian problem that one person's wielding of another's powers violates the universal principle of right. A civil condition empowering and burdening fiduciary officials can be supervised by a 'trustee' court. See Alec Stone Sweet and Eric Palmer, 'A Kantian System of Constitutional Justice: Rights, Trusteeship, Balancing' (2017) 6 *GlobCon* 377.

[11] Leading work includes Ernest J. Weinrib, *The Idea of Private Law* (rev. ed., Oxford University Press 2012), and concise engagement with conventional and critical conceptions of the private sphere appears in Hanoch Dagan and Avihay Dorfman, 'Just Relationships' (2016) 116 *Colum L. Rev.* 1395. This work explores relations between individual persons and relies heavily on accounts of individual autonomy. We mean to be provocative in adopting private law's relationality to treat the relation between state and Indigenous authorities as one between formally independent and equal parties. Compare Arthur Ripstein, *Private Wrongs* (Harvard University Press 2016): 'To be entitled to act on behalf of everyone, the state must stand in the right relation to each citizen over whom it exercises power. This vertical relation is different in kind from the horizontal relations between private persons that are governed by the principle that no person is in charge of another.' Our argument is that the right relation of the state to Indigenous citizens is not one of sovereign–subject; rather, it shares the governing principle that Ripstein articulates for private relations.

[12] To the extent that equity displays greater sensitivity to the interests of third parties and the public, it may also display greater potential sensitivity to a pluralist conception of the public interest.

(and in some contexts routinely) overridden by matters of public interest, particularly in conditions of necessity or emergency. To characterize fiduciary duties as private duties is to acknowledge that doctrinal limits and conditions (including rules governing expropriation and compensation) accompany regimes of private rights. Our argument is not that Indigenous interests invariably either trump or outweigh contending 'public' interests within that structure; it is arguably more significant. Invocations of an overriding public interest depend for their justification on the singularity and inclusivity of the public whose interests are being asserted against members of *that* public. In the case of the settler states, however, the very idea and composition of the public is contested, and assumptions built on its underlying premise of popular sovereignty are precarious.[13] For a 'public interest' to justifiably limit or outweigh Indigenous private rights, it would need to be directly justified in accordance with the authority and independent interests of the relevant Indigenous public (including in its interaction with other publics). Our account therefore does not import the content of the existing doctrinal limits that public interest imposes on private rights; rather, it imports that structure while inviting greater plurality into its content.

A better model, then, situates settler societies as made up of more than one public, constituted by multiple peoples and containing multiple legal authorities and public interests.[14] These features together challenge the notion that Indigenous peoples are subjects of the state, or at least challenge the extent, degree and conditions of any subjection. Central to these settler state–Indigenous relationships is the core principle that unlike in standard relationships between state and subject in public law, these are relationships between public authorities and between the polities they represent. This in turn matters to any characterization of the state–Indigenous relationship as one regulated by public law, for it suggests instead that the relevant legal tools must be designed to regulate inter-public or inter-authority relationships. It also suggests that the 'public' in public interest is plural, and that this is relevant to the form and content of justifications given for interferences with private interests in 'the' public interest. Seen in light of these ideals, the standard models of 'public fiduciary' relationships seem insufficiently pluralist.

In light of this, and given the public statuses of Indigenous peoples and states, a better model of the relationships might be located in international law and relations;[15]

[13] See, e.g., Steven Curry, *Indigenous Sovereignty and the Democratic Project* (Ashgate Publishing 2004); James Tully, *Strange Multiplicity: Constitutionalism in an Age of Diversity* (Cambridge University Press 1995); Ludvig Beckman, Kirsty Gover and Ulf Mörkenstam, 'Popular Sovereignty in Multi-people States: The Challenge from Indigenous Peoples to Conceptions of Popular Sovereignty as Democratic Participation' (manuscript on file with authors).

[14] See, e.g., Tully (n. 13); Duncan Ivison, 'Pluralising Political Legitimacy' (2017) 20 *Postcolonial Studies* 118; James [Sákéj] Youngblood Henderson, 'Empowering Treaty Federalism' (1994) 58 *Sask. L. Rev.* 241; Duncan Ivison, 'Justification Not Recognition' (2017) 8(24) *ILB* 12; P. Patton, 'The Limits of Decolonization and the Problem of Legitimacy' in David Boucher and Ayesha Omar (eds.), *Decolonisation: Evolution and Revolution* (Wits University Press 2019) (forthcoming); Nicole Roughan, 'Polities and Relative Authorities' (2018) 16 *ICON* 1215.

[15] Ivison, for example, refers to the Indigenous–state relationship as one entailing 'quasi-international relations'. Duncan Ivison, 'The Logic of Aboriginal Rights' (2003) 3 *Ethnicities* 321, 332.

Indigenous–state treaties and treaty-implementing agreements are, in any case, approached in settler state public law in a way that bears striking similarity to the treatment of international treaties.[16] In practice the judicial methods deployed to give effect to an inter-public model may also bear resemblance to those used in private international law, where choice-of-law decisions are to be made based on prior agreement or general jurisdictional principles.[17] Formally, however, settler states and their courts have emphatically rejected any proposition that Indigenous–state relations treaties, and disputes about treaties, should be governed by international law or addressed in international adjudicatory fora.[18] While state sovereignty continues to be framed doctrinally as an absolute, admitting of no contender, the (self-imposed) formal and doctrinal constraints operating on settler state institutions mean that the international law analogy can only be understood as an ideal, not within the practical reach of settler courts as currently mandated.

In its private conception of fiduciary duties, our account does not foreclose the prospect (indeed likelihood) of mutual influence between the public and the private spheres, or the entanglement of private and (plural) public interests. As the experiences of Indigenous polities attest, self-governance and lawmaking are intrinsically embedded in communal property rights, and recognition of these rights in settler law is a powerful tool for enabling and protecting Indigenous jurisdictional capacities. In this legally plural context, putatively private interests in property take on a decidedly public character as the basis for Indigenous authority. Moreover, communal property rights recognized in settler common law derive their content from the 'traditional laws and customs' that empower and obligate members of the property-holding community, and so include recognition (albeit tacit and limited) of the continuing import of Indigenous law in the settler states.

Furthermore, even within settler law, fiduciary duties in state–Indigenous relationships attach not only to Indigenous property interests (which may in appropriate cases be freighted with private fiduciary burdens in the forms of express, resulting and constructive trusts), but also, by default if not design, encompass interests in autonomy, authority, self-determination and forms of public ordering not confined within the rubric of property. Even while existing jurisprudence on the state–Indigenous fiduciary relationship and its attendant duties requires the identification of independent Indigenous *property* interests (whether pre-existing or substituted), there are lines of reasoning within this body of jurisprudence that identify broader procedural duties, including obligations to seek and receive instruction from Indigenous interest holders,[19] to accommodate Indigenous preferences[20] and to give effect to Indigenous

[16] See, e.g., Kirsty Gover, 'The Politics of Descent: Adoption, Discrimination and Legal Pluralism in the Treaty Claims Settlements Process' [2011] *NZL Rev.* 261, 286–93.

[17] For an overview of private international law as one example of variegated forms of legal pluralism, see Robert Wai, 'The Interlegality of Transnational Private Law' (2008) 71(3) *LCP* 107.

[18] The existing government-to-government relationships pertaining between recognized tribes and the federal US government is closer in substance and its historic conception to an international relations model than are the Indigenous–state relationships in the Commonwealth settler states.

[19] *Guerin* (n. 2); *Blueberry River Indian Band* v. *Canada* [1995] 4 SCR 344.

[20] *Wewaykum Indian Band* v. *Canada* [2002] 4 SCR 245 (*Wewaykum*).

law and decision-making.[21] Conceptions of fiduciary duty appear most prominently in public law reasoning as part of the constitutional principle of the honour of the Crown, which finds purchase in Canadian judicial interpretations of s. 35 of the Constitution protecting Aboriginal and treaty rights,[22] and in judicial constructions in New Zealand of the 'partnership' and 'good faith' principles of the Treaty of Waitangi.[23] In this guise, fiduciary conceptions entail, among other duties, procedural obligations such as the duty to make informed decisions, including by consultation with Indigenous peoples on matters that affect their claimed or proven property interests.[24]

For now the connection between the Crown's property-based duties and more procedural and constitutional obligations is contested, and we leave the bulk of this conversation for consideration in a separate paper.[25] The question we ask is whether (and how) this combination of private and public duties can support an account of the state–Indigenous relationship as one that pertains between polities rather than between the state and its subjects. For the time being, the fiduciary classification may supplement, shape and support the interpretation of procedural duties in public law, but does not repair the inadequacies of public law's content, structure and reasoning. It certainly does not approach what is required to found a genuinely inter-public and inter-authority conception of the state–Indigenous relationship.

These procedural and constitutional duties appear in contradistinction to general settler public law, which operates in ways that are typically ahistorical and often punishingly distributive. These use more or less symmetrical models of equality and non-discrimination that take the settler state apparatus as their temporal and institutional baseline for measures of equality and distributive justice. In doing so they fail to properly recognize or accommodate the pre-existing and continuing interests of Indigenous peoples. In contrast, an account of the state as an actor owing private fiduciary duties, we think, requires the Crown to diligently perform its obligations as an interlocutor and (where necessary) act as a bulwark between Indigenous peoples and both third parties and the public. This distinctive role as intermediary, and the priority it can secure, is of crucial importance. Case law from Australia[26] and Canada[27] indicates that where resort to fiduciary duty or other constitutional

[21] *Tsilhqot'in Nation* v. *British Columbia* [2014] 2 SCR 256 (on management of aboriginal title and economic uses to which the land can be put).

[22] *R.* v. *Sparrow* [1990] 1 SCR 1075, at 1108 ('In our opinion, *Guerin*, [. . .] ground[s] a general guiding principle for s 35(1)'); and at 1109 ('There is no explicit language in [s. 35 of the Canadian constitution] that authorizes this Court or any court to assess the legitimacy of any government legislation that restricts aboriginal rights. Yet, we find that the words "recognition and affirmation" incorporate the fiduciary relationship referred to earlier and so import some restraint on the exercise of sovereign power.').

[23] See, e.g., *Te Runanga o Wharekauri Rekohu Inc.* v. *Attorney-General* [1993] 2 NZLR 301, 304, 306 (Cooke P); *New Zealand Māori Council* v. *Attorney-General* [1987] 1 NZLR 641, 664. For the texts of the treaty, see Treaty of Waitangi Act 1975 (NZ).

[24] *Haida Nation* v. *British Columbia (Minister of Forests)* [2004] 3 SCR 511.

[25] Kirsty Gover and Nicole Roughan, 'The Authority of the Indigenous Principal: State–Indigenous Fiduciary Relationships in Constitutional Law' (manuscript on file with authors).

[26] *Gerhardy* v. *Brown* (1985) 159 CLR 70; *Maloney* v. *the Queen* (2013) 252 CLR 168.

[27] *R.* v. *Kapp* [2008] 2 SCR 483.

protections is not available, Indigenous claims are shoehorned into the narrow and inhospitable space provided by affirmative action or substantive equality measures in legislative or constitutional bills of rights.[28] If the claims and underlying interests cannot be protected as measures designed to further substantive equality, they remain vulnerable to the challenge that they are prohibited forms of racial discrimination. In the United States, for example, the landmark 1974 Supreme Court case of *Morton* v. *Mancari*[29] drew on the federal trust doctrine as a basis for deflecting equal protection claims aimed at 'preferences' for Indians, by casting the beneficiaries of those trust responsibilities as the members of recognized polities rather than members of a racial group.[30] Indigenous communities in the United States who are not similarly beneficiaries of federal trust duties are vulnerable to third-party challenges alleging racial preference in violation of the equal protection clause.[31]

The US example suggests that the designation of Indigenous communities as beneficiaries or principals of distinctive trust or fiduciary duties, rather than as racial groups, offers an important corrective to public law logics.[32] Nevertheless, and in addition to other criticisms made of that doctrine,[33] it is an inadequate protection that depends on state unilateralism in recognition practices. Where Indigenous peoples cannot be classified as beneficiaries of the state's fiduciary or trust duties because they, or the interests they assert, are not recognized in settler law, they likewise cannot be understood as political communities, appearing instead in settler public law as racial communities whose members cannot be preferred over those of other races.[34]

Alongside but apart from other critics of the 'fiduciary state', therefore, we worry that, to the extent that public fiduciary conceptions replicate the equality-based reasons that underpin administrative and constitutional law, they do not appropriately model

28 See, e.g., Kirsty Gover, 'Indigenous–State Relationships and the Paradoxical Effects of Antidiscrimination Law: Lessons from the Australian High Court in *Maloney v the Queen*' in Jennifer Hendry and others (eds), *Indigenous Justice: New Tools, Approaches, and Spaces* (Palgrave Macmillan 2018) 27–52.

29 *Morton* v. *Mancari*, 417 US 535 (1974).

30 Ibid., finding that '[r]esolution of the instant issue turns on the unique legal status of Indian tribes under federal law and upon the plenary power of Congress, based on a history of treaties and the assumption of a "guardian-ward" status, to legislate on behalf of federally recognised tribes': at 550. 'As long as the special treatment can be tied rationally towards Congress' unique obligation towards the Indians, such legislative judgments will not be disturbed': at 554–5.

31 *Rice* v. *Cayetano*, 528 US 495 (2000). Here the state of Hawaii had enacted legislation restricting voting for elections to the Office of Hawaiian Affairs to the descendants of pre-annexation residents and native Hawaiians, and sought to defend this preference by drawing an analogy with the federal trust responsibilities owed to recognized tribes by the US federal government. The majority rejected this analogy: 'To extend *Mancari* to this context would be to permit a State by racial classification, to fence out whole classes of its citizens from decision-making in critical state affairs. The fifteenth amendment forbids this result': at 522. For a recent and potentially transformative federal court decision, see *Brackeen* v. *Zinke*, 338 F. Supp. 3d 514 (ND Tex., 2018), issuing an order (based on the non-application of *Morton* v. *Mancari* (n. 29)) striking down the Indian Child Welfare Act as unconstitutional in its application to Indian children who were not members of federally recognized tribes (children eligible for membership are also included within the act's remit). These issues and cognates in other settler states are explored further in Gover and Roughan (n. 25).

32 Gover and Roughan (n. 25).

33 See, e.g., Seth Davis, 'The False Promise of Fiduciary Government' (2014) 89 *Notre Dame L. Rev.* 1145.

34 *Rice* v. *Cayetano* (n. 31).

the state–Indigenous relationship. Most treacherously, it seems possible that the principles offered to guide a 'fiduciary state' when called on to resolve competing private and public claims will replicate the injustices wrought against Indigenous peoples by the 'balancing' and 'proportionality' methods used to effect equality principles in public law. Concepts such as 'fairness, even-handedness and impartiality',[35] premised on concepts of the inherent and equal dignity of individuals an understanding those persons as subject to common, singular authority,[36] do not supply what is crucially needed, which is a method to insulate Indigenous interests from competing public and third-party claims. This in turn requires recognition that distinctive Indigenous rights and interests are not premised on the entitlement of those peoples to a fair and equitable share of primary and public goods, but to the *particular* interests held by their predecessors, which in conditions of justice they would have inherited.[37] These interests may appear in Western taxonomies as both public (governance) and private (property), but in Indigenous legal traditions, these distinctions may have little significance or relevance.[38] In what follows we discuss the ways in which the distinctiveness of Indigenous interests has been accommodated via judicial applications of state–Indigenous fiduciary duties.

3 A Closer Look at the Key Cases: *Guerin*, *Wewaykum* and *Wakatū*

In the section that follows, we revisit some of the core cases on the Indigenous–state fiduciary relationship. Our aim here is to set out the foundational features of that relationship, as constructed by the peak appellate courts of Canada and New Zealand, in order to draw attention to those characteristics most relevant to the two arms of the argument presented here. Those arms are (1) that the duties described could usefully be understood as private ones, notwithstanding the public status of the parties, and that this would better support the justice-promoting aspects of the relationship (as a set of duties that differ in quality, enforceability and application from those found in public law) and (2) that where third-party and public interests have been at stake in disputes involving Indigenous claims based on fiduciary duties, the courts have not qualified the resulting duties by reference to third-party or public interests, but instead they have kept the justifications for those interests separate in their judicial analysis. Both arms of our argument are directed towards the aim of showing that moves towards a general political theory of public fiduciary duty, at best, do not advance Indigenous interests, and at worst undermine Indigenous claims to the distinctive

[35] See, e.g., Fox-Decent, 'The Fiduciary Nature of State Legal Authority' (n. 6) 265.

[36] Ibid.

[37] Our commitment to a model of inter-public relationships does not sit easily with monistic distributive theories in which members of a community are similarly situated in respect of entitlement, vis-à-vis each other, in their relation to monistic public authority. It is not our aim here to offer a comprehensive theory in which the concerns of both distributive and corrective justice are worked out in the richly pluralist context of state–Indigenous authority and legal ordering.

[38] See, e.g., Mary Graham, 'Some Thoughts about the Philosophical Underpinnings of Aboriginal Worldviews' (2008) 45 *Australian Humanities Review* 181, 192.

protections available to Indigenous peoples (and only to Indigenous peoples) by virtue of the Indigenous–state fiduciary relationship. Here we outline the salient aspects of the cases before turning our attention to the ways that the cases have been used (and possibly misused) in accounts of public fiduciary theory.

Guerin marked the beginning of a line of jurisprudence in Canadian law that re-characterized relationship between Indigenous peoples and the Canadian Crown from a 'political trust' to one yielding legally enforceable fiduciary duties. We outline here the use made of the *Guerin* innovation in two further decisions: *Wewaykum* (Canadian Supreme Court, 2002) and *Wakatū* (New Zealand Supreme Court, 2017). Both include an elaboration of the Crown's duties to Indigenous people as duties that stand in contrast to its governmental duties to the public at large and to third parties.

A Guerin *(Canadian Supreme Court, 1984)*

In the facts giving rise to the Supreme Court's decision in *Guerin*, the Musqueam First Nation (formerly the Musqueam Band) had surrendered surplus reserve lands to the Crown so that they could be leased to a third party. The lease was subsequently concluded by the Crown in terms less favourable than those communicated to the First Nation prior to the surrender.[39] The Crown's powers were enabled by the legislative framework set out in the federal Indian Act, which provided a statutory confirmation of the discretion exercised by the executive branch over dispositions of land reserved to Indians.[40] The crucial factor in the reasoning of the majority judges, however, is that like the Aboriginal title on which they are based, First Nations' property interests in reserved lands do not derive from a Crown grant, from legislation or from treaty, and further, are inalienable except as surrenders to the Crown. Hence the relationship did not fall into the category of a 'political trust' in the way that earlier engagements had.[41] While the Indian Act obliged the Crown to exercise its discretions for the 'benefit of the Band',[42] the fiduciary obligation of the Crown did not arise from the relevant provisions of the Act, but instead '[had] its roots in the Aboriginal title of Canada's Indians',[43] and arose from the inalienability of that title. The long history of pre-emption in imperial and colonial law, guaranteeing to settler crowns a monopoly on acquisitions of aboriginal title rights, finally found purchase in *Guerin* as the source of a distinctive, legally enforceable set of fiduciary duties.

Critically, the majority judges held, these duties could not be classified usefully as public law obligations. Nor did they satisfy the requirements of trust law ('a highly-developed, specialised area of the law'[44]) that would enable the relationship to be described as an express trust (due to the lack of requisite certainties and the lack of a trust property following the surrender). Nor, in the absence of unjust enrichment on

[39] Fox-Decent, 'The Fiduciary Nature of State Legal Authority' (n. 6) 265.
[40] Indian Act, RSC 1985, c I-5, s 18. See, e.g., *Guerin* (n. 2) 348–49 (Wilson J).
[41] *Guerin* (n. 2) 379 (Dickson J).
[42] Indian Act 1985, c. I-5, s. 18(1).
[43] *Guerin* (n. 2).
[44] Ibid., 386 (Dickson J, Beetz, Lamer, McIntyre and Couinard JJ concurring).

the part of the Crown, was this an appropriate case for a constructive trust;[45] and though the relationship bore 'a certain resemblance to agency', the Crown was not strictly an agent.[46] The court's ambivalence is usefully illustrated in Dickson J's judgment:

> [T]he Indians' interest in land is an independent legal interest. It is not a creation of either the legislative or executive branches of government. The Crown's obligation to the Indians with respect to that interest is therefore not a public law duty. While it is not a private law duty in the strict sense either, it is nonetheless in the nature of a private law duty. Therefore, in this *sui generis* relationship, it is not improper to regard the Crown as a fiduciary.[47]

Elsewhere in the same judgment, Dickson J expressed the view that the Crown's obligation 'does not amount to a trust in the private law sense. It is rather a fiduciary duty',[48] albeit one that is 'trust-like in character'.[49] He thought, however, that the distinction was not determinative of remedies, noting that '[i]f [...] the Crown breaches this fiduciary duty it will be liable to the Indians in the same way and to the same extent as if such a trust were in effect'.[50] In *Guerin*, then, the Crown's fiduciary obligations derived from the particular vulnerability of Indigenous peoples and their property to the power exercised over them by the state.

In *Guerin*, it is the distinctive *source* of the Indigenous property rights in question that distinguishes the state–Indigenous fiduciary relationship from those regarded as 'political trusts'. The distinction is sufficiently important to be quoted here at some length:

> That principle [that the acquisition of sovereignty does not extinguish Aboriginal property rights] supports the assumption implicit in *Calder* that Indian title is an independent legal right which, although recognized by the Royal Proclamation of 1763, nonetheless predates it. For this reason *Kinloch v Secretary of State for India in Council; Tito v Waddell [No 2]* and the other 'political trust' decisions are inapplicable to the present case. The 'political trust' cases concerned essentially the distribution of public funds or other property held by the government. In each case the party claiming to be beneficiary under a trust depended entirely on statute, ordinance or treaty as the basis for its claim to an interest in the funds in question. The situation of the Indians is entirely different. Their interest in their lands is a pre-existing legal right not created by Royal Proclamation, by s 18(1) of the Indian Act, or by any other executive order or legislative provision.[51] [references omitted]

[45] Ibid.

[46] '[N]ot only does the Crown's authority to act on the Band's behalf lack a basis in contract, but the Band is not a party to the ultimate sale or lease, as it would be if it were the Crown's principal': at ibid. Compare Estey J (concurring), who would have relied directly on the Crown's breach of its duties of agency: at 394.

[47] Ibid., 388–9 (Dickson J, Beetz, Lamer, McIntyre and Couinard JJ concurring).

[48] Ibid., 376.

[49] Ibid., 335, 386–7. Our purposes here do not include an evaluation of the majority's position on the availability of an express or resulting trust.

[50] Ibid., 376.

[51] Ibid., 378–9 (Dickson J). See also Wilson J's opinion: 'the "political trust" line of authorities is clearly distinguishable from the present case because Indian title has an existence apart altogether from s 18(1) of the Indian Act 1985, c. I-5. It would fly in the face of the clear wording of the section to treat that interest as terminable at will by the Crown without recourse by the Band': at 352.

Crucially, then, while the Supreme Court in *Guerin* confirmed that the Crown in its regulatory 'legislative or administrative' functions was not normally viewed as a fiduciary, the fact that the Indian property interests were 'independent legal interest[s]' and 'existing' interests that were 'not a creation of either the legislative or executive branches of government' meant that the relationship could be characterized as one entailing duties 'of a private nature'. The emphasis in *Guerin*, therefore, is on the necessity of protecting Aboriginal interests from the competing claims or interests of third parties, and the role of the Crown in protecting Indigenous peoples from exploitation by third parties (in this case prospective purchasers or lessees).

B Wewaykum *(Canadian Supreme Court, 2002)*

Wewaykum applies the *Guerin* principle in a situation where two First Nations held competing interests in reserve lands. The Cape Mudge Band (the Wewaikai) and the Campbell River Band (the Wewaykum) were each erroneously assigned reserve lands intended for the other, and so came to occupy reserve lands not allocated to them as a matter of law. They claimed equitable interests in each other's reserve lands or financial compensation for the lands occupied by the other. They further claimed that these remedies were owed because the Crown had breached its fiduciary duty to each of them by misallocating their respective reserve lands.

The process of creating reserves required a complex set of consultation and consent mechanisms to be deployed between officials of the provincial and federal governments. In the case in question, this process was more than fifty years in duration, reaching a final conclusion in 1938. In the view of the court, 'from at least 1907 onwards, the Department treated the reserves as having come into existence, which, in terms of actual occupation, they had',[52] so that fiduciary duties were owed from that date: 'It cannot reasonably be considered that the Crown owed no fiduciary duty during this period to bands which had not only gone into occupation of provisional reserves, but were also entirely dependent on the Crown to see the reserve-creation process through to completion.'[53]

In 1888, before the reserves had been surveyed and approved under the federal Indian Act, a dispute arose between one of the bands and their non-Indigenous neighbours. As the boundaries of the reserve were at that stage not settled, there was no 'identifiable' Indigenous property interest yet at stake. The court had this set of third-party interests in their sights when discussing the Crown's obligations to non-Indians, as discussed in detail below. As will become clear, questions about whether the idea of a state–Indigenous fiduciary relationship can maintain its integrity in the face of competing individual and public interests has given judges pause, and intrigued proponents of public fiduciary duties. The consequences of this pressure for theories of public fiduciaries are discussed below.

[52] *Wewaykum* (n. 20) 291.
[53] Ibid.

C Wakatū *(New Zealand Supreme Court, 2017)*

The New Zealand courts have long been acutely aware of the Canadian jurisprudence on state–Indigenous duties and the need to 'lean against any inference that in this democracy the rights of the Māori people are less respected than the rights of aboriginal peoples are in North America'.[54] The Treaty of Waitangi had been described in landmark Court of Appeal cases as offering 'major support' for a fiduciary duty,[55] and the relationship it established was held to entail 'responsibilities analogous to fiduciary duties',[56] in 'a relationship of a fiduciary nature akin to a partnership'.[57] Later cases, however, decided by the Court of Appeal after it became a lower court (the Supreme Court was established in 2004), also emphasized that the treaty relationship was fiduciary 'by analogy' rather than by direct application[58] and, in addition, invoked concerns about the possibility of conflicting duties:

> [W]e see difficulties in applying the duty of a fiduciary not to place itself in a position of conflict of interest to the Crown, which, in addition to its duty to Māori under the Treaty, has a duty to the population as a whole. The present case illustrates another aspect of this problem: the Crown may find itself in a position where its duty to one Māori claimant group conflicts with its duty to another. If [the lower court judge] was saying that the Crown has a fiduciary duty in a private law sense that is enforceable against the Crown in equity, we respectfully disagree.[59]

In 2014, the new Supreme Court clarified that an enforceable fiduciary duty *could* be found in an appropriate New Zealand case,[60] preparing the ground for its 2017 decision in *Wakatū*, where a four-to-one majority held that the Crown owed a fiduciary duty to the Māori claimants with respect to land it had promised but failed to reserve for their benefit.[61] The particular dispute concerned Māori customary land at Wakatū (including modern Nelson and surrounds), purportedly sold in 1839 to the New Zealand Company on the condition that one-tenth of the land be reserved for the benefit of the customary owners and that occupied lands be excluded from the sale. In 1840, the signing of the Treaty of Waitangi committed the Crown to leave 'undisturbed' Māori rights in property, and rendered suspect pre-treaty private land sales. By operation of the Land Claims Ordinance 1841, all prior land sales were rendered void until an independent commission had investigated their circumstances, after which title vested in the Crown and could be granted to private settlers. After some delay the commission approved the sale of the land at Wakatū, noting the

[54] *Te Runanga o Muriwhenua Inc.* v. *Attorney-General* [1990] 2 NZLR 641, 655. The view was endorsed by Elias CJ in *Paki* v. *Attorney General [No. 2]* [2015] 1 NZLR 67, 124 (*Paki [No. 2]*).

[55] *Te Runanga o Wharekauri Rekohu Inc* v. *Attorney-General* (n. 23) 306.

[56] *New Zealand Māori Council* v. *Attorney-General* (n. 23) 664.

[57] *Te Runanga o Wharekauri Rekohu Inc.* v. *Attorney-General* (n. 23) 304.

[58] *New Zealand Māori Council* v. *Attorney General* [2008] 1 NZLR 318, 338.

[59] Ibid. Compare *Wewaykum* (n. 20) 293–4.

[60] *Paki (No. 2)* (n. 55). In that case, the claimants were found to have failed to establish the ownership interest which they claimed had triggered a fiduciary breach.

[61] The full facts of the case receive lengthy treatment in the judgment of Elias CJ and engage matters of contention among legal historians. For a leading analysis of the legal regimes applying to pre-treaty land sales, see Richard Boast, *Buying the Land, Selling the Land* (Victoria University Press 2008).

conditions that the 'Tenth reserves' be given effect, and occupied lands excluded. Both conditions were replicated in the subsequent Crown grant to the New Zealand Company, and by agreement between the Crown and the company, reserve lands were to vest in the Crown. In practice, however, the reserve lands were never identified, and occupied lands were not adequately excluded. The claimants argued that a trust had been created over those lands and/or that the Crown's undertakings generated fiduciary obligations, which had been breached. In the Supreme Court, two of five judges would have found a trust (and breach of trust), and as noted, the majority upheld the claim for breach of fiduciary duty.[62]

4 Public Fiduciary Law or Private Fiduciary Obligations of Public Actors?

A Independent Legal Interests

Both *Guerin* and *Wakatū* make the key point that the 'independent legal interests'[63] protected by the state–Indigenous fiduciary relationship are declared by, but not constituted or granted by, settler law. More precisely, those rights are understood as determined by independent Indigenous law and by Indigenous historic use and occupation, and then selectively recognized as common law property rights encompassed within the doctrine of aboriginal title. The doctrine of aboriginal title shows that such recognition is possible, and the state–fiduciary relationships show how pre-existing governance structures and property of Indigenous peoples can be recognized and enforced by a legal order other than the one that generates them. We see within this logic the possibility that other independent Indigenous rights could form the object of recognition within the fiduciary relationships described in these cases, and that these could extend to inherent rights to exercise authority and self-governance alongside the institutions of the state.[64]

In *Wakatū*, where the claim did not depend on doctrines of Aboriginal title, the chief justice (approving *Guerin*) further endorsed the view that the legal interests at stake were 'proprietary and exclusive, including as against the Crown',[65] on the basis that they were 'pre-existing and independent property interests'[66] arising in Indigenous systems of property.

[62] The case was remitted back to the High Court for evidence as to the extent of the breach, and argument on defences and remedies.

[63] *Guerin* (n. 2) 385; *Wakatū* (n. 3) 391.

[64] Some nascent movement on this point is discernible in Canadian law, where judges of the supreme courts have acknowledged the 'pre-existing sovereignty' of Indigenous peoples (*Haida Nation* (n. 24) 524) and have tentatively considered the possibility that self-government could be one of the 'treaty and aboriginal title rights' protected by section 35 of the Constitution (*R.* v. *Pamajewon* [1996] 2 SCR 821). At least one judge left open the possibility that aboriginal peoples and Canadian governments exercise a 'merged' and 'shared sovereignty', in which Indigenous sovereignty in Canada was not 'lost', only 'impaired' (*Mitchell* v. *MNR* [2001] 1 SCR 911, 988 (Binnie J)). As a point of comparison, New Zealand courts continue to rule out arguments based on continuing sovereignty but have offered limited forms of recognition to tikanga Māori (Māori law) as part of the law of New Zealand. See Natalie Coates, 'The Recognition of Tikanga in the Common Law of New Zealand' [2015] *NZL Rev.* 1; Joseph Williams, 'Lex Aotearoa: An Heroic Attempt to Map the Māori Dimension in Modern New Zealand Law' (2013) 21 *Waikato L. Rev.* 1.

[65] *Wakatū* (n. 3) 390.

[66] Ibid., 391.

These invocations of pre-existing and independent Indigenous legal interests are notable for entailing a (limited) recognition of legal plurality. Quite unlike other interests to which state undertakings might apply, the Indigenous property interests protected in the state–Indigenous fiduciary relationship inhere in systems of Indigenous property and authority. While these recognitions of rights and interests are not fully realized endorsements of legal plurality (as discussed in Section 4 below), they are crucially central aspects of the *distinctive* justification for the private fiduciary duties arising in state–Indigenous relationships.

B Protection of Private Independent Interests, Distinct from Public and Third-Party Interests

The key departure from the 'political trust' cases has been to position specifically protected interests as legally enforceable rights, and not mere matters of political or moral obligation, nor precluded by obligations of public governance. Significantly, in cases where fiduciary duties are owed to an Indigenous community, by virtue of their identifiable interests, judges have not weighed these protections against the Crown's public interest obligations. The cases of *Guerin*, *Wewaykum* and *Wakatū* all contain important indications of the conceptual distinction between the Crown's public functions on the one hand, and its private duties to Indigenous peoples on the other. In this section we elaborate on these aspects of the cases, in order to show the importance of private fiduciary duties as a device to protect Indigenous interests from encroaching public and third-party claims.

The importance of the protection for private interests, distinct from governmental responsibilities, takes on most significance when there are interests of third parties (Indigenous or non-Indigenous) at stake, as they were in *Wewaykum*, or when private duties could be pressured by public interests, as in *Wakatū*. These issues collide whenever the presence of competing claims is used to argue that an overarching governmental responsibility or public interest preludes private fiduciary duties altogether.

The landmark case of *Wewaykum* addresses the duties owed by the Crown in circumstances where more than one Indigenous party asserts an interest in the land in question, and where a non-Indigenous third party also claims an interest in that land. Crucially, the third-party interests are treated as matters to which the Crown should 'have regard' in the exercise of its 'ordinary governmental powers', but those interests are not themselves couched as competing claims arising within a fiduciary relationship; nor is the public interest directly referenced as entailing fiduciary duties.[67]

Instead, the sequence of events in *Wewaykum* required the court to articulate two standards of fiduciary duty, one pertaining to the period before the reserves were created (when the bands' property interests did not exist), and one that came into force once those reserves had been allocated:

[67] *Wewaykum* (n. 20) 245.

2. Prior to reserve creation, the Crown exercises a public law function under the Indian Act – which is subject to supervision by the courts exercising public law remedies. At that stage a fiduciary relationship may also arise but, in that respect, the Crown's duty is limited to the basic obligations of loyalty, good faith in the discharge of its mandate, providing full disclosure appropriate to the subject matter, and acting with ordinary prudence with a view to the best interest of the aboriginal beneficiaries.
3. Once a reserve is created, the content of the Crown's fiduciary duty expands to include the protection and preservation of the band's quasi-proprietary interest in the reserve from exploitation.[68]

The court was careful to note that the situation was not one involving the Crown's duty to conduct itself as a fiduciary when accepting a surrender of reserve lands for disposition to non-Indian purchasers; nor was the land subject to Aboriginal title or treaty rights (unlike the facts in *Guerin*).[69] The Crown was instead carrying out a number of mandated discretions enabled by federal legislation and confirmed in federal–provincial agreements. Accordingly, the court was of the view that

> [w]hen exercising ordinary government powers in matters involving disputes between Indians and non-Indians, the Crown was (and is) obliged to have regard to the interest of all affected parties, not just the Indian interest. [...] The Crown can be no ordinary fiduciary; it wears many hats and represents many interests, some of which cannot help but be conflicting. [...] In resolving the dispute between Campbell River Band members and the non-Indian settlers named Nunns, for example, the Crown was not solely concerned with the band interest, nor should it have been. The Indians were 'vulnerable' to the adverse exercise of the government's discretion, but so too were the settlers, and each looked to the Crown for a fair resolution of their dispute. At that stage, *prior to reserve creation*, the Court cannot ignore the reality of the conflicting demands confronting the government, asserted both by the competing bands themselves and by non Indians.[70] [emphasis in original]

The court then quoted from Dickson J's assessment in *Guerin* to affirm that '[p]ublic law duties, the performance of which requires the exercise of discretion, do not *typically* give rise to a fiduciary relationship'[71] (emphasis added by *Wewaykum* court), suggesting that in this phase of the dispute, before the reserves had been allocated, both public law and fiduciary duties existed alongside one another, and that the interests of all stakeholders were relevant considerations.

Considering the competing claims of the First Nations during the creation of the reserves, however, the court held that the Crown had a fiduciary duty arising from its

[68] Ibid., 290 (Binnie J). The nature of pre-reserve fiduciary obligations is of special significance in this case. Binnie J was careful to explain that the fiduciary relationship pertaining between the bands and the Crown did not yield fiduciaries' duties covering every aspect of that relationship, stating that 'even in the traditional trust context not all obligations existing between the parties to a well-recognized fiduciary relationship are themselves fiduciary in nature': at 291–2. See also *Haida Nation* (n. 24) 523: '"Fiduciary duty" does not connote a universal trust relationship encompassing all aspects of the relationship between the Crown and Aboriginal peoples.'

[69] *Wewaykum* (n. 20) 291.

[70] *Wewaykum* (n. 20) 293–4 (emphasis in original).

[71] Ibid., quoting *Guerin* (n. 2) 385.

role as intermediary between the First Nations and others, including the province.[72] This duty required it to 'act with respect to the interest of the aboriginal peoples with loyalty, good faith, full disclosure appropriate to the subject matter and with "ordinary" diligence in what it reasonably regarded as the best interest of the beneficiaries'.[73] With respect to their competing interests in one another's formally assigned reserves, the Crown had a duty to be 'even-handed towards and among the various beneficiaries' of that duty.[74] This duty, the court held, had been fulfilled by the Crown in the course of action it took.

The presence of multiple beneficiaries of fiduciary duties does not reduce in scale the extent of the duties owed to those beneficiaries, nor rule them out on the basis of their conflict. The interest of one does not, and it appears, should not, qualify the interest of the other, unless that interest is already susceptible to inherent limits. In *Wewaykum*, for example, the allocation of interests between the two bands did not have a zero-sum character; their allocations were determined in ways designed to be comparable in scope, and even given the technical error, neither had acquired reserve land at the expense of the other. As the court acknowledged, this situation was not one in which First Nations made competing claims to exclusive and non-fungible title: '(In the case of rival bands asserting overlapping claims to s 35 aboriginal title over the same land, for example, the Crown is caught truly and unavoidably in the middle, but that is not the case here.)'[75]

Under the circumstances, the Crown was obliged to give full effect to the interest held by each band. The presence of more than one beneficiary did not reduce its obligation to either:

> [T]he trial judge and the Federal Court of Appeal adopted, with respect, too restricted a view of the content of the fiduciary duty owed by the Crown to the Indian bands with respect to their existing quasi-proprietary interest in their respective reserves. In their view, the Crown discharged its fiduciary duty with respect to existing reserves by balancing 'the interests of both the Cape Mudge Indians and the Campbell River Indians and to resolve their conflict regarding the use and occupation of the [...] reserves ...

[72] *Wewaykum* (n. 20) 294.

[73] Ibid., 294.

[74] Ibid.

[75] Ibid., 292. It is difficult to imagine circumstances in which the exclusive possessory title could be found simultaneously to vest in two separate groups. There has been only one positive determination of Aboriginal title in Canada, the Supreme Court's decision in *Tsilhqot'in Nation* (n. 22), but this entailed no cross-claims. Note the different issues that arise where the interests are not held as Aboriginal *title* (which amounts to exclusive possession of land) but as Aboriginal rights to use land and waters in a way consistent with the groups' customary practices: see *R.* v. *Gladstone* [1996] 2 SCR 723, 769–70 ('Certainly the holders of such aboriginal rights must be given priority, along with all others holding aboriginal rights to the use of a particular resource; however, the potential existence of other aboriginal rights holders with an equal claim to priority in the exploitation of the resource, suggests that there must be some external limitation placed on the exercise of those aboriginal rights which lack internal limitation. Unless the possibility of such a limitation is recognized, it is difficult to see how the government will be able to make decisions of resource allocation amongst the various parties holding prioritized rights to participate in the fishery.').

> [without favouring] the interests of one band over the interest of the other' [. . .] . With respect, the role of honest referee does not exhaust the Crown's fiduciary obligation here. The Crown could not, merely by invoking competing interests, shirk its fiduciary duty.[76]

The interests of the third parties and the public affected by the transactions in *Guerin* and *Wewaykum* were not in those cases thought relevant to the fulfilment of the fiduciary duties owed to the Indigenous parties. A similar approach, separating the Crown's public governance duties from its private fiduciary ones, is evident in the reasoning of the majority in *Wakatū*. Importantly, that distinction arises even where a specific governance function itself already requires protection of Indigenous interests or special obligations not owed to the wider public. It was striking that the specific clause by which the Crown assumed the responsibility to reserve lands for the customary Māori owners explained that obligation as being additional to and distinctive from general governmental obligations the Crown owed to Māori in respect of land. As discussed by Arnold and O'Reagan JJ (in the majority):

> [T]he clause drew a clear distinction between:
>
> (a) the Government's role in ensuring that the Company's commitments to Māori in respect of the reservation and management of land were honoured; and
> (b) the Government's role in making arrangements in respect of other lands for the benefit of Māori in exercise of its general governmental responsibilities.[77]

There were thus two layers of protection in the relationship, the first arising as a consequence of the Māori landowners' general vulnerability and dependence on the Crown resulting from policies of Crown pre-emption, and the second arising from the specific undertakings to the customary landowners in respect of the specific transaction. The court divided over whether one or both (or for the dissenting judge neither) entailed fiduciary obligations enforceable in equity.

The chief justice, who with the majority found there were fiduciary duties, but was in a minority in further finding an express trust, thought that both the specific undertakings (regarding the lands at Wakatū) and the general undertakings (via Crown pre-emption) separately generated trust and fiduciary obligations. On the fiduciary duty analysis, it seemed to matter less whether a general protective relationship would have sufficed on its own, but her minority position that the Crown was a trustee two times over leaves open the more general proposition that both trust and fiduciary duties could arise from pre-emption doctrines and practices, even without the specific factual matrix of express land reservations:

> In addition to the trust that arose from the circumstances of the Crown's exclusive power to obtain surrender of the property of Indigenous peoples (grounded in the fiduciary obligations accepted in *Guerin*), I consider that the Crown in its dealings with the tenths reserves constituted itself a trustee by reason of its own assumption of responsibility in relation to the reserves.[78]

[76] *Wewaykum* (n. 20) 297–8. Some elisions in original.
[77] *Wakatū* (n. 3) 639.
[78] Ibid., 410.

Arnold and O'Reagan JJ considered that the Crown

> acted in two capacities. In its governmental capacity the Crown was concerned to ensure that pre-1840 purchases were fair. The Crown took it upon itself to provide the promised consideration. . . . In doing so, the Crown was not called upon to balance the interests of settlers and Māori or to take any decision of a political or governmental nature – it was simply performing, or ensuring the performance of, promises made to the original customary owners by the Company in the context of land sales.[79]

Glazebrook J, endorsing that approach, confirmed that the specific protection for the customary landowners was not touched by general governmental obligations nor complicated by competing loyalties, and that the specificity of the obligations did not depend on a more general state–Indigenous fiduciary duty:

> I do not accept that the Crown was unable to give its undivided loyalty to the customary owners because of its general governmental obligations including to the settlers. The Tenths reserves were to be held for the benefit of the customary owners and the settlers had no claim on those reserves. They were to be administered for the benefit of the customary owners and were thus not available for any general governmental purposes.[80]

5 The Use of Fiduciary Jurisprudence in Fiduciary Political Theory

A Assimilation of the State–Indigenous Example into Theories of the 'Fiduciary State'

The clearest and most express justificatory argument connecting the state–Indigenous fiduciary relationship with the projects advanced by fiduciary political theory is offered by Evan Fox-Decent. In his landmark work 'Sovereignty's Promise', Fox-Decent finds utility in the Canadian jurisprudence on the state–Indigenous fiduciary relationship in two ways: one indirect and generic, and the other drawing force from more precisely stated aspects of the doctrine articulated by courts.

The first strand of connection identified by Fox-Decent lies in what he understands to be a core hurdle for political theory: the deficits of accounts that source the state's legitimacy in the consent of its subjects. Fox-Decent draws a parallel between the difficulty of showing the consent of those subject to the unilateral power of the state, and the lack of consent in the unilateral assertion of sovereignty over the sovereign peoples in occupation of what is now Canada. In his words: '[t]he justification of Crown sovereignty over First Nations just makes explicit the fiduciary requirements of the ordinary justification of sovereign authority.'[81] More directly, Fox-Decent draws on Canadian jurisprudence to bolster his argument that a comprehensive public fiduciary relationship between a state and its subject is feasible and desirable '[b]ecause the Crown exercises the same kinds of powers over all its subjects, the Crown-Native case supplies a rich precedent from which to extend the idea of the

[79] Ibid., 785.
[80] Ibid., 582. References omitted.
[81] Fox-Decent, *Sovereignty's Promise* (n. 6) 78.

state as fiduciary to every person subject to state power'.[82] Fox-Decent acknowledges the strands in Canadian jurisprudence that emphasize the 'independence' of the pre-existing Indigenous legal rights at stake, but goes on to suggest that in accounts of the state–Indigenous fiduciary relationship, 'prior occupation and pre-existence are incidental rather than necessary to the fiduciary relationship. What really does the work for the court is the unilateral manner in which the Crown has asserted sovereignty over First Nations.'[83] This enables him to conclude that 'the special content of those duties does not undermine the broader idea that the state is a fiduciary of every person subject to its power'.[84]

Significantly, Fox-Decent suggests that the consideration of third-party claims in cases involving the state–Indigenous fiduciary relationship provides evidence in support of his fiduciary state model. These claims, he argues, show that the state–subject fiduciary duty is not rendered normatively or doctrinally incoherent by dint only of the pressure these claims put on orthodox concepts of fiduciary loyalty. He first makes the point that 'from the standpoint of fiduciary doctrine, it is not immediately apparent that the state can be said to be a fiduciary of both the individual and the general public, because the duties owed to each may conflict'.[85] But, he goes on to say:

> [J]urisprudence on First Nations may supply a counter-example to this objection to public fiduciary duties, since the Supreme Court has long recognised that a fiduciary relationship exists between the Crown and Canada's First Nations... The leading judgments are [*Guerin*] and [*Sparrow*]. These cases, I believe demonstrate that public fiduciary duties are possible. Indeed, the Court has recently said that the Crown's fiduciary duty remains intact even when the duty is owed to aboriginal groups with competing claims against one another.[86]

In these circumstances, 'where there are multiple beneficiaries with conflicting interests'[87], he argues that 'the fiduciary duty of loyalty may assume the content of public law duties of fairness and reasonableness'.[88]

The crucial problem with this analysis, insofar as it is premised on doctrine drawn from the court's approach in *Wewaykum*, is revealed in the analysis above. The only *beneficiaries* in the fiduciary relationship in that case were Indigenous.[89] There is no

[82] Ibid., 85.
[83] Ibid., 81.
[84] Ibid.
[85] Fox-Decent, 'The Fiduciary Nature of State Legal Authority' (n. 6) 264.
[86] Ibid., n. 5. See also Fox-Decent, *Sovereignty's Promise* (n. 6) 75: 'A further objection relates not to the desirability of deploying the fiduciary principle in this context, but to the question of whether the Crown can act as a loyal fiduciary of First Nations at all, since in some cases the interests of distinct First Nations are bound to conflict (to say nothing of First Nations' interests vis-a`-vis the interests of non-Aboriginals).'
[87] Fox-Decent, *Sovereignty's Promise* (n. 6) 75.
[88] Fox-Decent, 'The Fiduciary Nature of State Legal Authority' (n. 6) 261 and 265.
[89] Imprecise terminology employed to characterize both parties may further obscure the cases and commentaries. The more technical terminology distinguishing fiduciary–principal from trustee–beneficiary relationships may ameliorate some of the paternalism of the fiduciary category, as well as highlighting distinctions between trust and fiduciary duties: See Nicole Roughan, 'Public/Private Distortions' (n. 7).

suggestion in the court's reasoning that the non-Indigenous third parties, let alone the public at large, were similarly entitled to draw on fiduciary principles to advance their claims to the lands in question. In any case, as between the First Nation beneficiaries, the court was of the view that 'even-handedness', in the sense of impartiality, would not suffice to satisfy the performance of the Crown's fiduciary duties to the First Nation parties. Fox-Decent sees in *Wewaykum*'s reference to 'even-handedness' a fiduciary duty to the non-aboriginal stakeholders who had an interest in the Crown's decision about reserve allocations. He concludes from the court's reference to multiple and third-party interest holders that fiduciary duties can plausibly be owed to a diverse public without running afoul of loyalty commitments. In our view, as is outlined above, the case supports a conception of the Crown's fiduciary duty as one primarily concerned with securing the priority of Indigenous interests when these are under threat from competing claims.[90]

The point we make above is not confined to competing interpretations of *Wewaykum*, but has normative implications for the place of state–Indigenous exemplars in fiduciary political theory and for the justificatory force of that theory. The risk we see is that if the basis for the fiduciary *relationship* is identical for Indigenous peoples and for the public at large, there is no secure premise for a claim that the *duties* generated by these relationships differ, let alone a claim that in a conflict of duties, Indigenous interests should be accorded a degree of priority. If everyone has fiduciary protection, then perhaps no one has it.

Could requisite differentiation be supplied by a principle of 'fairness and reasonableness'? In Fox-Decent's account, he draws on Kantian principles familiar to those deployed in justifications of human rights,[91] arguing that 'the fiduciary principle can be understood to authorize the use of fiduciary power only to the extent that such power may be exercised in a manner consistent with each person's equal dignity'.[92] Otherwise, he suggests, arbitrariness enters the relationship, so that the fiduciary's mandate could be unilaterally altered to the prejudice of others who are 'similarly situated'. The key constraint operating on states faced with conflicting interests, according to Fox-Decent, is to ensure that the law 'does not and cannot, discriminate between legal persons conceived of as free and self-determining agents equally capable of have rights and acquiring obligations'. He concedes, in a footnote, the following:

> There may be some cases in which a fiduciary has a reason to treat distinct classes of beneficiaries differentially (eg a trustee may be required by the terms of the trust to project the interest of an infant beneficiary above all others). But these are not problem cases because the presence of a reason implies that the differential treatment is not arbitrary.[93]

[90] It is thus consistent with a fairly orthodox account of loyalty, notwithstanding sophisticated variants of the doctrine or dismissals of its significance. For a survey and analysis, see Andrew S. Gold, 'The Loyalties of Fiduciary Law' in Andrew S. Gold and Paul B. Miller (eds.), *Philosophical Foundations of Fiduciary Law* (Oxford University Press 2014).

[91] Fox-Decent draws elsewhere on other foundations in political theory. A sketch of the difficulties surrounding these other engagements is offered in Nicole Roughan, 'Public/Private Distortions' (n. 7).

[92] Fox-Decent, 'The Fiduciary Nature of State Legal Authority' (n. 6) 265.

[93] Ibid., n. 8.

Part of the puzzle of the reasoning presented above is that Fox-Decent seems to suggest (albeit obliquely) that the question of equal treatment between Indigenous and other individuals or legal persons can be deftly dealt with by invoking a reason that supports the need for differential treatment. Further, he may argue, there is nothing in his account that would prevent a settler state from assuming distinctive obligations to Indigenous peoples as differently situated groups of persons. The problem is that in public law and political reasoning, these reasons are far and few between. Much more prevalent in public law reasoning (especially that of Canada and Australia, but also the United States) is the idea that differential treatment of Indigenous peoples is suspect precisely because it appears as a form of impermissible preferential treatment, offered to groups on the basis of their race or ethnicity. Unfortunately for Indigenous peoples, in settler jurisprudence there is no shortage of examples in which the principles they have invoked to show that they are differently situated, and to justify their right to historic property and independent lawmaking authority, have been rejected by settler governments and courts.

What Indigenous peoples have secured through the narrow wedge of rights protected by fiduciary obligations is not simply a measure of loyalty, but a measure of priority. The relationship serves as a justification for much-needed differential treatment, necessary precisely because public law has failed to convincingly provide one, and as case law shows, the distinctive interests of Indigenous peoples remain imperilled by this failure. In this context, if the aim of fiduciary political theory, as Fox-Decent has explained, 'is not to affix new labels to familiar public law doctrines, but rather to offer an explanation of those doctrines that is attractive in its own right and responsive to criticism of the explanations that have come before',[94] then the explanations on offer are not any more attractive than the (unattractive) approaches currently available in public law. We suspect that as the law now stands, the only people who stand to lose anything in models of a comprehensively public fiduciary state are Indigenous peoples.

Notwithstanding the elasticity (and perhaps redundancy) of the 'fairness and reasonableness' standard, fiduciary political theory is sometimes presented as a way to accommodate settler state political and legal pluralists. Fox-Decent, for example, suggests that fiduciary duties can be calibrated to the scale of the interest held (or lost):

> As in the Canadian case, fiduciary concepts can help explain why Indigenous peoples benefit from such a duty while non-Indigenous citizens do not: the sovereignty of Indigenous people alone is threatened by and vulnerable to the sovereignty asserted by the formal state. The legal and political model suggested by these reflections is legal pluralism in which the pluralist fiduciary state has a duty to recognize, in some form or another, the right to self-determination of Indigenous peoples.[95]

[94] Fox-Decent, 'Challenges to Public Fiduciary Theory' (n. 5) 7. See also at 10: 'The second objection is more sweeping, and potentially devastating: if the results of the fiduciary theory are not pernicious, this is because the theory merely restates non-fiduciary doctrine that is already on the books, and therefore, at the level of doctrine and practice, the theory is superfluous.'

[95] Ibid., 11–12.

The question we pose in response, however, is not whether the approach proposed by Fox-Decent is plausible as a way to condition the exercise or legitimacy of state authority, but whether it would yield results for Indigenous peoples that are *more* just than the various public law avenues currently available to them. These include substantive equality or affirmative action measures, protections for members of minorities, treaties and, most importantly for this present project, private legal relationships that yield remedies in some cases, including of course the state–Indigenous fiduciary relationship.

We suspect the answer to our question is no. Consequently, Fox-Decent's approach seems to offer no more than extant public law mechanisms, which have not so far adequately accounted for the interests of Indigenous peoples. Further, by reconfiguring the private Indigenous–state relationship as one that can be extended wholesale to all relations between subjects and the state, Fox-Decent's characterization threatens to undermine the (modest) advantage that the relationship currently accords to Indigenous peoples. As it stands, it is the private nature of the relationship (analogous or otherwise) that serves to secure its benefits for Indigenous peoples against competing public or third-party claims. It is the non-generalizable nature of the relationship that positions it as an *augmentation* of general public law. It is among the very few legal mechanisms that have been drawn on to protect distinctive Indigenous interests (the others being treaties and other Indigenous-specific constitutional guarantees).

We further suspect that a public fiduciary theory, like public law more generally, could undermine the utility of the existing private law avenues by bringing Indigenous interests into direct conflict with third-party and public interests. The competition between these interests would thereby be resolved within the same body of law and principle, without (in the model proposed) a compelling account of Indigenous difference supporting their distinctive rights. Indigenous peoples are not similarly situated to settler populations, and settler state officials and settler state law have so far struggled to embrace a theory that could justify what would otherwise be impermissible preferential treatment of Indigenous peoples as racial communities. State–Indigenous fiduciary duties are a crack in door, very helpfully premised ultimately on inherited property rights (and so safe from the most difficult distributive elements of liberal democratic justice) but also capable of providing a model for duties that could attach to other cognizably inherent interests held by Indigenous peoples – that is, any interest that derives from their own authority as sovereign peoples.

For completeness, we note that our critique of the way that fiduciary political theory seeks to enlist the state–Indigenous fiduciary in its justificatory project differs to that offered in Seth Davis's important body of work. Davis includes reference to the Indigenous–state fiduciary relationship as part of his broader critique of fiduciary political theory and fiduciary theories of the state. As we understand Davis's complaint, the Indigenous–state example (illustrated in his work by reference to the US federal government's trust obligations to tribal nations) has enabled types of coercion and neglect that run counter to the doctrine's purported aims. He further argues that even if that relationship is given effect in compliance with its own aims and premises, it carries with it a justificatory frame for violence, paternalism and settler supremacy.[96] We agree with Davis that the concept of a fiduciary state responsible in that capacity to all members of the public could have pernicious effects. Our focus in this chapter, however, is narrower. We are concerned that Indigenous peoples could lose the ground they have gained by virtue of the fiduciary duties owed to them by states, were the same duties to be extended to all. This comparative 'advantage' is in any case meagre at best when viewed against the scale of the injustices on which it is premised, which include the continuing lack of legal avenues through which to pursue the redress for those injustices.

Davis may allow that we three agree on at least one central point: fiduciary and trust conceptions on offer are by no means the optimal model of state–Indigenous relations in the settler states.[97] However, as Davis notes, in the United States the trust doctrine nonetheless supplies some constraints on governmental interference with tribal self-governance and property, albeit inconsistently applied and often overlooked. In his words: 'It remains an open question whether Indian tribes would be better off without the trust doctrine than with it, but not because fiduciary government can fulfil the promises made in its name.'[98]

Here we are left with the uncertainty generated by the unavailable counterfactual, as well as persistent tensions between principle and pragmatism, incrementalism and wholesale change, about which we as co-authors have elsewhere differed.[99] Yet we have suggested that the existence of the federal trust doctrine, in part at least, protects the federal–tribal relationship from equal protection challenges. It does so by taking fiduciary responsibility away from public law, rather than embedding it in. Where that responsibility does not apply, as in the case of the native Hawaiian community served by the Office of Hawaiian Affairs, in *Rice* v. *Cayetano*, laws giving effect to independent Indigenous interests in collectively held property and self-governance could be struck down for non-compliance with the Constitution's equal protection clause. Given the range of federal and state laws recognizing Indigenous interests in the United States, the stakes are very high indeed.

6 Conclusion

Through the imprecision and ambivalence of jurisprudence on the state–Indigenous fiduciary duty, it is possible to discern a primary emphasis on the priority of Indigenous interests as against those of non-Indigenous third parties and the public.[100] It may

[96] 'Fiduciary theorists respond to this potential embarrassment by distinguishing that use of fiduciary government as rhetorical and racist. But postcolonial scholarship has charted the ways in which the fiduciary idea was productive of a racist colonial project and not simply reflective of it': see Davis (n. 33) 1187.

[97] Fox-Decent, *Sovereignty's Promise* (n. 6) 78.

[98] Davis (n. 33) 1188. Compare Fox-Decent: 'the relatively recent recognition of fiduciary duties owed by the Crown to Canada's First Nations was an achievement that has lent a measure of protection that was not available before'. See also Fox-Decent, 'Challenges to Public Fiduciary Theory' (n. 5) 11, and Monture-Angus (n. 9) 44–5.

[99] Roughan, 'Public Private Distortions' (n. 7); Kirsty Gover, 'The Honour of the Crowns: State–Indigenous Fiduciary Relationships and Australian Exceptionalism' (2016) 38 *Syd. LR* 339.

[100] Compare Fox-Decent, *Sovereignty's Promise* (n. 6) 62–3.

be possible to evolve a theory of 'even-handedness' and 'fairness' that accommodates this priority, but it does not seem to us that such a theory has satisfactorily been provided from within fiduciary political theory, and so far has not been plausibly advanced in statist public fiduciary law.

Instead, though, as the cases have made less than clear, the burden upon the state as a private fiduciary owing duties to Indigenous people *that it does not owe to others* ensures that actions that would constitute a private person a fiduciary will bear consequences even where that person is the state. For the time being, this remains possible because of the distinctive place of Indigenous peoples in the settler states, as pre-state polities holding continuing rights to property and authority that are not held by others. The state as fiduciary is accordingly responsible for securing those interests against the competing claims of third parties, the public and itself.

11

Political (Dis)Trust and Fiduciary Government

PAUL B. MILLER*

1 Introduction

The idea of fiduciary government stands in something of a curious relationship with ideas about trust in politics. Some have suggested that modern variants on the notion of fiduciary government represent an unfortunate juridification of a broader and more supple conception of political trust.[1] Others have suggested that theories of fiduciary government embed a political naivete through their association with political trust (and the, by turns, dangerous and quaint embrace of government paternalism and the notion that citizen trust in government is desirable).[2] In turn, advocates of fiduciary government have appealed to philosophical accounts of political trust as providing indirect support for the plausibility of a fiduciary conception of the state and of public office.[3] Thus have the fate of two sets of ideas – one of political philosophy, the other of legal theory – been joined.

For reasons that I shall explain, it is natural to link ideas of fiduciary government and political trust. It is not for nothing that critics and supporters of fiduciary government alike have been inclined to draw connections, each for their own purposes and to conflicting ends. The thought that the idea of fiduciary government might promote – by rendering more articulate – a political morality of trust seems only to be strengthened by an extensive literature that suggests a symbiosis between the personal morality of trust and the formation and flourishing of private fiduciary relationships.[4] If an interpersonal ethic of trust underlies and/or is promoted by private fiduciary relationships, it seems reasonable to think that political trust might have some normative salience for fiduciary government, and vice versa.

* I am grateful for comments from Evan Criddle, Evan Fox-Decent, Andrew Gold, Matthew Harding, Carolyn McLeod, James Penner and Gerald Postema.

[1] See, for example, Timothy Endicott, "The Public Trust" in Evan J. Criddle et al. (eds.), *Fiduciary Government* (Cambridge University Press 2018).

[2] See, for example, Seth Davis, "The False Promise of Fiduciary Government" (2014) 89 *Notre Dame L. Rev.* 1145, and Seth Davis, "Pluralism and the Public Trust" in Evan J. Criddle et al. (eds.), *Fiduciary Government* (Cambridge University Press 2018).

[3] Evan Fox-Decent, *Sovereignty's Promise: The State as Fiduciary* (Oxford University Press 2011) 3–4; Evan J. Criddle, "Fiduciary Foundations of Administrative Law" (2006) 54 *UCLA L. Rev.* 117, 124; and D. Theodore Rave, "Institutional Competence in Fiduciary Government" in D. Gordon Smith and Andrew S. Gold (eds.), *Research Handbook on Fiduciary Law* (Elgar 2018) 418.

[4] With mind, of course, to conditions requisite to realization of symbiosis. See especially Matthew Harding, "Trust and Fiduciary Law" (2013) 33 *OJLS* 81.

I say *might* advisedly. And that is because despite a tendency toward free association of ideas of political trust and fiduciary government, the precise relationship(s) between them have yet to analyzed. Discussions of political trust by political theorists sometimes make passing mention of "fiduciary" relationships and duties. And likewise, fiduciary theorists have made different things – constructive and critical – of apparent similarities between notions of political trust and fiduciary government. But neither body of work takes extended notice of the other.

In this chapter I aim to clarify the relationship between ideas of political trust and fiduciary government. I do so by examining several facets of political trust and what I take to be associated dimensions of fiduciary government. The overarching ambition is to clarify the relevance of each idea to the other. But my primary focus will be on explaining ways in which reflections on political trust shed new light on the moral and political significance of the idea of fiduciary government.

The chapter will unfold as follows. Section 1 provides a brief introduction to the idea of fiduciary government, distinguishing normatively thick variants on the idea favored by others from the normatively thin variant that I have articulated elsewhere. Section 2 introduces the idea of political trust, explaining the relational structure of trust and the distinction between subjective and objective forms of political trust. Sections 3–5 explore links between specific facets of political trust and fiduciary government, respectively. Section 3 compares and contrasts objective political trust with the conceptualization of public fiduciary mandates and the formation of fiduciary relationships. Section 4 considers the elements of political trustworthiness in comparison with what counts as compliance with public fiduciary norms. And Section 5 examines republican political theorists' suggestion that robust political trust requires a posture of citizen distrust and argues that the rationale for political distrust supports significant reframing of the idea of fiduciary government.

2 Fiduciary Government, Thick and Thin

As noted earlier, the idea of fiduciary government is sometimes attributed to figures who spoke or wrote of trust in government in broad terms. Thus, the lineage of the idea has been traced to the writings of Cicero, the political philosophy of John Locke and the vision of republican government held by America's founding fathers.[5] But I wish presently to focus on recent scholarship that elaborates *specifically fiduciary* conceptions of government; that is, the legal or juridical basis – doctrinal and/or theoretical – for fiduciary characterization of government functions or offices.[6]

[5] See works cited, *supra* note 3.

[6] Ibid. See also Paul Finn, "The Forgotten Trust: The People and the State" in Malcolm Cope (ed.), *Equity: Issues and Trends* (Federation Press 1995); Evan Fox-Decent, "Fiduciary Authority and the Service Conception" in Andrew S. Gold and Paul B. Miller (eds.), *Philosophical Foundations of Fiduciary Law* (Oxford University Press 2014); Evan J. Criddle, "Fiduciary Administration: Rethinking Popular Representation in Agency Rulemaking" (2010) 88 *Texas L. Rev.* 441; D. Theodore Rave, "Politicians as Fiduciaries" (2013) 126 *Harv. L. Rev.* 671; Sung Hui Kim, "The Last Temptation of Congress: Legislator Insider Trading and the Fiduciary Norm against Corruption" (2013) 98 *Cornell L. Rev.* 845; Ethan J. Leib et al., "A Fiduciary Theory of Judging" (2013) 101 *Calif. L. Rev.* 699; Ethan J. Leib et al., "Mapping Public

As I will explain, there are important differences between theories of fiduciary government. Some differ in their construal of the fiduciary character of government (for example, whether they think that there is a doctrinal basis for construing government in fiduciary terms or instead think the basis for the characterization to be legal-theoretical). They also differ in the account given of the normative implications of a fiduciary conception of government. However, there is also common ground.

One point of common ground is the conviction that fiduciary law – in doctrinal or legal-theoretical terms – supports a fiduciary characterization of government. It is, for example, widely accepted that government offices and functions are fiduciary insofar as they entail the possession and exercise of discretionary powers for other regarding purposes. As I have explained elsewhere, one legal-theoretical way of understanding the common relational structure of private and public administration is to recognize that *both* are fiduciary precisely insofar as they entail *representation* – i.e., relationships in which one person or group of persons personates, and so represents, another person or group through the exercise of legal power on their behalf.[7] The fiduciary characterization of a relationship or mandate signals and reflects the fundamentally representative nature of private and public administration; i.e., that fiduciaries just are persons legally authorized to act for others and that fiduciary relationships are relationships in which representation is given effect in the interests, or for the ends, of those represented by the fiduciary.

Another point of common ground is that the fiduciary characterization of a relationship, private or public, is normatively consequential in broadly uniform ways. The representative nature of a mandate is secured by a set of norms that require the fiduciary to respect its representative or other-regarding character. Compliance with these norms is necessary, perhaps even sufficient, to make one a good – or reasonably decent – representative. Violation of one or more of them marks particular failures or imperfections of representation. As I have explained elsewhere, fiduciary norms ramify differently in private and public law.[8] It is a mistake to refer in broad brush to "fiduciary duties," with the implication that private and public fiduciaries are held to identical standards, and that the standards applicable to public fiduciaries are necessarily (or even usually) legal. Nevertheless, it is possible – and instructive – to elucidate a broad set of principles that underlie and inform fiduciary standards in

Fiduciary Relationships" in Andrew S. Gold and Paul B. Miller (eds.), *Philosophical Foundations of Fiduciary Law* (Oxford University Press 2014); Paul B. Miller and Andrew S. Gold, "Fiduciary Governance" (2015) 57 *Wm. & Mary L. Rev.* 513; Evan J. Criddle et al. (eds.), *Fiduciary Government* (Cambridge University Press 2018); Ethan J. Leib and Stephen Galoob, "Fiduciary Principles and Public Offices" in Evan J. Criddle, Paul B. Miller and Robert H. Sitkoff (eds.), *The Oxford Handbook of Fiduciary Law* (Oxford University Press 2019); and D. Theodore Rave, "Fiduciary Principles and the State" in Evan J. Criddle, Paul B. Miller and Robert H. Sitkoff (eds.), *The Oxford Handbook of Fiduciary Law* (Oxford University Press 2019).

[7] Paul B. Miller, "Fiduciary Representation" in Evan J. Criddle et al. (eds.), *Fiduciary Government* (Cambridge University Press 2018).

[8] Paul B. Miller, "Principles of Public Fiduciary Administration" in Anat Scolnicov and Tsvi Kahana (eds.), *Boundaries of State, Boundaries of Rights* (Cambridge University Press 2016).

private law, public law and beyond.[9] The set includes principles of fidelity and prudence that require fiduciaries to respect the other-regarding purposes that underlie their mandates and principles of consensualism and candor that require fiduciaries to respect residual control interests of those whom they represent.[10]

I have said that there is broad consensus on the basis for fiduciary characterization of government functions and offices, and on the abstract implications of the characterization. However, there is a divergence of views on the wider implications of the idea of fiduciary government, including, especially, its implications for basic questions of political morality, of constitutional interpretation and structure, and of justice. Put simply, there is nascent difference of opinion on the implications of fiduciary government for a wide range of issues of normative political theory. As yet, these differences have not ripened into debate. But the issues loom large. Among them: Is fiduciary government primarily a legal or juridical idea, or one of political morality? How much normative weight can the idea of fiduciary government bear? Which normative questions – in law and in politics – might it illuminate or help to resolve? Recognizing that they have yet to be threshed out, we can get a handle on the positions likely to be staked on questions like these by distinguishing normatively *thick* from *thin* accounts of fiduciary government.

Thick accounts of fiduciary government treat it primarily as a legal or juridical idea and make bold and broad claims as to its normative significance. The work of Evan Fox-Decent is a leading example. According to Fox-Decent, a properly sorted theory of fiduciary government – i.e., one such as his own – may be an "ecumenical theory of everything" for public law.[11] By ecumenical, Fox-Decent means to suggest that fiduciary government has no particular political valence and so should be as appealing to liberals as it is to conservatives. Fox-Decent does not show that fiduciary government is per se ecumenical. It seems more plausible to suggest that theorists of different political stripes can find – or can highlight – different things in the idea. More to the point, though, is the suggestion that fiduciary government is, or could be, a "theory of everything." This rather arresting claim may not be meant to be taken literally – but nearly so, nonetheless. After all, in a large body of work drawn on broad canvass, Fox-Decent has made several strong claims about the normative implications of the idea of fiduciary government. In *Sovereignty's Promise*, he suggests that recognition of the fiduciary nature of state legal authority resolves (entirely or in part) the problem of political authority – i.e., that of justifying the authority the state claims over a public, absent meaningful consent.[12] In other work, Fox-Decent and Criddle suggest that the state's fiduciary obligations extend to – and thus explain and justify – the legal recognition and protection of various human rights.[13] Elsewhere, Fox-Decent has

[9] Ibid.

[10] Ibid.

[11] Evan Fox-Decent, "New Frontiers in Public Fiduciary Law" in Evan J. Criddle, Paul B. Miller and Robert H. Sitkoff (eds.), *The Oxford Handbook of Fiduciary Law* (Oxford University Press 2019) 909, 910.

[12] *Supra* note 3, at 89–112.

[13] Evan Fox-Decent and Evan J. Criddle, "The Fiduciary Constitution of Human Rights," (2009) 15 *Legal Theory* 301; Evan J. Criddle and Evan Fox-Decent, "Human Rights, Emergencies, and the Rule of Law," (2012) 34 *Hum. Rts. Q.* 39.

argued that the state has a fiduciary duty to present and future generations to take action on climate change.[14] And he and Criddle have made several arguments about the normative implications of the idea of fiduciary government for questions of constitutional structure, substantive law and institutional practice that bear on the roles and responsibilities of legislators, judges, administrative agencies and members of the executive branch.[15] On this rendering, plainly, the idea of fiduciary government is expected to bear very considerable normative freight within public law proper and beyond.

In other work, I have questioned whether the idea of fiduciary government can do all that has been asked of it.[16] My settled view is that it cannot; the idea sounds primarily in political morality rather than in law, and the contribution that it makes to normative political theory, while important, is relatively modest. I do not mean to press the point here. However, because I propose presently to explore the relationship between political trust and fiduciary government, I should clarify that the variant that I will be discussing is my own *thin* conception of fiduciary government. In my view, if the idea of fiduciary government is truly ecumenical, it can have achieved that only in virtue of its normative thinness. As I understand it, the idea does not resolve the problem of political authority, has no bearing on the resolution of inherently morally and politically divisive questions of public policy, and has only indirect[17] bearing on contentious questions of public law – including questions about constitutional structure, human rights and justice. For the most part, these questions – ones the answers to which shape the doctrinal content and contours of public law – are to be debated and resolved through the usual mechanisms of political decision-making.

The more modest normative contribution of the idea of fiduciary government is that of articulating conditions under which public governance (i.e., affairs of state) may be judged as a matter of political morality to have been conducted in a genuinely representative way.[18] Fiduciary government supplies a normative theory of the means rather than the ends of public governance. It suggests that a government and its officials can be understood as personifying a public and as exercising prerogative powers in an authentically public way, only to the extent that it respects the other-regarding purposes attached to these powers for the benefit of the public – whatever those purposes might happen to be, however prerogative power might happen to have been assumed or devolved upon a sitting government or government agent, and however political debates over the special or general ends of government and limitations on the authority of the state might be resolved.

Happily for our purposes, the central thematic concern of the thin conception of fiduciary government (i.e., determining what follows, morally, from the devolution of public powers to representative government) aligns quite nicely with the core

[14] Evan Fox-Decent, "From Fiduciary States to Joint Trusteeship of the Atmosphere: The Right to a Healthy Environment through a Fiduciary Prism" in Ken Coghill et al. (eds.), *Fiduciary States and the Atmospheric Trust* (Ashgate 2012).

[15] *Supra* notes 3 and 6.

[16] *Supra* note 8.

[17] Indirect in the sense of ruling out rather than ruling in or arbitrating between various answers to these questions.

[18] *Supra* note 7.

preoccupation of those interested in political trust (i.e., determining whether and if so when and in what sense a public joined in political community can be said to place trust in those who enjoy and exercise governmental power).

3 Trust: General and Particular, Subjective and Objective

In the decades following the publication of Annette Baier's landmark essay, philosophical interest in trust has burgeoned.[19] Moral philosophers have provided sophisticated accounts of the morality of interpersonal trust.[20] Political theorists have provided equally nuanced accounts of the ethics and politics of political trust.[21] And this is to say nothing of the voluminous social science literature on the subject, including a robust body of work in economics, psychology, sociology and management. While most of the social science work is not philosophically motivated, it does have implications for philosophical analyses of trust. The sheer volume and variety of work on trust and the different – sometimes sharply divergent – conclusions drawn about the nature of trust and its moral, social, political and economic significance lends the topic a somewhat mesmerizing quality. Much ground has been covered, and little of it is common or the subject of learned consensus.

Obviously, I cannot presently canvass all that might be of potential interest to proponents of the idea of fiduciary government in the literature on trust. Nor can I even do justice to the literature on political trust as a species of the broader genus. But I can and will highlight aspects of the literature on the genus and species that hold lessons for future development of the idea of fiduciary government. In many cases, I will be reduced to making stipulative definitions of my own or endorsement of those of others in the interest of presenting a coherent and tractable concept of political trust. Though I regret that the discussion must be truncated, I am comforted by the recognition that we have already to hand excellent philosophical accounts of the significance of trust to fiduciary law,[22] including other chapters in this volume.

A Trust: General and Particular

Unfortunately, if illustratively, one cannot even begin to relate something philosophically interesting about trust without landing in controversy. Philosophers agree that trust is a relational concept, even if they disagree about the possibility – and the sense of relationality – of self-trust. As a relational concept, trust marks out something about the character of the relationship(s) between two or more persons. But what exactly? And

19 Annette Baier, "Trust and Antitrust" (1986) 96 *Ethics* 231.

20 For recent analysis, see the papers collected in Paul Faulkner and Thomas Simpson (eds.), *The Philosophy of Trust* (Oxford University Press 2017). See also Eric M. Ulsaner, *The Moral Foundations of Trust* (Cambridge University Press 2002).

21 See especially Mark E. Warren (ed.), *Democracy and Trust* (Cambridge University Press 1999); Valerie A. Braithwaite and Margaret Levi (eds.), *Trust and Governance* (Russell Sage 2003); and Eric M. Ulsaner, *The Oxford Handbook of Social and Political Trust* (Oxford University Press 2018).

22 *Supra* note 4. See also Matthew Harding, "Manifesting Trust" (2009) 29 *OJLS* 245; and Matthew Harding, "Responding to Trust" (2011) 24 *Ratio Juris* 75.

how broad or narrow is, or might, trust be? We shall have to put off the former question, for it goes to the meaning of trust, and as we shall see, there is reason to think that personal and political trust have (or can have) divergent meanings and (fortunately, for us) that the meaning of personal trust is more ambiguous than is that of political trust.

Turning, then, to the question of the scope of trust: the literature marks out two possibilities. One view, increasingly prominent, is that trust should be understood as generalized relational property.[23] Trust marks an encompassing stance of one person to another, or broad construal of another. We trust in something stable and therefore reliable in the trusted person's character, behavior, or manifest motivations or intentions. The notion that trust is generalized in relationships in which it obtains is captured in the claim that trust should be analyzed formally as a *two-part* relation: A trusts B, where "trusts" marks A's inclination to consider and to treat B as a trustworthy *in general* and to distinguish him from others *in general* (i.e., as a person who deserves or merits trust) on that basis.[24]

The notion that trust might be *generalized* makes sense in accounting for personal trust between intimates and close associates. It captures something of the specialness of ideal types of relationships between spouses, parents and children, friends, and others in long-term relationships that involve repeat interactions that imply mutual dependence. Often, if we are to realize value in these relationships, it will be because we recognize our counterpart as trustworthy in general, place trust in them on that basis and aim to prove trustworthy in general ourselves in return.

However, if trust could *only* be properly understood as a generalized way of relating to others, it would have little direct bearing on fiduciary law or on the formation and flourishing of fiduciary relationships in everyday life. The same is true of trust in other kinds of legal relationship, from trust in contracts to trust in (or under) organizational governance. For in these cases, we are primarily interested in trust between strangers that is *purposive*. Here, usually, if there is trust at all, it will be *particularized* and so comparatively narrow or focused.

Fortunately, the conventional view of personal trust treats it in a particularized way. The starting point is Baier's suggestion that trust should be understood formally as a three-part relation in which the third element is the object of trust. Particularized trust arises where *A trusts B to do (or with) C*. The object of trust could be any of a number of things. For example, it could be a particular task or assignment. It could involve the care or custody of a person or thing, or some specific aspect of the affairs or a person or handling of a thing. Or it could simply involve the trusted person being present, or being present toward, another in a certain manner (i.e., adopting a certain attitude or behaving in a particular way). However one understands the range of possible objects of trust, it should be evident that particularized trust is the more salient variety of trust in politics and for private and public fiduciary relationships.

23 Jacopo Domenicucci and Richard Holton, "Trust as a Two-Place Relation" in Paul Faulkner and Thomas Simpson (eds.), *The Philosophy of Trust* (Oxford University Press 2017) 149; Paul Faulkner, "The Problem of Trust" in Paul Faulkner and Thomas Simpson (eds.), *The Philosophy of Trust* (Oxford University Press 2017) 109, 118–23.

24 Ibid.

As to the first point, while it is not inconceivable to imagine generalized citizen trust in government, it would be unusual and might even be defective and so something to be discouraged. Broad trust in government is suggestive of naivete – an *unduly* trusting passivity – about politics, about what government is for (i.e., what kinds of functions are properly entrusted to government, as contrasted with those that should be left to individuals, markets and mediating institutions) and about forces that shape the functioning of government institutions and the behavior of public officials. If we are to trust in government, it is better to be clear and specific about what we are trusting government to do.

As to the second point, I think it fairly obvious that the variety of trust most pertinent to fiduciary relationships is particularized. Sometimes a fiduciary might be granted a mandate on the basis of a close personal bond – one indicative of generalized trust – between him and the grantor (e.g., the selection of friends or family members to serve as guardians, trustees or executors). However, this is rare: fiduciary relationships are more commonly established between strangers, and so their personal and social utility turns on the possibility of trust between strangers. Furthermore, whatever the nature of the preformation bond (or lack thereof) between parties to a particular fiduciary relationship, it remains the case that general characteristics of fiduciary relationships are such as to call for particularized trust. Fiduciaries are called upon – trusted, if you will – to do *something in particular* for the grantor and his appointed beneficiaries. Namely, they are to undertake and exercise legal powers devolved by way of mandate in pursuit of other-regarding purposes expressly or impliedly attached to the mandate.[25] Thus, a trustee is trusted to perform the trust according to its terms and for the purposes identified by the settlor. The lawyer is trusted to provide specific legal services in the interests of her client in a matter in respect of which she has been retained.

The specificity of trust implied by a fiduciary relationship holds also in respect of fiduciaries appointed on the basis of generalized trust. Generalized trust in these circumstances reflects a purely personal condition or expressed preference of the grantor (i.e., given the choice, the grantor preferred to extend a mandate to someone they knew well enough to regard with general trust). It does no violence to one's thinking to say that, based on the general esteem in which they were held, these individuals were extended particularized trust to perform a fiduciary mandate, and so to do something for another.

B Trust: Subjective and Objective

As one turns from the relational character of trust to the meaning of trust, the dissensus deepens. There are by now several distinct plausible explanations of what trust consists in. The literature can again be cleaved in two. One the one hand are

[25] See generally Paul B. Miller, "The Fiduciary Relationship" in Andrew S. Gold and Paul B. Miller (eds.), *Philosophical Foundations of Fiduciary Law* (Oxford University Press 2014). See also Paul B. Miller, "Dimensions of Fiduciary Loyalty" in D. Gordon Smith and Andrew S. Gold (eds.), *Research Handbook on Fiduciary Law* (Elgar 2018).

accounts that treat trust as a subjective state of mind taken toward another.[26] And on the other are those that treat trust as a mode of relating to another through one's behavior.[27] Some characterize the former as trust properly so called and the latter as a "trusting response" or kind of "entrustment."[28] But in order to avoid begging questions about the parameters of trust, and for the sake of perspicuity, we can say that accounts of the former sort explain trust in *subjective* terms, while the latter explain it in *objective* terms.

What does, or might, trust consist in, if understood in subjective terms? There are a variety of views on offer. Some cognitivist accounts treat trust as a calculative assessment (resulting in a belief, opinion or prediction) of the probability that another will prove trustworthy by behaving in accordance with one's expectations. Trusting behavior is therefore understood as the product of considered decision-making in conditions of endemic uncertainty. Other cognitivist accounts frame trust as a belief about the motivations or intentions of the person in whom trust is placed (e.g., the trusting person believes the trusted to be well intentioned or properly motivated toward them). By contrast, some have argued that cognitivist theories provide an unduly thin or partial rendering of trust. Trust, they say, is not always – and not paradigmatically – calculative. Rather, in many circumstances, trust is automatic, or if not automatic, then relatively unreflective. It springs up, and waxes and wanes, as a result of deeper psychological drives and forces – some reflecting our self-conception, others our perceptions of other people. Thus, it has been argued that trust is an *affective* state. For example, Becker has argued that trust is a matter of noncognitive security about the motives of another.[29] Others have emphasized reactive attitudes that arise upon discovery of a betrayal of trust.[30] Our tendency to experience negative moral emotions when our trust is betrayed suggests that trust itself involves a positive moral-emotional investment in, and attachment to, another.[31]

Subjective accounts are most at home as explications of personal trust. That is because, whether framed in cognitive or affective terms, they assume relationships of close familiarity. The truster personally knows the trusted – or relies on the testimony of those who do – and so is in a position to form beliefs constitutive of trust. Alternatively, and more demandingly, the truster is close enough to the trusted to make an emotional investment in them. Partly because subjective accounts assume

[26] See, for example, Karen Jones, "Trust as an Affective Attitude" (1996) 107 *Ethics* 4; Lawrence C. Becker, "Trust as Noncognitive Security About Motives" (1996) 107 *Ethics* 43; Bernd Lahno, "On the Emotional Character of Trust" (2001) 4 *Ethical Theory & Moral Practice* 171; Stephen Darwall, "Trust as a Second-Personal Attitude (of the Heart)" in Paul Faulkner and Thomas Simpson (eds.), *The Philosophy of Trust* (Oxford University Press 2017) 35; Richard Holton, "Deciding to Trust, Coming to Believe" (1994) 72 *Aust J. Phil.* 63; Russell Hardin, "The Street-Level Epistemology of Trust" (1992) 21 *Pol. & Soc'y* 505; Benjamin McMyler, "Deciding to Trust" in Paul Faulkner and Thomas Simpson (eds.), *The Philosophy of Trust* (Oxford University Press 2017) 161.

[27] Baier, *supra* note 19. See also Thomas W. Simpson, "What Is Trust?" (2012) 93 *Pacific Phil. Q.* 550.

[28] Pamela Hieronymi, "The Reasons of Trust" (2008) 86 *Aust. J. Phil.* 213.

[29] *Supra* note 26.

[30] Katherine J. Hawley, "Trust, Distrust, and Commitment" (2014) 48 *Noûs* 1.

[31] Colin O'Neil, "Betraying Trust" in Paul Faulkner and Thomas Simpson (eds.), *The Philosophy of Trust* (Oxford University Press 2017) 70.

intimacy or familiarity in relationships of trust, some have doubted whether these accounts can be extended to relationships where that is atypical, including relationships of political trust.[32] Political trust is prototypically a kind of trust between strangers. The state is a faceless monolith; if it can be a recipient of trust at all, it cannot be on the basis of personal familiarity and beliefs or emotional investments premised on same. Likewise, public officials are usually strangers to the average citizen. These considerations suggest that subjective accounts of trust – and the phenomena they describe – are generally foreign to politics. But it should be noted that the point is not analytic. Some citizens likely do, if rarely, trust in government and in public officials by holding requisite beliefs and by making appropriate emotional investments, taking them to be trustworthy. So: we should hold open the possibility that political trust might encompass subjective trust, even if that is unusual.

We may turn now to objective conceptions of trust. What does, or might, trust consist in if understood in objective terms? The focus here is on *manifestations* of trust, or trusting behavior, whether or not it reflects trust in a subjective (cognitive and/or affective) sense.[33] Given the interest in trust as relational behavior, special attention is also paid to ways in which trust can be cultivated, invited and, where manifested, accepted, resulting in a mutual bond of trust. How, exactly, is trust manifested? Here one is again confronted by a variety of views. Some adopt a simple reliance-based conception of trust, according to which one manifests trust by relying on others in circumstances where one willingly places one's own interests at risk.[34] Others espouse a narrower powers-based account, according to which one manifests trust by granting another power over one's person or property, knowingly rendering oneself vulnerable to their misuse or abuse of power.[35]

Objective accounts were initially devised in order to explain personal trust in bilateral interactions between strangers and in group activity. They are especially valuable because they show how trust supports cooperation in small- and large-scale transactional and organizational contexts. Indeed, scholars have made a compelling case for thinking that personal trust is manifested (i.e., is reflected in individual and group behavior) in many of relationships of social and economic interdependence.[36] But objective accounts also hold obvious appeal for the analysis of political trust. As Pettit has shown, political trust is most readily understood as objective, and the phenomena that may be described as trust is plain for all to see.[37] Citizens invariably rely on the state and public officials for the provision of law, essential public goods

[32] Rom Harré, "Trust and Its Surrogates: Psychological Foundations of Political Process" in Mark E. Warren (ed.), *Democracy and Trust* (Cambridge University Press 1999).

[33] See generally Harding, *supra* note 22.

[34] Philip Pettit, "Trust, Reliance and the Internet" (2004) 26 *Analyse & Kritik* 108. See also Simon Blackburn, "Trust, Cooperation, and Human Psychology" in Valerie Braithwaite and Margaret Levi (eds.), *Trust and Governance* (Russell Sage 2003).

[35] Baier, *supra* note 19.

[36] See generally Ernest Gellner, "Trust, Cohesion, and the Social Order" in Diego Gambetta (ed.), *Trust: Making and Breaking Cooperative Relations* (Blackwell 1988), and Oliver E. Williamson, Calculativeness, Trust, and Economic Organization (1993) 34 *J. L. & Econ.* 453.

[37] Philip Pettit, "Republican Theory and Political Trust" in Valerie Braithwaite and Margaret Levi (eds.), *Trust and Governance* (Russell Sage 2003).

and important services. Equally, it cannot escape notice that, at least in democratic societies such as our own, government is made effective through rituals involving the conferral, undertaking and exercise of power for public purposes. The synchronicity is such that one is tempted simply to say that, though levels of subjective political trust wax and wane, democratic government entails political trust in an objective sense. And, indeed, Pettit has said as much. In his view, the reality is that we have no choice but to manifest political trust insofar as our subjection to government power is inescapable.[38] Our political agency is a matter of our capacity to decide *whom* to trust, recognizing that we must trust *someone* to govern.

In what follows, I will analyze the relationship between the thin conception of fiduciary government, on the one hand, and Pettit's *particularized* and *objective* conception of political trust, on the other. Independently of the fact that both present plausible interpretive accounts of relevant considerations of law and politics, each idea is the direct analogue of the other and so mutually illuminating of the normativity of a trust-based view of the law and politics of public representation.

4 Political Trust and Fiduciary Government

An advantage of understanding political trust as Pettit does is that it enables us to see consistency in the structure of trust relationships, from the personal to the political. In everyday life, we manifest trust reciprocally by giving and receiving other-regarding discretionary power, and we respect the expectations and emotional investments that accompany these rituals by restraining self-interest in favor of conduct calculated to benefit those who have shown us trust.[39] As Pettit observes, we are similarly bound up in demonstrations of political trust in government and in public officials.[40] Political trust, so understood, captures something essential about our political facticity. We have no choice but to place trust in government. And this is not merely a trite observation about our having inherited rule by (and so subjection to) government. We are collectively needful of sound government, and governing entails possession and discretionary exercise of the prerogative powers of state.

For those fortunate to live under democratic government, citizens decide where to place their political trust by electing representatives. In acting on political participatory rights, citizens often both (a) manifest trust (whether in candidates, fellow citizens and/or political processes) and (b) place or enforce conditions on their investiture of trust. As is true of relationships of personal trust, so through the investiture of political trust we rely on others to represent our interests, recognizing that they might well disappoint our expectations by ignoring imperatives that attach to their powers. In this, we face a collective political vulnerability that corresponds in its basic character with the personal vulnerability that we must accept whenever we trust others in bilateral relationships of representation.

[38] Ibid., 299–304. See also John Dunn, "Trust and Political Agency" in Diego Gambetta (ed.), *Trust: Making and Breaking Cooperative Relations* (Blackwell 1988).

[39] Baier, *supra* note 19.

[40] *Supra* note 37.

Another attraction of Pettit's republican framing of political trust is that it dovetails nicely with the idea of fiduciary government and suggests a broader conceptual continuity between objective trust and fiduciary relationships. From personal and political trust, to private and public fiduciary administration, we are concerned with a specific form of relationship that operates on personal and political levels: that of representation.[41] As is true of the thin conception of fiduciary government, so too the republican conception of political trust emphasizes that the prerogative powers of democratic states are held on a representative basis, having been entrusted to government for the good of a political community. As is also true of the thin conception of fiduciary government, the republican conception of political trust implies that public officials can live up to the representative nature of their office only by acting in accordance with the terms of a trust reposed. Ordinarily, this will be a matter of respecting the other-regarding purposes and pledges, promises or other commitments that attach to their office. Under both accounts, respect will be shown through abidance and active pursuit of these purposes and commitments, by action that shows due care and consideration of the gravity of decisions made and actions taken while in office, by a posture of self-restraint and by recognition of the political agency of constituents and their standing to demand accountability.

One understandable worry might be that the synchronicity of political trust and fiduciary government is suggestive of their redundancy. It might be thought that there are not two distinct ideas here. Instead, there is a single idea, and the only question is whether it is more illuminatingly framed in terms of trust or fiduciary obligation. However, as I will explain, ideas of political trust and fiduciary government dovetail without proving duplicative. Important differences obtain on descriptive and normative planes.

First, it should be noted that each idea is addressed to a different explanandum. Parallels in the descriptive claims made about the explananda are a function of the fact that they are integrated. Allow me to explain.

I take it that, insofar as the republican conception of political trust advances descriptive claims, it is engaged in a project of characterizing elements of an underlying political reality (or set of realities). More specifically, having stipulated assumptions of democratic government and collective aspiration to popular sovereignty for a polity, the republican conception advances claims about how we ought to understand democratic franchise, party politics, deliberative political processes and political institutions. It claims, for example, that popular election of representatives entails objective trust (i.e., a collective manifestation of political trust). It suggests that campaign promises are intended to, and do, induce constituent trust. And it suggests that political checks-and-balances mechanisms in government should be understood as trust securing or reinforcing. Put simply, the suggestion is that much *political activity*, within and beyond political institutions, is underlain by political trust or involves ongoing negotiation over the terms of a trust reposed and undertaken.

[41] Miller, *supra* note 7.

By contrast, the descriptive claims of fiduciary government are addressed to the character and implications of the investment of prerogative powers of state in government and in public officials. The thin conception of fiduciary government has nothing to say about political activity in general, other than to clarify what ought, as a matter of political morality, be understood to be the *effect* of the establishment of democratic government, elevation of an individual to public office and the performance of governmental functions through the exercise of the prerogative powers of the state.[42] Where a government and/or an official has emerged from the melee of electoral politics and assumes power, the proper interpretation of what obtains as a matter of law – according to the thin conception of fiduciary government – is that the government or official has undertaken a legally effective mandate of representation.[43] Setting aside cases involving electoral irregularities or other bases for challenging the legal validity of a mandate to govern, we – lawyers and legal theorists – are left with the challenge of explaining how political representation should be understood as a matter of *law*. And the descriptive claim central to fiduciary government is that the possession and exercise of prerogative powers of the state by a government or official is inherently fiduciary inasmuch as legal representation is itself inherently fiduciary.[44] Accordingly, one might say that electoral manifestations of political trust confer the burden of fiduciary government on those who emerged victorious in a contest for the power to govern.

Second, turning to normative claims, it may be noted that arguments advanced by theories of political trust and fiduciary government are directed at different facets of political representation and articulate different kinds of reasons germane to a varying cast of actors engaged in different kinds of activities.

Political trust ramifies normatively in the political realm, articulating reasons of political morality that should weigh on citizens and public officials alike as they navigate bonds of trust through political activity. For example, considerations of political trust factor in scrutiny of the political trustworthiness of political parties and their leaders as well as candidates for office. Considerations of political trust give reasons to prefer – and to advocate for – some institutional arrangements over others. And these considerations give constituents reason to take action in holding politicians to high standards of transparency and accountability, whether or not a trust reposed has been disappointed or betrayed. Furthermore, considerations of political trust should be front of mind to governmental officials as they perform their functions, especially where they find their focus or integrity challenged. Given the different, and wider, dispersion of reasons of political morality generated by political trust, theories like Pettit's capture salient expectations that the idea of fiduciary government does not (for example, justified feelings of having been betrayed by a politician who made false promises in order to get elected).

42 I underscore "ought." The thin conception of fiduciary government does not claim that the idea of fiduciary government *is* given legal effect (i.e., is recognized as a matter of law, much less in a way that parallels the juridical expression given to fiduciary principles in private law).

43 Miller, *supra* note 7.

44 Ibid.

By contrast, normative claims made by the thin conception of fiduciary government are relatively narrow. They are narrow partly in that they bear only upon the manner in which prerogative powers of the state are exercised after a government or official has assumed power. But they are also narrow because they highlight outside limits – or de minimis conditions, if you prefer – for political representation that are, and/or should be, expressed by law. The narrowness of the limits implied by fiduciary government is revealed not in the principles of political morality that it engenders – principles of fidelity, prudence, candor and the like – which are admittedly quite capacious but rather in the sporadic and generally thin expression given to these principles in law and policy (e.g., regulatory conflict rules that constrain self-dealing, and criminal sanctions for corruption and breach of trust). The narrowness of fiduciary constraints does not imply their triviality or unimportance. Rather, it reflects the delicate balance that must be struck between facilitation and constraint in the practice of representation, and recognition that accountability for poor representation is usually understood as a matter of pure political trust to be resolved through political rather than legal processes.

5 Political Trustworthiness and Fiduciary Government

The philosophical literature on trust reveals as much interest in trustworthiness as in trust.[45] And for good reason. After all, we ordinarily assume that trust is responsive to the trustworthiness of a person or group in whom trust is placed. That responsiveness is shown in the initial willingness to trust, or feeling of trust. It is also shown in reactions to new evidence pertinent to ongoing assessments of trustworthiness, and so the warrant or justification for continued trust. Untrustworthy behavior will usually destroy or compromise trust, ultimately causing it to be withdrawn. Correlatively, vindication of trust will generally foster a deepening of trust.

This being allowed, it might be thought that trustworthiness is rather less important to political trust and to other varieties of automatic or unwilling trust. If, for example, one has no choice but to manifest trust because one is compelled by one's circumstances to do so, in what sense can it matter whether a person in whom trust is placed is – or could be – judged trustworthy? It cannot matter to the inclination to trust, because here such inclinations are immaterial. Trust is simply a feature of the context in which one finds oneself.

There is some truth in this, but it is too quick. To begin with, political trust is not wholly automatic. Though we don't have a choice but to trust in *a* government, in democratic societies we have meaningful choice in deciding whom to trust to form *our* government and to carry out elected public offices. And one might hope that these decisions will, at least to some extent, be informed by assessments of trustworthiness. Furthermore, even in respect of automatic trust, there is reason to be concerned about

[45] See, for example, Russell Hardin, "Trustworthiness" (1996) 107 *Ethics* 26; Russell Hardin, *Trust and Trustworthiness* (Russell Sage 2002); Karen Jones, "Trustworthiness" (2012) 123 *Ethics* 61; and Onora O'Neill, "Trust, Trustworthiness, and Accountability" in Nicholas Morris and David Vines (eds.), *Capital Failure: Rebuilding Trust in Financial Services* (Oxford University Press 2014).

trustworthiness. And that is because, whether or not we are able to do anything with it, we ought to be able to say whether and if so in what sense we judge someone deserving of our trust. These assessments are pivotal to our practices of moral evaluation of the character and conduct of those in whom we have placed trust, independently of the significance they hold for our assessment of the rationality of decisions of whom to trust where trust is willing rather than automatic. Furthermore, evaluations of trustworthiness figure in our reactive attitudes where our trust is vindicated or disappointed (e.g., positive attitudes of praise and contentment, and negative ones of blame and indignation).[46] Regardless how we've come to trust another, we think it possible and important to evaluate their behavior, character and motivation in respect of our trust – e.g., whether they've proven themselves worthy of trust by acting in an appropriately trust-responsive way.[47]

Recognizing its importance, how is political trustworthiness to be understood? And what contribution, if any, does fiduciary government make to it? As we will see, there is a tight relationship between conditions requisite to political trustworthiness and compliance with norms of fiduciary government. The tightness of the relationship is a function of the fact that each is directed toward our evaluation – here in the arena of politics, there in light of law – of the behavior of government and of public officials in terms of their fitness to serve representatively. Put otherwise, and more elaborately: our evaluations of trustworthiness in this context are largely a product of our observations about proven or potential *character* for office (*dignitary fitness*, or suitability to serve faithfully and honorably as a representative) and *competence* for office (*fitness for performance*, or capability to execute the functions of government or of an office well).

The usual approach is to draw conclusions on political trustworthiness inferentially from tendencies revealed by the behavior of parties and public officials, as well as verbal and other communications that predict how the party or official is likely to act.[48] The inferences in question collate factors pertinent to the likelihood that a party or official will prove robustly responsive to the representative nature of their mandate, including the general and specific public purposes that are to animate and guide their work. Pertinent factors include evidence of personal integrity (e.g., honesty and probity), the nature of commitments (e.g., policy promises) made and demonstrated competence. It should be noted that judgments of political trustworthiness are not politically neutral. Indeed, they may often be politically informed and even politically charged. The decision whether to trust a party or person with the responsibility to govern, being central to political activity as such, is itself inherently political. Accordingly, judgments of political trustworthiness will in the end be made on the basis of the citizen's own political preferences and personal values. A party or candidate whose

46 Holton, *supra* note 26; Darwall, *supra* note 26; and Hawley, *supra* note 30.

47 Philip Pettit, "The Cunning of Trust" (1995) 24 *Phil. & Pub. Aff.* 202; Victoria McGreer and Philip Pettit, 'The Empowering Theory of Trust' in Paul Faulkner and Thomas Simpson (eds.), *The Philosophy of Trust* (Oxford University Press 2017) 14, 29–33.

48 Margaret Levi and Laura Stoker, "Political Trust and Trustworthiness" (2000) 3 *Ann. Rev. Polit. Sci.* 475; and Margaret Levi, "A State of Trust" in Valerie A. Braithwaite and Margaret Levi (eds.), *Trust and Governance* (Russell Sage 2003).

platform a citizen does not endorse, or positively rejects, might be considered trustworthy in the sense that they can be taken at their word and trusted to behave representatively (for and on behalf of the community, on the basis of a platform pledged). Yet they may not be trusted, and indeed be deemed untrustworthy, on the basis of substantive disagreement. This citizen will refuse to extend trust precisely because she rejects the party or candidate's platform and worries about the prospect of associated policies being realized.

How does fiduciary government relate to political trustworthiness, so understood? The first thing that might be noted is that compliance with fiduciary norms (particularly where there is a pattern of such compliance) will usually evidence and so support the political trustworthiness of a public official. A person who proves loyal, competent, open and honest in their work of representation shows that they can be trusted to serve representatively (allowing that they might still not be trusted on the basis of substantive political disagreement). It should be remembered that many fiduciary standards recognized at law are (relative to broader fiduciary principles) minimally demanding. So, bare compliance with these standards provides only weak evidence of political trustworthiness. However, an official who shows a more robust commitment to the deeper moral sense of the principles underlying enforceable standards (supposing there are same in a given legal system) will be prima facie trustworthy on that account.

Relatedly, it may be noted that fiduciary norms have, by virtue of expressive effects, the potential to strengthen political trustworthiness systemically. To the extent that these norms are taken seriously as a matter of political culture, there is reason to think that public officials will be inclined to internalize them. Furthermore, public notice and enforcement of fiduciary norms may have a salutary impact on subjective citizen trust in government. McGreer and Pettit have suggested that one of the most important mechanisms for creating a virtuous cycle of escalating trust and trustworthiness is the willing risking of trust.[49] Mere demonstration of trust supports trust-responsive behavior, inasmuch as it engages the dignitary interests of the trust recipient in maintaining the status and associated benefits of being reputed trustworthy. If this is true, robust fiduciary norms may buttress trustworthiness by facilitating citizen trust.

6 Political Distrust and Fiduciary Government

I have just suggested that norms of fiduciary government might contribute to political trustworthiness, and so in turn to subjective trust by citizens in government and/or public officials. Whether and to what extent this occurs will depend on the strength of fiduciary norms in a polity, the extent of observance of them, and whether and how they have been violated in the past. If compliance is generally good and damaging breach rare, there is reason to think that fiduciary norms might be partly responsible for supporting political trustworthiness and subjective citizen trust.

[49] *Supra* note 47.

I wish now to introduce a suggestion that might seem paradoxical in light of the conclusions drawn thus far. The suggestion is not mine; it is Pettit's.[50] And it is that, notwithstanding the centrality of objective political trust in our political system and that levels of subjective political trust might be diagnostic of its relative health, we have good reason to make provision – institutionally, and culturally – for moderate subjective political *distrust* on the part of citizens.[51]

This suggestion is admittedly jarring. We usually think of subjective distrust as a bad thing: a consequence of betrayals of trust or of corrosive cynicism (or both), and a precipitant of the decay of personal bonds and group cohesion.[52] Indeed, we tend to think that if distrust is acute, it will result in the breakdown of relationships that depend on trust, resulting in mutual alienation. In turn, if acute distrust becomes pervasive within groups or society more generally, widespread social alienation, strife and self-serving behavior seem likely to follow. Entrenched subjective distrust might show up in widespread withdrawal from group engagement and activity, including civic and political activity.

From this perspective, the suggestion that we should want more rather than less subjective political distrust – and that we may have reason to cultivate it – might even seem foolish, something that bespeaks the fallen state of those so habituated in their distrust that they are blind to its harms. One might think that rather than encourage subjective distrust, we ought to quell it and to engage in projects aimed at building or restoring civic and political trust.

This reaction is natural and appropriate in relation to the most familiar form of distrust; namely, acute and corrosive distrust that arises in response to betrayals of trust. But as Pettit[53] and Braithwaite[54] have shown, there is another, socially beneficial variety of distrust.[55] Let's call it *socially and politically constructive distrust* (or *constructive distrust*, for short). Constructive distrust is best understood as a corollary of cognitive – and more specifically, calculative – subjective trust. Unlike corrosive distrust, constructive distrust is not the product of negative reactive attitudes or the habits of emotion and thought borne of betrayals of trust. Instead, it is an open, searching form of distrust – one that is the flip side of the inherently critical posture of calculative trust. Borne not of betrayal but instead a sensible wariness, constructive distrust is manifested in awareness of risks of untrustworthy behavior, the taking of steps to minimize or mitigate these risks and a readiness to act appropriately in response to evidence of disappointment or betrayal of trust.

Where a person afflicted by corrosive distrust might refuse to demonstrate trust even where it would be rational to do so and might resent having to trust where it is

50 *Supra* note 37.

51 Ibid., 308–11.

52 Some of the harms of distrust are discussed in Jason D'Cruz, "Humble Trust" (2019) 176 *Phil. Stud.* 933.

53 *Supra* note 37.

54 John Braithwaite, "Institutionalizing Distrust, Enculturating Trust" in Valerie A. Braithwaite and Margaret Levi (eds.), *Trust and Governance* (Russell Sage 2003).

55 See also Mark E. Warren, "Democratic Theory and Trust" in Mark E. Warren (ed.), *Democracy and Trust* (Cambridge University Press 1999) and Deborah Welch Larson, "Distrust: Prudent, If Not Always Wise" in Russell Hardin (ed.), *Distrust* (Russell Sage 2004).

unavoidable, one who adopts a posture of constructive distrust recognizes the potential value of subjective trust and, where apt, the value or inevitability of objective trust. But she doesn't consider trust an all-or-nothing investment, much less a blind one. Rather, she remains open to evidence of the utility and rationality of trust and likewise its potential disutility and irrationality. Her posture is one of willingness to trust, and to maintain investments in trust, balanced by alertness to associated risks. Given that she responds to evidence of the value of trust, she is also inclined to respond to untrustworthy behavior not by immediately withdrawing trust – unless that is the rational thing to do – but rather by finding ways to reallocate, to restore or to strengthen trust. To the extent that personal trust depends for its effectiveness on an environment of collective trust – as will be true for investments in group projects – she will also be inclined to support conditions favorable to the development and maintenance of collective trust.

One can now better appreciate why Pettit and Braithwaite would write approvingly of political distrust. Constructive political distrust is an element of civic virtue: it is the mark of the citizen who is critically engaged in her political participation, mindful of the stakes and concerned to hold government to its promise to govern representatively. This individual maintains a posture of constructive subjective distrust by calibrating her beliefs about the trustworthiness of government and public officials in response to evidence that supplies her with reasons to trust or not to trust, and by seeking out this evidence. She maintains a posture of constructive objective distrust by acting appropriately on reasons to trust or to withdraw trust and by acting to buttress political trustworthiness (e.g., by supporting improvement of background conditions for political trustworthiness).

I have already suggested that fiduciary government supports political trustworthiness to the extent that fiduciary norms are robust and are generally complied with. What is the relationship between fiduciary government and constructive political distrust? I'll offer two observations.

The first is that our discussion of constructive political distrust holds important lessons for ongoing work on fiduciary government. More specifically, it suggests the importance of greater care in the choice of analogues in framing the relationship between government and the governed. Elsewhere, I have criticized the tendency to characterize the state as a fiduciary by analogy to fiduciary relationships in which the beneficiary is a minor or other incapable person.[56] While fiduciary theorists have rightly emphasized the practical inevitability of citizens' subjection to the authority of the state, they have neglected to discuss franchise and other participatory rights, many of which have parallels in the typical private fiduciary relationship (i.e., that in which the beneficiary is a person of full capacity). The literature on constructive political distrust serves as a useful reminder that in modern democracies, the condition of the citizen is not one of bare subjection; it is, rather, one under which sovereign power is checked by legal *and* political accountability mechanisms designed to ensure that representative government is responsive to citizen interests and concerns as voiced by citizens themselves.

[56] *Supra* note 8.

The second observation is that fiduciary norms can, and likely do, contribute to constructive political distrust. As Pettit and Braithwaite have observed, constructive distrust can be stymied or made to flourish depending on the presence and vitality of institutional mechanisms for meaningful citizen engagement. These mechanisms promote or compel: disclosure, resolving information asymmetry problems; a culture of public justification (e.g., formal or informal reason giving); publicity (e.g., public meetings); participation (e.g., plebiscites, polls and referenda); and regular formal (e.g., legal or electoral) accountability. The mere recital of these mechanisms is indicative of the contribution that fiduciary norms make to constructive political distrust. After all, each mechanism may be fairly said to reflect an implicit commitment to fiduciary norms in government. More specifically, they reflect norms of candor, honesty and consensualism.[57] And then too: the primary norm of answerability entailed by the undertaking and the claim – made by *all* fiduciaries – to serve and to act representatively.

7 Conclusion

In this chapter, I have clarified the relationship between ideas of political trust and fiduciary government. The perception that the ideas are redundant is mistaken. Clarity on their relationship is most readily achieved if one adheres to a thin conception of fiduciary government, according to which fiduciary norms generate legitimacy conditions for the manner in which prerogative powers are exercised. Fiduciary norms – reflected in familiar principles of fidelity, prudence and candor – bespeak aspects of the quality and integrity of representation. Matters of political trust are broader, encompassing manifestations of trust and trustworthiness by political actors across the full spectrum of political activity. I have suggested that fiduciary norms play a narrow but important supporting role in the dynamics of political trust. To the extent that fiduciary norms are robust, widespread compliance will support subjective and objective political trust. To the extent that they include empowering norms (e.g., disclosure rules and participatory rights), they will also support constructive political distrust. In these ways, far from being duplicative or redundant, fiduciary government promises important contributions to political trust in theory and in practice.

[57] Ibid., 265–70.

12

Trust, Distrust and the Rule of Law

GERALD J. POSTEMA

As there is a degree of depravity in mankind which requires a certain degree of circumspection and distrust, so there are other qualities in human nature which justify a certain portion of esteem and confidence.[1]

1 A Strategy of Distrust

"Political writers have established it as a maxim," Hume observed, "that, in contriving any system of government, and fixing the several checks and controuls of the constitution, every man ought to be supposed to be a *knave*, and to have no other end, in all his actions, than private interest."[2] In the same vein, Thomas Jefferson wrote, "In questions of power, then, let no more be heard of confidence in man, but bind him down from mischief by the chains of the Constitution." For, he explained, "free government is founded in jealousy, and not in confidence; it is jealousy and not confidence which prescribes limited constitutions, to bind down those whom we are obliged to trust with power."[3]

Jefferson speaks of "confidence" versus "jealousy"; others, more typically, speak of trust versus distrust. Bentham, for example, made distrust central to his strategy of constitutional design. He proposed a carefully engineered system of "securities against misrule" to counteract the pervasive threat of abuse of power by officials. Security against misrule, he insisted, requires maximal "responsibility" of government officials. "For security against breach of trust, the sole apt remedy is … constant responsibility." For this, the primary and most effective tool is "on every occasion and at all times, the strictest and most absolute dependence" on the public.[4] "Publicity is the very soul of justice," he argued. "It is through publicity alone that justice becomes the mother of security."[5] Publicity entails both transparency and vigorous, vigilant public

[1] Publius (James Madison), "Federalist No. 55," in *The Federalist Papers* (Ian Shapiro ed., Yale University Press 2009) 285.

[2] David Hume, "Of the Independency of Parliament," in *Essays Moral, Political and Literary* (Eugene F. Miller ed., LibertyClassics, 1985), 42–43. Hume adds that, regarded as an empirical generalization this principle is false; nevertheless it is indispensable as a practical maxim of institutional design.

[3] Thomas Jefferson, "Resolutions Relative to the Alien and Sedition Acts," in *The Founders' Constitution* (Philip Kurland and Ralph Lerner eds., University of Chicago Press 1987), vol. 1, 292–93.

[4] Jeremy Bentham, *The Works of Jeremy Bentham* (John Bowring ed., W. Tait 1838–43), vol. ix, 6. See Gerald J. Postema, "The Soul of Justice: Bentham on Publicity, Law, and the Rule of Law," in *Bentham's Theory of Law and Public Opinion* (Xiaobo Zhai and Michael Quinn eds., Cambridge University Press 2014), 40–62.

[5] Jeremy Bentham (n. 4), vol. iv, 316–17.

accountability holding. Security "depends upon the spirit, the intelligence, the vigilance, the alertness, the intrepidity, the energy, the perseverance, of those of whose opinions Public Opinion is composed."[6] However, Bentham asked, isn't this system of *public responsibility* nothing more than "a system of *distrust*"? Yes, indeed, he replied, but "every good political institution is founded upon this base," for "whom ought we to distrust, if not those to whom is committed great authority, with great temptations to abuse it?"[7]

This theme has remained strong in contemporary constitutional thinking.[8] Philip Pettit, echoing eighteenth-century republican theory, insists that eternal vigilance is the price of liberty and that vigilance is a "sustained manifestation of distrust."[9] Yet a serious tension lurks in this cold, sober embrace of the suspicion of power and those who wield it. It is evident at the margins of Bentham's thought and Jefferson's. We are, after all, "obliged [i.e., we have no choice but] to trust government," Jefferson wrote. At least, it is widely thought that government, especially democratic government, cannot function well in civic soil poisoned by suspicion and distrust. Onora O'Neill, for example, warned that the culture of accountability that gained a foothold in Britain's public life had engendered a culture of suspicion that threatened to corrode and distort the very institutions and officials that accountability was meant to control.[10] Some writers add paradox to this tension by arguing that institutionalized distrust is a (perhaps the only) route to trust in government.[11]

These concerns bear on our understanding of the content and feasibility of the rule-of-law ideal. On the account of the rule of law I have defended elsewhere,[12] an *ethos* of *fidelity* complements the demands of institutional *legality*, an ethos in which members of a political community, citizens and officials alike, take responsibility for holding each other accountable under the law. Moreover, I have argued, since the rule of law concerns the mode of association in the political community, as well as its mode of governance, accountability holding that is meant to serve the rule of law has a horizontal (citizens holding each other accountable) as well as vertical (citizens holding officials accountable) dimension. However, if vigilance manifests distrust and accountability creates suspicion and poisons the social order, the rule of law would seem to threaten bonds of trust that are arguably essential to social and

6 Jeremy Bentham, *Securities against Misrule and Other Constitutional Writings for Tripoli and Greece* (Philip Schofield ed., Clarendon Press 1990), 139. Bentham regarded the efforts of the public, exercised through informal and quasi-formal associations of civil society as a kind of court. He called it the "public opinion tribunal."

7 Jeremy Bentham, *Political Tactics* (Michael James et al. eds., Clarendon Press 1999), 37.

8 See, for example, Russell Hardin, "Liberal Distrust" (2002), 10 *European Review* 73–89; Margaret Levi, "A State of Trust," in *Trust and Governance* (Valerie Braithwaite and Margaret Levi eds., Russell Sage Foundation, 1998), 81.

9 Philip Pettit, "Republican Theory and Political Trust," Braithwaite and Levi (eds.) (n. 8), 309.

10 Onora O'Neill, *A Question of Trust* (Cambridge University Press 2000), chs. 1–2.

11 Piotr Sztrompka, *Trust: A Sociological Theory* (Cambridge University Press 2000), 140; John Braithwaite, "Institutionalizing Distrust, Enculturating Trust," in Braithwaite and Levi (n. 8), 343–75.

12 Gerald J. Postema, "Law's Rule: Reflexivity, Mutual Accountability, and the Rule of Law," in Zhai and Quinn (n. 4), 7–39, and "Fidelity in Law's Commonwealth," in *Private Law and the Rule of Law* (Dennis Klimchuk ed., Oxford University Press 2014), 17–40.

political life and to its own effective functioning. Call this the "Trust Challenge" to the rule of law.

We might think, likewise, that the strategy of institutionalized distrust threatens the rule of law as defended by the fiduciary theory of government.[13] The rule of law, on this view, holds that principles of fairness and reasonableness bind those who exercise political power in the administration of law. Fiduciary theory regards the relationship between citizen and public officials as a relationship of trust. However, if "chains of [law and] the Constitution" hold public officials to their obligations of fairness and reasonableness, and these chains manifest distrust and suspicion, then, again, we might reasonably worry that trust at the heart of the rule of law is under threat by our deployment of devices that are crucial to the rule of law.

However, the thesis of this essay is that vigilant and responsible accountability holding does not threaten the rule of law on either understanding.[14] I shall argue that vigorous accountability holding is not a threat to but an important support for political and civic trust. Both trust romantics and trust cynics uncritically adopt a particular form of personal trust as their paradigm and draw unwarranted inferences from this paradigm. To pull the sting from the Trust Challenge, we need a nuanced understanding of trust and distrust as they occur in civic and political contexts and the ways in which being held to account engages these attitudes. But, first, we need better to understand the ideal of the rule of law and accountability fitted up for its task of serving the rule of law.

2 Fidelity, Accountability and the Rule of Law

The core idea of the rule of law, I contend, is that *when law rules in a political community, it provides protection and recourse against the arbitrary exercise of power through the distinctive instrumentalities, powers and capacities of law*. The thought is that a polity is well ordered when its members are secured against the arbitrary exercise of power and that law, because of its distinctive features, is especially if not uniquely capable of providing such security. This normative ideal focuses on all exercises of power in a polity, whether political, wielded by public officials over the governed, or social, wielded by individuals or group members over other members. The rule of law advocates both a *mode of governance*, ordering the exercise of political power, and a *mode of association*, a distinctive way in which members of a polity regard, recognize and relate to each other.

A Fidelity

It is customary to identify the rule of law ideal with a range of principles and institutions – for example, generality and prospectivity of laws, judicial independence, and impartiality, fairness and reasonableness in the administration of law. These are

[13] See, for example, Evan Fox-Decent, *Sovereignty's Promise* (Oxford University Press 2011), ch. IV.

[14] This essay builds on, and revises, an earlier version, "Fidelity, Accountability, and Trust: Tensions at the Heart of the Rule of Law" (forthcoming).

familiar principles of *legality*. I argue that these formal principles and institutions of legality must be complemented by an *ethos* of *fidelity*.

The need for this ethos is evident if we take seriously the idea that the rule of law is all about ruling – about the *law's* ruling. The rule of law obtains in a polity when law alone rules. And it rules, I argue, only when all those who exercise power are subject to a rich network of robust accountability. The *fidelity thesis* holds that law rules in a political community when its members, official and lay members alike, take responsibility for holding each other accountable under the law. Adam Ferguson captured the fidelity thesis well. The law's capacity to rule, he argued, lies in "the influence of men resolved to be free; of men, who, having adjusted in writing the terms on which they are to live with the state, and with their fellow-subjects, are determined, by their vigilance and spirit, to make these terms be observed." Only if this vigilance is pursued with "a spirit [of] . . . refractory and turbulent zeal" can the effects of the rule of law be secured.[15] Ferguson suggests that fidelity is expressed not only in compliance with law and standards of legality but also in the active taking of responsibility for law's rule. In particular, it involves taking responsibility for holding partners in the relationship to their respective duties. Fidelity involves mutual accountability as well as reciprocal compliance.

The idea that fidelity and trust travel together is ancient. An anonymous Sophist from the fourth century BCE observed that the result of lawfulness (*eunomia*) is trust.[16] Indeed, fidelity not only seems to underwrite trust but also to depend on it. Theorists of "social capital" have argued that trust is a condition of effective government.[17] Trust also lies at the center of law's ethos. Fidelity in the horizontal dimension depends on a shared standing to hold each other accountable that involves entrusting to each other the authority to one to account. Likewise, fidelity in the vertical dimension, which inter alia involves people holding those who exercise political power accountable to the law, depends on the combined efforts of the people, which can be effective only if individual citizens can trust others to join them in the effort.

However, if Hume, Jefferson, Bentham and hosts of constitution designers after them are to be believed, institutionalized structures of accountability enact and manifest not trust but distrust and suspicion. This assessment reflects an apparent aversion to accountability in interpersonal relations. "Being called to account for one's actions and claims," Jonathan Wolff observes, "gives the impression that one is not trusted, that one is an object of suspicion and hence is not being respected."[18]

15 Adam Ferguson, *An Essay on the History of Civil Society* (1767) (Fania Oz-Salzberger ed., Cambridge University Press 1995), 249, 160.

16 *Early Greek Political Thought from Homer to the Sophists* (Michael Gagarin and Paul Woodruff eds., Cambridge University Press 1995), 293, 294.

17 See Robert Putnam, *Bowling Alone: The Collapse and Revival of American Community* (Simon & Shuster, 2000); see the range of essays on aspects of "social capital" in *The Handbook of Social Capital* (Dario Castiglione et al. eds., Oxford University Press 2008).

18 Jonathan Wolff, "Fairness, Respect and the Egalitarian Ethos" (1998) 27 *Philosophy and Public Affairs* 108. However, Wolff qualifies his observation, adding that being called to account manifests distrust when one is "called too often or in circumstances where others are not, or when the depth of the investigation seems out of proportion."

Close monitoring, it is thought, is poisonous to interpersonal relationships of value. This brings us face to face with the Trust Challenge. We understand trust to be a key ingredient in effective governance as well as a necessary condition of effective efforts at holding power accountable. However, the challenge argues, accountability thrives on distrust and drives out trust. This tension, the challenge alleges, lies at the heart of the rule of law: the rule of law demands accountability; accountability depends on trust; yet, accountability manifests distrust and drives out trust, thereby jeopardizing the rule of law.

B Accountability Fit for the Rule of Law

To answer the Trust Challenge, we need a clear understanding of trust and distrust in its many forms. We also need an understanding of accountability – in particular, of accountability appropriate to its task of enabling law to rule. I turn the task of providing the latter first.

For our purposes, we can understand accountability holding in its generic form as an interpersonal, normatively structured, discursive activity. Accountability is an *interpersonal* activity: two parties – an accountability holder and an account giver – engage in an asymmetrical relationship with respect to a domain of the giver's activity. The holder calls on the giver to provide, in a setting not of his choosing,[19] an account of the giver's activity in the domain, and the holder offers an assessment of the account given. The relationship is *discursive* in that the account makes public (at least to the holder) the activities of the giver in the domain and seeks to explain or justify them; and the holder assesses the giver's actions in light of the reasons the giver offers for them. The relationship is *normatively structured* in that the holder is entitled to call for the account from the giver; and the giver is normatively liable to be called and owes an obligation to the holder to provide the account to the holder. A set of norms defines the powers, claims and obligations of the accountability relationship, structures the domain of the giver's activities and consequently structures the giver's account and the holder's assessment. Thus, the holder's activity, as well as the giver's, is subject to the norms of the relationship, and the holder is liable to be held accountable for that activity.

Accountability fit for the rule of law is a special case of accountability understood in this way. Rule-of-law accountability (1) is a public activity; that is, the account is given *in* public, regarding public matters, and given to officers of the public or to the public generally (usually, through the mediation of civic associations, organizations or institutions). Moreover, (2) the norms defining the relationship and the domain of the giver's activity are the laws of the political community. (3) The discursive, reason-giving activity is governed and given content by the deliberative discipline of law. (4) Individual instances of accountability holding, on the fidelity thesis, take place within a network of mutual accountability practices. Each party subject to law submits to and participates in a network of mutual accountability. Although each occasion of

[19] Jeremy Waldron, *Political Political Theory* (Harvard University Press 2016), 169.

accountability holding is asymmetrical between the holder and the giver, on other occasions the holder is liable to give an account to some other holder, perhaps for his calling the initial giver to account. These connections form a network, rather than a hierarchical chain.

Finally, (5) sanctions are not in the foreground of this model of accountability. The holder's power to call the giver to account is normative, not physical. While some means of compelling the giver to provide an account may lie in the background,[20] it is not necessary that there be some means of enforcing the holder's judgment, other than issuing the judgment itself. There is nothing defective or incomplete about an accountability mechanism that does not build in sanctions to enforce the judgments of accountability holders; we must not equate the giver's subjection to the holder's *judgment* with the giver's liability to suffer *punishment* at the holder's hand. Sanctions are adventitious relative to the activity of demanding and assessing an account; they are external incentives to encourage or compel compliance. (Moreover, the normative structure of accountability alone does not settle whether there are good reasons to add them.) The requirement to provide reasons for the exercise of power appeals to common norms of law and to the presumed commitment the giver and the holder make to these norms effective. Consequently, the holder's judgment engages the giver's integrity, or at least the giver's concern for the holder's esteem or good offices (or those of the public). These motivations connect with the giver's presumed commitment to law. The giver may find the holder's adverse and public judgment painful and unwelcome, but that is because the giver takes seriously her commitment to the law, and the holder's judgment implicates this commitment and may cast unfavorable light on it.

We can contrast this model of accountability fit for the rule of law with other modes of accountability holding. A limiting case would be exercises of power, or threats of them, intended to give a person incentive to act in certain ways – for example, exercises of market power against business enterprises (boycotts or public protests) or exercises of coercive power by police. In these cases, the primary aim is to secure compliance with some norm. Accountability that focuses solely on providing external incentives (especially coercive incentives) for compliance leaves out of the picture the crucial discursive element of law and fails to appreciate and make use of the full range of the offices of the law. The incentives involved in rule-of-law accountability are meant to be internal to the norms to which parties are held accountable or to their mutual commitments to fidelity.

Bureaucratic forms of accountability also contrast with rule-of-law accountability. "Managerial accountability," Onora O'Neill observed, controls performance by setting targets and measuring success or failure in terms of meeting these targets, or rough (but clear and "objective") proxies for success or failure, and sanctioning failure and rewarding success.[21] These methods, typically imposed top down, leave little room for individual judgment or expert discretion, and there need be no opportunity for

[20] See John Braithwaite (n. 11), 355.

[21] Onora O'Neill, "Trust, Trustworthiness, and Accountability," in *Capital Failure: Rebuilding Trust in Financial Services* (Nicholas Morris and David Vines eds., Oxford University Press 2014), 174.

discursive interaction between the giver and the holder. Moreover, often, bureaucratic norms are not fully public; they are in-house norms determined by the mission of the bureaucratic organization. One finds this deficiency also in principal–agent accountability.[22] In this form of accountability, although the domain of the agent's activities is structured by norms, the norms are determined by the principal (perhaps within a larger legal framework of the relationship), and the agent's account is owed to the principal just because the agent is doing the principal's business. Also, the activity of holding accountable on the principal–agent model is hierarchical; reciprocity is not a key element.

From this swift survey, we can see that accountability fit for the rule of law is a distinctive kind of accountability, reflecting distinctive features of law and the aims and values of fidelity. As we shall see presently, this reciprocal character of accountability can also be found in other relationships – in interpersonal moral relationships but also in some commercial partnerships.[23]

3 Trust – Contexts and Contraries

To assess the Trust Challenge, we also need a nuanced understanding of trust. Trust, paradigmatically, concerns a kind of relationship, the nature of which can vary as the contexts in which that kind of relationship thrives vary. The different contexts bring some features to the foreground and move others to the background. The Trust Challenge concerns the effect of widespread practices of accountability on trust in political and in civic contexts, so to assess the challenge, we need to understand political and civic trust. Philosophical discussions of trust in recent years have focused largely on trust in the context of interpersonal relations. I, too, will begin with this paradigm but then adjust this understanding to fit trust in the rather different political and civic contexts. We must avoid taking trust in thick interpersonal relations as our model, but we must also take care not to exaggerate the differences between trust in personal and impersonal contexts. A careful assessment of both is the key to answering the Trust Challenge.

A Interpersonal Trust

Trust, in general and especially in the interpersonal context, involves a personal stance of one party toward another, involving a complex of attitudes and dispositions to act.[24] To bring interpersonal trust into focus, I begin with stances that approximate, but do not fully realize, trust.

[22] See Waldron's discussion of the principal–agent model in Waldron (n. 11), ch. 8.

[23] I am grateful for Matthew Harding's suggestion on this point.

[24] This view is widely held by contemporary philosophers. See, e.g., Richard Holten, "Deciding to Trust, Coming to Believe" (1994) 72 *Australian Journal of Philosophy* 63–76; Pamela Hieronymi, "Reasons of Trust" (2008) 86 *Australasian Journal of Philosophy* 214. In this section, I summarize some major themes in recent philosophical literature on trust. I do not attempt to adjudicate significant disagreements among contributors to this literature.

a Prototrust

Trust involves, at a minimum, the stance of *reliance* directed to some other party. This involves not only a confident belief but also a readiness to act. Prototrust, we might call it, is an asymmetrical relation between two parties in a certain kind of circumstance. Relative to some domain, A is *vulnerable* to B's action affecting something, X, that A values or cares about, and A *relies* on B (at a minimum) not to damage X. Because B is not entirely under the control of A, A believes there is some uncertainty or risk that B will not act as predicted.

Prototrust falls short of trust. One reason is that one could take this attitude toward human, animate or even inanimate parties – toward nature, for example, or one's bicycle. Trust, however, involves two parties, both of whom are capable of agency.[25] First, trust involves, to some degree, an exercise of agency by the trusting party. A makes herself vulnerable, or willingly accepts her vulnerability, to B's action regarding X.[26] If A literally has no choice but to rely on B, there is no need – there is no room – for proper trust. Indeed, A may actively distrust B and may seek any way she can to avoid relying on B, and yet have no choice but to rely on him. Likewise, second, if trust is possible, B must be a free agent, acting on his own, not coerced or compelled to act in ways that affect X.[27] B is free to act competently and has a degree of discretion regarding the exercise of that competence. B is free within limits to decide how to act in response to A's trust. Thus, at a minimum, if A trusts B, then A submits something she values to B's care; she makes herself vulnerable to the discretion and actions of a free agent.

Trusting B, A relies on B's motivation to act in ways that promote, respect or at least do not damage X. These motivations may include B's self-interest, or B's moral or other commitments, B's character or even B's good will toward people like A.[28] However, if A bases her reliance only on predictions of B's competence and motivation, then, again, A's stance approximates, but does not yet reach, trust. Some theorists call this stance *predictive reliance*.[29] Although such reliance has a free agent as its target, and is a commitment of a free agent, the nature of the relation between the parties is not necessarily *personal*. It is not substantially different from the relation one has to nature or one's bike; only the bases of predictions are different. However, trust is, paradigmatically, an interpersonal relation. One typical personal dimension of a relation between two parties involves mutual recognition. Missing from predictive reliance is an interactive, *recognitional* dimension. What is important for trust between A and B is that A relies on B because of how B stands to A, not merely

25 Generally, see Karen Jones, "Trustworthiness" (2012) 123 *Ethics* 61–85.

26 Karen Jones, "Trust and Terror," in *Moral Psychology: Feminist Ethics and Social Theory* (Peggy DesAutels and Margaret Urban Walker eds., Rowman & Littlefield 2004), 4, 6; Pettit (n. 9), 298.

27 Philip Pettit, "The Cunning of Trust" (1995) 24 *Philosophy and Public Affairs* 208; Baier, "What Is Trust?" in *Reading Onora O'Neill* (David Archard et al. eds., Routledge 2013), 178.

28 Russell Hardin, *Trust and Trustworthiness* (Russell Sage Foundation 2002), ch. 1; Katherine Hawley, "Trust, Distrust and Commitment" (2012) 48 *Nous* 9–12; Annette Baier, "Trust and Anti-trust" (1986) 96 *Ethics* 234.

29 Robert Stern, "Trust is Basic," in *The Philosophy of Trust* (Paul Faulkner and Thomas Simpson eds., Oxford University Press 2016), 275; Thomas Simpson, "What Is Trust?" (2012) 93 *Pacific Philosophical Quarterly* 565.

because of how B stands to something that A values,[30] and that fact is recognized by both parties.

One recognitional dimension involves nested cognitive expectations of behavior and the consequent interdependence of practical deliberation. A's expectations concerning B's conduct are available to B as are B's attitudes toward A, which may include B's expectations of A; likewise, A may recognize B's recognition of A's attitude, etc. In such cases, the deliberation of the two parties will be to some degree interdependent. Russell Hardin casts his understanding of trust as "encapsulated interest" in this mold.[31] On Hardin's account, A trusts B because A recognizes that her interest (in X) is "encapsulated" in B's interest, which in some way depends on doing what serves A's interest with respect to X. Where the kind of expectations involved remains strictly cognitive – expectations *that* B will act in certain ways – we have a closer approximation to proper trust – we might call it *predictive trust*[32] – but it is not full-fledged trust even yet.

b Robust Recognitional Trust

Genuine interpersonal trust has a different and more complex recognitional dimension. The difference is signaled by the fact that when B does not act as expected, does not perform as trusted, A is not merely disappointed; she feels that the party trusted has to some degree failed her. Often, she may legitimately feel betrayed. It is the *trusted party* who fails, not the trusting party (by mistakenly assessing the evidence of B's reliability); moreover, the trusted party fails *the trusting party.* A's expectations may be defeated, but the expectations are normative, not merely prediction-based. A expected B *to* behave in a certain way; she did not merely expect *that* he would.[33] Responsibility for the failure lies, in the first instance, in the conduct of the trusted, not in the cognitive performance of the trusting party, and responsibility, rather than merely rational performance, is a salient feature of this interpersonal dimension. The stance is interpersonal rather than objective, a stance taken by a person engaging another person, recognizing his key moral features.[34]

The following features characterize this relationship of trust. First, trust has distinctive normative dimensions. Some are inclined to think of these in quasi-juridical terms, marking out the rights, duties and powers of the parties, but others find a closer analogue in relationships of love and attachment.[35] In either case, as we have seen, A's expectations are normative in nature, not merely predictive. What A expects B to do

[30] Daniel Weinstock, "Building Trust in Divided Societies" (1999) 7 *The Journal of Political Philosophy* 293.

[31] Hardin (n. 28), ch. 1.

[32] See, e.g., Raimo Tuomela and Maj Tuomela, "Cooperation and Trust in Group Context" (2005) 4 *Mind and Society* 73; see also Jones, "Trustworthiness" (n. 25), 65, and Jones, "But I Was Counting on You!" in Faulkner and Simpson (n. 29), 93–94.

[33] Jones (n. 26), 6.

[34] Holten (n. 24) draws on Strawson's distinction between participant and objective stances. Peter Strawson, "Freedom and Resentment," in P. F. Strawson, *Freedom and Resentment and other Essays* (Methuen, 1974), 1–28.

[35] Stephen Darwall, "Trust as a Second-Personal-Attitude (of the Heart)," in Faulkner and Simpson (n. 29), 35–49.

will involve caring for something A values, usually in some specific domain, but what exactly she expects B to do may vary with the circumstances. A may trust B to care for her child, feeding him, keeping him safe on the playground, but not, perhaps, to make medical decisions affecting the child's life. In many cases, B's actions will be properly responsive to A's trust if his conduct is good enough, even if not optimal.[36] Indeed, B may fail to act as A trusted him to act and yet not betray A's trust; for B's acting as trusted might, in the circumstances, have involved doing a greater wrong to another person or may have required B to shoulder costs or burdens far greater than A could reasonably ask B to bear. B does not show himself to be untrustworthy if, in these circumstances, he does not act as trusted.

Certain normative expectations apply also to A's behavior. A's trusting B involves, within limits, acknowledging that B must exercise discretion, that B's conduct is not entirely within A's control. Accordingly, at the least, A will forego taking extensive precautions to prevent B's failing to act as trusted. Acknowledging the discretion accorded to B, A will not engage in close monitoring.[37] Likewise, A should recognize that there are moral limits to properly trust-responsive behavior. And, in light of the personal nature of the relationship, A should be willing to forgive B's failing to live up to her expectations[38] and to act in ways that encourage B's trustworthiness in the future.

Second, the recognitional dimension of robust interpersonal trust is critical. The trusting party not only expects certain behavior, but she invites reciprocation. She invites the trusted party to accept her trust and actively engages his agency.[39] Pettit's notion of "trust responsiveness" helps us explain this dimension of the trusting relationship.[40] A person is trust responsive if he takes the fact that another person manifestly relies on him to do something in her behalf as a salient reason itself for acting as trusted. Trust responsiveness is different from sensitively responding to another's need or even to that person's dependency on one. A trust-responsive person responds appropriately to another person's *manifested* reliance, to her counting on him. This fact explains why it is possible for B to act as A trusts him to act and yet betray A's trust. A might feel her trust was betrayed, or at least not properly honored, if the circumstances make clear to A that the fact that B's action would fulfill A's trust in no way figured in B's motivation. What B did might be consistent with fulfilling A's trust but *not responsive* to A's trust.

The recognitional dimension of trusting also works in the reverse direction. Trusting behavior may, and in some circumstances perhaps should, be responsive to trustworthiness. A may trust B based solely on B's general reputation as trustworthy, but if B signals his trustworthiness, gives some assurance of it, A would

[36] Jacopo Domenicucci and Richard Holten, "Trust as a Two-Place Relation," in Faulkner and Simpson (n. 29), 151.

[37] Baier (n. 27), 176; Jones (n. 26), 4.

[38] Victoria McGeer, "Trust, Hope and Empowerment" (2008) 86 *Australasian Journal of Philosophy* 247; Jones (n. 26), 6, 11.

[39] Darwall (n. 35), 38; Jones (n. 25), 65; McGeer (n. 38), 245.

[40] Philip Pettit (n. 27), 205–07; Victoria McGeer (n. 38), 237–54, and Victoria McGeer and Philip Pettit, "The Empowering Theory of Trust," in Faulkner and Simpson (n. 29), 14–34.

properly respond to this invitation with trust in B. The responsive dimension of this phenomenon is evident in the fact that, in some circumstances, B, having signaled his trustworthiness, might take A's refusal to trust him as an affront. It might be too much to say that B is entitled to A's trust or that A is duty bound to trust B; nevertheless, her refusal is a kind of moral failing. A falls short of what B has some moral reason to hope for. Of course, A's refusal may be entirely justified if she has good reason to suspect that B's invitation is insincere and potentially manipulative.

In sum, we can reasonably say that *A trusts B when A manifestly relies on B, intending (or believing) that manifesting her reliance will trigger B's reasons to do what A trusts him to do*. A counts on B's responsiveness to A's manifested counting on him.[41] A manifestly depends on B, expecting (or hoping or intending) in part that her doing so will trigger B's motivation. B's recognition of this manifested trust engages his antecedent reasons for fulfilling A's trust. A's trust manifests her recognition of B as potentially trust responsive and hence trustworthy.[42] It invites B's recognition of A's vulnerability and of the valued thing A put in B's care. It also engages B's commitments, his sense of integrity, his sense of himself as trustworthy. Robust trust involves mutual recognition of a morally interesting sort. It is not surprising that we often think (sometimes, perhaps, mistakenly) that trust of this kind engenders an obligation on the trusted party, and why we might resist or even regard the trust as unwelcome.

Thus, the trusting party looks to trust responsiveness, not to the general good will, honesty or decency of character of the trusted party, or likelihood that he will follow social norms or a shared moral code.[43] Of course, the trusted party's trust responsiveness may be motivated by further considerations. Pettit argues that the typical motivation is *esteem*: B's desire to be regarded as trustworthy by A and perhaps others who observe his conduct. He may desire this either because he values or seeks their good opinion or because he wishes to draw on their good offices in future.[44] Other motivations are also familiar: B may wish to build or maintain a strong relationship with A that B values for its own sake, or he may especially care about A and wish to enable her to make use of his competence; or, like the Good Samaritan, B may simply respond to manifested need. What is critical for robust trust is only the trusted party's trust responsiveness – his taking the manifested fact that the trusting party counts on him as a salient and significant reason to act as trusted.[45]

Third, there is a characteristic cognitive dimension, or perhaps consequence, of interpersonal trust. Trusting, we have seen, involves more than an anticipatory guess about the likely behavior of another person, or even secure confidence regarding that

[41] Jones (n. 25), 66–67, 78.

[42] Trust responsiveness is trustworthiness in the context of robust trust relationships. We may talk of trustworthiness also with respect to less robust forms of trust.

[43] As several writers have maintained. See, e.g., Eric Uslaner, *The Moral Foundations of Trust* (Cambridge University Press 2002), 18; Kevin Vallier, *Must Politics Be War? Restoring Trust in the Open Society* (Oxford University Press 2019), 27–37.

[44] Pettit (n. 27) 212–17.

[45] Jones (n. 25), 66–67, 77–78.

behavior. Trust inevitably affects the way the trusting party evaluates evidence.[46] "The world looks different when viewed with trust from how it looks when viewed with distrust or neutrality," writes Karen Jones. "Trust is a lens that changes how agents understand their situation and the reasons it affords."[47] The trusting party is inclined, within some limit, to view evidence in a light favorable to the trusted party. This is neither irrational, nor "prerational";[48] rather, it is typical of the cognitive attitudes that people take toward their attachments and the people involved in them. The evidence of the risk that the other party will not prove trustworthy is bracketed, Jones maintains, not because other evidence outweighs this evidence, but rather because weighing it seems inconsistent with the relationship the trusting party has and values, or seeks to establish.[49] This is especially true of what we might call "intrarelational" trust – that is, trust that is embedded in rich interpersonal relationships. Those attachments would not have the intrinsic value they have for us, and could not survive, without such attitudes.

c Proleptic Trust

This understanding brings trusting and entrusting close together, because A means to engage in conduct that is visible to B and is intended to trigger B's trust-fulfilling behavior. However, in some cases, A may *entrust* something of value to the care of B while not entirely *trusting* him – that is, without fully believing in advance that B is fully trustworthy. A may do so hoping (possibly intending) that B will take the opportunity to show himself trust responsive.[50] A's conduct will *communicate* trust, by virtue of the public meaning such conduct typically has, without thereby *manifesting* A's *trust*, which A does not yet have. We might call it anticipatory, or *proleptic*, trust.[51] There need be nothing sinister, manipulative or insincere about A's entrusting behavior. Entrusting something of value to another *invites* a certain kind of mutual recognition and interaction rooted in it.

Proleptic trust, and perhaps robust trust more generally, can work only if certain conditions obtain between trusting party and the trusted party and in the environment in which they interact.[52] First, whether B's motivation in such cases proves trust responsive depends on the reasons that lie behind this motivation. These reasons may be various, but they must be relatively hearty, in the sense that it must not easily yield to countervailing motivations.[53] Second, A's conduct must communicate A's trust to B and others. Consequently, it must have the public significance

[46] McGeer (n. 38), 240; Patti Tamara Lenard, *Trust, Democracy and Multicultural Challenges* (University of Pennsylvania Press 2012), 31; Bernd Lahno, "Institutional Trust: A Less Demanding Form of Trust?" (2001) 15 *Revista Latinoamericana de Estudios Avanzados* 29; Karen Jones, "Trusting Interpretations," in *Trust: Analytic and Applied Perspectives* (Pekka Mäkelä and Cynthia Townley eds., Brill 2013), 15–29.

[47] Jones (n. 46), 15.

[48] Lahno (n. 46), 31.

[49] Jones (n. 46), 20–21.

[50] McGeer (n. 38), 242, 247–48; Pettit (n. 27) 212–17.

[51] Karen Jones calls it "therapeutic trust" (n. 26), 5, but that suggests, unfortunately in my view, that there is something morally unhealthy about B or B's character.

[52] I here build on Pettit's discussion of the phenomena of "trust-responsiveness" (n. 27) 220–25.

[53] McGeer and Pettit (n. 40), 16.

of signaling A's reliance and vulnerability and her (normative) expectation of B's trust responsiveness. Consequently, the meaning of A's action *as trusting or entrusting* and B's action *as trust responsive* must be available to each other and some relevant range of third parties. Similarly, B will be able effectively to signal his *trustworthiness* only if his actions or words convey his sincere invitation to trust. For these communications to take place, there must be enough entrusting, trust-fulfilling, and trust-inviting conduct in the social environment in which A and B interact that their actions can reasonably be understood as entrusting, trust fulfilling, and trust inviting. In social climates poisoned by cynicism or a pervasive assumption that everyone is out only for his or her own private good, proleptic trust, and possibly robust trust itself, will be difficult to achieve.

Third, proleptic trust is not likely to succeed where there are sharp divisions between B and A, or in the social environment in which they interact. Where sharp divisions obtain, B may not care about A's opinion of his trustworthiness or may not care about the opinions of others like A. Moreover, for proleptic trust to elicit trust-responsive behavior, the relationship between A and B must not be such that A's reliance on B is reasonably seen by B and others as motivated by something other than B's potential trust responsiveness; for, in that case, A's reliance would not be viewed as entrusting conduct. This would be true, for example, if B were forced by some third party to act in A's behalf. Similarly, the relationship must not be such that there is a significant manifest inequality of power between A and B. If A holds B in her power, B's action will reasonably be regarded as ingratiating or sycophancy rather than trust responsive, or A's conduct will be seen as hypocritical rather than trusting. If B holds A in his power, A's reliance and vulnerability will lack the necessary dimension of voluntariness, and A will lack the opportunity to engage B's trust-responsive behavior. Her reliance will reasonably be read as acquiescence, not trust. Thus, the manifest presence of strong sanctions for B's behavior and manifest inequalities of power between A and B can make entrusting impossible and can turn otherwise trust-responsive behavior into mere compliance. In sum, *the social context of potentially trust-relevant behavior, and the social meanings available in that context, can materially affect the possibilities for trusting and trust-responsive conduct.*

B Varieties of Nontrust

With this extended discussion of interpersonal trust in hand, we can deal more quickly with contraries and contradictories of trust. Although trust and distrust are mutually exclusive, they are not exhaustive of the trust domain. Some interactions among people may not be trust relevant at all;[54] they fall outside the trust spectrum. Along this spectrum fall clear, all-in cases of trust, at one end, and similarly full-fledged cases of distrust, with mistrust occupying a band between them. Moreover, cases of trust may share only some features of trust or share them to the robust degree of all-in cases. For example, one's trust in another may be limited in scope (A may

[54] Edna Ullmann-Margalit, "Trust, Distrust, and in Between," in *Distrust* (Russell Hardin ed., Russell Sage Foundation 2004), 60–82; Lenard (n. 46), ch. 3.

trust B in some matters but not others) or in intensity (willing to forego monitoring generally but not completely) and the like. Trust may shade into mistrust as mistrust may shade into distrust. There are cases that fall into zones of clarity on this spectrum, but there are also shades of gray on either side of mistrust. We impoverish our understanding of the moral, psychological and social landscape if we insist on considering only those cases that fall into the zones of clarity. The tendency to insist that all the space beyond all-in trust is the domain of distrust lies at the center of the Trust Challenge.

We may be inclined to think of a person's lack of trust in another person to be equivalent to distrust. In some contexts, "I just don't trust him!" is a clear expression of distrust. However, context can make all the difference. Where trust is expected, encouraged or actively invited, to say one does not trust another may express distrust. But it is also possible for one's attitude to occupy a position entirely off the trust spectrum; one may take no trust-relevant attitude to another person. Absence of trust is not a way of regarding another person; it involves the absence of any such regard. Likewise, A may rely on B but for reasons that have nothing to do with B, B's motivation or B's potential responsiveness to A's reliance.

Distrust, however, is a distinctive personal stance located at the opposite end of the spectrum of trust-relevant attitudes and dispositions. Distrust involves not merely a lack of reliance on another but rather the intentional *withholding* of reliance, a *refusal* to make oneself vulnerable to another person, either on some occasion or in general. If she has no choice but to rely, the reliance of a distrusting person will be unwilling, diffident and possibly defiant. Whether she also manifests these attitudes will depend, in part, on the costs to her of doing so. She will be disposed to withdraw her reliance at the first safe opportunity or will take all feasible measures to protect herself from the harm that she fears may eventuate. The distrusting person bases her withholding of reliance or diffidence on deep and active *suspicion* of the other party's competence or motivation.[55] If A distrusts B, A believes that B would (or does) treat any entrusting by A with indifference, if not contempt. A not only believes B to be unreliable but believes that, if given the chance, B is likely to act out of ill will against A or manifest indifference to A's interests or well-being. She believes that B will answer any trust she might place in him by exploitation or domination. Moreover, distrust, like trust, colors A's interpretations of B's conduct, insofar as it bears on A's interests, except with the opposite valence. A is strongly inclined to see B's motivations as sinister even when, to others, they might appear entirely innocent. In this respect, the distrusting person tends to be resistant to and discount evidence of the other party's cooperativeness or benign motivation. We might call this the "Othello effect" of distrust.[56]

On the spectrum between trust and distrust lie doubt and *mistrust*. A's trust-relevant stance regarding B may vary in two dimensions. First, A may have more or less confidence in, or more or less doubt about, B's competence, motivation or trust responsiveness. Second, depending on her confidence or doubt, A may adjust how much of what she values she is willing put in B's hands. At some indeterminate point,

[55] Lenard (n. 46), 56.
[56] Jones (n. 46), 18; see also Lenard (n. 46), 57.

A's less-than-full trust shades into a region of mistrust, characterized by some degree of doubt, which is still distinct from distrust. A, who mistrusts B, may still be willing to rely on B to some extent, still harboring doubt to some degree. Her reliance will be correspondingly cautious and tentative, perhaps taking some precautions against a worst-case scenario and taking care about what she puts in B's hands. She may hedge her bets, without closing off opportunities for B to demonstrate his trustworthiness. Thus, one who mistrusts another person is open to further evidence regarding the other party's trustworthiness and trust responsiveness. She may be willing to give the other party the benefit of the doubt she still harbors.[57]

Falling short of *mistrust*, one might harbor some doubts about the other party's trust responsiveness and yet *hope* that, by manifestly counting on him, she may engender trust-responsive behavior and plant a seed that could grow into trustworthiness. She may even be willing to *entrust* something of value to the care of the other person trusting them proleptically.[58]

C *Beyond the Interpersonal Paradigm*

It would be a mistake to leave our discussion of the salient features of trust and varieties of nontrust distrust at this point, since we find in other contexts trust-like phenomena that we are not inclined to dismiss as something other than trust properly understood. These contexts differ markedly from the philosophical paradigm interpersonal context and the differences inevitably affect the salient features of the trust phenomena we find in them. Our primary focus will be on trust-impersonal contexts, but first I want to consider briefly another kind of interpersonal context that deviates from the paradigm we have been considering.

a Ur Trust

Some philosophers have suggested that there is a more fundamental form of interpersonal trust. In some contexts, the trusting party does not willingly put her trust in another, making herself vulnerable to the trusted party's discretion, but rather simply *finds* herself in such a relationship – or, if that makes the matter still too much a matter of the trusting party's awareness, we might say that she simply *is*, in some fundamental, liminal way, deeply reliant on the other party.[59] Others have suggested that the "basic" form of interpersonal trust, whether conscious and willing or not, is the trust one person places *in* the other *person*, not limited to any relatively specific domain that she trusts to the other party's care.[60] That is to say, the trust of one person in another may be unarticulated, psychologically elemental and not fixed to a specific valued something. One example of this "ur trust"[61] is that between infant and parent. However, this case stands at a distance from the typical kind of

57 Lenard (n. 46), 59.
58 McGeer (n. 38) develops this theme in detail.
59 Stern (n. 29), 276.
60 Domenicucci and Holten (n. 36), 155–57; Baier (n. 27), 179.
61 The notion to which I give this name is different from "Ur-trust" discussed by Simpson (n. 29) 557–58.

interpersonal trust we have been discussing, and I am inclined to think of it as, at best, a limiting case. Not only is the vulnerability unchosen by the infant, but also the child lacks the capacity to grasp in even the most elementary way the nature of the relationship. The child's behavior does not even manifest confidence in the good will and care of the parent.

b Basic Trust

Other philosophers have thought that interpersonal trust often comes in less articulated, calibrated or calculated forms than the recognitional trust we discussed above. They maintain that trust lies in the background of relationships, giving them a distinctive shape, and, although they are unarticulated, they influence the more specific forms of interaction available and meaningful to participants in the relationships. They call this "basic trust" since they regard it as more fundamental than, and basic to, the more immediately observable recognitional trust.[62] This trust, they argue, does not call attention to itself because it is an unquestioned horizon of the meaningful interactions within the relationship. Indeed, they argue, if someone asks whether, why or how far to trust another in such circumstances, the other party could reasonably take the query as an insult, perhaps a failure of respect, or at least a failure to understand the nature of their relationship. Such questions, they observe, come up only when the relationship itself is not entirely healthy.

Something like this interpersonal phenomenon is familiar; we should not ignore it. However, for the purposes of this essay, its social, rather than elemental psychological, form is of greater significance. In a (happy) community, people may relate to each other against a general background of such "basic trust." Presently, I will explore some of the salient features of this "climate of trust."

c Impersonal Contexts

Impersonal contexts in which we find trust phenomena may be informal or to various degrees formally structured or institutionalized. In informal contexts, people may encounter other individuals – persons may interact with two or more other persons – but their interactions or relationships are mediated and at a distance. One person may encounter another knowing only that the other person is a member of a more or less familiar group or occupant of a recognized social role. The trust may be directed not at any particular individual but rather at unassignable members of a social group. In cases like this, trust can shade off into a general confidence regarding the likely competence or motivations of people in the group, but some significant features of trust may remain.

In more formally structured contexts, institutions can figure in trust relations in either of two different ways. The institution itself may be the trusted agent – people put trust *in* the institution. They trust the institution to perform as designed or advertised, believing that it is likely to be fair, to serve their interests or to serve important principles or values to which they are committed.[63] Call this "institutional

[62] Simpson (n. 29), 560; Stern (n. 29), 284.
[63] Ullmann-Margalit (n. 54), 72.

trust." Although people who have meaningful opportunities to participate in the institution may be more likely to trust it, nonparticipants may also trust social or political institutions that they judge are likely to serve their needs or interests. Sometimes this trust amounts to little more than unforced reliance, but it might involve significant normative expectations. People who are more actively engaged in the institution may look for something closer to trust responsiveness of the institution or the officials they encounter.

Alternatively, the institution may be the incubator or underwriter of trust – either robust interpersonal trust or more distant impersonal trust of an individual occupying an institutional role. Call this "institution-dependent" trust. A's trust in B is institution dependent when A trusts B, who holds an official position in an institution C, in part based on what A knows about how the C's processes and procedures underwrite B's competence and motivations. On that basis, A can count on B, within certain parameters, to act in A's interest, or at least to act fairly when it comes to matters of A's interests. A's trust is akin to personal trust, but more distant and mediated by the institution. A's trust in B depends on her confidence in the institution in which B is an official, but it extends to something approximating personal trust in B acting in his official capacity.

Impersonal contexts, whether formal or informal, in which trust exists differ from paradigm interpersonal contexts of trust in several respects. First, the trusted or distrusted party is not an individual with whom the trusting party is familiar. The candidate for trust might be a collectivity, an organization or an institution. In that case, the trust involved will be akin to predictive reliance. Trusting parties rely on the design of structures, constitution and procedures of the institution to produce outcomes that serve their interests or values. Alternatively, the candidate for trust may be an individual. In that case, the individual will be anonymous or, as Bentham put it, an "unassignable" stranger to trusting party. The individual might be a member of a group, known to the trusting party only by virtue of commonly recognized characteristics of members of that group, rather than personal experience. If the individual occupies a formally defined institutional role, or a recognized social role, the trusting party will know the individual through the recognized features, powers and obligations of incumbents in that role. If the trusting party is herself a member of the group, she may have some insider, participant attitude that warrants her attributing a degree of trustworthiness to the individual.

Thus, second, there is likely to be little opportunity for direct, shared personal experience between the trusting and trusted parties. Personal encounters between individuals, if they occur, will be episodic and mediated. The parties will appear to each other as abstracted individuals, representatives of roles or groups, rather than concrete persons. Thus, the second-personal aspects of the relations may still exist, but in a changed or thinned-out form; and the recognitional aspects of trust, while possibly still present, will be less concrete, depending on background social conventions and practices known to the parties. In interpersonal contexts, parties can customize such background understandings and public meanings, but in impersonal contexts, recognitional resources will be generic and off the rack. Information available to the parties will be general, mediated and not personalized. Some theorists hold that trust in a robust sense is not possible among strangers, but this overlooks the resources we have for understanding and interpreting the behavior of others in a wider shared, or overlapping, culture. Broadly available social meanings of behavior, rather than meanings born in intimacy, will play a dominant role in trust encounters.

Third, the meaning of efforts to give trusting parties some assurance that the trusted party will be trustworthy may change. Especially where the reasonableness of placing trust in certain agents depends on the willingness of others also to put their trust in the agent, public assurances of the trustworthiness of the potentially trusted party will have a larger role to play than in paradigm interpersonal contexts; so too will the climate in which people who are more or less strangers encounter each other.

Fourth, the nature of the reliance is also likely to be different in impersonal contexts. The range of options open to the trusting party are likely to be more limited, narrowing the scope for the trusted party's voluntarily entrusting something of value to the care of another. Where trust is possible in these contexts, it may not involve a robust undertaking or entrusting, but rather some form or other of willing acceptance.

Fifth, the normative dimensions of the trusting relationship may differ in significant ways. For example, the parties to the relationship are not likely to regard the relationship as intrinsically valuable. Likewise, failure or betrayal of a trust that would deeply rock an intrapersonal relationship may do far less damage to a relatively impersonal one; on the other hand, the stakes involved in the impersonal relationship may be much higher. Similarly, responses to failures in impersonal encounters are less likely to include forgiveness and more likely to involve efforts to reform faulty institutional mechanisms. Further, in impersonal contexts, nontrust may be the normal default, rather than trust, and this will shape the public meanings of trust-giving and trust-responsive conduct. A wary response to signaled trustworthiness might be viewed as more reasonable, less likely to strike one as offensive or a lack of respect, among strangers than between persons well known to each other. The same may be true regarding the extent to which monitoring of the trusted party by the trusting party is tolerated or regarded as reasonable. Again, while desire for the esteem or good opinion of others might be a motivation for trust responsiveness that, if known, could damage a relatively close interpersonal relationship,[64] it may be regarded as entirely appropriate in impersonal contexts, especially those of institution-dependent trust. Trust-fulfilling behavior may be important to B because it implicates his integrity or his commitment to certain principles, and the good opinion of others reflects back to him an assessment of his integrity or of the commitments he is inclined to take seriously.

4 Trust – Civic and Political

Mindful of the nature of robust interpersonal trust and of the effects that differences of context can have on the nature and dynamics of trust, we can proceed to explore more directly civic and political trust, which are the primary targets of the Trust Challenge.

[64] As McGeer argues; see McGeer (n. 38) and McGeer and Pettit (n. 40).

A Civic Trust

Civic trust is the form of trust that members of a political community have in other members of their community, or groups of members, or in the associations and institutions that structure their civic life. Civic trust is a special case of impersonal trust. It concerns public matters, but its modality is "horizontal" – looking to other members – rather than "vertical" – looking to public officials and representatives of government. The trusting parties are not merely external observers of conduct of members of the community; rather, they are participants in the political community, engaging regularly with other participants. The scope of civic trust in a political community can be relatively wide, potentially encompassing the entire political community, and community's members are likely to be quite diverse. Because the context for such trust is impersonal, the relationships in which trust is offered and accepted may be relatively thin and distant, and they are typically mediated by institutions or more or less formally structured associations. So, if A has trust in B in this civic context, A is unlikely personally to encounter B and is unlikely to have any personal knowledge of B's character, commitments, loyalties, general cooperativeness or trust responsiveness. Nevertheless, as we have seen, the second-personal, recognitional aspects are not necessarily eliminated; rather, they take on a different form.

a Climate of Trust

In some cases, members of the political community may consciously undertake to put trust in other members, but it often functions in the background, as the milieu in which members of the political community interact. Where that is true, civic trust is a special case of the phenomenon of a climate of trust – it is the climate of trust in the political community as a whole.

David Hume observed that "a good natured man finds himself in an instant of the same humour with his company; and even the proudest and most surly take a tincture from their countrymen and acquaintance."[65] Confirming Hume, recent social scientists have observed that a given individual's level of trust is often influenced by the trust levels of others around them.[66] People observe or sense, without being able to describe accurately, the climate of trust in a community.

The climate of trust (or mistrust or distrust) in a community is a social rather than personal phenomenon. It has an "objective," or rather a nonsubjective and public, dimension that supervenes on those attitudes and dispositions of individual members; it is not reducible to them. The climate of trust in a community is a kind of commons – a "commons of the mind," in Annette Baier's useful phrase[67] – that people draw on, add to, sustain or weaken through their trusting activities, interactions, practices and engagements with other members of the community and their

[65] David Hume, *A Treatise of Human Nature* (David Fate Norton and Mary J. Norton eds., Oxford University Press 2000), 206.

[66] Kenneth Newton, Dietlind Stolle and Sonja Zmerli, "Social and Political Trust," in *The Oxford Handbook of Social and Political Trust* (Eric M. Uslaner ed., Oxford University Press 2018), 49.

[67] Annette Baier, *The Commons of the Mind* (Open Court 1997).

reflections on them. These trust-related activities include trust-responsive conduct but also failures of trust, betrayals and abandonments of trust, and challenges to, corrections of and attempts to repair such failures. This trust commons typically may be articulated in informal norms at work in the community, norms to which members of the community hold each other by informal means.[68] The trusting relationship and the attitudes and dispositions rooted in it are made concrete in these informal norms and expressed in conduct shaped by them. Generic trusting is simultaneously expressed and nourished, enacted and reproduced, through compliance with informal norms of self-restraint, mutual respect, fairness and decency, and challenges or corrections to perceived deviations from them. Public behaviors can nourish or poison the climate, enrich or impoverish the publicly available "language" of impersonal trust.

This complex of interactions and interdependent expectations, attitudes and dispositions is broadly a matter of common knowledge, although this knowledge may be only implicit for many members of the community. They sense the climate and live in it, rather than observe, study or manage it. Their trusting and entrusting – and their mistrusting and distrusting – take shape in it. In this climate, conduct gets its public meaning as trust giving or trust withholding, trust fulfilling or trust betraying. Individual members draw from this commons to anticipate and assess the conduct of nonintimate fellow members; they depend on it for the public meaning of their behavior. It is also from this commons that they draw resources to reinforce social bonds within their circle and to extend trust to those beyond the limits of their narrow circle. It is an important component of what social theorists call "social capital."

This climate can be rich and robust or thin, fragile, partial or incomplete. The climate of trust in a community can be narrowly circumscribed, limited to small subgroups of a political community, or broad and community wide, embracing many diverse subgroups in the community. Civic trust, as I have characterized it, depends on a wide-scope climate of trust. Depending on the scope of trusting, the climate in a political community as a whole can be both trusting and distrusting – trust within a subgroup can feed or respond to distrust of the wider community. Wide-scope trust is likely to encourage, enable and support generalized trust in subcommunities. But breakdowns in the climate of trust in a political community as a whole can result in a rise of distrust of members of the community generally and, simultaneously, an intensification of trust in members of smaller subgroups that provide refuge from the larger political community.[69] Breakdown of civic trust often leads to fragmentation of the community and intense, sometimes destructive, small-group trust and loyalty. Similarly, it is reasonable to expect that intense small-group trust, especially among social or political elites, can create equally intense, but more widespread, civic and political distrust if the elites ignore or alienate large portions of the wider community.[70]

[68] See Geoffrey Brennan and Philip Pettit, *The Economy of Esteem* (Oxford University Press 2004), ch. 14.

[69] Martin Krygier, "Virtuous Circles: Antipodean Reflections on Power, Institutions, and Civil Society" (1997) 11 *East European Politics and Societies*, 71; Baier (n. 27), 178.

[70] Matthew Harding offered this plausible suggestion. It deserves serious empirical study beyond the scope of this essay.

B Political Trust

Political trust, for our purposes, is the trust that those who are subject to political power place in those who exercise that power. It involves trust either in governmental institutions or institution-dependent trust of in public officials. The political trust that citizens may have is typically mediated by civil associations or institutions. Consider, first, citizens' trust *in* government or its constituent institutions.

Citizens who trust in their government rely on its constitution, structure, procedures and institutions. They take confidence in the design and real-time operation of government institutions. They regard the guiding principles and values of the institutions as benign and believe that they align generally with their own interests and values and that government institutions tend to function according to design. Good institutional design deploys mechanisms to provide citizens with dependable evidence of the performance of public officials and safeguard against abuse of public power. In virtue of the evaluative dimension, their expectations are not merely predictive but also normative. Citizens may take an internal point of view with regard to the institutions of government. In that case, they do not see government as an alien force but as an entity, perhaps even an agent, on which they can make normative demands. Citizens *expect* government and public officials *to* perform as required by the constitution and laws, which, they assume, broadly conform to the principles and values underlying them. Nevertheless, compared to trusted parties in personal contexts, government is a very different kind of trusted agent, and the trust that citizens put in it is decidedly impersonal. The kind of attitudes trusting citizens adopt are appropriate to the kind of agent that government is.[71] Citizens place their trust in formal institutions, and their relations to individual public officials that occupy positions of authority are correspondingly formal. Formality in this context is a virtue. Governmental institutions are trusted, in part, because we can expect them to function according to design, even though the people staffing them constantly change. The performance of governmental institutions is impersonal.[72]

Trust in institutions does not entirely close off some form of quasi-personal trust in officials; rather, it may make such trust possible and actually underwrite it. Such trust of officials is institution mediated and institution dependent. Parties do not meet on a personal basis but rather as occupants of institutionally defined roles or positions. Government institutions define and structure the encounters and secure competent and properly oriented performance. Such structures, procedures and safeguards are not incidental to the operation of the institutions; rather, they are intrinsic to their design and proper functioning. Something approximating interpersonal trust is possible, but an impersonal, institution-mediated form of trust is more common.

Indeed, in the political domain, robust personal trust – or something that mimics it – in public officials can be very dangerous. Authoritarian leaders and certain forms of populism seek to generate a robustly personal relationship of trust between the leader and the people, unmediated by political institutions or civic associations.

[71] Daniel Weinstock, "Trust in Institutions," in David Archard (n. 27), 214.
[72] Ullmann-Margalit calls this "the principle of substitutability" (n. 54), 77.

The formality and distance of the kind of political trust we have just considered is anathema. The people – or rather individuals en masse – on this view must feel a direct, emotional connection with the leader. Of course, the elimination of distance is only virtual or imagined, rooted in the feeling that he is *like me* and reinforced by the sense that he is speaks directly *to me* and *for me*, unmediated by representative institutions. This form of trust – or trust manqué – is especially useful for the ruler because it sets him free from any genuine form of accountability. Leaders who aspire to attract this kind of trust are proper objects of deep suspicion and distrust. And mechanisms that weaken this kind of trust are not troubling to the rule of law.

5 Responses to the Trust Challenge

Political trust, then, combines trust in governmental, legal institutions with institution-dependent trust. Civic trust is a kind of general, social trust, perhaps with elements of more robust personal trust, depending on a background climate of trust. Contraries of political and civic trust are also now recognizable. Trust-relevant attitudes across the spectrum are possible, from robust trust to weaker forms of trust through the range of mistrusting attitudes and conduct to full and deep distrust. We are now in a position to assess the strength of the Trust Challenge. That challenge, recall, was directed against two understandings of the rule of law, one defended by the *fiduciary theory* of government, the other resting on the *fidelity thesis*. Consider, first, the challenge to the *fiduciary theory*.

A Juridical Trust

We can deal with this challenge briefly. The Trust Challenge poses no problem for the fiduciary theory for the possibly unwelcome reason that the notion of trust on which the fiduciary theory relies is only a distant cousin of the notion we have been entertaining. The latter is a relational notion of trust, although the relationships vary widely, and consequently the core elements of trust vary as well. In contrast, the notion of trust that the fiduciary theory invokes is the *juridical* notion. The juridical notion concerns a certain kind of legal (and, by extension, moral) duty that arises from facts of dependency and subjection to power. We have no reason to think that a constitutional strategy institutionalizing some form of relational distrust is likely to threaten the juridical trust on which the fiduciary relationship between subjects and the state allegedly is built. This happy outcome comes with a rather high price tag for fiduciary theory, however, because the significant difference between these two notions makes the relational notion unfit to do the theoretical work fiduciary theorists have assigned it. I must explain.

To talk about the relationship between citizens and public officials in terms of juridical trust is to characterize a certain duty of those officials that is (or ought to be) recognized and enforced by law. The special ground of this duty determines its content. It is imposed on certain agents to act in ways that specifically benefit another party – the beneficiary – rather than the agents (or third parties) on the ground that the beneficiary is in a deep and pervasive way dependent on the agent, subject to the agent's power and at the agent's mercy. Evan Fox-Decent seeks to construe this relationship in terms of the relational trust we explored above. The state–subject relationship, he suggests, rests on a "presumption of [relational] trust."[73] This, I think, is a mistake. Facts of dependency, broadly construed, are sufficient to trigger or ground the fiduciary duty of trust, and that duty requires agents to act only with the interests and good of the beneficiary in view. Nothing about the beneficiary except her subjection to the power of the agent need play a role in generating this duty. Thus, no relationship other than that constituted by the fact of dependency is involved; in particular, no *trusting* relationship need be involved.

Not only is it not necessary for the beneficiary actively and intentionally to *entrust* something of value to the discretion of the agent; it is not even necessary that the beneficiary trust the agent in any way. In fact, the juridical trust – that is, the fiduciary duty – can survive fully intact despite the beneficiary's full, active and manifest relational *distrust* of the agent. If there is willing reliance, it is externally (that is, legally) secured reliance, not any mode of reliance more personal than that. Thus, prototrust, if there is such, is not a ground but rather a consequence of an expectation that the agent will honor the dependency. Relational trust, and the lack or even the opposite of it, is irrelevant to the ground of the fiduciary duty. Juridical trust and relational trust are conceptually and normatively distinct.

Evan Fox-Decent appeals to what I earlier called "Ur trust" – modeled by the relationship between infant and caregiver – in an attempt to ground juridical trust in relational trust.[74] However, this is an unfortunate gambit. "Ur trust" is an especially unattractive model for the subject–state relation because it infantilizes citizens and encourages a dangerous self-understanding among public officials that approximates contempt and domination.

The attempt to employ the relational notion of trust in the service of the fiduciary theory of government has another unfortunate consequence. While fiduciary theorists are keen to argue that trust relationships do not necessarily invoke anything akin to consent, or active engagement by the beneficiary in the relationship, they still are inclined to talk of *entrusting*. However, the entrusting agent is *the law*.[75] Of course, this talk is entirely innocent if we take it to mean simply that the law underwrites or enforces fiduciary duties. However, if we take the use of the notion of entrusting seriously, fiduciary theorists must accept a most unwelcome consequence. For strictly speaking, the law cannot entrust anything; the law is not an agent. The law can authorize – that is, legal norms can ground – actions or grant powers to agents who can do so, but the law does not – it cannot – entrust. The state and its agents entrust through the law. However, it follows that fiduciary theory is committed to the view that the state entrusts the well-being, interests and good of the beneficiary *to itself*. That, surely, is an understanding of the state's obligations that few of us (including fiduciary theorists) will find attractive. Moreover, it again casts citizens in an entirely passive, unengaged role. On the relational model, the entrusting agent is the

73 Fox-Decent (n. 13), ch. IV.
74 Ibid., 106–08.
75 Ibid., 106.

beneficiary; but on this proposal, the entrusting agent is not the beneficiary but the trusted party itself. In addition, on this model, the state's obligations are not owed to the beneficiary but to the state. Finally, there is no advantage in selecting international law rather than domestic law as the entrusting agent.[76] Although it avoids the embarrassment of the state entrusting itself, it still leaves the beneficiary in an entirely passive position and misdirects the duties owed by the state. In this case, they are owed not to the beneficiary but to international law or the international community. Fiduciary theory surely does not want to embrace these consequences, but then it must acknowledge that the notion of trust it employs is the strictly juridical notion, not the relational notion. Fiduciary theory avoids the Trust Challenge by playing on a different conceptual field.

B Accountability and Civic Trust

Consider now the argument that robust accountability is a threat to civic trust. Recall it was argued that being called to account (under some circumstances) may reasonably be experienced as an insult, expressing distrust and hence a failure of basic respect. By extension, the Trust Challengers argue that accountability undermines the civic climate of trust. This objection is fundamentally mistaken. I will argue, on the contrary, that mutual accountability in the context of interpersonal relations presupposes and expresses trust, rather than distrust or even mistrust, and it is likely to build and reinforce trust; and that this fact informs our more distant, less personal civic relations and the social meanings of our actions available to us in our civic interactions.

The centrality of mutual accountability to moral life and the moral community is a common view among moral philosophers. In the first edition (1759) of his *Theory of Moral Sentiments*, Adam Smith wrote:

> A moral being is an accountable being . . . a being that must give an account of its actions to some other, and that consequently must regulate them according to the good-liking of this other. . . . But tho' he is, no doubt, principally accountable to God, in the order of time, he must necessarily conceive of himself as accountable to his fellow creatures.[77]

Kant extended this thought when he wrote, "no one can bind another to something without also being subject to a law by which he in turn can be bound in the same way by the other."[78] That is, to submit to moral law is, necessarily, to submit to *reciprocal* (or at least *mutual*) accountability. If A claims to bind B and to hold B accountable to this obligation, A is also subject to a network of accountability to others in which

[76] Criddle and Fox-Decent write, "International law entrusts states with authority based upon their assumption of public powers held for the benefit of their people." Evan Criddle and Evan Fox-Decent, *Fiduciaries of Humanity: How International Law Constitutes Authority* (Oxford University Press 2016), 50.

[77] Adam Smith, *A Theory of Moral Sentiments* (D. D. Raphael and A. L. MacFie eds, LibertyClassics 1982), 111.

[78] Immanuel Kant, "Perpetual Peace," in Kant, *Practical Philosophy* (M. J. Gregor trans. and ed., Cambridge University Press 1996) 323 n. † (emphasis deleted).

B also participates. Echoing Kant, Stephen Darwall has argued that deontic notions like duty and obligation are categorically different from the idea of a good moral reason for action. Agents who violate their duties or do not fulfill their obligations are liable to moral blame, and "moral blame comes with ... an implicit demand for accountability and acknowledgment of the legitimacy of this demand." Likewise, "guilt reciprocates blame by acknowledging the legitimacy of its implicit demand, and it is itself a form of holding oneself accountable for complying with this demand."[79] To hold someone accountable for his actions with respect to his obligations to others is not, at the first level of normative communication, to threaten or apply some external incentive to conformity to that obligation. It is, rather, a demand on the obligation bearer to give an account of his actions and an encouragement to hold *himself* accountable, to take responsibility for his actions.[80] Darwall characterizes all of morality in these Smithian-Kantian terms; he calls it "morality as equal accountability."[81] "Moral norms," he writes, "regulate a community of equal, mutually accountable, free and rational agents as such, and moral obligations are the demands such agents have standing to address to one another and with which they are mutually accountable for complying."[82]

Far from giving insult or denying respect, accountability is an expression of respect, provided it is reciprocal. "Holding someone responsible involves commitment to a form of mutual respect," Darwall observes, "since it commits the holder to the idea not just that he has an authority to hold the other responsible, but also that the other can hold himself and others [including the one holding him responsible] responsible as well."[83] Morality so understood is not as a matter of every person subjected to an externally imposed, impersonal code of norms but rather as a norm-structured practice in which each person is and regards himself as accountable to others and they to him. To purport to hold another accountable, under these conditions, is not to exercise unilateral authority over the other person but to acknowledge common participation in the practice of mutual accountability to common governing norms.

We have seen that in the fidelity practice, unlike in structures of bureaucratic or managerial accountability, trust plays a key role. For in holding another accountable, one acknowledges the authority of the other party to hold oneself accountable. One puts oneself in the hands of the other party, makes oneself vulnerable to her freely exercised judgment, to her "good-liking," as Smith put it. This entrusting is reciprocal. Acts of accountability holding may have the properties Trust Challengers allege when the norms are externally imposed or where there is no recognizable community between the holder and the giver, and especially where the accountability holding is not mutual. In such circumstances, holding another person accountable amounts to

[79] Stephen Darwall and Brandan Dill, "Moral Psychology as Accountability," in *Moral Psychology and Human Agency: Philosophical Essays on the Science of Ethics* (Justin D'Arms and Daniel Jacobson eds., Oxford University Press 2014), 43.

[80] Ibid., 44.

[81] Stephen Darwall, *The Second-Person Standpoint* (Harvard University Press 2006), 100–04.

[82] Ibid., 101.

[83] Stephen Darwall, "Respect and Honor as Accountability," in Stephen Darwall, *Honor, History, and Relationship: Essays in Second-Personal Ethics II* (Oxford University Press 2013), 12–13.

subjecting that person to one's unilateral power or demonstrating to her the fact and burden of that subjection. However, the accountability at the center of fidelity is not like this. It is and must be reciprocal. Civic trust is a condition and a consequence of mutual accountability in the civic association. Where each is the guardian of each, there is no reason for one to regard being called to account as an insult or the expression of distrust.

Reciprocal accountability holding, then, can be a form of participation in a climate of civic trust. Moreover, it provides a means of publicly signaling one's trustworthiness. It can enhance, rather than threaten, trusting activity in the community. Thus, we may conclude that, regarding the practice of accountability at the civic level, as long as the practice involves mutual submission to and mutual participation in the practice, the practice presupposes and expresses trust rather than threatening it.

Of course, social conditions can undermine or threaten this practice. In a culture otherwise dominated by distrust, it may not be possible for the morality of equal accountability to gain a foothold. In the absence of widely recognizable examples of mutual accountability holding, where normative requirements are impersonal and imposed from above and demands for compliance are unilateral, it may not be possible to read attempts to hold persons accountable as trust involving. If the soil of the community's civic culture is poisoned, mutual accountability characteristic of fidelity cannot take root. We must concede, then, that, under some social conditions, accountability may be read as nothing more than the exercise of externally imposed power; but also, in this climate, fidelity in general could not get a foothold, and, sadly, robust rule of law could not long exist. Under these conditions, law itself can survive, if at all, only by depending on the use of coercive force beyond levels few could regard as tolerable.

C Accountability and Political Trust

It remains for us to address the Trust Challenge to accountability in the political domain. As we have seen, political trust (or its contraries) can take as its object either the political institutions themselves – various agencies of government or the regime as a whole – or public officials. I will focus on the latter, "institution-dependent" trust, and the alleged challenge to robust accountability of officials. Recall, political theorists and constitution writers, following the lead of Hume, Jefferson and Bentham, insist that those who exercise political power must be subject to systematic accountability, institutionalized in "the chains of the Constitution" and other legal devices. They have called attention to two constant dangers of political life. One danger is the potential for abuse of power and corruption of human motivation that is an inevitable feature of putting great power in the hands of human beings. The other is the danger of unguarded and unquestioning trust in officials by citizens. We recognized the wisdom in these worries when we highlighted the danger of implicit trust in leaders modeled on intimate, intrarelational trust. Acknowledging these dangers, clear-eyed institutional designers proposed systematic measures of control and accountability, which they were happy to characterize as devices of *institutionalized distrust*.

Trust challengers seize on this characterization, arguing that, indeed, mechanisms of accountability are motivated by, publicly express and effectively nurture political distrust, but they see this as a threat to good government and the rule of law, rather than, as Bentham put it, means of security against misrule. The technologies of distrust, they argue, are rooted in a deep suspicion of power and of those who exercise it and an expectation, resistant to counter evidence, that they are irredeemable "knaves." Motivated in this way, systematic accountability undermines effective government in several ways, they argue. First, mechanisms of accountability stifle the necessary exercise of reasonable judgment, making official decision-making rigid and inflexible.[84] This obviates trust, they argue, since trust necessarily confers an important degree of discretion on the trusted party. Second, accountability undermines desirable motivations of public officials. Pervasive accountability mechanisms make it difficult for officials to demonstrate their trustworthiness because their actions will reasonably be seen not as taking the fact that trust has been placed in them as a reason for performing their official duties but only as responding to external sanctions. Subjecting officials to external sanctions crowds out desirable internal motivations, including a sense of integrity, concern for the public good and trust responsiveness.[85] It signals that external intervention is the controlling factor in official decision-making. Third, they argue, frequent, publicly visible operation of accountability mechanisms undermine the confidence of people in government institutions and public officials. While general confidence of citizens in a regime and its institutions is enhanced by knowledge of the existence and availability of mechanisms of accountability, as these mechanisms are deployed, confidence in public officials declines. "The potential availability" of such check and controls, writes Piotr Sztompka, "must be matched by their very limited actualization."[86]

I regard these concerns as important, and I agree that political distrust, if pervasive in the polity, is corrosive of good government and of robust rule of law. But we need to take a more careful measure of political distrust and of the nature and consequences of mechanisms of accountability. This more careful measure will allow us to pull the sting of the Trust Challenge and assure us of the integrity and effectiveness of accountability fit for the rule of law. The lesson we should draw from observation of potential costs of deploying mechanisms of accountability is not to retreat from rule-of-law demands for effective accountability devices, nor to concede that accountability and political trust are incompatible. Rather, we should conclude that we must design accountability devices and practices to avoid or reduce to a minimum these potential effects.

To begin our response to the Trust Challenge, we should recall that distrust lies at the opposite end of the trust spectrum. It involves active withholding of reliance on the distrusted party, a refusal rooted in deep suspicion that the other party, given the opportunity, will treat one's interest with indifference or contempt. It is subject to

[84] Roderick M. Kramer, "Trust and Distrust in Organizations: Emerging Perspectives, Enduring Questions" (1999) 50 *Annual Review of Psychology* 591–92; Lahno (n. 49), 47; O'Neill (n. 24), 175–77.

[85] Bruno S. Frey, "A Constitution for Knaves Crowds Out Civic Virtue" (1997) 107 *The Economic Journal* 1043–53; Brennan and Pettit (n. 69), 260–63, and works cited there.

[86] Piotr Sztompka, *Trust: A Sociological Theory* (Cambridge University Press 2000), 146. See also Paul C. Bauer and Matthias Fatka, "Direct Democracy and Political Trust: Enhancing Trust, Initiating Distrust – or Both?" (2014) 20 *Swiss Political Science Review* 49–69.

what we called "the Othello effect": the distrustful person is closed to new evidence of potential good will or trustworthiness of the other party and tends to read all evidence in a light unfavorable to that party. In the political context, distrust tends to produce in those who harbor it cynicism, alienation, despair and, as a result, disengagement from political life, or radical rejection of and opposition to its institutions. Distrust is, indeed, corrosive to political life. It represents the danger opposite to that of naive political trust that motivated designers of "the chains of the Constitution." However, mistrust, while it acknowledges doubt, is willing to engage, even perhaps to rely, on the other party, perhaps taking precautions. A mistrustful party is open to evidence of the trustworthiness of others, willing to respond with trust to credible signals of trust responsiveness. A sober assessment of political power and its institutionalization should lead us to avoid both naive trust and deep distrust. An open, if somewhat wary, mistrust seems more reasonable. It also leaves open a degree of proleptic trust.

Next, recall that the political trust in view here is institution dependent. Rarely do citizens address officials directly. Governmental institutions and civic associations of many kinds mediate their encounters; and these associations themselves are organized in different ways for different kinds of accountability and for holding accountable different kinds and levels of governmental officials. Thus, for the most part, we will consider matters of trust and its contraries in impersonal contexts. The personal attitudes that individual citizens or officials take will not be at the center of our concern; rather, we will focus on their trust-relevant conduct, their entrusting conduct, their conduct-withholding reliance and their trust-responsive conduct. Accordingly, we must consider the publicly recognized meanings of the conduct involved in public accountability-holding activities that are available in the civic climate and reasonable inferences from them. Moreover, the normative expectations in these impersonal contexts are different from, and not plausibly modeled on, more intimate personal contexts. The questions we must consider, then, are (1) what attitudes and dispositions along the trust–distrust spectrum accountability-holding activities signal or communicate and (2) what effect these are likely to have on the conduct and motivations of government officials.

Starting with the first question, we can uncover the plausible public meanings of these activities by looking at their publicly acknowledged aims and presuppositions and the reasonable associations that are likely to be drawn between these activities and others seen as similar in motivation and upshot. Accountability mechanisms are meant to make good the rule of law's promise of protection and recourse against the arbitrary exercise of power. They are meant to give concrete shape to the partnership between those who wield political power and those who are subject to it. This partnership involves not only mutual commitments to comply with the law but also common commitments to hold each other accountable to its terms. Although the relations between individual officials and individual laypersons will ordinarily be perceived as unequal, there is still a publicly recognized mutuality or reciprocity between officials and the public. Moreover, the operative assumption animating the design of institutions of accountability is not that all human beings are inherently malevolent or by nature untrustworthy ("knaves"), but rather that ordinary human beings are at their motivationally weakest in circumstances where they wield power over the lives and fortunes of other human beings and where the temptation to use that power for private gain is great. The law regularly and reasonably makes concessions to predictable, all-too-human weaknesses. The law of criminal excuses offers several examples; the rule of law does the same. Finally, we noted earlier that the public meaning of trust-relevant conduct takes shape against the background of certain default assumptions. In interpersonal contexts, some degree of trust or at most tempered circumspection is the default, but this default assumption often is suspended in circumstances where the stakes of relying on another person are very high, typical temptations are very strong or the parties are engaged in innocent competition. We can expect, then, that the same would be true in impersonal, especially political, contexts.

With these considerations in mind, it is reasonable to think that the accountability-holding actions of citizens say publicly something like the following to officials:

> We agreed to submit to the law and your execution of it on the condition that you also submit to law and regard it as the guide and judge of our actions and of yours. Moreover, although we recognized that concentrated governing power is in many respects far greater than the dispersed power of individuals and civic associations, we entrusted this power to you, making ourselves vulnerable to your actions as free agents and to your judgments of us. We did so because you also submitted to the law and our judgment of your best efforts to comply with and enforce it. Our holding you accountable for actions in the domain of your power as defined by the law provides to you opportunities to show your good faith in acting out your commitment in circumstances that might otherwise appear to compromise that good faith. We do not expect that you will deceive us or abuse your power or act against our legally protected interests from malevolent motives. But we do know that the temptations of power are significant. Routine calls for you to give account of your exercise of the powers entrusted in you protect you from those temptations and from otherwise not unreasonable interpretations of your actions as ultra vires, taken in bad faith and inconsistent with your commitment.

If this is the prevailing message, and coercive sanctions only lie in the background, then the appeal to the integrity and public spirit of officials, or at least to their interest in the good opinion of others, will be in the foreground. The demand for accountability on a routine, and not personally directed, basis can then reasonably be seen as an invitation to the official to hold himself accountable and to connect the execution of his official duties to values and commitments important to him.

Do accountability mechanisms thus characterized presuppose or express distrust in any significant way? Clearly, they do not. They may be motivated by and possibly even express caution based on realism about the dynamics of power and its temptations, and a willingness to take certain precautions to avoid some worse-case scenarios. At most, this underlying stance is one of moderate mistrust and may look more like a modest form of trust, wary perhaps but open to evidence of the good faith and trust responsiveness of public officials. Moreover, such moderate mistrust, if that is what it is, leaves open the option of genuine proleptic trust. Indeed, the activities described above look more like exercises of proleptic political trust than resolute refusals to trust and withdrawals of reliance. They engage rather than constrain the exercise of judgment by public officials; they recognize publicly the autonomy and moral capacities of officials and put in play the concerns of public good, justice and law's substantive demands on which we want official judgment to focus.

Accordingly, we have good reason to think that accountability-holding activities will not drive out intrinsic motivations of integrity or concern for the public good. Rather, they are open to, and seek to encourage, trust-responsive behavior on the part of officials, behavior that not only publicly demonstrates officials' good faith but also allows officials to act in ways that maintain their own integrity. There is nothing essentially punitive about holding to account a person to whom great power is entrusted. Accountability just makes manifest that exercises of power are subject to the deliberative forces of law and provides a public forum for those deliberative forces to work.

Of course, the desire for esteem may lie behind trust responsiveness,[87] but, as we have seen, trustworthiness is primarily about trust responsiveness, not the reasons that motivate it. In this respect, trust in impersonal contexts may differ from trust in more intimate settings. Hume, one of philosophy's most penetrating observers of human motivation, wrote "to love the fame of laudable actions approaches so near the love of laudable actions for their own sakes, that these passions are more capable of mixture, than any other kinds of affections."[88] If Hume's observation is sound, desire for esteem – desire for the good opinion of others regarding proper, just, equitable decision-making – may be indistinguishable to the official from finding these considerations themselves intrinsically compelling.

We can conclude, I believe, that well-designed mechanisms of accountability are not properly characterized as institutions of distrust but rather mechanisms of proleptic political trust or at least of mitigated moderate mistrust. They represent institutions and practices of active and engaged vigilance, not sullen, alienated disengagement. This also suggests a response to the problem of the alleged trust-depressing effect of the visible use of such mechanisms. This effect can be mitigated through education of citizens' normative expectations of official behavior and public recognition of concessions to human weakness manifest in the mechanisms of accountability, and more through active engagement of citizens in the mechanisms of accountability.

However, we must concede that this public meaning and its effects may be unavailable in political communities characterized by a climate-pervasive cynicism about human motivations, especially motivations of public officials. That is, rule-of-law accountability devices express and support modest trust in a moderately healthy climate of civic trust. Where the only publicly salient examples of official conduct are actions manifestly insensitive to, or contemptuous of, norms of trust and trustworthiness, it will be difficult for people reasonably to read official conduct except through distrustful lenses. A special case of this poisoned climate of civic trust is evident in societies deeply polarized by partisan political, religious, racial or ethnic differences. Where fellow citizens are treated with deep suspicion, distrust or worse just because of their membership in rival groups, it will be difficult to sustain robust political trust, or

[87] Brennan and Pettit (n. 68), 260–63.

[88] David Hume, "Of the Dignity or Meanness of Human Nature," in *Essays Moral, Political and Literary* (Eugene F. Miller ed., LibertyClassics 1985), 86.

even moderate mistrust, of political officials who will inevitably be associated with some such groups to the exclusion of others. This is not a problem caused by devices of accountability, but it will undermine their effectiveness and jeopardize law's rule. Of course, it is possible that in this climate accountability mechanisms may be misused or even "weaponized" for partisan political purposes. No devices – constitutional, legal or civic – can guarantee their own purity or success in protecting against the arbitrary exercise of power.

Yet, in a climate of moderately healthy civic trust, and when the accountability mechanisms work reasonably well and are known to do so, and the institutional checks and balances are also doing their work, room is opened up for genuine if moderated institution-dependent political trust. Effective and publicly functioning accountability mechanisms enhance and support political trust. Well-calibrated accountability devices are not expressive of distrust and may in fact carry public meanings of trust (possibly proleptic) and promise to enhance rather than undermine political trust.

6 Conclusion

The fidelity thesis embraces James Madison's insight expressed in the epigraph to this essay. An understanding of the kind of accountability invoked by the fidelity thesis, and the subtle dimensions of civic and political trust and their contraries, enables us to answer the Trust Challenge. There is not after all a deep tension at the heart of our ideal of the rule of law. Vigorous efforts at accountability do not drive out trust of an important and valuable kind. Rather, such trust is a condition and reasonably hoped-for consequence of it. The rule-of-law ideal does not assume that all power holders are knaves, but it does recognize that even the best of us are at our weakest in conditions that allow or encourage arbitrary exercises of that power. Constraints on the exercise of power recognize and capitalize on the "other qualities in human nature" that inspire our confidence.

PART IV

Trust and Fiduciary Law in Context

13

For-Profit Managers as Public Fiduciaries

A Neoclassical Republican Perspective

ROB ATKINSON*

> The Social Responsibility of Business Is to Increase Its Profits.
>
> Milton Friedman[1]

> The enjoyment of property and the direction of industry are considered, in short, to require no social justification, because they are regarded as rights which stand by their own virtue, not functions to be judged by the success with which they contribute to a social purpose.
>
> R. H. Tawney[2]

> All is, if I have grace to use it so,
> As ever in my great task-master's eye.
>
> John Milton[3]

1 Introduction: On Bees and Hives (and Beekeepers and Hive Builders)

"What is good for the hive is good for the bee."[4] So Marcus Aurelius reminded himself and eventually us. As he very well knew, this adage raises as many questions as it answers; much depends on what kind of hive and what kind of bees and what kind of honey the keepers want to have. And, of course, on what kind of keepers we want to be.[5]

* Special thanks to Kacey Heekin, Young Kang, and Joseph McGehee for their excellent research assistance. Considerations of space have required me to drop from this chapter important material that can be found in an article of the same title at *Florida State Business Review* (Rob Atkinson, "For-Profit Managers as Public Fiduciaries: A Neo-classical Republican Perspective," 19 *Fla. St. U. Bus. Rev.* 1 (2020)). I cannot thank my friend Matthew Harding enough for working out this arrangement and for inviting me to participate in this project.

1 Milton Friedman, "The Social Responsibility of Business Is to Increase Its Profits," *The N.Y. Times* (New York City, September 13, 1970) (quoting title, with original capitalization).

2 R. H. Tawney, *The Acquisitive Society* 24 (first published in 1920, Peter Smith Publisher Inc. 1962).

3 John Milton, *On Being Arrived at the Age of 23*.

4 Marcus Aurelius, *Meditations* (CreateSpace Independent Publishing Platform 2019).

5 Gibbon, of course, gave these emperors their greatest compliment, which neoclassical republicanism has to see as richly deserved: "The forms of the civil administration were carefully preserved by Nerva, Trajan, Hadrian, and the Antonines, who delighted in the image of liberty, and were pleased with considering themselves as the accountable ministers of the laws. Such princes deserved the honor of restoring the republic had the Romans of their days been capable of enjoying rational freedom." Edward Gibbon, *The Decline and Fall of the Roman Empire* (first published 1776, Sagwan Press 2015).

Marcus Aurelius, of course, was thinking of human society as a whole; our focus is on the duties of managers of business enterprise in modern liberal society. To understand the proper conduct of our managers, we must first notice that these two levels of analysis are fundamentally related: the "suite" of managerial duties we think appropriate will vary with the kind of modern liberal society we think best.

As my three epigraphs suggest, the possible duties of for-profit managers range across a very wide spectrum, from minimal to maximal suites of duties. On closer inspection, we will see that each of the points on the spectrum that corresponds to a particular set of managerial duties also corresponds to a particular kind of liberal society. The minimalist position, at the right pole of the spectrum, has for-profit managers focus solely on owners' profits. This corresponds to the social model of natural law, Lockean liberalism. The mediating position insists that for-profit managers see not only profit making but also private ownership itself as serving public functions to which both owners and managers should properly subordinate their pursuit of profit. This correspondents to descriptive models of consumerist capitalism and liberal democracy. The maximalist position has managers see both property and profit as serving the most expansive possible vision of the common good, the advancement of which is the proper task of owners as well as managers. This corresponds to the neoclassical republicanism of my title.

This paper suggests that we, as students of fiduciary duty, should see this last view of managerial duties as also the best. More precisely, this paper suggests not merely that we *should* see the last as the best but also that we actually *do* see it that way already. This follows from our own function and the perspective from which we perform our function. We are the fiduciaries of fiduciary duty; our standard is the good of all, determined by our own assessment of all alternatives.

From that perspective, this is what I think we will see. On the one hand, each of our three ideal societies requires a much broader set of managerial duties than those that managers are now generally thought to owe investors. This is because each regime requires a basic commitment to the common good, not just to the private good of owners. On the other hand, the scope of the common good differs in each of the regimes. This difference, in turn, means that managers' duties will differ across regimes, both in terms of what the duties are and in terms of how – to whom and from whom – they run.

These findings, I'm afraid, will come both as a bit of a surprise and a bit of an embarrassment. The surprise will be that our modern liberal society, once we recognize the fuller range of managerial duties that it implies, is already better than we let ourselves believe it could be. The embarrassment will be that we will see ourselves as very much a part of what makes our society as good as it is. We are the fiduciaries of fiduciary duty, because the eye of Milton's "great task-master" is ours, even as it was his (although, we will have to admit, not necessarily his, much less ours, alone). Which will make for a final surprise, and embarrassment: Our society would be a great deal better still if we could get past our embarrassment. We could, I believe, make global capitalism great again. That, indeed, is our fiduciary duty, as academic students of the fiduciary duties of for-profit managers in a modern liberal society.

Our analysis moves from the regime that entails the fewest and thinnest managerial duties to the regime that entails the most and the thickest, from the libertarian state, through the modern liberal state, to the neoclassical republic. As we find deficiencies in one, we seek to address them in the next. This process will lead us, ultimately, to the set implied by neoclassical republicanism.

2 Lockean Libertarian Society: What's Good for the Bee Is Good for the Hive (and "Good" Is Either God's Will or a Quasi-Newtonian Normative Gravity)

Our epigraph from R. H. Tawney nicely captures the Lockean notion of private property and private economic enterprise: "The enjoyment of property and the direction of industry are considered, in short, to require no social justification, because they are regarded as rights which stand by their own virtue, not functions to be judged by the success with which they contribute to a social purpose."[6] I follow Tawney's lead in beginning with the Lockean version of liberalism for essentially the reasons Tawney himself gave: "To-day that doctrine, if intellectually discredited, is still the practical foundation of social organization."[7] If anything, the case for starting with Locke is stronger in our time and place than in his.[8] Locke's interlocking theories of property and politics, already intellectually dubious in Tawney's time, have enjoyed a robust revival in our own.[9] Given the continuing appeal of Locke's model (or, perhaps more precisely, the continuing appeals *to* Locke's model), we need to see that this model itself implies a wider and more robust range of managerial duties than is generally recognized.

We look first at the appeal of Locke's ethics and politics to those who take the narrowest possible view of managers' fiduciary duties. We then notice that Locke's ethics and politics imply a more robust set of managerial duties than they, or we, tend to recognize. Even so, we note, finally, that the fiduciary duties found in Locke may well not satisfy us and that Locke's foundations of his ethics and politics give us ample warrant to look elsewhere.

6 R. H. Tawney (n. 2). Tawney does not explicitly mention Locke, and the libertarian theory of property that Tawney outlines could, quite conceivably, have non-Lockean foundations. Indeed, as Tawney points out, it very much needs them. It is this reference to shaky foundations of the popular understanding of libertarian property that makes me sure he's alluding to Locke.

7 Ibid.

8 In the English-speaking world beyond the British Isles, particularly in the United States, Lockean notions of property and politics are even more thoroughly rooted in the popular notions of proper social order. See also Louis Hartz, *The Liberal Tradition in America* 9–11 (1955) ("There never has been a 'liberal movement' or a real 'liberal party' in America: we have had the American Way of Life, a nationalistic interpretation of Locke which usually does not know that Locke himself was involved."). See also P. S. Atiyah, *The Rise and Fall of Freedom of Contract* 47 (1979) ("But what was prescriptive in England became descriptive in the United States, where the Federal Constitution embodies Locke's ideas concerning the relationship of Government to property."); Morton J. Horowitz, *The Transformation of American Law 1870–1960* ("the orthodox idea of property was that it was a pre-political, Lockean natural right not created by law").

9 *See* Martin S. Flaherty, "History 'Lite' in Modern American Constitutionalism," 95 *Colum. L. Rev.* 523, 528 (1995) ("Theorists such as Richard Epstein, committed to at least one version of foundational rights, claim to look at the American past but see little more than John Locke.").

A Locke's Appeal to Laissez-Faire Fiduciary Minimalists

In our time as in Tawney's, efforts to expand private property rights to their maximum and to reduce conceptions of the common good to its minimum tend naturally to settle on something like Lockean foundations.[10] As Tawney suggests, this is because Locke's system shifts the burden of proof on two critical questions so radically as to essentially beg those questions: What are the respective functions of private property and political society? For Locke, even as Tawney recalls, private property is a sort of a priori entitlement, part and parcel of human rights in a fundamental if far-off state of nature, and the basic function of political society is to protect those rights. From explicitly Lockean foundations, if not by the most compelling of steps, modern liberals of the libertarian stripe derive their minimalist, night watchman state.[11]

In classical terms, Locke explicitly subordinates politics to ethics – what is more, to an ethics that is radically individualistic. Every person has "natural" rights to life, liberty, and property; each person has a reciprocal duty not to interfere with the equal "natural" rights of every other person. The state is, essentially, a kind of joint venture the sole legitimate purpose of which is to protect these individual rights better than individuals themselves could protect them through purely private means in the "state of nature." There is, it is important to see, a common good in Locke's politics, even as Aristotle said there must be in all political systems, almost as a matter of logic.[12] But Locke's common good is little more than the protection of everyone's private rights. Even Locke's notion of "the commons," the great store of resources beyond individuals' bodies, is really just a place where individuals can take what they will, virtually whenever they want. In that state, the fiduciary duties of for-profit managers find their lowest ebb.

B Lockean Limits on Friedman's Profit-Making Mandate

On first reflection, the minimalist, property-protective society of Locke's liberalism seems an ideal fit for the minimalist, owner-oriented view of managerial duties of Friedman's titular epigraph: "The Social Responsibility of Business Is to Increase Its Profits." But as soon as Friedman himself begins to unpack that slogan, we see that this cannot be all:

[10] *See, e.g.*, Richard Epstein, *Takings* (Harvard University Press 1985)(arguing that the modern welfare state, even in its most modest US form, violates sound Lockean principles of property and politics); Robert A. Goldwin, "Locke and the Law of the Sea," *Commentary* (New York, June 1981) (opposing on Lockean grounds the provisions of the UN Law of the Sea Treaty that recognize the seabed as the common heritage of humankind); D. F. Libling, "The Concept of Property: Property in Intangibles," 94 *LQR* 103, 104 (arguing that the common law includes the principle that "any expenditure of mental or physical effort, as a result of which is there is created an entity, whether tangible or intangible, vests in the person who brought the entity into being, a proprietary right to commercial exploitation of that entity, which right is separate and independent from the ownership of that entity.").

[11] *See, e.g.*, Epstein (n. 10).

[12] Aristotle, *Politics* (R. F. Stalley ed., Ernest Barker trans., reissue ed., Oxford University Press 2009).

> In a free-enterprise, private-property system, a corporate executive is an employee of the owners of the business. He has direct responsibility to his employers. That responsibility is to conduct the business in accordance with their desires, which generally will be to make as much money as possible while conforming to the basic rules of the society, both those embodied in law and those embodied in ethical custom.[13]

Even as Friedman asserts that the manager's primary duty is to increase owners' profits, he admits two telling social limits: law and ethical custom. As soon as we elaborate those two limits from Locke's liberalism, we find that each limit is far more extensive than Friedman's statement of business duties would have us believe.

Both Locke's ethics and his politics, radically individualistic though they are, imply important duties from for-profit manager to others besides their employers and, even more significantly, for those owner–managers themselves. These are profoundly significant for the function of all three of society's public sectors, the economic, the legal and the cultural.

This is both most obvious and most relevant in the *economic* sector. Owners' use of their private property for profit is, in Locke's system, subject to their ethical duty not to harm others.[14] This is an ethical duty, strictly speaking; it is a matter of "natural law" even when not supported by state sanctions in Locke's ideal political regime.[15] On this basis, one could found a fair number of seriously restrictive obligations of business owners themselves, rather like our common law torts of product liability and fraud and misrepresentation. These ethical limits on owners would doubly apply to managers; principals must not do through agents what they must not do themselves. And under Locke's basic ethical principles, managers as individuals operate under their own direct "no-harm" obligation to other individuals.

This ethical obligation of business owners and managers in the economic sector implies parallel limits on profit making in the *legal* sector. The same Lockean ethical principles that limit the rights of business owners in the economic sector justify the state itself in taking on a fairly robust regulatory role. Libertarians tend to think of the Lockean state as a night watchman, limited to protecting owners from criminal harm to their persons and property. But the state might also legitimately enforce private rights against a wide range of tortious harms as well.[16]

What is more, the legitimacy of these laws implies additional duties of owners and managers. Because legislation to enforce these rights of consumers is in accord with the basic function of the state, business owners and managers could not, as a matter of both ethics and politics, legitimately oppose such legislation. More specifically, they could not

13 Friedman (n. 1). See also Milton Friedman, *Capitalism and Freedom* 133 (first published in 1962, University of Chicago Press 2002) (in a "free economy," "there is one and only one social responsibility of business – to use its resources and engage in activities designed to increase its profits so long as it stays within the rules of the game, which is to say, engages in open and free competition, without deception or fraud.").

14 John Locke, *The Second Treatise of Government; and, A Letter Concerning Toleration* paras. 6–7 (Mark Goldie ed., 1st ed., Oxford University Press 2016). In which Locke explains that natural law constrains all men, and the use of their property, from causing harm to one another.

15 *See* ibid.

16 *See, e.g.*, Epstein (n. 10), on the grounding of torts and contracts in Lockean property rights.

lobby legislators to vote against such legislation, and they could not campaign against legislators on the basis of their voting for such legislation. They could, of course, argue that state money spent here might better be spent somewhere else. But that line of argument would take them, ultimately, from the expenditure side of the ledger to the revenue side. And on that side, Locke himself imposes a very real limit.

If it is hard to find a principled limit in Locke for business's antiregulatory lobbying, it is easy to find a limit for their antitax lobbying. Indeed, as soon as we "map" Friedman's "increase profits" business mandate onto Locke's ethical and political theory of taxation, we notice a conflict of interests. Paying taxes is, of course, a legal obligation, and Freidman admits that business's pursuit of profit must be legal. But behind this legal obligation lies a business opportunity. Even as the legal obligation to pay taxes inevitably reduces net profits, so the possibility of lowering taxes offers an opportunity to increase profits – an opportunity that, in Friedman's system, would be a right of owners and hence an obligation of managers. It is entirely legal to lobby to convince legislators to lower taxes or to campaign to convince voters to elect legislators who will lower taxes. But how much lower? Friedman's "increase profits" mandate suggests the answer is asymptotic toward zero; the lower taxes are, the higher profits will be.

Here Locke's political and ethical theory, individualist though it is, imposes a very different limit (albeit with a bit of embarrassment): "It is true, governments cannot be supported without great charge, and it is fit that every one who enjoys his share of the protection, should pay out of his estate this proportion for the maintenance of it."[17] Like everyone else who enjoys its benefits, business owners have a duty to pay their fair share of the cost of government; government only exists, remember, as their joint venture with other citizens for the mutual protection of private property and other individual rights. If business owners try to lower their legal tax burden below their fair share, then those owners are, in effect, breaching their original private contract with their fellow citizens in forming the state and their ongoing obligation under that contract to both their fellow citizens and the state itself. And notice, this is not a garden-variety buyer–seller business contract but the very contract on which the entire political community rests. A business manager who assisted in that effort would, in Locke's society, be assisting in the breaching of just that contract.

That said, we must notice the other side to the coin of the owner–manager relation. Even if managers' duty to owners is, for soundly Lockean reasons, secondary to their duties to the public, managers' duties to owners are, of course, prior to managers' own economic self-interest. That, after all, is what they are basically for. When we think of "capitalists," we must be careful to avoid what in America is a false dilemma often posed as "Wall Street versus Main Street." Advanced capitalism offers markets for

[17] Locke (n. 14), para. 140. What goes for "estate" goes also for other "natural rights," including both liberty and labor. See also Locke, ibid., para. 130 ("he . . . engages his natural force . . . to assist the executive power of the society, as the law thereof shall require: for being now in a new state, wherein he is to enjoy many conveniences, from the labor, assistance, and society of others in the same community, as well as protection from its whole strength; he is to part also with as much of his natural liberty, in providing for himself, as the good, prosperity, and safety of the society shall require; which is not only necessary, but just, since other members of the society do the like.").

capital itself. As a result, those who are consumers on one side of the market are often "investors" on the other.[18] Those who produce and consume on Main Street also invest on Wall Street, particularly through retirement plans. In fact, of course, the savings of many state employees (myself included) are largely invested in private enterprises. With this in mind, we can now appreciate another problem: managers themselves lobbying to have their fiduciary duties to owners "lowered" in their own interest. Lockean principles would seem to forbid this; good evidence suggests that has happened, rather close to home for some of us.[19]

All of this means that we must, on Locke's own principles, expand managers' fiduciary duties beyond those that run to owners, to include duties running from both managers and owners to both fellow citizens and the state. Notice, too, that breaching these latter duties is more serious than breaching the former. Breaching duties to fellow citizens and the state undermines the Lockean social contract itself; it is subversion, if not treason. Modern Lockeans of a libertarian stripe must know that this is perverse, even as they also know that it is pervasive.

But again, it may not be, perhaps cannot be, illegal. Even if, on Lockean principles, the state could not legitimately outlaw these tax-shirking efforts, they would still, on a strictly Lockean normative analysis, be both ethically and politically wrong. That brings us to the third public sector, the *cultural.* For Locke, as for all liberals, this sector is, as a matter of positive law, both voluntary and pluralistic. The state cannot adopt an official ideology of its own; nor can it impose sanctions on the expression of private opinions, including opinions on ethics and politics. This, for Locke, is a basic "natural" liberty that individuals cannot "cede" to the state.[20] Individual expression in a Lockean society must, as a matter of ethics and politics, be legally free.

But, quite significantly for our analysis, that does not make legally protected individual expression free of either ethical or political duties. As we have seen, Locke's ethics and politics forbid misleading others for one's own benefit in both the economic and legal spheres,[21] even if that misrepresentation cannot be legally prohibited. And the same conclusion should apply in the cultural sphere as well: in our ordinary discourse with our fellow folk, we harm them when we mislead them; the more serious the subject of our discourse, the more serious their harm. And if the harm is intentional, or even careless, then it is also wrong. Thus, even under strictly Lockean principles, business owners and their agents are ethically and politically bound not to mislead their fellows. The temptation will be great where the potential gain is great: in general, gaining adherents to the view that what is profitable for business is good for the public; more specifically, promoting opposition to legitimate taxation and regulation. The Koch brothers and their agents, it is safe to say, read their Locke either very differently or much more selectively.

18 And even as "investors" are often consumers, so "managers" are, in a very significant industry, often "owners": the financial services industry.

19 *See* Alex Etson and Michael L. Shakman, "The ALI Principles of Corporate Governance: A Tainted Process and a Flawed Product," 49 *The Business Lawyer* 1761 (1994).

20 *See* Locke (n. 14), para. 135.

21 *See* ibid., paras. 6–7.

All these for-profit managerial duties inferable from Lockean principles suggest that a particular pair of virtues would be appropriate for managers: the intellectual virtue of knowing the public good and the political virtue of commitment to that good. These are, you may notice, the shared virtues of all professionals. In addition to their specific "occupational knowledge" – management or medicine or law[22] – and the garden-variety virtues of care and loyalty to their clients, professionals must also know how the good of the public limits what they can properly do for their private clients.[23]

These professional virtues are not something for which principals are likely to pay a premium; properly professional virtues benefit the public, not the principal. Nor are they virtues that the law can practically impose, because they involve personal commitments that are hard to police in practice and improper to impose in principle. And yet, from the perspective of the functioning of a complex social system, they are political, not just "personal," virtues: they don't just make professionals ethically better people, in terms of their own personal values; they also make the system better, in the narrow "inside" sense of better serving its own self-defined purposes. This is true, we can now see, even in a system as fundamentally individualistic as Locke's liberalism.[24]

This suggests a final, truly expansive possibility: if professional virtue were in short supply (for reasons that modern economics neatly explains, as we shall see), then it would seem that the Lockean state would need to take affirmative steps to shore it up. The Lockean state, as a liberal state, could not say that these virtues were good absolutely, but it could say that they are necessary if the Lockean state is to function best. And again, if these virtues are in short supply, this is not merely something the Lockean state *could* say but something that, by its own principles, it *should* say.

The Lockean system, systematically examined, requires more expansive managerial duties than either its supporters or its opponents might have thought. The difference between Milton Friedman and R. H. Tawney is not as great as our epigraphs suggest, because even Locke's liberal principles move Friedman's profit-maximizing maxim closer to Tawney.

But it does not close the gap. We examine the remaining gap in the following section.

C *Limits on Locke's Limits on Profit Making (and His Ethics and His Politics)*

Locke's ethical theory of individual rights, as we have seen, constrains the content of Locke's politics, his norms for all three public sectors. This ensures that, across a wide range of job-related activity, managers who are performing their occupational duties

22 Even the more thoroughgoing of modern libertarians, it is worth noting, concede the legitimacy of state regulation to ensure this kind of knowledge. See, e.g., Charles Fried, *Modern Liberty* 182 (W. W. Norton 2006) (acknowledging "the reasonable demand that doctors, pharmacists, lawyers, accountants, and many others be competent and that the government certify that competence").

23 See, e.g., Eliot Friedson, *Professionalism: The Third Logic* (1st ed., University of Chicago Press 2001).

24 On this theory they are not state-sponsored cartels, as Friedman argues; see Freidman, *Capitalism and Freedom* (n. 13), ch. 9, "Occupational Licensure." Nor are they merely a means of protecting the "buyers" of professional services from incompetent "pseudoprofessionals." Beyond that, and more basically, professional regulation ensures that professionals know the public good they are obliged to serve.

are also acting in accord with their ethical duties. But, we now to need to notice, the sum of both sets of Lockean norms, the ethical and the political, is remarkably "thin." These are almost exclusively negative, about exercising one's freedom without harming others. They are very seldom positive, about exercising one's freedom to help one's neighbor, or even to improve oneself.

To get a sense of this, notice something peculiar about Lockean professionalism: although Locke's politics requires managerial professionalism to ensure the proper function of all three of his public sectors, Locke's ethics requires professionalism only in a distinctly derivative, conditional way. If you decide to become a manager, you must not do a range of ethically and politically "bad" things; to avoid doing those bad things, you must become a properly educated and committed professional.

But deciding to become a manager, as opposed to pursuing some other career path, is entirely optional, as an ethical matter. Nothing in Locke's ethics commends the managers' work or, for that matter, any other. Locke's ethics does, somewhat surprisingly, have self-regarding duties. Locke's ethical duties to one's self are neatly congruent with his ethical duties to others: as you may not deprive others of their liberty by enslaving them or their life by killing them, so you may not deprive yourself of your liberty by enslaving yourself or your life by committing suicide.[25] Beyond that, you are own your own, left to your own ethical lights.

This takes us to a more basic point: Locke's ethics itself is peculiarly limited, and this peculiarity marks, and mars, not merely Locke's professionalism but also the entire political system that he builds upon his ethics. Both his ethics and his politics are fundamentally "negative." This is notoriously true of Lockean politics; his version of liberalism is perhaps the paradigm of Berlin's "negative liberty," freedom from state interference.[26]

But, we need to remember, Locke's politics of negative liberty is founded, ultimately, on his more basic ethical liberty. Being an ethical person clearly entails not harming your fellow folk, but it does not clearly entail helping them. Cain, in Locke's state of nature, is surely forbidden to kill Abel; Jacob, in the same state, seems also free to withhold porridge from Esau until his starving brother agrees to give up his birthright in return. In Locke's world, we are, indeed, our brother's keepers, but we are not required to keep them very well. Locke's liberalism, often faulted for being long on liberty and short on equality, has in fairness an equality perfectly matched to its liberty. What it really lacks is the third value in the liberal triad, fraternity.

We are, of course, free to adopt a more "siblingly" ethic toward our fellow folk; that, as we have seen, is an aspect of the voluntary pluralism of Locke's cultural sector. We can make our motto, in all aspects of our life, the good of others or the good of all, including ourselves.

Here, indeed, we must not be too hard on Locke himself. He, presumably, assumed that those who followed his politics would also be following the ethics of the pervasive

[25] Locke (n. 14), 10–14.

[26] *See* Philip Pettit, *Republicanism: A Theory of Freedom and Government* (Oxford University Press 1999), on "noninterference" versus "nondomination."

Christianity of his time, which was at least nominally other regarding.[27] He did not need to supplement that religious ethic in his political theory; he simply needed not to impose any political obligations in conflict with it. Modern libertarians, of course, operate against a very different ethical background, from which at least some of them feel free to choose radically self-regarding ethical systems.[28] Even so, as we have just seen, Locke's political and ethical theories themselves impose a more robust range of managerial duties than his latter-day libertarian-leaning enthusiasts seem to appreciate.[29]

But notice that, on this very important point, Friedman's profit-maximizing mandate presents a problem to which Locke's system offers no solution. The problem is a potential conflict of interest. If we are business managers, any additional ethical duties we adopt and apply in our business life are, strictly speaking, exogenous and in that sense "personal," even idiosyncratic. On the other hand, any purposes that our employer wants to advance or indulge, within the political and ethical limits we have identified, are his prerogative.

This presents a rather dark side to Friedman's observation that "their desires ... generally will be to make as much money as possible while conforming to the basic rules of the society, both those embodied in law and those embodied in ethical custom."[30] Your bosses might, as Friedman suggests, be generally inclined to make as much profit as is legitimate under Lockean principles. Then again, they might be willing to sacrifice a bit of their net gain to engage in a bit of free expression. They might, for example, buy every employee a bright gold cross or star or crescent. And they might insist that employees wear those gold symbols at work or work elsewhere. The less religiously inclined might require a measure of feudal obeisance. What we would call quid pro quo sexual harassment would become a contractually grounded *droit de seigneur*.

Matching business owners' freedom to hire is their freedom to sell. Even as owners may decline, for purely personal reasons, to hire employees, so they may decline, also for purely personal reasons, to sell to customers. They might, in the exercise of this aspect of their inherent freedom, reject customers who wear different religious

[27] Indeed, James Penner argues that Locke himself invoked just such limits in another work, *Venditio* (1695), to produce his own version of "just price" theory in the tradition of Aristotle and Aquinas. James Penner, "Rights, Distributed and Undistributed: On the Distributive Justice Implications of Lockean Property Rights, Especially in Land," in James Penner and Michael Otsuka (eds.), *Property Theory: Legal and Political Perspectives* (Cambridge University Press 2018) 153.

[28] Each house of the US Congress offers a notable example: libertarian Speaker of the House of Representatives Paul Ryan's declared Ayn Rand his favorite philosopher; libertarian senator Rand Paul is her namesake as well as her admirer.

[29] And, we must note, not all of Locke's latter-day enthusiasts are at all libertarian leaning. Some, happily, lean distinctly left; these left-Lockeans tend to find, to various degrees disputed among themselves, limits within Locke's own theory on the more extravagantly private-property-protective implications that libertarian Lockeans insist on drawing from the same source. See Penner (n. 27), 153 (arguing for an expansive reading of "Locke['s] famous[] claim[] that first appropriations of the material resources of the world was subject to a proviso, that there be 'enough and as good' left for others similarly to appropriate").

[30] Friedman (n. 1).

symbols, customers who exercise different "lifestyle preferences" and customers of a different gender or nationality or race.[31]

And even as owners could, in these ways, exercise their freedom of contract to limit their profits, so too they could exercise their freedom of contract to increase their profit. In particular, they could agree with other producers not to hire any workers above an agreed wage, not to buy from suppliers above a set price or not to sell to any consumers below an agreed price. Not only was this widely done;[32] it was widely objected that it was beyond the state's power to forbid that it be done.[33] In the United States, this gave "trust" a rather unsavory secondary meaning, synonymous with artificial monopoly.

If we find these corollaries objectionable, we are forced back to two prospects. We can question whether they are properly derived from the system's basic premise, the priority of individual liberty, or we can question that basic premise itself. The first alternative, I'm afraid, is more than we have time for; what's more, if we've gotten it wrong, we haven't gotten it by way of parody. The conclusions we reached are the same that modern Lockeans reach.[34] The other direction is thus likely to be a more fruitful line of inquiry: Where does Locke get the primacy of individual liberty in the form on which he bases his entire social system?

All the objectionable features of the array of managerial duties implicit in Locke's regime trace back to the sole end of that regime: protecting individual liberty. That, in turn, presses us back to that liberty itself (both epistemologically and ontologically): How do we know that this is the ultimate human good? Here we find two bases that, in Locke's theory, seem to complement each other.[35]

The first basis is God,[36] and a distinctly sovereign, and Christian, God. How do we know that each person's life and liberty and labor are inalienably their own? Because God set things up that way. How do we know that the world is a commons, open to all for unilateral acquisition as private property? Because God said so, in the first chapter of Genesis.[37] To Locke's credit, we are inclined to think, he generally shows how God's otherwise inscrutable arrangements make eminent human sense. Perhaps, for all we know, Locke's theological arguments were more rhetorical than real; in any case, we do know that Locke's current fans tend to claim that his system, with a minimum of adjustment, can rest on a thoroughly secular foundation.[38]

[31] *Masterpiece Cakeshop, Ltd.* v. *Colorado Civil Rights Comm'n* 138 S.Ct. 1719, 1723 (2018); *Katzenbach* v. *McClung* 379 US 294, 297 (1964); *Heart of Atlanta Motel Inc* v. *US* 379 US 241.

[32] See P. S. Atiyah, *The Rise and Fall of Freedom of Contract* 618 (1979) ("The reality of the economy was that oligopoly and monopoly and anti-competitive Trade Associations existed in almost every industry throughout the length and breadth of the country [England].").

[33] See ibid., 619–20 (noting English courts' repeated refusal, in deference to "freedom of contract," to invalidate various anti-competitive agreements).

[34] Epstein (n. 10).

[35] "Proponents of natural right theories, on the other side, derive the legitimacy of positive law immediately from a higher moral law. . . . [N]atural law, which is explained in metaphysical or religious terms." Jurgen Habermas, "Between Facts and Norms: An Author's Reflections," 76 *Denv. U. L. Rev.* 937 (1999).

[36] See Atiyah (n. 32), 48 ("Locke is none too specific about the source of Natural Law, but it is clearly associated with the laws of God.").

[37] Locke (n. 14), 14–16.

[38] Epstein (n. 10).

This second, secular foundation is a special kind of reasoning, which Robert Nozick describes as "knock-down" arguments; as he notes, this kind of argument, on this kind of issue, has come into distinct disfavor.[39] This is, no doubt, the kind of disfavor that H. R. Tawney alluded to in the passage with which we began. You yourself may have independently concluded the same; I must say – with neither shame nor pride – that I have.

What matters for our analysis is that a profoundly important line of thinking turned away from Locke on this fundamental point and tried to build a normative vision of our modern liberal society on different foundations. What is more, this new vision tried to redress the unacceptable results that Locke derived from his foundation. We need to examine that vision not only because it is a sensible response to Locke but also because it is well ensconced in all three public sectors of our modern liberal society. That model, like Locke's, has important implications for the scope and content of for-profit managers' duties.

3 Modern Liberal Society: What's Good for the Bees Is Good for the Hive (and What's Good Is an Aggregation of Individual Desires)

Modern impatience with the metaphysics of traditional natural law theories like Locke's is nowhere better captured than in Bentham's famous fulmination: "Natural rights is simple nonsense: natural and imprescriptible rights, rhetorical nonsense – nonsense upon stilts."[40] Bentham, of course, offered his alternative, hedonistic utilitarianism, as a universal solvent for all the problems he associated with the likes of Locke. As we will need to remind ourselves, this raised at least as many questions as it answered; it might fairly be argued that it begged the very basic "natural law" questions it intended to avoid. But in its effort to avoid those questions, if not answer them, it gave a radically new, and profoundly useful, way of looking at all three public sectors of liberal society. The implications of Bentham's liberalism for the economic sector are both the most relevant to our analysis and most different from Locke's theory. We will look at that sector first, then turn to the legal sector and, finally, to the cultural.

A *The Economic Sector: The Sovereignty of Aggregate Consumer Satisfaction*

We need to look first at Bentham's critique of Locke's economics, then at modern economists' modification of Bentham and, finally, at the implications of modern economics for the fiduciary duties of for-profit managers.

a Bentham's Shifting of Locke's Foundations (and Foundationalism)

The better to appreciate Bentham's revolutionary effect on Lockean economics, we must step back a generation, to Adam Smith's *Wealth of Nations* (not coincidentally,

[39] See Robert Nozick, *Philosophical Explanations* 4–5, 8 (1981) (recommending "philosophical explanations," which make "[v]arious philosophical things ... coherent and better understood," over the "[c]oercive philosophy" of "knockdown argument[s]").

[40] Bentham, *Anarchical Fallacies* (1843).

the go-to text for much of modern laissez-faire opposition to expanding both government regulation generally and for-profit managers' fiduciary duties in particular). Smith offers two insights critical to our analysis. First, Smith makes explicit what in Locke was only implicit: capitalist producers supply our wants out of concern, not for our welfare but for their own.[41] Second, and more important, Smith implicitly refocuses the functionalist analysis of capitalism itself. From Smith on, economics focuses on the satisfaction of our desires, not the property rights of the capitalist. His very title tips his hand: what concerns us is the wealth of nations, not the private property rights, much less the individual profits, of capitalists themselves.

In Bentham's hands, this shift of focus is radicalized: both private property and capitalist enterprise are to be justified only in turns of their social function. More famously, Bentham radicalized the function of society itself. For Locke, it was to protect individual "natural" rights; for Bentham, it was to promote the greatest good of the greatest number. Reduced to its essence, Bentham's argument comes to this: everyone desires his own happiness, even as Locke's theory acknowledges. The next step is a marvelous trick of legerdemain at least as old as sophism itself: happiness is what all people desire; therefore, happiness is desirable. Bentham famously, if unfortunately, tried to equate happiness with pleasure and to make all pleasures equal: "Prejudice apart, the game of push-pin is of equal value with the arts and sciences of music and poetry."[42] That leveling is a serious problem, to which we'll return. But that leveling hugely simplifies economic analysis, to which we now turn. All measurements will be quantitative, not qualitative.[43] All that Bentham's analysis required was a "felicific calculus." That, alas, proved as elusive as the philosopher's stone.

b From Bentham's Utilitarianism to Orthodox Modern Economics

What Bentham, alas, failed to find, classical economics provided: another simplifying assumption. People's satisfaction, damned difficult to measure directly, might be equated with what they are both willing and able to pay for.[44] Human desires could thus be measured in dollars (or, if less alliteratively, any other standard currency unit). This simplifying move itself raises as many problems as the Benthamite assumptions on which it rests. We will have to examine some of them shortly. But what we need to remember is that this is the foundation of modern economic analysis, and that modern economic analysis, with Bentham, stands Lockean economics on its head: private property fundamentally, and capitalist's profits derivatively, are not ends in themselves but merely means to satisfying aggregate consumer demand.

Modern economic analysis essentially rewrites the social contract between capitalists and society. With respect to property itself, capitalists no longer come to the table

[41] Adam Smith, *Wealth of Nations* (first published 1776, Bantam Classics 2003).

[42] Jeremy Bentham, "The Rationale of Reward' (*The Works of Jeremy Bentham*, 1843), http://oll.libertyfund.org/title/1921/113884/2342588, accessed February 14, 2019; see also Jeremy Bentham, "An Introduction to the Principles of Morals and Legislation" (1789), http://econolib.org/library/Bentham/bnthPML1.html, accessed February 14, 2019.

[43] See Arthur A. Leff, "Economic Analysis of Law: Some Realism about Nominalism," 60 *Va. L. Rev.* 451 (1974) (reviewing Richard Posner's *Economic Analysis of Law*).

[44] See ibid.

with preexisting ownership of the means of production; instead, society recognizes private property interests in the means of production only insofar as it suits society's primary economic end, maximum aggregate consumer satisfaction. With respect to the profits from capitalist property, capitalists are no longer entitled to all but their pro rata share in the cost of government; instead, they are entitled to only so much as is necessary to get them to engage in producing the goods and services consumers want. On Lockean principles, property is a right, and its fruits belong to its owners; on modern economic principles, property is a trust,[45] and profits no more than the price paid for its management.

c Modern Economics' Implications for Manager's Duties

This inversion of Locke's theory of private property, and with it the economic system that libertarians try to derive from that theory, has huge implications for our analysis of the duties of for-profit managers. We have time and space only to look at these implications in broadest outline. We begin with the areas of agreement between Locke and modern economists. Even here, we see that the new foundations alter the arrangement, generally pressing toward the expansion of duties that Locke recognized. Then we turn to the areas of disagreement, focusing on a few of the problems we have identified with those duties as derived from Locke's theory.

The areas of overlap are both large and significant. Modern economics, like Lockean ethics, nicely underpins the basic managerial duties to enterprise owners: loyalty and care. And modern economics, like Locke, implies a general duty on both owners and managers not to harm others. Beyond that, modern economics offers useful insights into how harm might be understood. Locke's theory of property, for example, required individuals to take from the common, but only so long as good enough is left for all; modern economics explains why rational self-maximizing individuals, acting independently, tend to overuse common resources to the tragic detriment of all, including themselves.[46] And this, in turn, implies additional legitimate functions of the state, which, again, business owners and managers cannot legitimately resist.

So, too, with taxation. Modern economics sees the state's legitimate "take" not only as the business owner's fair share of a "night watchman" state but also as any profit beyond the minimum necessary to encourage optimal production.[47] This, you will notice, is nothing more at the Laffer curve from a different direction.[48] Even as this

[45] This insight offers the prospect of expanding Criddle's modern republican theory to include a much larger range of fiduciary duties. See Evan J. Criddle, "Liberty in Loyalty: A Republican Theory of Fiduciary Law," 95 *Tex. L. Rev.* 993, 1032 (2017)(arguing that "a defining feature of any fiduciary relationship is entrusted power" and noting that "[p]ower may be entrusted ... by the independent operation of law").

[46] See Garrett Hardin, "The Tragedy of the Commons," 162 *Science* 1243 (1968).

[47] Paul Krugman "The Economics of Soaking the Rich," *The N.Y. Times* (New York City, January 5, 2019), www.nytimes.com/2019/01/05/opinion/alexandria-ocasio-cortez-tax-policy-dance.html; Peter Diamond and Emmanuel Saez, "The Case for a Progressive Tax: From Basic Research to Policy Recommendations," 25 *J. Economic Perspectives* 165, 171 (2011) (on optimal top tax rate of 73 percent).

[48] Will Kenton, "The Laffer Curve" (*Investopedia*, April 4, 2018), www.investopedia.com/terms/l/laffercurve.asp, accessed February 14, 2019.

larger tax bill is legitimate, so owners' and managers' efforts to reduce that bill below this new, higher level is illegitimate.

And so, finally, with the professionalism of managers. The duties that Locke's system imposed on managers, as we have seen, implied that they would have to know and serve the common good, as do all proper functionalist professions. What distinguishes each is their serving the public good through the application of their particular area of expert knowledge. The modern economists' perspective requires not only that the manager learn and serve a very different view of the common good but also that they have a much more elaborate set of technical tools specific to their managerial task.[49]

Here modern economic theory both requires and explains a basic institution of modern liberal society, the university. For reasons that modern economic theory also explains, the university is essentially an institution of the culture sector, where we will consider it in more detail.

In all these areas of agreement with Lockean theory as to proper imposition of fiduciary duties on owners and managers, modern economic theory tends to produce duties that are "bigger" than their Lockean counterparts. Even where Locke checks the same boxes as modern economic theory, that theory builds much bigger "cubes."

The more dramatic differences from Locke's liberalism, though, lie in the new duties that modern economics would impose on owners and managers. All these differences derive, we need to remember, from modern economics' radical reversal of Locke's theory of property. For Locke, private property is an irreducible, prepolitical natural right; for modern economics, it is a social institution to be shaped to fit social functions.

To begin with the starkest difference, recall the Lockean position on price-raising agreements among capitalist producers. For Locke, they are implicitly permitted because capitalists are free to sell at whatever prices they like. For modern economists, they are implicitly forbidden because their manifest purpose is to decrease consumer satisfaction by raising prices above the minimum required to cover production costs and keep capitalists in business. Owners are forbidden to engage in price-fixing agreements, and their managers are forbidden to help them.

This prohibition, in turn, is but a corollary of a more basic, and more positive, obligation: owners directly, and managers by derivation as their agents, have a duty to consumers to supply goods and services at market prices (because market prices tend to be the lowest possible cost-covering prices). Other corollaries are less obvious but equally important. One is a dramatic limit on discrimination toward employees and consumers. Replacing the basis of Lockean economics, protecting the owner's right to freedom of contract, with the basis of modern economics, maximizing aggregate consumer satisfaction, directly undermines the basis for owners' discriminating against consumers. And it undermines owners' discrimination against employers only a little less directly. Owners' indulgence of any private preferences at the expense of cost-effective production tends to mean costlier products and thus less consumer

49 Rob Atkinson, "An Elevation of Neo-classical Professionalism in Law and Business," 12 *Georgetown J. L. & Policy* 621 (2014).

satisfaction. Owners of business, under modern economic theory, are no longer lord and ladies of their Lockean manors; now they themselves are but managers of the estate – more precisely, the public's estate.

In light of this expansion of the duties of owners and managers, we need to underscore two important points. The first is that this entire set of rights and duties is based on modern liberal economics, market capitalism. They derive not from the rights of either owners or managers, whatever the source of those rights might be, but from the rights of consumers, grounded in economic theory. We will see, in the next section, that consumers' rights, in modern liberalism, rest on a legal foundation of democratic politics. What we need to see here is that consumers' rights are derived, as a functional matter, from entirely orthodox economics.

This is the second point: the economic system that implies these rights is a capitalism market system, understood in its own terms. This view of capitalism is the prevailing capitalist view of capitalism. In the United States, it is called the Chicago school; nowhere is it called the school of Athens or Jerusalem, much less Leningrad or even Geneva. This is not Marx's dialectical materialism or Tawney's "democratic socialism." It is, rather, a thoroughly orthodox neoclassical account of the (merely instrumental) virtues of (properly regulated and supplemented) capitalism.

Capitalism, on this view, is a goose that has reliably laid golden eggs. It is a domestic animal; it is neither a sacred cow nor a lapdog, and it needn't be a tribal totem. Take it on the testimony of a rural veterinarian's son and sometime assistant: geese are always messy and sometimes mean, especially when you go to collect "their" eggs.

d The Floating Foundation of Modern Economics

Modern economic analysis has built, on Benthamite foundations, a liberal theory of capitalist property and profit radically at odds with Lockean liberal theory. And modern economic theory, in turn, produces a set of managerial duties that is much more robust than that of Lockean theory. Even as it recognizes the need for a duty of care and loyalty to managers, it insists that these duties are subordinate to owners' own expanded duty to consumers – not only a negative duty not to cheat or physically hurt them but also an affirmative duty to give them maximum possible return on their consumer dollars (at minimum necessary return to the capitalist's own private investment).

But this impressive edifice, for better or worse, rests on a most peculiar foundation. Even as modern economic analysis jettisons the a priori natural rights foundation of Locke's theory, it substitutes a doubly questionable foundation of its own. It is questionable, in one sense, from "outside" the theory; we can call into question Bentham's hedonistic utilitarianism as easily as we can call into question Locke's natural law foundations. And so we will, a little later. But, we need to notice now, the foundations of economic analysis are questionable in another way, and this way is "inside" the theory itself.

In modern economic theory, as we have seen, the purpose of capitalist markets is to satisfy aggregate consumer demand (at the lowest possible cost). But, we need to notice, this purpose itself is conditional, not absolute. In Kantian terms, the basic structure of the economic theory of capitalism is a hypothetical, not a categorical, imperative:[50] if you want to maximize aggregate consumer satisfaction, and if you find that capitalist production more or less often performs that function best (as compared with production in any one of the other social sectors), then you should establish and maintain capitalism.

The conditional nature of this imperative takes us to the basic problem of modern liberal political theory: Who is to say whether we should build an economy on the basis of aggregate consumer satisfaction? The answer, in the law of modern liberal democratic states, is "We, the People" (in the aggregate).

B *The Legal Sector: The Sovereignty of Majority Voter Preference*

Like its economic system, modern liberalism's legal system reflects a major inversion of Locke. For him, liberal political regimes exist to protect preexisting individual rights, which Locke conveniently subsumed under the heading "property."[51] Political majoritarianism is nothing more than a balance wheel in that system, a necessary means to avoid electoral and legislative deadlocks.[52] Political majorities cannot override natural, prepolitical rights, which include private property rights as well as rights to life and liberty. In Locke's version of liberal democracy, then, democracy is the handmaid of liberalism, in both economics and law.

For modern liberal economists, as we have seen, the entire edifice of capitalism exists only to maximize aggregate consumer satisfaction. The decision to have an economy with the goal of consumer satisfaction is left, in modern liberal political systems, to the will of political majorities. Rights to capitalist property and profit are limited, then, by majoritarian politics. But so, too, are the rights of life and liberty as well. In modern liberal legal systems, in other words, liberalism itself is the handmaid of democracy, in law as well as in economics.

Unlike modern liberal economic theory, which has a principled way of coordinating its two key elements, "capitalist" and "market," modern liberal legal theory has no generally accepted theory for accommodating its two key elements, "liberal" and "democratic." No liberal politics, it is safe to say, have satisfactorily "squared the circle" of liberal democracy.[53] What we need to notice is that, as a strictly legal matter, all actual democracies tend, in their very foundational laws, to subordinate liberalism to democracy. This has, of course, huge implications for the liberalism of our law, particularly in an era of resurgent populist nationalism. What we need examine now, admittedly more modestly, are its implications for the duties of for-profit managers.

[50] Immanuel Kant, *Foundations of the Metaphysics of Morals* (first published 1785, Lewis White Beck trans. 2nd ed., Pearson), on hypothetical imperatives.

[51] This is a foundation that at least some modern libertarians are themselves willing both to concede and to question. See Fried (n. 22), 79–80 (conceding Locke's reliance on prepolitical, natural rights to property); ibid., 183 (conceding that conflicts between other basic commitments "and individual liberty cannot be definitively resolved by any formula or deduction from first principles").

[52] Locke (n. 14), 66–71.

[53] See Habermas (n. 35) (noting the difficulty of reconciling popular sovereignty with liberal versions of human rights).

We have already noted the most basic economic implication of modern liberal law: the people could, by entirely legal means, abolish the entire system of private property and capitalist production. That, of course, is not in the cards. But a kind of lesser included prospect is far more likely, if not actually in evidence: the people could accept the premise of modern economics – "yes, we want maximum consumer satisfaction" – without heeding the mandate that follows from that premise, "then you should establish and maintain a capitalist system of production." The people and their legislative representatives, most basically, could fail to enact and maintain the kind of legal infrastructure that the optimal, or even minimal, functioning of capitalism requires. This would, of course, be irrational. But it would not, notice, be undemocratic. And, not to put too fine a point on it, this seems to be what electorates in liberal democracies around the world are actually doing.

Remember, in this connection, that the traditional source of both basic property law and basic business law is common-law adjudication. There is good, if disputed, evidence that common law judges "made" much of this law with an eye, however theoretically unenlightened, toward the goal of modern liberal economics: the maximization of aggregate consumer satisfaction. There is also good, if disputed, evidence that at least some of the legal infrastructure of capitalism would better be made wholesale, in the way of legislation or agency rulemaking, rather than retail, as in the case-by-case adjudications of the common law.

But notice that this latter argument contains an important, but only implicit, premise: law made by legislatures and administrative bodies can only improve over judge-made law if legislators and administrators both know how to run a capitalist system properly and are committed to that function. And remember that, even as modern liberalism subordinates liberalism, both economic and legal, to democracy, so it also subordinates judge-made common law to statutes and rules made by legislators and administrators. And remember, finally, that the liberal legal protection of free speech permits capitalists to fund campaigns for political office in both the legislative and executive (in some places, even the judicial) branches of government.

This, of course, poses a huge problem for modern liberalism, both in practice and in theory: capitalists can as a matter of law, and do as a matter of fact, secure legislation and regulation that undercuts the function of capitalism as defined by economists. They could, and do, attack a host of regulatory arrangements that were designed, in a more "progressive" era, to internalize many of the costs of capitalist production and limit many of the whimsical prerogatives of for-profit owners and managers. Pollution is the most salient example, not least because, if unabated, it may destroy the very possibility of life on earth. And they have, of course, restructured tax regimes to ensure that their after-tax returns on investments are far above what economists say is an appropriate minimum, the level that achieves an optimal level of production.[54]

[54] The most obvious, if not the most egregious, example is the Trump-inspired round of tax relief to the rich in the United States, grounded (to the extent that it can be said to be grounded at all) on a "trickle-down" theory of economics that virtually no serious economists actually believe. See Krugman (n. 47).

C The Cultural Sector

The cultural sector of modern liberalism, like that of Lockean liberalism, is both voluntary and pluralistic. Basically, the state cannot forbid individuals to hold any set of beliefs, and the state cannot promote any of its own beliefs as ultimately true or good. But it does, and in theory it legitimately could, point out that certain beliefs underlie its own proper function. This, too, is subject to democratic lawmaking. Just as democracy might fail to provide the legal infrastructure for capitalism, so it might fail to provide the cultural infrastructure.

This latter prospect is especially important in light of the importance of universities in liberal societies, even, as we have seen, in strictly economic terms. Locke's system implied a very limited kind of professionalism; modern liberalism implies a very much broader professionalism. And that broader professionalism implies a very much more significant academy. It is, after all, the academy that has given us the theory of capitalism with which we are now working. As we have seen, this theory is a sort of "owners' guide" to capitalism: If you want a thriving capitalist economy, then here's what you should do. Similarly, academic lawyers who specialize in the legal infrastructure of capitalism must explain the relative advantages and disadvantages, the costs and benefits, of various technical alternatives: when, for example, bright-line "rules" produce better, more efficient results than flexible "standards." And this particular institution thus implies a very significant value: the truth.[55] If academics are to do their job well, they must explain the economy as it best functions. (This functionally true importance of truth is perhaps self-evident; in an era of "alternative truths," you will pardon the emphasis.)

The rise of modern economics and its displacement of both Bentham and Locke points to a second critical function of academics in modern society. Modern academics not only showed us practical problems with Bentham and how to get around them. They also showed us fundamental theoretical problems with both Bentham and Locke. Nor, of course, was theirs the first example of that second academic function. Locke, himself an academic, had displaced an earlier political theory of absolute monarchy with his own liberal theory. The volume of Locke we focus on is the second; we are able to focus on it because no one now sees the need to revisit the first volume's task, theoretically dethroning absolute monarchism.[56] (This points to the paradox Clinton Rossiter long ago observed about American conservatives: to the extent that they are conserving the likes of Locke, they are conserving a radical tradition.)[57] Ultimately, of course, that process of critical social analysis goes back at least to Plato's own academy, where he wrote the original integrated study of ethics and politics.

And, of course, that process of critical social analysis goes forward as well as backward. Modern economists did not just show us the flaws in Bentham and Locke; nor did they merely give us, as a technical matter, the owners' manual of their refurbished capitalism. They and other scholars also remind us that the basic premise

[55] Friedson (n. 23) on truth as a core value of the professionalism of scientists, both "physical" and "social."
[56] *See* Christie and Martin, *Jurisprudence* 289.
[57] Clinton Rossiter, *Conservatism in America* 67–70 (Alfred A. Knopf 1955).

of capitalism, satisfying aggregate consumer demand, is open to question. And that, of course, poses our own question: What are the alternatives?

Those alternatives are the "products" on which Socrates worked, ethics and politics.[58] That work was the crime for which Athenian democrats executed him. Both the theory and the history of modern liberal economics strongly suggest that they would have done better to impose the sentence Socrates himself suggested: a lifetime meal-ticket.[59]

D Modern Liberalism's Ethics

Within the limits of liberal politics, including the obligations imposed by liberal law and the functional requirements of for-profit management, individual managers are free, in modern liberal society as in Locke's, to do as they like. The modern liberal cultural sector gives many ethical options, but few are well integrated with liberal politics. In particular, liberal professional ethics tends to treat ethics and politics as ultimately incommensurate; this means that managers and other professionals must choose to elevate either their ethics or their politics over the other. The basic problem is that liberal professional ethicists tend to accept a modern view of economics and law in which clients are entitled to do what is unethical but legal and profitable, and try to reconcile it with the professional's obligation to be ethical.[60] Beyond that, modern liberalism offers professionals little guidance on how to live their lives outside the requirements of their work or how to choose that work itself. Republicanism is fairly seen as an offer to fill these twin gaps.

4 Neoclassical Republican Society: What's Good for the Bee and Good for the Hive Is Good (Which Is – No Spoiler Alert Necessary! – Socrates, Satisfied)

Even as reservations with Locke's liberalism led us to examine the alternative of modern liberalism, so reservations about modern liberalism press us on to our third and final liberal alternative, neoclassical republicanism. As in our two earlier analyses, we begin with its politics, its view on how to organize the best society, looking at what that politics implies for all three public sectors, the economic, the legal and the cultural. We then turn to its ethics, its view on how to be the best possible person. All through we will be looking particularly for the light that republicanism sheds on the proper fiduciary duties of for-profit managers.

A The Economic Sector

Our analysis of republican economics must focus on its points of agreement and disagreement with modern liberal economics. The basic division is this: on the one

[58] *See* Plato, "Apology," in *Dialogues of Plato* 401, 403 (Benjamin Jowett trans., Oxford University Press 1892) ("Is there anyone who understands human and political virtue?").

[59] Ibid., 419.

[60] This is, admittedly, a very tight summary of a huge, and hugely helpful, literature; the fault, as it tries to show, lies not in the scholars but in the system.

hand, republicanism takes the economic theory that modern liberalism built on Bentham's foundations as essentially sound; if you want to satisfy aggregate consumer preferences, market capitalism is a fine means to that end. Republicanism admits, with modern liberals, that modern economic theory may be flawed in its details, but republicanism nonetheless holds, like modern liberalism, that those can be corrected within the general framework of neoclassical economists. On the other hand, republicanism radically questions the basic economic premise of both Bentham and modern liberal economics: that all consumer preferences are to be treated as equal. We discuss, first, republicanism's areas of agreement with modern liberalism, then its differences.

a Areas of Agreement

This topic deserves a separate heading for the same reason that some sentences deserve a separate paragraph: republicanism accepts all the working principles of neoclassical economics and all that these principles imply for both the fiduciary duties of for-profit managers and the functions of the liberal state.

b Areas of Disagreement

As the areas of agreement between republicans and modern liberals are extremely wide, so the area of their disagreement is very narrow. But, alas, it is also very deep. To understand that depth, and the difference it makes for managerial duties, we must look briefly back at the foundations of modern liberal economics. As you recall, both Bentham and the modern economists who modified his system decline to rank different pleasures, though they come to this position from very different directions. Bentham refused to distinguish among pleasure because he believed he had proved them all equal. He, again, famously pronounced that the pleasures of poetry are ultimately no better than those of pushpin. Modern economists, on the other hand, refuse to distinguish among pleasures not because they believe they are all equal but because that refusal avoids the problem of finding an accepted, or acceptable, standard. By different paths, then, and for somewhat different reasons, Bentham and the founders of modern liberal economics came to the same basic conclusion, which they make the basic premise of their entire economic system: all consumer satisfaction counts the same.

Republican economics emphatically rejects that premise, over both Bentham and modern economists. In this we are not alone; indeed, I believe we are in better company: Bentham's heretical disciple, John Stuart Mill (who was no mean modern economist himself). According to Mill, "It is better to be a human being dissatisfied than a pig satisfied; better to be Socrates dissatisfied than a fool satisfied. And if the fool, or the pig, are a different opinion, it is because they only know their own side of the question."[61] Mill could, alas, have made his point more charitably; greater charity must, perforce, be part of the mandate of republicanism. But he could not have put his

[61] John Stuart Mill, *Utilitarianism* (first published 1863, CreateSpace Independent Publishing Platform 2010).

point more accurately, and on that point republican economics rests (as, we will see, does the rest of its politics, its law and its culture, and all of its ethics).

We who know both sides of the question know that some pleasures are better than others, and we know why. We moderns mock Milton's party on many points, not least because, we say, they banned bearbaiting, not because it gave pain to the bears but because it gave pleasure to the spectators.[62] A mere moment's reflection reveals the truth: it must have been both, the bear's pain and the spectator's pleasure. This is no way for humans to treat an animal, because it is worse than beastly, because it lowers humans below animals.

c Implications for the Duties of For-Profit Managers

From the perspective of republican economics, the mandate of liberal economics cannot get us where we need to go because it heads us in the wrong direction. Owners' and managers' merely pursuing maximum profits, even under the consumer-regarding constraints that modern liberalism imposes, will not ensure that they produce the socially optimal mix of goods and services. To approach that optimal mix, owners and managers must seek to produce not those goods and services that most satisfy consumers (at a sustainable rate of return on investment) but instead those goods and services that, at the minimum, harm consumers least and, at the optimum, benefit consumers the most.

Lest this basic republican economic goal seem utopian, we must focus first on its minimum, doing the least harm. Although this standard is emphatically not a part of our current economic theory, it is deeply rooted in widely shared social norms. That, presumably, is why we tend to look askance at pornographers, cigarette manufacturers and vendors of cheap intoxicants. It is not because selling these products is not profitable; it is because these profits come, by our best lights, at real harm to consumers themselves.

Nor is it hard to find evidence of the optimal end of the republican goal, doing consumers the most good. Henry Ford seemed less interested in increasing his personal wealth than in making automobiles affordable to people of modest means, the better to enhance their lives. (The suit against him by his coinvestors, the founders of a competing motor company, reminds us that you can do that sort of thing with your own money, but not with the money of unconsenting investors.)[63] And even in our own postindustrial age, we still hear echoes of Ford's sentiment: Mark Zuckerberg says the real point of Facebook is to connect people in a radically new, and better, way; Apple announces every new i-thing as the key to opening bright new avenues of human achievement. Quite likely, of course, these great humanitarian goals are exaggerated, if not fabricated. The point here is not that the entrepreneurs are virtuous but rather that, even at their most hyperbolic and

[62] "The Puritan hated bear-baiting, not because it gave pain to the bear, but because it gave pleasure to the spectators." – Thomas Babington Macaulay (1800–59).

[63] See *Dodge* v. *Ford Motor Co.*, 170 N.W. 668 (Mich. 1919), which held in Ford's favor, on the thoroughly republican principle that what was good for Ford's consumers, at least in this case, was also good for Ford's investors.

hypocritical, they are paying homage to what we ourselves recognize as a virtuous motive: doing good, as they say, while doing well.

This is not to say, of course, that virtuous motive is enough under the republican economic norm. Henry Ford had some notoriously obnoxious ideas, anti-Semitism most salient among them, and the more we see of Mark Zuckerberg, the scarier he seems. But this cuts for, rather than against, the basic republican model: we have shared standards by which we can measure the good that capitalists purport to do. By their fruits, we can judge them – and, on republican principles, so we should. And our judgment, we need to note, is not idiosyncratic; we are not acting arbitrarily, like Locke's lords of the manor. It is principled, and that principle is a corollary of the basic mandate of republican economics: do not just satisfy consumer preferences, agnostic to the good of those preferences; do consumers as much good (including as little harm) as you can, by shared standards of human need and human excellence.

But who, in the last analysis, is to say what those standards are? That question is best answered under the heading of republican culture. But, even as we defer that question, we need to note that if republican managers are to function properly under republican economic principles, they must know what that answer is. Learning it, accordingly, must be a part of their basic professional training. As modern liberalism requires of managers more training than Locke, so neoclassical republicanism requires yet more again. Here, though, we come to a limit, because neoclassical republicanism requires the broadest and deepest education we have yet imagined, the "classical" ideal of liberal education.

This Millian position on the economic sector has profound consequences for the republic's legal sector, its balancing of democracy and liberalism, which in turn has profound effects on its cultural sector.

B The Legal Sector

Republicanism is famous, of course, not for its position on the economic system but for its prescription for the legal system: in the just state, the wise rule for the good of all. In the latter half of the last century, alas, the republican tradition came to be associated – paradoxically, more in the academic than in the popular mind[64] – with totalitarianism rather than with either liberalism or democracy. Even if I were the person, this would still not be the place to rehabilitate republicanism tout court.[65] But we must, within the limits of our task, notice that republicanism is, in fact, consistent with both liberalism and democracy in their modern forms. And we must notice that the form of republican law is just the form of the managerial professionalism we have already identified in modern liberalism's economic sector.

Here the most basic point, and the point most easily made, is that many of the founders of modern liberal democracy built on explicitly republican foundations. The

64 The standard citation here is Karl Popper, *The Open Society and Its Enemies* (first published 1945, Princeton University Press 2013), where Plato is made the father of totalitarianism in both its fascist and its communist forms.

65 See Pettit (n. 26).

most prominent promoters of the US Constitution were, for example, remarkably republican on this essential point: "The aim of every political constitution is, or ought to be, first to obtain for rulers men who possess most wisdom to discern, and most virtue to pursue, the common good of society; and in the next place, to take the most effectual precautions for keeping them virtuous whilst they continue to hold the public trust."[66] Here we have, in barest outline, a way to accommodate republicanism and democracy. The people's will is not the source of the good, as in popular sovereignty, but the people's voice is the means by which the rulers are both chosen and kept to their task: ruling for the good of all.

Here, too, we find a familiar pattern: those who should rule, in the vision of the authors of one of the most durable modern liberal constitutions, are those with the most basic virtues of the kind of professionalism we have already identified, the highest virtue of the mind, knowledge of the common good, wedded to the highest virtue of the heart, commitment to that good. The Federalists' statesman, like our proper business managers, are thus cast in the same mold.

Noticing this common professional stamp points to an even deeper compatibility of republicanism and democracy, of which the Federalists were quite well aware. The actual drafting of their constitution, like the ideal development of our fiduciary duties, was in the hands of the wise, committed to ruling for the good of all. In the actual operation of their law, as we have seen, democracy was reduced to the best means to the best end, rule of the wise for the good of all. But in the inauguration of their law, the Federalists gave not just democracy but something like popular sovereignty pride of place: their Constitution begins with the words "We, the People of the United States"; their regime began when elected members of conventions in each of the states ratified their Constitution.

When it was founded, the United States was something very like a neoclassical republic; that we have lapsed from that arrangement of late is rather, I think, to be lamented than celebrated. On the Federalist view, liberal democratic law, like capitalist market economics, works best in the hands of proper professionals. It is no insult, but rather the reverse, to believe that the people themselves, if properly led, will themselves see it that way. Republicanism is not merely compatible with modern, post-Enlightenment democracy; it is, rather, that very democracy in its most fully functioning form.

But what of liberalism, the other element of liberal democratic law? Does republicanism not pose a threat to liberalism analogous to the threat that democracy poses? A fuller theoretical answer will have to await our discussion of republican ethics, where we see the kind of person that the republic is not only to protect but also to foster. Here we can only point back to the regime of rights the Federalists established in the United States, and even further back to the fate of Socrates: In the republic, those found to have criticized the very foundations of the state will not be punished with death, as the popular party in Athens successfully argued; they will be rewarded, even as Socrates suggested, with a life pension.

[66] *Federalist No. 57*, ML ed., 370 (Hamilton or Madison).

Republicanism is thus more liberal than modern liberalism's fraternal twin, democracy. What is more surprising is that republicanism is more liberal than modern liberalism. Republicanism undertakes to teach the values and virtues of liberty to the people; republicanism trusts that, properly tutored, the people will not only respect liberal values and virtues but make those values their own. But if they reject them, republicans neither console themselves that the people's will is nonetheless being done nor fumble with the gordian knot of liberal rights and popular sovereignty. Republicanism cuts that knot. It places liberal values in the hands of those who will hold them most firmly, be they ever so few, not those who will let them lapse, be they urged on by ever so many. If the people take an illiberal path, republicanism condemns their turn as wrong and urges them to follow the better angels of their nature. To be a republican is to make that your job; more precisely, your job is to recognize yourself as a fiduciary of liberal values, even as you are a fiduciary of fiduciary duties.

C The Cultural Sector

Even as our neoclassical republican society must have a legal sector that is both liberal and democratic, so it must have a cultural sector that is both voluntary and pluralistic. Poets will not be banned, as Socrates is said to have insisted,[67] and books will not be censored, even though Milton himself once wielded the stamp. But the state, as in modern liberalism, will be free to educate its citizens in its own values, which they must always be free to embrace or reject.

The main difference with modern liberalism will be this: the education of children will not be the state's option; it will be the state's most basic function. Even as Socrates says in *The Republic*, the primary task of the guardians must be educate all of the republic's children equally.[68]

In part, we can now see, this is because both of the republic's other two public sectors, the economic and the legal, cannot function properly unless staffed by professionals who know and serve the common good. But that is only half the story because, as we said at the outset, politics, the norms of the ideal social order, is fully integrated with ethics, the norms of the ideal individual life.

D The Integration of Politics and Ethics

For present purposes, the ethics of neoclassical republicanism is best seen in comparison with the Lockean and modern liberal alternatives. Like Locke's ethics, the ethics of neoclassical republicanism is "structurally" integrated with its politics. In each system, the goal of politics is to guard the highest individual ethical value, and, conversely, the limit of the state's power is interference with that individual value. But when we examine what that value is, the difference could hardly be greater.

67 See Plato, *The Republic* bk. X (A. D. Lindsay trans., Everyman's Library 1993).

68 Ibid., 95 ("Therefore the first and weightiest command of God to the rulers is this – that more than aught else they be good guardians of and watch zealously over the offspring").

For Locke, the highest individual good is "negative liberty," freedom as nonconstraint.[69] From this it follows that the state's primary function is defensive, protecting each individual's freedom from other's wrongful interference. For neoclassical republicans, the ultimate individual value is human excellence, being the best human being that one can possibly be; from this it follows that the state's primary function is enabling, creating the conditions under which the excellence of each citizen can be most thoroughly realized. Here, on account of this difference, neoclassical republicanism is able to offer a level of ethical and political integration that Lockean liberalism cannot match. The highest individual excellence in the republican system is the willingness and ability to engage in the governance of the republic itself (the "positive liberty" that Isaac Berlin rather too quickly dismissed).

This brings us to the most significant implication of neoclassical republicanism for the fiduciary duties of for-profit managers. Meeting the full range of their managerial obligations and being the best individuals they can be comes, ultimately, to the same thing: being, in their particular sphere, a committed servant of the common good, a proper guardian, in their chosen work, of the republic itself.

5 Conclusion

Our search has been for the right mix of for-profit managers' fiduciary duties: not too restrictive, and not too permissive, either, but just right. But "just right" for what? To find that Goldilocks point (or, if you prefer, Aristotelian mean), we have looked at the most basic aims of three ideal type modern societies: Lockean liberalism, modern liberalism and neoclassical republicanism. Locke's system subordinates the common good to the individual good by defining the public good as the protection of individual rights, from both other individuals and the state. Modern liberal states subordinate the individual good to the common good by instituting popular sovereignty, even as modern liberal theorists try to reconcile the two. Neoclassical republicanism tries to coordinate the individual good and the public good, ethics and politics, by making each the complement of the other: the best person is the one best suited to rule for the good of all; the best state is the one best suited to produce just such individuals.

Each system, we have seen, implies a distinctive role for the business manager, with a distinctive set of duties. For Locke, managers are the servants of businesses owners, and they, with business owners themselves, have only a negative duty not to harm. For modern liberals, managers are still the servants of business but with a mandate to produce what the consumers want, constrained by whatever laws voters approve. For republicans, managers are, in effect, subagents of the republic itself, charged by its politics to produce what is best for its people, even as they are charged by its ethics to be, themselves, the best people that the republic can produce.

Our first epigraph, the title of Milton Friedman's famous essay, offered a decidedly individualistic view of the fiduciary duties of for-profit managers: The social responsibility of business is to increase its profits. But even there, in that effort to cash out the

[69] See Pettit (n. 26).

common good in terms of private profit, lay the seed of something very much larger. When we followed Tawney's lead and traced business's social responsibility back to its social function, we found a far wider range of options, all well within the meaning of liberalism. If we, capitalism's ultimate managers, are to make it great again, we must keep it close to its entrusted task: serving the common weal as we understand it. Under our watchful eyes, business's bounties can be everyone's blessings.

Not least among those blessings will be liberty, the same liberty that Milton imagined when he was de facto foreign minister for the first English-speaking republic:

> I imagine myself to have set out upon my travels, and that I behold from on high, tracts beyond the seas, and wide-extended regions; that I behold countenances strange and numberless ... from the columns of Hercules to the farthest borders of India, that throughout this vast expanse, I am bringing back, bringing home to every nation, liberty, so long driven out, so long an exile.[70]

In the republican vision, that liberty would be positive, not negative. Neoclassical republicanism believes, with Dr. King, "I have the audacity to believe that peoples everywhere can have three meals a day for their bodies, education and culture for their minds, and dignity, equality and freedom for their spirits." [71]

And so, I believe, do you.

[70] John Milton, *The Second Defense of the English People* (1654).

[71] Martin Luther King Jr., "Nobel Prize Acceptance Speech," in *I Have a Dream: Writings and Speeches That Changed the World* (HarperCollins 1992) 107, 110.

14

Fiduciary Law and the Preservation of Trust in Business Relationships

BRIAN J. BROUGHMAN, ELIZABETH POLLMAN
AND D. GORDON SMITH

1 Introduction

Fiduciary law has remarkably wide application, as scholars have shown in recent years, extending the fiduciary principle to elected officials, jurors, voters and other public law contexts. This chapter explores the application of fiduciary law in the more traditional private law context of business relationships, specifically examining the preservation of trust between business parties as an underexplored justification for fiduciary obligations.

It does so by engaging in a simple thought experiment, first inquiring into what the relationship between an entrepreneur and investor would look like without fiduciary law, where the parties rely solely on contract to govern their interactions. Because contracts are inevitably incomplete, after investment there is a risk of opportunistic behavior by whichever party controls the business. While the parties could try to draft a more detailed agreement prohibiting various forms of opportunism, the very act of drafting such an agreement and requesting such protections can undermine whatever trust existed between the parties at the outset of their relationship. Against this backdrop, a vulnerable party may decide to forgo important protections against opportunism rather than signal its distrust of the other party.

From there, we introduce state-imposed fiduciary law into the business relationships to see its impact on both the contract and underlying trust that exists between the parties. Our analysis highlights an overlooked point: the development of trust between contracting parties may depend on whether the parties are required to negotiate for protection against opportunism or whether that protection is provided by the legal system. Negotiation over protection may signal distrust, eliciting costly reactions (defensive measures/hedging/lack of intrinsic motivation) in the counterparty. By contrast, a prohibition limiting opportunism in state-imposed fiduciary obligations removes the invocation of distrust by either party to the agreement. We further observe that while fiduciary protections can help prevent distrust among a small number of contracting parties, fiduciary protections may prove inadequate in some settings, especially in addressing horizontal conflicts between beneficiaries.

This chapter unfolds as follows. Section 2 examines contractual incompleteness, using as an example the relationship between an entrepreneur and an outside investor to explore how parties cannot contract for all future contingencies, and governance arrangements will still leave noncontrolling parties vulnerable to opportunism due to the exercise of ex post discretion. Further, the relationship between trust and contract is not straightforward. Trust and contract sometimes function as economic substitutes in that the need for contractual detail may arise because the business parties lack sufficient trust at the outset of the relationship, while at other times a party's attempt to push the boundary of contractual completeness can itself undermine trust. Section 3 introduces fiduciary law, first demonstrating its traditional purview in business settings and then explaining how mandatory fiduciary obligations can preserve trust between contracting parties. This section concludes by exploring areas in which fiduciary law is unable to provide effective protection, including situations in which there is a horizontal conflict among vulnerable parties and settings where a fiduciary has other business interests or operates within overlapping roles. The chapter concludes by observing that the limits of contract and fiduciary law leave a residual zone of vulnerability in which trust and other mechanisms of risk reduction play a significant role.

2 Contract and Incompleteness

To isolate the role of trust in business relationships, it is helpful to first imagine a world without fiduciary law. For purposes of this thought experiment, assume the primary parties – an entrepreneur and an outside investor – can enter into a contract to govern their relationship but that such agreement is not backstopped by fiduciary protections. The investor's primary concern is that the financing terms provide sufficient protection to assure the investor that it will – at least in expectation – get a sufficient economic return to justify the original outlay of capital.[1] Payout to the investor, however, is indeterminate at the time of contracting as it depends on future events and strategies pursued by the firm's management sometime after investment. This setting is a classic agency problem, in which the investor wants to design a contract that causes the agent (i.e., management) to take actions that maximize the investor's economic return.[2]

In a frictionless world with perfect information, the parties might draft a complete contract that specifies exactly what the firm will do and each party's cash flow entitlement for each possible contingency that could arise. With a complete contract, there would be no need for trust because the agreement (by assumption) would anticipate every contingency, and neither the entrepreneur nor the investor would be vulnerable to opportunistic behavior by the other.

Unfortunately, real-world contracts are incomplete. Many future situations cannot be foreseen ex ante, and relevant events (even if anticipated) may be unverifiable to a

1 See, e.g., A. Shleifer and R. W. Vishny, "A Survey of Corporate Governance" (1997) 52 *J. Fin.* 737 (describing the basic problem of corporate governance).

2 See generally Michael C. Jensen and William H. Meckling, "Theory of the Firm: Managerial Behavior, Agency Costs and Ownership Structure" (1976) 3 *J. Fin. Econ.* 305 (noting that the value of a firm is not fixed but depends on management's consumption of nonpecuniary benefits at the expense of economic returns to investors).

judicial fact finder ex post and consequently cannot be the subject of a legally enforceable contract. Furthermore, the real world is not frictionless and drafting a more detailed contract brings with it increasing transaction costs.

Instead of trying to contract directly over *actions* that a business will take in future scenarios, a more realistic approach is to contract over governance structure, namely *who* gets to make decisions when unplanned contingencies arise. As noted by Oliver Hart: "The financial contracting literature takes the view that although the contracting parties cannot specify what decisions should be made as a function of (impossible) hard-to-anticipate-and-describe future contingencies, they can choose a decision-making process in advance."[3] For example, an equity financing contract may give the investor voting rights. An investor can contract for representation on the board of directors and the ability to replace the entrepreneur as CEO. Similarly, the investor may insist on protective provisions (or negative covenants), requiring investor consent before the firm can take specified actions. Indeed, empirical research documenting financing agreements shows that parties actively bargain over governance rights and that such rights are sometimes decoupled from the underlying financial claims.[4]

Despite the ability to contract over the governance process, the resulting agreement remains incomplete, and the parties remain vulnerable to abuse of discretion by whoever holds decision-making power. The best a contract can hope to accomplish is to assign residual control (i.e., decision-making power) for an issue to the party whose interests are most closely aligned with collective welfare.[5] But it may often be the case that neither the entrepreneur's nor the investor's preferred outcome is the best choice for the firm as a whole. If the entrepreneur is assigned control, she has an incentive to cause the firm to pursue strategies that benefit her personal interest, possibly to the detriment of the investor and other constituents of the firm. If the contract were to instead assign control to the investor, this would merely flip the problem, making the entrepreneur vulnerable to the investor's choice of action. To be sure, various shared control arrangements – such as sharing control with an independent third party – may reduce the risk of opportunistic holdup by a controlling party.[6]

Even so, because of contractual incompleteness, the core problem remains. Ex post, someone must decide on actions for the firm for any contingency not contemplated by the contract.[7] The party (or parties) assigned decision-making rights will often

[3] Oliver Hart, "Financial Contracting" (2001) 39 *J. Econ. Lit.* 1079, 1084.

[4] Steven N. Kaplan and Per Strömberg, "Financial Contracting Theory Meets the Real World: An Empirical Analysis of Venture Capital Contracts" (2003) 70 *Rev. Econ. Studies* 281.

[5] For the purpose of discussion, we use interchangeably the terms "control rights," "governance rights," and "decision-making rights."

[6] For a discussion of how sharing control of the board with a third-party independent director could improve outcomes and reduce ex post holdup, see Brian Broughman, "Independent Directors and Shared Board Control in Venture Finance" (2013) 9 *Rev. L. & Econ.* 41; Brian J. Broughman, "The Role of Independent Directors in Startup Firms" (2010) *Utah L. Rev.* 461; D. Gordon Smith, "The Exit Structure of Venture Capital" (2005) 53 *UCLA L. Rev.* 315; William W. Bratton, "Venture Capital on the Downside: Preferred Stock and Corporate Control" (2002) 100 *Mich. L. Rev.* 891.

[7] Margaret Blair and Lynn Stout described the role of the board of directors as a mediating hierarchy that would resolve disputes between corporate stakeholders. Margaret M. Blair and Lynn A. Stout, "A Team Production Theory of Corporate Law" (1999) 85 *Va. L. Rev.* 247.

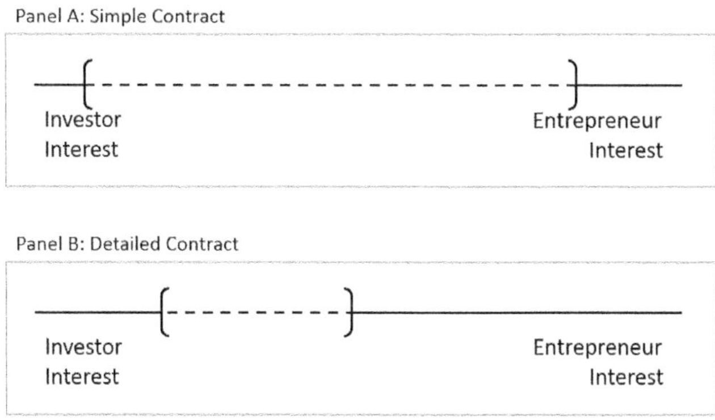

Figure 14.1 Zone of discretion allowed by contract

have considerable discretion in the choice of action, highlighting vulnerability for noncontrolling parties.

Figure 14.1 illustrates the issue of ex post discretion under a hypothetical contract between an entrepreneur and an investor. The horizontal line represents a set of strategies/actions that a firm might pursue, arranged from left to right, with strategies on the left benefiting the investor's interests and strategies on the right benefiting the entrepreneur's interest. In both Panel A and B, the dashed line between the brackets represents a "zone of discretion." The controlling party (or parties) can choose any action within the zone of discretion but cannot choose actions that fall outside the bracketed area, as these would be prohibited by contract. For example, the agreement may prohibit the entrepreneur from causing the firm to issue additional debt (or equity) that is senior to (or on par) with the claims held by the original investor without first obtaining the consent of the original investor, or the agreement may prevent substantial changes in the type of assets held by the firm without prior investor consent.

We can think of more detailed contracting as an effort to shrink or reshape the zone of discretion by prohibiting certain actions or putting the entrepreneur on an incentive scheme that reduces the conflict between actions favored by one party as opposed to the other. Panel A represents a simple contract that does little to constrain the controlling party's exercise of its discretion, while Panel B represents a detailed contract that attempts to limit the zone of discretion by prohibiting actions that might benefit one party (especially the entrepreneur) at the expense of the other.

The zone of discretion helps illustrate the role of trust in contract settings. Trust occurs when a party in a position of vulnerability willingly places its fate or well-being in the hands of another (the controlling party).[8]

[8] On this limited conception of trust, see Larry E Ribstein, "Law v. Trust" (2001) 81 *BU L. Rev.* 553, 555 ("'Trust' differs from the decision to rely. It refers to the willingness to make oneself vulnerable to another without costly external constraints. Trust is socially valuable, and thus society should encourage it. Law relates only to the external constraints that lead to the decision to rely, rather than to trust."); ibid. at 568–71 (arguing that law can "crowd out" trust); D. Gordon Smith, "The Critical Resource Theory of Fiduciary Duty" (2002) 55 *Vand. L. Rev.* 1399, 1418 ("[T]o the extent that parties rely on legal constraints

The interaction between trust and contract is complex. On the one hand, trust and contract function as economic substitutes that are both used to facilitate a business transaction.[9] Trust can remove the need to draft detailed contracts, and a detailed contract can reduce the need for trust by narrowing the zone of discretion and thereby reducing the risk of opportunistic conduct. As noted by Larry Ribstein, "[t]rust is a kind of social glue that allows people to interact at low transaction cost."[10] A trusting counterparty may to decide to use a simple contract with few legal protections. Trust does not remove the risk of opportunism (especially in a world without fiduciary duties), but it does facilitate simpler contracts and can reduce transaction costs.

On the other hand, the act of drafting, interpreting and enforcing a contract can interfere with trust, suggesting that trust and contract are not merely economic substitutes but different modes of analyzing a problem. To illustrate, consider the challenges in drafting an earn-out clause for a merger agreement. An earn-out is a contingent payment made to the shareholders of a target company based on defined performance measures (earnings, net income, units sold, etc.) or defined milestones (creating a market-ready product, passing regulatory hurdles, etc.), which are observed postclosing. For example, management of a target firm may argue that their firm is worth $30 million, while a prospective acquirer believes the business is only worth $20 million. Rather than simply *trusting* that the target management forecasts are accurate, the acquirer could offer to pay $20 million at closing and draft an earn-out clause that will pay up $10 million extra to the target firm (or an escrow account set up for this purpose) a couple of years after the transaction closes based on a defined measure of postclosing performance.

In theory, an earn-out is a great strategy for addressing price disagreements and solving bargaining problems related to asymmetric information.[11] Yet in practice, earn-outs can magnify postclosing disputes. Control over how the seller's business is operated after closing may affect the defined performance measure, and consequently the earn-out payment can be manipulated by the controlling party.[12] Contracting over how a business will be run postclosing reflects deep distrust of the acquirer and consequently drafting a detailed earn-out clause to constrain the acquirer's actions or

for protection, they are not trusting at all, but instead relying on the law of fiduciary duty for protection. Such reliance displaces trust."); Oliver E. Williamson, "Calculativeness, Trust, and Economic Organization" (1993) 36 *JL & Econ.* 453, 463 (It "can be misleading to use the term 'trust' to describe commercial exchange for which cost-effective safeguards have been devised in support of more efficient exchange. Calculative trust is a contradiction in terms."). Of course, contracts are not merely used to regulate ex post behavior in settings of vulnerability but can also clarify shared understandings and even illustrate topics on which the contracting parties do not feel vulnerable. To illustrate, the existence of a contract itself may be predicated (in part) on a shared belief that the parties to the agreement are law abiding.

9 To be sure, while they are substitutes, trust and contract are not mutually exclusive. For a given transaction, a party may elect to contract over certain issues/risks, while at the same time trusting that their counterparty will not abuse its discretionary power on other topics left unaddressed by the contract.

10 Larry E. Ribstein, "Law v. Trust" (2001) 81 *BU L. Rev.* 553. See also Margaret M. Blair and Lynn A. Stout, "Trust, Trustworthiness, and the Behavioral Foundations of Corporate Law" (2000) 149 *U. Pa. L. Rev.* 1735.

11 Albert H. Choi, "Facilitating Mergers and Acquisitions with Earnouts and Purchase Price Adjustments" (2017) 2 *J. L. Fin. & Acctg.* 1.

12 See ibid.

to verify accounting inputs can quickly destroy any trust the parties may have had going into the deal. Practitioners caution that earn-outs "are a nightmare to draft, negotiate and . . . to live with" and suggest that often everyone will be better off if the parties "simply compromise on the price."[13]

As the above example illustrates, attempts to push the boundary of contractual completeness can introduce "distrust." Indeed, scholars have noted that the extent of contractual incompleteness is hard to explain based on standard optimal contracting models:

> According to standard results in contract theory, an optimal contract should be conditional on all verifiable information containing statistical information about an agent's action or type. Most real world contracts, however, condition only on few contingencies, and often no explicit contract is signed at all. The costs of writing a complete contract, or the limited ability to foresee all relevant contingencies, can only partially explain the observed contractual incompleteness. There remain many relationships in which a simple contract could help to avoid potentially severe incentive problems at relatively low costs. Nonetheless, many people abstain from writing a complete contract.[14]

While seeming less than optimal, this contractual incompleteness can be understood in the context of the crucial importance of trust in relationships. Because lengthy and detailed contracts, particularly with punishments and other explicit incentives, may signal distrust and add cost or risk, parties may prefer to propose a less complete contract.[15] Of course, social norms surrounding the contracting process also matter, and we think the signal of distrust is likely to be strongest when the proposed changes deviate from market norms.

The notion of distrust as an added cost associated with drafting a detailed contract is also consistent with common intuition in a variety of settings. To illustrate, a prenuptial agreement may be a sensible way to limit vulnerability upon entering into a marriage, but proposing such an agreement (without regard for specific terms) could be very damaging to trust that might otherwise exist between the individuals.

Various related arguments are sometimes given for why a detailed contract can undermine trust. First, if a contract party requests detailed language to cover certain risks, this may have undesirable signaling effects on the other party. In particular, it may cause the other party to worry that such risks are much greater than originally thought and may even cause the other party to take countermeasures to insure against such risks. Kathryn Spier shows that this can cause the original concerned party to leave such terms out of the agreement, increasing the level of contractual incompleteness rather than signaling its concern and distrust to the other party.[16] Second, a number of experimental studies suggest that adding detailed incentives and prohibitions to a

[13] L. Kling and E. Nugent, *Negotiated Acquisitions of Companies, Subsidiaries and Divisions* (LJ Press 2013).
[14] Florian Herold, "Contractual Incompleteness as a Signal of Trust" (2010) 68 *Games & Econ. Behav.* 180. See also M. Halonen-Akatwijuka and O. D. Hart, "More Is Less: Why Parties May Deliberately Write Incomplete Contracts" (2013) *Nat'l Bureau Econ. Res.* (No. w19001) ("Transaction costs and bounded rationality cannot be a total explanation since states of the world are often describable, foreseeable, and yet are not mentioned in a contract.").
[15] Florian Herold, "Contractual Incompleteness as a Signal of Trust" (2010) 68 *Games & Econ. Behav.* 180.
[16] K. E. Spier, "Incomplete Contracts and Signalling" (1992) 23 *RAND J. Econ.* 432–43.

contract can crowd out intrinsic motivations,[17] and – particularly relevant for the current project – the risk of crowding out is heightened if one of the parties to the contract created the particular scheme of sanctions and prohibitions.[18]

3 Fiduciary Law and Incompleteness

What can be done to improve upon a world of incomplete contracts and distrust? This is where fiduciary law enters the picture. As noted in the introduction, one underappreciated benefit of fiduciary law is that it is imposed by the state. This fact allows the contracting parties to have some protection against opportunism without either party having to specifically ask for the protection and thereby reveal its distrust of the other. This section first examines the traditional realm of fiduciary law in business relationships and then lays out our core argument for how state-imposed mandatory fiduciary obligations can help solve the distrust problem in an incomplete contract setting. Finally, this section concludes by acknowledging the limitations of fiduciary law as a solution to distrust. Just as contracts are limited in the effectiveness of their protection, and gaps or incompleteness are inevitable, so too fiduciary law solves some trust-related problems yet ultimately leaves others outside its reach.

A The Traditional Realm of Fiduciary Law in Business

Certain relationships are not contractual in nature or are not purely contractual, but are "fiduciary."[19] Every fiduciary relationship has two parties, a fiduciary and a beneficiary, each of which may be an individual, an organization or a group of individuals or organizations. Scholars have set forth numerous theories of the fiduciary relationship.[20] As one of us has argued, "fiduciary relationships form when one party (the 'fiduciary') acts *on behalf of* another party (the 'beneficiary') while exercising *discretion* with respect to a *critical resource* belonging to the beneficiary."[21]

[17] E. Fehr and B. Rockenbach, "Detrimental Effects of Sanctions on Human Altruism" (2003) 422 *Nature* 137–40; E. Fehr and K. M. Schmidt, "Adding a Stick to the Carrot? The Interaction of Bonuses and Fines" (2007) 97 *Amer. Econ. Rev.* 177–81; B. Frey, *Not Just for the Money: An Economic Theory of Personal Motivation* (Edward Elgar 1997); U. Gneezy and A. Rustichini, "A Fine Is a Price" (2000a) 29 *J. L. Stud.* 1; U. Gneezy and A. Rustichini, "Pay Enough or Don't Pay at All" (2000b) 115 *Q. J. Econ.* 791.

[18] See Florian Herold, "Contractual Incompleteness as a Signal of Trust" (2010) 68 *Games & Econ. Behav.* 180.

[19] D. Gordon Smith, "The Critical Resource Theory of Fiduciary Duty" (2002) 55 *Vand. L. Rev.* 1399, 1402, 1487–91 (explaining that fiduciary duty requires loyalty to the beneficiary, whereas good faith and fair dealing requires loyalty to the deal); Deborah DeMott, "Beyond Metaphor: An Analysis of Fiduciary Obligation" (1988) *Duke LJ* 878, 880 (arguing that equating fiduciary obligation with contract law is erroneous).

[20] See, e.g., Paul D. Finn, *Fiduciary Obligations* (Federation Press 1977); Tamar Frankel, "Fiduciary Law" (1983) 71 *Cal. Rev.* 795; Tamar Frankel, *Fiduciary Law* (Oxford University Press 2011); Deborah DeMott, "Beyond Metaphor: An Analysis of Fiduciary Obligation" (1988) *Duke LJ* 878; Frank H. Easterbrook and Daniel R. Fischel, "Contract and Fiduciary Duty" (1993) 36 *J. L. & Econ.* 425; Robert Cooter and Bradley J Freedman, "The Fiduciary Relationship: Its Economic Character and Legal Consequences" (1991) 66 *NYU L. Rev.* 1045; Paul B. Miller and Andrew S. Gold, "Fiduciary Governance" (2015) 57 *Wm. & Mary L. Rev.* 455.

[21] D. Gordon Smith, "The Critical Resource Theory of Fiduciary Duty" (2002) 55 *Vand. L. Rev.* 1399, 1402.

In such relationships, the fiduciary acts primarily for the benefit of another and exercises discretion in carrying out an assigned task.[22] The fiduciary may have greater expertise or more time to devote.[23] However, in carrying out the task, the possibility arises that the fiduciary may act opportunistically in exercising discretion or abuse the power bestowed.[24] Furthermore, the beneficiary may lack the time or skill to monitor the fiduciary.[25] With an incomplete contract between the parties, the beneficiary is vulnerable.

Rooted in equity, fiduciary law steps into this relationship to assert certain duties are owed by the fiduciary to the beneficiary.[26] Most importantly, the fiduciary owes the beneficiary a duty of loyalty, a distinctive legal obligation that requires a fiduciary to sacrifice her own self-interest on behalf of her beneficiary, which scholars have described as an obligation to behave in an "other-regarding" fashion.[27] The duty of loyalty does not require complete selflessness on the part of the fiduciary,[28] but it requires that the fiduciary "refrain from self-interested behavior that constitutes a wrong to the beneficiary as a result of the fiduciary exercising discretion with respect to the beneficiary's critical resources."[29]

[22] Some scholars define the fiduciary relationship in terms of trust and entrustment. See, e.g., Tamar Frankel, "Fiduciary Law in the Twenty-First Century" (2011) 91 *BU L. Rev.* 1289, 1293 ("[F]iduciary relationships involve a crucial component of entrustment."); Deborah DeMott, "Breach of Fiduciary Duty: On Justifiable Expectations of Loyalty and Their Consequences" (2006) 48 *Ariz. L. Rev.* 925, 940 (arguing a fiduciary relationship arises when "the course of the parties' dealings over time should justify an expectation of loyalty when the relationship has deepened into one in which one party is invited to and does repose substantial trust in the other's fidelity to the trusting party's interests or joint interests of the parties.").

[23] Frank H. Easterbrook and Daniel R. Fischel, "Contract and Fiduciary Duty" (1993) 36 *JL & Econ.* 425, 437.

[24] See Tamar Frankel, "Fiduciary Law" (1983) 71 *Cal. L. Rev.* 795, 809 ("[W]hile the fiduciary must be entrusted with power in order to perform his function, his possession of the power creates a risk that he will misuse it and injure the entrustor.").

[25] Larry E. Ribstein, "Fencing Fiduciary Duties" (2011) 91 *BU L. Rev.* 899, 904.

[26] Deborah DeMott, "Beyond Metaphor: An Analysis of Fiduciary Obligation" (1988) *Duke LJ* 878, 880–81 (discussing the equitable origins of fiduciary obligation); Henry E. Smith, "Why Fiduciary Law Is Equitable" in Andrew S. Gold and Paul B. Miller (eds.), *Philosophical Foundations of Fiduciary Law* (Oxford University Press 2014) (discussing equity as a safety valve to counter opportunism and as the historical root of fiduciary law).

[27] Margaret M. Blair and Lynn A. Stout, "Trust, Trustworthiness, and the Behavioral Foundations of Corporate Law" (2000) 149 *U. Pa. L. Rev.* 1735, 1783; see also *Guth* v. *Loft, Inc.*, 5 A.2d 503, 510 (Del. 1939) ("[A]n undivided and unselfish loyalty to the corporation demands that there shall be no conflict between duty and self-interest.").

[28] Perhaps the most cited judicial formulation of the duty of loyalty is Justice Cardozo's opinion in *Meinhard* v. *Salmon*, in which he described the "duty of finest loyalty" owed by one joint venturer to another in terms of selflessness: "Salmon had put himself in a position in which thought of self was to be renounced, however hard the abnegation." 164 NE 2d 545, 548 (NY 1928). As one of us has noted elsewhere, this statement of the duty of loyalty goes too far. See D. Gordon Smith, "The Critical Resource Theory of Fiduciary Duty" (2002) 55 *Vand. L. Rev.* 1399, 1410 n. 43. Indeed, the notion of loyalty may imply something quite the opposite of selflessness – namely, an egocentric motivation for action. See Andrew Oldenquist, "Loyalties" (1982) 79 *J. Phil.* 173, 175 ("Normative judgments based on egoism and normative judgments based on loyalties share the characteristic of containing uneliminable egocentric particulars").

[29] D. Gordon Smith, "The Critical Resource Theory of Fiduciary Duty" (2002) 55 *Vand. L. Rev.* 1399, 1407.

In the business context, persons with managerial power – partners, directors, officers and so forth – are fiduciaries because they exercise discretion over the resources that belong to the business organization.[30] Through statutory and judge-made law, fiduciaries owe the duties of care and loyalty, to act with certain standards of care and to avoid self-interested conduct that wrongs the beneficiary.[31]

In light of this ability of fiduciary law to address the spaces that contracts leave incomplete, business law scholars and economists have described fiduciary duties as "gap fillers."[32] In business relationships, this gap-filling role of fiduciary law can act as a fail-safe that ex ante specifies standards of fiduciary obligation that will apply in future states of the world that the parties may not foresee.[33] It plays a special role in protecting against vulnerabilities and harms that the beneficiary cannot protect against through contract, regulation or other means.[34]

B Fiduciary Law as Trust Preservation

The notion of fiduciary obligations as a "gap filler" is inherently a contractual mode of analysis and often leads to discussion of whether fiduciary duties are a default term that the parties can modify if they desire.[35] Even for noncontractarian scholars,

30 Ibid. at 1412 (describing "formal" and "informal" fiduciary relationships).

31 See, e.g., James D. Cox and Thomas Lee Hazen, 2 *Treatise on the Law of Corporations* § 10 (2018). Some scholars have distinguished the duty of care as not distinctively fiduciary in nature. Deborah DeMott, "Beyond Metaphor: An Analysis of Fiduciary Obligation" (1988) *Duke LJ* 878, 915; Larry E. Ribstein, "Fencing Fiduciary Duties" (2011) 91 *BU L. Rev.* 899, 908.

32 See, e.g., John C Coffee Jr., "Privatization and Corporate Governance: The Lessons from Securities Market Failure" (1999) 25 *J. Corp. L.* 1, 28 ("[T]he common law's concept of fiduciary duty both enables and instructs the common law judge to fill in the gaps in an incomplete contract."); Frank H. Easterbrook and Daniel R. Fischel, "Contract and Fiduciary Duty" (1993) 36 *J. L. & Econ.* 425, 429 ("To say that express contracting is allowed is to say that the law is designed to promote the parties' own perception of their joint welfare. That objective calls for filling gaps in fiduciary relations the same way courts fill gaps in other contracts."); Johnathan R. Macey, "An Economic Analysis of the Various Rationales for Making Shareholders the Exclusive Beneficiaries of Corporate Fiduciary Duties" (1991) 21 *Stetson L. Rev.* 23, 25 ("[F]iduciary duties should properly be seen as a method of gap-filling in incomplete contracts."). For a discussion of fiduciary law as "terms which are expressed or implied into voluntary (contractual and non-contractual) undertakings," see James Edelman, "When Do Fiduciary Duties Arise?" (2010) 126 *L. Quarterly Rev.* 302.

33 Robert H. Sitkoff, "The Economic Structure of Fiduciary Law" (2011) 91 *BU L. Rev.* 1039, 1044 ("[T]he loyalty and care standards empower the court to complete the parties' contract as regards the facts and circumstances as they in fact unfolded . . . the fiduciary obligation fills the gap.").

34 Tamar Frankel, "Fiduciary Law" (1983) 71 *Cal. L. Rev.* 795, 811 ("If the entrustor can protect himself from abuse of power, there is no need for the intervention of fiduciary law."); D. Gordon Smith, "The Critical Resource Theory of Fiduciary Duty" (2002) 55 *Vand. L. Rev.* 1399, 1424–25.

35 Scholars have examined the elimination or waiving of fiduciary duties in a variety of contexts, including LLCs, director exculpation of the duty of care and corporate opportunity carve-outs. See Andrew S. Gold, "On the Elimination of Fiduciary Duties: A Theory of Good Faith for Unincorporated Entities" (2006) 41 *Wake Forest L. Rev.* 123; Leo E. Strine Jr. and J. Travis Laster, "The Siren Song of Unlimited Contractual Freedom" in Robert W. Hillman and Mark J. Lowenstein (eds.), *Research Handbook on Partnerships, LLCs and Alternative Forms of Business Organization* (Edward Elgar 2015); R. Franklin Balotti and Mark J. Gentile, "Elimination or Limitation of Director Liability for Delaware Corporations" (1987) 12 *Del. J. Corp. L.* 5; E. Norman Veasey and Christine T. Di Guglielmo, "What Happened in Delaware Corporate Law and Governance from 1992–2004: A Retrospective on Some Key Developments" (2005) 153 *U. Pa.*

fiduciary duties are often premised on the idea that the beneficiary is unable to adequately protect herself through contract or other means.[36] In either case, inadequacy of contract is part of the story. Traditional accounts of fiduciary law as a gap filler rely on transaction costs, inability to foresee future contingencies or lack of verifiable information as reasons that the underlying contract is incomplete and thus in need of a fiduciary backstop.

By contrast, our analysis shows that even if transaction costs are low and relevant events are foreseeable, the parties may nonetheless leave important protections out of the agreement to avoid signaling distrust of their counterparty. It is important to note that our argument for fiduciary law as a device that preserves trust between contracting parties does not depend on contract being *unable* to address the risk of opportunism; rather, it depends on distrust that could arise if the parties were to bargain over provisions designed to limit opportunism. This distinction helps explain why fiduciary protection needs to be mandatory if it is to preserve trust.[37]

The following example is illustrative. In settings where fiduciary obligations are simply default rules – as in an LLC – an awkward conversation comes up. Imagine an LLC is formed between two parties: A and B. Party A suggests that they opt out of all fiduciary obligations in their operating agreement. B would prefer to keep the duty of loyalty as part of the agreement, as she is concerned that A may use his discretion to benefit himself at her expense. Further suppose that B's preference for keeping the duty of loyalty is stronger than A's preference for opting out.

If this were an optimal contract, the parties would agree to keep the duty of loyalty in the operating agreement. Yet, if B insists on retaining the duty of loyalty, that could emphasize to A that she does not trust him and thinks of him as the sort of person who takes advantage of others. Signaling this type of distrust is damaging as it (i) can crowd out intrinsic motivations to work on behalf of someone else[38] and (ii) may cause the distrusted party to update his beliefs regarding the character/trustworthiness of his counterparty in return. Following the logic in Spier (1992), B may simply concede to A's request to opt out of the duty of loyalty rather than revealing her distrust. Paradoxically, the freedom of contract (i.e., the ability to opt out) can lead to suboptimal contract terms. The parties are better able to reach a truly optimal agreement if the state makes fiduciary obligations mandatory.[39]

L. Rev. 1399; Gabriel Rauterberg and Eric Talley, "Contracting Out of the Fiduciary Duty of Loyalty: An Empirical Analysis of Corporate Opportunity Waivers" (2017) 117 *Colum. L. Rev.* 1075.

36 Tamar Frankel, "Fiduciary Law" (1983) 71 *Cal. L. Rev.* 795, 811.

37 To be sure, other arguments have been proposed for why some aspects of fiduciary law are mandatory. See, e.g., John C Coffee Jr., "The Mandatory/Enabling Balance in Corporate Law: An Essay on the Judicial Role" (1989) 89 *Colum. L. Rev.* 1618. Our analysis here focuses exclusively on distrust as a separate reason for making (at least some) fiduciary duties mandatory.

38 See, e.g., Ernst Fehr and Simon Gächter, "Do Incentive Contracts Undermine Voluntary Cooperation?" (2002), Zurich IEER Working Paper No. 34, available at http://dx.doi.org/10.2139/ssrn.313028; Dirk Sliwka, "Trust as a Signal of a Social Norm and the Hidden Costs of Incentive Schemes" (2007) 97 *American Economic Rev.* 999.

39 This suggests that fiduciary opt-outs may be overused in LLC agreements because no one wants to signal distrust. Whether that in fact occurs is an empirical question that (to our knowledge) has not yet been explored by scholars.

Returning to the illustration in Figure 14.1, mandatory fiduciary obligations can be understood as an alternative way to narrow the zone of discretion. The controlling party (i.e., the fiduciary) is prohibited from engaging in self-dealing or other conduct that might violate the duty of loyalty. To be sure, fiduciary protections are a crude mechanism. Because of the business judgment rule and challenges in bringing a derivative claim in the corporate context, management retains considerable discretion, suggesting that even with mandatory fiduciary obligations, the zone of discretion may be closer to the "simple contract" pictured in Panel A than the "detailed contract" in Panel B.[40]

Nonetheless, business parties benefit from this arrangement to the extent that common-law fiduciary obligations approximate a set of protections that the parties would have requested but for concerns about introducing distrust into the relationship. Our sense is that fiduciary law works quite well at preserving interparty trust in simple settings. For example, fiduciary law is a generally good fit for situations in which there is a single beneficiary or where all beneficiaries have the same interest (e.g., a single class of liquid stock owned by holders with the same terms and without other affiliations with the corporation). State-imposed duties are likely to closely resemble what the parties would have bargained for if they could do so without costs and without damaging trust. Notably, however, many business settings involve horizontal conflicts between beneficiaries or a fiduciary with multiple business interests. The next section addresses this challenge to the ability of fiduciary law to preserve interparty trust.

C Limitations of Fiduciary Law as a Solution to Incomplete Contracts and Trust Preservation

As the above discussion explores, fiduciary law plays a foundational role in business law, which many see as filling gaps in an incomplete contract and which we suggest can help to preserve trust in business relationships. Fiduciary protections are incomplete in some regards, however, and do not provide a perfect solution. In particular, although fiduciary duties can usefully constrain opportunism and protect the development of trust in vertical relationships, such as in a simple principal–agent arrangement, other situations involve complexity that fiduciary duties cannot easily resolve.

Returning again to our example of an entrepreneur and an outside investor, imagine the latter is a venture capital firm that uses a portfolio model for its investments, deploying capital from a fund into multiple start-up companies.[41] Investing in risky innovative start-ups involves problems of uncertainty, information asymmetry,

[40] See Melvin Aron Eisenberg, "The Divergence of Standards of Conduct and Standards of Review in Corporate Law" (1993) 62 *Fordham L. Rev.* 437; William T. Allen et al., "Realigning the Standard of Review of Director Due Care with Delaware Public Policy: A Critique of Van Gorkom and Its Progeny as a Standard of Review Problem" (2002) 96 *Nw. U. L. Rev.* 449.

[41] See Ronald J. Gilson, "Engineering a Venture Capital Market: Lessons from the American Experience" (2003) 55 *Stan. L. Rev.* 1067, 1071.

incomplete contracting and agency costs.[42] In response, venture capitalists typically engage in a range of mechanisms to screen, monitor and control their start-up investments.[43] As part of these efforts, venture capitalists often negotiate for designated board seats.[44]

This common practice gives rise to the well-known "dual fiduciary" problem: the venture fund directors have fiduciary duties to the fund itself and its partners, as well as to the start-up corporation and its shareholders.[45] Strategic investors in start-ups that take board seats likewise confront conflicting fiduciary duties. When acting in their roles as directors sitting on the start-up board, courts hold these outside investors to their fiduciary duties owed to the corporation and its shareholders.[46]

A key area of vulnerability is left regarding other business that investors may pursue, which has the potential to affect the start-up's success. To the extent that an opportunity arises to which the start-up corporation itself has a claim, directors have a fiduciary duty of loyalty not to take it for their own purposes. Fiduciary law does not provide a remedy if the opportunity is not one that belongs to the corporation but rather concerns investment in an entirely different corporation. For example, the duty of loyalty would not constrain a venture capital firm that sits on company A's board from investing in company B, even if both companies were in the same industry and even if it meant that company B might be advantaged.[47]

A related issue that commonly arises is the fiduciary with multiple obligations. Although a fiduciary is prohibited from taking a position adverse to her beneficiary, the law does little to constrain an individual from entering multiple fiduciary relationships with different beneficiaries that are not in direct conflict. The time and resources of the fiduciary are, however, naturally limited. The fiduciary's loyalties may be formally undivided, but she still must make decisions about how to deal with each of the separate beneficiaries, whose interests are competing for her

[42] See, e.g., William A. Sahlman, "The Structure and Governance of Venture-Capital Organizations" (1990) 27 *J. Fin. Econ.* 473; Paul Gompers and Josh Lerner, "The Use of Covenants: An Empirical Analysis of Venture Partnership Agreements" (1996) 39 *JL & Econ.* 463, 465; Steven N Kaplan and Per Strömberg, "Financial Contracting Theory Meets the Real World: An Empirical Analysis of Venture Capital Contracts" (2003) 70 *Rev. Econ. Studies* 281.

[43] For example, venture capitalists stage their financing, use convertible preferred stock that comes with protective terms and contract for covenants to guard against certain unfavorable outcomes. D. Gordon Smith, "The Exit Structure of Venture Capital" (2005) 53 *UCLA L. Rev.* 315, 318–55; Paul A. Gompers, "Optimal Investment, Monitoring, and the Staging of Venture Capital" (1995) 50 *J. Fin.* 1461, 1464; Michael Klausner and Kate Litvak, "What Economists Have Taught Us about Venture Capital Contracting" in Michael J. Whincop (ed.), *Bridging the Entrepreneurial Financing Gap* (Ashgate Pub. Ltd. 2001); William W. Bratton and Michael L. Wachter, "A Theory of Preferred Stock" (2013) 161 *U. Pa. L. Rev.* 1815, 1878–82.

[44] D. Gordon Smith, "The Exit Structure of Venture Capital" (2005) 53 *UCLA L. Rev.* 315, 318–19.

[45] Steven E. Bochner and Amy L. Simmerman, "The Venture Capital Board Member's Survival Guide: Handling Conflicts Effectively While Wearing Two Hats" (2016) 41 *Del. J. Corp. L.* 1.

[46] *In re Trados Inc. Shareholder Litigation* 73 A.3d 17 (Del. Ch. 2013).

[47] Michael Blanding, "What Happens When the Interests of the VC and the Startup Don't Align?" (*Forbes*, June 16, 2016), www.forbes.com/sites/hbsworkingknowledge/2016/06/16/what-happens-when-the-interests-of-the-vc-and-the-startup-dont-align/ - 388f031ee048 (discussing examples).

time and attention. One recent report identified twenty-four venture capitalists who hold nine or more directorships at technology start-ups, including one VC who sits on eighteen boards.[48]

Furthermore, the "dual fiduciary" problem also leads to conflicts of interest that do not fit within the traditional framing of loyalty claims. For example, because venture capital is based on a business model that depends on having a few "home runs" in the portfolio,[49] in some instances a venture capital firm would prefer a suboptimal sale or liquidation of a company rather than its continued operation, which would take ongoing time and resources without providing a large-enough return from the venture capital firm's perspective. Abraham Cable has termed the incentive to withdraw human and financial capital for redeployment an "opportunity–cost conflict."[50] In a similar vein, William Bratton and Michael Wachter have highlighted the conflicts that can arise between the common and preferred shareholders in the "moderate downside" scenario, in which a start-up is not a huge success nor hopelessly insolvent.[51]

These examples of fiduciaries with other business arising from their overlapping roles as investors, the multiple obligations of dual fiduciaries and opportunity–cost conflicts could be characterized as horizontal in nature as they are not traditional, vertically oriented principal–agent relations. A further expansion of fiduciary duties to attempt to solve these kinds of horizontal conflicts is likely undesirable because there is no compelling reason to favor one vulnerable party over the other. In contrast to vertical principal–agent relationships in which mandatory state-imposed duties can approximate what the parties would have bargained for absent cost or concern about signaling distrust; in the horizontal setting, with webs of relationships, it is less clear how to do so. Instead, a significant risk exists that any trust-preserving benefit that the state might provide is potentially outweighed by the possibility of forcing the parties away from the agreement they would have reached in a frictionless world.

An important Delaware decision, *In re Trados*, illustrates the difficulties of applying fiduciary law to business relationships with horizontal conflicts.[52] The case arose in the context of a start-up board composed of two company executives, three venture capital directors with dual fiduciary duties and preferred stock, one preferred stock investor with ties to one of the venture capital directors and one industry expert. The

[48] See Alfred Lee, "How Many Board Seats Is Too Many?" (*The Information*, Jan. 17, 2018), www.theinformation.com/articles/how-many-board-seats-is-too-many; see also Bob Zider, "How Venture Capital Works' (*Harv. Bus. Rev.*, Nov.–Dec. 1998), https://hbr.org/1998/11/how-venture-capital-works ("The popular image of venture capitalists as sage advisors is at odds with the reality of their schedules. The financial incentive for partners in the VC firm is to manage as much money as possible. The more money they manage, the less time they have to nurture and advise entrepreneurs.").

[49] Bob Zider, "How Venture Capital Works" (*Harv. Bus. Rev.*, Nov.–Dec. 1998), https://hbr.org/1998/11/how-venture-capital-works ("Given the portfolio approach and the deal structure VCs use, however, only 10% to 20% of the companies funded need to be real winners to achieve the targeted return rate. . . . In fact, VC reputations are often built on one or two good investments.").

[50] Abraham J. B. Cable, "Opportunity–Cost Conflicts in Corporate Law" (2015) 66 *Case W. Res. L. Rev.* 51, 53.

[51] William W. Bratton and Michael L. Wachter, "A Theory of Preferred Stock" (2013) 161 *U. Pa. L. Rev.* 1815; William W. Bratton, "Venture Capital on the Downside: Preferred Stock and Corporate Control" (2002) 100 *Mich L. Rev.* 891.

[52] 73 A.3d 17 (Del. Ch. 2013).

company had neither failed nor succeeded, and the board decided to enter into a transaction to sell the company at a price that returned capital to the preferred shareholders and funded a management incentive plan, leaving no return for the common shareholders. The court held that directors owe a fiduciary duty to the common shareholders as the residual claimants and applied this rule despite the fact that the preferred shareholders had negotiated ex ante for board seats as constituency directors.[53] This ruling could have the effect of constraining a director's opportunism against certain shareholder beneficiaries, but it potentially comes at the expense of enterprise value maximization, which reflects the interests of all participants.[54] Furthermore, in the start-up context that has evolved past our simple thought experiment of an entrepreneur and an investor in a vertical agency relationship, it is not clear that a fiduciary duty to the common shareholders represents the optimal contract that would be arrived at absent a desire to avoid creating distrust through the bargaining context. Venture-capital-backed start-up companies typically involve founders, executives, investors and employees that have diverging interests in light of their equity with different terms and other affiliations with the corporation.[55] The *Trados* ruling goes beyond filling gaps in an incomplete contract and instead mandates a set of fiduciary obligations that do not fit easily with the bargains made and the aggregate value of interests represented by the corporation.

4 Conclusion

In this chapter, we have examined the traditional realm of fiduciary law in business relationships, and we suggest a new explanation for such fiduciary protections being supplied on a mandatory basis by the law – the preservation of trust that might otherwise be eroded through the bargaining process. Fiduciary protections do not provide a perfect solution in all business relationships, however. Although fiduciary duties can usefully constrain opportunism and preserve trust in vertical business relationships, such as in a simple principal–agent arrangement, other situations involve complexity that pose challenges for fiduciary duty law. We illustrate this observation with examples of various horizontal conflicts, or diverging interests, in the venture-capital-backed start-up context. To the extent that contract and fiduciary law are each incomplete, a residual domain for trust and other mechanisms for risk reduction or self-help remains.

53 Ibid. at 40–41.

54 William W. Bratton and Michael L. Wachter, "A Theory of Preferred Stock" (2013) 161 *U. Pa. L. Rev.* 1815, 1885–87, 1904–06; Robert P. Bartlett III, "Shareholder Wealth Maximization as Means to an End" (2015) 38 *Seattle U. L. Rev.* 255.

55 Elizabeth Pollman, "Startup Governance" (2019) 168 *U. Pa. L. Rev.* 155.

15

How Much Trust Do Trusts Require?

THOMAS P. GALLANIS*

"Now faith is the assurance of things hoped for, the conviction of things not seen."[1] So we may read in the Letter to the Hebrews, as translated in the Revised Standard Version. The word here translated as "faith" is the Greek word πίστις (*pistis*),[2] often translated as "faith" in the many places in which the word appears in the New Testament.[3] In Greek mythology, Pistis – or, to use her Roman name, Fides – was the personified spirit (δαίμων, *daimon*) of trust, honesty and good faith.[4] Thus perhaps we may say that *trust* is the assurance of things hoped for, the conviction of things not seen. A related definition is found in the *Oxford English Dictionary*: trust is "confidence or faith in a person or thing, or in an attribute of a person or thing."[5]

What exactly *is* trust? The question is not a small one, and much scholarly ink has been spilled on it.[6] Perhaps a reason for the complexity is that trust "is at the centre of a whole web of concepts: reliability, predictability, expectation, cooperation, goodwill, and – on the dark side – distrust, insincerity, conspiracy, betrayal, and incompetence."[7] This paper is not the right venue – nor am I the right person – to attempt a philosophically rigorous definition of "trust" nor to parse the distinctions that can be

* This paper was prepared for the conference Fiduciaries and Trust: Ethics, Politics, Economics and Law, held at the University of Melbourne Law School in December 2018. I acknowledge with gratitude the helpful comments received at that conference and, earlier, in August 2018 at a Legal Studies Workshop at the University of Iowa. It is also a pleasure to thank my student Katlyn Bay for research assistance.

Disclosure: I served as an associate reporter for the *Restatement Third of Trusts* and currently serve as executive director of the Uniform Law Commission's Joint Editorial Board on Uniform Trust and Estate Acts. However, I emphasize that the views in this paper are mine alone. I am speaking neither for the American Law Institute nor for the Uniform Law Commission.

1 Hebrews 11:1 (Revised Standard Version).

2 For a recent scholarly discussion of the meaning of *pistis* in this verse, see Teresa Morgan, Roman Faith and Christian Faith: *Pistis* and *Fides* in the Early Roman Empire and Early Churches (Oxford University Press 2015) 338–40.

3 For a different translation – *pistis* as "loyalty" or "allegiance" – see N. T. Wright, *Paul: A Biography* (HarperOne 2018) 90. I am grateful to Professor Gordon Smith for this reference.

4 Other personified spirits (*daimones*) included Dike (justice), Eros (love), Hypnos (sleep), Mnemosyne (memory), Nike (victory), Phobos (fear) and Thanatos (death).

5 "Trust" (*Oxford English Dictionary*), def. 1a, www.oed.com. For an argument that trust is different from confidence and different from faith, see Matthew Harding, "Contract, Fiduciary Relationships and Trust," in this volume.

6 For recent studies of trust from various disciplinary perspectives, see, e.g., Geoffrey Hosking, *Trust: A History* (Oxford University Press 2014); Peter Schröder, *Trust in Early Modern International and Political Thought 1598–1713* (Cambridge University Press 2017); Paul Faulkner & Thomas Simpson (eds), *The Philosophy of Trust* (Oxford University Press 2017).

7 Katherine Hawley, *Trust: A Very Short Introduction* (Oxford University Press 2012) 3.

made among "trust" and its synonyms. Instead, I can offer four observations by way of modest elaboration. First, in this paper when I speak of trust in the nonlegal (hereinafter "general") sense, I am speaking of *interpersonal* trust. When there is interpersonal trust, there is a person who trusts and a person who is trusted.[8] (I am not speaking, for example, of trust in inanimate objects, such as trust in my alarm clock to wake me at the time I desire.) Second, interpersonal trust involves more than reliance, as the philosopher Katherine Hawley perceptively observes. "When we trust people, we rely on them," writes Professor Hawley, though she proceeds to emphasize that there is "an extra dimension to that reliance, something which differentiates true interpersonal trust from mere reliance."[9] As she explains, "the difference between trusting someone and just mechanically relying on them has something to do with your heightened expectations in trusting, and your reactions if the trustee lets you down."[10] We should "understand trust in terms of *commitment*: when we trust people, we rely on them to meet their commitments."[11] She gives an arresting example: "When we rely on a crowd as a windbreak, we realize that the crowd has made no commitment to shelter us, indeed they don't even know that's what we want. And that's why this isn't a matter of trust."[12] Interpersonal trust depends on a commitment made by the trusted person to or on behalf of the person who trusts. Sociologists Paul Bauer and Markus Freitag explain that "trust is situation-specific": "When speaking about trust, we essentially speak about truster *A* that trusts (judges the trustworthiness of) a trustee *B* with respect to some behavior *X* in context *Y* at time *t*."[13] Thus, to use parts of the Bauer–Freitag formulation, trust stems from the commitment by trustee B to or on behalf of truster A. Third, the placement of trust is demonstrated by behavior. To the extent that there is trust, the person who trusts is not constantly verifying the performance of the person who is trusted. A husband who constantly checks the whereabouts of his wife does not trust her. The trust placed in the trusted person might turn out to be justified or alternatively might result in betrayal and harm. But while there is trust, there is not constant verification. Thus, international relations scholar Nicholas Wheeler defines trust as "the expectation of no harm in contexts where betrayal is always a possibility."[14] Fourth, when I speak of a person "having" to trust another, or of a situation or arrangement "requiring" trust, I am speaking as ordinary people regularly do. Consider the following dialogue:

PERSON A Can you prove to me that you are telling the truth?
PERSON B No, you will have to trust me.

[8] The crucial nouns in this sentence appear in the singular for simplicity only; they are meant to include the plural. The reference to "person" also includes entities such as corporations and nations, which act through persons.

[9] Hawley (n. 7) 4.

[10] Ibid., 5.

[11] Ibid., 5–6 (emphasis in original).

[12] Ibid., 6.

[13] Paul C. Bauer & Markus Freitag, "Measuring Trust" in Eric M. Uslaner (ed.), *The Oxford Handbook of Social and Political Trust* (Oxford University Press 2018) 16 (italics supplied).

[14] Nicholas J. Wheeler, *Trusting Enemies: Interpersonal Relationships in International Conflict* (Oxford University Press 2018) 2.

In a literalistic sense, Person A never *has* to trust anyone. Irrespective of Person A's behavior, Person A's mental state can be one of *dis*trust. However, this cramped sense of never "having" to trust is not how ordinary people speak. When ordinary people speak of "having" to trust another person, or of a situation or arrangement "requiring" trust, what is meant is that the most realistic course of action is to behave as if one trusts another – in other words, to press forward despite the risk of betrayal and harm.

Some interpersonal interactions involve substantial trust, while others do not. The interaction between an infirm, elderly parent who needs personal care or management of assets and an adult child who undertakes to provide it is an example of a relationship that typically involves substantial trust. The child has undertaken to provide personal care or to serve as the parent's attorney in fact, and the parent trusts the child to do so – typically without a written contract formalizing the child's undertaking and the parent's expectations, other than, perhaps, a standard-form document granting a power of attorney. Some other interactions, however, even long-term interactions or those between repeat players, can require much less trust because the terms of the arrangement are specific and entail strong verification protocols. For example, two nations might sign an agreement committing themselves to reductions in nuclear weapons without much, if any, trust between them,[15] in the expectation that on-site inspections will verify whether the agreement is being honored.[16]

This paper focuses on *the trust*, in the precise legal sense of that term, and the relationship between the trustee of the trust and the trust's beneficiaries and settlor. To what extent does trusteeship in the legal sense require trust in the general sense? Is the relationship between the trustee and the trust's beneficiaries and settlor more akin to the relationship between a family caregiver and a dependent care recipient, typically entailing a high degree of trust, or more akin to the relationship between nations signing an arms-reduction treaty with verification protocols, requiring very little trust? (Note, of course, that the position of the settlor often is different from the position of the beneficiaries. In a typical case, the settlor might have more reason to trust the trustee than the beneficiaries do, given that it is typically the settlor who selects the trustee. Yet many settlors have been betrayed by their chosen trustees. Nor are the beneficiaries all in alignment themselves. The interests of some beneficiaries often differ from the interests of other beneficiaries.)

[15] This is interpersonal trust. Persons negotiate treaties; persons vote to ratify treaties; persons take actions that are consistent with or that violate treaties.

[16] This low level of trust was captured by US President Ronald Reagan's repeated invocation, in disarmament talks with General Secretary of the Communist Party of the Soviet Union Mikhail Gorbachev, of the Russian maxim Доверяй, но проверяй (*Doveryai, no proveryai*), meaning "trust, but verify." See Jack F. Matlock Jr., *Reagan and Gorbachev: How the Cold War Ended* (Random House 2004) 114–15; Richard Reeves, *President Reagan: The Triumph of Imagination* (Simon & Schuster 2005) 436; Andrew H. Kydd, *Trust and Mistrust in International Relations* (Princeton University Press 2005) 3. For an empirical study of the relationship between trust and verification in a commercial setting, see George Gundlach & Joseph P. Cannon, "'Trust but Verify?' The Performance Implications of Verification Strategies in Trusting Relationships" (2010) 38 *J. of the Academy of Marketing Science* 399 (finding that, depending on the specific verification strategy, the use of verification can enhance or reduce trust in commercial relationships).

Before tackling all these questions, I want to make three preliminary points about the trusts in the legal sense that are the subject of this paper. First, the trusts analyzed in this paper are trusts governed by US law. The law of trusts is not uniform across all the nations that recognize the trust, nor even within the family of common-law nations; for example, trust law in the United States differs in important respects from the trust law of England.[17] This paper concerns the law of trusts in the United States. Second, this paper focuses on trusts created expressly – not on constructive or resulting trusts, which arise by operation of law. In so doing, this paper follows the emphasis of the American Law Institute's Restatements on trust law. In the words of the *Restatement Third of Trusts* (hereinafter, the *Restatement Third*): "When the term 'trust' is used in this Restatement without any qualifying adjective or description, it denotes . . . an express trust rather than a resulting or constructive trust."[18] Essentially similar words appear in the first and second Restatements on trusts.[19] The same limiting principle applies here: the trusts that are the subject of this paper are express trusts, not resulting or constructive trusts. Third, the person who accepts the office of trustee of an express trust makes a commitment, willingly, to the trust's settlor and beneficiaries. As stated in the *Restatement Third*: "A person who has not accepted the office cannot be compelled to act as trustee."[20] The commitment to act as a trustee – to behave as a trustee ought to behave – is made by choice. This relates to an aspect of trust in the general sense: interpersonal trust entails a commitment. If there is a commitment, then we can have "true" interpersonal trust, as Professor Hawley puts it, not "mere reliance."[21] The trustee's commitment to act as a trustee meets this description.

Let us now turn to the central question: To what extent does a trust in the legal sense require trust in the general sense? To answer this question, we need to identify the features of the trust that particularly bear on the extent to which trust is required.

There are three features of the trust under modern US law and practice that would seem to require there to be a significant degree of trust in the trustee by the trust's beneficiaries and settlor.

First, the modern US trust is a vehicle for the active management[22] of a portfolio of assets held by the trustee for the benefit of the beneficiaries.[23] This separation of

17 For discussion of some of the differences, see Thomas P. Gallanis, "The New Direction of American Trust Law" (2011) 97 *Iowa LR* 215, 219–22, 226–29, 234–37.

18 *Restatement Third of Trusts* (American Law Institute 2003) s. 2 comment a.

19 See *Restatement of Trusts* (American Law Institute 1935) s. 2 comment a; *Restatement Second of Trusts* (American Law Institute 1959) s. 2 comment a.

20 *Restatement Third of Trusts* (American Law Institute 2003) s. 35 comment a. The situation is different with respect to a person who accepted the trusteeship and subsequently wishes to resign it. A person who accepted the trusteeship may resign it only "(a) in accordance with the terms of the trust; (b) with the consent of all beneficiaries or (c) upon terms approved by a proper court." Ibid., s. 36.

21 Hawley (n. 7), 4.

22 On the transformation of the trust from "a device for the conveyancing of land" to "a management device for holding a portfolio of financial assets," see John H. Langbein, "Rise of the Management Trust" (2002) 143 *Trusts & Estates* 52.

23 The phrase "for the benefit of the beneficiaries" focuses the reader's attention on private (i.e., noncharitable) trusts. For the rule that a private trust and its terms must be for the benefit of the trust's beneficiaries, see *Restatement Third of Trusts* (American Law Institute 2003) s. 27(2); Unif. Trust Code

management (by the trustee) and ownership (by the beneficiaries) presents a classic problem.[24] The powers of trust administration are held by the trustee, who has no personal stake in the effect of decisions regarding the trust and who may be tempted to gain personally from the trusteeship; conversely, the beneficiaries who have the ownership of the trust's assets, and thus who bear the risk of loss to, or underperformance of, the trust's portfolio, have little control over the trust's administration. In the language and literature of law and economics, this is known as the problem of "agency cost,"[25] but the problem can be described readily without resort to economic jargon. The problem of lack of control over the trust's administration affects not only the beneficiaries but also the settlor, who ceases to be the owner of the assets once they are placed in trust.[26] The settlor can guide the trust's administration by prescribing the terms of the trust,[27] but the management of the trust's portfolio of assets within the boundaries of those terms rests in the hands of the trustee. A trustee who is not worthy of being trusted can inflict great damage.

Second, the interests of the beneficiaries in modern US trusts are typically discretionary interests.[28] This means that while the trust is in existence, the decision whether to make a distribution – and how much, if any, to distribute – to a beneficiary rests within the trustee's discretion. The artificially simple "income to A for life, then corpus to B" trust, in which A is entitled to all of the trust's income, is rarely seen today. Instead, the interests of trust beneficiaries in income or principal, other than an income interest held by a surviving spouse[29] or distributions on trust termination, typically rest within the trustee's discretion. The trust instrument might express a standard to limit or guide the exercise of that discretion – for example, the trust instrument might provide that distributions are to be made for a beneficiary's "health, education, maintenance, and support" – or there might be no such limiting standard. In either case, a court "will not interfere with a trustee's

§ 404 (Unif. Law Comm'n 2000). However, the problem described in this paragraph also affects charitable trusts, wherein the trustee manages the trust's assets for the trust's charitable purposes. See *Restatement Third of Trusts* (American Law Institute 2003) s. 28.

24 This sentence and the remaining sentences in this paragraph draw freely on Thomas P. Gallanis, "The Trustee's Duty to Inform" (2007) 85 *North Carolina LR* 1615, without further citation.

25 Michael C. Jensen & William H. Meckling, "Theory of the Firm: Managerial Behavior, Agency Costs, and Ownership Structure" in Roberta Romano (ed.), *Foundations of Corporate Law* (Oxford University Press 1993) 7–8.

26 This is technically true even for revocable trusts, although the power to revoke gives the settlor substantial control over the trust's management. Indeed, while a trust is revocable, the trustee owes fiduciary duties to the settlor, not to the beneficiaries. See Unif. Trust Code § 603(b) (Unif. Law Comm'n, amended in 2018); see also *Restatement Third of Trusts* (American Law Institute 2007) s. 74.

27 On the meaning of "terms of the trust," see *Restatement Third of Trusts* (American Law Institute 2003) s. 4; Unif. Trust Code § 103(18) (Unif. Law Comm'n, amended in 2018).

28 This is also true outside the United States. See Lionel Smith, "Massively Discretionary Trusts" (2017) 70 *CLP* 17.

29 An income interest given to a surviving spouse cannot be discretionary if it is to qualify for the federal transfer tax marital deduction. See, e.g., 26 USC § 2056(b)(5) (requiring the surviving spouse to be "entitled for life to all the income from the entire interest, or all the income from a specific portion thereof, payable annually or at more frequent intervals"); 26 USC § 2056(b)(7)(B)(ii)(I) (requiring the surviving spouse to be "entitled to all the income from the property, payable annually or at more frequent intervals").

exercise of a discretionary power when that exercise is reasonable and not based on an improper interpretation of the terms of the trust."[30] Some trust instruments give the trustee even further discretion, describing the trustee's discretion as "absolute" or "uncontrolled." A court will interfere with such "extended" discretion only if the trustee "act[s] in bad faith or for some purpose or motive other than to accomplish the purposes of the trust."[31]

An example will serve to illustrate the range of a trustee's discretion under modern US law and practice.[32] Suppose that A and B are a married couple with two adult children, X and Y. A is a professor of law earning $200,000 per year, and B is a self-employed music teacher earning $50,000 per year. X and Y are undergraduates at a private university; the annual cost for both children's education is $170,000. The family's total annual income is $305,000, and the total annual expenses are $326,000. The family's one major liability is a mortgage of $400,000 on the family home. A's mother died last year. Her will devised $4.2 million in trust. The trustee is directed to pay so much of the income, principal or both as the trustee determines to be needed for A's support and maintenance; unexpended income is to be added to principal. Upon A's death, the principal and any accumulated income are to be distributed to X and Y. The trustee has invested the $4.2 million so that it produces income of $165,000 a year. How much should the trustee distribute to A this year? Just a few of the many possible answers include (1) $0, because A's income is sufficient for all expenses other than the children's university education, and there is no duty in US law to support adult children; (2) $21,000, which is the difference between the family's annual expenses and annual income; (3) $71,000, which is the difference between the family's annual expenses and annual income if B's income is disregarded; (4) $165,000, which is all of the trust's annual income and (5) $400,000 – in other words, $165,000 of income and $235,000 of principal – in order to eliminate the mortgage on the family home. Each of these possible distributions, ranging from $0 to $400,000 or potentially even more, would be upheld by a court.

Another example of the trustee's discretion with respect to the beneficiaries' interests in the trust arises in the context of trust decanting. "Decanting" is the word used to describe the distribution of property from one trust to another. The word

> provides a rich metaphor to help us understand exactly what decanting a trust is all about. The word 'decant' literally means to pour a liquid from one vessel to another, leaving unwanted sediment in the first vessel. When we decant a trust, the liquid is the trust principal, the first vessel is the original trust instrument, the second vessel is the new trust instrument, and the unwanted sediment is the unwanted terms and conditions in the original trust instrument.[33]

[30] *Restatement Third of Trusts* (American Law Institute 2003) s. 50 comment b.

[31] *Restatement Third of Trusts* (American Law Institute 2003) s. 50 comment c.

[32] This example draws freely on Thomas P. Gallanis, *Family Property Law: Cases and Materials on Wills, Trusts, and Estates*, (7th ed., Foundation Press 2019) 582–84, without further citation.

[33] Anne Marie Levin & Todd A. Flubacher, "Put Decanting to Work to Give Breath to Trust Purpose" (2011) 38 *Estate Planning* 3.

Decanting is authorized in approximately half the states in the United States by statute[34] and in some other states by judicial decision.[35] In 2015, the Uniform Law Commission approved a Uniform Trust Decanting Act. Under that act, a trustee with "expanded distributive discretion"[36] – defined as "a discretionary power of distribution that is not limited to an ascertainable standard or a reasonably definite standard'"[37] – has broad powers when decanting assets into a new trust, including the power to delete discretionary beneficiaries of the old trust from the new trust; the only beneficiaries who must be retained in the new trust are those with a "vested interest," meaning those who are entitled to "mandatory" distributions or otherwise have a "noncontingent right . . . to some or all of the trust property."[38] Of course, this power to delete discretionary beneficiaries, like any other of the trustee's powers, must be exercised in good faith.[39]

Put simply: the discretionary nature of the beneficial interests in modern US trusts gives great latitude to a trustee. This creates a significant risk of harm and betrayal. (Of course, the beneficiaries can sue the trustee for breach of fiduciary duty, but litigation is costly and imperfect.)

A third feature of modern US trust law and practice pointing in the direction of requiring substantial trust in the general sense is that modern US trusts often include as beneficiaries persons who are unborn or unascertained when the trust is created. The example two paragraphs above, in which the trust's beneficiaries are all living and named individually – A, the law professor; B, the music teacher; and X and Y, their children – is hardly the only pattern. Also prominent are trusts with beneficial interests held by persons identified not by name but by a group designation; for example, the settlor's "children" or "descendants." Beneficial interests so held are known as "class gifts."[40] A good definition appears in the *Restatement Third of Property: Wills and Other Donative Transfers*: "A class gift is a disposition to

[34] See Ala. Laws 2018-519 (HB 163, Unif. Trust Decanting Act); Alaska Stat. § 13.36.157–13.36.159; Ariz. Rev. Stat. § 14-10819; Colo. Rev. Stat. § 15-16-901 et seq. (Unif. Trust Decanting Act); 12 Del. Code § 3528; Fla. Stat. § 736.04117; Ga. Code § 53-12-62; 760 Ill. Comp. Stat. 5/16.4; Ind. Code § 30-4-3-36; Ky. Rev. Stat. § 386.175; Mich. Comp. Laws § 700.7820a; Minn. Stat. § 502.851; Mo. Rev. Stat. § 456.4-419; Nev. Rev. Stat. § 163.556; NH Rev. Stat. § 564-B:4-418; NM Stat. §46-12-101 et seq. (Unif. Trust Decanting Act); NY EPTL §10-6.6(b)–(s); NC Gen. Stat. § 36C-8B-1 et seq. (Unif Trust Decanting Act); Ohio Rev. Code § 5808.18; RI Gen. Laws §18-4-31; SC Code §62-7-816A; SD Cod. Laws §55-2-15 et seq.; Tenn. Code §35-15-816(b)(27); Tex. Prop. Code §112.071 et seq.; Va. Code §64.2-779.1 et seq. (Unif. Trust Decanting Act); Wash. Rev. Code § 11.107.010 et seq. (Unif. Trust Decanting Act); Wisc. Stat. § 701.0418; Wyo. Stat. §4-10-816(a)(xxviii).

[35] See, e.g.. *Morse* v. *Kraft* 992 NE 2d 1021 (Mass. 2013).

[36] See Unif. Trust Decanting Act § 11 (Unif. Law Comm'n 2015).

[37] Unif. Trust Decanting Act § 2(11) (Unif. Law Comm'n 2015). The definitions of "ascertainable standard" and "reasonably definite standard" are found in Unif. Trust Decanting Act §§ 2(2), 2(21) (Unif. Law Comm'n 2015).

[38] Unif. Trust Decanting Act §§ 11(a)(4), 11(c)(3) (Unif. Law Comm'n, 2015).

[39] See *Restatement Third of Trusts* (American Law Institute 2007) s. 76(1); Unif. Trust Code § 105(b)(2) (Unif. Law Comm'n, amended in 2018).

[40] On the interpretation of class gifts in donative documents, see *Restatement Third of Property: Wills and Other Donative Transfers* [hereinafter *Restatement Third of Property*] (American Law Institute 2011) ch. 13–16.

beneficiaries who take as members of a group. Taking as members of a group means that the identities and shares of the beneficiaries are subject to fluctuation."[41] If the class is "subject to increase," then new members can enter the class after the creation of the class gift.[42] For example, a beneficial interest in trust in favor of the settlor's "children" is subject to increase as long as the settlor is alive because the settlor could have or adopt a child; a beneficial interest in favor of the settlor's "grandchildren" is subject to increase as long as at least one child of the settlor is alive because that child could have or adopt a child; and a beneficial interest in favor of the settlor's "descendants" is subject to increase as long as the settlor or at least one descendant of the settlor is alive because the settlor or that descendant could have or adopt a child. Indeed, each of these classes might be subject to increase even longer, given the possibility of posthumous assisted reproduction.[43]

Whether there is an outer limit on how long a class gift can remain open depends on the law of each US state. The rule governing this outer limit is the Rule Against Perpetuities. The classic formulation of the Rule Against Perpetuities in American common law was provided near the beginning of the twentieth century by Professor John Chipman Gray: "No [contingent future] interest is good unless it must vest, if at all, not later than twenty-one years after some life in being at the creation of the interest."[44] The Rule Against Perpetuities governs class gifts because the interest of an unborn or unascertained person in a class gift is a future interest contingent upon the person becoming a member of the class (e.g., by birth, adoption or ascertainment).[45] By the late twentieth century, the formulation of a perpetuity period[46] as "twenty-one years after some life in being" meant, on average, approximately ninety years.[47] In 1986, the Uniform Law Commission approved a Uniform Statutory Rule Against Perpetuities containing a perpetuity period of ninety years.[48] This Uniform Rule used to be the law in more than half the states in the United States, but a lobbying effort to repeal or extend the Rule Against Perpetuities has been successful in many state legislatures. Today, twenty states and the District of Columbia have statutes allowing

41 *Restatement Third of Property* (American Law Institute 2011) s. 13.1(a).

42 See *Restatement Third of Property* (American Law Institute 2011) s. 13.1 comment h.

43 On posthumous assisted reproduction and class gifts, see *Restatement Third of Property* (American Law Institute 2011) s. 15.1 comment j.

44 John Chipman Gray, *The Rule against Perpetuities* (2nd ed., Little, Brown 1906) 166.

45 For discussion, see Thomas P. Gallanis, *Estates, Future Interests, and Powers of Appointment* (Nutshell Series, 6th ed., West Academic 2018) 79–85. An example of a class gift in which the members are unascertained (and some or all might also be unborn) is a future interest in favor of a living person's "heirs." A person's heirs typically are ascertained at the person's death. On class gifts to heirs, see *Restatement Third of Property* (American Law Institute 2011) ch. 16.

46 Actually, there is no "perpetuity period" at common law because the common-law Rule Against Perpetuities requires initial certainty; the common-law Rule is either satisfied or not at the moment of the future interest's creation. The reference here to "perpetuity period" is a reference to the period of time allowed under a modification of the common-law Rule known as "wait and see." For discussion, see Gallanis, *Estates, Future Interests, and Powers of Appointment* (n. 41) 159–61.

47 See Lawrence W. Waggoner, "The Uniform Statutory Rule Against Perpetuities: The Rationale of the 90-Year Waiting Period" (1988) 73 *Cornell LR* 162, 166–68.

48 Unif. Statutory Rule Against Perpetuities § 1(a)(2) (Unif. Law Comm'n 1986).

trusts to last forever,[49] and eleven states have statutes allowing trusts to last for a century or more – up to 1,000 years in Colorado, Utah and Wyoming.[50] The American Law Institute has taken an official position against this movement to allow perpetual or near-perpetual trusts, denouncing the statutes as "ill advised,"[51] but the ALI's criticism has been ignored.

To the extent that a trust's beneficiaries are unborn or unascertained (or underage or incapacitated), they will be unable to supervise a trustee's performance or enforce a trustee's fiduciary duties, unless their interests are defended by the living adult beneficiaries with legal capacity, by a cotrustee or successor trustee or by a representative, perhaps court appointed.[52] A trustee who is not worthy of trust will have far too much room to maneuver if there is no effective supervision or enforcement.

So far, this paper has examined three features of the trust under modern US law and practice that seem to require a significant degree of trust in the trustee by the trust's beneficiaries and settlor. The paper now turns to three features of modern US trust law and practice that attempt to protect the trust's settlor and beneficiaries so that they need not place worryingly high levels of trust in the trustee.

First, the fiduciary rules of US trust law are stricter in important respects than their counterparts in other branches of US fiduciary law, such as corporate law. For example, the duty of loyalty in US trust law requires the trustee to act in the "sole" interests of the beneficiaries,[53] whereas the duty of loyalty (or "fair dealing"[54]) in US corporate law requires the corporation's directors and officers to act in the corporation's "best" interests.[55] The distinction between sole interests and best interests has important consequences.[56] Transactions creating a conflict between fiduciary and personal interests

[49] Alaska, Delaware (for trusts of personal property), the District of Columbia, Hawaii, Idaho, Illinois, Kentucky, Maine, Maryland, Michigan (for trusts of personal property), Missouri, Nebraska, New Hampshire, New Jersey, North Carolina, Ohio, Pennsylvania, Rhode Island, South Dakota, Virginia and Wisconsin.

[50] Alabama (360 years), Arizona (500 years), Colorado (1,000 years), Delaware (110 years, for trusts of real property), Florida (360 years), Georgia (360 years), Nevada (365 years), Tennessee (360 years), Utah (1,000 years), Washington (150 years) and Wyoming (1,000 years).

[51] *Restatement Third of Property* (American Law Institute 2011) 564, vol. 3, "Introductory Note" to ch. 27.

[52] See *Restatement Third of Trusts* (American Law Institute 2012) s. 94(1) ("A suit against a trustee of a private trust to enjoin or redress a breach of trust or otherwise to enforce the trust may be maintained only by a beneficiary or by a co-trustee, successor trustee, or other person acting on behalf of one or more beneficiaries"); Unif. Trust Code § 305(a) (Unif. Law Comm'n 2000) ("If the court determines that an interest is not represented . . . the court may appoint a [representative] to receive notice, give consent, and otherwise represent, bind, and act on behalf of a minor, incapacitated, or unborn individual, or a person whose identity or location is unknown").

[53] See *Restatement Third of Trusts* (American Law Institute 2007) s. 78(1).

[54] See *Principles of Corporate Governance: Analysis and Recommendations* (American Law Institute 1994) 200, vol. 1, "Introductory Note" to pt. V ("Part V avoids the use of the term 'duty of loyalty,' when dealing with the obligations of a person who acts with a pecuniary interest in a matter, and instead uses the term 'duty of fair dealing'").

[55] See *Cede & Co. v. Technicolor Inc.*, 634 A.2d 345, 361 (Del. 1993) ("the duty of loyalty mandates that the best interest of the corporation and its shareholders take precedence over any interest possessed by a director, officer or controlling shareholder and not shared by the stockholders generally").

[56] For an argument that trust law should adopt the "best interest" standard, see John H. Langbein, "Questioning the Trust Law Duty of Loyalty: Sole Interest or Best Interest?" (2005) 114 *Yale LJ* 929. For a rebuttal, see Melanie B. Leslie, "In Defense of the No Further Inquiry Rule: A Response to Professor John Langbein" (2005) 47 *William & Mary LR* 541.

by a trustee are subject to a rule of strict liability called the "no-further-inquiry rule."[57] This rule flatly prohibits such transactions, which are "voidable by a beneficiary affected by the transaction."[58] As the *Restatement Third of Trusts* states, "it is immaterial that the trustee may be able to show that the action in question was taken in good faith, that the terms of the transaction were fair, and that no profit resulted to the trustee."[59] US corporate law used to have a "sole" interests rule but "changed course, rejected the trust law solution, and developed a regime for accommodating such conflicts to the interests of the corporation."[60] Modern US corporate law

> emphasizes three principles for dealing with conflicted-director transactions: disclosure, delegation, and fairness.
>
> (1) The conflicted director must disclose the conflict and all the material circumstances to his or her fellow directors.
> (2) The decision whether to approve the conflicted transaction is delegated to the nonconflicted directors.
> (3) In making their decision, the participating directors are required to test the transaction against a standard of fairness to the corporation.[61]

Another example concerns the standard of review[62] of alleged violations of the duty of "prudence" as it is called in US trust law, or "care" as it is called in US corporate law. The duties themselves are similar. The trust-law duty of prudence requires a trustee "to administer the trust as a prudent person would, in light of the purposes, terms, and other circumstances of the trust."[63] The corporate-law duty of care requires a director or officer to act "in good faith, in a manner that he or she reasonably believes to be in the best interests of the corporation, and with the care that an ordinarily prudent person would reasonably be expected to exercise in a like position and under similar circumstances."[64] A crucial difference between prudence in trust law and care in corporate law lies in the standard of review applied by the courts. US corporate law has the "business judgment rule," which creates a strong presumption in favor of the validity of a corporate decision. A classic formulation of this rule appears in the Delaware Supreme Court's decision in *Aronson* v. *Lewis*:

> The business judgment rule . . . is a presumption that in making a business decision the directors of a corporation acted on an informed basis, in good faith and in the honest belief that the action taken was in the best interests of the company. Absent an abuse of discretion, that judgment will be respected by the courts. The burden is on the party challenging the decision to establish facts rebutting the presumption.[65]

[57] See *Restatement Third of Trusts* (American Law Institute 2007) s. 78 comments a & b.
[58] Unif. Trust Code § 802(b) (Unif Law Comm'n 2000).
[59] *Restatement Third of Trusts* (American Law Institute 2007) s. 78 comment b.
[60] Langbein, "Questioning the Trust Law Duty of Loyalty" (n. 52) 959.
[61] Ibid.
[62] On the distinction between a standard of conduct and a standard of review, see Melvin A. Eisenberg, "The Divergence of Standards of Conduct and Standards of Review in Corporate Law" (2007) 62 *Fordham LR* 437.
[63] *Restatement Third of Trusts* (American Law Institute 2007) s. 77(1).
[64] *Principles of Corporate Governance: Analysis and Recommendations* (American Law Institute 1994) s. 4.01.
[65] *Aronson* v. *Lewis* 473 A.2d 805, 812 (Del. 1984) (citations omitted).

As the Delaware Supreme Court explained in its subsequent decision in *Brehm v. Eisner*, "[c]ourts do not measure, weigh or quantify directors' judgments. We do not even decide if they are reasonable in this context. Due care in the decision-making context is *process* due care only. Irrationality is the outer limit of the business judgment rule."[66] There is no equivalent of the business judgment rule in trust law. The normal burden of proof applies, of course; a plaintiff alleging a violation of the duty of prudence must prove the claim by a preponderance of the evidence. Additionally, a court must be careful not to use hindsight in evaluating the prudence of a trustee's action or inaction.[67] But the extremely heavy thumb on the scale in favor of the due care of a business decision combined with the limitation of the court's review to the process rather than the substance of the business decision has no equivalent in the law of trusts.

Second, the US law of trusts places a duty on the trustee to provide information to the trust's beneficiaries, or at least to some of them, about the trust and its administration so that the beneficiaries can monitor and enforce the trustee's performance. This duty is articulated in the *Restatement Third* as follows:

> (1) Except as provided in § 74 (revocable trusts) or as permissibly modified by the terms of the trust, a trustee has a duty:
> (a) promptly to inform fairly representative beneficiaries of the existence of the trust, of their status as beneficiaries and their right to obtain further information, and of basic information concerning the trusteeship;
> (b) to inform beneficiaries of significant changes in their beneficiary status;
> (c) to keep fairly representative beneficiaries reasonably informed of changes involving the trusteeship and about other significant developments concerning the trust and its administration, particularly material information needed by beneficiaries for the protection of their interests.
> (2) Except as provided in § 74 or as permissibly modified by the terms of the trust, a trust also ordinarily has a duty promptly to respond to the request of any beneficiary for information concerning the trust and its administration, and to permit beneficiaries on a reasonable basis to inspect trust documents, records, and property holdings.[68]

The Uniform Trust Code contains similar rules, though with different terminology: the relevant term of art is "qualified beneficiaries" rather than "fairly representative beneficiaries." Section 813(a) of the Uniform Trust Code provides that "[a] trustee shall keep the qualified beneficiaries of the trust reasonably informed about the administration of the trust and of the material facts necessary for them to protect

[66] *Brehm* v. *Eisner* 746 A.2d 244, 264 (Del. 2000) (emphasis in original), citing *Sinclair Oil Corp.* v. *Levien* 280 A.2d 717, 720 (Del. 1971), for the proposition that "decisions will not be disturbed if they can be attributed to any rational business purpose."

[67] See *Restatement Third of Trusts* (American Law Institute 2007) s. 77 comment a ("the prudence of a trustee's conduct is to be judged on the basis of circumstances at the time of that conduct, not with the benefit of hindsight or by taking account of developments that occur after the time of the action or decision").

[68] *Restatement Third of Trusts* (American Law Institute 2007) s. 82.

their interests. Unless unreasonable under the circumstances, a trustee shall promptly respond to a beneficiary's request for information related to the information of the trust."[69] The term "qualified beneficiary" is defined in the Uniform Trust Code as

> a beneficiary who, on the date the beneficiary's qualification is determined:
>
> (A) is a distributee or permissible distributee of trust income or principal;
> (B) would be a distributee or permissible distributee of trust income or principal if the interests of the distributees described in subparagraph (A) terminated on that date without causing the trust to terminate; or
> (C) would be a distributee or permissible distributee of trust income or principal if the trust terminated on that date.[70]

The duty to inform helps to align the interests of the trustee with those of the beneficiaries by shedding light on the otherwise hidden decisions made by the trustee in the course of trust administration.[71] Providing this information is important in order to achieve trust management in the interests of the beneficiaries. The duty to inform deters the trustee from committing a breach of fiduciary duty by giving the beneficiaries access to the information needed to monitor the trustee's performance. The duty also assists the beneficiaries in remedying a fiduciary breach after it has occurred by giving them the information needed to prove the breach. Providing the information to the beneficiaries is important because the assets at stake are theirs. The beneficiaries, and only the beneficiaries, have the full incentive to supervise and enforce the trustee's fiduciary obligations.

An important question is whether the duty to inform should be framed at least to some extent as a mandatory rule of trust law or whether it should be a default rule, which the settlor can modify or waive in the terms of the trust. The *Restatement Third* takes the position that the duty has a mandatory core that cannot be waived: "Furthermore, although subject to modification by trust provision, the duty to provide information to certain beneficiaries under Subsection (1), Clauses (a) through (c), may not be dispensed with entirely or to a degree or for a time that would unduly interfere with the underlying purposes or effectiveness of the information requirements."[72] The Uniform Trust Code similarly provides in section 105(b)(8) and (b)(9) that the following aspects of the duty to inform are mandatory and prevail over any contrary terms of the trust:

> (8) the duty . . . to notify qualified beneficiaries of an irrevocable trust who have attained 25 years of age of the existence of the trust, of the identity of the trustee, and of their right to request trustee's reports;
> (9) the duty . . . to respond to the request of a [qualified] beneficiary of an irrevocable trust for trustee's reports and other information reasonably related to the administration of a trust; . . . .[73]

[69] Unif. Trust Code § 813(a) (Unif. Law Comm'n 2000).
[70] Unif. Trust Code § 103(13) (Unif. Law Comm'n 2000).
[71] This paragraph draws freely on Gallanis, "Trustee's Duty to Inform" (n. 23) 1616–17 without further citation.
[72] *Restatement Third of Trusts* (American Law Institute 2007) s. 82 comment a(2).
[73] Unif. Trust Code § 105(b)(8), (b)(9) (Unif. Law Comm'n, amended in 2004).

The position of *Restatement Third* and the Uniform Trust Code that the duty to inform should have a mandatory core has proven controversial.[74] Of the thirty-two US jurisdictions that have enacted all or most of the Uniform Trust Code, sixteen have eliminated section 105(b)(8) and (b)(9),[75] with the effect that the duty to inform in those jurisdictions is a default rule entirely waivable by the settlor. Of the remaining sixteen Uniform Trust Code jurisdictions, nine have a mandatory duty to inform that is substantially narrower than in the official version of the code.[76]

A third feature of modern US trust law and practice that might reduce the need for trust in the general sense is that modern US trust law facilitates the appointment of a trust director – also known as a trust protector or trust adviser – to safeguard the intentions of the settlor and the interests of the beneficiaries. As stated in the *Restatement Third*:

> The terms of a trust may reserve to the settlor or grant a designated person the authority to control the trustee in certain matters, by direction or by withholding a required consent. The person who holds a directory or veto power may be designated by name, by class or other description, or by inclusion in the trust provision of a list of persons to serve in the role concurrently or in sequence.[77]

A sizeable majority of the states in the United States have statutes authorizing a trust director. Some of these statutes are enactments of section 808 of the Uniform Trust Code, which provided in pertinent part:

(b) If the terms of the trust confer upon a person . . . power to direct certain actions of the trustee, the trustee shall act in accordance with an exercise of the power unless the attempted exercise would constitute a serious breach of a fiduciary duty that the person holding the power owes to the beneficiaries of the trust.

. . .

(d) A person, other than a beneficiary, who holds a power to direct is presumptively a fiduciary who, as such, is required to act in good faith with regard to the purposes of the trust and the interests of the beneficiaries. The holder of a power to direct is liable for any loss that results from a breach of a fiduciary duty.[78]

[74] See Unif. Trust Code § 105, Comment (Unif. Law Comm'n, amended in 2004) ("These subsections [(b)(8) and (b)(9)] have generated more discussion in jurisdictions considering enactment of the UTC than have any other provisions of the Code").

[75] See Ark. Code § 28-73-105; Kans. Stat. § 58a-105; Mass. Gen. Laws ch. 203E § 105; Minn. Stat. § 501C.0105; Mont. Code § 72-38-105; NH Rev. Stat. § 564-B:1-105; NC Gen. Stat. § 36C-1-105; ND Cent. Code § 59-09-05; SC §.62-7-105; Tenn. Code § 35-15-105; Utah Code § 75-7-105; 14A Vt. Stat. § 105; Va. Code § 64.2-703; W. Va. Code § 44D-1-105; Wisc. Stat. § 701.0105; Wyo. Stat. § 4-10-105.

[76] See Ala. Code § 19-3B-105; Ariz. Rev. Stat. § 14-10105; Ky. Rev. Stat. § 386B.1-030; 18-B Me. Rev. Stat. § 105; Mo. Rev. Stat. § 456.1-105; NJ Stat. § 3B:31-5; NM Stat. §§ 46A-1-105, 46A-8-813; Ohio Rev. Code § 5801.04; 20 Pa. Cons. Stat. §§ 7705, 7780.3. An additional state worth mentioning is Texas, which has a nonuniform trust code with a mandatory duty to inform that is substantially narrower than in the Uniform Trust Code. See Tex. Prop. Code § 111.0035.

[77] *Restatement Third of Trusts* (American Law Institute 2007) s. 75 comment a.

[78] Unif. Trust Code § 808 (2000, deleted in 2018).

The first legislation in the United States on directed trusts was enacted in Delaware in 1986.[79] Since then, statutes on directed trusts (other than Uniform Trust Code section 808) have been enacted in more than a dozen other states.[80] The Uniform Law Commission approved a Uniform Directed Trust Act in 2017[81] and as a consequence deleted section 808 from the Uniform Trust Code. The Uniform Directed Trust Act is well summarized in the act's prefatory note:

> The Uniform Directed Trust Act addresses an increasingly common arrangement in contemporary estate planning and asset management known as a "directed trust". In a directed trust, the terms of the trust grant a person other than a trustee a power over some aspect of the trust's administration. There is no consistent vocabulary to describe the person other than a trustee that holds a power in a directed trust. Several terms are common in practice, including "trust protector", "trust adviser", and "trust director". There is much uncertainty in existing law about the fiduciary status of a nontrustee that has a power over a trust and about the fiduciary duty of a trustee, sometimes called an 'administrative trustee' or 'directed trustee', with regard to actions taken or directed by the nontrustee. . . .
>
> Under the Uniform Directed Trust Act, a trust director has the same default and mandatory fiduciary duties as a trustee in a like position and under similar circumstances. In complying with a trust director's exercise of a power of direction, a directed trustee is liable only for the trustee's own "willful misconduct". The logic behind these rules is that in a directed trust the trust director functions much like a trustee in an undirected trust. Accordingly, the trust director should have the same duties as a trustee in the exercise or nonexercise of the director's power of direction, and the fiduciary duty of the directed trustee is reduced with respect to the director's power of direction. . . .
>
> Compared with a non-directed trust in which a trustee holds all power over the trust, a directed trust subject to this act provides for more aggregate fiduciary duties owed to a beneficiary. All of the usual duties of trusteeship are preserved in the trust director, and in addition the directed trustee has a duty to avoid willful misconduct.[82]

One of the prominent trust companies in the United States advertises directed trusts with the following slogan: "When you need a trust, but want to or must maintain control."[83] This is the aim of a directed trust, to enable the use of the trust as a flexible device for wealth planning but to cabin the trustee's exercise of authority and discretion.

79 Del. Laws 1986, ch. 422 § 5. For the current version, see 12 Del. Code § 3313.

80 See, e.g., Alaska Stat. § 13.36.370; Ariz. Rev. Stat. § 14-10818; Colo. Rev. Stat. § 15-16-801; Ga. Code § 53-12-500 et seq.; Idaho Code § 15-7-501; 760 Ill. Comp. Stat. 5/16.3; Ind. Code § 30-4-3-9; Mich. Comp. Laws § 700.7809; Miss. Stat. § 91-8-1201 et seq.; Nev. Rev. Stat. § 163.553 et seq.; NH Rev. Stat. § 564-B:12-1201 et seq.; NC Gen. Stat. § 36C-8A-1 et seq.; RI Gen. Laws § 18-9.2-2(9)(iii); SD Cod. Laws §55-1b-1 et seq.; Tenn. Code § 35-15-1201 et seq.; Tex. Prop. Code § 114.0031; Wash. Rev. Code § 11.100.130; Wisc. Stat. § 701.0818; Wyo. Stat. § 4-10-710.

81 Unif. Directed Trust Act (Unif. Law Comm'n 2017). The first enactment was in New Mexico. See NM Laws 2018 ch. 63 (SB 101).

82 Unif. Directed Trust Act, Prefatory Note (Unif. Law Comm'n 2017).

83 See Carol G. Kroch & Jeffrey C. Wolken, "The Flexibility and Freedom of a Delaware Directed Trust" (Wilmington Trust, March 2018), https://library.wilmingtontrust.com/wealth-planning/the-flexibility-and-freedom-of-a-delaware-directed-trust, accessed June 30, 2018.

These features of modern US trust law prompt two striking observations. The first observation is that US trust law is moving in *both* directions. Some aspects of the modern law require greater trust in the trustee, for example by allowing the settlor to create a perpetual or near-perpetual trust and to restrict or eliminate the information rights of the beneficiaries. Other aspects of modern US law reduce the need for trust in the trustee, for example by facilitating the appointment of a trust director. This does not mean that the modern law is schizophrenic. One often sees the same individuals advocating for statutes authorizing perpetual trusts and a fully waivable duty to inform *and also* advocating for statutes authorizing directed trusts. The developments are connected and are part of a desire to achieve the right balance in the trust law, although there is a range of views on where the right balance is to be struck.[84]

The second, and related, observation is that, to the extent that US state legislatures have enacted rules of trust law different from the trust law promulgated by the Uniform Law Commission or the American Law Institute, the divergent rules typically have the effect of increasing – rather than decreasing – the need for trust in the trustee. Examples here include the evisceration of the Rule Against Perpetuities (a move condemned by the American Law Institute as "ill advised"[85]) and the rejection of the Uniform Trust Code's provision that the trustee's duty to provide information at least to some of the beneficiaries should be a matter of mandatory law.[86] These outcomes in state legislatures are not the product of faith in the trustee but rather of a desire to cater to the supposed preferences of settlors in order to attract trust business into the enacting state. Nonetheless, one of the effects is to push the state's law in the direction of requiring greater trust in the trustee.

"Put not your trust in princes,"[87] says the psalmist, using in the original Hebrew a form of the word בָּטַח (*baṭaḥ*, *batach*), meaning "to trust." But to what extent must we put our trust in trustees?

The answer depends on the terms of the trust and the governing state law. More trust in the general sense is needed if the trust is irrevocable than if it can be revoked. More is needed if the beneficiaries' access to information about the trust and its administration is curtailed than if it is mandatory. More is needed if the beneficial interests are held by unborn, unascertained, underage or incapacitated persons than if the beneficial interests are held by living adults with full legal capacity. More is needed if the trustee has wide discretion than if the trustee is directed.[88]

In the opening scene of one of Shakespeare's most well-known plays, the Countess of Roussillon gives the following advice to her son, Bertram, on his departure for the

[84] For some recent academic commentary, see Gallanis, "New Direction" (n. 16); Lionel Smith, 'Give the People What They Want? The Onshoring of the Offshore' (2018) 103 *Iowa LR* 2155.

[85] See n. 50.

[86] See nn. 73–75 and accompanying text.

[87] Psalm 146:3 (Revised Standard Version).

[88] This requires trust in the trust director, of course. Turtles all the way down? For discussion, see Gregory Alexander, "Trust Protectors: Who Will Watch the Watchmen?" (2006) 27 *Cardozo LR* 2807.

French court: "Love all, trust a few." Her words are sage counsel in almost all contexts. They also have relevance for the settlor and beneficiaries of a trust under modern US law. Depending on the terms of the trust and the governing state law, the settlor and beneficiaries will need to put their trust – often substantial trust – in the trustee. Whether that trust is justified will determine whether all is well during the trust's administration and whether the trust ends well with its final distributions.[89]

[89] For the Countess of Roussillon's advice to her son, see William Shakespeare, *All's Well That Ends Well* act 1, scene 1.

INDEX